1763

Wash. Co. Md.

adam
amon
Henry
Ruth
mary
Rachel
Benedict
Elizabeth (Betsy)
nancy
amon massena
amelia (ameley)

MARYLAND RECORDS

COLONIAL, REVOLUTIONARY, COUNTY AND CHURCH

FROM

ORIGINAL SOURCES

BY

GAIUS MARCUS BRUMBAUGH, M.S., M.D., Litt.D.

WASHINGTON, D. C.

VOLUME II

GENEALOGICAL PUBLISHING CO., INC.

BALTIMORE 1975

Originally Published
Lancaster, Pennsylvania
1928

Reprinted
Genealogical Publishing Co., Inc.
Baltimore, 1967

Baltimore, 1975

Library of Congress Catalogue Card Number 67-24374
International Standard Book Number 0-8063-0059-0

Made in the United States of America

PREFACE

Volume I of this publication appeared in 1915. Since that time there has been a frequently repeated demand for the publication of the existing remainder of the Maryland Colonial Census of 1776, and the same is here made available (pp. 79–230, partly in facsimile). The other facsimile records of West St. Mary's Manor (pp. xi) and the State of His Lordship's Manors (Frontispiece and pp. 4–78) contain the names and ages of settlers of yet earlier periods and all these records will be found valuable. The Colonial Census and the Lord Baltimore records are so large in size and often so indistinct in preservation, and of such varying construction, that special code treatment has been necessary. A careful study of the explanation given at the beginning of each of these sections is necessary and will quickly enable the reader to understand and use the materials as published.

Many of the names of the Colonial period were phonetically and otherwise poorly spelled. The spellings found in the original records have been followed and an effort to assist the reader is made throughout the comprehensive index. Page 184, "Shurlotter Mitchel" is evidently Charlotte Mitchel; page 185, "Elexander Larance" is probably Alexander Lawrence; page 259, Charles "Ginings" is probably Jennings; etc. The searcher should constantly keep in thought the possible phonetic variations of the names being sought in the index.

Negative and positive photostatic copies and the original records themselves, and a reading glass, were used in preparing this volume. In cases of extreme importance to the reader, or of doubt as to the published spelling, it may be well to refer to the original record the location of which is usually mentioned throughout the volume. Photostatic copies of many of these original records may be obtained from the Maryland Historical Society, custodian of the State Archives, or from the author.

The last section of page 136, as deciphered by means of a reading glass appears to be:

James Mather	53	Mary Mather	20
Jemimah (?) Mather	57	Jeremiah Mather	—
Michael Mather	25	Darby Dwur	40
Thomas Mather	23	Lucy Morgan, Svts.	25

The indistinct portion of page 300 has been supplied on page 308.

The number of times a name appears upon a given page is often indicated thus: "(2)." However, it is well to glance through the entire page as the name may appear as "Sr." and "Junr." yet be indexed only once on the page. The reader will be much interested in tracing the same person through several classes of records at different ages of the person.

Numerous co-workers who secured and suggested important source records for this volume since its preparation began, have passed to the other life, and it is a pleasure to record full appreciation for their assistance. The Right Reverend Alfred Harding, D.D., Bishop of Washington, mentioned in the Preface to Vol. I, gave direction to my first researches and frequently expressed his continued interest and approval. The "Broad Creek Records," etc., are as a result ready for publication in Vol. III. Governor Edwin Warfield who died in April, 1920, and who, as President of the Md. Historical Society, placed many of its historical treasures at my disposal. Mr. James Walter Thomas kindly and freely granted copyright use (p. 208) from his important "Chronicles of Maryland." Mr. George W. Hodges carefully transcribed the Anne Arundel Co. Marriages (p. 415) and the Worcester Parish Records (p. 579), and the late Dr. Wm. Tayloe Snyder materially assisted in securing various Episcopal Church Records.

Among the numerous living helpers it is a pleasure to acknowledge the coöperation of the officers of the Maryland Historical Society, and especially the continuous interest and active assistance of Mr. Charles Fickus, acting Librarian, and, recently, of Dr. J. Hall Pleasants, Chairman of its Publication Committee. Mr. Francis Barnum Culver, Registrar General, N. S. Sons of American Revolution, and also prominent officer in various other national patriotic societies, has closely followed the progress of the work and has kindly written the Introduction. Mr. Arthur Sullivan Browne, Register of Rock Creek Parish has shown his active coöperation throughout the years, and the materials to be published in Vol. III will more fully show the results of his interest. To all those mentioned and to the various other Church and County officers and to all the friends who have assisted in making this volume possible, including my wife who extensively assisted in the preparation of the index, and to the Lancaster Press, Inc., printers, I express most cordial thanks.

Gaius Marcus Brumbaugh

WASHINGTON, D. C.,
January 11, 1928.

INTRODUCTION

Men generally are satisfied with a superficial brand of knowledge and usually that knowledge is confined to a few subjects of common interest. Their attitude is based for the most part upon the practical value of material things, and whatever seems less likely to yield profit or personal advantage is consistently ignored.

There are some minds however, which delight in probing beneath the surface and in exploring neglected by-paths in search of hidden treasures. For those who are so inclined, the Maryland Historical Society of Baltimore provides a fertile field, a veritable mine of historical lore.

In this volume of Maryland Records and in the volume which preceded it, Dr. Gaius M. Brumbaugh, the compiler and author, has culled from a mass of material in the Society's possession, and from numerous other original sources, a prodigious amount of data heretofore little known and not generally accessible.

The contents of this work are remarkably interesting and valuable in every respect; particularly, from the genealogical view-point. An examination of the Table of Contents of this volume will show how extensive the field is, and a study of the text will reveal a discerning and discriminating sense on the part of the compiler.

The lists of Maryland marriages, the transcripts of the church records of various counties of the State, the census reports of the inhabitants, the data from the early Rent Rolls and Land Books, and perhaps most interesting to patriotic societies, the section devoted to Maryland Revolutionary War pensioners, constitute a collection of historical material which will make Dr. Brumbaugh's work indispensable as a book of reference. A voluminous index adds to the value of the whole.

Francis B. Culver

WASHINGTON, D. C.,
December 17, 1927.

Contents of Volume II

West St. Mary's Manor

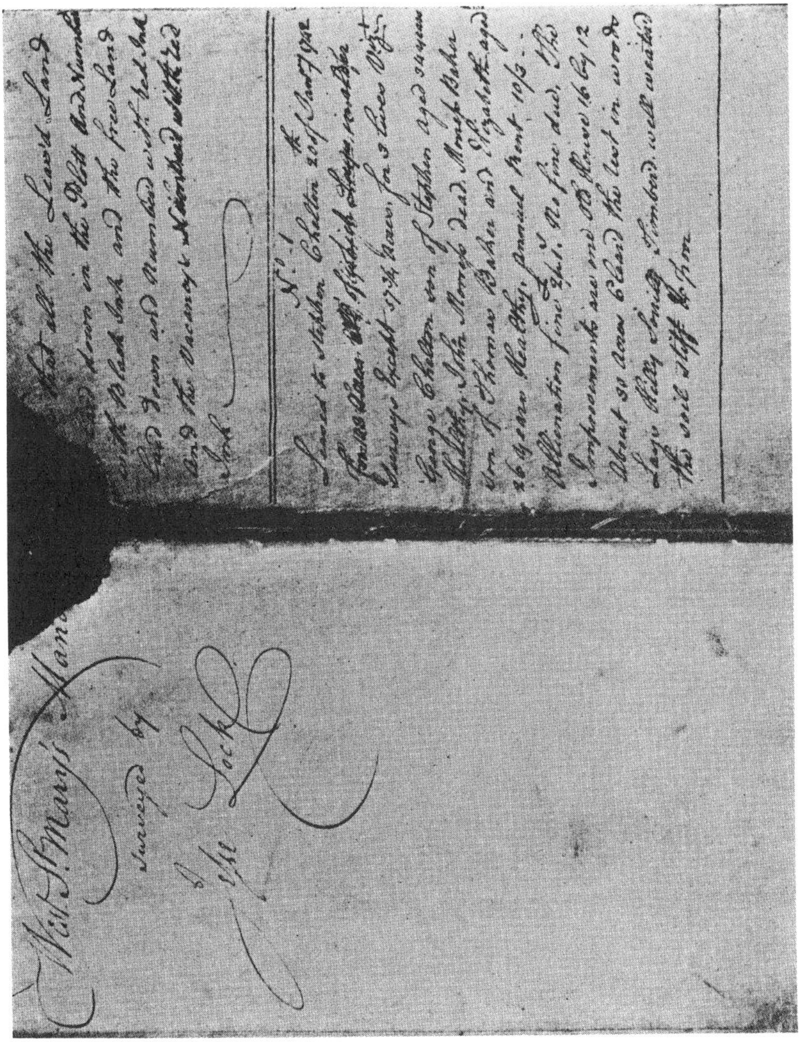

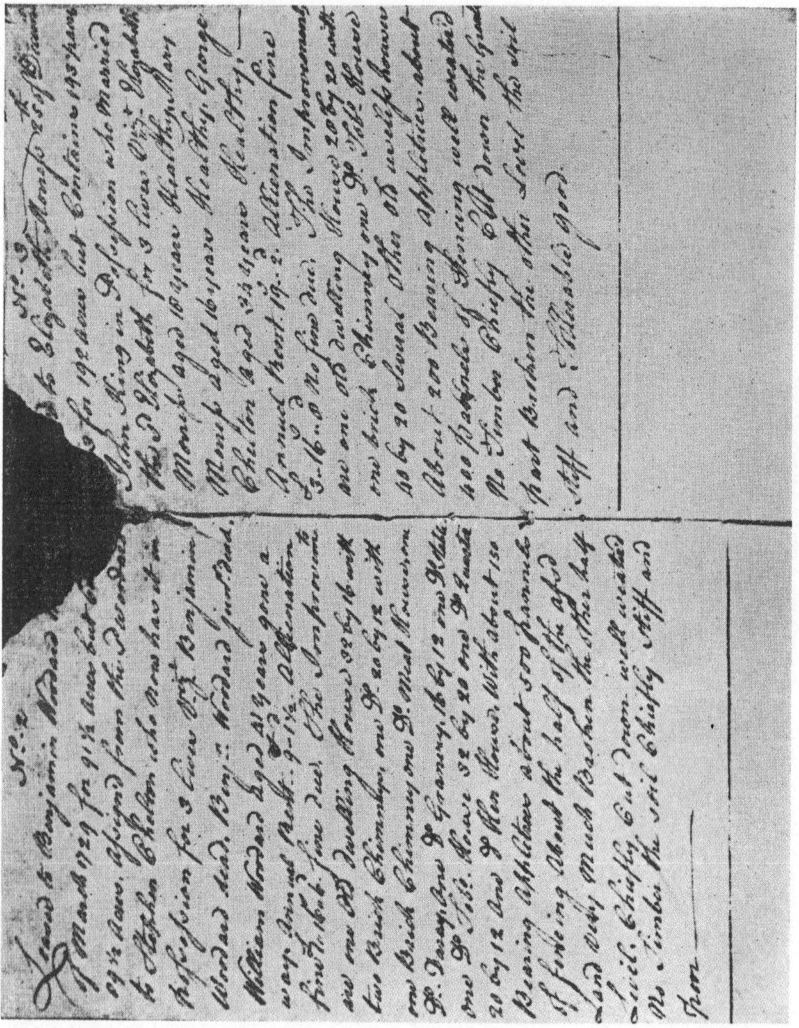

No. 2

Leased to Benjamin Woodard [illegible] of March 1729 for 91½ acres but [illegible] 69½ acres. Assigned from the sd Woodard to Stephen Chelton who now has it in possession for 3 lives Viz. Benjamin Woodard dead. Benjn. Woodard junr. dead. William Woodard aged 41 years gone a way. Annual Rent .. 9 - 1½. Allienation fine to 16 ob. fine due. The Improvemts are one old dwelling House 32 by 16 with two Brick Chimneys, one Do. 20 by 12 with one Brick Chimney one Do. Meat House one Do. Dary. one Do Granery 16 by 12 one Do. Stable one Do. Tobo. House 32 by 20 one Do Quarter 20 by 12 one Do Hen House. With about 150 Bearing apple trees about 500 pannels of fencing About the half of the afsd Land very much Broken the other half Level. Chiefly Cut down well watered No Timber the soil Chiefly Stiff and poor ——

No. 3

[illegible] to Elizabeth Money 25th of Decem[illegible] for 192 acres but Contains 193 [illegible] John King in Possession who married the sd Elizabeth for 3 lives Viz. Elizabeth Money aged 18 years Healthy. Mary Money aged 16 years Healthy. George Chelton aged 34 years Healthy. — Annual Rent 19 .. 2. Allienation fine £3 - 16 - 8 No fine due. The Improvements are one old dwelling House 20 by 20 with one brick Chimney one Do. Tobo. House 40 by 20 Several other old useless houses About 200 Bearing apple trees about 400 pannels of fencing well watered No Timber Chiefly Cut down the great part Broken the other Level the soil stiff and Tollerable good.

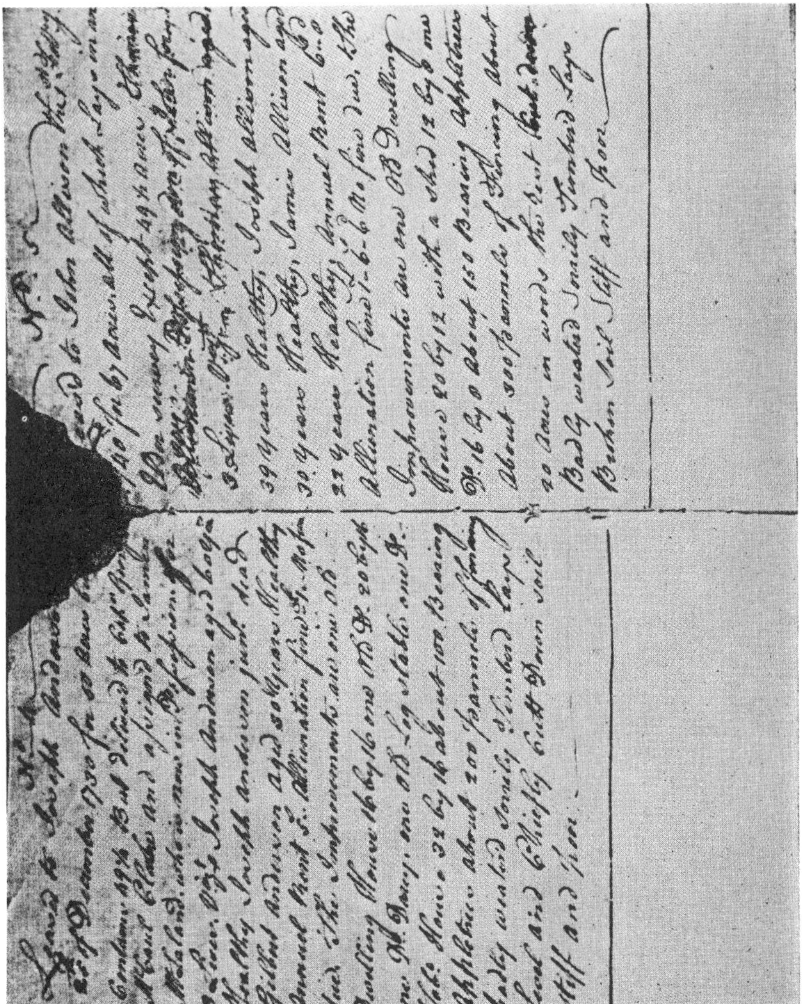

No. 4

Leased to Joseph Anderson [illegible]
25 of December 1730 for 50 Acres [illegible]
Contains 49½ But delivered to Capt. Geo[illegible]
McCaul Clarke and assigned to James
McLaland. who is now in Possession for
3 Lives. Viz.t Joseph Anderson aged 60 years
Healthy Joseph Anderson jun.r dead
Gilbert Anderson aged 30 years Healthy
Annual Rent 5/. Allienation fine 2/1. No fine
due. The Improvements are one Old
Dwelling House 16 by 16 one Old D.o 20 by 16
one D.o Dairy. one Old Log stable and D.o
Tob.o House 32 by 16 about 100 Bearing
Appletrees about 200 pannels of fencing
badly watered Sorrily Timbered Lays
Level and Chiefly Cutt Down soil
Stiff and poor.

No. 5

Leased to John Allison the [illegible] of
1740 for 67 Acres. all of which Lays in an
Elder survey Except 49½ Acres [illegible]
[illegible] Possession [illegible] for
3 Lives. Viz.t [illegible] Allison aged
39 years Healthy, Joseph Allison aged
30 years Healthy, James Allison aged
22 years Healthy, Annual Rent 6.s 8d
Allienation fine 1-6-6 No fine due, The
Improvements are one Old Dwelling
House 20 by 12 with a shed 12 by 8 one
D.o 16 by 8 about 150 Bearing Appletrees
about 300 pannels of Fencing about
40 Acres in woods the rest [illegible]
Badly watered Sorrily Timbered Lays
Broken Soil Stiff and poor.

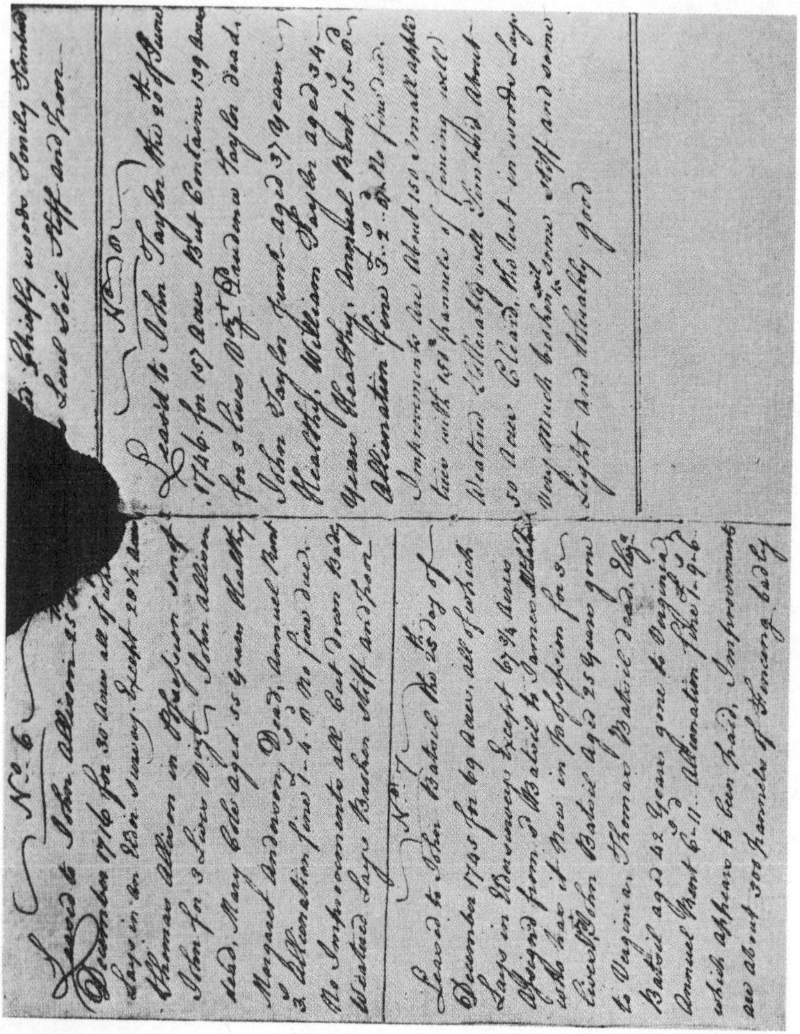

No. 6

Leased to John Allison 25 [illegible] December 1716 for 30 Acres all of which Lays in an Eder Survey Except 20½ Acres [illegible] Thomas Allison in Possession son of John for 3 Lives Vizt John Allison dead, Mary Cole aged 55 Years Healthy Margaret Anderson Dead, Annual Rent 3s Allienation fine 1-4-0 No fine due. No Improvements all Cut down Badly Weatered Lays Broken stiff and poor

[illegible] Chiefly woods Sorily Timbered [illegible] Level Soil Stiff and poor—

No. 7

Leased to John Batsil the 25th day of December 1745 for 69 Acres, all of which Lays in Eder survey Except 67¾ Acres Assigned from sd Batsil to James McSal[illegible] who has it Now in Possession for 3 lives Vizt John Batsil Aged 25 Years gone to Virginia, Thomas Batsil dead. Eliza Batsil aged 42 Years gone to Virginia Annual Rent 6-11. Allienation fine 1-9-6 which appears to been paid, Improvements are about 300 pannels of Fencing badly

No. 8

Leased to John Taylor the 20th of June 1746 for 157 Acres But Contains 139 Acres for 3 lives Vizt Prudence Taylor dead, John Taylor Junr aged 37 Years Healthy, William Taylor aged 34 Years Healthy, Annual Rent 15-0 Allienation fine 3-2-0 No fine due. Improvements are About 150 small apple tree with 150 pannels of fencing well Weatered Tollerably well Timbered About 50 Acres Cleard, the rest in woods Lays Very Much broken soil some stiff and some Light and tollerably good

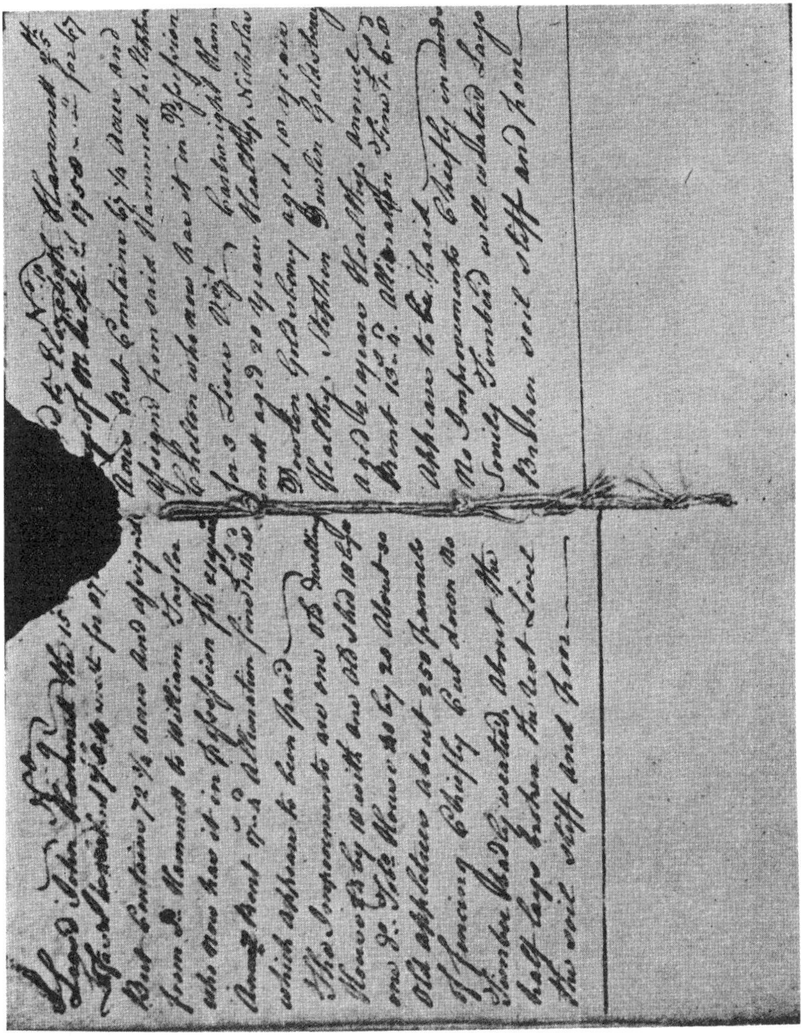

No. 9
Leased John Hammett the 15 [illegible]
[illegible] 17[illegible] [illegible] for 07 [illegible]
But Contains 72 1/2 Acres And assigned
from Do. Hammett to William Taylor
who now has it in possession [illegible]
Annual Rent [illegible] Allienation fine [illegible]
which appears to been paid
The Improvements are one Old dwelling
House 16 by 10 with one Old shed 10 by [illegible]
one Do. Tob. House 20 by 20 About 30
Old appletrees about 250 pannels
of fencing Chiefly Cut down No
Timber badly watered About the
half lays broken the rest Level
the soil stiff and poor

No. 10
[illegible] to Elizabeth Hammett [illegible]
[illegible] of March [illegible] 1750 [illegible] for 67
Acres But Contains 67 1/4 Acres and
Assigned from said Hammett to Stephen
Chelton who now has it in Possession
for 3 Lives Vizt. Cartwright Ham-
mett aged 20 years Healthy, Nicholas
Dowlin Goldsberry aged 10 years
Healthy. Stephen Dowlin Goldsberry
aged [illegible] years Healthy. Annual
Rent [illegible] Allienation Fine [illegible]
Appears to be paid
No Improvements Chiefly in woods
Lonily Timbered well watered Lays
Broken soil stiff and poor

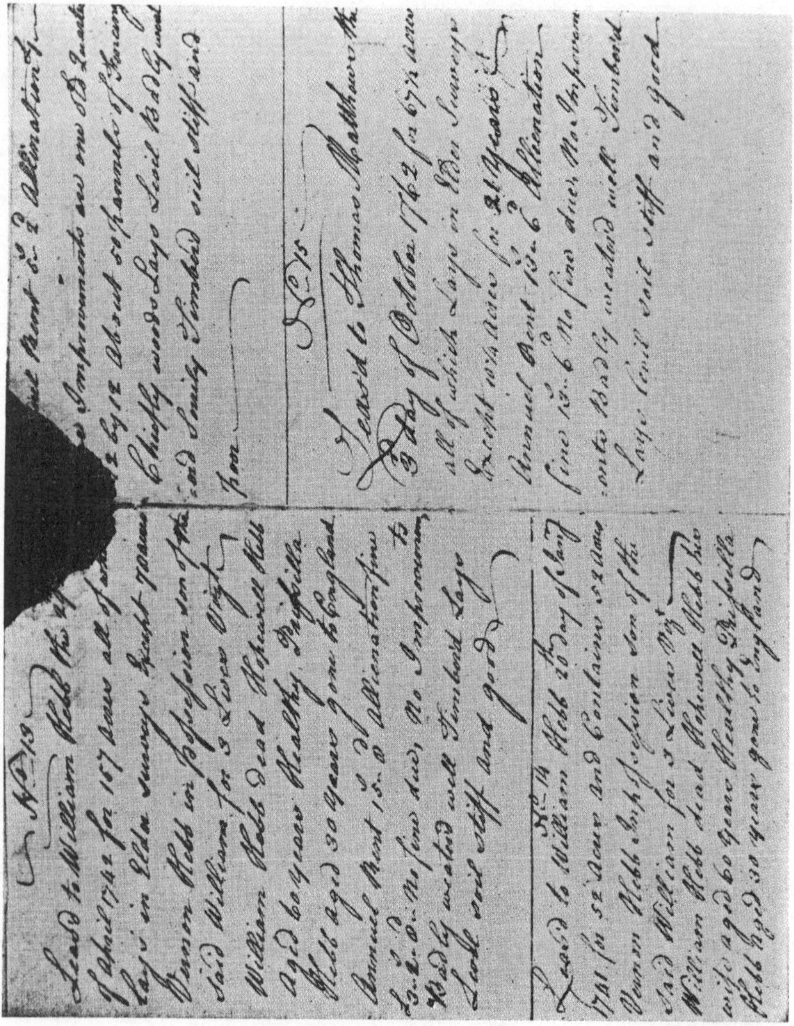
No. 13
Leased to William Hebb the 4th of April 1742 for 167 Acres all of which Lays in Elder Swamps Except 70 Acres
Vernon Hebb in possession son of the said William for 3 Lives Vizt
William Hebb Dead Hopewell Hebb Aged 60 years Healthy Priscilla Hebb aged 30 years gone to England
Annual Rent 15.0 Alienation fine £3.2.0. No fine due, No Improvements
Badly wasted well Timbered Lays Low and stiff and good

No. 14
Leased to William Hebb the 20 day of Jany 1751 for 52 Acres and Contains 52 Acres
Vernon Hebb in possession son of the said William for 3 Lives Vizt
William Hebb dead Hopewell Hebb his wife aged 60 years Healthy Priscilla Hebb aged 30 years gone to England

Annual Rent 2.2 Alienation fine
The Improvements are one old Quarter 12 by 12 about 50 pannels of fencing
Chiefly wood Lays Soil Badly and Sandy Timbered soil stiff and poor

No. 15
Leased to Thomas Matthews the 3 day of October 1762 for 67½ Acres all of which Lays in Elder Swamps
Except 21 Acres
Annual Rent 13.6 Alienation fine 13.6 No fine due, No Improvements
Badly wasted well Timbered Lays Low and stiff and good

"State of His Lordship's Manors," 1766, 1767, 1768. Rent Rolls—Partial Census

"Frederick the sixth, last Lord Baltimore, was born Feb. 6, 1731/2. His guardians, during the brief period of his minority which remained after his succession to the title, were John Sharpe, Esq., a barrister, and the Right Honorable Arthur Onslow, Speaker of the House of Commons." *

"——, Frederick, it was admitted, enjoyed from this heritage at the time of his marriage in 1753 [to Lady Diana Egerton, who d. Aug. 1758] a yearly revenue of £9,500, and at the time of his death in 1771, the amount had increased to £12,000." †

Mr. Arthur Trader, C. C. Land Commissioner's Office, Annapolis, Md., writes: "We have never published a list of Manors as recorded in our records, as the office has always considered them to be private estate of the Lords Baltimore, and would properly belong to the separate estate of the Proprietary."

"All of these lands were either sold by private sale, before the Revolution, or by the Intendent of the Revenue, as confiscated British property. They were not sold under their Manor names, but as seated farm lands."

The following reports are carefully prepared for printing from photostatic copies of the original unbound and much worn record book, extending across 2 pp. each $12^1/_2'' \times 17^1/_2''$, and from a few separate sheets. It has seemed impractical to here reproduce these large sheets in facsimile, and they represent the discoveries to date amongst the historical treasures of this character in the Maryland Archives. They are published through the coöperation and courtesy of the Maryland Historical Society.

Abbreviations Adopted for Column Headings to Conserve Space.

[1], [2], etc.—"No. of Lot or Plat."
(A)—"Date of Lease."
(B)—"To Whom Leased."
(C)—"No. of Acres."
(D)—"Tenant in Pofsefsion."
(E)—"Annual Rent."
(F)—"Alien^a. Fine," "Fines Due."
(G)—"Quality of the Land."
(H)—"Improvements."
(K)—"Price per Acre."
(L)—"On What Lives or Term of Years," "now held."
(M)—"Ages of the Persons mentioned in the Lease & other remarks."
(M [1])—"Incumbrances or Lives and Ages."

* "*The Lords Baltimore and the Maryland Palatinate,*" Clayton Colman Hall, p. 162.

† *Ibid.*, pp. 166, 167.

2

Note:

"Dead" and "Expired," wherever written in "(M)" appear in a handwriting different from the excellent writing of the various reports.

The ages of the Lessees, see "(L)," "(M)," (M^1), appear to be calculated as for 1766, 1767, 1768, as given on each Manor List. This is valuable genealogical source material. G. M. B.

SUMMARY OF THE STATE OF LORD BALTIMORE'S MANNOURS, 1766–'68.

The half sheets 12 × $19\frac{1}{4}$ in great detail present the report of Hor^o. Sharpe and Danl. Dulany.

"Bills of Exchange Remitted"	Sterling.
1766, Nov. 1, By the Ship Baltimore	107. 13. 9
November 20, By the Ship Matthias	125. 4. 9
December 7, By the Ship Brandon	49. 4. $1\frac{1}{2}$
1767, March 11, By the Ship Leeds	3. 9. 0
June 14, By the Ship Elizabeth	27. 0. 0
July 30, By the Ship Betsey	71. 2. 0
Sept. 3, By the Ship S——	46. 14. 5
Sept. 14, By the Ship Neptune	1766. 14. $9\frac{1}{2}$
Sept. 15, By the Ship Samuel	15. 8. $9\frac{1}{4}$
Novem. 2, By the Baltimore Packet	1363. 18. $5\frac{1}{2}$
Novem. 24, By the Ship Lord Legonier,	284. 11. $6\frac{1}{4}$
1768, Apr. 19, By John Morton Jordan, Esqr.	2569. 3. $11\frac{3}{4}$
Total	£6510. 5. $6\frac{1}{2}$

This report covers a total of £10,341. 14. 5 and the following "Mannours" in the order as reported: *

Ann Arundel,	$10,680\frac{7}{8}$ acres.
Conegocheague,	11,586 acres.
Queen Anne,	6,000 a.
Gunpowder,	$7,265\frac{2}{8}$ a.
Chaptico,	18,546 a.
Collington,	$1,297\frac{2}{8}$ a.
Calverton,	7,230 a.
Kent,	8,000 a.
Beaverdam,	7,680 a.
Zachariah,	9,637 a.
Nanticoke,	5,449 a.
West St. Mary's,	3,091 a.

* Those desiring further details are referred to the originals preserved by the Maryland Historical Society, which kindly furnished the photostatic copies from which these records are taken.

Mill,	2,696 a.
Woolsey,	$3{,}131\,^{3}/_{8}$ a.
Snow Hill, St. John's, St. Barbara's,	$982\,^{4}/_{8}$.
Manockacy,	Plat not yet returned.
North East,	Ditto.
Elk,	Ditto.
Wecomico,	Not yet surveyed.
My Ladys,	Suit depending about this.

Connaught, This is the Man^{r}. that was granted Col^{o}. Talbot.
Woolcote, 200 a. Cut off by the Divisional Line.
White Plains, 812 a. Escheat.
Abbington, 109 a. Escheat.

Total contents on Survey $114{,}633\,^{6}/_{8}$ a.;—Quantity now for Sale $69{,}736\,^{2}/_{8}$ a.; Quantity Sold, $17{,}015\,^{1}/_{4}$ a. for 1834l. 14. 5; etc.

State of His Lordships Manor in Kent County, 1766. (I)

[12]. (A) 1731, Septr. 9th.; (B) John Keeting; (D) William Keeting; (C) 100; (E) 0. 10. 0; (L) William & Mary Keeting.

[36]. (A) Ditto; (B) Samuel Norris; (D) Rachel Hynson; (C) 56; (E) 0. 5. 7$^{1}/_{2}$; (L) Saml. & Rich^{d}. Norris. This Lease was for 95 acres, 39 acres of which runs into other lands.

[48]. —— Septr. 29; (B) Rebecca Taylor; (D) Bartus Piner; (C) 133; (E) 0. 13. 4; (L) Bartus Piner.

[11]. (A) 1738, Novr. 7; (B) James Wallace; (D) John Beesley; (C) 64; (E) 0. 6. 6; (L) Mary Beesley.

[41]. (A) 1742, June 5; (B) Anthony Camron; (D) John Maxwell; (C) 130; (E) 0. 13. 0; (L) William Maxwell & And^{w}. Jemison.

[47]. (A) Ditto; (B) John Burgan; (D) William Merrit; (C) 30; (E) 0. 3. 0; (L) James & Benjamin Burgin.

[54]. (A) ——, July 9; (B) John Greenwood; (D) John Greenwood; (C) 98; (E) 0. 9. 11; (L) John Greenwood, Senr. [& Joseph Greenwood is crossed out].

[4]. (A) ——, Augt. 20; (B) John Cove; (D) William Waters; (C) 96; (E) 0. 9. 7$^{1}/_{2}$; (L) Elizabeth Cove & Job Cove, Junr. [Crossed out "John —— Job Cove, quere if all alive."]

[42]. (A) Ditto; (B) Isaac Ridgrave; (D) Isaac Ridgrave; (C) 134; (E) 0. 13. 6; (L) Isaac Ridgrave, Junr., Danniell [?] & Eliz: Ridgrave.

[25]. (A) 1744, July 26; (B) Thos. Perkins; (D) Thos. Perkins; (C) 140; (E) 0. 14. 0; (L) Thos. & Isaac Perkins & Mathias Harris.

[46]. (A) 1743, Feby. 6; (B) John Page; (D) Robt. Maxwell; (C) 11; (E) 0. 1. 1; (L) William Thornton [Crossed out but legible] "Lessor removed from —— 29, 1762 or 21 years.

[46]. (A) 1745, June 10; (B) John Page; (D) Ditto; (C) 30; (E) 0. 3. 0; (L) Jeremiah Luther "Burchmall."

[46]. (A) Ditto; (B) John Page; (D) Ditto; (C) 50; (E) 0. 5. 0; (L) Aquilla & Mary Page.

[30]. (A) —— Dec. 20; (B) John Gleaves; (D) John Gleaves; (C) 400; (E) 2. 0. 0; (L) John Gleaves.

[18]. (A) Ditto; (B) John Wallace, Senr.; (D) Phil Warner; (C) 53; (E) 0. 5. 4; (L) John Wallace, Junr.

[5]. (A) 1746, April 18; (B) Geo. Garnet; (D) Dennis "Thahon" [Shahon?]; (C) 114; (E) 0. 11. 5; (L) George Thomas & George Garnet, Junr.

[2]. (A) —— Sepr. 29; (B) William Walls; (D) Henry Bodien; (C) 114; (E) 0. 11. 6; (L) William & Saml. Walls.

[55]. (A) ——, Ditto; (B) James Greenwood; (D) Saml. Groome; (C) 160; (E) 0. 16. 0; (L) Jane Greenwood.

[31]. (A.) ——, Ditto; (B) Eliz: Hickman; (D) Thos. Gilbert; (C) 90; (E) 0. 9. 0; (L) John & Eliz: Hickman.

[46]. (A) ——, Ditto; (B) Eliz: Hickman; (D) Robert Maxwell; (C) $15^{3}/_{4}$; (E) 0. 1. $7^{3}/_{4}$; (L) John & Eliz: Hickman.

[3]. (A) 1747, April 7; (B) Henry Brooke; (D) Henry Bodun; (C) 184; (E) 0. 18. 5; (L) Robert Peacock [& Mary Brooks, quere Mary Brooke, stricken out].

[16]. (A) ——, May 15; (B) Sarah Dier; (D) Ditto; (C) 90; (E) 0. 9. 0; (L) Tenant at will.

[No. 37]. (A) 1753, April 10th; (B) William Walls; (D) William Walls; (C) 120; (E) 0. 12. 0; (L) Elizabeth, Samuel & Eliz: Walls, Junr.

[10]. (A) 1747, May 15; (B) John Graham; (D) John Graham; (C) 31; (L) John & James Graham.

[57]. (A) Ditto; (B) Suttor [?] Burger; (D) John Burger; (C) 13; (E) 0. 1. 4; (L) One Life Sarah Burger ["Two Lives John Moris Burger &" are stricken out]. "Lease 18 acres."

[26]. (A) 1743, Augt. 5; (B) John Shawhan; (D) John Shawhan; (C) 130; (E) 0. 13. 0; (L) John, Elizabeth & John Shawhan, Junr.

[51]. (A) 1748, Jany. 25; (B) Mary Dining; (D) Annas Glenn; (C) 100; (E) 0. 10. 0; (L) Mary, James & John Dining.

[40]. (A) 1751, May 9; (B) Susannah Hudson; (D) J —— Jobson; (C) 83; (E) 0. 8. 4; (L) Moses & Mary Hudson.

[28]. (A) Ditto; (B) James Hudson; (D) —— Hudson; (C) 50; (E) 0. 5. 0; (L) Moses & Sarah Hudson, "quere."

[44]. (A) ——, October 24; (B) John Tilden; (D) W —— Tilden; (C) 190; (E) 1. 1. 0; (L) William Blay Tilden & John Withered.

[38]. (A) 1752, Augt. 20; (B) Peirce Lamb; (D) Peirce Lamb; (C) 197; (E) 0. 19. 8; (L) Peirce, George & John Lamb.

[11]. (A) 1753, Feby. 1; (B) John Maxwell; (D) —— Maxwell; (C) ——; (E) 0. 4. $10^{3}/_{4}$; (L) John & Robt. Maxwell, Junr. & Robt. Maxwell, younger.

[29]. (A) ——, April 20; (B) John Maxwell; (D) John Maxwell; (C) 200; (E) 1. 0. 0; (L) James [torn].

[50]. (A) ——, April 6; (B) Robert Guy; (D) Robert Guy; (C) 80; (E) 0. 8. 0; (L) Robert, Penelope & John Guy, Son of Robt.

[20]. (A) Ditto; (B) John Graham; (D) John Graham; (C) 142; (E) 0. 14. 3; (L) John, James & Andrew Graham.

[49]. (A) ——, April 10; (B) Andrew Hynson; (D) Bartus Piner; (C) 38; (E) 0. 3. $9^{1}/_{2}$; (L) Andrew, Sarah & Thomas Hynson.

[19]. (A) Ditto; (B) Ebenezer Reyner; (D) Ebenezer Reyner; (C) 360; (E) 1. 16. 0; (L) Eben^{r}. Reyner [Amilia & Maynard are stricken out].

[46]. (A) Ditto; (B) John Page; (D) Robert Maxwell; (C) 146; (E) 0. 14. 6; (L) Aquilla Page.

[46]. (A) ——, August 10; (B) John Page; (D) Ditto; (C) 25; (E) 0. 2. 6; (L) Aquilla & Mary Page.

[51]. (A) 1753, April 10; (B) Mary Thear; (D) Annas Glenn; (C) 15; (E) 0. 2. 0; (L) Richard & John Scago & Lessee.

[43]. (A) 1747, June 25; (B) William Rasin; (D) Wm. Wothered; (C) 230; (E) 1. 3. 0; (L) William & John Wothered.

[17]. (A) 1740, Novr. 6; (B) Corn^{s}. Rain; (D) Jacob Falkner; (C) 79; (E) 0. 7. 11; (L) Lives unknown, gone away many years ago Lives Corn^{s}. Rain & Joseph & Ruth his Son & Daughter. Corn^{s}. Rain seen ab^{o}. 2 years ago.

[6]. (A) 1745, Decr. 20; (B) John Gilbert; (D) John Gilbert; (C) $180^{1}/_{2}$; (E) 0. 19. $8^{1}/_{2}$; (L) John & Thos Gilbert & Sam. Merrit. Leased for 200 acres but by order of the agent resurveyed & found to contain $180^{1}/_{2}$ acres.

[30]. (A) 1735, Sepr. 1st.; (B) Job Cove [Cave?]; (D) John Gleaves; (C) 50; (E) 0. 5. 0; (L) Lives unknown, gone away many years ago, supposed to be Dead.

[9]. (A) 1746, June 7; (B) Henry Spencer; (D) Sarah Mullin; (C) 24; (E) 0. 2. 5; (L) Tenant at will.

[13]. (A) 1760, Aug^{t}. ——; (B) John Wallace; (D) John Wallace; (C) 104; (E) 1. 0. 10; (L) John & Mary Wallace & Ja^{s}. Graham.

[53]. (A) ——, Aug. 12; (B) Francis Lamb; (D) Francis Lamb; (C) 214; (E) 2. 2. 10; (L) Francis, John & Thos. Lamb.

[54]. (A) ——, Ditto; (B) John Greenwood; (D) John Greenwood; (C) 5; (E) 0. 0. 11; (L) John Greenwood, Senr. John Greenwood, Junr. & Fc [Jo?] Greenwood son of John, Junr. The last Life gone away, not been found.

[1]. (A) ——, Augt. 14; (B) Thos. Perkins; (D) Isaac Perkins; (C) 62; (E) 0. 12. 6; (L) Isaac Perkins, John Brooks & Saml. Mansfield.

[7]. (A) ——, Ditto; (B) John Wallace; (D) Philip Warner; (C) 13; (E) 0. 2. 6; (L) John & Francis Wallace, Sons of Lessee.

[24]. (A) ——, Augt. 18; (B) Hezekiah Cooper; (D) Hez^{h}. Cooper; (C) 170; (E) 1. 14. 0; (L) Hez^{h}. & Peregrine Cooper their son. [Ft appears likely that Mary Cooper is written above "&" and is crossed out. "Wm Jones" is also crossed out].

[14]. (A) ——, Ditto; (B) Hannah Billis; (D) Alphonso Cornegys; (C) 30; (E) 0. 6. 0; (L) Lives in Being, unknown, ["all alive," in different handwriting].

[No. 8]. (A) ——, Augt. 19; (B) George Little; (D) George Little; (C) 195; (E) 1. 19. 0; (L) George, Mary his wife & Ann Little.

[No. 8]. (A) ——, Ditto; (B) George Little; (D) Ditto; (C) 9; (E) 0. 2. 0; (L) Same Lives.

[6]. (A) 1760, Augt. 14th.; (B) John Gilbert; (D) John Gilbert; (C) 18; (E) 0. 4. 0; (L) John, Ann & John Gilbert, Junr.

[33]. (A) 1764, Feby. 18; (B) Stephen Dening; (D) Stephen Dening; (C) 86; (E) 0. 17. 4; (L) 21 years. 84 acres in all.

[22]. (A) 1763, Septr. 10; (B) John Wallace; (D) John Wallace; (C) 163; (E) 1. 12. $7^{1}/_{2}$; (L) 21 years.

[35]. (A) 1764, Feby. 18; (B) John Day; (D) Bartus Piner Guard^{n}. of J. Day; (C) 141; (E) 1. 8. 3; (L) 21 years.

[34]. (A) ——, Ditto; (B) Arim^{a}. Day; (D) Bartus Piner; (C) 121; (E) 1. 4. 3; (L) 21 years.

[27]. (A) ——, March 2^{d}.; (B) John Hudson; (D) Ruth Hudson; (C) 62; (E) 0. 12. $5^{1}/_{2}$; (L) 21 years.

[23]. (A) ——, 3d; (B) John Graham; (D) John Graham; (C) $18^{3}/_{4}$; (E) 0. 3. 9; (L) 21 years.

[52]. (A) ——, June 9; (B) George Lamb; (D) George Lamb; (C) 57; (E) 0. 11. 6; (L) 21 years.

[15]. (A) ——, Octr. 24; (B) John March; (D) John March; (C) $247^{1}/_{2}$; (E) 2. 9. 6; (L) 21 years.

[——]. (C) 6; (E) 0. 1. 4; (L) Not under Lease, Church Land p^{d}. by the Vestry.

[39]. (A) 1747, Augt. 1; (B) Robert Hart; (D) Robert Hart; (C) 450; (E) 2. 5. 0; (L) Held by Robert Hart of Cecil County. Terms of the Lease not known to the Steward.

Totals: (C) $7015^{1}/_{2}$; (E) 43. 17. $19^{1}/_{2}$.

[32]. (A) 1752, April 1; (B) Beale Bordley; (D) Said Bordley; (C) 75; (E) 0. 7. 6; (L) Said Beale Bordley, Margaret Beardley & Loyd Dulany.

"—— Kent County, November, 1766." (II)

"This Manor Laid off May 1," ——.*

(L) William Keeting & Mary Keeting, his Son & Daughter; (M) William 50 & Mary about 53 years of age. Mary Dead.

(L) Samuil Norris & Richard Norris; (M) Saml. ab^{o}. 48 & Richard 40. Leased for 95 acres, 39 acres in other ——.

(L) Bartus Piner; (M) Bartus Piner 47—assigned Apr. 12, 1743. Capons due.

(L) Robt. [?] Jeremiah & John Cove, all left this Province many years ago; (M) quere, Alienations due.

(L) Mary Beesley, Daughter of the Lessee; (M) Mary Beesley aged about 30.

(L) Lessee, Joseph & Ruth Rain his Son & Daughter; (M) Father bought from John Walls & Walls from the Lessee, no assignment from the Lessee to Walls. Lives all moved to Carolina about 15 years ago.

(L) William Maxwell, Son of Robt. & Andrew Jemeson; (M) Wm. Maxwell 47, A. Jemeson 30, left by will from Camron to Maxw—.

(L) James & Benjamin Burgan, Sons of the Lessee; (M) James ab^{o}. 25 & Benj^{a}. ab^{o}. 24—Vide the Date of the Lease.

(L) Lessee; (M) Aged upwards of 70 years.

(L) Lessee, Job Cove Junr. & Eliz: Cove; (M) Lives all left the Province quere gone & if Dead or Living.

(L) Damsell, Eliz: & Isaac Ridgrane, Wife, Son & Daughter of Lessee; (M) Damsell ab^{o}. 50, Eliz: 28, Isaac 26.

(L) Lessee, Elizabeth his Wife & John Shawhon his Son; (M) Lessee 51, wife 50 & son about 27.

(L) Lessee, Isaac Perkins, Son of Ebenezer & Mathias Harris (dead); (M) Lessee 42 (Dead), Isaac Perkins 25, & Math^{s}. Harris 50.

(L) Aquila Page & William Burchnell; (M) Aquila Page, 22, Wm. Burchnell 30.

(L) [Je]remiah Luther Burchnell; (M) Aged about 30 years.

(L) John Gleaves; (M) John Gleaves about 28.

(L) John Wallace; (M) John Wallace about 22. Dead & the Land Sold.

(L) Lessee, Thomas & George Garnett his Sons; (M) Lessee, 60, Dead, Thomas 30, Dead, George 28, Quere Fine. 2 Lives Dead.

(L) Lessee & Samuel Walls his Son; (M) Lessee about —. Dead, Samuel 33. Quere Fine.

* But the right half of the record survives,—torn and irregular. See Frontispiece.

(L) Jane Greenwood; (M) Aged 25 yrs. Assign[d]. 3[d] Feby. 1755, Consideration £20 ——.

(L) John & Elizabeth Hickman, Son & Daughter of Lessee; (M) John 25, Eliz: ab[o]. 30, quere Fine.

(L) Same Lives.

(L) Tenant at will.

(L) Robert Peacock Jun[r]. & Mary Brooks; (M) Peacock ab[o]. 23, Mary Brooks abo —— Dead, Bodier Guard. 1 Life dropt.

(L) Tenant at will.

(L) Lessee & his Son James Graham.

(L) John Morris Burgan & Sarah Burgan; (M) J. M. Burgan Dead. Lives both under 30. N. B. Lease mentions 18 acres.

(L) William Wethered & John Wethered.

(L) Lessee & his Son, James Hart; (M) Lessee about 60, James about 30, Dead.

(L) Lessee, Thomas Gilbert & Samuel Merritt; (M) Lessee ab[o]. 40, Thomas 30 & Samuel 22, Leased for 200 acres but resuryey'd & contains only 180$^1/_2$ by order of the Agent.

(L) Lessee & his Sons James & John Deming; (M) Lessee 40 Dead, James 23, John 21. N. B. Glenn holds 12 acres on his lease & another for 15 acres.

(L) Moses & Mary Hudson, children of the Lessee; (M) Moses 16, Mary 20, by assignment consid[n]. £130 —— Capons in ——.

(L) Moses & Sarah Brother & Sister of the Lessee; (M) Moses 16, Sarah 17.

(L) William Blay [May?] Tilden & John Wethered.

(L) Lessee, Margaret his Wife & Loyd Dulany.

(L) Lessee, George & John Lamb, his Brothers; (M) Lessee 34, George 30, John 27.

(L) Lessee, Robert Maxwell Son of Robert & Robert Maxwell Son of Wm.; (M) Lessee 40, Robert, Son of Robert 30, Robert, Son of Wm. 13.

(L) Lessee, Penelope his Wife & John Guy his Son; (M) Lessee 45, Penelope 40, John the Son 16.

(L) John Graham, James & Andrew his Sons; (M) John 48, Dead, James 24 Dead, Andrew 21.

(L) Lessee, Thomas & Sarah his Children; (M) Lessee 40, Thomas 30, Sarah 15. Wrong Information abo. Lives.

(L) Lessee & Emelia Reyner his Daughter; (M) Lessee 40, Emelia 18.

(L) Aquila Page.

(L) Lessee, Richard & John Scaggs; (M) Mary Thear 60; Richard 29, John 25.

(L) Lessee, Robert Maxwell, Son of Robt. & Robert Maxwell, Son of Wm.; (M) Lessee 40, Robt. Son of Robert 30, Robert Son of Wm. 13.

(L) Elizabeth his Wife, Samuel his Son & Elizabeth his Daughter; (M) Wife 54, Samuel 33, Eliz:th Daughter 23.

(L) Aquila & Mary Page; (M) Aquila 22, Mary 25.

(L) Lessee, his Wife Mary & James Graham; (M) Lessee 28, his Wife 27, James Graham 25.

(L) Francis, John & Thomas Lamb; (M) Francis 78, John 21, Thomas 10.

(L) Lessee, John his Son & Joseph the Son of John his Son.

(L) "Isaac Perkins, Son of Eben^r^. John Brooks, Son of Philip & Saml. Mansfield Junr."

(L) John & Francis Wallace, Sons of the Lessee; (M) John about 21 Dead, Francis 16.

(L) Lessee, his Wife & John Gilbert Son of Thomas; (M) Lessee 40, Wife 35, John Son of Thomas 13 ——.

(L) Lessee, *Martha his Wife* & Son Peregrine; (M) Lessee 37, Wife 30 Dead, Son very Young.

(L) Lessee, Peregrine Cooper, Son of Hez^h^. & James Jones, Son of Peter; (M) Lessee 26, the others very young, quere Fine.

(L) Mary his Wife & Ann his Daughter; (M) Lessee 40, Wife 50, Daughter 8.

(L) Term of twenty one years.

(L) Ditto; (M) Renewed Lease.

(L) Ditto; (M) Stephen Denning hold 86 acres & M^r^. Wicks an^o^. pay 17/4 Rev.

(L) Ditto. [60]. (L) Ditto. [61]. (L) Ditto. [62]. (L) Ditto. [63]. (L) Ditto.

(L) Ditto. [65]. (L) Not under Lease. Rent p^d^. by the Vestry.

(L) Cirtified Septm^r^. 16th. 1706; (M) Rented.

"State of His Lordships Manor in Kent County," 1766. (III)*

[1]. (M [1]) 3 Lives, Ages from 16 to 24; (C) 62; (G) Good Land, but all cleared except one corner where remains some timber; (H) None; (K) 22/.

[15. 5. 02]. (M [1]) 2 Lives, Ages 33 & 60; (C) 114; (G) Good Land, but little or no Timber—not quite so good as No. 1; (H) Of no great value; (K) 25/6, quere Fine.

[15. 10. 03]. (M [1]) 1 Life, age 23; (C) 184; (G) Good Land equal to No. 1; (H) good; (K) 27/.

[4]. (M [1]) 3 Lives, left the province, quere 2 alive; (C) 96; (G) Indifferent Land, Sandy & but little Timber; (H) pretty good; (K) 22/.

[23. 9. 05]. (M [1]) 1 Life, Age 28 ["60" and "30" are crossed out "3 Lives"]; (C) 114; Good white clay land, sandy, something better than No. 4, very little Timber; (H) good; (K) 21/6, quere Fine.

[6]. (M [1]) 3 Lives, ages 40, 30 & 22; (C) 180½; (G) Rather better than No. 1, very little Timber; (H) Pretty good. 1 Life only, left 30 years.

[6 do]. (M [1]) 3 Lives, ages 40, 35, 13; (C) 18; (G) As good as No. 6, but cleared of Timber; (H) Pretty good; (K) for both [6] & [6 do] 24/.

[7]. (M [1]) 2 Lives, ages 21 & 16; (C) 13; (G) The same as No 6, cleared of Timber; (H) None.

[8]. (M [1]) 3 Lives, ages 40, 30 & 8; (G) About 9 acres Timber, equal to No 6, the whol quantity of little value; (K) 24/.

[9]. (M [1]) None; (C) 24; (G) Middling good Land, but Clear'd; (H) None; (K) 30/.

[19. 1. 010]. (M [1]) 2 Lives, Ages 50 & 25; (C) 31; (G) Full as good as No 6, with plenty of Timber to support it; (H) None; (K) 24/.

[13. 9. 011]. (M [1]) 1 Life, age 30; (C) 64; (G) Middling Land, worn & no Timber; (H) 1 dwell'g, H°. 20 X 30, good repair, 50 apple trees; (K) 27/.

[12]. (M [1]) 1 Life, age 50; (C) 100; (G) Pretty good Land, much worn & very little Timber; (H) Tollerably good; (K) 27/.

[13]. (M [1]) 3 Lives, ages 28, 27 & 25; (C) 104; (G) Nearly the same as No 12; (H) of little value; (K) 23/6 Sold.

[14]. (M [1]) 3 Lives, ages 26, 22 & 10; (C) 30; (G) Poor Land & little or no Timber; (H) pretty good; (K) 20/ quere Fine.

* Apparently discriptive of the first list. Note the agreement of acres and the ages for "Lives" mentioned in the leases.—G. M. B.

[15]. (M [1]) 18 years; (C) 247$\frac{1}{2}$; (G) Good Land, with some Timber equal to No 6; (H) very good; (K) 28/.

[16]. (M [1]) None; (C) 90; (G) Middling Land, with a small parcel of Wood; (H) None; (K) 30/.

[17]. (M [1]) Lives gone to Carv^a. 15 years. Leasd. 1740; (C) 79; Poor Land & Sandy, no Timber; (H) pretty good; (K) 24/2 Fines due.

[15. 11. 018]. (M [1]) 1 Life, age 22; (C) 53; (G) Middling Land, with little or no Timber; (H) none; (K) 25/.

[19]. (M [1]) 1 Life, age 40; (C) 360; (G) pretty good Land with Timber sufficient & some Meadow; (H) pretty good; (K) 28/.

[20]. (M [1]) 3 Lives, ages 48, 24 & 21; (C) 142; (G) poor Land & very little Timber; (H) of very little value; (K) 20/.

[21]. (C) 484; (G) Bennetts Bridge, very good Land & plenty of Timber; (K) 31/6.

[22]. (M [1]) 17 years; (C) 163; (G) Indifferent Land & very little Timber; (H) None; (K) 24/. 3 acres Sold at 25/.

[23]. (M [1]) 17$\frac{1}{2}$ years; (C) 18$\frac{3}{4}$; (G) Middling Land & no Timber; (H) of very little value; (K) 24/6. Sold.

[24]. (M [1]) 2 Lives, ages 37, 10. The others very young. (C) 170; (G) very Indifferent, quere Timber; (H) good; (K) 20/.

[25]. (M [1]) 3 Lives, ages 42, 25 & 50; (C) 140; (G) middling Good Land with some Timber; (H) of no great value; (K) 24/.

[22. 10. 15. 26]. (M [1]) 3 Lives, ages 51, 50 & 27; (C) 130; (G) pretty good Land, but scarce of Timber; (H) pretty good; (K) 25/6.

[27]. (M [1]) 17$\frac{1}{2}$ years; (C) 62; (G) middling good Land with some Timber; (H) of very little value; (K) 25/.

[28]. (M [1]) 2 Lives, ages 16 & 17; (C) 50; (G) poor Land & no Timber; (H) 1 small old Log House; (K) 21/.

[29]. (M [1]) 3 Lives, ages 40, 30 & 13; (C) 200; (H) John Maxwell's; (K) 26/6 together with No 41. Sold.

[14. 3. 030]. (M [1]) 1 Life age 28; (C) 400; (G) Good Land with some Timber but scarce for the quantity; (K) 27/6, better than J. Maxwell's.

[Same No]. (M [1]) 3 lives, left the province many years; (C) 50; (G) Middling Land, much worn & no Timber; (H) for these two tracts—of no great value; (K) 28/6. quere alienations.

[21. 11. 15. 31]. (M [1]). 2 Lives, ages 25 & 30; (C) 90; (G) middling good, but worn & no Timber; (K) 23/. quere aliena. Fine.

[32]. (M [1]) J [F?]. B. Bordley, wife & Loyd Dulany; (C) 75; (G) Indifferent & broken with a small parcel of Timber; (H) of very little value; (K) 20/6.

[33]. (M [1]) 17$\frac{1}{2}$ years; (C) 84; (G) poor, having been much worn & little or no Timber; (H) of no great value; (K) 24/.

[34]. (M [1]) $17^{1}/_{2}$ years; (C) 121; (G) middling Land with some little Timber; (H) pretty good; (K) 26/.

[35]. (M [1]) $17^{1}/_{2}$ years; (C) 141; (G) pretty good Land, with some Timber; (H) of very little Value; (K) 27/.

[15. 7. 15. 36]. (M [1]) 2 Lives 38 & 40; (C) 56; (G) Middling Land with some Timber; (H) none; (K) 24/.

[26. 8. 22. 37]. (M [1]) 3 Lives, 54, 33 & 23; (C) 120; (G) Middling Land with very little Timber; (H) of no great value; (K) 22/.

[38]. (M [1]) 3 Lives, 34, 30 & 27; (C) 197; (G) Good Land with some Timber; (H) pretty good; (K) 23/6.

[39]. (M [1]) 2 Lives, ages 60 & 30; (C) 450; (G) Middling Land with some Timber; (H) pretty good; (K) 27/. Tenanted in part.

[40]. (M [1]) 2 Lives, 16 & 20; (C) 83; (G) pretty much worn, with no Timber; (G) pretty good; (K) 22/. Sold assigned. Cons^{n}. £130.

[18. 20. 41]. (M [1]) 2 Lives, ages 47 & 30; (C) 130; (H) very good.

[41]. (M [1]) 3 Lives, 40, 30 & 13; (C) 49; (H) very good. (K) 26/6. This and the previous tract with No. 29 Sold.

[25. 11. 042]. (M [1]) 3 Lives, 50, 28 & 26; (C) 134; (H) Middling Land, with some Timber; (K) 24/.

[43]. (M [1]) 2 Lives, Wm. & Jno. Wethered ab^{o} 21 & 26; (C) 230; (G) Good Land, with some Timber; (H) 1 Fram'd Dwell'g House 18 × 25, good repair; (K) 25/6.

[44]. (M [1]) 2 Lives, Wm. B. Tilden 26 & Jno. Wethered 21; (C) 190; (G) Good Land with some Timber; (H) of not much value; (K) 25/6. Church on this Land.

[45]. (G) Old Land called Ivingo.

[22. 9. 15. 46]. (M [1]) 2 Lives, ages 22 & 30; (C) 30; (K) 27/.

[13. 9. 0. 46]. (M [1]) 1 Life, age 30, (C) 50; (H) Robt. Maxwell's; (K) 28/.

[21. 11. 15. 46]. (M [1]) 2 Lives, 25 & 30; (C) $15^{3}/_{4}$; (H) good Improvements on the $277^{3}/_{4}$ acres but on what part not distinguished; (K) 27/.

[15. 11. 0. 46]. (M [1]) 1 Life, age abo. 22; (C) 146; (K) 28/.

[23. 5. 15. 46]. (M [1]) 2 Lives, ages 22 & 25; (C) 25; (K) 27/.

[Same No]. (M [1]) 16 yrs.; (C) 11; (K) 28/.

(G) For the preceding 6 tracts good Land with some Timber.

[22. 11. 047]. (M [1]) 2 Lives, ages 25 & 24; (C) 30; (G) Middling Land & very little Timber; (H) of no great value; (K) 23/. vide Date of Lease.

[8. 9. 048]. (M [1]) 1 Life 47; (C) 133; (G) Middling good Land with some Timber; (H) none; (K) 26/. Sold. Fine chag^{d}. £5. 6. 8.

[49]. (M [1]) 3 Lives, ages 40, 30 & 15, vide min.; (C) 38; (G) Middling Land & some Timber; (K) 23/. Sold. Fine chd. 0. 9. 6.

[50]. (M [1]). 3 Lives 45, 40 & 16; (C) 80; (G) Middling Land, scarce any Timber; (H) pretty good; (K) 23/.

[29. 3. 15. 51]. (M [1]) 3 Lives, 40, 23 & 21. N. B. a man Gleen (?) hold 120 acres by the plat in these Leases; (C) 100; (G) Middling Land but little Timber; (H) of not much value; (K) 22/.

[Ditto] 3 ditto, 60, 29 & 25; (C) 15; (G) The same; (K) 22/.

[52]. (M [1]) $17^{3}/_{4}$ years; (C) 57; (G) pretty good Land with Timber to support; (H) good; (K) 25/6.

[53]. (M [1]) 3 Lives 78, 27 & 10; (C) 214; (G) Middling good Land. quere Timber?; (H) very good; (K) 23/6.

[26. 054]. (M [1]) 1 Life, upwards 70; (C) 98; (G) Middling Land, but very little Timber; (H) of no great value; (K) 28/6.

[Same]. (M [1]) 3 Lives, 70, 50, 20; (C) 5; (G) a little Branch for Water; (K) 28/6.

[18. 1. 055] (M [1]) 1 Life age 25 years; (C) 160; (G) pretty good but little or no Timber; (H) of no great value; (K) 27/6. Ap^{d}. 3^{d} Feby. 1755, Cons^{n}. £200.

[56]. (G) old Land calld. Blays Range.

[16. 0. 057]. (M [1]) 1 Life under 30; (C) 13; (G) Medm. Land & no Timber; (H) pretty good.

[Unnumbered]. (M [1]) none; (C) 6; (G) Church Land. Rent pd. by the Vestry; (H) Church. Included in No. 44.

Total acres $7554^{1}/_{2}$.

ANNE ARUNDEL COUNTY

"State of His Lordship's Manor of Ann Arundel, 1767"

Lot 1. (A) March 25th, 1755; (B) William Coale; (C) $114^{3}/_{4}$; (D) John Coale; (E) 5–15–0; (F) 11–10–0; (G) $12^{1}/_{2}$; (H) $127^{1}/_{4}$; (K) John Coale.

Lot 2. (A) ——; (B) Expired; (C) $33^{1}/_{2}$; (D) George Simmons; (E) 1–18–6; (F) 3–17–0; (G) ——; (H) $45^{3}/_{4}$; (K) Joseph Hill.

Lot 3. (A) ——; (B) Expired; (C) 100; (D) John Norris; (E) 5–0–0; (F) 10–0–0; (G) $105^{1}/_{4}$; (K) ——.

Lot 4. (A) ——; (B) Expired; (C) 100; (D) Franklin & Gott; (E) 5–0–0; (F) 10–0–0; (H) $105^{1}/_{4}$; (K) Joseph Hill.

Lot 5. (A) ——; (B) Expired; (C) $59^{1}/_{2}$; (D) Benj^{a}. Ward; (E) 2–19–6; (F) 5–19–0; (H) 57; (K) George Simmons.

Lot 6. (A) Dec. 10th 1747; (B) Henry Hall; (C) 112; (D) Isaac Hall; (E) 4–4–0; (G) $17^{5}/_{8}$; (H) $140^{7}/_{8}$; (K) Isaac Hall.

Lot 7. (A) Feby. 6th. 1746; (B) George Stewart; (C) 150; (D) Lessee; (E) 5–12–6; (F) —— (H) $165^{1}/_{4}$; (K) George Stewart.

Lot 8. (A) Mch. 25, 1751; (B) Ditto; (C) 13; (D) Ditto; (E) 0–13–0; (F) 1–6–0 (K) George Stewart.

Lot 9. (A) Jany. & Feb. 7, 1748; (B) Coale & Gott; (C) 90; (D) Walter Gott; (E) 3–7–6; (F) 6–15–0; (H) $82^{1}/_{2}$; (K) Walter Gott.

Lot 10. (A) Mch. 25, 1760; (B) Walter Gott; (C) 100; (D) Lessee; (E) 5–0–0; (F) 10–0–0; (G) 6; (H) 106; (K) Walter Gott.

Lot 11. (A) Sept. 29th. 1755; (B) Robt. Gott's Exec^{rs}.; (C) $62^{1}/_{2}$; (D) Walter Gott; (E) 3–2–6; (F) 6–5; (H) $57^{1}/_{4}$; (K) Walter Gott.

Lot 12. (A) Sept. 29th. 1755; (B) Isabella Franklin; (C) 100; (D) Lessee; (E) 5–0–0; (F) 10–0–0; (H) $98^{3}/_{4}$; (K) Stephen Steward.

Lot 13. (A) Sept. 29th. 1755; (B) Stephen Love; (C) 115; (D) John & Ezekiel Gott; (E) 5–15–0; (F) 11–10–0; (H) $117^{1}/_{2}$; (K) Ezekiel Gott.

Lot 14. (A) Sept. 29th. 1755; (B) Ezekiel Gott; (C) 78; (D) Lessee; (E) 3–18–0; (F) 7–16–0; (G) $6^{1}/_{2}$; (H) $80^{1}/_{4}$; Ezekiel Gott.

Lot 15. (A) Sept. 29th, 1761; (B) Ann Thomas; (C) 250; (D) Lessee; (E) 12–10–0; (F) 25–0–0 (H) 266; (K) John Thomas.

Lot 16. (A) ——; (B) Stewards Lotte; (C) $199^{7}/_{8}$; (D) John Thomas.

Lot 17. (A) Sept. 29th, 1756; (B) John Thomas; (C) 166; (D) Lessee; (E) 8–6–0; (F) 16–12–0; (H) $177^{1}/_{2}$; (K) John Thomas.

Lot 18. (A) Sept. 29, 1755; (B) Rachel Sherbutt; (C) 50; (D) Lessee; (E) 2–10–0; (F) 5–0–0; (H) $52^{1}/_{2}$; (K) John Thomas.

Lot 19. (A) Sept. 29, 1755; (B) William Hollyday; (C) 100; (D) Lessee; (E) 5–0–0; (F) 10–0–0; (H) 106$^1/_8$; (K) Henry Plummer.

Lot 20. (A) Sept. 29th. 1763; (B) Geo. Stewart; (C) 224; (D) Lessee; (E) 11–4–0; (F) 22–8–0.

Lot 21. (A) Sept. 29, 1755; (B) Geo. Stewart; (C) 78; (D) Lessee; (E) 3–18–0; (F) 7–16–0.

Lot 22. Included in No. 20, (H) Lots 20, 21, 22 313$^3/_4$; (K) George Stewart, Esq.

Lot 23. (A) Sept. 29th. 1755; (B) Thomas Norris; (C) 83; (D) Leasee; (E) 4–3–0; (F) 8–6–0; (H) 83; (K) Stephen Steward.

Lot 24. (A) Sept. 29, 1755; (B) Henry Child; (C) 73; (D) Lessee; (E) 3–13–0; (F) 7–6–0; (G) 7; (H) 82$^1/_4$; (K) Henry Child.

Lot 25. (A) Sept. 29, 1755; (B) Isaac Owens; (C) 187; (D) Lessee; (E) 9–7–0; (F) 18–14–0; (G) 10; (H) 197$^1/_2$; (K) Isaac Owens.

Lot 26. (A) Sept. 29, 1755; (B) James Cowley; (C) 90; (D) Lessee; (E) 4–10–0; (F) 9–0–0; (H) 93$^1/_4$; (K) James Cowley.

Lot 27. (A) Sept. 29, 1755; (B) Joseph Cowman; (C) 150; (D) Lessee; (E) 7–10–0; (F) 15–0–0; (H) 149$^3/_4$ (K) ——.

Lot 28. (A) Sept. 29, 1755; (B) Thomas Deale; (C) 232; (D) Cowley & Welsh; (E) 11–12–0; (F) 23–4–0; (H) 242$^1/_4$ (K) John Welsh, Son of Robt.

Lot 29. (A) Sept. 29, 1755; (B) Wm. & Elenr. Barrett; (C) 100; (D) Eler. Barrett & Sons; (E) 5–0–0; (F) 10–0–0; (H) 105$^1/_4$; (K) John Barrett.

Lot 30. (A) Mch 25th. 1758; (B) Joseph Ward; (C) 196; (D) Lessee; (E) 9–16–0; (F) 19–12–0; (H) 193$^3/_4$; (K) Joseph Ward.

Lot 31. (A) Mch. 10th. 1747; (B) John Galwith; (C) 131; (D) McDaniel & Carr; (E) 4–18–0; (F) 9–16–0; (H) 117$^3/_4$; (K) Benjamin Carr.

Lot 32. (A) Mch. 25, 1755; (B) Richd. Richardson; (C) 127$^1/_2$; (D) Lessee; (E) 6–7–6; (F) 12–15–0.

Lot 33. (A) Sept. 29, 1756; (B) Ditto; (C) 80$^1/_2$; (D) Lessee; (E) 4–0–6; (F) 8–1–0; (H) Lots 32, 33, 212$^3/_4$; (K) Richd. Richardson [Both].

Lot 34. (A) Sept. 29, 1756; (B) Dinah Sparrow; (C) 117; (D) Benj. & Wm. Sherbutt; (E) 5–17–0; (F) 11–14–0; (G) 11$^1/_2$; (H) 128$^1/_8$; (K) Philip Pindell.

Lot 35. (C) 55$^3/_4$; (D) Nathan Brashiers; (E) 3–3–0; (H) 55$^3/_4$; (K) Nathan Brashiers.

Lot 36. (A) Sept. 29, 1755; (B) Nichs. Watkins; (C) 137$^1/_2$; (D) Gassaway Watkins; (E) 6–17–6; (F) 13–15–0; (H) 152; (K) Gassaway Watkins.

Lot 37. (A) Sept. 29, 1755; (B) John Sappington; (C) 120; (D) Robert Norris; (E) 6–0–0; (F) 12–0–0; (H) 110¼; (K) Robert Norris.

Lot 38. (A) Sept. 29, 1755; (B) Edwd. McDaniel; (C) 118; (D) Lessee; (E) 5–18–0; (F) 11–16–0; (H) 122¾.

Lot 39. (A) Sept. 29, 1755; (B) John Battey; (C) 105; (D) Lessee; (E) 5–5–0; (F) 0–10–0; (H) 105.

Lot 40. (A) Mch. 10, 1747; (B) Benj^{a}. Carr; (C) 100; (D) Lessee; (E) 3–15–0; (F) 7–10–0; (H) 112½; (K) Benj^{a}. Carr.

Lot 41. (A) Sept. 29, 1756; (B) Joseph Hill; (C) 137; (D) Lessee; (E) 6–17–0; (F) 13–14–0; (H) 135¾; (K) Thomas Cowley.

Lot 42. (A) Sept. 29, 1757; (B) Rich^{d}. Sheckell; (C) 157½; (D) Lessee; (E) 7–17–6; (F) 15–15–0; (H) 169¾; (K) Richard Sheckell.

Lot 43. Lease expired Nov. 1766; (C) 100; (D) "Rich^{d}. Sheckells;" (E) 3–15–0; (F) ——; (H) 108½; (K) "Rich^{d}. Sheckell."

Lot 44. (A) Mch. 25, 1756; (B) "John Shickell;" (C) 93; (D) Lessee; (E) 4–13–0; (F) 9–6–0; (H) 105⅞; (K) "John Sheckell."

Lot 45. (A) Sept. 29, 1755; (B) Benj^{a}. Cheney; (C) 102½; (D) Lessee; (E) 5–2–6; (F) 10–5–0; (H) 103⅞.

Lot 46. (A) Sept. 29, 1757; (B) Nich^{s}. Nicholson; (C) 74½; (D) Lessee; (E) 3–14–6; (F) 7–9–0; (H) 77½; (K) Nicholas Nicholson.

Lot 47. (A) Mch. 25, 1760; (B) Jonas Galwith; (C) 154½; (D) Lessee; (E) 7–14–6; (F) 15–9–0; (H) 156⅜; (K) Abraham Simmons.

Lot 48. (A) Mch. 25, 1759; (B) Abraham Simmons; (C) 155; (D) Lessee; (E) 7–15–0; (F) 15–10–0; (H) 164⅜; (K) Abraham Simmons.

Lot 49. (A) Sept. 29, 1756; (B) Abraham Sheckells; (C) 110; (D) Richard Hopkins; (E) 5–10–0; (F) 11–0–0; (H) 113⅛; (K) Richard Hopkins.

Lot 50. (A) Mch. 25, 1762; (B) John Sheckells; (C) 60; (D) Lessee; (E) 3–0–0; (F) 6–0–0; (H) 62; (K) John Sheckells.

Lot 51. (A) Mch. 25, 1757; (B) Jno. Cheney, Son of Jno.; (C) 100; (D) Mary Cheney; (E) 5–0–0; (F) 10–0–0; (H) 107¾; (K) John Sheckells.

Lot 52. (A) ——; (B) ——; (C) 30; (D) Mary Cheney; (E) 1–10–0; (F) 3–0–0; (H) 22½; (K) John Sheckells.

Lot 53. (A) Mch. 25, 1762; (B) Benjn. Cheney; (C) 20; (D) Lessee; (E) 1–0–0; (F) 2–0–0; (H) 20; (K) John Sheckells.

Lot 54. (A) Sept. 29, 1761; (B) William Thomas; (C) 153; (D) William Taylor (followed by undecipherable—Sr? Jr?); (E) 7–13–0; (F) 15–6–0; (H) 153; (K) John Sheckells. Lots 51, 52, 53, 54 are all "assigned I. T. Augustus Prigg."

Lot 55. (A) Mch. 25, 1755; (B) Isaac Simmons; (C) 124; (D) Lessee; (E) 6–4–0; (F) 12–8–0; (H) 127⅛; (K) Isaac Simmons.

Lot 56. (A) Sept. 29, 1760; (B) Samuel Ward; (C) 153; (D) Lessee; (E) 7–13–0; (F) 15–6–0; (H) 129; (K) Samuel Ward.

Lot 57. (A) Sept. 29, 1756; (B) Saml. Ward; (C) $142^1/_2$; (D) Lessee; (E) 7–2–6; (F) 14–5–0; (H) $142^1/_8$; (K) Samuel Ward.

Lot 58. (A) Sept. 29, 1755; (B) Rachel Moone; (C) 250; (D) Lessee; (E) 12–10–0; (F) 25–0–0.

Lot 59. (A) Sept. 29, 1758; (B) Rachel Moone; (C) 87; (D) Lessee; (E) 4–7–0; (F) 8–14–0; For Lots 58, 59 (G) 27; (H) $388^1/_4$.

Lot 60. (A) Sept. 29, 1758; (B) James Owens; (C) $136^1/_4$; (D) Lessee; (E) 6–16–3; (F) 13–12–6; (H) $140^3/_4$; (K) James Owens.

Lot 61. (A) Mch. 25, 1756; (B) Rich[d]. Green; (C) $163^1/_2$; (D) Lessee; (E) 8–3–6; (F) 16–7–0; (H) 187; (K) Richard Green.

Lot 62. (A) Sept. 29, 1756; (B) Sarah Widow of Chas. Connant; (C) $312^1/_2$; (D) Richard Green; (E) 15–12–6; (F) 31–5–0; (H) $301^3/_4$; (K) Richard Green.

Lot 63. (A) Sept. 29, 1757; (B) Thomas Owens; (C) 100; (D) Lessee; (E) 5–0–0; (F) 10–0–0; (H) $107^3/_4$; (K) Richard Green.

Lot 64. (A) Sept. 29, 1757; (B) Edward Cole; (C) 150; (D) Lessee; (E) 7–10–0; (F) 15–0–0; (G) $13^1/_4$; (H) $167^1/_4$; (K) Edward Cole.

Lot 65. (A) Mch. 25, 1759; (B) Gerard Hopkins; (C) 67; (D) Lessee; (E) 3–7–0; (F) 6–14–0; (G) $34^3/_4$; (H) $106^1/_4$; (K) Gerard Hopkins,Son of Philip.

Lot 66. (A) Sept. 29, 1758; (B) James Owens; (C) 50; (D) Lessee; (E) 2–10–0; (F) 5–0–0; (H) $50^1/_2$; (K) James Owens.

Lot 67. (A) Sept. 29, 1761; (B) James Owens; (C) 37; (D) Lessee; (E) 1–17–0; (F) 3–14–0; (H) $41^3/_4$; (K) James Owens.

Lot 68. (C) 34; (D) John Owens, Tenant; (E) 1–14–0; (F) 3–8–0; (H) 34; (K) Richard Green.

Lot 69. (A) Mch. 25, 1759; (B) Martha Tillard; (C) 100; (D) Lessee; (E) 5–0–0; (F) 10–0–0; (H) $101^1/_2$; (K) Martha Tillard.

Lot 70. (A) Mch. 25, 1759; (B) Martha Tillard; (C) 50; (D) Lessee; (E) 2–10–0; (F) 5–0–0; (H) $54^1/_2$; (K) Martha Tillard.

Lot 71. (G) 36; (H) 36; (K) Martha Tillard.

Lot 72. (A) Mch. 25, 1759; (B) Rich[d]. Simmons; (C) $121^1/_4$; (D) Lessee; (E) 6–1–6; (F) 12–3–0; (H) $128^1/_4$; (K) Richard Simmons.

Lot 73. (A) Sept. 29, 1756; (B) Jacob Macceney; (C) 131; (D) Lessee; (E) 6–11–0; (F) 13–2–0; (H) 137; (K) Jacob Macceney.

Lot 74. (A) Sept. 29, 1756; (B) Jacob Macceney; (C) 117; (D) Lessee; (E) 5–17–0; (F) 11–14–0; (H) $114^1/_2$; (K) Jacob Macceney.

Lot 75. (A) Sept. 29, 1756; (B) Charles Owens; (C) $75^1/_2$; (D) Rich[d]. Wells; (E) 3–15–6; (F) 7–11–0; (H) $77^1/_2$.

Lot 76. (A) Sept. 29, 1756; (B) Peter Dowell; (C) 100; (D) Rich[d]. Windfield; (E) 5–0–0; (F) 10–0–0; (G) 18; (H) 108.

Lot 77. (A) Sept. 29, 1760; (B) "Saml. Sheckell;" (C) 112; (D) Lessee; (E) 5–12–0; (F) 11–4–0; (G) 57½; (H) 165¼; (K) "Samuel Sheckells."

Lot 78. (A) Dec. 1, 1747; (B) John Bogler; (C) 100; (D) Lessee; (E) 3–15–0; (F) 7–10–0; (H) 105½; (K) Benja. Cheney.

Lot 79. (C) 26¼; (D) John Bogler; (E) 1–6–3; (F) 2–12–6; (H) 25⅜; (K) Benja. Cheney.

Lot 80. (A) Mch. 25, 1761; (B) Ann Belt; (C) 90¼; (D) Lessee; (E) 4–10–3; (F) 9–0–6; (H) 89⅜; (K) Thomas Belt.

Lot 81. (C) 46¾; (D) Thos. Lawson, Tent. (E) 2–6–9; (H) 46¾; (K) Thomas Belt.

Lot 82. (A) Mch. 25, 1758 (B) Joseph Yeates; (C) 50; (D) Lessee; (E) 2–10–0; (F) 5–0–0; (G) 134½; (H) 176.

Lot 83. (A) Mch. 10, 1758; (B) John Brashiers; (C) 250; (D) Lessee; (E) 12–10–0; (F) 25–0–0; (G) 46¼; (H) 284½; (K) John Brashiers.

Lot 84. (A) Mch. 25, 1761; (B) Geo. Gardner; (C) 50; (D) Lessee; (E) 2–10–0; (F) 5–0–0.

Lot 85. (A) Mch. 10, 1758; (B) Geo. Gardner; (C) 100; (D) Lessee; (E) 5–0–0; (F) 10–0–0.

Lot 86. (A) Mch. 25, 1762; (B) Geo. Gardner; (C) 23¾; (D) Lessee; (E) 1–3–9; (F) 2–7–6. For Lots 84, 85, 86 (G) 10; (H) 188½; (K) George Gardner.

Lot 87. (A) Mch. 25, 1760; (B) John Brown (C) 50; (D) Lessee; (E) 2–10–0; (F) 5–0–0; (G) 163½; (H) 217; (K) Joseph Allen.

Lot 88. (A) Mch. 25, 1758; (B) John Brown; (C) 65; (D) Lessee; (E) 3–5–0; (F) 6–10–0; (G) 8; (H) 73½; (K) Joseph Allen.

Lot 89. (C) 213½; (D) Benjamin Allen; (E) 10–13–6; (F) 21–7–0; (G) 23; (H) 236½.

Lot 90. (G) 44¾; (H) 44¾; (K) John Brashiers.

Lot 91. (G) 153¾; (H) 153¾; (K) Thomas Belt, 3d.

——. (G) 3¼; (H) 3¼.

——. (G) 7½; (H) 7½.

——. (G) 26¼; (H) 26¼; (K) Bennitt Darnall.

N. B. The above Manor laid off March 16, 1667.

"A List of the unsold Part of Anne-Arundel Manor, Augt. 16th. 1770"

21/3. (A) March 25th 1755; (B) John Norris; Sold to "R. Norris per I. Hall"; (C) 101 1/4; Price per Acre 21/6; Amt. of 6^d per Acre, 2–10–7 1/4.

24/27. (A) Septr. 29, 1755; (B) Joseph Cowman 6; Sold to Joseph Cowman; (C) 149 3/4; Per Acre 24/6; Amt. of 6^d. per Acre, 3–14–10 1/4.

28/38. (A) Ditto; (B) Edward McDaniel; Sold to Robt. Norris; (C) 122 3/4 Per Acre 20/6; Amt. of 6^d. per Acre, 3–1–4 1/2.

20/39. (A) Ditto; (B) John Battey 6; (C) 105.

21/45. (A) Ditto; (B) Benjamin Cheney—6; Sold to Ben^a. Cheney; (C) 103 1/2; Per acre 21/6; Amt. of 6^d. per Acre, 2–11–11 1/4.

20/75. (A) Sept. 29, 1756; (B) Richard Wells—7; (C) 77 1/2.

20/76. (A) Ditto; (B) Rich^d. Windfield 7; (C) 108.

18/82. (A) March 25, 1758; (B) Joseph Yeates; Sold to R^d. Sprigg; (C) 176; Amt. of 6^d. per Acre, 4–8–0.

15/89. (B) Benj. Allen; (C) 236 1/2.

25/6. (C) 3 1/4.

25/6. C 7 1/2. Total Acres, 1191 3/5; Gross Amt. of Sales 189–4–0, Disct. 8–6–3, 180–17–9.

CHARLES COUNTY

"State of His Lordship's Manor of Calverton, Charles County, 1767"

Plat 1. (A) Decem^{r}. 22, 1748; (B) George Maxwell; (C) 383; (D) Lessee; (E) 0–10–0; (F) 0–10–0; (L) George Maxwell & Letice Wardrop; (M) Geo. 46, Letice 46. Leased for 102 acres or thereabout.

2. (B) Patent Land; (C) 1210; (D) Chas. Saml. Smith.

3. (A) March 28th. 1767; (B) Basil Brooke; (C) 740; (D) Lessee; (E) 1–0–0. Leased for 21 years & "Renewable to the end of the World." "Leased for 500 Acres."

4. (A) May 31, 1763; (B) Joseph Anderson; (C) 145; (D) Lessee; (E) 1–9–0. Leased for 21 years only.

5. (A) Decem^{r}. 1st. 1714; (B) Gabriel Moran; (C) 118; (D) John Moran; (E) 0–3–6; (F) 1–8–0; (L) Elizabeth Moran; (M) Elizabeth 76. Decd. Leased for 35 acres.

6. (A) Decem. 25th. 1753; (B) George Maxwell; (C) 111; (D) Lessee; (E) 0–11–1; (F) 2–4–4; (L) George Maxwell & Lettice Wardrop; (M) George 46, Lettice 46.

7. (A) October 18, 1752; (B) Richard Estep; (C) 147; (D) John Hammitt; (E) 0–14–8; (F) 2–18–8; Fines due, 5–17–4; (L) Richard Estep, Alex^{r}. Estep & Mary Estep; (M) Richard 21, Alex^{r}. 22, Mary 25.

8. (A) Ditto; (B) Nehemiah Wilson; (C) 172; (D) Susan^{h}. Willson; (E) 0–17–2; (F) 3–8–0; (L) Abraham Wilson & Catharine Wilson (M) Abraham 15, Catharine, 16.

9. (A) Ditto; (B) Jonathan Wilson; (C) 105; (D) John Hammitt; (E) 0–10–6; (F) 2–2–0; Fines due 6–6–0; (L) Jonathan Wilson & John Wilson; (M) Jonathan 50, John ——.

10. (A) July 25th. 1750; (B) Mary Stone; (C) 215; (D) John Moran; (E) 0–10–0; (F) 2–0–0; Fines due 4–0–0; (L) Jonathan Stone, Mary Stone, Junr. & Catharine Stone; (M) Jonathan 25, Mary 23, Catharine 20; "This land appears to be held by a lease for 100 a to Mary Stone & an old Lease for 35 acres."

11. (A) Decem. 24th. 1739; (B) Elizabeth Morris; (C) 157; (D) William Pitney; (E) 1–0–0; (F) 3–0–0; Fines due, 3–0–0; (L) Margaret Spriggs Daughter of Osburn Spriggs; (M) Margaret 36. "Leas'd for 80 acres to Eliz. Morris."

12. (A) May 31st. 1758; (B) John Wheatley; (C) 40; (D) Lessee; (E) 0–8–0; (F) 0–8–0; Leased for 21 yrs.

13. (A) Octo^{r}. 23^{d}. 1747; (B) John Estep; (C) 169; (D) Lucy Estep,

widow; (E) 0–17–0; (F) 3–8–0; (L) Alexander Estep, Richard Estep & Walter Smith; (M) Alex^r^. 22, Rich^d^. 21, Walter 28, if alive, but gone away from these parts.

14. (A) Octo^r^. 17, 1752; (B) Richard "Addams;" (C) 260; (D) Charles Venables; (E) 1–6–0; (F) 5–4–0; Fines due 5–4–0; (L) John Rouss "Adams"; (M) John Rouse Adams 21.

15. (A) March 25, 1742; (B) John "Willson"; (C) 363; (D) James Forbes; (E) 1–16–0; (F) 7–4–0; Fines due 7–4–0; (L) William "Wilson"; (M) William Wilson 27. "Dead."

16. (A) Decem^r^. 11, 1751; (B) Allen Davis; (C) 57; (D) George Maxwell; (E) –5–8; (F) 0–11–4; (L) James Davis & James Lyon; (M) James Davis 24, James Lyon 24. N. B. Davis out of the province.

17. (A) Ditto; (B) Edward Burch; (C) 65; (D) Mary Burch, widow; (E) 0–5–4; (F) 1–5–4; (L) Jessee Burch, Edward Burch, Junr. & Catharine Burch; (M) Jessee 31, Edward 17, Catharine 22.

18 Vacant.

19. (A) May 4th. 1761; (B) John Rouse Adams; (C) 210; (D) Lessee; (E) 2–2–0; (F) 2–2–0; (L) 21 years.

20. (A) May 16, 1721; (B) Joseph Johnson; (C) 57; (D) Sarah Harrison, Wid^w^.; (E) –5–6; (F) 2–4–0; (L) Joseph Johnson, Junr.; (M) *Joseph 50, if alive*, but out of these parts. Expired.

21. (A) Jan. 1, 1753; (B) George Venables; (C) 85; (D) Ann Venables, Widow; (E) 0–8–6; (F) 1–14–0; (L) Ann Venables & Josias Venables; (M) Ann 40, Josias ——.

22. (A) Jan. 1, 1753; (B) Thomas Canter; (C) 115; (D) William Canter, Junr.; (E) –11–6; (F) 2–6; (L) Thomas Canter & Isaac Canter; (M) Lessee 50, out of the parts if alive. Isaac 20.

23. (A) Dec. 25, 1753; (B) Francis Oden; (C) 90; (D) Lessee; (E) 0–9–0; (F) 1–16–0; (L) Mary Oden, Rebecca Oden & Prissilla Packer Oden; (M) Mary 18, Rebecca 16, Prissilla 14.

24. (A) Octr. 2^d^. 1760; (B) Francis Oden; (C) 118; (D) Lessee; (E) 1–3–6; (F) 1–3–6; (L) 21 years.

25. (A) Sept. 11, 1765; (B) ——; (C) 22; (D) John Wheatley.

26. (A) Decem^r^. 25th. 1753; (B) William Ogden; (C) 93; (D) Francis Oden; (E) –9–3; (F) 1–17–0; Fines due 3–14–0; (L) Philimon Ogden & Mary Ogden; (M) Philimon 30, Mary 14.

27. (A) Novem. 15, 1727; (B) Nicholas Yoe; (C) 80; (D) William Canter, Junr.; (E) –8–0; (F) 3–4–0; Fines due 6–8–0; (L) Robt. Yoe & James Yoe; (M) Robert 60, James 50. N. B. Both out of the parts if alive.

28. (A) Decem. 1, 1758; (B) William Wallace; (C) 36; (D) William Wallace; (E) 0–7–2; (F) –14–4; (L) 21 years.

29. (A) Feb. 15, 1727; (B) Samuel King; (C) 38; (D) William Wallace; (E) 0–4–1; (F) 1–12–8; Fines due, 6–10–8; (L) Samuel King; (M) Samuel King 50 or 60.

30. (A) Ditto; (B) William King; (C) William Wallace; (D) –4–0; (E) 1–12–0; Fines due, 1–12–0; (L) Elizabeth King, Samuel King; (M) Elizabeth 50, Samuel King, Junr. N. B. Sam: was born 11 years after date of [torn—lease?].

31. (A) May 22^d. 1728; (B) John King; (C) 40; (D) Henry Lyon; (E) 0–12–8; (F) 1–12–0; Fines due 3–4–0; (L) John King & Jonathan Lyon; (M) John 47, Jonathan 36.

32. (A) July 7th. 1739; (B) John Parker; (C) 57; (D) Abraham Parker; (E) –5–8; (F) 1–2–8. N. B. This Lease must be fallen, a false An^r. given.

33. (A) February 8, 1764; (B) Edward Burch; (C) 24; (D) Mary Burch, Widow; (E) –5–0; (F) –5–0; (L) 21 years.

34. (A) Octr. 2^d. 1718; (B) George Plater; (C) 250; (D) Mary Burch, Widow; (E) 1–5–0; (F) 10–0–0; Fines due, 8–15–0; (L) Thomas Cothell; (M) Thos. Cothell supposed by everybody to be dead, 25 shs. of this Al^a. p^d. young Pairan.

35. (A) August 21, 1760; (D) Doct^r. James Bate.

36. (A) Aug. 21, 1760; (B) Edward Burch; (C) 14½; (D) Mary Burch, Widow; (E) 0–2–10; (L) 21 years.

37. (A) May 25, 1758; (B) Joseph Walls; (C) 132; (D) John Wheatley; (E) 1–16–4; (F) 2–12–8; Fines due, 2–12–8; (L) Joseph Walls, Eliz: Walls & Sarah Walls; (M) Joseph 40, Eliz: 36, Sarah 10.

38. (A) April 11th. 1761; (B) John Wheatley; (C) 139½; (D) Lessee; (E) 1–8–0; (F) 1–8–0; (L) 21 years.

39. (A) Septem^r. 13, 1718; (B) Mary Lyon; (C) 94; (D) Henry Lyon; (E) –9–5; (F) 3–15–6; (L) John Lyon; (M) John Lyon 63. Expired.

40. (A) Decr. 25th. 1746; (B) William Canter; (C) 139; (D) William Canter; (E) 0–5–10; (F) 2–7–2; (L) William Canter, James Canter & Jonathan Canter; (M) W^m. 45, James 26, Jonathan 30.

41. (A) Decm^r. 25, 1753; (B) George Ross; (C) 158; (D) George Ross; (E) 0–15–9; (F) 3–3–0; (L) Lessee, George Ross & W^m. Ross his Children.

42. (A) July 25th. 1742; (B) Allen Davis; (C) 273; (D) Robert Glading; (E) 1–7–4; (F) 5–9–4; Fines due 5–9–4; (L) Allen Davis, Jonathan Davis & James Davis; (M) Allen 65, Jonathan 40, James 24. Vide Date of Lease for James' Age, taken from Counterpart, Northern P——.

43. (A) Octr. 20, 1749; (B) John Wheatley; (C) 206; (D) John Wheatley; (E) –10–0; (F) 1–0–0; (L) John Wheatley, Middleton Smith & Elias Smith; (M) John 51, Middleton 26, Elias 24. N. B. Leas'd for 100 acres.

44. (A) Augt. 20, 1745; (B) Allice Walls; (C) 181; (D) Henry Lyon, Junr.; (E) 0–18–0; (F) 3–12–0; Fines due, 10–16–0; (L) Allice Walls, Joseph Walls & Monaca Walls; (M) Allice 80, Joseph 40, Monaca 35.

(C) Total 7149 acres.

State of His Lordships Manor of Pangaiah in Charles County, January, 1768

3. (C) 16½, Vacancy. 5. (C) 13, Ditto. 12. (C) 3½, Ditto. 17. (C) 44½, Ditto. 20. (C) 77½, Ditto. 24. (C) 40½, Ditto; 30. (C) 3½, Ditto; 37. (C) 10, Ditto. 39. (C) 2½, Ditto. 42. (C) 16, Ditto. 46. (C) 10, Ditto. 48. (C) 16, Ditto. 51. (C) 25¼, Ditto. 59. (C) 9, Ditto. 62. (C) 35½, Vacancy.

25. (A) March 25, 1744; (B) Alexander McPherson; (C) 72¾; (D) Henry McPherson; (E) 0–8–0; (F) 1–12–0; (L) Mack McPherson & Priscilla McPherson; (M) Mack 45, Priscilla 25.

29. (A) May 1, 1763; (B) William Clements; (C) 5¼; (D) William Clements.

33. (A) Octor. 21, 1706; (B) Benj. Adams; (C) 14; (D) Thomas Adams; (E) 0–10–5; (F) 4–2–0; (L) Lodowick Adams; (M) Lodowick 63 Dead, Cons. 137 acres—123 acres of this Land lies without the Manor.

34. (A) Sepr. 2d. 1743; (B) Joseph Gainer; (C) 26½; (D) Joseph Gainer; (E) 0–4–4; (F) 1–15–2; (L) Wm. Gainer, Joseph Gainer, Junr. & John Gainer; (M) Willm. 40, Jos. 31, John 28. Leasd. for 44 acres the rest without the Manor.

36. (A) Decr. 17th. 1762; (B) George Clements; (C) 23¾; (D) George Clements; (E) 0–5–2; (F) 0–5–2; (L) 16 years.

38. (A) June 1st, 1758; (B) William Clements; (C) 70; (D) William Clements; (E) 0–14–8; (F) 1–9–4; (L) 3 Lives, Edwd., William & Eleanor Clements, Children of Lessee. quere their Ages, all Living.

41. (A) Decemr. 10th, 1743; (B) William Clements; (C) 127½; (D) George & Elizh. Clements; (E) 0–15–11; (F) 3–3–8; (L) Oswell Clements, B. Hanson Clements & Edd. Clements; (M) Oswell 39, Hanson 36, Edward 26.

43. (A) Decr. 25, 1743; (B) Thos. Mathew Sanders; (C) 196; (D) Dan Jenifer & B. H. Clements; (E) 1–0–6; (F) 4–2–0; (L) Thos. Mathew Sanders, Hena. Sanders & Sarah Sanders; (M) Thos. 26, Henrietta 30, Sarah 46.

44. (A) Decr. 25, 1743; (B) William McPherson; (C) 22; (D) William McPherson; (E) 0–2–11; (F) 0–11–8; (L) Thomas McPherson, Danl. McPherson, Henry McPherson; (M) Thos. 40, Henry 31, Danl. 38.

47. (A) Decr. 25, 1743; (B) Edmund Maggottee; (C) 114; (D) Thomas Maggottee; (E) 0–11–4; (F) 2–5–4; (L) George Clements; (M) George 37.

49. (A) Jany. 15, 1714; (B) Anthony Neale; (C) 256½; (D) Elizabeth Clements; (E) 1–0–0; (F) 8–0–0; (L) Bennett Neale; (M) Bennett 54 Dead.

58. (A) June 1st, 1758; (B) Francis Clements; (C) 29¼; (D) Elizabeth Clements; (E) 0–7–6; (F) 0–15–0; (L) Thomas Clements & Henry Clements; (M) Thomas 22, Henry 19.

60. (A) Augt. 30, 1765; (B) John & Thos. Maggotte; (C) 104; (D) Mary Maggotte; (E) 1–6–2; (F) 1–6–10; (L) 18½ yrs.

61. (A) Augt. 30, 1765; (B) Ann & Abedo. Maggottee; (C) 59½; (D) Ann Maggottee; (E) 0–13–2; (F) 0–13–2; (L) 18½ yrs.

63. (C) 6; (D) Vacancy, Thos. Maggottee [different handwriting]; (E) 0–0–4.

State of His Lordships Manor of Zachaiah in Charles County, February, 1768

1. (A) Decemr. 25th, 1741; (B) William Simms; (C) 92½; (D) Wm. Simms; (E) 1–0–8; (F) 4–2–8; (L) William Simms, Sarah Simms, David Osborn; (M) William 60, Sarah 30, David 36.

2. (A) Decemr. 25, 1753; (B) William Simms; (C) 42¼; (D) Wm. Simms; (E) 0–6–8; (F) 1–6–8; (L) William Simms, Sarah Simms & Walter Kerrick; William 60, Sarah 30, Walter 16.

3. (A) July 17th, 1763; (B) William Simms; (C) 16½; (D) Wm. Simms; (E) 0–4–9; (F) 0–4–9; (L) 16½ yrs.

4. (A) June 1st, 1758; (B) James Keech; (C) 91; (D) James Keech; (E) 1–0–0; (F) 2–0–0; (L) James Keech, John Keech & John Smith Keech; (M) James 58, John 32, John Smith 10.

5. (A) Jany. 1st, 1753; (B) Paul Howell; (C) 40; (D) Paul Howell; (E) 0–4–0; (F) 0–18–0; (L) Paul Howell, Samuel Howell & Sarah Howell; (M) Paul 43, Samuel 15, Sarah 20.

6. (A) Novemr. 1, 1755; (B) William Moreland; (C) 113; (D) Wm. Moreland; (E) 1–9–0; (F) 2–18–0; (L) William Moreland & Jacob Moreland; (M) Wm. 50, Jacob 18.

7. (C) 1333; Patent Granted out of the Manor July 10th. 1705. Called His Lordships Favor.

8. (A) July 10th, 1740; (B) Michael Hines Roby; (C) 70; (D) Thos. Owens & Eliz: Roby; (E) 0–6–0; (F) 1–4–0; Fines due, 1–4–0; (L) Thos. Roby, John Taylor Roby & Hines Roby; (M) Thomas 37, John 35, Hines 33.

9. (C) 753; Patent Land calld. Baltimores Bounty.

10. (A) Decemr. 25th, 1743; (B) Samuel Roby; (C) 54; (D) Saml. Roby; (E) 0–6–0; (F) 1–4–0; (L) Samuel Roby & Berry Roby; (M) Samuel 59, Berry 26.

11. (A) May 3d, 1728; (B) Peter Roby; (C) 86¼; (D) 0–10–0; (E) 4–0–0; (L) John Roby & John Henly; (M) John 43, John Henly 40.

12. (A) July 25, 1750; (B) William Roby; (C) 84½; (D) Wm. Roby; (E) 0–15–0; (F) 3–0–0; (L) William Roby, Mary Roby & Ann Roby; (M) Wm. 52, May 49, Ann 25.

13. (A) June 23d, 1762; (B) John Roby Junr. (C) 42; (D) Thomas Luckett; (E) 0–8–4; (F) 0–8–4; Fines due, 0–8–4; (L) 15 years & 4 months.

14. (A) June 29th, 1728; (B) Michael Hines Roby; (C) 123¼; (D) Thos. Owens & Eliz: Roby; (E) 0–12–0; (F) 4–16–0; Fines due, 2–8–0; (L) 1 Life Sarah Roby; (M) Sarah 40.

15. (A) July 5th, 1764; (B) Thomas Owen; (C) 97¼; (D) Thomas Owen; (E) 0–16–2; (F) 0–16–2; (L) 17½ years.

16. (A) July 6th, 1739; (B) John Moreland [Mouland?]; (C) 50½; (D) Paul Howell; (E) 0–5–0; (F) 1–0–0; (L) Patrick Moreland & John Moreland Junr.; (M) Patrick 34, John 32.

17. (C) 12; Vacancy.

18. (A) Augt. 25th, 1745; (B) Thos. & Wm. "McDaniel"; (C) 208; (D) Smith Middleton & others; (E) 1–1–7; (F) 4–6–4; (L) William "Mcdaniel" & Esther "Mcdaniel"; (M) William 39, Esther 36.

19. (A) Jany. 25th, 1753; (B) Ditto; (C) 38½; (D) Ditto; (E) 0–4–2; (F) 0–4–2; (L) Wm. Mcdaniel, Drusila Mcdaniel & Allen Mcdaniel; (M) Wm. 39, Drusila 17, Allen 16.

20. (A) June 1st, 1758; (B) William Moreland; (C) 19; (D) Wm. Moreland; (E) 0–4–0; (F) 0–8–0; (L) Wm. Moreland, Walter Moreland & Jacob Moreland; (M) Wm. 50, Walter 20, Jacob 18.

21. (A) July 3d, 1764; (B) Smith Middleton; (C) 19; (D) Smith Middleton; (E) 0–4–1; (F) 0–4–1; (L) 17½ yrs.

22. (A) Novemr. 30, 1714; (B) John Pigeon; (C) 92¾; (D) Mary Pigeon; (E) 0–11–7; (F) 4–12–9; (L) John Vincent, William Perkins; (M) John 60, Wm. 55.

23. (A) May 3d, 1728; (B) Benjamin Roby; (C) Wm. Roby; (D) 0–9–4; (E) 3–15–0; (L) William Roby; (M) William 68.

24. (C) 59; Vacancy.

25. (A) Augt. 20th, 1745; (B) Benjamin Downs; (C) 94; (D) John Nally Roby; (E) 0–9–6; (F) 1–18–0; (L) Benjamin Downs & Mary Downs; (M) Benjamin 54, Mary 52.

26. (A) July 10th, 1740; (B) Benjamin Downs; (C) 101; (D) John

Nally Roby; (E) 0–10–0; (F) 2–0–0; (L) Benja. Downs, Mary Downs & John Griffin; (M) Benja. 54, Mary 52, John 30.

27. (A) Octr. 23d, 1747; (B) William Roby, Senr. (C) 6; (D) William Roby; (E) 1–0–0; (F) 4–0–0; (L) Wm. Roby & Pryor Smallwood Roby; (M) William 34, Pryor 30.

28. (C) 615½; Vacancy, 30. Vacancy, 32. (C) 76; Vacancy.

29. (A) Decemr. 21st, 1748; (B) Thomas Owen; (C) 81¾; (D) Thomas Owen; (E) 0–8–0; (F) 1–12–0; (L) Thomas Owen, Owen Roby & Thos. Kenedy; (M) Thomas 44, Owen 22, Thomas Kennedy 25.

31. (A) Decemr. 25, 1753; (B) Thomas Owen; (C) 123¼; (D) Thomas Owen; (E) 0–12–9; (F) 2–11–0; (L) Thomas Owen & Joseph Owen; (M) Thomas 44, Joseph 15.

33. (A) Decemr. 25, 1741; (C) 12¼; (D) John Loveless; (E) 0–1–2; (F) 0–4–8; (L) Saml. Lovelass & Luke Lovelass; (M) Saml. 36, Luke 32.

34. (A) Decr. 25, 1750; (B) Philip Key; (C) 290; (D) Philip Key; (E) 1–10–0; (F) 6–0–0; (L) Francis Key; Francis 40 Dead.

35. (C) 2144; Patent Land called Jourden Tract Granted 1695.

36. (A) Decemr. 11th, 1751; (B) Thomas & Edwd. Mcdanniel; (C) 132; (D) Thomas Darnall; (E) 0–14–10; (F) 2–19–4; (L) Thomas Darnall & Sarah Darnall; (M) Thomas 54, Sarah 54.

37. (A) April 8th, 1762; (B) Thomas Owens; (C) 12¾; (D) Thos. Owens; (E) 0–2–7; (F) 0–2–7; (L) 15 yrs.

38. (A) Decemr. 25, 1721; (B) John Lovelass; (C) 59½; (D) John Lovelass; (E) 0–6–4; (F) 2–11–6; (L) John Lovelass; (M) John 70.

39. (A) Septr. 2d, 1765; (B) Thomas Arvin; (C) 15; (D) Thos. Arvin; (E) –3–10½; (F) 0–3–10½; (L) 18½ yrs.

40. (A) Augt. 20th, 1745; (B) John Lovelass; (C) 78; (D) John Lovelass; (E) 0–9–0; (F) 1–16–0; (L) Samuel Lovelass & Luke Lovelass; (M) Samuel 36, Luke 32.

41. (A) June 29th, 1728; (B) Ralph Roby; (C) 104½; (D) Ralph Roby; (E) 0–10–0; (F) 4–0–0; (L) Ralph Roby & Sarah Roby; (M) Ralph 60, Sarah 45.

42. (A) April 27th, 1727; (B) Edward Darnall; (C) 113; (D) Thomas Darnall; (E) 0–11–3; (F) 4–10–0; (L) Thomas Darnall; (M) Thos. 54.

43. (A) Octr. 1st, 1740; (B) George Askin; (C) 13; (D) Hezekiah Rieves; (E) 0–1–3; (L) Rebecca Asken & John Asken; (M) Rebecca 50, John 40.

44. (A) Decemr. 25, 1749; (B) Elizabeth Askin; (C) 80; (D) Hezekiah Rieves; (E) 0–8–3; (F) 1–12–0; (L) Andra Askin; (M) Andra 26.

45. (C) 76; Vacancy (Supposed).

46. (A) Decemr. 25, 1739; (B) James Middleton; (C) 69½; (D) James Middleton; (E) 0–10–0; (F) 2–0–0; Smith Middleton, Jas. Middleton &

Ig^{s}. Middleton; (M) Smith (44), James 41, Ignatius 26. N. B. Ig^{s}. must be more.

47. (A) Decem^{r}. 25, 1728; (B) George Askin; (C) 79$^{3}/_{4}$; (D) Hezekiah Reeves; (E) 0–7–6; (F) 3–0–0; (L) John Askin & Rebecca Askin; (M) John 40, Rebecca 50.

48. (A) May 3^{d}, 1763; (B) Richard Vincent; (C) 12; (D) 0–3–9; (E) 0–3–9; (L) 16$^{1}/_{4}$ yrs.

49. (A) Novm^{r}. 8th, 1739; (B) Philip Moreland; (C) 49$^{1}/_{2}$ & 122; (D) Philip Moreland; (E) 0–4–4 & 0–10–0; (F) 2–0–0; (L) Philip Moreland & John Moreland; (M) Philip 64, John 32.

50. (C) 60, Vacancy.

51. Totals Brought Over (C) 8272$^{1}/_{4}$; (E) £20–12–8$^{1}/_{2}$; Fines due 4–0–4.

52. (A) Decem^{r}. 11th, 1751; (B) John Hindly; (C) 67$^{1}/_{4}$; (D) James More; (E) 0–7–9; (F) 1–11–0; (L) John Hindly, Ruth Hindly & John Hindly, Junr., (M) John 40, Ruth 40, John Hindly Junr. 18.

53. (A) June 1st, 1758; (B) Thomas Cawood; (C) 40; (D) Thomas Cawood; (E) 1–2–0; (F) 2–3–4; (L) Stephen Cawood & Mary Cawood; (M) Stephen 18, Mary 20.

54. (A) Jany. 1st, 1754; (B) Edward Darnall; (C) 48; (D) Thomas Boarman; (E) 0–7–0; (F) 1–8–0; Fines due, 1–8–0; (L) Pricilla Darnall & Lizzie Darnall; (M) Pricilla 32, Lizzie 16.

55. (A) May 1st, 1758; (B) John Vincent; (C) 96$^{1}/_{2}$; (D) James Marshall; (E) 0–11–9; (F) 2–7–0; (L) John Pidgion Vincent, Philip Vincent & Joanna Vincent. quere their ages & which are alive.

56. (A) Decem^{r}. 25, 1746; (B) John Moreland; (C) 76; (D) John Moreland; (E) 0–7–7; (F) 1–10–4; (L) Zachariah Moreland & Zephaniah Moreland; (M) Zachariah 25, Zephaniah 23.

57. (C) 91, Vacancy.

58. (A) Decem^{r}. 25th, 1746; (B) Andrew Cambrun; (C) 125; (D) Thos. Wedding & John Moreland; (E) 0–15–6; (F) 3–2–0; Fines due, 7–15–0; (L) John Smith More, James More & Hezekiah More; (M) John 40, James 36, Hezekiah 24.

Vacancies; 59. (C) 39$^{1}/_{2}$; 60. (C) 76; 62. (C) 48; 63. (C) 53$^{1}/_{2}$; 66. (C) 30; 68. (C) 51$^{1}/_{4}$ & Sundry Vacancies (C) 131$^{1}/_{4}$.

61. (A) March 25th, 1742; (B) William Ogden; (C) 89; (D) Edward Jenkins; (E) 0–10–5; (F) 2–1–0; Fines due, 1–0–8; (L) Hen^{a}. Jenkins, Edwd. Jenkins & Sarah Jenkins; (M) Henrietta 35, Edward 32, Sarah 30.

64. (A) Decem^{r}. 26th, 1746; (B) Edward Jenkins; (C) 54$^{1}/_{2}$; (D) Edward Jenkins; (E) 0–5–8; (F) 1–2–8; (L) Edwd. Jenkins, Sarah Jenkins, & John Boon; (M) Edward 32, Sarah 30, John 36.

65. (A) April 27th, 1753; (B) John Moor; (C) 43$^{1}/_{2}$; (D) James Marshall; (E) 0–5–8; (F) 1–2–8; (L) James Moor, Hezekiah Moor & John Moor.

67. (A) Decem^{r}. 25th, 1746; (B) John Baggott; (C) 78; (D) John Baggott; (E) 0–8–6; (F) 1–14–0; (L) John Baggott, John Bowling Baggott & Sam: Baggott; (M) John 67, John Bowling 32, Samuel 27.

69. (A) Decem^{r}. 25, 1749; (B) Thomas Speake; (C) $40\frac{1}{2}$; (D) Thomas Speake; (E) 0–9–0; (F) 1–16–0; (L) Jane Speake & John Speake; (M) Jane 54, John 35.

70. (A) Decem^{r}. 5th, 1737; (B) John Vincent; (C) 86; (D) James Marshall; (E) 0–8–7; (F) 1–14–4; (L) John Vincent, Elizabeth Vincent & Rich^{d}. Vincent. quere their Ages & which are alive.

Totals: (C) 9637; (E) 26–12–$1\frac{1}{2}$; Fines due, 14–4–0.

DORCHESTER COUNTY

State of His Lordships Manor of Nanticoke in Dorchester County, November, 1767

I. (A) June 12th, 1747; (B) Henry Hooper, Son of Col°.; (C) 187; (D) Lessee; (E) 0–18–9; (L) Lessee & Ann his Wife; (M) Lessee 40, his Wife 38. Improved agreeable to Lease. Good Land.

II. (A) June 12, 1747; (B) Henry Hooper, Son of Col°.; (C) 170; (D) Lessee; (E) 0–17–0; (L) Ditto; (M) Ditto. Some improvements & soil.

III. (A) June 7, 1757; (B) Joshua Edmondson; (C) 168¾; (D) Lessee; (E) 1–13–10; (L) 21 years; Improved agreeable to Lease. Tollerable good low swampy land.

IV. (A) July 5, 1760; (B) Mary Jones; (C) 31; (D) Lessee; (E) 0–6–3; (L) 21 yrs. Low swamp.

V. (A) February 5th, 1760; (B) Elizabeth Foster; (C) 80; (D) Lessee; (E) 0–16–0; (L) 21 yrs. Improved agreeable to Lease. Tollerable good low Lands.

VI. (A) February 5th, 1760; (B) James Jones, Junr.; (C) 54; (D) Lessee; (E) 0–10–10; (L) 21 yrs. Chiefly low Swamp.

VII. (A) Aug. 17, 1760; (B) Daniel Jones, Junr.; (C) 92; (D) Lessee; (E) 0–18–6¾; (L) 21 yrs. Tollerable good Land.

VIII. (A) Apr. 25th, 1760; (B) Henry Hooper; (C) 14; (D) Lessee; (E) 0–2–11; (L) 21 yrs. Marsh, Water & Strand point.

IX. (A) Apr. 16, 1761; (B) Ditto; (C) 138¾; (D) Ditto; (E) 1–8–2; (L) 21 yrs. Good Swamp.

X. (A) Apr. 18, 1761; (B) Ditto; (C) 158; (D) Ditto; (E) 1–11–7; (L) 21 yrs. Poor Swamp.

XI. (A) Apr. 18, 1761; (B) William Jones; (C) 53¾; (D) Lessee; (E) 0–10–9; (L) 21 yrs. Good low Land.

XII. (A) Apr. 17, 1761; (B) John Wheeler; (C) 207; (D) Lessee; (E) 2–1–5; (L) 21 yrs. Improved agreeable to Lease. Chiefly broken poor Swamp.

XIII. (A) Apr. 21, 1761; (B) Gilbert Huffington; (C) 46½; (D) Lessee; (E) 0–9–4½; (L) 21 yrs. A Marsh.

XIV. (A) Aug. 24th, 1762; (B) William Smith; (C) 174; (D) Lessee; (E) 1–14–9¾; (L) 21 yrs. Improved agreeable to Lease. Part good Land & part low Swamp.

XV. (A) Ditto; (B) Ditto; (C) 46½; (D) Lessee; (E) 0–9–4; (L) 21 yrs. A Marsh.

XVI. (A) Feb. 7th, 1762; (B) William Jones; (C) 77; (D) Lessee; (E) 0–15–5; (L) 21 yrs. Good Swamp.

XVII. (A) April 13th, 1762; (B) John Pike; (C) 91; (D) Lessee; (E) 0–18–1½; (L) 21 yrs. Broken Land with small Ridges.

XVIII. (A) Oct. 29th, 1762; (B) Alexander Lang; (C) 150; (D) Lessee: (E) 1–10–0; (L) 21 yrs. Broken Swamp.

XIX. (A) Aug. 25th, 1762; (B) James Jones; (C) 100; (D) Lessee; (E) 1–0–0; (L) 21 yrs. Poor Swamp chiefly over the Manor Line.

XX. (A) June 25th, 1762; (B) John Charles Craft; (C) 50; (D) Lessee; (E) 0–10–0; (L) 21 yrs. Deep Swamp without Improvement.

XXI. (A) May 12th, 1763; (B) William Jones; (C) 25; (D) Lessee; (E) 0–5–0; (L) 21 yrs. All Marsh.

XXII. (A) May 11th, 1763; (B) Michael Holland; (C) 176; (D) Lessee; (L) 21 yrs. Broken Swamp some of which is very low.

XXIII. (A) May 12, 1763; (B) Alexander Lang; (C) 30; (D) Lessee; (E) 0–6–0; (L) 21 yrs. Poor Marsh.

XXIV. (A) June 12, 1763; (B) Levin Charlescraft; (C) 50; (D) Lessee; (E) 0–10–0; (L) 21 yrs. Very poor white Clay Swamp.

XXV. (A) May 14th, 1764; (B) Joshua Edmondson; (C) 261½; (D) Lessee; (E) 2–12–3; (L) Lessee. Improved as per Lease. Great part is low Swamp.

XXVI. (A) Ditto; (B) Zacharias Campbell & Co. (C) 3½; (D) Lessee; (E) 0–0–8; (L) 21 yrs. Improved as per Lease.

XXVII. (A) Sept. 29th, 1764; (B) Levin Bistpitch; (C) 103; (D) Lessee; (E) 1–0–7; (L) 21 yrs. Tollerable good low Land.

XXVIII. (A) Ditto; (B) John Bistpitch; (C) 288; (D) Lessee; (E) 2–17–7; (L) 21 yrs. Tollerable good low Land.

XXIX. (A) April 15th, 1766; (B) Jonathan Charlescroft; (C) 49; (D) Lessee; (E) 0–10–0; (L) 21 yrs. Poor white Clay Swamp.

XXX. (A) Ditto; (B) William Wheland; (C) 208; (D) Lessee; (E) 2–1–7; (L) 21 yrs. Improved as per Lease. Chiefly good low Land.

XXXI. (A) May 20th, 1762; (B) Charles Muir; (C) 432; (D) Lessee; (E) 3–12–0. Improved as per Lease. Lease not Executed per Cert. 360 a. Chiefly poor white Clay Swamp.

XXXII. (C) 50; (D) Edward White; (E) –10–0. Part good high Land & part Marsh, held per Certe.

XXXIII. (C) 25; (D) John Charlescraft; (E) 0–5–0. All marsh, held p. Certe.

XXXIV. (A) Dec. 11th, 1733; (B) Tranus Money; (C) 195; (D) Gilbert Huffington; (L) Life of John "Hodson" son of John "Hudson" *Quartus*, aged 45. N. B. Govr. & Agent granted this Lease clear of Rent. Tollerably good low Land.

XXXV. (C) 200; (D) John Leatherberry. held by Certificate. N. B. Leatherberry is pray[s]. Pattent. Tollerably good Land.

Total Annual Rent £35–8–11 3/4.

No.
A. (C) 66, Vacancy Joining No VIII & Nanticoke River.
B. (C) 42, ditto do No III & Manor Line.
C. (C) 223, ditto do Nanticoke River.
D. (C) 12, ditto do No V & X.
E. (C) 63, ditto do No XVIII & Manor Line.
F. (C) 43, ditto do No XIV & XXXIV.
G. (C) 238, ditto do Manor Line, XVII, XIX, XX, XXXI & XXXIV.
H. (C) 126, ditto do Manor Line, XXII, XXVII & XXVIII.
I. (C) 380, ditto do Nanticoke River, XXXI & XXXV.
K. (C) 71, ditto do Manor Line, XXVII & XXVIII.

Total acres 5449 1/4. N. B. The whole Manor is much Pillaged of Timber.

"State of His Lordship's Mannor of Gunpowder March, 1767. This Manor Certificate Dated Maie" ——.

Platt 1. (A) September 30th, 1736; (B) George Elliott; (C) 100; (D) John Chamberlain; (E) 1–0–0; (F) 2–0–0; (L) Ann Elliot & Susanna Westwood; (M) Ann about 75, Susana. ab[o]. 45.

Platt 2, 3, 4. (A) January 10th, 1745; (B) Jacob Wright; (C) 157; (D) Sarah Wright; (E) 1–11–4 3/4; (F) 3–2–9 1/2; (L) Ezekiel Wright & Solomon Watkins; (M) Ezekiel ab[o]. 39, Solomon ab[o]. 40.

5. (C) 143; (D) John Chamberlain; (E) 1–8–7 1/4; (M) held by a Certificate July 29th, 1762.

6. (A) January 14th, 1743; (B) John Chamberlain; (C) 106; (D) John Chamberlain; (E) 1–1–1; (F) 2–2–2; (L) Tho[s]. Chamberlain, Eliz. Chamberlain & Mary Chamberlain; (M) Thomas 25, Eliz: 26, Mary 20—Vide Date of the Lease.

7. (A) January 24, 1756; (B) Joseph Frost; (C) 100; (D) Mary Frost; (E) 1–0–0; (F) 2–0–0; (L) Twenty one years.

8. (A) March 2[d], 1737; (B) Thomas Gittings; (C) 153; (D) James Gittings; (E) 1–10–0; (F) 3–0–0; (L) Susanna Gittings, Tho[s]. Gittings & James Gittings; (M) Susanna 39, Thomas 36, James 31.

9. (A) January 1, 1738; (B) Thomas Gittings; (C) 108; (D) Ja[s]. Gittings & John Chamberlain; (E) 1–1–7 1/2; (F) 2–3–3; (Fines due) 1–11–

2; (L) Thomas Gittings, James Gittings & Azael Gittings; (M) Thos. 36, James 31, Azael 28. Vide Date of Lease. Fine due or ——.

10. (A) March 7, 1721 (B) Thomas Gittings (C) 155; (D) John Chamberlaine; (E) 2–5–0; (F) 10–0–0; (L) Margaret Chamberlaine Daughter of Thos. Gittings; (M) Margaret Chamberlaine 47.

(A) March 7, 1755; (B) Thomas Gittings, New Lease; (C) 295; (D) James Gittings; (E) 3–5–0; (F) 6–10; (L) Ja^{s}. Gittings, Azael Gittings & Thos. Son of Thos. Gittings; (M) James 31, Azael 28, Thomas 14. In this Lease is included the Lea ——.

11. (C) 80; (D) James Gittings; (E) 0–16–0; (M) held by Certificate.

12. (A) December 28, 1728; (B) John Diggs; (C) 150; (D) James Moore; (E) 0–15–0; (F) 6–0–0; (L) Philip Diggs, Edward Diggs & William Diggs; (M) Philip 50, Edward 48, William 46, pays 2 Capons.

13. (C) 120; (D) John Miller; (E) 1–4–0; (M) held by Certificate.

14. (A) February 25, 1742; (B) Charles Baker; (C) 115; (D) Charles Baker; (E) 1–3–0; (F) 2–6–0; (L) Charles Baker & Charles Baker his Son; (M) Charles Senr. 63, Charles Junr. 26.

15. (A) March 20, 1720; (B) William Deason; (C) 100; (D) Charles Baker; (E) 0–10–0; (F) 4–0–0; (L) Saml. Deason, W^{m}. Deason Junr. & John Deason; (M) Saml. 63, W^{m}. 60, John 58. Gone to Virg^{a}. ab^{o}. 15 years ago.

16. (C) 33; (D) Charles Baker; (E) 0–6–$7^{1}/_{2}$; (M) held by Certificate.

17. (A) August 29, 1761; (B) John James; (C) 73; (D) John James; (E) 0–14–7; (F) 1–9–2; (L) Twenty One years.

18. (C) 100; (D) Michael Jenkins; (E) 1–0–0; (M) held by Cirtificate.

19. (A) February 25, 1742; (B) William Standeford; (C) 220; (D) William Standeford; (E) 2–4–0; (F) 4–8–0; (L) William Standeford & Anila Standeford; (M) William 58, Aquila 25.

20. (A) Septem^{r}. 30, 1736; (B) Darby Hernley; (C) 100; (D) Michael Jenkins; (E) 1–0–0; (F) 2–0–0; (Fines due) 2–0–0; (L) Mary Hernley, Darby Hernley & Edmund Hernley; (M) Mary 40, Darby 35, Edmund 33, all gone to Carolina 4 y ——.

21. (A) March 20, 1720; (B) John Fuller; (C) 120; (D) Michael Jenkins; (E) 0–12–0; (F) 4–0–0; (Fines due) 4–0–0; (L) Henry Fuller, Nehemiah Fuller; (M) Henry 50, Nehemiah 48, pays 2 Capons. Gone to Carolina.

22. (A) January 1, 1738; (B) Thomas Gittings; (C) 98; (D) Thomas Gittings; (E) 0–19–$7^{1}/_{2}$; (F) 1–19–3; (L) Thos. Gittings, James Gittings & Azael Gittings; (M) Thomas 36, James 31, Azael 28. Vide Date of Lease.

23. (A) April 15, 1749; (B) James Moore, Junr.; (C) 200; (D) Geo. Hunter & Ja^{s}. Gittings; (E) 2–0–0; (F) 4–0–0; (L) James Moore, Rezin Moore & Mary Moore; (M) James 46, Rezin 22, Mary 24.

24. (A) Septem^{r}. 29, 1756; (B) James Moore; (C) 200; (D) George Hunter & Ja^{s}. Gittings; (E) 2–0–0; (F) 4–0–0; (L) Rezin Moore, Ja^{s}. Frances Moore & Nicholas Ruxton Moore; (M) Rezin 22, Ja^{s}. Francis 15, Nic^{s}. Ruxton 12.

25. (A) January 29, 1762; (B) Rezin Moore; (C) 125; (D) George Hunter; (E) 1–5–0; (F) 2–10–0; (L) Twenty one years.

26. (A) December 15, 1742; (B) James Demmit; (C) 200; (D) Arthur Croskery; (E) 2–0–0; (F) 4–0–0; (Fines due) 4–0–0; (L) Ja^{s}. Demmit, Athaliah Demmit & Eliz: Demmit; (M) James 60, Athaliah 29, Eliz: 27. Gone to Carolina, ab^{o}. 1 year.

27. (A) March 20, 1720; (B) William Demmit; (C) 100; (D) James Demmit; (E) 0–10–0; (F) 4–0–0; (L) James 60, William 56. Pay 2 Capons. Ja^{s}. gone to Carolina.

28. (A) March 7, 1755; (B) Thos. Gittings; (C) 50; (D) James Gittings; (E) 0–10–0; (F) 1–0–0; (L) James Gittings, Azael Gittings, & Thos. Son of Thos. Gittings; (M) James 31, Azael 28, Thomas 14.

29. (C) 166; (D) James Demmitt; (E) 1–13–2$^{1}/_{2}$; (M) held by Certificate April 10, 1755.

30. (A) Sept. 11, 1728; (B) Darby Hernley; (C) 100; (D) Joseph Lewis; (E) 0–10–0; (F) 4–0–0; (Fines due) 4–0–0; (L) Darby Hernley, Ann Hernley, Mary Hernley; (M) Darby 63, Mary 40, Ann 42. "Quere all gone to Carolina."

31. (C) 156; (D) Joseph Lewis; (E) 1–11–2$^{1}/_{2}$; (M) held by Certificate March 25th, 1761.

32. (C) 14; (D) Arthur Croskery; (E) 0–2–10$^{3}/_{4}$; (M) held by Certificate Sep^{t}. 29, 1762.

33. (A) Jan. 1, 1738; (B) Thos. Gittings; (C) 36; (D) Ja^{s}. Gittings & John Chamberlaine; (E) 0–7–2$^{1}/_{2}$; (F) 0–14–5; (L) Thos. Gittings, James Gittings, Azael Gittings; (M) Thos. 36, James 31, Azael 28. Vide Date of Lease, same Land as No. 3 ——.

34. (A) Jan. 1, 1738 —— record duplicates Platt 33 ——; (L) "same lives."

35. (C) 76; (D) William Sandeford; (E) 0–15–2$^{1}/_{2}$; (M) held by Certificate Feb. 25, 1754. This & No. 19 are the same Land & make together 2 ——.

36. (C) 22; (D) Benjamin Guiton; (E) 0–4–4$^{3}/_{4}$; (M) held by Certificate.

37. (A) July 7, 1743; (B) Abraham Enlows; (C) 41; (D) Robert Cummings; (E) 1–8–2; (F) 2–16–6; (L) Mary Enlows & Benj^{a}. Enlows; (M) Mary 56, Benj^{a}. 28.

38. (C) 143; (D) Edward Bussey; (E) 1–8–7$^{1}/_{4}$; (M) held by Certificate.

39. (C) 15$^{1}/_{4}$; (D) Jeremiah Chance; (E) 0–2–$^{1}/_{2}$; (M) held by Certificate.

40. (C) 140; (D) William Bryan; (E) 1–8–0; (M) held by Certificate, Dec. 15, 1750.

41. (C) 52; (D) Abraham Bryan; (E) 0–10–4$^{3}/_{4}$; (M) held by Ditto Aug. 30, 1762.

42. (A) May 10, 1748; (B) Abraham Ditto; (C) 100; (D) Abraham Ditto; (E) 1–0–0; (F) 2–0–0; (L) Abraham Ditto, Mary Ditto & Diana Ditto; (M) Abraham 50, Mary 45, Diana 27.

43. (A) Dec. 17, 1742; (B) John Legett; (C) 125; (D) Thomas Butler; (E) 1–5–0; (F) 2–10–0; (Fines due) 2–10–0; (L) John Legett; (M) John Legett 56.

44. (C) 13; (D) Samuel Watkins; (E) 0–2–7$^{1}/_{4}$; (M) held by Certificate Aug. 16, 1762.

45. (C) 152; (D) Samuel Watkins; (E) 1–10–4$^{3}/_{4}$; (M) held by Certificate May 21, 1750.

46. (C) 100; (D) Colding Coombs; (E) 1–0–0; (M) held by Certificate June 20, 1753.

47. (A) Sept. 29, 1748; (B) Cornelius Lynch; (C) 120; (D) Cornelius Lynch; (E) 1–4–0; (F) 2–4–0; (L) Winifred Lynch, Catharine Lynch & Hugh Brady; (M) Winifred 26 [?], Catharine 22, Hugh Brady 24.

48. (A) May 28, 1761; (B) Cornelius Lynch; (C) 140; (D) Cornelius Lynch; (E) 1–8–0; (F) 2–16–0; (L) Twenty one years.

49. (A) Dec. 16, 1742; (B) William Dimmit; (C) 200; (D) Benjamin Guiton; (E) 2–0–0; (F) 4–0–0; (L) William Dimmit, James Dimmit & W^{m}. Dimmit, Junr.; (M) William 56, James 50, William, Junr. 26.

50. (A) Nov. 10, 1733; (B) Abraham Enlows; (C) 100; (D) Robert Cummings; (E) 1–0–0; (F) 2–0–0; (Fines due) 2–0–0; (L) Mary Enlows & Benjamin Enlows; (M) Mary 55, Benj. 28.

51. (A) May 30, 1744; (B) "Edward Busey"; (C) 100; (D) "Edward Bussey"; (E) 1–0–0; (F) 2–0–0; (L) Jessie Bussie & Thomas Bussey; (M) Jessie 29, Thomas 24.

52. (C) 116; (D) Thomas Atkinson; (E) 1–3–2$^{1}/_{2}$; (M) held by Certificate April 30, 1753.

53. (A) March 25, 1742; (B) William Coal; (C) 100; (D) Edward Rose; (E) 1–0–0; (F) 2–0–0; (Unpaid fines) 2–0–0; (L) William Coal, Mary Coal & Broad Coal; (M) William 45, Mary 43, Broad 34.

54. (A) July 7, 1748; (B) Peter Mallanee; (C) 100; (D) Abraham Wright; (E) 1–0–0; (F) 2–0–0; (L) John Mallanee; (M) John Mallanee 30.

55. (A) Dec. 25, 1743; (B) John Lawson; (C) 152; (D) Jeremiah Chanee; (E) 1–10–2$^{1}/_{2}$; (F) 3–0–5; (L) John Lawson, Ann Lawson & Eliz: Lawson; (M) John 42, Ann 28, Eliz: 27.

56. (A) Sept. 22, 1761; (B) Jeremiah Chanee; (C) 18; (D) Jeremiah Chanee; (E) 0–3–7; (F) 0–7–2; (L) Twenty one years.

57. (C) 104; (D) James Elliot; (E) 1–0–9$^{1}/_{2}$; (M) held by Certificate March 31, 1746.

58. (A) March 2^{d}, 1737; (B) Robert Gott; (C) 100; (D) Mary Gudgeons; (E) 1–0–0; (F) 2–0–0; (L) Richard Gott & Elizabeth Gott; (M) Richard 31, Eliz: 42.

59. (C) 44; (D) Abraham Wright; (E) 0–8–9$^{1}/_{2}$; (M) held by Cirtificate, 60. (A) March 2^{d}, 1737; (B) Richard Cox; (C) 100; (D) Henry McCastlin; (E) 1–0–0; (F) 2–0–0; (Unpaid fines) 6–0–0; (L) Ann Cox & Elizabeth Cox; (M) Ann 55, Eliz: 33, remov^{d}. from Virg^{a}. to S^{o}. Carolina ab^{o}. 3 years.

61. (A) Sept. 9, 1761; (B) Groombright Bailey; (C) 175; (D) Groombright Bailey; (E) 1–15–0; (F) 3–10–0; (L) Twenty one years.

62. (A) March 7th, 1746; (B) William Wilson; (C) 240; (D) John & Benjamin Thidd Wilson; (E) 2–8–0; (F) 4–16–0; (L) John Wilson & Benjamin Thidd Wilson; (M) John 46, Benjamin 36.

63. (A) January 12, 1746; (B) Richard Harriot; (C) 100; (D) Richard Harriot; (E) 1–0–0; (F) 2–0–0; (L) Richard Harriot, Ann Harriot & Mary Harriot; (M) Richard 60, Ann 28, Mary 26.

64. (C) 72; (D) John Wilson; (E) 0–14–4$^{3}/_{4}$; (M) held by Certificate May 25th, 1762.

65. (A) Sept. 13, 1734; (B) John Lawson; (C) 100; (D) George Smith; (E) 1–0–0; (F) 2–0–0; (Unpaid fines) 2–0–0; (L) John Lawson, Thomas Lawson & Moses Lawson; (M) John 42, Thomas 39, Moses 38.

66. (C) 62; (D) Michael Jenkins; (E) 0–12–4$^{3}/_{4}$; (M) held by Certificate May 19th, 1754 for 162, the 100 acres ——.

State of His Lordships Manor [Conegocheague?] 1767— Surveyed October 25th. 17—

1. (A) July 21, 1762; (B) Joseph Williams; (C) 233; (D) George Ross Ex^{r}. of Lessee; (E) 2–6–8; (E) 5. 13. 4; (L) 21 yrs.

2. (A) June 23, 1762; (B) George Ross; (C) 300; (D) George Ross; (E) 3–0–0; (F) 6–0–0; (L) 21 yrs.

3. (A) June 23, 1762; (B) Aaron More; (C) 128; (D) Aaron More; (E) 1–5–7; (F) 2–11–2; (L) 21 yrs.

4. (A) Octob^{r}. 17, 1737; (B) Van Swearingen Senr.; (C) 103; (D) Van Swearingen Junr.; (E) –11–0; (F) 0–11–0; Fines due, 0–11–0; (L) Joseph Swearingen, John Swearingen & Van Swearingen, Sons of Lessie; (M) Joseph 42, John 36, Van 34. Quere if this fine is due.

5. (A) Septem^{r}. 17, 1762; (B) Van Swearingen Junr.; (C) 165; (D) Van Swearingen, Junr.; (E) 1–13–0; (F) 3–6–0; (L) 21 yrs.

6. (A) June 28, 1762; (B) Arnest Cremer; (C) 111; (D) Arnest Cremer, Lessee; (E) 1–2–2$^{1}/_{2}$; (F) 2–4–5; (L) 21 yrs.

7. (A) Septem^{r}. 7, 1762; (B) Basil Williams; (C) 300; (D) Basil Williams; (E) 3–0–0; (F) 6–0–0; (L) 21 yrs.

8. (A) Decem^{r}. 9, 1752; (B) Col^{o}. Thomas Prather; (C) 214; (D) Thomas Prather; (E) 1–1–4$^{3}/_{4}$; (F) 2–2–9$^{1}/_{2}$; (L) Thomas Prather; (M) Thomas Prather 60, Elizabeth & Thomas Clegett Prather, both Dead.

9. (A) Septem^{r}. 30, 1765; (B) Martin Vasner; (C) 65; (D) Martin Carner; (E) 0–13–0; (F) 1–6–0; (L) 21 yrs.; (M) held by Certificate dated March 30, 1765. Lease executed.

10. (C) 100; (D) Edward Gaither; (E) 1–0–0; (F) 2–0–0; (L) 21 yrs. held by Certificate dated March 4th, 1763 made to Danl. Williams & sold to present Possessor.

11. (C) 100; (D) Valentine Lytle; (E) 1–0–0; (F) 2–0–0; (L) 21 yrs.; (M) held by Certificate dated Feb. 28, 1765.

12. (C) 100; (D) Zephaniah Walker; (E) 0–13–7$^{1}/_{2}$; (F) 1–7–3; Fines due, 1–7–3; (L) 21 yrs.; (M) held by Certificate dated Mch. 14th, 1765 for Joseph Wells & sold to the present Possessor.

13. (A) Decem^{r}. 23^{d}, 1762; (B) Richard Lucas; (C) 100; (D) Lawrence Swoop; (E) 1–0–0; (F) 2–0–0; (L) 21 yrs.

14. (A) March 5th, 1763; (B) James Kendall; (C) 100; (D) Jacob Pryliman; (E) 1–0–0; (F) 2–0–0; (L) 21 yrs.

15. (A) Feby. 10, 1763; (B) Joseph Wells; (C) 150; (D) Joseph Wells; (E) 1–10–0; (F) 3–0–0; (M) held by Certificate dated Feb. 10th, 1763.

16. (A) Jany. 30, 1737; (B) Jonathan "Symmonds" Senr.; (C) 200; (D) John Swearingen; (E) 1–0–0; (F) 2–0–0; (L) Elizabeth "Symonds" & Jonathan "Symonds"; (M) Lessee dead, Elizabeth 52, Jonathan 31.

17. (C) 56; (D) Samuel Lucas; (E) 0–11–2$^{1}/_{2}$; (F) 1–2–5; (L) 21 yrs.; (M) held by Certificate dated March 14th, 1765.

18. (A) May 4th, 1749; (B) Peter Bell; (C) 72; (D) Samuel Lucas Tenant of Lessee; (E) –7–2$^{1}/_{2}$; (F) –14–5; (L) Peter Bell Lessee & Samuel Lucas; (M) Peter 75, Samuel 35, Eliz: wife of Lessee Dead.

19. (C) 100; (D) George Fry; (E) 1–0–0; (F) 2–0–0; (L) 21 yrs.; (M) held by Certificate dated Jan. 13th, 1764. Lease Exc^{d}.

20. (C) 100; (D) John Mane; (E) 1–0–0; (F) 2–0–0; (L) 21 yrs.; (M) held by Certificate dated March 14th, 1765.

21. (C) 100; (D) Jacob Houser; (E) 1–0–0; (F) 2–0–0; (L) 21 yrs.; (M) held by Certificate dated Jany. 13th, 1764.

22. (C) 100; (D) John Morndaller; (E) 1–0–0; (F) 2–0–0; (L) 21 yrs.; (M) held by Certificate dated Decem^{r}. 9th, 1764.

23. (C) 94; (D) William Miller; (E) 0–18–10; (F) 1–17–8; (L) 21 yrs.; (M) held by Certificate dated July 20th, 1765. Lease Executed.

24. (A) June 26th, 1765; (B) Peter Settee; (C) 105; (D) Peter Settee; (E) 1–1–0; (F) 2–2–0; (L) 21 yrs. as appears by Counterpart; (M) held by Certificate dated June 26th, 1765.

25. (C) 70; (D) John Varner; (E) 0–14–0; (F) 1–8–0; (L) 21 yrs.; (M) held by Certificate dated June 26, 1765. Lease Excd.

26. (A) October 6th, 1763, (B) John Layman; (C) 125; (D) Adam Miller; (E) 1–5–0; (F) 2–10–0; (L) 21 yrs.

27. (C) 118; (D) Joseph Leaman; (E) 1–3–7; (F) 2–7–3; (L) 21 yrs.; (M) held by Certificate dated Feb. 25th, 1765. Lease Excd.

28. (A) July 21st, 1762; (B) John Laymon; (C) 160; (D) Joseph Burley; (E) 1–12–0; (F) 3–4–0; (L) 21 yrs.

29. (C) 120; (D) Frederick Shaveley; (E) 1–4–0; (F) 2–8–0; (L) 21 yrs.; (M) held by Certificate dated Feby. 26th, 1765. Lease Excd.

30. (C) 120; (D) John Upperhizer; (E) 1–10–7½; (F) 3–1–3; (L) 21 yrs.; (M) held by Certificate dated Feby. 27th, 1765.

31. (A) Decemr. 24th, 1762; (B) John Belt, Son of Higginton; (C) 100; (D) Jeremiah Lackland; (E) 1–0–0; (F) 2–0–0; (L) 21 yrs.

32. (A) June 13, 1763; (B) James Stockwell; (C) 115; (D) Jacob Priliman; (E) 1–3–0; (F) 2–6–0; Fines due 2–6–0; (L) 21 yrs.

33. (C) 68; (D) John Bowslaw; (E) 0–13–7½; (F) 1–7–3; (L) 21 yrs.; (M) held by Certificate dated Decemr. 31st, 1765. Lease Excd.

34. (A) Septr. 29th, 1743; (B) Thomas Waller; (C) 100; (D) Christian Miller; (E) 0–10–0; (F) 1–0–0; (L) Lessee, Mary, Lessee's wife & John their Son; (M) Lessee 86, Mary 70, John 29.

35. (A) April 4, 1763; (B) Christian Miller; (C) 132; (D) Christian Miller, Lessee; (E) 1–6–5; (F) 2–12–10; (L) 21 yrs.

36. (A) June 18, 1763; (B) Nicholas Rhodes; (C) 126; (D) Nichs. Rhodes, Lessee; (E) 1–5–2½; (F) 2–10–5; (L) 21 yrs.

37. (A) June 19th, 1763; (B) Ezekiel Rhodes; (C) 100; (D) Ezekiel Rhodes, Lessee; (E) 1–0–0; (F) 2–0–0; (L) 21 yrs.

38. (A) Augt. 25, 1763; (B) James Butcher; (C) 100; (D) James Butcher, Lessee; (E) 1–0–0; (F) 2–0–0; (L) 21 yrs.

39. (A) Septmr. 29th, 1737; (B) Van Swearingen; (C) 278; (D) Van Swearingen, Lessee; (E) 1–7–9½; (F) 1–7–7; (L) Lessee, Samuel & Charles; (M) Lessee 76, Samuel 37, Charles 32. N. B. This fine is less than the ann. Rent.

40. (A) Augt. 26, 1763; (B) Charles Swearingen; (C) 92; (D) Charles Swearingen, Lessee; (E) 0–18–5; (F) 1–16–10; (L) 21 yrs.

41. (A) Septr. 6, 1763; (B) Charles Neal, Junr. (C) 130; (D) Eleanor Midley; (E) 1–6–0; (F) 2–12–0; (L) 21 yrs.

42. (A) Feby. 26, 1739; (B) John Hallam; (C) 100; (D) Leonard Smith; (E) 0–15–0; (F) 1–10–0; (L) Lessee, Mary his wife & William their son; Lessee 65, Mary 55, William 36. Quere if all alive. Vide Minutes.

43. (C) 128; (D) Leonard Smith; (E) 1–5–7½; (F) 2–11–3; (L) 21 yrs.; (M) held by Certificate dated Septr. 10th, 1765.

44. (A) Octr. 17th, 1737; (B) Van Swearingen; (C) 99; (D) Christ^{o}. Plunk or Brunk; (E) 0–10–0; (F) 0–10–0; (L) Van Swearingen's Son & Elizabeth Wife of Lessee; (M) Van 40, Elizabeth 70. N. B. The names of the Lessee & Lives in this Lease & Coun [?] are erased & other inserted.

45. (A) July 27, 1762; (B) Joseph Rench; (C) 172; (D) Christopher Plunk; (E) 1–14–5; (F) 3–8–10; (L) 21 yrs.

46. (A) July 26, 1762; (B) Joseph Crable; (C) 185; (D) Adam Coodle & Jacob Grove; (E) 1–17–0; (F) 3–14–0; (L) 21 yrs.

47. (A) Augt. 5, 1762; (B) Jacob Miers; (C) 100; (D) John Judy; (E) 1–0–0; (F) 2–0–0; (L) 21 yrs.

48. (A) March 16, 1761; (B) David Miller; (C) 148; (D) David Miller; (E) 1–9–6; (F) 2–19–0; (L) 21 yrs.

49. (A) Septr. 19, 1761; (B) William Miller; (C) 108; (D) George Huver; (E) 1–1–7½; (F) 2–3–3; (L) 21 yrs.

50. (A) [Torn] em 7, 1761; (B) Jacob Yeakill; (C) 107; (D) Jacob Yeakill, Lessee; (E) 1–1–5; (F) 2–2–10; (L) 21 yrs.

51. (A) [Torn] tem^{r}. 30, 1763; (B) Robert Jackson; (C) 150; (D) Robert Jackson, Lessee; (E) 1–10–0; (F) 3–0–0; (L) 21 yrs.

52. (A) Septmb^{r}. 29, 1760; (B) James Hinthorn; (C) 171; (D) Jacob Plunk; (E) 1–3–5; (F) 2–6–10; (L) 21 yrs.

53. (C) 177; (D) John Craig; (E) 1–15–5; (F) 3–10–10; (L) 21 yrs.; (M) held by Certificate dated Octo^{r}. 1st, 1763. Ed^{d}. Nichols has a Lease for Lives on this but he never [improved?]

54. (A) [Torn] 29th, 1759; (B) Rich^{d}. Carter; (C) 70; (D) Richard Carter, Lessee; (E) 0–14–0; (F) 1–8–0; (L) 21 yrs; (M) In this Lease there is a great mistake in the Courses. Vide Plat & Minutes.

55. (A) [Torn] 1745; (B) Joseph Lashier; (C) 120; (D) Joseph Lashier, Lessee; (E) 0–12–0; (F) 1–4–0; (L) Lessee, Thomas Lashier & John Lashier his Sons; (M) Joseph 40, Thomas 26, John 24.

56. (A) [Torn] 1754; (B) John Little; (C) 138; (D) Rich^{d}. Carter, Ex^{r}. of Lessee; (E) 0–13–9; (F) 1–7–6; (L) Frances, Widow of Lessee & Mary his Daughter; (M) Frances 40, Mary 16. Frances is now married to R. Carter present Tenant.

57. (A) [Torn] 1754; (B) Peter Malott; (C) 106; (D) Peter Malott; (E) 0–10–7; (F) 1–1–2; (L) Lessee, Sarah his Wife & Thomas their Son; (M) Lessee 40, Sarah 34 & Thomas 16.

58. (A) [Torn] 1737; (B) George Gordon; (C) 500; (D) Doc^r. Charles Neale; (E) 2–10–0; (F) 5–0–0; (L) Mary Gordon & John children of Lessee & James Forbes Son of John of St. Mary's Co. (M) Mary 35, John 32, James 40. Quere if all alive.

59. (A) [Torn] 1759; (B) Doc^r. Charles Neale; (C) 200; (D) Doc^r. Charles Neale; (E) 2–0–0; (F) 4–0–0; (L) 21 yrs.

60. (C) 144; (D) Ralph Neale; (E) 1–8–10; (F) 2–17–8; (L) 21 yrs.; (M) held by Certificate dated Septr. 17, 1765. Lease Executed.

61. (C) 100; (D) Christian Traxall; (E) 1–0–0; (F) 2–0–0; (L) 21 yrs.; (M) held by Certificate dated Septr. 15, 1765. Lease Executed.

62. (C) 164; (D) Ralph Neale; (E) 1–12–10; (F) 3–5–8; (L) 21 yrs.; (M) held by Certificate dated Septr. 16, 1765. (Lease Executed).

63. (A) June 16th, 1761; (B) Edward Henesch; (C) 57; (D) Edward Henesch; (E) 0–11–5; (F) 1–2–10; (L) 21 yrs.

64. (C) 100; (D) Martin Carner; (E) 1–2–0; (F) 2–4–0; (M) held by Certificate dated March 10th, 1760.

65. (C) 240; (D) Martin Varner; (E) 2–8–0; (F) 4–16–0; (L) 21 yrs.; (M) held by Cirtificate dated November 9th, 1764. Lease Exc^d.

66. (A) July 19, 1763; (B) Martin Trout [Frout]; (C) 85; (D) Martin Trout [Frout?]; (E) 0–17–0; (F) 1–14–0; (L) 21 yrs.

67. (A) June 30, 1762; (B) Hans Millar; (C) 156; (D) Hans Millar; (E) 1–11–2½; (F) 3–2–5; (L) 21 yrs.

68. (C) 92; (D) John Fry [Try?]; (E) 0–18–5; (F) 1–16–10; Fines due 1–16–10; (L) 21 yrs.; (M) held by Cirtificate dated Novr. 12th, 1764, made out for Jos. Davis & sold to the present [Torn].

69. (A) June 13, 1762; (B) Ephraim Skyles; (C) 122; (D) Ephraim Skyles; (E) 1–4–5; (F) 2–8–10; (L) 21 yrs.; (M) this Lot lies almost without the Manor Lines.

70. (C) 104; (D) Thomas South; (E) 0–10–5; (F) 1–0–10; (L) Thomas South age about 50; (M) Certificate dated Septr. 29, 1763, but whether held by it or not uncertain vide ——.

71. (C) 76; (D) Joseph Malott; (E) 0–15–2½; (F) 1–10–5; (L) 21 yrs.; (M) held by Certificate dated July 20, 1765. Leese executed.

72. (C) 51; (D) Benjamin Malott; (E) 0–10–2½; (F) 1–0–5; (L) 21 yrs; (M) held by Cirtificate dated Feby. 25, 1766. Lease Executed.

73. (C) 200; (D) George Ross; (E) 2–0–0; (F) 4–0–0; (L) 21 yrs.; (M) held by Cirtificate dated Septr. 29, 1765. Lease Executed.

74. (C) 170; (D) George Ross; (E) 1–14–0; (F) 3–0–0; (L) 21 yrs.; (M) held by Cirtificate dated Sep^t. 29, 1765. Ditto.

75. (A) Oct^r. ——; (B) John Swan; (C) 100; (D) John Swan; (E) 0–10–0; (F) 1–0–0; (L) Lessee, Elizabeth his Wife & Thomas their Son; (M) Lessee 45, Wife 43, Son 20.

76. (B) Thomas Cresap; (C) 106; (D) Col°. Thomas Cresap; (D) 0–10–8; (E) ——; (L) Lessee, Thomas his Son & Michael his Son. (M) tis said Cresap has a Leese for this.

77. (C) 200; (D) Thomas Powell; (E) 2–0–0; (F) 4–0–0; (L) 21 yrs.; (M) held by Cirtificate June 14th, 1765. Lies in the Reserve, is part of Helmes' Reston Widows Mito [Caveat?]

78. (C) 50; (D) John Powell; (E) 0–10–0; (F) 1–0–0; (L) 21 yrs.; (M) held by Cirtificate June 12, 1765. Lies in the Reserve. Lease Executed.

79. (C) 100; (D) Jeremiah Foster; (E) 1–0–0; (F) 2–0–0; (L) 21 yrs.; (M) held by Cirtificate June 16, 1765. Lies in the Reserve.

80. (C) 100; (D) Anthony Higer [?]; (E) 1–0–0; (F) 2–0–0; (L) 21 yrs.; (M) held by Cirtificate dated June 15, 1765. Lies in the Reserve. Leese Excd.

Note: Conegocheague (?) Manor, pages 43–48, probably belongs in Frederick County, following.

FREDERICK COUNTY, 1767-1768

"State of His Lordship's Manor of Monococy, Monococy, 1767."*

Lot or Plat No. 1. (A) Leased Nov. 1, 1752 to (B) Simon Shover, (C) 54 acres; (D) tenant in possession, Simon Shover, lessie; (E) annual rent, –10–10; (F) "aluna. fine," 1–1–10; fines due, none; (L) leased on lives of Simon Shover, Adam son of Simon, Peter Shover; (M) ages of persons named in the lease, Simon 55, Adam 20, Peter 21.

No. 2. Leased Aug. 23, 1741 to John Biggs, 203 acres; tenant in possession Caspar Devil; annual rent, 1–0–4; aluna. fine, 2–0–8; fines due, none; leased on 2 lives, Benjamin Biggs & Wife, Benjamin Biggs & William Biggs; Ages Benjamin 43, William [?]0. [Note: the latter age is indistinct as to the first figure—the "O" is heavy, as in correction. Following is the addition of 43 and 15, or 58, and after the "58" appears "55".]

No. 3. Leased March 30, 1745 to Daniel Pattinger, 186 acres; tenants in possession, George, David and Christn. Miller; annual rent, 0–18–7; aluna. fine, 1–17–2; fines due, none; leased on 3 lives. Daniel Pattinger, John Pattinger & Elizabeth Pattinger; ages Daniel 55, John 27 & Elizabeth 50.

No. 4. Leased Nov. 28, 1743 to George Devil, 125 acres; tenant in possession Caspar Devil; annual rent 0–12–6; aliena. fine 1–5–0; fines due, none; leased on 2 lives, George and John Devil's; ages, George 55, John 27.

No. 5. Leased Febry. 25, 1743 to Peter Evelant, 99 acres; tenant in possession George Devil, Junr.; an. rent 0–9–11; aliena. fine 0–19–10; fines due, none; leased on 3 lives, John Hoffman, Barbara Hoffman & George son of George Devil; ages John 55, Barbara 56, George 22.

No. 6. Leased Oct. 8, 1741 to William Wilson, 100 acres; tenant in possession William Wilson, lessie; an. rent 0–10–0; aliena. fine 1–0–0; leased on 3 lives, John Wilson, William Wilson, Thomas Wilson; ages John 42, William 37, Thomas 26.

No. 7. Leased June 25, 1761 to Robert Whitnall, 33 acres; Robert Whitnall lessee in possession; an. rent 0–6–7; aliena. fine, 0–13–2; fines due, none; leased for 21 years.

No. 8. Leased Decr. 6, 1743 to Handell Hann, 120 acres; tenant in possession Frederick Baker; an. rent, 0–12–0; aliena. fine, 1–4–0; fines due, none; leased on lives of Handel Hann, Mary Hann, & Catherine

* This information is given in 2 sheets 12½ in. x 17½ in.

Hann; ages Handel 45, Mary 40, Catherine 13, all gone to Carolina 8 years.

No. 9. Leased March 12, 1754 to Richard Cooke, 240 acres; tenant in possession George Devil; an. rent, 1–4–0; aliena. fine, 2–8–0; fines due, none; leased on lives of Richd. Cooke [Mary Magdale crossed out] & Richard Donaldson Cooke; ages Richard 50, [Mary Magdalene 46], Richard Donaldson 20.

No. 10. Leased Augst. 26, 1748 to Joseph Hedge, 150 acres; tenant in possession Charles Hedge, Junr.; an. rent, 0–15–0; aliena. fine, 1–10–0; leased on life of Solomon Douther age of person named in the lease Solomon 40, gone to Carolina 14 years. Que. if alive.

No. 11. Leased Decr. 22, 1741 to Thomas Ebthorp, 100 acres; tenant in possession Charles Hedge, Senr.; an. rent, 0–10–0; aliena. fine, 1–0–0; fines due 3–0–0; leased on life of Peter Numbers; age Peter. Que. if alive.

No. 12. Leased Novr. 8, 1752 to Kennedy Farrell, 250 acres; tenant in possession William Crume; an. rent, 1–5–0; aliena. fine, 2–10–0; fines due, 2–10–0; leased on life of John Farrell; age of John 30. Que. if alive.

No. 13. Leased Octr. 29, 1751 to Christian Rodebaugh, 132 acres; tenant in possession Jacob Cremer; an. rent, 0–13–$2\frac{1}{4}$; aliena. fine, 1–6–$4\frac{1}{2}$; fines due, none; leased on life of Christian Rodebaugh, Elisabeth Rodebaugh, Valentine Wisecup [Winecup?]; ages of persons named in lease, Christian 60, Elisabeth 50, Valentine 22. Gone to Raestown 12 years. Que. if alive.

No. 14. Leased ——, to ——, 50 acres; tenant in possession Christian Berg—held by Certificate dated May 12th, 1761.

No. 15. Leased Octor. 10, 1764 to George Devil, 103 acres; George Devil lessie in possession; annual rent, 1–0–$7\frac{1}{4}$; aliena. fine, 2–1–$0\frac{1}{2}$; leased for 20 years. Also written "19 yr. lease."

No. 16. Leased Septr. 30, 1765 to William Smith, 77 acres; William Smith lessie in possession; an. rent, 0–15–$5\frac{1}{2}$; aliena. fine, 1–10–11. Leased for 18 years.

No. 17. Leased Septr. 29, 1764 to Simon Shover, 18 acres; Simon Shover in possession; an. rent, 0–3–7; aliena. fine, 0–7–2; leased for 19 years.

No. 18. Leased Febry. 24, 1743 to John Christian Smith, 100 acres; John Christian Smith lessie in charge; an. rent, 0–10–0; aliena. fine, 1–0–0; leased on 3 lives John Christian Smith 53 yrs., William Smith 30, Peter Berg, Junr. 28.

No. 19. Leased Octor. 29, 1764 to Jacob Keller, $11\frac{1}{2}$ acres; Jacob Keller lessie in charge; ann. rent, 0–2–2; aliena. fine, 0–4–4; fines due, none; leased for 19 years.

No. 20. Leased Octr. 29, 1751 to Jacob Keller, 120 acres; Jacob Keller lessie in charge; an. rent, 0–12–0; aliena fine, 1–4–0; leased on lives of Jacob Keller and Mary Keller; ages Jacob 38, Mary 17.

No. 21. Leased June 3, 1763 to Isaac Ritchy, 100 acres; Isaac Ritchey lessie in charge; an. rent, 1–0–0; aliena. fine, 2–0–0; 21 years' lease.

No. 22. 85 acres; tenant in charge John Beard; held by Certificate dated Novr. 25, 1763.

No. 23. Leased Febry. 9th, 1763 to Christian Shutter, 100 acres; Christian Shutter in charge; an. rent, 1–0–0; aliena. fine, 2–0–0; lease for 12 years.

No. 24. Leased April 11, 1742 to Frederick Clapbough, 150 acres; Peter Hedge tenant in charge; an. rent, 0–15–0; aliena. fine, 1–10–0; leased on lives of Mary Clapbough, age 66, John Clapbough, age 35.

No. 25 (first). Leased to Peter Berg, in possession, 100 acres; an. rent, 0–10–0; aliena. fine, 1–0–0; leased on lives of Peter Berg, Catherine Berg, William Berg; ages of persons named in lease Peter 55, Catherine 48, William 27.

No. 25. 257 acres, Peter Berg in possession; held by certificate May 3, 1753.

No. 26. Leased Febry. 25, 1743 to Johannes Berg, 150 acres; Johannes Berg lessie in charge; an. rent, 0–15–0; aliena. fine, 1–10–0; leased on lives of Johannes Berg, age 53, Judith Berg, age 49, John, age 29.

No. 27. Leased Septr. 29, 1752 to John Berg, 100 acres; "Johnie (Johannes)" Berg lessie in charge; an. rent, 1–0–0; aliena. fine, 2–0–0; lease for 21 years.

No. 28. Leased Febry. 24, 1743 to Christian Berg, 122 acres; Christian Berg, lessie in charge; an. rent, 0–12–3; aliena. fine, 1–4–6; leased on lives of Christian Berg, age (?) 7, William 25, John 28.

No. 29. Leased July 22, 1753 to Martin Adams, 136 acres; Andrus Adams tenant in charge; an. rent, 0–13–7; aluna. fine, 1–7–2; leased on lives of Mary Adams, Henry Adams; Mary 50 years, "Henry, Que. if there is any such Person."

No. 30. Leased July 25, 1742 to William Elrod, 100 acres; tenant in charge Christian Creger; an. rent, 0–10–0; alina. fine, 1–0–0; leased on lives of James Read, age 50, Mary Read, age 49, Henry Read, age 27.

No. 31. Leased May 6th, 1761 to Henry Hoover, 90 acres; Henry Hoover lessie in possession; an. rent, 0–18–0; aluna. fines, 1–16–0; leased for 21 years.

No. 32. Leased Octr. 10, 1759 to Valentine Creger, 153 acres; Valentine Creger in possession; an. rent, 1–10–8; aliena. fine, 3–1–4; leased for 21 years.

No. 33. Leased June 10, 1749 to Johannes Kooper, 140 acres; Johannes Kooper, lessee in possession; an. rent, 0–14–0; aliena. fine, 1–8–0; leased on lives of Johannes Kooper, age 47, Mary Kooper, age 37, Charity Kooper, 21.

No. 34. Leased May 6th, 1761 to Anthony Abell, 160 acres; John Cress tenant in possession; an. rent, 1–12–0; aliena. fine, 3–4–0; lease for 21 years.

No. 35. Leased Octr. 1st, 1742 to John Henn [Kenn?], 200 acres; Jacob Cremer tenant in possession; an. rent, 1–0–0; aliena. fine, 2–0–0; leased on lives of Sarah Henn, age 48, Elizabeth Henn, age 28 —— "in Carolina 16 years."

No. 36. Leased April 4, 1745 to Nathan Gregg, 230 acres; Robert Fulton tenant in possession; an. rent, 1–3–0; aliena. fine, 2–6–0; leased on life of William Gregg, age 40.

No. 37. Leased Decr. 22, 1741 to John Bell, 113 acres; Charles Springer tenant in possession; an. rent, 0–11–4; aliena. fine, 1–2–8; leased on lives of John Bell, age 60, Elizabeth Bell, age 50, John Bell, age 27.

No. 38. Leased June 5, 1750 to John Silver, 40 acres; John Silver, lessee in possession; an. rent, 0–4–0; aliena. fine, 0–8–0; leased on lives of John Silver age 45, and Susannah Silver age 18.

No. 39. Leased Octr. 23, 1762 to Samuel Matthews, 83 acres; Samuel Matthews lessee in possession; an. rent, 0–16–7$^1/_2$; aliena. fine, 1–3–3; leased for 21 years.

No. 40. Leased Octr. 26, 1762 to John Matthews, 94 acres; Frederick Rumbirts [?] tenant in possession; an. rent, 0–18–10; aliena. fine, 1–17–8; fines due, 1–17–8; leased for 21 years.

No. 41. Leased Septr. 29, 1765 to George Humbert, for 18 years, 200 acres; George Humbert, lessee in possession.

No. 42. Leased Octr. 26, 1762 to William Berg, for 21 years, 100 acres; William Berg, lessee in possession; an. rent, 1–0–0; aliena. fine, 2–0–0.

No. 43. Leased Octr. 20, 1762 to Handel Berg for 21 years, 75 acres; Handel Berg, lessee, in possession; an. rent, 0–15–0; aliena. fine, 1–10–0.

No. 44. Leased Jany. 22, 1742 to William Berg, 250 acres; William and Handel sons of lessee; an. rent, 1–5–0; aliena. fine, 2–10–0; leased on lives of William Berg age 40, and John Berg age 22, sons of Handel Berg.

No. 45. Leased March 12, 1754 to Catherine Crouse, 80 acres; Martin Smith tenant in possession; an. rent, 0–8–0; aliena. fine, 0–16–0; leased on lives of Catherine Crouse age 50, and Christian Crouse age 22.

No. 46. Leased June 4, 1763 to Martin Smith for 21 years, 38 acres; Martin Smith lessee in possession.

No. 47. Leased Septr. 30, 1763 to Jabez Jarvis for 18 years, 150 acres; Stephen Miller tenant in possession; an. rent, 1–10–0; aliena. fine, 3–0–0.

No. 48. Leased March 31, 1763 to Luke Bernard for 21 years, 100 acres; Luke Bernard lessee in possession; an. rent, 1–0–0; aliena. fine, 2–0–0.

No. 49. Leased March 30, 1763 to Nathanael Bernard for 21 years, 90 acres; Catherine Hartman tenant in possession; an. rent, 0–18–0; aliena. fine, 1–16–0; fines due, 1–17–0.

No. 50. 45 acres, tenant in possession Robert Wood; held by Certificate dated Septr. 29, 1764.

No. 51. Leased Septr. 28, 1762 to Robert Swan for 21 years, 180 acres; George Yost tenant in possession; an. rent, 1–16–0; aliena. fine, 3–12–0; fine due, 3–12–0.

No. 52. Leased Decr. 24, 1751 to Nathaniel Wickham, 94 acres; tenant in possession John Carver; an. rent, 0–9–4$^3/_4$; aliena. fine, 0–18–9$^1/_2$; leased on the lives of Samuel Wickham, John Wickham & Nathaniel Wickham; ages Nathaniel 38, Samuel 32, John 20.

No. 53. Leased June 20, 1749 to Thomas Perkinson, 47 acres; Adam Miller tenant in possession; an. rent, 0–4–8$^1/_4$; aluna. fine, 0–9–4$^1/_2$; leased on lives of Edward Perkinson, age 30, John Perkinson, age 27.

No. 54. Leased June 1, 1763 to Adam Miller, for 21 years, 33 acres; Adam Miller in possession; an. rent, 0–6–7; aliena. fine, 0–13–2.

No. 55. Leased Nov. 12, 1747 to Philip Howard, 150 acres; Christian Hufferd tenant in possession; an. rent, 0–15–0; aliena. fine, 1–10–0; leased on lives of Philip Howard Senr. age 66, Philip Howard Junr. age 41 [?], John Howard age 37.

No. 56. Leased Septr. 2, 1741 to Joseph Wood, 100 acres; Joseph Wood lessee in possession; an. rent, 0–10–0; aliena. fine, 1–0–0; leased on lives of Joseph Wood age 58, and Robert Wood age 31.

No. 57. Leased June 3, 1763 to Joseph Wood for 21 years; an. rent, 0–6–6; aliena. fine, 0–13–0.

No. 58. Leased Feb. 25, 1744 to John Harland, 125 acres; an. rent, 0–12–6; aliena. fine, 1–5–0; leased on lives of John Howland age 50, Joel Howland age 27, John Howland, Junr. 24.

No. 59. Leased Septr. 18, 1754 to Jacob Barton, 114 acres; Michael Crouse tenant in possession; an. rent, 0–11–5; aliena. fine, 1–2–10; fine due, 2–5–8; leased on lives of Henrietta Barton, age 46, Jacob Barton, age 20.

No. 60. Leased Feby. 28, 1748 to Zacheriah Albough, 224 acres; Ann Albough tenant in charge; an. rent, 1–2–6; aliena. fine, 2–5–0; leased on lives of John Albough, age 36 and Peter Albough, age 28.

No. 61. Leased June 4, 1763 to Zacheriah Albough for 21 years, 22 acres; Ann Albough tenant in possession; an. rent, 0–4–5$^1/_2$; aliena. fine, 0–8–11.

No. 62. Leased June 16, 1763 to Zacheriah Albough for 21 years, $77^{1}/_{2}$ acres; Ann Albough tenant in possession; an. rent, 0–13–6; aliena. fine, 1–7–0.

No. 63. Leased June 20, 1763 to Robert Wood for 21 years, 16 acres; Robert Wood lessee in possession; an. rent, $0–1–7^{1}/_{2}$; aliena. fine, 0–3–3. "Que. if this rent is right."

No. 64. Leased Novr. 4, 1762 to Christian Hufferd for 21 years; 10 acres; an. rent, 0–2–0; aliena. fine, 0–4–0.

No. 65. Leased Septr. 29, 1759 to Peter Hertzog, 100 acres; Margaret Hertzog tenant in possession; an. rent, 0–10–0; aliena. fine, 1–0–0; leased on lives of Margaret Hertzog age 55, & Nicholas Hertzog 32.

No. 66. Leased June 9, 1749 to Philip Smith, 69 acres; Philip Smith lessee in charge; an. rent, $0–6–10^{3}/_{4}$; aliena. fine, $0–13–9^{1}/_{2}$; leased on lives of Philip Smith, age 60, Johannes Smith, age 23 & Peter Smith, age 21.

No. 67. Leased Septr. 29, 1764 to Philip Smith for 21 years, 133 acres; Philip Smith lessee in charge; an. rent, $1–6–7^{1}/_{4}$; aliena. fine, $2–13–2^{1}/_{2}$.

No. 68. Leased June 9, 1749 to Christian Gross, 115 acres; Christian Gross lessee in possession; an. rent, 0–11–6; aliena. fine, 1–3–0; leased on lives of Christian Gross, age 55, Mary Gross, age 43 & Jacob Gross, age 25.

No. 69. Leased Septr. 29, 1764 to Conrod Creger for 19 yrs; an. rent, 0–8–7; aliena. fine, 0–17–2.

No. 70. Leased Septr. 29, 1764 to Christian Miller for 21 yrs., 4 acres; Christian Miller lessee in possession; an. rent, 0–0–10; aliena. fine, 0–1–8.

State of His Lordships Manor of Monocosy in Frederick County April 1768.

1. (A) Novr. 1st, 1752; (B) Simon Shover; (C) 49; (D) Simon Shover; (E) 0–10–10; (F) 1–1–10; (L) Simon Shover, Adam Shover & Peter Shover; (M) Simon 55, Adam 23, Peter 21.

2. (A) Augt. 23^{d}, 1741; (B) John Biggs; (C) $175^{1}/_{2}$; (D) Caspar Devel biss; (E) 1–0–4; (F) 2–0–8; (L) Benjamin Biggs & W^{m}. Biggs; (M) Benjn. 43, W^{m}. 40.

3. (A) March 30, 1745; (B) Daniel Pattinger; (C) $173^{1}/_{4}$; (D) Geo. Devilbiss & C. Miller; (E) 0–18–7; (F) 1–17–2; (L) Daniel Pattinger, John Pattinger & Elizabeth Pattinger; (M) Daniel 55, John 27, Eliz: 50.

4. (A) Novr. 28th, 1743; (B) George Divilbiss; (C) 138; (D) Caspar Divilbiss; (E) 0–12–6; (F) 1–5–0; (L) George Divilbiss & John Devilbiss; (M) George 55, John 27. (Written both Divilbiss & Devilbiss).

5. (A) Feby. 25, 1743; (B) Peter Evelant; (C) $94^{3}/_{4}$; (D) George

Devilbiss, Junr.; (E) 0–9–11; (F) 0–19–10; (L) John Hoffman, Barbarah Hoffman & Geo. Son of Geo. Devilbiss; (M) John 55, Barbarah 56, Geo. 22.

6. (A) Octo^{r}. 8th, 1741; (B) William Wilson; (C) $100^{1}/_{2}$; (D) W^{m}. Wilson; (E) 0–10–0; (F) 1–0–0; (L) John Wilson, W^{m}. Wilson & Thomas Wilson; (M) John 42, W^{m}. 37, Thomas 26.

7. (A) June 25, 1761; (B) Robert Whitnall; (C) $29^{3}/_{4}$; (D) Robt. Whitnall; (E) 0–6–7; (F) 0–13–2; (L) 21 yrs.

8. (A) Decr. 6th, 1743; (B) "Handell" Hann; (C) $137^{1}/_{4}$; (D) Frederick Baker; (E) 0–12–0; (F) 1–4–0; (L) "Handel" Hann, Mary Hann & Catharine Hann; (M) Handel 45, Mary 40, Catharine 13. All Gone to Carolina 8 years. Vide Date.

9. (A) March 12th, 1754; (B) Rich^{d}. Cooke; (C) 183; (D) George "Debilbiss"; (E) 1–4–0; (F) 2–8–0; (L) Richard Cooke & Richard Donaldson Cooke; (M) Rich^{d}. 50, Richard Donaldson Cook 20.

10. (A) Augt. 26, 1748; (B) Joseph Hedge; (C) $158^{1}/_{2}$; (D) Charles Hedge, Junr.; (E) 0–15–0; (F) 1–10–0; (L) Solomon Douthet; (M) Solomon 40. Gone to Carolina 14 years, quere if alive.

11. (A) Decr. 22, 1741; (B) Thomas Ebthorp; (C) $100^{1}/_{2}$; (D) Charles Hedge, Senr.; (E) 0–10–0; (F) 1–0–0; Fines due, 3–0–0; (L) Peter Members; (M) Peter 40. Quere if alive.

12. (A) Novr. 8, 1752; (B) Kenedy Farrell; (C) 172; (D) William Crumb; (E) 1–5–0; (F) 2–10–0; Fines due, 2–10–0; (L) John Farrell; (M) John 20. Quere if alive.

13. (A) Octo^{r}. 29, 1751; (B) Christian Rodebaugh; (C) $128^{3}/_{4}$; (D) Jacob Cremer; (E) 0–13–$2^{1}/_{4}$; (F) 1–6–$4^{1}/_{2}$; (L) Christian Rodebaugh, Eliz: Rodebaugh, Valentine Wisecup; (M) Christian 60, Eliz: 50, Valentine 22. Gone to Rays Town 12 years. Quere if alive.

14. (C) $51^{3}/_{4}$; (D) Christian Berge; held by Certificate dated May 12th, 1761.

15. (A) Octr. 10, 1764; (B) George "Divillbiss"; (C) 103; (D) George "Devilbiss"; (E) 1–0–$7^{1}/_{4}$; (F) 2–1–$^{1}/_{2}$; (L) 21 yrs.

16. (A) Sepr. 30, 1765; (B) William Smith; (C) $85^{1}/_{2}$; (D) W^{m}. Smith; (E) 0–15–$5^{1}/_{2}$; (E) 0–15–$5^{1}/_{2}$; (F) 1–10–11; (L) 18 yrs.

17. (A) Sepr. 29, 1764; (B) Simon Shover; (C) 22; (D) Simon Shover; (E) 0–3–7; (F) 0–7–2; (L) 19 yrs.

18. (A) Feby. 24, 1743; (B) John Christian Smith; (C) 106; (D) John Chris^{n}. Smith; (E) 0–10–0; (F) 1–0–0; (L) John Chris^{n}. Smith, W^{m}. Smith & Peter Berg Junr.; (M) John Christian 53, W^{m}. 30, Peter 28.

19. (A) Octr. 29, 1764; (B) Jacob Keller; (C) $11^{1}/_{2}$; (D) Jacob Keller; (E) 0–2–2; (F) 0–4–4; (L) 19 yrs.

20. (A) Octr. 29, 1751; (B) Jacob Keller; (C) 120; (D) Jacob Keller; (E) 0–12–0; (F) 1–4–0; (L) Jacob Keller (torn); (M) Jacob 38, Mary 17.

21. (A) June 3^{d}, 176 (torn) Rit (torn).

22. (C) $96\frac{1}{4}$; (D) John Beard; (L) (Torn) & John Clapbaugh; (M) Mary 66, John 35.

23. (A) Feby. 9th, 1765; (B) Christian Shutter; (C) $85\frac{1}{2}$; (D) Christian Shutter; (E) 1–0–0; (F) 2–0–0; (L) 12 yrs.

24. (A) April 11th, 1742; (B) Frederick Clapbough; (C) 144; (D) Peter Hedge; (E) 0–15–0; (F) 1–10–0; (L) Mary Clapbaugh & John Clapbaugh; (M) Mary 66, John 35.

25. (A) Feby. 25, 1743; (B) Peter "Berge"; (C) $11\frac{3}{4}$ & 243; (D) Peter "Berge"; (E) 0–10–0; (F) 1–0–0; (L) Peter "Berg," Catharine Berg & W^{m}. Berg; (M) Peter 55, Catharine 48, W^{m}. 27.

26. (A) Feby. 25, 1743; (B) Johannes Berg; (C) 149; (D) Johannes Berg; (E) 0–15–0; (F) 1–10–0; (L) Johan^{s}. Berg, Judith Berg & John Berg; (M) Johannes 53, Judith 49, John 28.

27. (A) Sep^{t}. 29, 1762; (B) John Berg; (C) $100\frac{1}{2}$; (D) John Berg; (E) 1–0–0; (F) 2–0–0; (L) 21 yrs.

28. (A) Feby. 24th, 1743; (B) Christian Berg; (C) $119\frac{1}{2}$; (D) Christian Berg; (E) 0–12–3; (F) 1–4–6; (L) Christian Berg, W^{m}. Berg & John Berg; (M) Christian 47, W^{m}. 35, John 28.

29. (A) July 22^{d}, 1753; (B) Martin Adams; (C) $138\frac{1}{4}$; (D) Andrew Adams; (E) 0–13–7; (F) 1–7–2; (L) Mary Adams & Henry Adams; (M) Mary 50. Quere if any such person as Henry.

30. (A) July 25, 1742; (B) William Elrod; (C) 95; (D) Christian Cregar; (E) 0–10–0; (F) 1–0–0; (L) James Read, Mary Read & Henry Read; (M) James 50, Mary 49, Henry 27.

31. (A) May 6th, 1761; (B) Henry Hoover; (C) $86\frac{1}{4}$; (D) Henry Hoover; (E) 0–18–0; (F) 1–16–0; (L) 21 yrs.

32. (A) Octo^{r}. 10th, 1759; (B) Valentine Cregar; (C) $124\frac{3}{4}$; (D) Valentine Cregar; (E) 1–10–8; (F) 3–1–4; (L) 21 yrs.

33. (A) June 10th, 1749; (B) Johannes Hooper; (C) $140\frac{1}{2}$; (D) Johannes Hooper; (E) 0–14–0; (F) 1–8–0; (L) Johan^{s}. Hooper, Mary Hooper & Charity Hooper; (M) Johannes 47, Mary 37, Charity 21.

34. (A) May 6th, 1761; (B) Anthony Abell; (C) $142\frac{1}{4}$; (D) John Cross; (E) 1–12–0; (F) 3–4–0; (L) 21 yrs.

35. (A) Octo^{r}. 1st, 1742; (B) John Henn; (C) $203\frac{1}{2}$; (D) Jacob Cremer; (E) 1–0–0; (F) 2–0–0; (L) Sarah Henn, Elizabeth Henn; (M) Sarah 48, Elizabeth 28—in Carolina 16 years.

36. (A) April 4th, 1745; (B) Nathan Greg; (C) 228; (D) Robert Fulton; (E) 1–3–0; (F) 2–6–0; (L) W^{m}. Greg; (M) W^{m}. 40.

37. (A) Decr. 22^{d}, 1741; (B) John Bell; (C) $114\frac{1}{4}$; (D) Charles Springer; (E) 0–11–4; (F) 1–2–8; (L) John Bell, Elizabeth Bell & John Bell; (M) John 60, Eliz: 50, John 27.

38. (A) June 5th, 1750; (B) John Silver; (C) $41^{1}/_{2}$; (D) John Silver; (E) 0–4–0; (F) 0–8–0; (L) John Silver, Susannah Silver; (M) John 45, Susannah 18.

39. (A) Octo^{r}. 23^{d}, 1762; (B) Saml. Mathews; (C) $84^{3}/_{4}$; (D) Samuel Mathews; (E) 0–16–$7^{1}/_{2}$; (F) 1–3–3; (L) 21 yrs.

40. (A) Octo^{r}. 26th, 1762; (B) John Mathews; (C) $95^{3}/_{4}$; (D) Frederick Humbert; (E) 0–18–10; (F) 1–17–8; Fines due, 1–17–8; (L) 21 yrs. Lease dated 3^{d} June, 1763, vide countreps.

41. (A) Sep^{t}. 29, 1765; (B) George Humbert; (C) $148^{1}/_{2}$; (D) George Humbert; (E) 2–0–0; (F) 4–0–0; (L) 18 yrs.

42. (A) Octr. 26th, 1762; (B) W^{m}. Berg; (C) $73^{3}/_{4}$; (D) W^{m}. Berg; (E) 1–0–0; (F) 2–0–0; (L) 21 yrs.

43. (A) Octo^{r}. 20th, 1762; (B) Handel Berg; (C) $52^{3}/_{4}$; (D) Handle Berg; (E) 0–15–0; (F) 1–10–0; (L) 21 yrs.

44. (A) Jany. 22, 1742; (B) William Berg; (C) 252; (D) W^{m}. & Handel Berg; (E) 1–5–0; (F) 2–10–0; (L) W^{m}. Berg, John Son of Handel Berg; W^{m}. 40, John 22.

45. (A) March 12, 1754; (B) Catharine Crouse; (C) 64; (D) Martin Smith; (E) 0–8–0; (F) 0–16–0; (L) Catharine Crouse & Christian Crouse; (M) Catharine 50, Christian 22.

46. (A) June 4th, 1763; (B) Martin Smith; (C) $34^{3}/_{4}$; (D) Martin Smith; (E) 0–7–8; (F) 0–15–4; (L) 21 yrs.

47. (A) Sep^{t}. 30th, 1765; (B) Jabez Jarvis; (C) 150; (D) Stephen Miller; (E) 1–10–0; (F) 3–0–0; (L) 18 yrs.

48. (A) March 31, 1763; (B) Luke Bernard; (C) $102^{1}/_{4}$; (D) Luke Bernard; (E) 1–0–0; (F) 2–0–0; (L) 21 yrs.

49. (A) March 30, 1763; (B) Nathl. Bernard; (C) $87^{1}/_{2}$; (D) Catharine Hartmane; (E) 0–18–0; (F) 1–16–0; (L) 21 yrs.

50. (C) $45^{1}/_{2}$ (D) Robert Wood, held by Certificate dated Sep^{t}. 29, 1764.

51. (A) Sep^{t}. 28, 1762; (B) Robert Swann; (C) $177^{1}/_{4}$; (D) George Yost; (E) 1–16–0; (F) 3–12–0; (L) 21 yrs.

52. (A) Decr. 24th, 1751; (B) Nathl. Wickham; (C) 88; (D) John Carver; (E) 0–9–$4^{3}/_{4}$; (F) 0–18–$9^{1}/_{2}$; (L) Saml. Wickham, John Wickham & Nathl. Wickham; (M) Nathaniel 38, Samuel 32, John 20.

53. (A) June 20, 1749; (B) Thomas Perkinson; (C) $44^{1}/_{2}$; (D) Adam Miller; (E) 0–4–$8^{1}/_{4}$; (F) 0–9–$4^{1}/_{2}$; (L) Edward Perkinson & John Perkinson; (M) Edward 30, John 27.

54. (A) June 1st, 1763; (B) Adam Miller; (C) 32; (D) Adam Miller; (E) 0–6–7; (F) 0–13–2; (L) 21 yrs.

55. (A) Novr. 12, 1747; (B) Philip Howard; (C) 160; (D) Christian Hufferd; (E) 0–15–0; (F) 1–10–0; (L) Philip Howard, Philip Howard, Junr. & John Howard; (M) Philip, Senr. 66, Philip, Junr. 44, John 37.

56. (A) Septr. 2^{d}, 1741; (B) Joseph Wood; (C) 101; (D) Joseph Wood; (E) 0–10–0; (F) 1–0–0; (L) Joseph Wood, Robert Wood; (M) Joseph 58, Robert 31.

57. (A) June 3^{d}, 1763; (B) Joseph Wood; (C) 35; (D) Joseph Wood; (E) 0–6–6; (F) 0–13–0; (L) 21 yrs.

58. (A) Feby. 25, 1744; (B) John Harland; (C) 135; (D) John Harland; (E) 0–12–6; (F) 1–5–0; (L) John Harland, Joel Harland, John Harland, Junr.

59. (A) Sepr. 18, 1754; (B) Jacob Barton; (C) $115\frac{3}{4}$; (D) Michael Crouse; (E) 0–11–5; (F) 1–2–10; Fines due, 2–5–8; (L) Hen^{a}. Barton & Jacob Barton; (M) Henrietta 46, Jacob 28.

60. (A) Feby. 28, 1748; (B) Zach^{h}. Albaugh; (C) $239\frac{1}{2}$; (D) Ann Albaugh; (E) 1–2–6; (F) 2–5–0; (L) John Albaugh & Peter Albaugh; (M) John 36, Peter 28.

61. (A) June 4th, 1763; (B) Ditto; (C) $28\frac{1}{2}$; (D) Ditto; (E) 0–4–$5\frac{1}{2}$; (F) 0–8–11; (L) 21 yrs.

62. (A) June 16, 1763; (B) Ditto; (C) $70\frac{1}{2}$; (D) Ditto; (E) 0–13–6; (F) 1–7–0; (L) 21 yrs.

63. (A) June 20th, 1763; (B) Robert Wood; (C) 16; (D) Robert Wood; (E) 0–1–$7\frac{1}{2}$; (F) 0–3–3; (L) 21 yrs.

64. (A) Novr. 4th, 1762; (B) Christian Hufferd; (C) 12; (D) Christian Hufferd; (E) 0–2–0; (F) 0–4–0; (L) 21 yrs.

65. (A) Sepr. 29, 1759; (B) Peter Hertzog; (C) 101; (D) Margaret Hertzog; (E) 0–10–0; (F) 1–0–0; (L) Margaret Hertzog & Nicholas Hertzog; (M) Margaret 55, Nicholas 32.

66. (A) June 9th, 1749; (B) Philip Smith; (C) $70\frac{3}{4}$; (D) Philip Smith; (E) 0–6–$10\frac{3}{4}$; (F) 0–13–$9\frac{1}{2}$; (L) Philip Smith, Johannes Smith & Peter Smith; (M) Philip 60, Johannes 23, Peter 21.

67. (A) Sep^{t}. 29, 1764; (B) Philip Smith; (C) 133; (D) Philip Smith; (E) 1–6–$7\frac{1}{2}$; (F) 2–13–$2\frac{1}{2}$; (L) 21 yrs.

68. (A) June 9th, 1749; (B) Christian Gross; (C) $117\frac{1}{2}$; (D) Christian Gross; (E) 0–11–6; (F) 1–3–0; (L) Christian Gross, Mary Gross & Jacob Gross; Christian 55, Mary 45, Jacob 25.

69. (A) Sepr. 29, 1764; (B) Conrad Creger; (C) 44; (D) Conrad Creger; (E) 0–8–7; (F) 0–17–2; (L) 19 yrs.

70. (A) Sepr. 29, 1764; (B) Christian Miller; (C) $7\frac{1}{2}$; (D) Christian Miller; (E) 0–0–10; (F) 0–1–8; (L) 21 yrs.

Totals (C) 7521. Deduct for No. [?] $45\frac{1}{2}$ acres, part of N°. 395 acres, part of [torn] $113\frac{1}{2}$ acres, or $159\frac{3}{4}$,—$7365\frac{1}{4}$ under Lease. Sundry Vacancies $1870\frac{1}{4}$. Contents of the Manor $9231\frac{1}{2}$ acres.

ST. MARY'S COUNTY

State of His Lordships Manor of Beaverdam in St. Mary's County, March, 1768.

1. (A) Decemr. 25, 1741; (B) John Raley; (C) 84½; (D) George Plater; (E) 0–10–0; (F) 2–0–0; (L) Jane Raley, Gabriel Raley & John Mitchel Raley; (M) Jane 34, Gabriel 31, John 28.

2. (A) Decemr. 25, 1741; (B) Jonathan "Seale"; (C) 113½; (D) George Plater; (E) 0–12–0; (F) 2–8–0; (L) Ann "Seall"; (M) Ann 33.

3. (A) Decemr. 25, 1743; (B) Robert Goldsberry; (C) 161¾; (D) Jane Goldsberry; (E) 0–16–8; (F) 3–6–8; (L) Margr. Goldsberry & John Baptist Goldsberry; (M) Margaret 32, John 24, gone away. Quere his Age if Living.

4. (A) May 30, 1761; (B) Henry Goldsberry; (C) 14; (D) Jane Goldsberry; (E) 0–4–0; (F) 0–4–0; (L) 14 yrs.

5. (A) Decemr. 25, 1741; (B) William Stone; (C) 46; (D) Ignatius Stone; (E) 0–4–9; (F) 1–0–0; (L) Ignatius Stone; (M) Ignatius 27.

6. (A) July 10th, 1741; (B) William Stone; (C) 110; (D) Ignatius Stone; (E) 0–10–10; (F) 2–4–0; (L) Ignatius Stone; (M) Ignatius 27.

7. (A) Decemr. 25, 1719; (B) Wm. Stone; (C) 58¾; (D) Ignatius Stone; (E) ——; (F) 2–8–10; (L) Wm. Stone, Junr.; (M) William 53.

8. (A) Decemr. 11, 1751; (B) William Stone, Junr.; (C) 50¾; (D) William Stone, Junr.; (E) 0–5–10; (F) 1–3–4; (L) William Stone Junr, Inonia Stone & Mary Stone; (M) William 53, Inonia 24, Mary 22.

9. (A) April 9, 1729; (B) Francis "Harbert"; (C) 100¼; (D) Ignatius Fenwick; (E) 0–10–3; (F) 4–4–4; (L) Elizabeth "Herbert"; (M) Elizabeth 39.

10. (A) Sepr. 10th, 1742; (B) Francis Harbert; (C) 63; (D) Ignatius Fenwick; (E) 0–6–8; (F) 1–6–0; (L) Francis Herbert & Michael Herbert; (M) Francis 29, Michael 31.

11. (A) Decr. 25, 1746; (B) Jonathan "Seale"; (C) 90½; (D) Ignatius Fenwick; (E) 0–9–10; (F) 2–0–0; (L) Elizabeth "Seall" & John Baptist Goldsberry; (M) Elizabeth 22, John 24.

12. (A) June 27, 1761; (B) John Dorsey; (C) 6; (D) John Dorsey; (E) 0–1–6; (F) 0–1–6; (L) 14¼ yrs.

13. (A) June 10th, 1743; (B) Thomas Blackman; (C) 211; (D) John Dorsey; (E) 1–4–4; (F) 4–17–4; (L) Tabitha Dent; (M) Tabitha 25.

14. (A) Decemr. 25, 1741; (B) John Lucas; (C) 119; (D) Enoch Fenwick; (E) 0–14–4; (F) 2–17–4; (L) John Lucas, Ignatius & Thos. Lucas; (M) John 50, Ignatius 27, Thomas 29.

15. (A) May 1st, 1737; (B) Enoch Fenwick; (C) 268; (D) Enoch Fenwick; (E) 1–6–2; (F) 5–5–0; (L) Enoch Fenwick, Ignatius Fenwick & John Miles; (M) Enoch 54, Ignatius 37, John 31.

16. (A) Decem^{r}. 25, 1741; (B) W^{m}. & Charles King; (C) 133; (D) Enoch Fenwick; (E) 0–13–3; (F) 2–13–0; (L) Charles King & James King; (M) Charles 48, very sickly. James 31.

17. (A) May 29, 1760; (B) Enoch Fenwick; (C) 29; (D) Enoch Fenwick; (E) 0–4–8; (F) 0–4–8; (L) 13 yrs.

18. (A) Decr. 25, 1741; (B) John Miles; (C) 165; (D) Levin Cracraft; (E) 0–16–0; (F) 3–4–0; (L) Josias Miles; (M) Josias 28 years.

19. (A) March 29, 1762; (B) Henry Jewell; (C) 12; (D) Levin Cracraft; (E) 0–1–8; (F) 0–1–8; (L) 15 yrs.

20. (A) June 30, 1760; (B) Lazarus Ross; (C) 82; (D) Lazarus Ross; (E) 0–16–6; (F) 0–16–6; (L) $13\frac{1}{4}$ yrs.

21. (A) June 30, 1760; (B) John Raley; (C) 79; (D) John Raley; (E) 0–18–9; (F) 0–16–6; (L) $13\frac{1}{4}$ yrs.

22. (A) March 28, 1726; (B) Paul Peacock, Junr. (C) $45\frac{3}{4}$; (D) Lessee; (E) 0–4–8; (F) 1–16–0; (L) Saml. Abell, Junr. & John Abell; (M) Sam 49, John 47.

23. (A) June 28, 1760; (B) Paul Peacock; (C) 7; (D) Lessee; (E) 0–1–4; (F) 0–1–4; (L) $13\frac{1}{4}$ yrs.

24. (A) March 26, 1726; (B) Samuel Abell, Senr.; (C) 134; (D) Samuel Abell, Junr.; (E) 0–13–6; (F) 5–8–8; (L) Sam Abell, Junr. & John Abell; (M) Sam 49, John 47.

25. (A) April 2^{d}, 1741; (B) Samuel Abell; (C) 62; (D) Samuel Abell, Junr.; (E) 0–6–5; (F) 1–5–0; (L) Lidia Abell & Philip Abell; (M) Lidia 32, Philip 27.

26. (A) March 25, 1762; (B) Samuel Abell; (C) $68\frac{1}{2}$; (D) Samuel Abell, Junr.; (E) 0–18–6; (F) 0–18–6; (L) 15 yrs.

27. (A) May 29, 1762; (B) Samuel Abell; (C) 34; (D) Samuel Abell, Junr.; (E) 0–8–9; (F) 0–8–9; (L) 15 yrs.

28. (A) March 25, 1762; (B) Samuel Abell; (C) $7\frac{3}{4}$; (D) Samuel Abell, Junr.; (E) 0–1–10; (F) 0–1–10; (L) 15 yrs.

29. (A) Decem^{r}. 21, 1762; (B) Samuel Abell; (C) $7\frac{1}{2}$; (D) Samuel Abell, Junr.; (E) 0–2–0; (L) 74 years. Condemn'd for a Mill.

30. (A) Augt. 20, 1745; (B) Ignatius Joy, Senr.; (C) 135; (D) Ignatius Joy, Junr.; (E) 0–13–9; (F) 2–14–0; (L) John Raley, Enoch Joy & Atha^{s}. Joy; (M) John 33, Enoch 26, Atha^{s}. 23.

31. (A) Decr. 11, 1751; (B) Abell Magill; (C) $54\frac{1}{4}$; (D) Ignatius Joy, Junr.; (E) 0–10–0; (F) 2–0–0; (L) Ann Magill; (M) Ann 26.

32. (A) May 2^{d}, 1743; (B) John Goddard; (C) 82; (D) Mary Goddard; (E) 0–8–8; (F) 1–14–0; (L) Ignatius Goddard, Monaca Goddard & John Goddard; (M) Ign^{s}. 26, Monaca 35, John 32.

33. (A) Augt. 21, 1745; (B) Enoch Joy; (C) $75^{1}/_{4}$; (D) Teakler Joy; (E) 0–8–0; (F) 1–12–0; (L) Enoch Joy & Ann Joy; (M) Enoch 26, Ann 33. N. B. Enoch gone away.

34. (A) Decem^{r}. 17, 1714; (B) Mary Chamberlain; (C) 28; (D) James Drury; (E) 0–3–0; (F) 1–4–0; (L) Eleanor Chamberlain & Mary Chamberlain; (M) Eleann 62, Mary 54.

35. (A) June 20th, 1746; (B) John "Makintach"; (C) 143; (D) John Mugg; (E) 0–14–3; (F) 3–0–0; (L) Walter Mugg, John & James "Mackintosh"; (M) Walter 29. John & James both old & gone away.

36. (A) Decem^{r}. 25, 1743; (B) Martin "Yates"; (C) 122; (D) Martin Yates; (E) 1–2–8; (F) 2–10–0; (L) Martin "Yeates," Edward "Yates" & Martin "Yates" Junr.; (M) Martin 68, Edward 39, Martin, Junr. 33.

37. (A) Sep^{t}. 1st, 1742; (B) John Campbell; (C) $103^{1}/_{2}$; (D) Martin Yates; (E) 0–11–1; (F) 2–4–4; (L) Eleanor Campbell; (M) Eleanor 26.

38. (A) Octr. 20, 1747; (B) Peter Mugg; (C) $38^{3}/_{4}$; (D) John Mugg; (E) 0–4–1; (F) 0–16–4; (L) John Mugg, Thos. Mugg & Peter Mugg, Junr.; (M) John 31, Thos. 27, Peter, Junr. 25.

39. (A) April 26, 1727; (B) Henry Grenwell; (C) 131; (D) Ignatius Greenwell; (E) 0–7–8; (F) 3–2–4; (L) Eleanor Grenwell & Edmond Grenwell; (M) Eleanor 41, Edmond 42.

40. (A) March 25, 1744; (B) Sarah "Cecell"; (C) $95^{1}/_{2}$; (D) Sarah "Secill"; (E) 0–10–0; (F) 2–0–0; (L) John "Cefsell," Thomas "Cefsell" & Ann "Cefsell"; (M) John 29, Thomas 30, Ann 27.

41. (A) Decem^{r}. 25, 1741; (B) Peter Drury; (C) 111; (D) Peter Drury; (E) 0–10–9; (F) 2–0–0; (L) Nich^{s}. Drury, Peter Drury & W^{m}. Drury; (M) Nich^{s}. 30, Peter 28, W^{m}. 31.

42. (A) Decem^{r}. 4, 1743; (B) John Ford; (C) 63; (D) Althanatius Ford; (E) 0–6–4; (F) 1–5–0; (L) Althanasius Ford & John Ford Junr.; (M) Altha^{s}. 40, John 26.

43. (A) Decem^{r}. 5, 1741; (B) William Lucas; (C) 201; (D) Althanatius Ford; (E) 0–19–11; (F) 4–0–0; (L) Charles Lucas; (M) Charles 35.

44. (A) April 3^{d}, 1762; (B) Altha^{s}. Ford; (C) $18^{1}/_{4}$; (D) Althanatius Ford; (E) 0–5–8; (F) 0–5–8; (L) 15 yrs.

45. (A) Decem^{r}. 25, 1741; (B) Thomas Howard; (C) $80^{1}/_{4}$; (D) Althanatius Ford; (E) 0–8–9; (F) 1–14–0; (L) W^{m}. Howard, Thos. Howard & Nich^{s}. Howard; (M) W^{m}. 40, Thomas 28, Nich^{s}. 30.

46. (A) March 25, 1726; (B) W^{m}. Bryan; (C) 59; (D) James Greenwell; (E) 0–7–2; (F) 2–17–8; (L) John Abell, Junr., Ignatius Bryan; (M) John 57, Ignatius 40.

47. (A) April 15, 1714; (B) John Miles; (C) $38^{1}/_{2}$; (D) James Greenwell; (E) 0–4–0; (F) 1–12–0; (L) Expired.

48. (A) Decem^r. 25, 1741; (B) Thomas Spalding; (C) 225 1/4; (D) Thomas Spalding; (E) 1–3–3; (F) 4–13–0; (L) Thos. Spalding, Elictious Spalding & Clem-Joseph; (M) Thos. 62, Elections 30, Clement 62, Dead.

49. (A) Decem^r. 25, 1743; (B) Elizabeth Spalding; (C) 124; (D) Theodorita Key; (E) 0–13–3; (F) 2–15–8; (L) Edm^d. Spalding, James Spalding & Ben^tt. Spalding; (M) Edmund 40, James 42, Bennitt 25.

50. (A) Decem^r. 20, 1743; (B) Henry Bryan; (C) 119; (D) Elenor Bryan; (E) 0–13–5; (F) 2–14–0; (L) Edm^d. Grenwell, Ign^s. Abell & Eliz: Abell; (M) Edmund 42, Ign^s. 27, Elizabeth 25.

51. (A) Feby. 20, 1742; (B) John Raley; (C) 88; (D) Joseph Stone; (E) 0–10–2; (F) 2–0–0; (L) Henry Raley, Zach^y. Forrest, Ann Raley; (M) Henry 40, Zach^y. 25, Ann 30.

52. (A) May 2^d, 1737; (B) Cuthbert Fenwick; (C) 231; (D) Bennitt Fenwick; (E) 1–3–9; (F) 4–15–0; (L) Bennett Fenwick; (M) Bennitt 40. Expired.

53. (A) Decem^r. 25, 1741; (B) Henry Spalding; (C) 107 1/4; (D) Henry Spalding; (E) 0–12–7; (F) 2–11–0; (L) Henry Spalding, Elec^s. Spalding & Edm^d. Spalding; (M) Henry 43, Elec^s. 30, Edmund 34. The last gone away.

54. (A) Decem^r. 25, 1742; (B) William Spalding; (C) 156 1/2; (D) Thomas Forrest; (E) 0–17–9; (F) 3–11–0; (L) (Torn) Spalding; (M) Basil 5 (Torn).

55. (A) Decem^r. 25, 1768 [?]; (B) William More; (C) 129; (D) Nicholas More; (E) 0–12–6; (F) 5–0–0; (L) Nicholas More & James More; (M) Nicholas 56, James 42. Expired.

56. (A) June 10, 1743; (B) John Brewer; (C) 147 3/4; (D) John Brewer; (E) 0–14–5; (F) 2–17–8; (L) George Brewer, Ann Brewer & Susannah Brewer; (M) Geo. 23, Ann 29, Susanna 25.

57. (A) Decm^r. 25, 1743; (B) James Wilkinson; (C) 57; (D) James Wilkinson; (E) 0–5–6; (F) 1–1–9; (L) William Wilkinson, David Wilkinson & Aquilla Wilkinson; (M) William 32, David 25, Aquilla 27.

58. (A) Decem^r. 25, 1741; (B) Charles Joy; (C) 357 1/2; (D) Charles Joy; (E) 1–16–8; (F) 7–6–8; (L) [Vacant; (M) Vacant].

59. (A) June 10th, 1743; (B) George Bowles; (C) 79 1/2; (D) Edward Stone; (E) 0–8–3; (F) 1–13–0; (L) Mary Seale, —— Seale & Lydia Seale. Quere their Age & if alive.

60. (A) Decr. 25, 1742; (B) Abram Clarke; (C) 129 1/2; (D) Abram Clarke; (E) 0–13–8; (F) 2–14–8; (L) Abram Clarke, Robert Clarke; (M) Abram 50, Robert 40.

61. (A) Decr. 25, 1719; (B) Richard Hazle; (C) 77; (D) Sam Abell, Junr. (E) 0–7–6; (F) 3–0–0; (L) Rich^d. Hazle, Junr., John Hazle; (M) Richard 37, John 56.

62. (A) Decr. 25, 1741; (B) Wm. Wimsatt; (C) 115¾; (D) Joshua Jarbeo; (E) 0–12–6; (F) 0–12–6; (L) James Wimsatt & Tenison Wimsatt; (M) James 45, Tenison 43.

63. (A) Decr. 25, 1742; (B) Richd. Wimsatt; (C) 200; (D) Robert Wimsatt; (E) 1–4–1; (F) 4–16–4; Henry Wimsatt, Ignatius Wimsatt; Henry 30, Ignatius 27.

64. (A) March 25, 1742; (B) John Raley; (C) 171; (D) James Brown; (E) 0–16–8; (F) 3–6–8; (L) John Raley & Gabriel Raley; (M) John 59, Gabriel 31.

65. (A) Feby. 1st, 1742; (B) James Brown; (C) 125; (D) James Brown; (E) 0–13–7; (F) 2–14–0; (L) John Baptist Brown & Leonard Brown; (M) John 35, Leonard 30.

66. (A) March 24, 1762; (B) John Abell; (C) 151; (D) John Abell; (E) 1–11–4; (F) 1–11–4; (L) 15 yrs.

67. (A) Decr. 25, 1745; (B) John "Nevett"; (C) 59½; (D) Ignatius Joy, Senr.; (E) 0–6–10; (F) 1–7–6; (L) John "Nevit," John Baptist "Nevit" & Mary "Nevit"; (M) John 55, John Baptist 25, Mary 23.

68. (A) Sepr. 10, 1742; (B) Bennitt Fenwick; (C) 80; (D) Bennitt Fenwick; (E) 0–8–0; (F) 1–10–0; (L) Bennitt Fenwick & Francis Harbert; (M) Bennitt 44, Francis 28.

69. (A) Decr. 25, 1719; (B) John More, Senr.; (C) 71; (D) John More, Junr.; (E) 0–7–6; (F) 3–0–0; (L) Eleanor More; (M) Eleanor More 62.

70. (A) Decr. 25, 1742; (B) Edward Spalding; (C) 175; (D) Edward Spalding; (E) 0–18–0; (F) 3–12–4; (L) Edward Spalding & Edward Barton Smith; (M) Edward 77, Edward Barton 28 gone away.

71. (A) June 25, 1761; (B) Ignatius Fenwick; (C) 55; (D) Edward Spalding; (E) 0–16–2; (F) 0–16–2; (L) 14¼ yrs.

72. (A) July 4th, 1740; (B) Elizabeth Spalding; (C) 120½; (D) Michael Spalding; (E) 0–17–16; (F) 3–10–0; (L) James Spalding, Michael Spalding & Edmund Spalding; (M) James 42, Michael 41, Edmund 40.

73. (A) Augt. 8th, 1739; (B) Henry Grenwell; (C) 84; (D) Edmond Grenwell; (E) 0–9–8; (F) 1–8–9; (L) "Edmund" Grenwell, Ignatius Grenwell, John Ross; (M) Edmond 40, Ignatius 31, John 22.

74. (A) April 26, 1728; (B) Thos. Spalding; (C) 53; (D) Thos. Spalding; (E) 1–1–2; (F) 2–2–4; (L) Thos. Spalding, Peter Spalding & James Spalding; (M) Thos. 53, Peter 48, James 45.

75. (A) Decr. 10, 1714; (B) (Vacant); (C) 461; (D) William Spalding; (L) Patent Land.

76. (A) Decr. 25, 1741; (B) William Spalding; (C) 189½; (D) William Spalding; (E) 1–1–0; (F) 4–8–8; (L) ——; (M) ——.

77. (A) June 12, 1761; (B) James Wimsatt; (C) 89½; (D) James Wimsatt; (E) 0–17–0; (F) 0–17–0; (L) 14¼ yrs.

78. (A) Octr. 23, 1747; (B) Henry Spalding; (C) 92; (D) W^{m}. & Thos. Spalding; (E) 0–11–8; (F) 1–16–8; (L) Henry Spalding, Electious Spalding, Henry Spalding, Junr.; (M) Henry 43, Electious 30, Henry, Junr. 22.

79. (A) June 25, 1761; (B) Edward Cole; (C) 87; (D) Ignatius Fenwick; (E) 0–17–6; (F) 0–17–6; (L) 14¼ yrs.

80. (C) 44; (D) Joshua Jarbeo; (E) 0–4–8.

81. (A) Octr. 1st, 1740; (B) Thomas Taney; (C) 141¼ & 35; (D) Raphael Taney; (E) 1–2–0; (F) 4–8–0; (L) Raphael Taney; (M) Raphael 40.

82. (A) Mch. 10, 1694; (B) Henry Lowe; (C) 90; (D) Raphael Taney; (L) Patented.

—. (C) 917½ Sundry Vacancies part of which, 'tis said, lies in Delabrook & Fenwick Manors. Total, (C) 9578¼.

State of His Lordships Manor of Chaptico, in S^{t}. Mary's County, January, 1768.

1. (A) Decem^{r}. 11, 1751; (B) Tenison Cheshire; (C) 163; (D) Lessee; (E) 0–16–4; (F) 3–5–4; (L) Tenison Cheshire, Barbara his Wife & Benj^{a}. Burch Cheshire; (M) Tenison 42, Barbara 40, Benj^{a}. 17.

(2). (A) Decr. 25, 1749; (B) Stephen Cawood; (C) 28½; (D) Lessee; (E) 0–2–7; (F) 0–10–0; (L) Stephen Cawood, Son of Lessee & Thomas Cawood; (M) Stephen, 29, Thomas 23.

(3). (A) Decem^{r}. 25, 1719; (B) Thomas Nichols; (C) 73; (D) Philip Key; (E) 0–3–3; (F) 1–11–0; Fines due 1–11–0 Pd.; (L) Mary Nichols & Susannah Nichols; (M) Mary 60, Susannah 51.

4. (A) Feby. 1762; (B) Edward Pratt; (C) 194; (D) Edward Pratt; (E) 1–18–8; (F) 3–17–4; (L) 21 yrs.

5. (A) Decem^{r}. 20, 1741; (B) Thomas Nichols; (C) 106; (D) Thomas Nichols, Junr.; (E) 0–10–9; (F) 2–4–0; (L) Thomas Nichols; (M) Thomas aged 34 years.

6. (A) Septr. 29, 1756; (B) Rich^{d}. Brown; (C) 89¼; (D) Philip Briscoe; (E) 0–11–6; (F) 1–3–0; Fines due, 2–6–0 Pd.; (L) Alexander Brown & William Bailey Clark Brown; (M) Alexander 21, William 19.

7. (A) July 13, 1740; (B) Williamson Hays; (C) 141; (D) Philip Briscoe; (E) 0–13–6; (F) 2–14–0; Fines due, 2–14–0, Pd.; (L) Samuel Miscar; (M) Samuel 31.

8. (A) Septemr. 29, 1742; (B) Leonard Clarke; (C) 266; (D) John Higgs; (E) 1–10–6; (F) 6–2–0; Fines due, 6–2–0; (L) Charles Sothoron Clark & Leonard Clark, Son of the Lessee; (M) Charles 26, Leonard 28.

9. (A) March 25, 1758; (B) John Eden; (C) 86; (D) Philip Briscoe; (E) 0–9–2; (F) 0–18–4; Fines due, 0–18–4 Pd.; (L) John Eden, James Eden & Townsend Eden; (M) John 40, James 19, Townsend 12.

10. (A) ——, 1718; (B) John Donaldson; (C) 305 1/4; (D) Ditto & Molly Key; (E) 2–9–6; (F) 19–19–5; Fines due, 39–18–10; (L) Elizabeth Daughter of John Donaldson; (M) Elizabeth 50, Sold Philip Briscoe pd. y Parran [?] £3–8–6.

11. (A) April 16, 1740; (B) William Bond; (C) 247 1/2; (D) Philip Briscoe; (E) 1–14–10; (F) 5–0–0; Fines due, 10–0–0, Pd.; (L) Zachh. Bond Son of William Zachh. Bond, Son of Thos. & Jerh. Bond; (M) Zachh. Son of William 29, Zachh. Son of Thos. 33, Jeremiah 31.

12. (A) June 16, 1752; (B) Zachy. Bond; (C) 243 1/2; (D) Lessee; (E) 1–7–0; (F) 5–16–0; (L) Samuel Bond & Samuel Edilin; (M) Sam Bond 20, Samuel Edilin, 17.

13. (A) June 29, 1739; (B) Zachy. Bond; (C) 229; (D) Lessee; (E) 1–10–0; (F) 9–5–4; (L) Jeremiah Bond; (M) Jeremiah 31.

14. (A) Jany. 25, 1753; (B) N. Warren & Jane "Vadry"; (C) 167 3/4; (D) Zachariah Bond; (E) 1–10–0; (F) 6–0–0; (L) Notley Warren, Jane Warren & Jane "Vaudry"; (M) Notley 32, Jane 30, Jane Vaudry 25.

15. (A) Augt. 20, 1745; (B) Zach & Zephy. Bond; (C) 164 1/2; (D) Zephaniah Bond; (E) 1–10–0; (F) 6–0–0; (L) Zachariah Bond, Zephaniah Bond & Jeremiah Bond; (M) Zach. 29, Dead; Zeph. 26, Dead, Jeremiah 31.

16. (A) Ditto; (B) Ditto; (C) 109 1/4; (D) Zach. & Zeph. Bond; (E) 0–11–0; (F) 2–4–0; (L) Same as above; (M) Ditto.

(17). (A) Ditto; (B) Anthony Sims; (C) 203 1/4; (D) Lessee; (E) 1–4–6; (F) 5–1–0; (L) Bennett Sims Dead & Jane Sims; (M) Bennett 25, Jane 27.

18. (A) Decemr. 25, 1742; (B) John Johnson Sothoron; (C) 354 1/2; (D) James Thomas; (E) 1–18–6; (F) 7–14–0; Fines due, 7–14–0; (L) Henry Greenfield Sothoron, Richd. Sothoron, John Sothoron; (M) Henry 36, Richard 26, John 25.

19. (A) Decemr. 25, 1750; (B) Edward Rion; (C) 189; (D) Jane Rion; (E) 0–18–10; (F) 3–15–4; (L) Mary Rion; (M) 29.

20. (A) Jany. 10th, 1742; (B) Francis "Clarke"; (C) 132 1/4; (D) Samuel Higgs; (E) 1–8–6; (F) 5–14–0; Fines due, 5–14–0; (L) Susanah "Clarke," Francis "Clark" son of Lessee; (M) Susanah 50, Francis 28.

21. (A) Augt. 20, 1745; (B) Dr. Richd. Cook; (C) 103; (D) Richd. Ward Keys Heirs; (E) 0–14–8; (F) 2–18–8; Fines due, 2–18–8; (L) Dr. Richd. "Cooke" & Mary Magdalen Stoddart; (M) Richard 50, Mary Magdalen 20. Sold Philip Briscoe.

22. (A) March 13, 1762; (B) Elizabeth Higgs; (C) 59 1/2; (D) Lessee; (E) 0–13–8; (F) 0–13–8; (L) 21 yrs.

23. (A) Feby. 10th, 1742; (B) Henry Williamson; (C) 132; (D) Leonard Briscoe; (E) 0–15–4; (F) 3–1–0; Fines due, 3–1–0 P^d.; Rachel Williamson & Sarah Williamson; (M) Rachel 65, Sarah 25.

24. (A) Feby. 5th, 1742; (B) Benj^a. Williamson; (C) 44 1/4; (D) Leon^d. Briscoe; (E) 0–4–6; (F) 0–18–0; Fines due, 0–18–0, P^d.; (L) Nathan Williamson & William Williamson; (M) Nathan 28, William 25.

25. (A) March 25, 1743; (B) Leonard Briscoe; (C) 214; (D) Lessee; (E) 1–2–0; (F) 4–8–0; (L) Leonard Briscoe & George Briscoe; (M) Leonard 47, George 35.

26. (A) Decem^r. 25, 1718; (B) Henry Williamson; (C) 39 3/4; (D) Philip Briscoe; (E) 0–3–10; (F) 1–10–6; Fines due, 1–10–6; (L) Rachel Williamson; (M) Rachel 65.

27. (C) 310 1/4; (D) George Briscoe; (M) One Life as supposed, about 45.

28. (A) March 25, 1749; (B) Bullet Gardner; (C) 139 3/4; (D) "Bullet" Gardner; (E) 0–12–9; (F) 2–6–0; (L) "Bullett" Gardner & John Gardner; (M) "Bullet" 48, John 25.

29. (A) Feby. 13, 1748; (B) Rich^d. Wainwright; (C) 181; (D) Lessee; (E) 0–18–1; (F) 3–12–0; (L) Richard Wainwright, Dead, & William Wainwright; (M) Richard 65, William 40.

30. (A) Mch. 25, 1749; (B) James Watson; (C) 19; (D) Lessee; (E) 0–1–10; (F) 0–8–0; (L) Mary Watson, Eliazer Watson & Azariah Watson; (M) Mary 38, Eliazer 21, Azariah 19.

31. (A) Jany. 20, 1742; (B) James Compton; (C) 104 1/2; (D) William Wainwright; (E) 0–10–6; (F) 2–2–0; Fines due, 2–2–0, p^d.; (L) Elianor Compton, Elizabeth Compton, John Compton; (M) Elianor 50, Eliz: 28, John 26.

32. (A) Septr. 29, 1742; (B) Joseph Bloxam; (C) 97; (D) Robt. Slye Wood; (E) 0–11–3; (F) 2–5–0; Fines due, 2–5–0 p^d.; (L) Ann Bloxam & Joseph Stephens; (M) Ann 45, Joseph 43.

33. (A) March 11th, 1762; (B) John Swan; (C) 53 1/4; (D) Basil Smith; (E) 0–13–4; (F) 0–13–4; Fines due, 0–13–4 p^d.; (L) 21 yrs.

34. (A) June 27, 1739; (B) Mary Haw; (C) 200 1/2; (D) Christopher Haw; (E) 1–1–2; (F) 4–4–0; (L) Christopher Haw Dead; (M) Christopher 32, expired.

35. (A) Jany. 20, 1742; (B) James Swan; (C) 121 1/2; (D) 0–13–7; (E) 2–14–0; (L) John Swan & James Swan; (M) John 46, James 42.

36. (A) Decr. 25, 1743; (B) John Branson; (C) 157; (D) John Branson, Junr.; (E) 0–16–0; (F) 3–4–0; (L) John Branson Dead, John his Son & John his Grandson; (M) John 83 Dead, his Son 56, his Grandson 28.

37. (A) Jany. 16, 1752; (B) Lydia Vadry; (C) 376$^{3}/_{4}$; (D) Maj^{r}. Zach^{h}. Bond; (E) 2–1–2; (F) 4–2–4; (L) Lydia Vadry, Thos. Cartwright & Gustavus Cartwright; (M) Lydia 36, Thomas 46, Gustavus 28.

38. (A) March 25, 1726; (B) George Witter; (C) 86$^{3}/_{4}$; (D) Corn^{s}. Barber; (E) 0–12–0; (F) 4–16–0; Fines due, 4–16 p^{d}.; (L) Mary Witter & William Witter; (M) Mary 48, William 45.

39. (A) Decr. 25, 1739; (B) Thomas Morris; (C) 153$^{3}/_{4}$; (D) Henry Morris; (E) 0–17–5; (F) 3–10–0; (L) Expired.

40. (A) Decr. 25, 1718; (B) Jane Price; (C) 82$^{1}/_{4}$; (D) Catharine Chunn; (E) 0–11–5; (F) 4–12–0; (L) Catharine Price 56.

41. (A) Decr. 25, 1762; (B) Elizabeth Price; (C) 51$^{3}/_{4}$; (D) Catharine Chunn; (E) 0–7–1; (F) 1–8–0; Fines due, 1–8–0, p^{d}.; (L) Ann Price 39.

42. (A) Decr. 26th, 1746; (B) Edward Rion; (C) 88$^{1}/_{4}$; (D) Jane Rion; (E) 0–9–4; (F) 1–17–4; (L) Mary Rion; (M) Mary 29.

43. (A) Feby. 10, 1742; (B) Mathew Compton; (C) 200; (D) Lessee; (E) 0–19–7; (F) 4–0–0; (L) Rachel Compton, W^{m}. Compton & Stephen Compton; (M) Rachel 52, William 34, Stephen 32.

44. (A) Decem^{r}. 25, 1719; (B) Benj^{a}. Chun; (C) 53; (D) Rebecca Chun; (E) 0–5–3; (F) 2–2–4; (L) Expired.

45. (A) Decem^{r}. 25, 1753; (B) Thomas Nash; (C) 37$^{1}/_{4}$; (D) Lessee; (E) 0–3–4; (F) 0–13–4; (L) Thomas Nash, Barnett Nash & Elizabeth Nash; (M) Thomas 57, Barnett 15, Eliz: 17.

46. (A) April 25, 1757; (B) Robert Horner; (C) 103; (D) Robert Horner; (E) 1–0–6; (F) 2–1–0; (L) 21 yrs.

47. (A) Decem^{r}. 25, 1753; (B) William Scott; (C) 25; (D) Lessee; (E) 0–2–6; (F) 0–10–0; (L) William Scott, Christian Scott & Elianor Scott; (M) William 41, Chris^{n}. 38, Elianor 16.

48. (A) July 29th, 1764; (B) James Wood; (C) 32; (D) James Wood; (E) 0–6–8; (F) 0–6–8; (L) 21 yrs.

49. (A) Decr. 25, 1746; (B) Ann Scott; (C) 52$^{3}/_{4}$; (D) Elizabeth Love; (E) 0–5–0; (F) 1–0–0; (L) Elizabeth Scott & Walter Burch; (M) Elizabeth 42, Walter 23.

50. (A) June 29, 1764; (B) Philip Wood; (C) 28; (D) Lessee; (E) 0–3–4; (F) 0–3–4; (L) 21 yrs.

51. (A) Decr. 25, 1746; (B) John Slye; (C) 52; (D) Lessee; (E) 0–4–9; (F) 0–19–0; (L) Mary Slye & Robert Slye; (M) Mary 32, Robert 21.

52. (A) May 19, 1749; (B) Francis Painham; (C) 104; (D) Heirs of Francis Painham; (E) 0–10–0; (F) 1–0–0; (L) Mary Painham, Ann Painham Junr.; (M) Mary 53, Ann 26.

53. (A) Decr. 25, 1753; (B) Robert Horner; (C) 7; (D) Lessee; (E) 0–0–8; (F) 0–2–8; (L) Robert Horner, John Briscoe & Alexander Henson; (M) Robert 45, John 24, Alexander 22.

(C) 1669$^{1}/_{2}$ Vacancies.

State of His Lordships Manor of Mill in S^{t}. Mary's County, January, 1768.

1. (A) January 25, 1741; (B) James Armstrong; (C) 155; (D) Diana Armstrong; (E) 0–16–8; (F) 3–0–0; (L) Diana Armstrong, Catharine Armstrong & Hellen Armstrong; (M) Diana 51, Catharine 32, Hellen 28.

2. (A) March 25th, 1744; (B) James Armstrong; (C) 60; (D) Diana Armstrong; (E) 0–7–2; (F) 1–8–8; (L) Same Lives; (M) Ditto.

3. (A) March 5th, 1742; (B) John Warren; (C) 102; (D) Mathew Hagar; (E) 0–10–3; (F) 2–1–0; Fines Due, 2–11–3; (L) Thomas Warren, Ann Warren & Mary Warren; (M) Thomas 40, Ann 38, Mary 35.

4. (A) May 14th, 1762; (B) Francis Hilton; (C) 8½; (D) Francis Hilton; (E) 0–1–10; (L) 15½ yrs.

5. (A) Sep^{t}. 29, 1742; (B) Martha Wheatley; (C) 109½; (D) William Coombs; (E) 0–10–10; (F) 2–3–0; (L) Martha Wheatley Joseph Wheatley, Winifred Wheatley; (M) Martha 50, Joseph 30, Winifred 26.

6. (A) March 25, 1744; (B) Henry Nowell; (C) 70½; (D) Henry Nowell, Junr.; (E) 0–1–¼; (F) 1–8–1; (L) Henry Nowell Junr. & Ann Nowell; (M) Henry 27, Ann 23.

7. (A) Feby. 1st, 1740; (B) Thomas Cook; (C) 95; (D) Thomas Cook; (E) 0–9–6; (F) 1–18–0; (L) Josiah Cook, Thomas Cook & Ignatius Cook; (M) Josiah 34, Thomas 32, Ignatius 28.

8. (A) March 24, 1744; (B) John Warren; (C) 5¼; (D) William Coombs; (E) 0–0–8; (F) 0–2–6; (L) Thos. Warren, Ann Warren & Mary Warren; (M) Thomas 40, Ann 36, Mary 35.

9. (A) July 5, 1742; (B) Thomas Baker; (C) 198½; (D) William Gaither, Junr.; (E) 1–0–0; (F) 4–0–0; (L) Thomas Baker; (M) Thomas 50.

10. (A) July 4th, 1714; (B) Francis Cole; (C) 110; (D) Susannah Cole; (E) 0–7–4; (F) 2–19–2; (L) Ann Cole; (M) Ann Aged 60.

11. (A) April 10th, 1738; (B) Francis Cole; (C) 29; (D) Susannah Cole; (E) 0–3–0; (F) 0–12–0; (L) Francis Cole, Junr., Judith Cole, Junr. & James Wheatley; (M) Francis 32, Judith 28, James 34.

12. (A) March 10th, 1743; (B) Jonathan Seale; (C) 326½; (D) Thomas Key; (E) 1–12–4; (F) 6–9–4; (L) Monaca Seale & Lidia Seale; (M) Monaca 30, Lidia 28.

13. (A) Augt. 24, 1758; (B) Joseph Jenkins; (C) 140; (D) Joseph Jenkins; (E) 1–8–0; (F) 1–8–0; (L) 11½ yrs.

14. (B) Patented to W^{m}. Jenkins; (C) 89½; (D) Joseph Jenkins; (L) Patent Land younger than the Manor.

15. (A) Augt. 20th, 1745; (B) John Silanee; (C) 170; (D) John Silanee; (E) 0–17–0; (F) 3–8–0; (L) John Silanee & John Silanee Junr.; (M) John 50, John Silanee Junr. 28.

16. (A) April 24th, 1762; (B) John Silanee Junr. (C) 46; (D) John Silanee Junr. (E) 0–9–2; F 0–9–2; (L) 15$^{1}/_{4}$ yrs.

17. (A) Augt. 6th, 1739; (B) John Edwards; (C) 44; (D) Zachariah Forrest; (E) 0–4–9; (F) 0–19–2.

18. (A) Decr. 25, 1743; (B) Joseph Cullison; (C) 75$^{1}/_{2}$; (D) James Tailton; (E) 0–7–7; (F) 1–10–4; Fines due, 3–8–3; (L) Joseph Cullison, William Cullison & Ignatius Cullison; (M) Joseph 45, W^{m}. 42, Ignatius 28.

19. (A) Decem^{r}. 25, 1750; (B) Joseph Cullison; (C) 30; (D) James Tailton; (E) 0–3–0; (F) 0–12–6; Fines due 1–8–0; (L) Joseph Cullison, James Cullison & Joseph Cullison Junr.; (M) Joseph 45, James 20, Joseph Junr. 18.

20. (A) Augt. 20, 1761; (B) Ditto (C) 53; (D) Ditto; (E) 0–10–6; (F) 0–10–6; Fines due 1–1–0; (L) 14$^{1}/_{2}$ yrs.

21 & 22. (A) April 25th, 1729; (B) John Tailton; (C) 50 & 22$^{3}/_{4}$; (D) Michael Beverley; (E for both tracts) 0–7–6; (F) 3–0–0; (L) John Tailton 80, Dead.

23. (A) April 10th, 1738; (B) James Tailton; (C) 35; (D) John Tailton; (E) 0–3–6; (F) 0–14–0; (L) John Tailton Junr. 30.

Totals: (C) 2025$^{1}/_{2}$; (E) £10–17–7$^{1}/_{4}$; (F) £8–8–6.

Sundry Vacancies not yet ascertained.

N. B. Mill Manor only Contains within the Lines according to the Resurvey 1921$^{3}/_{4}$ acres, the rest lies without the Manor.

State of His Lordships Manor of Snow Hill, Including S^{t}. Barbaras and S^{t}. Johns Freeholds, January, 1768.

1. (A) July 25th, 1750; (B) Capt. John Hicks; (C) 378; (D) William & Geo. Hicks; (E) 1–17–9; (F) 7–11–0; (L) W^{m}. Hicks now of White Haven; (M) William 36.

2. (A) Decem^{r}. 25, 1746; (B) Roger Tolle; (C) 143; (D) Rev^{d}. Moses Fabbs; (E) 0–14–4; (F) 3–11–8; (L) Jonathan Tolle, John Tolle & Roger Tolle; (M) Jonathan 33, John, 31, Roger 26.

3. (A) Decem^{r}. 25, 1749; (B) James Watts; (C) 190; (D) Mary Morris; (E) 0–19–0; (F) 4–0–0; (L) Roger Tolle, Son of Roger; (M) Roger 26.

4. (A) July 1st, 1740; (B) John Baker; (C) 97½; (D) John Baker; (E) 0–10–4; (F) 2–1–7; (L) John Baker & Thomas Baker; (M) John 45, Thomas 48.

5. (A) August 30, 1761; (B) John Baker; (C) 41¾; (D) John Baker; (E) 0–12–2; (F) 0–12–2; (L) 14½ years.

7. Land held by an ancient Deed, from a certain Gerard Miller.

8. (A) March 25th, 1750; (B) Thomas Williner; (C) 80¼; (D) Thomas Williner; (E) 0–8–7; (F) 1–14–4; (L) Thos. Williner, Thomas his Son & Miriam Williner; (M) Thomas 65, Thomas Junr. 20, Miriam 25.

Totals: (C) 982½; (E) £5–7–5.

State of His Lordships Manor of West St. Marys Lying in St. Marys County February 1768, Recorded 1666.

1. (A) Jany. 20th, 1742; (B) Stephen Chilton; (C) 57¾; (D) Stephen Chilton; (E) 0–10–3; (F) 2–1–0; (L) George Chilton, Morris Baker, Dead; (M) George 34, Morris 26.

2. (A) March 16, 1729; (B) Benjamin Woodard; (C) 89½; (D) Stephen Chilton; (E) 0–9–1½; (F) 1–16–6; Fines due 1–16–6; (L) William Woodard; (M) William 41. N. B. Gone away several years.

3. (A) Decemr. 25, 1750; (B) Elizabeth Morris; (C) 193½; (D) John King; (E) 0–19–2; (F) 3–16–8; (L) Elizabeth Morris, Mary Morris & George Chilton; (M) Elizabeth 18, Mary 16, George 34.

4. (A) Decemr. 25, 1730; (B) Joseph Anderson; (C) 49¼; (D) James McLaland; (E) 0–5–0; (F) 1–0–0; (L) Joseph Anderson & Gilbert Anderson; (M) Joseph 60, Gilbert 30—quere the Age if the Last & Vide Date of Lease.

5. (A) Feby. 1, 1740; (B) John Allison; (C) 49½; (D) Thomas Allison; (E) 0–6–8; (F) 1–6–8; Thomas Allison, Joseph Allison & James Allison; (M) Thomas 39, Joseph 30, James 22. Vide Date of Lease for the Last Life.

6. (A) Decemr. 25, 1716; (B) John Allison; (C) 28¼; (D) Thomas Allison; (E) 0–3–0; (F) 1–4–8; (L) Mary Cole (M) Mary 55.

7. (A) Decemr. 25, 1745; (B) John Batsell; (C) 67¾; (D) James McLaland; (E) 0–6–11; (F) 1–9–6; (L) John Batsel & Elizabeth Batsel; (M) John 25, Eliz: 42, both gone to Virginia.

8. (A) June 20, 1746; (B) John Taylor; (C) 139; (D) John Taylor; (E) 0–15–8; (F) 3–2–8; (L) John Taylor, Junr. & William Taylor; (M) John 37, William 34.

9. (A) June 15th, 1754; (B) John Hammett; (C) $72^{3}/_{4}$; (D) William Taylor; (E) 0–17–4; (F) 1–14–8; (L) $7^{3}/_{4}$ yrs.

10. (A) March 25, 1758; (B) Elizabeth Hammett; (C) $67^{1}/_{4}$; (D) Stephen Chilton; (E) 0–13–4; (F) 1–6–8; (L) Cartwright Hammitt, Nich^{s}. Dowlin Goldsborough & Stephen Dowlin Goldsborough; (M) Cartwright 20, Nicholas 18, Stephen 21.

13. (A) April 29, 1742; (B) William Hebb; (C) 78; (D) Vienon [Virnon?] Hebb; (E) 0–15–8; (F) 3–2–8; (L) Hopewell Hebb Dead, & Precilla Hebb; (M) Hopewell 60, Precilla gone to England 30.

14. (A) Jany. 20, 1741; (B) William Hebb; (C) 52; (D) Vienon Hebb; (E) 0–5–2; (F) 1–0–0; (L) Same Lives as above; (M) Same as 13.

15. (A) Octo^{r}. 3^{d}, 1762; (B) Thomas Mathews; (C) $10^{1}/_{4}$; (D) Lessee; (E) 0–13–6; (F) 0–13–6; (L) $15^{3}/_{4}$ yrs. Leased for $67^{1}/_{2}$ acres, but lies in older Surveys except $10^{1}/_{4}$.

23. (C) $3^{1}/_{4}$; (D) Vienon Hebb.

Total (E) £7–0–$9^{1}/_{2}$. Vacancies: 1. $166^{1}/_{2}$; 2. $176^{3}/_{4}$; 3. $10^{1}/_{4}$; 4. $18^{1}/_{4}$; 5. 3; 6. $34^{3}/_{4}$; 7. $2^{1}/_{2}$; 8. $^{1}/_{4}$; Total $1370^{1}/_{4}$, $1720^{3}/_{4}$ Patented Lands, Making 3091 acres in the Manor.

State of His Lordships Manor of Woolsey in S^{t}. Mary's County, December, 1767.

1. (A) Novr. 10th, 1739; (B) John Williams; (C) $100^{3}/_{8}$; (D) Susanna Williams; (E) 0–10–1; (F) 2–0–0; (L) Susannah Williams; (M) Susan. 30. Expired.

2. (A) April 11th, 1763; (B) Susanna Williams; (C) $18^{1}/_{8}$; (D) Lessee; (E) 0–3–10; (F) 0–7–8; (L) 21 yrs.

3. (A) Decem^{r}. 25th, 1742; (B) Thomas Welman; (C) $133^{1}/_{4}$; (D) Thomas Cecil; (E) 0–13–2; (F) 2–12–8; Fines due, 5–5–4; (L) Thomas Welman & John Welman; (M) Thos. 29, gone away. John 27.

4. (A) April 9th, 1763; (B) Thomas Cecil; (C) 52; (D) Lessee; (E) 0–11–9; (F) 0–11–9; (L) 21 yrs.

5. (A) May 1st, 1761; (B) Clement Jacbo [Jaibo]; (C) $59^{3}/_{8}$; (D) Thomas Cecil; (E) 0–12–4; (F) 0–12–4; Fines due, 0–12–4; (L) 21 yrs.

6. (A) Decr. 25th, 1746; (B) Thomas Dogin; (C) $67^{5}/_{8}$; (D) Lessee; (E) 0–8–0; (F) 1–12–0; (L) Thos. Dogin & John Michael Raley; (M) Thos. 48, John 26, but gone away.

7. (A) Novr. 10th, 1739; (B) Thomas Watt; (C) $40^{1}/_{2}$; (D) Jeremiah Rhoades; (E) 0–4–0; (F) 0–16–0; Fines due, 1–12–0; (L) Mary Watt; (M) Mary Watt 70.

8. (A) Decr. 25th, 1719; (B) Joseph Milbourn; (C) 61; (D) Henry King; (E) 0–6–0; (F) 2–8–0; Fines due, 2–8–0; (L) Stephen Milburn, Junr., Peter Milburn; (M) Stephen 42, gone away. Peter 39. Vide Date of Leese.

9. (A) July 5th, 1729; (B) Francis Hilton; (C) 85 1/2; (D) John Hilton; (E) 0–7–4; (F) 2–19–0; (L) Francis Hilton, Junr. & Wm. Hilton; (M) Francis 42, William 38.

10. (A) Sept. 20th, 1742; (B) Robert Alexander; (C) 27 1/4; (D) Robert Alexander; (E) 0–2–9; (F) 0–11–0; (L) Robert Alexander, Dead, Christian Alexander, Jas. Alexander; (M) Robt. 64, Christian 29, James 27.

11. (A) Feby. 22d, 1763; (B) Ditto; (C) 37 1/2; (D) Ditto; (E) 0–8–6; (F) 0–8–6; (L) 21 yrs.

12. (A) Decr. 25th, 1742; (B) Francis Hilton; (C) 42; (D) William Hilton; (E) 0–5–0; (F) 1–0–0; (L) John Hilton, Stepn. Hilton & Thos. Hilton; (M) John 40, Stephen 33, Thomas 28.

13. (A) Decr. 25th, 1719; (B) Ditto; (C) 53 5/8; (D) Ditto; (E) 0–5–0; (F) 2–0–0; (L) Mary Harlow; (M) Mary 50.

14. (A) Decr. 25th, 1758; (B) Ephraim Adams; (C) 87 1/4; (D) William Hilton; (E) 0–17–0; (F) 1–12–0; Fines due, 1–12–0; (L) Ephraim Adams, Reb: Adams & Robt. Adams; (M) Ephraim 40, Reb: 36, Robert 16—all gone away.

15. (A) Decr. 25th, 1720; (B) John Milbourn; (C) 34 3/8; (D) Henry Jenkins; (E) 0–3–3 1/2; (F) 1–4–6 1/2; Fines due, 6–2–8 1/2; (L) John Milburn, Dead, & Ann Milburn, Dead; (M) John 47, Ann 49, expd.

16. (A) Decr. 25th, 1740; (B) Robert Clarke; (C) 100 7/8; (D) Robert Clarke; (E) 0–13–2; (F) 2–12–8; (L) Robt. Clarke & Ann Clarke; (M) Robt. 45, Ann 40.

17. (A) May 25th, 1758; (B) Charles Dillian; (C) 36 1/8; (D) Ann Dillian; (E) 0–7–6; (F) 0–14–0; (L) 21 yrs.

18. (A) Sept. 15th, 1742; (B) John Milburn; (C) 40 1/8; (D) Sarah Breeden; (E) 0–3–10; (F) 0–15–0; Fines due, 0–15–0; (L) Mary Milburn & Ann Milburn; (M) Mary 40, Ann 26.

19. (A) Feby. 29th, 1742; (B) Francis Kirby; (C) 53 5/8; (D) Ignatius Bryan; (E) 0–5–6; (F) 1–5–0; (L) Frans. Kirby, Mary Kirby & Wm. Kirby; (M) Francis 45, Mary 41, William their Son 22. Vide Date of Lease.

20. (A) Sept. 7th, 1763; (B) Ignatius Bryan; (C) 49 1/4; (D) Ignatius Bryan; (M) held by Cirtificate.

21. (A) Decr. 25th, 1719; (B) Stephen Milburn; (C) 48 3/8; (D) Mathew Wise; (E) 0–4–8; (F) 1–17–6; (L) Stephen Milburn Dead, Stephen Milburn Junr. Peter Milburn; (M) Stephen 70, Stephen Junr. 49 but gone away, Peter 47. Vide No. 8. Same Lives but ages difft.

22. (A) Decr. 25, 1720; (B) Ditto; (C) $75\frac{5}{8}$; (D) Mathew Wise; (E) 0–7–9; (F) 3–2–7; (L) Steph^{n}. Milburn, Rebecca Milburn; (M) Stephen 70, Rebecca 46.

23. (A) April 26th, 1743; (B) John Lewis; (C) $48\frac{3}{4}$; (D) Adam Wise, Junr.; (E) 0–4–8; (F) 1–10–0; Fines due, 3–0–0; (L) Charles Lewis, Sarah Lewis & Eleanor Lewis; (M) Charles 29, Sarah 40, Eleanor 26.

24. (A) Novr. 13, 1743; (B) Adam Wise; (C) $62\frac{3}{4}$; (D) Adam Wise, Senr.; (E) 0–5–9; (F) 1–3–0; (L) Adam Wise, Senr., Diana Wise & Mathew Wise; (M) Adam 50, Diana 43, Mathew 25.

25. (A) Decr. 25th, 1741; (B) John Milbourn; (C) 81; (D) Richard Wise; (E) 0–8–2; (F) 1–12–9; Fines due, 1–12–9; (L) Ann Milburn, W^{m}. Milburn Son of Stephen; (M) Ann 49, William 30, gone away.

26. (A) March 25th, 1744; (B) William Howard; (C) 50; (D) John Hammott; (E) 0–4–9; (F) 1–8–8; Fines due, 1–8–8; (L) W^{m}. Howard, Ann Howard & Sarah Howard; (M) William 46, Ann 35, Sarah 20. Vide Date of Lease.

27. (A) Augt. 19th, 1761; (B) John Hammott; (C) $16\frac{1}{2}$; (D) John Hammott; (E) 0–4–0; (F) 0–4–0; (L) 21 yrs; (M) Expired.

28. (A) Mch. 5th, 1739; (B) Ditto; (C) $84\frac{3}{4}$; (D) John Hammott; (E) 0–8–5; (F) 1–14–0; (L) John Hammot, John Hammot, Son of Robt., Jno. Norris; (M) John 50, John Son of Robt. 28, John Norris 30.

29. (A) Novr. 13, 1743; (B) James Adams; (C) $52\frac{1}{2}$; (D) James Adams; (E) 0–5–5; (F) 1–0–0; (L) James Adams, Mary Adams, Eph^{m}. Adams; (M) James 51, Mary 51, Ephraim 40, the last gone away.

30. (A) June 24th, 1740; (B) James Farthing; (C) $91\frac{1}{2}$; (D) John Tarlton; (E) 0–9–8; (F) 1–19–0; Fines due, 1–19–0; (L) Mary Farthing & Robert Hurtle; (M) Mary 40, Robert 30.

31. (A) Decr. 25th, 1720; (B) Griffian Morris; (C) $42\frac{1}{8}$; (D) Robert Alexander; (E) 0–4–6; (F) 1–16–0; Fines due, 1–16–0; (L) Lessee Dead, Jane his Wife Dead & Monaca Morris; (M) Their ages cannot be learn't being gone away.

32. (A) April 2^{d}, 1761; (B) James Breeden; (C) $109\frac{1}{2}$; (D) Sarah Breeden; (E) 1–9–8; (F) 1–17–2; (L) 21 yrs.

33. (A) Decr. 11th, 1751; (B) John Frazier; (C) $183\frac{1}{8}$; (D) John Frazier; (E) 0–17–6; (F) 3–10–4; (L) John Frazir Dead, Leonard King; (M) John 40, Leonard (gone away) 25.

34. (A) Augt. 20th, 1761; (B) Ditto; (C) $12\frac{7}{8}$; (D) Ditto; (E) 0–6–0; (F) 0–6–0; (L) 21 yrs.

35. (A) Decr. 25th, 1741; (B) Theodore Jordan; (C) $148\frac{1}{8}$; (D) Henry Reeder; (E) 0–15–0; (F) 3–0–0; Fines due, 6–0–0; (L) Eliz: Jordan, Elizabeth Jordan Daughter of Lessee & Susannah his Sister; (M)

Eliz: 56, Eliz: Daughter of Lessee 29, Susannah 27. N. B. There is a Counterpart of a Lease for this Land dat^d. 1739 to Jno. Dyal on Lives.

Vacancies:
No. 1, (C) 110 3/4; No. 2, 565 3/4; No. 3, 50; No. 4, 15 1/4; No. 5, 106 1/2.
N. B. of the above quantity 27 Acres Lies in Mill Manor & ab^o. 21 1/2 in the Reserve Woolsey.

Caroline County, Bredge Town Hundred, Census of 1776.

"A Liste of the in Habbatance of Bredge Town Hundred Taking by Preson Goodwin." *

This Census is written upon 2 sheets 13¹/₄ in. × 16¹/₂ in., originally fastened together by red sealing wax.

"a" means "Under 16 years"; "b" means "From 16 to 50 years"; "c" means "Above 50 years" using the columns in the originals. "x" means males, "z" means females, "2ax" means 2 white males under 16 years, "3 az" means 3 white females under 16, etc.

Heads of Families:

Keed [?—Heed, Reed], William, 1 bx; 1 az, 1 bz—total 3.
Draper, Samuel, 1 ax, 1 bx; 1 az, 2 bz—5.
Hughs, Daniel, 1 bx; 2 az, 1 bz—4.
"Elaxandrio," Robert, 2 ax, 1 ax; 1 bz—4.
Reed, Charles, 1 ax, 1 bx; 1 bz—3.
More, William, 1 ax, 1 bx; 1 az, 1 bz—4.
Wilighboey, Richd., 6 ax, 1 bx; 1 az, 1 bz—9.
Founton, Thomas, 1 ax, 1 bx; 1 az, 1 bz—4.
Coox, Thomas, 1 ax, 1 bx; 2 az, 1 bz—5.
Bostick, James, 1 ax, 1 bx; 2 az, 2 bz—6.
Founton, Saml., 1 bx; 1 az, 1 bz—3.
Owins, William, 1 bx; 1 az, 1 bz—3.
Orrell, Thos., 1 bx—1.
Stradlee, Thos. Coox, 2 ax; 1 bx, 1 bz—4.
Walker, John, 1 ax, 1 bx; 2 az, 1 bz—5.
Comton, John Bablis, 1 bx; 2 az, 1 bz—4.
Hollis, Clark, 2 ax, 1 cx; 2 az, 3 bz—8.
Laine, Francis, 3 ax, 1 bx; 1 az, 2 bz—7.
Wyth, Daniel, 3 ax, 1 cx; 1 bz, 1 cz—6.
Brett, Damina, 1 bx, 1 cx; 1 cz—3.
Barwick, James, 2 ax, 1 bx; 1 az, 3 bz—7.
Carrill, Grace, 1 ax; 1 az, 2 bz—4.
Mason, Abraham, 1 ax, 1 bx; 3 az, 1 bz—6.
Eutt, Seth Hill, 1 bx; 1 az, 1 bz—3.

* "Preston Goodwin" is written in the enumeration in the bold handwriting of Benson Stanton, Chaⁿ·, but the actual signature is "Preson Goodwin."

Hill, Thomas Smith "Cat." [Captain?], 2 ax, 1 bx; 1 az, 1 bz—5.
Cullon, Davied, 1 ax, 1 bx; 1 az, 1 bz—4.
Wilkson, Henery, 3 ax, 1 bx; 1 az, 1 bz—6.
Allen, Ann, 1 bz, 1 cz—2.
Simson, Elijah, 1 bx; 1 az, 1 bz—3.
Cooper, Owin, 2 ax, 2 bx; 1 az, 3 bz, 1 cz—9.
Rogirs, William, 2 ax, 1 bx; 2 az, 2 bz, 1 cz—8.
Baynard, Mary, 1 bz—1.
Johnson, John, 2 ax, 2 bx; 1 az, 2 bz—7.
Hamblton, William, 1 bx—1.
Johnson, Henery, 2 ax, 1 bx; 1 az, 2 bz—6.
Hurd, William, 1 cx; 3 az, 1 bz—5.
Skinner, Francis, 2 bx; 1 bz—3.
Drapir, Gudall, 1 ax, 2 bx; 1 az, 2 bz—6.
Raws, Sarah, 2 az, 1 bz—3.
Williowbee, Solomon, 1 bx; 1 bz—2.
Williowbee, Absolomon, 1 bx; 1 cz—2.
Chanee, Aron, 1 ax, 2 bx; 7 az, 4 bz—14.
Mason, John, 2 ax, 1 cx; 1 az, 1 bz—5.
Emery [?], John, 1 ax, 1 bx; 1 bz—3.
Duglass, William, 5 ax, 1 bx; 1 az, 1 bz, 1 cz—9.
Lilley, William, 1 ax, 1 bx; 1 az, 1 bz—4.
Cook, William, 2 ax, 1 bx; 1 az, 1 bz, 1 cz—6.
Rogers, John, 3 ax, 1 bx; 1 az, 1 bz—6.
Sherrwed, Hugh, 2 ax, 2 bx, 1 cx; 3 az, 1 bz—9.
Sherrwed, Francis, 1 ax, 1 bx; 2 bz—4.
Baynard, John, 1 ax, 3 bx; 2 az, 2 bz, 1 cz—9.
White, John, 2 ax, 2 bx; 1 az, 1 bz—6.
Garrner, Parrish, 2 ax, 1 bx; 6 az, 1 bz—10.
Lammar, Nathan, 2 ax, 1 bx; 3 az, 1 bz—7.
Dickson, John, 1 bx; 1 bz—2.
Ingrum, John, 1 ax, 1 bx; 1 bz—3.
Garroot, John, 1 bx; 1 az, 1 bz—3.
Longe, Thomas, 3 ax, 1 bx, 1 cx; 3 az, 2 bz—10.
Longe, John, 1 ax, 1 bx; 3 az, 2 bz—7.
Glandin, William, 2 ax, 1 bx, 1 cx; 2 az, 1 bz—7.
Haress [Harris?], Benjamin, 2 ax, 1 bx; 3 az, 1 bz—7.
Smith, Edwd. 1 bx, 1 cx; 1 az, 1 cz—4.
Quinnily, Richd. 1 cx; 1 cz—2.
Talboy, Ann, 2 bx; 1 bz, 1 cz—4.
Wothers, Elijah, 1 ax, 2 bx; 1 az, 1 bz—5.
Currey, William, 1 ax, 1 bx, 1 cx; 4 bz—7.

Morgan, James, 1 bx—1.
Morgan, Solomon, 1 bx—1.
Gladston, Nathan, 1 bx—1.
Hobs, William, 1 bx—1.
Lecompt, Thos. 1 bx—1.
Wilson, Robt. 1 bx—1.
Turnner, John, 1 bx—1.
Hill, Nathan, 1 bx—1.
Swgat, Beneymon [Benjamin?], 1 bx—1.
Chanell [?], Eleey, 1 bx—1.
Green, Zariah, 1 bx—1.
Wothers, Ruban, 1 bx—1.
Wothers, John, 4 ax, 1 bx; 2 az, 2 bz—9.
Bland, Joseph, 1 bx; 2 az, 1 bz—4.
Bland, Joseph, Senr. 3 ax, 1 bx; 3 az, 1 bz—8.
Bright, Jonis, 2 ax, 1 bx, 3 az, 1 bz—7.
Everret, Joseph, 1 bx—1.
Brite, George, 1 bx—1.
Founton, William, 1 bx—1.
Jurdam, Batt, 1 bx, 1 cx; 2 az, 1 bz, 1 cz—6.
Black, Betty, 2 ax; 2 az, 1 cz—5.
Goodwin, Preston, 3 ax, 1 bx; 1 bz—5.
Warron, Solomon, 3 ax, 1 bx; 1 az, 1 bz—6.
Leventon, Mary, 1 bx; 1 az, 1 bz, 1 cz—4.
Cahill, William, 1 ax, 1 bx; 6 az, 1 bz—9.
Porter, Larnie, 2 bx; 3 az, 1 bz—6.
Thomas, Richard, 1 bx; 1 az, 1 bz—3.
Solsboury, Nemiah, 2 ax, 1 bx; 3 az, 1 bz—7.
Willighbouy, Edward, 4 ax, 1 bx; 3 az, 2 bz—10.
Fedmon, Batt, 4 ax, 1 bx; 3 az, 2 bz—10.
Cahill, John, 1 bx; 2 az, 1 bz, 1 cz—5.
Draper, William, 3 ax, 2 bx; 2 az, 2 bz—9.
Sordinge, Edward, 3 ax, 1 bx; 1 az, 1 bz—6.
Paine, Isaac, 5 ax, 2 bx; 2 az, 1 bz—10.
Maikmahn, William, 1 bx; 1 az, 1 bz—3.
Harper, William, 3 ax, 2 bx; 3 az, 1 bz—9.
Founton, John, 6 ax, 1 bx; 1 az, 1 bz—9.
Hudson, John, 1 bx; 1 bz—2.
Porter, Robt. 1 bx; 2 az, 1 bz—4.
Wilimson, Elijah, 3 ax, 1 bx; 3 az, 2 bz—9.
Swegatt, Thomas, 2 ax, 1 bx, 1 cx; 1 az, 2 bz, 1 cz—8.
Draper, Nemiah, 1 bx—1.

Smith, John, 3 ax, 1 bx; 1 az, 1 bz—6.
Munnett, William, 4 ax, 2 bx; 2 az, 1 bz—9.
Lester [Lister?], Joshua, 5 ax, 1 bx; 1 az, 1 bz—8.
Stevens, Azell, 2 ax, 1 bx; 1 az, 2 bz—6.
Bredinge, John, 1 ax, 2 bx; 2 bz, 1 cz—6.
Smith, John, Sennr. 3 bx, 1 cx; 1 az, 1 bz, 1 cz—7.
"Solsboy," Ebenezar, 1 ax, 1 bx; 2 az, 1 bz—5.
"Solsboury," James, 4 ax, 2 bx; 1 az, 4 bz—11.
"Joness," William, 2 ax, 1 bx, 1 cx; 4 bz—8.
Simson, John, 1 ax, 1 bx; 1 az, 2 bz—5.
Allen, Preseller, 2 az, 2 bz—4.
Morgan, Elesebeth, 1 ax, 1 bx; 2 bz, 1 cz—5.
Hoobes, Elesebeth, 1 bx; 1 az, 1 cz—3.
Raws, James, 1 ax, 1 cx; 1 az, 1 cz—4.
Harriss, James, 1 ax, 2 bx; 1 az, 1 bz—9.
Smith, Joshua, 2 ax, 2 bx; 4 az, 1 bz—9.
Hignutt, Daniel, 1 ax, 1 bx; 3 az, 1 bz—6.
Towirs, James, 2 ax, 1 bx; 4 az, 3 bz—10.
Chilrood, John, 2 ax, 1 bx; 3 az, 1 bz—7.
Dillion, John, 6 ax, 2 bx; 2 az, 2 bz—12.
Foster, Joseph, 1 ax, 2 bx; 3 az, 1 bz—7.
Harriss, Elsibeth, 1 ax; 2 bz—3.
Shinnee, Peter, 1 bx; 2 bz—3.
Mathers, Rose, 1 az, 2 bz—3.
Solsboury, John, 1 ax, 3 bx; 2 az, 1 bz—7.
Solsboury, Oliie, 2 ax, 1 bx; 1 az, 2 bz—6.
Swegatt, James, 2 bx; 1 az, 2 bz—5.
Hamblton, Jamis, 1 ax, 2 bx; 2 az, 1 bz—5.
Collilis, Robt. 1 ax, 1 bx, 1 cx; 3 az, 1 bz, 1 cz—8.
Fisher, Abraham, 1 ax, 1 bx; 2 az, 1 bz—5.
Horney, James, 1 bx—1.
Porter, Robert, Senr. 2 ax, 1 cx; 1 az, 2 bz, 1 cz—7.
Chafinch, John, 3 ax, 1 bx, 1 cx; 3 az, 1 bz—9.
Counton, Mary, 2 ax; 3 az, 1 bz—6.
Perrey, Mary, 2 ax, 1 bx; 1 az, 1 bz—5.
Howard, Joseph, 2 ax, 1 cx; 3 az, 1 bz—7.
Connelly, Jesa, 1 bx; 1 az, 1 bz, 1 cz—4.
Connely, William, 1 ax, 1 bx, 1 cx; 1 cz—4.
Rumbly, Smith, 1 ax, 1 bx; 1 bz—3.
Durell [Dunell?], Larrence, 1 ax, 1 bx; 1 az, 1 bz—4.
Smith, Thomas, 1 bx; 1 az, 1 bz—3.
Holbrook, Alaxandreo, 3 ax, 1 cx; 1 az, 1 bz—6.

Hoobs, Leblun, 3 ax, 1 bx; 2 az, 1 bz—7.
Hornny, Jiffery, 3 bx, 1 cx; 2 az, 1 bz, 2 cz—9.
Withers, Arron, 2 ax, 1 bx; 1 bz—4.
Kinord, Richard, 1 bx; 1 bz—2.
Killey, Batt, 1 ax, 1 bx; 1 az, 1 bz—4.
Greene, Edward, 4 ax, 2 bx; 2 az, 1 bz—9.
Griffind, John, 1 ax, 1 bx; 3 az, 3 bz—8.
Withers, Solomon, 1 ax, 1 bx; 1 az, 1 bz—4.
Staford, John, 4 ax, 2 bx; 1 az, 2 bz—9.
Chaniee Richd. 1 bx; 1 bz—2.
Swegott, Henery, 4 ax, 3 bx; 3 az, 2 bz—12.
Richardson, John, 2 ax, 1 bx; 3 az, 1 bz—7.
Stevens, William, 2 ax, 1 bx; 3 az, 2 bz—8.
Bushoope, Robart, 4 ax, 1 bx; 1 az, 1 bz—7.
Bushope, William, 2 ax, 1 bx; 1 az, 1 bz, 1 cz—6.
Smith, Leaven, 1 bx; 1 az, 2 bz—4.
Moberey, Arron, 1 ax, 1 bx; 2 az, 1 bz—5.
Harriss, William, 2 ax, 1 bx; 5 az, 2 bz—10.
Ward, Mary, 1 bx; 2 bz, 1 cz—4.
Barwick, Margrett, 1 ax, 3 az, 1 bz—5.
Grenholt [?], Johnathan, 3 ax, 1 bx; 1 bz—5.
Marthers, Darby, 1 bx; 1 az, 1 bz—3.
Row, Thomas, 1 ax, 4 bx; 5 az, 2 bz—12.
Earvin, Emmillis, 2 ax; 1 az, 1 bz—4.
Parson, Edward, 3 ax, 1 bx; 2 az, 2 bz—8.
Baynard, Leavin, 2 ax, 1 bx; 2 az, 1 bz—6.
Cooper, Mark, 4 ax, 2 bx; 3 az, 3 bz—12.
Total 954.

Owners of Blacks are grouped together, with the "a," "b," "c" classifications in the original lists but only the totals are here given and designated as "N," thus: "21 n," meaning 21 blacks.

Heads of Families:

Driver, Mathew, 1 ax, 2 bx; 3 az—6, and 21 n.
Hindson, Charles, 1 ax, 1 cx; 1 az, 3 bz—6, and 5 n.
Driver, Christopher, 1 ax, 3 bx; 1 az, 2 bz, 1 cz—8, and 7 n.
Cook, Thomas, 3 ax, 1 bx, 1 cx; 4 az, 2 bz—11, and 2 n.
Baynard, Gedion, 1 ax, 1 bx, 1 cx; 5 az, 3 bz—11, and 1 n.
Dickson, Obadiah, 1 ax, 1 bx, 1 cx; 2 az, 2 bz, 1 cz—8, and 10 n.
Merrick, Isaac, 4 bx; 1 az, 1 bz—6, and 3 n.
Rich, Peter, 2 bx; 2 az, 1 bz—5, and 6 n.
Smith, Abigail, 1 ax; 1 bz, 1 cz—3, and 6 n.

Smith, William, Junr. 1 ax, 2 bx; 1 az, 1 bz—5, and 5 n.
White, Cathrine, 1 cz—1, and 1 n.
Roodes, Jeremiah, 6 ax, 1 bx; 1 az, 1 bz—9, and 16 n.
Lucais, John, 1 bx; 2 bz—3, and 2 n.
Poselwatte, Robet. 2 ax, 1 bx; 1 az, 1 bz—5, and 3 n.
Dixon, Benjmon, 2 ax, 3 bx; 1 az, 1 bz—7, and 1 n.
Rumbley, Jacob, 2 ax, 1 bx; 2 az, 3 bz, 1 cz—9, and 7 n.
Willson, Jonathan, 3 ax, 1 bx, 1 cx; 4 az, 2 bz—11, and 3 n.
Shaw, William, 3 ax, 1 bx, 1 cx; 1 az, 4 bz—10, and 6 n.
Barwick, Joshua, 1 ax, 1 bx; 2 bz—4, and 3 n.
Whitee, Samuel, 1 ax, 1 bx; 5 az, 2 bz—9, and 1 n.
Hughins, James, 2 ax, 1 bx; 3 az, 1 bz—7, and 9 n.
Stockley, George, 1 bx; 3 az, 1 bz—5, and 11 n.
Onell, Thomas, 1 bx; 1 az, 1 bz—3, and 1 n.
Clemmer, Francis, 1 bx; 1 bz—2, and 1 n.
Rumbley, Edger, 3 ax, 1 bx; 5 az, 3 bz—12, and 1 n.
Barwick, James, 4 ax, 3 bx; 2 az, 3 bz—12, and 1 n.
Cooper, John, 1 bx; 1 bz—2, and 2 n.
Hasleitt, William, 1 ax, 2 bx; 2 az, 1 bz—6, and 3 n.
Lucais, Michill, 6 ax, 2 bx; 1 az, 2 bz—11, and 6 n.
Swording, Sarah, 1 cz—1, and 1 n.
Garrner, Joseph, 1 ax, 1 bx; 2 bz—4, and 4 n.
Willson, Christopher, 3 ax, 1 bx; 2 az, 1 bz—7, and 1 n.
Willowbeey, Saml. 1 bx; 2 az, 1 bz—4, and 3 n.
Hinds, Daniel, 2 ax, 4 bx; 1 cz—7, and 2 n.
Dillehay, William, 1 bx; 1 az, 1 bz—3, and 1 n.
Founton, Thomas, 1 ax, 2 bx, 1 cx; 1 bz—5, and 1 n.
Cooben, William, 1 ax, 1 bx; 2 az, 2 bz—6, and 1 n.
Orrill, John [Onill, Onell?], 2 ax, 1 cx; 1 az, 2 bz—6, and 6 n.
Stevens, John, 1 ax, 1 bx, 1 cx; 1 az, 2 bz—6, and 14 n.
Vaulx, Ebennezer, 1 cx—1, and 2 n.
White, John, 5 ax, 1 bx, 1 cx; 2 az, 1 bz—10, and 12 n.
Founton, Andrew, 3 ax, 3 bx; 3 az, 1 bz—10, and 7 n.
Founton, Merey, 2 bx, 1 cx; 1 cz—4, and 12 n.
Lecompt, James, 4 ax, 2 bx; 3 bz—9, and 4 n.
Lecompt, James, Senr. 1 ax, 4 bx, 1 cx; 2 bz—8, and 5 n.
Lecompt, Charles, 2 bx—2, and 1 n.
Juvel, William, 1 ax, 1 bx, 1 cx; 1 az, 1 bz, 1 cz—6, and 1 n.
Rich, William, 3 bx; 4 az, 1 bz—8, and 3 n.
Willson, John, 1 bx; 4 az, 2 bz—7, and 5 n.
Scoot, John, 1 bx; 4 az, 2 bz—7, and 7 n.
Scoot, James, 1 bx—1, and 1 n.

Baynard Thomas, [No age given] 1, and 2 n.
Wheatly, William, 1 ax, 2 bx; 1 az, 1 cz—5, and 14 n.
Dixon, Robert, [No age given]—1, and 3 n.
Peterkin, James, 1 cz—2 [Evidently 1 omitted], and 9 n.
Stanton, Benson, 1 bx; 1 az, 1 bz—3, and 25 n.
Totals 330 and 954, "Whites 1287" and 291 n.

Caroline County Scr. In Committee Jany. 6, 1777.

Preston Goodwin being appointed by this Committee to Assertain the number of Inhabitants in Bridge Town Hundred, made Oath that the within and above List contains the whole of the Inhabitants in Hundred.

Signed by Order,
BENSON STANTON, Cha^{n}.

DORCHESTER COUNTY

Dorchester County, Nantacoake Hundred, Census of 1776.*

"List of Inhabitants in Nantacoake Hundred, Dorchester County, anno 1776. No. 2033." †

"a" means 10 years of age and under; "b" means 10 to 16; "c" means 16 to 21; "d" means 21 to 30; "e" means 30 to 40; "f" means 40 to 50; "g" means 50 to 60; "h" means 60 to 70, "x" means white males; "z" means white females, and the prefixed figure means the number enumerated in the class indicated by the letter, thus "3 ax" means three males 10 years and under, "2 cz" means two females 16 years to 21, "n" means "blacks."

Heads of Families:

Abet, Sarah, 2 ax, 1 az, 1 dz.
Adams, Mcnamar, 1 ax, 1 az, 1 bz, 1 ex, 1 ez, 1 gz.
Ackman, Phillep, 2 ax, 2 az, 1 bz, 1 ex, 1 ez.
Abbet, Thomas, 2 ax, 2 bz, 1 cz, 1 ex, 1 ez.
Angel, William, 2 bz, 2 cz, 1 ex, 1 ez. "Also White man from 70 to 80."
Adkins, Rachel, 1 ax, 2 bx, 1 ez.

* First Division of Dorchester County into Hundreds:

The first political divisions of Dorchester County were hundreds, of which there is no official record to be found of their boundary lines, but the locations of the hundreds are recognizable by their names. They were laid out prior to 1698 when there were few roads through the vast forests which were only bounded by creeks, streams and other bodies of water.

The names of the hundreds were:

1. Great Choptank Hundred.
2. Nanticoke Hundred.
3. Transquaking Hundred.
4. Fishing Creek Hundred.
5. Little Choptank Hundred.
6. Hermitage (or Armitage) Hundred.
7. Straits Hundred.
8. Cambridge Hundred.

These divisions of the county were recognized in the appointment of constables, road overseers and other district officials, but were not election districts. They were retained as county divisions until 1829 when the county was divided into eight election districts herein named." *Hist. of Dorch. Co.*,—Elias Jones, 1902, pp. 142, 143.

† This record consists of 5 sheets, 12 in. x 14½ inches folded in the center and stitched together with an additional half sheet stitched to the side of the last sheet. The entire record is very yellow and worn and written upon both sides of the sheets.

Atter Son, Arter, 2 ax, 4 az, 1 dx, 1 dz, 1 ez, 1 fx.
Adley, William, 2 az, 1 cz, 1 dz, 1 ex.
Alexson, Alexander, 2 az, 1 bx, 2 bz, 1 cz, 1 dx, 1 fz, 1 gx.
Browhon, Patrick, 1 ax, 1 az, 1 bz, 1 cz, 1 dz, 1 ex, 6 n.
Bramble, Levina, 2 ax, 1 az, 2 bx, 1 bz, 1 cx,* 1 cz, 1 fz.
Badley, Christopher, 1 az, 1 bx, 1 cz, 1 fz, gx.
Badley, Richard, 1 dx, 1 dz.
Baker, John, 1 ax, 2 z, 1 dx, 1 dz.
Bonewill, Georg, 1 ax, 1 az, 1 bx, 1 bz, 1 ex, 1 ez, 4 n.
Brown, Sarah, 1 ax, 1 az, 2 ez, 3 n.
Ball, Precilla, 1 ax, 2 az, 1 bx, 2 bz, 1 cx, 1 ex, 1 fz, 25 n.
Bonersill, Mckeel, 2 az, 1 dx, 1 dz.
Bestpitch, William, 1 ax, 1 az, 1 ex, 1 ez.
Bramble, Edmon, 1 az, 1 bx, 1 bz, 1 cx, 1 fz, 1 gx.
Blesset, William, 1 az, 1 bx, 1 ex, 1 fz, 1 gz.
Bancks, Ann, 1 ax, 3 n.
Broks, Sarah, 1 ax, 2 az, 3 bz, 1 dz, 1 gz, 9 n.
Beard, John, 1 bx, 1 bz, 2 dz, 1 hx, 1 hz, 8 n.
Batey, Benjamin ("lived in Somerset"), 1 cx, 1 ex.
Beard, Thomas, 1 ax, 2 az, 1 bx, 1 bz, 1 cz, 1 ez, 1 fx, 3 n.
Beard, John, 1 ax, 1 az, 1 cz, 1 dz, 1 ex, 1 n.
Bestpitch, Levin, 3 ax, 1 bx, 2 bz, 1 ex, 1 ez, 4 n.
Brown, Georg, 2 ax, 3 az, 1 bz, 1 cx, 1 dz, 1 fx, 2 n.
Badley, Ezekel, 3 ax, 1 az, 1 bz, 1 ex, 1 ez.
Beard, Georg, 1 cz, 1 dx.
Ball, Benjamin, 3 az, 1 bz, 1 cx, 1 dz, 1 ez, 1 fx, 12 n.
Cantar, Isaac, 2 ax, 1 dx, 1 dz.
Cohon, Peter, 1 az, cz, 1 dx.
Cammel, Zacharas, 1 ax, 4 az, 1 cx, 1 ex, 2 ez, 13 n.
Canter, Sarah, 1 bx, 1 dx, 1 gx.
Cook, Elesabeth, 1 bx, 1 bz, 1 dx, 1 ez, 1 n.
Craft, Charles Levi, 1 ax, 1 dx, 1 dz, 2 n.
Coap, Jonathan, 1 ax, 2 az, 1 cz, 1 dz, 1 ex, 1 fz.
Clark, James, 1 az, 1 dx, 1 ez.
Callendar, William, 1 cz, 1 dx.
Craft, charls John, 1 ax, 1 ex, 1 ez.
Coap, Mary, 2 ax, 1 az, 2 bx, 2 bz, 1 dx, 1 gz.
Coap, John, 1 bx, 2 bz, 2 cz, 1 fx.
Cox, Joseph, 1 ax, 3 az, 1 bz, 1 ex, 1 gz.
Cane, Sarah, 1 ax, 1 az, 1 bx, 1 cz, 1 dz, 1 gz.
Church, Abraham, 2 n.

* "Lived to Isaac Canter."

Coap, Joseph, 2 az, 1 bx, 1 dx, 1 fx.
Craft, charls John, 2 ax, 1 bx, 1 cz, 1 ex, 1 ez, 1 n.
Craft, charls, John, Senr. 1 bx, 1 ez, 1 hx, 1 n.
Craft, charls Thomas, 1 ax, 1 az, 1 cz, 1 dz.
Craft, Aleas, 3 ax, 1 bz, 1 ez.
Craft, Jonathan, 1 dz, 1 ex.
Craft, Sarah, 1 cx, 1 gz.
Cook ——, "a black man 110 to 115."
Dorroty, Ezekel, 1 ax, 3 az, 1 bz, 1 cz, 1 dz, 1 fx.
Dudney, Aleas, 1 az, 1 bx, 2 bz, 1 cx, 1 ez.
Dudney, Mary, 4 ax, 3 az, 1 cx, 1 ez, 1 hz.
Deen, Charls, 1 dx, "love free."
Deen, Henry, 1 az, 1 dx, 1 dz.
Daffin, Joseph, 20 n.
Daniel, John, Senr. 2 ax, 1 az, 1 cz, 1 dz, 1 gx.
Daniel, John, 1 ax, 1 dx, 1 dz, 2 n.
Elett, John, 2 ax, 3 az, 1 bx, 1 ez, 1 gx, 15 n.
Ellett, Thomas, 4 ax, 1 az, 1 bx, 1 bz, 1 fz, 1 gx.
Elburd, William, 1 ez, 7 n.
Evins, Mary, 1 ax, 1 az, 1 bx, 1 bz, 1 dz.
Ellett, Thomas, 3 az, 2 bz, 1 ex, 1 ez, 1 n.
Evins, fisher Henry, 1 az, 1 cz, 1 dx, 1 gx.
Ellett, John, 4 ax, 1 az, 1 bz, 1 dz, 1 ex, 1 ez, 3 n.
Ennales, Henry 27 n.
Furrough, Jesse 1 n [Black man 21 to 30].
Fisher, John, 1 az, 1 dx, 1 dz.
Foster, Elesabeth, 1 ax, 1 bz, 1 ez, and "1 white woman 70 to 80."
Gambell, Sarah, 1 bx, 2 bz, 2 cz, 1 fz.
Green, Richard, 1 ax, 1 dz, 1 ex.
Goute, Shadrick, 2 ax, 2 az, 1 bx, 1 dx, 2 ez, 4 n.
Goute, Sophiah, 1 ax, 1 az, 1 dz.
Griffen, Joseph, 2 dx, 2 dz, 17 n.
Gardif, Christopher, 1 ax, 4 az, 2 bx, 1 cz, 1 ez, 1 hx, 2 n.
Goute, George, 1 ax, 3 az, 1 cx, 1 dx, 1 dz.
Gordon, James, 2 ax, 1 cx, 1 cz, 1 dx, 1 dz, 4 n.
Gray, Archable, 1 az, 1 dx, 1 dz.
Grinnan, Ann, 3 ax, 1 az, 1 ez.
Grayham, John, 3 ax, 1 az, 2 bx, 1 bz, 1 ex, 1 ez.
Gambell, John, 2 ax, 1 ex, 1 fz.
Harper, John, 2 ax, 2 bz, 1 cx, 1 cz, 1 dx, 1 fx, 1 fz, 2 n.
Harper, Ezekel, 2 ax, 3 az, 2 bz, 1 cx, 1 ez, 1 fx, 5 n.
Hodson, Thomas, 3 ax, 1 az, 1 bx, 2 bz, 1 cz, 1 dx, 1 fx, 1 fz, 7 n.

Hodson, Ann, 3 az, 3 bz, 2 ez, 2 n.
Hambleton, Mary, 1 ax, 1 az, 1 bx, 1 fz, 3 n.
Hambleton, Lilley 4 n.
Hicks, Thomas, 1 ax, 2 bx, 1 cx, 2 cz, 1 fx, 1 fz, 17 n.
Hicks, Mary, 2 ax, 1 ez, 1 gz, 13 n.
Holland, Rasmis, 1 ax, 3 az, 1 dz, and "1 white woman 70 to 80."
Hincks, Thomas, 2 ax, 2 az, 1 bx, 1 bz, 1 dz, 1 ex, 1 ez, 1 fx, 2 n.
Hicks, Tabitha, 1 ax, 1 ez.
Higgins, Sarah, 1 ax, 3 bx, 1 cz, 1 fz.
Hughs, Precilla, 2 az, 1 bz, 1 cz, 2 ez.
Hopkins, John, 1 az, 1 dz, 1 ex, 3 n.
Harvey, William, 3 ax, 1 dx, 1 dz.
Hust, Samuel, 1 az, 1 bz, 1 dz, 1 ex.
Hust, Archabel, 3 ax, 2 az, 1 bx, 1 bz, 1 dz, 1 ex.
Hurley, Edward, 1 bx, 1 bz, 2 fz, 1 hx.
Hust, James, 2 ax, 1 az, 2 bx, 3 cz, 1 ex, 1 ez.
Hubbart, Humphra, 1 ax, 1 az, 1 bz, 1 dz, 1 fz, 1 hx.
Hoppar, Henry, 11 n.
Hughs, James, "1 black man 40 to 50."
Henry, John, 1 az, 3 bx, 2 bz, 1 cx, 1 cz, 1 dx, 1 dz, 1 gx, 2 gz, 55 n.
Hammon, William, 1 ez, 1 fx.
Hughs, Edmon, 2 ax, 2 az, 1 cx, 1 cz, 1 dx, 1 fz, 1 gx.
Horsman, John, 1 ax, 1 az, 1 bx, 1 bz, 1 fz, 1 gx.
Horsman, Luke, 2 ax, 2 az, 1 bx, 1 bz, 1 fz, 1 gx.
Hurley, Mathew, 1 ax, 2 az, 1 bz, 1 dz, 1 fx.
Hurley, "Jan" [John?], 1 ax, 1 bx, 1 ez.
Hurley, Jacob, 1 ax, 2 az, 1 bx, 1 dz, 1 ez.
Hugins, Hezekiah, 3 az, 1 bx, 1 dz, 1 ez.
Hurley, Moses, 1 cz, 1 dx.
Hurley, Sophiah, 1 dz, 1 ez, 1 gz, 2 n.
Hurley, John, 2 ax, 2 az, 3 bx, 1 cz, 1 ez, 1 gx, 3 n.
Horsman, Henry,* 1 ax, 1 bx, 1 ez, 1 fz.
Hurley, Durbey, 2 ax, 3 bx, 1 fz, 1 gx.
Hurley, John, 3 az, 2 bx, 2 cz, 1 fx, 1 n.
Hurley, Thomas, 1 ax, 1 bx, 1 dx, 1 dz.
Hurley, Elijah, 4 ax, 1 az, 1 ex, 1 ez.
Hollan, Connar, 1 cz, 1 dx.
Hollan, Michal, 2 bx, 1 dz, 1 gx, 1 gz.
Hughe, John, 1 fx.
Harper, David, 2 az, 1 bx, 2 bz, 1 cz, 1 ez, 1 fx, 7 n.

* Also "White woman 70 to 80." "White woman 80 to 90." The second entry may perhaps apply to Henry Durbin, but the position seems to favor the Henry Horsman, family. G. M. B.

Hust, Joseph, 1 dx.
Huffington, John, 1 ex, 1 ez.
Hurley, Constantine, 2 ax, 1 az, 1 cz, 1 ex.
Haddan, Larance, cz ("with one leg of") [Enumerated twice, G. M. B].
Hollan, Connar, 1 cz, 1 dx.
Hollan, Michal, 2 bx, 1 dz, 1 gx, 1 gz.
Hughe, John, 1 fx.
Harper, David, 2 az, 1 bx, 2 bz, 1 cz, 1 ez, 1 fx, 7 n.
Hust, Joseph, 1 dx.
Huffington, John, 1 ex, 1 ez.
Hurley, Constantine, 2 ax, 1 az, 1 cz, 1 ex.
Jones, William, 1 ax, 2 az, 2 bx, 1 cz, 1 dx, 1 ez, 1 fz, 1 gx, 3 n.
Jones, Levin, 1 ax, 3 az, 2 bx, 1 cz, 1 dz, 1 ez, 1 fx, 8 n.
Jones, Mary, 1 ax, 1 az, 1 dz.
Jones, Levin, 2 ax, 1 bx, 1 bz, 1 cz, 1 dx, 1 ex, 1 ez.
Jones, Sarah, 3 az, 1 ez.
Johnson, Joseph, 1 bx, 2 bz, 1 cz, 1 fz, 1 hz, 5 n.
Jones, James, 2 ax, 3 az, 3 bx, 1 bz, 1 cx, 1 ex, 1 ez, 4 n.
Jones, William, 1 ax, 1 az, 1 dx, 1 dz.
Johnson, Nathan, 2 az, 1 cx, 1 ex, 1 fz, 1 n.
Jones, William, 4 ax, 1 az, 1 cz, 1 dx, 1 ez, 1 fx.
Jones, Levin, 1 cz, 1 dx.
Jones, Isaac, 2 az, 1 bx, 1 cz, 1 dx, 1 dz.
Jones, Frances, 1 az, 1 bx, 1 cz, 1 dx, 1 dz.
Kirkman, Levin, 3 ax, 1 az, 1 dz, 1 ex, 10 n.
Kirkman, Georg, 1 fx, 1 hx, 9 n.
Kirkman, Elisha, 1 az, 1 dx, 1 dz.
Kimmey, Henry, 3 ax, 2 az, 1 dz, 1 gx.
Killener, John, 2 bx, 1 ex, 1 ez.
Lewis, Glod, 1 ax, 1 cx, 1 ex, 1 ez.
Langfitt, Frances, 1 az, 1 bx, 1 cx, 1 cz, 1 gz, 1 hx.
Lines, Cornelus, 1 az, 1 dx, 1 dz.
Langfitt, Jarvis, 1 bx, 1 dx, 1 ez.
Langfitt, William, 2 cz, 1 hz, 7 n, also "1 white man 70 to 80."
Langfitt, John, 2 ax, 1 az, 1 bz, 1 cz, 1 dx, 1 gz, 10 n.
Langfitt, Levin, 1 az, 1 bx, 1 bz, 1 cz, 1 dx, 1 dz.
Lewis, Levin, 1 ax, 1 cx, 1 dx, 1 dz, 1 fx, 1 fz, 1 n.
Langurl, William, 1 ax, 1 az, 1 bx, 1 cx, 2 dz, 1 ex, 4 n.
Lingart, James, 1 cx, 1 gz, also "1 white man 80 to 90."
Lingurl, William, 3 ax, 1 cx, 1 cz, 1 ex, 1 ez.
Laton, James, 1 ax, 2 az, 2 bx, 1 bz, 1 dz, 1 ex, 11 n.
Laton, Daniel, 4 az, 1 cx, 1 dx, 1 dz, 1 n.

McCallester, William, 1 ax, 1 az, 1 bx, 1 bz, 1 cz, 1 ex, 1 fx, 1 fz.
McCallester, Easter, 1 az, 1 dz.
McCallester, Sarah, 1 ax, 1 ez.
Marcy, Mary, 1 ax, 1 dz, 2 n.
Minish, Elesabeth, 3 ax, 1 az, 1 bx, 1 bz, 1 cx, 1 cz, 1 dx, 1 fz.
Muir, James, 1 ax, 1 bz, 1 cx, 1 cz, 1 dx, 1 fx, 1 fz, 17 n.
McBrid, Hugh, 3 dx, 1 ex, 1 ez, 1 fx "lived in sumerset," 7 n.
Mears, Fisher, 3 ax, 1 bx, 1 ex, 1 ez.
Miars, John, 1 az, 1 bx, 1 bz, 1 cz, 1 dx.
Marign, Angel, 5 ax, 1 bz, 1 cx, 1 fz, 1 n.
McKell, Thomas, 1 dz, 1 ex, 5 n.
Moor, Elijah, 1 ax, 3 az, 1 bx, 1 dx, 1 dz.
McCallester, John, 1 bx, 1 cx, 1 cz, 1 ez, 1 fx, 1 hz.
McCallester, Andrew, 1 ax, 2 az, 1 bx, 2 bz, 1 cx, 1 cz, 1 ex, 1 ez.
Messack, James, 2 ax, 1 bx, 2 cz.
McCallster, Alceabeth, 1 bz, 2 cx, 1 gz.
Morgan, William, 1 ax, 3 az, 2 bx, 3 bz, 2 dx, 1 ez, 1 fx, 3 n.
Muir, Charls, 2 ax, 1 az, 1 bx, 1 bz, 1 dz, 1 ez, 1 fx, 29 n.*
Major, Levin, 2 ax, 1 az, 1 dz, 1 ex.
McCrary, Sarah, 1 ax, 1 az, 1 bx, 1 cx, 1 cz, 1 gz.
Moor, Thomas, 1 ax, 1 dx, 1 dz "lived in Somer Set."
Meddis, Thomas, 2 ax, 1 az, 1 bx, 1 dz, 1 ez.
Millar, Sarah, 1 az, 1 bz, 1 fz.
McCollester, Tabtha, 1 ax, 1 az, 1 bx, 1 ez.
Mabra, John, 1 dx "arised—enter in Quens ans."
Norman, Christophar, 2 ax, 1 az, 1 bz, 1 cz, 1 ez, 1 hx.
Neel, James, 2 az, 1 dz, 1 ex.
Oram, Levi, 2 ax, 2 az, 1 bx, 2 dz, 1 ex, 1 n.
Philleps, John, 1 ax, 1 az, 1 bx, 1 cz, 1 dx, 1 dz, 1 n.
Phillips, William, 1 dx, 1 dz.
Parris, Comfort, 1 ax, 1 bz, 1 fz, 2 n.
Parrish, John, 4 az, 1 dx, 1 dz.
Pely, William, 2 ax, 1 dz, 1 ex.
Roberson, John, 1 ax, 1 dx, 1 dz.
Rawley, James, 2 ax, 1 az, 1 cz, 1 dx, 1 dz.
Rawley, James, 2 ax, 1 cz, 1 dx.
Richards, Ann, 2 bx, 1 bz, 1 ex, 1 ez, 1 gz, 1 n.
Ragg, Andrew, 1 az, 1 bz, 1 cx, 1 ex, 5 n.
Regin, Tabitha, 1 ax, 1 dz.
Rawley, John, 2 ax, 1 bz, 1 ex, 1 ez.
Riggin, Edward, 1 ax, 1 ex, 1 dx, 1 dz, 1 n.

* "Of these 1 is blind and 1 love free."

Rawley, James, 1 az, 1 bx, 1 fx, 1 fz.
Reed, Joshua, 1 ax, 1 ex, 1 dx, 1 dz.
Staintors, Thomas, 1 ax, 2 az, 4 bx, 1 ex, 1 ez, 5 n.
Stoaks, Vollintin, 3 ax, 2 az, 2 bx, 1 fz, 1 gx.
Stinson, Samuel, 3 az, 2 bx, 1 ex, 1 fz.
Shaw, James, 2 ax, 2 dx, 1 dz, 1 fz, 4 n.
Sandars, John, 1 ez, 4 n.
Staton, Jacob, 2 ax, 2 az, 2 bx, 1 bz, 1 ex, 1 ez, 2 n.
Sweeting, Richard, 1 dx.
Sasorson, Daniel, 1 ax, 2 az, 1 cz, 1 dz, 1 fx.
Sturd, James, 1 ax, 1 bz, 1 ez, 1 fx.
Sward, Peter, 1 ax, 1 bz, 1 cz, 1 ex, 1 fz.
Sturd, James, 1 az, 1 ex, 1 ez, 1 n.
Steele, Henry, 2 ax, 1 az, 1 bx, 1 cx, 1 fx, 1 fz, 91 n.
Sackel, John, 2 ax, 2 az, 1 dx, 1 ex, 1 ez, 1 n.
Shanks, Abner, 2 ax, 1 az, 1 bx, 1 ez, 1 fx.
Sulivan, Nicll. 2 ax, 2 bx, 1 ez.
Sears, Peter, 1 ax, 1 az, 1 cx, 1 cz, 1 ez, 1 fx, 4 n.
Travers, Hicks John, 2 ax, 1 bx, 1 fx, 9 n.
Tickel, William, 1 az, 2 bx, 2 bz, 1 dz, 1 gx, 1 gz.
Tickel fletcher David, 1 az, 1 dx, 1 dz.
Tanar, batson Vinson, 1 ax, 1 az, 1 dz, 1 ex.
Thompson, Edwards, 2 ax, 1 az, 1 cz, 3 ez, 1 fx, 6 n.
Travers, Levin, 4 n.
Tilghman, Elijah 4 n.
Tommas, John, 1 bz, 1 cz, 1 fx, 1 fz.
Travers, Matthew, 4 ax, 3 az, 1 bx, 1 bz, 1 ez, 1 gx.
Thompson, Joseph, 1 ax, 1 cx, 1 cz, 1 ez, 1 fx, 2 n.
Thompson, Nickels John, 2 ax, 1 bx, 1 n.
Talor [Tabor?] James, 1 cz, 1 dx, 1 dz, 1 n.
Tommas, Elesabeth, 1 cx, 1 gz.
Tommas, Joseph, 1 ax, 1 dx, 1 dz.
Vickars, Soloman, 3 dx, 1 ez, 1 hz.
Vain, Henry, 1 ax, 2 az, 1 bx, 3 bz, 1 cz, 1 ez, 1 gx.
Vinson, John, 2 az, 1 bz, 1 dx, 1 dz.
Wallas, John, 1 bz, 1 hx, 1 hz, also "white woman 80/90."
Wallas, William, 3 az, 1 dx, 1 dz, 1 ez.
Windon, Charles, 3 ax, 3 az, 1 bz, 1 cx, 1 cz, 1 fx, 1 hz.
Woodards, Benjamin, 1 bz, 1 dz, 1 ex.
Wheelar, John, 1 ax, 1 az, 1 bx, 2 cz, 1 dz, 1 gx.
William, Levin, 4 az, 1 bx, 1 bz, 1 cx, 4 ez, 1 fx.
Willcox, Michal, 1 ax, 3 az, 1 bx, 1 cz, 1 dz, 1 ex, 1 fz.

Whalend, Jan [Jon?], 1 bx, 1 cx, 1 cz, 1 gz, 8 n.
Wille, Pritch, 2 ax, 1 az, 1 bx, 1 bz, 1 dx, 2 dz, 1 ex, 5 n.
White, John, 1 dx, 1 dz, 6 n.
Winget, Zebulon, 1 ax, 1 bz, 1 dx, 1 dz, 1 hz, 3 n.
Walter, Daniel, 1 ax, 4 az, 2 bx, 2 bz, 1 dz, 1 ex, 1 hz.
White, Sarah, 1 ax, 1 az, 1 bz, 1 dz, 1 gz, 12 n.
Webster, Catron, 1 ax, 1 bx, 2 bz, 1 ez.
Williams, Robert, 1 ax, 1 bx, 2 bz, 2 cx, 1 cz, 1 fz, 1 gx, 1 gz.
Williams, Thomas, 1 dx.
White, Mary, 1 az, 1 bx, 1 cx, 1 cz, 1 gz, 5 n.
White, Thomas, 1 bz, 1 dx.
White, John, 2 ax, 1 az, 1 dz, 1 fx.
Wale, John, 2 ax, 1 dx, 1 dz.
Winwright, Evins, 1 ax, 3 az, 1 bz, 1 ex, 1 ez, 1 hx ("White man 70/80").

Heads of Families [Summary]:

246 ax, 242 az, 131 bx, 113 bz, 48 cx, 86 cz, 87 dx, 102 dz, 68 ex, 98 ez, 39 fx, 41 fz, 18 gx, 25 gz, 13 hx, 9 hz, 638 n. Also enumerated: From 70 to 80 6 white men 1 white woman. From 80 to 90 2 white men and 3 blacks. One black man 110/115.

Dorchester County S[s]. Sep[tr]. 16th, 1776, Personally appeared Peter Sears before the Committee of Observation for the County aforesaid & made Oath on the Holy Evangels of Almighty God that the aforegoing is a true & perfect List to the best of his Knowledge of the Number of the Inhabitants of Nantacoake Hundred in the County and so fair forth as was in his power to obtain.

Signed P order of the afs[d]. Committee.
J[no]. C. Harrison Clk.

Dorchester County, Straight's Hundred, Census of 1776.

"A List of the inhabitants in Straights Hundred in Dorchester County in the year one Thousand Seven Hundred and Seventy Six"—1324 Persons.

This Census is written upon a continuous sheet 5 feet long by 13½ inches wide. The numbers of blacks are given in each division but are here omitted.

"a" means "10 years of age and under"; "b" means "From 10 to 16"; "c" means "From 16 to 21"; "d" means "From 21 to 30"; "e" means "From 30 to 40"; "f" means "From 40 to 50"; "g" means "From 50 years of age and upwards"; "x" means "White Boys" or "White Men"; "z" means "White Girls" or "White Women;" "n" means "Blacks;" 1 ax means 1 white boy 10 years or under, etc.

Heads of Families:

Mookin, Mark, 1 ax, 1 bx, 1 cz, 1 dx, 1 ez.
Mookin, Mary, 2 ax, 1 az, 1 ez.
Johnson, Ezekie, 2 ax, 1 cz, 1 dx.
Johnson, William, 3 ax, 3 az, 2 bx, 1 ex, 1 ez.
Wells, John, 1 dz, 1 fx.
Tigner, William, 1 ex.
Griffith, Lewes, 1 ax, 3 az, 1 bx, 1 cx, 2 cz, 1 fx, 1 fz.
Foxwell, John, 3 ax, 1 az, 1 dz.
Hart, Levin, 1 ax, 1 cx, 1 cz.
Woodling, John, 3 ax, 1 bz, 1 dx, 1 dz.
Holmes, John, 1 ax, 2 az, 2 bx, 1 bz, 2 cx, 1 dx, 1 ez.
Woodling [?] Richard, 2 ax, 2 az, 3 bz, 1 ex, 1 ez.
Coward, John, 2 ax, 1 az, 1 dz, 1 fx.
Pearson, Edward, 1 ax, 2 az, 1 dx, 1 dz.
Tyler, David, 3 ax, 1 bz, 1 cz, 1 dx, 1 dz.
Johnson, James, 1 ax, 1 az, 1 ex, 1 ez.
Foxwell, Rachel, 1 bz, 1 cx, 1 cz, 1 dz, 1 gx, 1 gz.
Foxwell, Eliz^a^. 1 gx, 1 gz.
Hughs, James, 1 ax, 2 az, 1 dx, 1 ez.
Tyler, John, 1 bx, 3 bz, 1 dz, 1 gx.
Carman, John, 1 bz, 1 dz, 1 gx.
Graham, Charles, 1 ax, 1 cx, 1 cz, 1 dx, 1 dz.
M. Nemara, John, 1 ax, 1 bx, 2 bz, 1 cx, 1 cz, 1 dx, 1 gx.
Barkley, James, 1 az, 1 bx, 1 cx, 1 dx, 1 dz.

Merideth, William, 1 cz, 1 dx, 1 gx, 1 gz.
Merideth, John, 2 ax, 1 bx, 2 bz, 1 cx, 1 ez, 1 fx.
Merideth, Rebecca, 1 ax, 2 az, 1 dx, 1 dz.
Starling, Elijah, 1 ax, 1 bx, 1 bz, 1 ex, 1 ez.
Wootten, Thomas, 1 dx, 1 ex, 1 gx, 1 gz.
Wootten, Hager, 3 az, 1 bx, 1 bz, 1 ex, 1 ez.
Adames, Salathal, 1 ax, 2 az, 1 dz, 1 ex.
Wootten, Prissilla, 1 bz, 1 dx, 1 dz.
Starling, Henry, 1 cz, 1 dx, 1 gx.
Woodling, John, 1 ax, 1 az, 1 dx, 1 gx.
Todd, John, 2 ax, 2 az, 1 cz, 1 dz, 1 ex.
Woodling, Solomon, 3 ax, 1 bx, 2 bz, 1 ex, 1 ez.
Misler, Abraham, 1 bx, 1 cx, 1 cz, 1 gx, 1 gz.
Parks, John, 3 ax, 2 az, 2 bx, 2 cz, 1 dx, 1 fz, 1 gx.
Adames, Thomas, 2 ax, 3 az, 1 dz, 1 ex.
Whitley, Thomas, 1 ax, 2 az, 2 bx, 1 bz, 1 ex, 1 fx.
Wootten, Thos. 3 ax, 1 az, 1 bx, 1 cx, 1 cz, 1 dx, 1 fz, 1 gx.
Wootten, Priss, 2 ax, 2 az, 1 cz, 1 dx.
Adames, Thos. 1 ax, 2 az, 1 bx, 1 cx, 1 dz, 1 gx, 1 gz.
Parks, John, 2 ax, 1 dx, 1 dz.
Shorter, William, 2 ax, 2 az, 1 dz, 1 ex.
Mesick, John, 2 ax, 3 az, 1 bx, 1 bz, 1 gx, 1 gz.
Lake, Henry, 3 ax, 2 az, 1 bz, 1 ex, 1 ez.
Whitley, Bridget, 1 ax, 1 az, 1 bx, 1 dz, 1 ex, 4 ez, 1 fz, 1 gx.
Paul, Jacob, 2 ax, 1 az, 1 fx, 1 fz.
Adames, Peter, 1 cz, 1 dx.
Insley, Bettey, 1 cx, 1 dx, 1 gz.
Paul, Mary, gz.
Simpson, Peter, 1 gx.
Wootton, Prissillah, 1 az, 1 dz, 1 ex, 1 ez.
Wootton, Mary, 1 ax, 2 az, 1 dx, 1 dz.
Ross, Robert, 2 bx, 1 cx, 1 cz, 1 gz.
Ross, Thomas, 2 ax, 3 az, 1 bx, 2 bz, 1 cz, 1 ex, 1 fx, 1 fz.
Wingate, Angelo, 1 ax, 1 bx, 1 fz, 1 gx.
Andrews, Joseph, 5 ax, 1 az, 2 bx, 1 cx, 1 ez, 1 fx.
Shors, Sarah, 1 ax, 1 dz.
Wildey, Molley, 1 ax, 1 az, 1 cx, 1 dz, 1 ex, 1 ez, 1 gx.
Todd, Benjamin, 2 ax, 1 bx, 2 cx, 1 cz, 2 dx, 1 ex, 1 fx, 1 fz, 1 gz.
Todd, David, 1 fx, 1 gz.
Drane, Sarah, 1 fz, 1 gz.
Sanders, Levin, 2 ax, 1 az, 1 dz, 1 fx, 1 gz.
Insley, Vallintine, 2 ax, 2 az, 3 bx, 1 cx, 1 fz, 1 gx.

Todd, Michael, 2 ax, 2 az, 1 bz, 1 fx.
Scott, Robert, 1 ax, 1 bx, 1 cz, 1 dx, 1 dz, 1 fz, 1 gx.
Wingate, Molley, 1 ax, 1 bz, 2 cz, 1 dx, 1 dz, 1 fz, 1 gx.
Wingate, John, 2 ax, 2 az, 1 ex, 1 ez.
Wingate, William, 2 bz, 1 dx, 1 ez, 1 gx.
Wingate, Robert, 1 az, 1 ez, 1 gx.
McNamara, Timothey, 3 ax, 1 az, 1 dx, 1 dz.
Lewis, Shadrick, 1 ax, 1 cz, 1 dx, 1 dz.
Insley, Jacob, 1 ax, 4 az, 1 bx, 1 cx, 1 ez, 1 gx.
Tobb, Job, 2 ax, 2 az, 1 bz, 1 dz, 1 ex.
Todd, Jonathan, 1 bx, 1 dx, 1 gz.
Moore, Thomas, 1 bx, 1 cz, 1 dx, 1 gz.
Robinson, John, 1 ax, 1 ex.
Robinson, Andrew, 1 ax, 2 az, 1 cz, 2 dx, 1 gx, 1 gz.
Robinson, Lake, 1 ax, 4 az, 1 bz, 1 cz, 1 ez, 1 fx.
Cannon, Bettey, 1 cz, 1 dx, 1 fz, 1 gx.
Johnson, Levi, 2 ax, 1 az, 1 dz, 1 ex.
Cannon, Susannah, 1 ax, 1 dx, 1 dz.
Robinson, Molley, 1 dx, 1 dz, 1 gx.
Jones, Jacob, 4 ax, 1 dz, 1 ex, 1 ez, 1 gx.
McNamara, Levin, 2 ax, 1 cz, 1 dx.
Bramble, John, 1 ax, 1 az, 1 dz, 1 ex.
Bramble, Lewis, 1 bz, 1 cx, 3 dx, 1 ex, 1 gx, 1 gz.
Johnson, Henry, 1 az, 1 bx, 1 cz, 1 fz, 1 gx.
Cannon, James, 2 ax, 3 az, 1 cx, 1 dx, 1 ex, 1 ez, 1 gz.
Cannon, William, 1 az, bx, 2 bz, 1 cx, 2 dz, 1 gx, 1 gz.
Cannon, Elizabeth, 1 bx, 2 bz, 2 cz, 4 dz, 1 ex, 1 gz.
Tyler, John, 1 ax, 3 az, 1 dz, 1 ex.
Todd, Jobe, 1 ax, 2 bz, 1 dx, 1 ez, 1 fx.
Pritchett, Zebulon, 2 ax, 1 dx, 1 dz.
Rumble, John, 1 bz, 1 cx, 1 dx, 1 fz, 1 gx.
Follen, Daniel, 1 ax, 5 az, 1 dz, 1 ex, 1 gz.
Pritchett, Thomas, 2 ax, 1 az, 2 dz, 1 ex.
Pritchett, Jabis, 1 cz, 1 ex.
Horner, Moses, 1 ax, 1 az, 1 bx, 2 bz, 1 cx, 1 dx, 1 dz, 1 fz, 1 gx.
Cope, Sarah, 4 ax, 2 az, 6 bx, 2 bz, 3 cz, 3 dx, 4 dz, 2 ex, 1 fx, 1 fz, 2 gx, 2 gz.
Whaland, Joseph, 1 ax, 1 az, 1 bz, 1 dz, 1 ex, 1 fz, 1 gx.
Hopkins, William, 1 cz, 1 dz, 1 gx, 1 gz.
Rumble, John, 2 ax, 1 az, 1 bx, 1 bz, 1 cx, 1 dz, 1 fx.
Willen, Levi, 1 ax, 3 az, 1 dx, 2 dz.
Johnson, Henry, 1 az, 1 dx, 1 dz.

Murphey, John, 1 ax, 1 az, 1 bz, 1 cx, 1 fx, 1 fz.
Bloodsworth, Robert, 1 ax, 1 az, 1 cz, 1 dx, 1 ex.
Pritchett, Arthur, 4 ax, 1 az, 1 bx, 1 bz, 1 cz, 1 fx, 1 gz.
Willson, Jobe, 1 ax, 2 az, 2 bx, 1 dz, 1 ex.
Follen, Barnebay, 1 ax, 2 dx, 1 dz, 1 gx.
McNemara, John, 2 ax, 1 dz, 1 ex, 1 fz.
Insley, Bettey, 5 az, 1 ex, 1 ez.
Deane, James, 1 az, 1 cz, 1 ex.
Deane, Henry, 1 az, 1 bx, 2 bz, 1 cx, 1 cz, 1 fx.
Hart, Naboth, 2 ax, 2 az, 2 bx, 1 cx, 1 ez, 1 fz, 1 gz.
Insley, Gabril, 1 bx, 1 cx, 1 dx.
Insley, Jos. 1 ax, 1 bx, 1 bz, 2 cx.
Foxwell, Levi, 1 az, 1 dx, 1 dz.
Street, Thomas, 1 ax, 1 az, 1 dx, 1 dz.
Foxwell, Roger, 4 ax, 1 az, 1 bx, 1 bz, 1 ex, 1 ez.
Hart, Henry, 1 ax, 1 bx, 1 cx, 1 cz, 1 ez.
Insley, Andrew, 1 bx, 1 dx, 1 dz, 1 ez, 1 gx.
Andrews, Isaac, 1 az, 3 bz, 2 cx, 1 fx.
Andrews, Keziah, 1 az, 1 bz, 1 cz, 1 dx.
Willey, Nelley, 1 ax, 2 az, 1 bx, 1 ez.
Willey, Jeane, 2 ax, 4 az, 2 bx, 1 ex, 1 ez.
Farguson, Bettey, 1 az, 1 dz.
Andrews, Nathal, 1 bx, 3 cz, 1 fx, 1 gx.
Willey, Indey, 1 ax, 2 az, 1 cx, 1 dz, 1 ex, 1 gz.
Andrews, Rubin, 1 cx, 1 cz, 1 dx.
Willey, William, 3 ax, 2 bx, 1 cz, 1 dx, 1 gz.
Insley, Elizabeth, 1 ez.
Phillips, Rachel, 2 az, 1 ez.
Moore, Susannah, 2 ax, 3 az, 2 bz, 1 ez, 1 gx.
Smith, John, 1 ax, 2 az, 1 ex, 1 ez.
Smith, Arthur, 1 ax, 1 bx, 1 gx, 1 gz.
Mookins, Ezekiel, 2 ax, 1 dx, 1 dz.
Hart, Arthur, 1 ax, 1 bz, 2 dx, 1 dz.
Moors, Samuel, 1 ax, 1 cx, 1 dx, 1 dz.
Smith, William, 1 ax, 1 bx, 1 bz, 1 cx.
Willey, Ezekiel, 1 ax, 1 az, 1 bx, 1 bz, 1 cx, 1 cz, 1 fx, 1 fz.
Sharom [?],* George, 1 fx, 1 fz, 1 gx, 1 gz.
Deane, Richard, 2 ax, 2 az, 1 bz, 1 ex, 1 ez.
Sharom [?],* Job, 2 ax, 1 bx, 1 bz, 3 cx, 1 cz, 1 dx, 1 dz, 1 fz, 1 gx.
Phillips, Jeane, 2 az, 2 bx, 1 bz, 1 ez.
Gootee, John, 3 bz, 1 cx, 1 dx, 1 ez, 1 gx.

* Sharom, Racom, Slacom [?]—indistinct.

Denike, Samuel, 2 ax, 1 az, 1 dz, 1 ex.
Gootee, Andrew, 4 ax, 1 bx, 1 dx, 1 dz, 1 ex, 1 gz.
Cole, Rachel, 1 az, 1 dz, 2 ex.
Booze, George, 1 az, 2 bx, 1 bz, 1 gz.
Bramble, Adam, 1 cz.
Booz George, 1 gx.
McGraw, John, 2 az, 1 bx, 1 ex, 1 ez.
Cole, Diannah, 2 ax, 1 bz, 1 cz, 1 ez, 1 gz.
Paul, Charles, 1 ax, 1 cz, 1 dx, 1 dz.
Wootten, John, 3 az, 1 ex, 1 ez.
Whitley, David, 1 ax, 1 az, 1 dz, 1 ex, 1 gz.
Bramble, Bettey, 1 az, 1 bz.
Buley, Stephen [no enumeration].
Edger, John, 1 ax, 1 az, 1 bx, 2 bz, 1 dx, 1 ez.
Edger, James, 1 ax, 1 az, 1 bz, 1 dz, 1 ex.
Insley, Solomon, 1 ax, 1 az, 1 dx, 1 dz.
Greenlief, James, 1 az, 1 dz, 1 fx.
Edger, James, 2 ax, 2 az, 1 bz, 1 dz, 1 ex.
Edger, William, 1 ax, 2 az, 1 bz, 1 dx, 1 dz, 1 ex.
Edger, Mary, 1 bx, 1 bz, 1 ez, 1 fx, 1 gz.
Bramble, John, 1 ax, 1 az, 2 bx, 1 cz, 1 ez, 1 fx.
Deane, Bettey, 1 az, 1 bx, 1 gz.
Booz, James, 1 cx, 1 cz, 1 dx.
Farguson, Molley, 1 ax, 2 az, 1 dz.
Deane, Uriah, 1 bz, 1 cz, 1 dz, 1 ez, 1 gz. [No male enumerated].
Reed or Rood [?], William, 1 ax, 1 dx, 1 dz.
Wingate, John, 1 gx, 1 gz.
Wingate, James, 1 ax, 4 az, 1 bx, 1 ex, 1 ez.
Todd, Jabis, 1 ax, 1 dx, 1 dz.
Wingate, John, 1 bx.
Carwan, Thomas, [No enumeration].
Barns, Thomas, 2 ax, 2 az, bx.
Davis, James, 1 ax, 2 az, 1 dz, 1 ex, 1 fx.
Woodling, Richard, 2 ax, 1 az, 1 bz, 1 cz, 1 ex, 1 ez.
Paul, Lewis G. 1 az, 1 cz, 1 dz, 1 ez, 1 fx.
Tyler, John, 1 ax, 1 bz, 1 dz, 1 ex, 1 ez.
Hall, Joseph, 2 ax, 2 az, 1 bz, 1 dz, 1 ez.
Wallace, Richard, 1 ax, 1 az, 1 ex, 1 ez.
Wootten, Aquiloe, 1 ax, 2 az, 1 dz.
Wallace, Rhode, 1 dz, 1 gz.
Hayard, Allen, 3 ax, 1 ex, 1 ez.
Clarkinson, Joseph, 2 ax, 1 bx, 3 bz, 1 cz, 1 dx, 1 ex, 1 ez, 1 gx.
Booth, —— hn, 1 az, 1 dx, 1 dz, 1 gx.

701 ax, 102 az, 83 bx, 82 bz, 46 cx, 62 cz, 80 dx, 92 dz, e——, 29 fx, 26 fz, 46 gx, 44 gz. No Whites 1099, No Blacks 225, No the Hole 1324.

Dorchester County SS. September 16, 1776 personalley Appeared Charles Sapleport (?) before the Committee of Observation for the County afs[d]. and Made Oath on the Holey Evangeles of Almighty god that the aforegoing is a True and perfect List to the best of his Knowledge of the Number of the inhabitants of Straights Hundred in the County afs[d]. so far —— as was in his power to Obtain.

Signed per order of the afs[d]. Committee
JOHN C. HARRISON Clk.

Dorchester County, Transquakin Hundred, Census of 1776

"List of Inhabitants in Transquakin Hundred, Dorchester County, Anno 1776. No. 2897"—315 "Heads of Families." *

"a" means 10 years of age and under; "b" means 10 to 16; "c" means 16 to 21; "d" means 21 to 30; "e" means 30 to 40; "f" means 40 to 50; "g" means 50 and upwards; "x" means males; "z" means females; "n" means "blacks."

Heads of Families:

Hooper, Henry, 2 d. 1 dx, 1 fx, 1 fz; 22 n.
Bromajim, John, 1 ax, 1 az, 1 bx, 2 bz, 1 ex, 1 ez; 5 n.
Hooper, Henry, Genrl. 1 bz, 1 cx, 1 cz, 2 dx, 2 ez, 1 gx, 1 gz; 59 n.
Pitt, Thomas, 1 ax, 1 az, 1 bx, 2 bz, 2 cx, 1 dz, 1 ez, 1 fx; 11 n.
Burk, Mary, 1 ez, 1 gz.
Lamb, John, 1 ax, 2 az, 1 bx, 1 cx, 1 dz, 1 ex; 1 n.
Mills, James, 2 ax, 1 bx, 1 bz, 1 ez, 1 dz, 1 ez, 1 fx; 2 n.
Wheelar, Mary, 3 ax, 1 az, 1 ez.
Smith, Nicolas, 2 ax, 1 az, 1 bx, 1 bz, 1 ez, 1 fx.
Sewel, John, 1 az, 1 bx, 1 bz, 1 cz, 1 dz, 1 gx.
Delihay, James, 1 ax, 2 bz, 2 cx, 1 dx, 1 fz, 1 gx; 1 n.
Davidson, Thomas, 1 ax, 2 az, 1 fx, 1 fz; 5 n.
Turner, Ann, 1 az, 1 fz.
Price, William, 1 bz, 1 cx, 1 cz, 1 gx; 4 n.
Harvey, David, 2 az, 1 cz, 1 dx, 1 dz.
Dorley, John, 3 ax, 1 az, 1 bx, 1 bz, 1 cx, 1 cz, 1 ex, 1 ez.

* This record is well preserved and consists of 4 sheets, each $16^1/_8 \times 13$ inches, fastened together end to end, written upon both sides.

Royley, Water, 2 ax, 1 az, 2 bx, 1 dx, 2 dz; 4 n.
Chaice, Frederick, 1 ex; 17 n.
Webb, Augustus, 1 az, 1 dx, 1 dz.
Ennalls, Barthow, Senr. 1 dx.
Moses [or Noble?], William, 1 ax, 1 bx, 1 dx [This line is much worn].
Windows, Thomas, 1 dx, 1 dz.
Tootle, John, 2 ax, 1 az, 1 bx, 1 bz, 1 cz, 1 ex, 1 ez; 4 n.
Hayward, Addling, 1 ax, 1 az, 1 bx, 1 bz, 1 cx, 1 fz.
Giffin, James, 2 ax, 2 az, 1 bx, 1 bz, 1 cx, 1 cz, 1 dx, 1 ez, 2 fx; 4 n.
Hayward, Francis, 1 az, 1 cz, 1 dx, 1 dz, 1 fz, 1 gx; 10 n.
Whittington, Stephen, 2 ax, 1 az, 1 bz, 1 ez, 1 fx; 5 n.
Hodson, Ann, 1 az, 1 bx, 2 cx, 1 dx, 1 fz; 14 n.
Ennalls, Thomas, 3d, 1 ax, 1 dx, 1 dz; 8 n.
Dent, George, 2 ax, 1 dx, 1 dz.
Ennalls, William, 1 cz, 1 ex; 22 n.
Ennalls, Coll, Barthow, 1 bz, 1 cz, 1 gx; 27 n.
Ennalls, Henry, 1 ex; 17 n.
Rue, Jessey, 2 ax, 1 az, 3 bz, 1 cx, 1 dx, 1 fz.
Morain, Moses, 1 cx, 1 cz.
Callender, Robert, 2 az, 2 bx, 1 cx, 1 cz, 1 ez, 1 fx.
West, Mary, 2 ax, 2 az, 1 bz, 1 cx, 1 cz, 1 ez.
Stewart, James, 1 az, 1 dx, 1 dz.
Griffin Joseph [Black], 9 n.
Vinson, Stephen, 1 ax, 1 az, 1 bz, 1 dz, 1 ex.
Ennalls, Joseph Magr. 5 ax, 2 az, 1 dz, 1 ex, 18.
Paul, Daniell, 2 az, 1 bz, 1 cz, 1 ex, 1 fz.
Knott, John, 1 ax, 1 az, 1 bx, 1 bz, 1 cx, 1 cz, 1 dx, 1 fx, 1 fz.
Sheppard, John, 1 az, 1 gx.
Ward, Lousey, 2 ax, 1 az, 1 bx, 1 bz, 1 cx, 1 cz, 1 dx, 1 fz.
Badley, William, 1 ax, 3 az, 1 bx, 1 cx, 2 cz, 1 dx, 1 dz, 1 fx, 1 fz.
Pike, Lewis, 2 bx, 1 cx, 1 cz, 1 fx.
Cook, Zeabulon, 2 ax, 1 ex, 1 fz.
Cook, Mary, 1 gz.
Clark, Robert, 1 az, 1 cz, 1 dx.
Killender, Thomas, 1 ax, 1 ex, 1 fz.
Phillips, William, 1 ax, 2 az, 1 cx, 2 dx, 2 dz.
Sherman, Benjamin, 4 ax, 2 bx, 1 cz, 1 ez, 1 fx.
Paul, Edward, 1 ax, 1 az, 1 bx, 2 cz, 1 dz, 1 fx, 1 fz.
Webb, John, 3 az, 1 bx, 1 ex, 1 ez.
Barnes, Sarah, 1 az, 1 bz, 1 dz.
Hayward, John, 1 ax, 1 bx, 1 bz, 1 cz, 1 ez, 1 gx.
Rogers, Thomas, 2 bx, 1 fz, 1 gx.

Nuton, Richard, 2 ax, 5 az, 2 bx, 1 dx, 1 ex, 1 ez; 5 n.
Hevens, Luke, 2 ax, 3 az, 2 bx, 1 cz, 1 fx, 1 fz; 1 n.
Hevens, Thomas, 1 ax, 1 cz, 1 dx.
Sweatten, Siney, 1 az, 1 cz; 1 n.
Morris, Edward, 1 ax, 2 az, 1 bx, 1 cz, 1 ex, 1 ez.
Plug, Rose [Black] 1 fz, 1 n.
M. Callister, Jeremiah, 2 ax, 1 bx, 1 dx, 1 dz.
Littleton, Southy, 1 ax, 3 az, 4 bz, 2 cx, 1 fz, 1 gx; 1 n.
Littleton, Mark, 1 ax, 1 cz, 1 dx.
Littleton, William, 2 ax, 1 az, 1 bx, 1 bz, 2 cz, 1 ex, 1 ez, 1 fx.
Sulivane, Daniel, Magr. 1 ex, 1 gx, 1 gz; 11 n.
Sulivane, Daniel, Junr. 2 ax, 1 az, 1 ex, 1 ez; 12 n.
M. Callister, Athilda, 2 ax, 1 dx, 1 dz.
M. Callister, Ezekiel, 1 az, 1 bx, 1 cx, 1 ex, 1 fz.
Badley, William, 1 bz, 1 gx, 1 gz.
Badley, Nathan, 1 ax, 1 az, 1 ex, 1 ez.
Woodards, Elizabeth, 1 ax, 1 cz, 1 ex, 1 gz.
Granger, William, 4 ax, 1 bx, 2 dz, 1 fx, 1 fz; 1 n.
Russum, Luke, 1 ax, 2 az, 1 bx, 1 bz, 1 cx, 1 ez, 1 gx.
Scott, John, 3 az, 1 bz, 1 cz, 1 ex, 1 ez.
Higens, Diana, 1 ax, 1 dx, 1 gz.
Wayford, John, 3 ax, 1 az, 1 bx, 1 cz, 1 ex, 1 ez.
Granger, Edward, 1 ax, 3 az, 1 bx, 1 cx, 1 ex, 1 ez.
Cook, Eliner, 1 ax, 1 cz, 1 ez.
West, Solomon, 4 ax, 1 cx, 1 cz, 1 ex, 1 ez.
Hicks Denward, 1 ax, 1 bx, 1 bz, 1 cz, 1 dx, 1 fz, 1 gx; 27 n.
Scott, Mary, 1 bz, 1 cx, 1 dz, 1 ez, 1 gz.
Brinsfield, James, 3 az, 2 bx, 1 bz, 2 cx, 1 fx, 1 fz; 6 n.
Handley, Leavin, 1 ax, 3 az, 1 bx, 1 bz, 1 cx, 1 dx, 1 ex, 1 ez.
Anderton, John, 1 az, 1 fx; 16 n.
Glanding, John, 1 ax, 1 az, 1 bz, 1 dz, 1 ex.
Sulivane, James, 2 ax, 3 az, 1 dz, 2 ex, 1, ez; 21 n.
Southerlin, James, Doctr. 2 dx; 1 n.
Smith, Francis, 2 ax, 1 az, 2 dz, 1 ez.
Scott, John, 1 ax, 2 az, 2 dz, 1 ex, 1 ez; 10 n.
Morain, Mary, 1 ax, 2 az, 2 bx, 1 bz, 2 cx, 1 fz; 1 n.
Stevens, John, 1 az, 1 bx, 1 dx, 3 dz, 1 ex; 3 n.
Shaw, Nancy, 1 ax, 1 bz.
Robinson, George, 1 ax, 1 cz, 1 dx; 1 n.
Adams, Mary, 1 bz, 1 cz, 1 gz.
Marshall, John, 2 ax, 2 az, 1 bx, 1 cz, 1 dx, 1 dz; 13 n.
Roylins, Hodson, 2 az, 1 cz, 1 dx, 1 dz.

Norman, Ester, 1 ax, 1 az, 2 bx, 1 bz, 1 cx, 1 fz.
Davis, Margrit, 3 bx, 2 bz, 1 cx, 1 cz, 1 fz.
Adams, Bettey, 1 ax, 1 az, 1 bz, 1 fz.
Saunders, William, 2 ax, 1 az, 1 bx, 2 dz, 1 fx; 6 n.
Rollisten, Richard, 2 ax, 1 bz, 1 dx, 1 dz.
Bramble, Aron, 1 az, 1 cx, 1 dx, 1 dz.
Bramble, Thomas, 1 ax, 1 dx.
Wright, Sarah, 2 bx, 1 cz, 1 gz.
Hardin, Mary, 2 ax, 1 dz.
Whitchits, Ezekiel, 1 dx; 3 n.
Billings, William, 2 ax, 1 bx, 2 bz, 1 dx, 1 fz.
Williams, Elizabeth, 1 ax, 1 bx, 1 dz, 1 gz.
White, John, 1 cz, 1 dx; 3 n.
White, Thomas, 1 az, 1 dz, 1 ex; 6 n.
Thompson, John, 3 ax, 1 fx, 1 fz.
Hubbart, John, 1 az, 1 bz, 1 dx, 1 dz, 1 ez.
Hooper, John, 1 az, 1 bx, 1 cz, 1 dz, 1 fx.
Wheelar, Solomon, 2 ax, 3 az, 1 bz, 1 ez, 1 fz, 1 gx.
Layton, Mary, 1 ax, 1 bx, 1 cx, 1 dx, 1 ez, 1 gz.
Williams, Phillip, 1 az, 1 dx, 1 dz.
Boudle, John, 1 bz, 1 dx, 1 fx, 1 fz; 6 n.
Boudle, Henry, 2 ax; 2 n.
Scotter, Edward, 1 az, 1 bx, 1 fx, 1 fz.
Lecompt, William, 2 bx, 1 bz, 2 ez, 1 gx; 19 n.
Ennalls, ——, 1 bz, 1 ez; 16 n.
Owens, Owen, 2 ax, 1 az, 1 bx, 1 cx, 1 cz, 1 dz, 1 ex.
Lecompt, Samuel, 1 ax, 1 dx, 1 dz.
Cavender, David, 1 az, 1 bx, 2 bz, 1 ex, 1 fx, 1 fz, 1 gz.
Dawson, John, 1 ax, 1 bx, 1 bz, 1 cx, 1 cz, 1 dx, 2 fz, 1 gx.
Cavender, Thomas, 1 ax, 1 cz, 1 dx.
Hooper, Henry, 3 ax, 3 az, 1 bx, 1 dz, 1 fx, 1 fz.
Wheelar, Thomas, 2 ax, 2 az, 1 ex, 1 ez.
Rose, Samuel, 2 bx, 1 cz, 1 dz, 1 gx, 1 gz.
Nuton, Nimrod, 1 ax, 1 bx, 1 cx, 1 dx, 2 dz.
Nuton, Willis, 1 ax, 2 az, 1 bx, 1 dx, 1 dz, 1 ex, 1 ez; 5 n.
Hicks, Joseph, 1 ax, 1 az, 2 bx, 1 cx, 2 dx, 1 dz, 1 fz, 1 gx.
Wright, Henry, 1 ax, 1 az, 2 bx, 1 dz, 1 ex; 3 n.
Ferguson, Collen, 1 dx.
Molix, Jimmimey [Black], 5 n.
Hooper, Roger A. 2 ax, 2 az, 2 bx, 2 cx, 1 ez, 1 gz; 12 n.
Linningham, Peatrick, 1 az, 1 cz, 1 dx, 1 dz.
Cummins, James, 2 ax, 2 az, 2 bx, 2 cz, 1 ex, 1 ez.

Brodess, Thomas, 2 az, 1 dx, 3 dz; 10 n.
Harrison, Mary, 1 ax, 1 cx, 1 dz, 1 ez; 1 n.
Ward, Joseph, 1 ax, 1 az, 1 cz, 1 dx.
Langfit, Francis, 1 ax, 1 az, 1 dx, 1 dz.
Heron, Elizabeth, 2 az, 1 bx, 2 cx, 2 cz, 1 dx, 1 ex, 2 gz; 8 n.
Jones, Mary, 3 ax, 2 az, 1 bz, 1 ez, 1 gz.
McDaniel, Leavin, 2 ax, 1 az, 1 ex, 1 ez.
Jones, Morgan, 4 az, 1 bx, 1 bz, 1 dz, 1 gx; 1 n.
Bird, Magor, 2 ax, 3 az, 1 bz, 1 cx, 1 dx, 1 dz; 10 n.
Lecompt, John, 3 ax, 3 bx, 1 bz, 1 cz, 1 dx, 1 dz, 1 fx, 1 fz; 17 n.
M[c]henry, Alexandr, 1 az, 1 bz, 1 ex, 1 fz.
Godding, Elizabeth, 2 az, 2 dx.
Kees, Francis, 1 ax, 1 bx, 1 bz, 1 ez.
Tripe, William, 2 ax, 1 dz, 1 ex; 8 n.
Darbey, John, 1 az, 1 bz, 1 fx, 1 fz; 12 n.
Dodson, George, 2 ax, 2 az, 1 cx, 1 dx, 1 dz, 1 ex, 1 ez; 2 n.
McDaniel, William, 2 ax, 2 az, 2 bz, 1 dx, 1 dz, 1 ex.
Hodson, Hoopes, 2 ax, 2 az, 1 bx, 1 bz, 1 dz, 1 fx; 6 n.
Manning, Anthony, 2 ax, 1 cz, 1 ex; 12 n.
Coopper, John, 2 ax, 1 ex, 1 ez; 5 n.
Noble, Mark, 2 ax, 5 az, 1 bz, 1 ex, 1 ez.
Hodson, John, 1 ax, 2 az, 2 bx, 1 bz, 2 cx, 1 dx, 1 ez, 1 gx; 28 n.
Hodson, Henry, 1 az, 1 cz, 1 dx; 8 n.
Cocklin, Thomas, 1 az, 1 gx, 1 gz.
Smith, Edward, 1 ax, 1 dx, 1 dz; 6 n.
Handley, Handy, 2 ax, 2 az, 2 bx, 1 ex, 1 ez; 1 n.
Brown, John, 2 ax, 1 az, 1 dz, 1 ex.
Alexandr, William, 1 ax, 1 az, 1 dz, 1 ex, 1 gx.
Monrow, Elizabeth, 1 ax, 1 az, 1 ez.
Warron, Beazil, 1 ax, 1 az, 1 dz, 1 ez, 1 gx.
Hubbart, Bettey, 1 bx, 1 bz, 1 cz, 1 fz.
Lecompt, Leavin, 6 ax, 1 bx, 1 dz, 1 ex.
Ross, James, 2 ax, 3 az, 1 bx, 1 bz, 1 dx, 1 ex, 1 fz; 1 n.
Owens, John, 1 cx, 1 cz, 1 dx; 5 n.
Jackson, Robert, 2 ax, 1 dz, 1 ex.
Lecompt, William, [Black] 3 n.
Adam, "free, negro" 2 n.
Cook, John, 3 ax, 1 bz, 1 dx, 1 dz.
Lecompt, Charles, 1 bz, 1 ex, 1 ez, 1 fz; 5 n.
Phillips, Pegey, 1 az, 1 cx, 1 dx, 1 ez.
Lecompt, James, 2 ax, 2 az, 1 bz, 1 dx, 1 ez, 1 fx.
Oggan, Peggey, 2 ax, 1 az, 1 bz, 1 dx, 1 ez.

Basset, Thomas, 1 ax, 1 az, 1 cx, 1 cz; 2 n.
Sulivane, Thomas, 1 ax, 1 az, 1 dx, 1 dz.
Covey, John, 1 ax, 2 dx, 1 dz, 1 fz.
Long, John, 2 ax, 1 az, 2 bx, 2 bz, 1 ez, 1 gx, 1 gz; 1 n.
Green, Ralph, 1 az, 1 bx, 1 dz, 1 ex; 13 n.
Brown, Elijah, 1 az, 1 cz, 1 dx, 1 ez.
Smith, Francis, 2 ax, 1 az, 2 bx, 2 cx, 1 dx, 1 ez.
Bruffit, Garner, 1 ax, 1 az, 1 bz, 1 dx, 1 dz; 1 n.
Traverse, Leavin, 3 ax, 1 az, 2 bx, 1 bz, 2 dz, 1 ez, 1 fx; 15 n.
Claridge, Elizabeth, 3 ax, 1 bx, 1 fz.
Goldsborough, Robert, Esqr.; 15 n.
Moore, Christopher, 2 az, 1 bx, 1 bz, 1 cz, 1 fx, 1 fz.
McClemmey, Samuel, 1 cx, 1 dx, 1 ex.
Hooper, John, 1 cx, 2 dx.
Vinson, Nehemiah, 1 az, 2 bx, 1 bz, 1 cz, 2 dx, 1 ez, 1 fx.
Ward, Summars, 2 az, 1 bz, 1 cx, 1 cz, 1 dz, 1 fx; 3 n.
Hamiltown, John, 2 ax, 2 bx, 1 bz, 1 cx, 1 cz, 1 ez, 1 fz; 3 n.
Greenwood, John, 1 ax, 2 az, 2 bx, 1 bz, 1 cx, 1 dx, 1 ex, 1 ez, 1 fx; 2 n.
Dickinson, Col. John, 3 ax, 1 az, 3 bx, 1 cx, 1 cz, 1 fx, 1 fz; 40 n.
Parker, Daniel, 2 ax, 1 az, 1 ex, 1 ez; 8 n.
Brodess, Edward, 2 ax, 1 az, 1 bx, 2 dx, 2 dz; 4 n.
Formar, William, 2 bz, 1 fx, 1 gz.
Notherwood, Joseph, 1 cx, 1 cz; 7 n.
Brodess, Tabitha, 1 cx, 2 dx, 2 dz, 1 gz; 4 n.
Ennalls, Coll, John, 1 ex; 38 n.
Harvey, Salathal, 2 ax, 2 az, 1 cz, 1 ex, 1 ez.
Burge, Ailse, 1 ax, 2 bx, 1 bz, ez.
Eccleston, Capt. Hugh, 2 az, 2 bx, 1 bz, 1 ez, 1 fx, 1 fz; 32 n.
Cullins, Isaac, 1 dz, 1 gx, 1 gz.
Denney, John, 1 ax, 1 bx, 1 bz, 1 dx, 1 dz.
Summars, Parks, 1 ax, 1 az, 1 dz, 1 ex.
Beotpich, John, 1 ax, 2 az, 1 bx, 1 cz, 1 dz, 1 ex, 1 ez; 2 n.
Becks, William, 2 ax, 1 az, 2 bx, 1 bz, 1 cx, 1 fz, 1 gx.
Evans, Samuel, 1 ax, 2 az, 3 bx, bz, 2 ez, gx.
Beotpitch, Jonathan, 2 ax, 4 az, 1 bx, 1 cz, 1 fx, 1 fz; 4 n.
Bacon, George, 2 ax, 2 az, 1 bz, 1 cz, 1 ez, 1 fx.
Saunders, William, 1 ax, 3 az, 1 gx, 1 gz.
Foxwell, Isaac, 2 ax, 1 az, 1 dx, 1 ez.
Slight, Joseph, 1 ax, 1 bz, 1 cz, 1 dx.
Lewis, William, 2 ax, 1 az, 1 dz, 1 fx.
Goutee, Jabus, 2 ax, 3 az, 1 dx, 2 ez.
Smith, Ann, 1 cx, 2 cz, 1 gz.

Lawson, Samuel, 3 bx, 1 dx, 1 fx, 1 fz.
Keene, Mary, 1 az, 1 bx, 1 gz; 2 n.
Copper, Gustavus, 1 dz, 1 ex.
Partridge, Isaac, 1 dz, 1 gx, 1 gz; 10 n.
Driver, Martin, 1 ax, 1 az, 1 bx, 1 ez, 1 fx.
Pattison, Atthow, 1 az, 2 cz, 1 dx, 1 dz, 1 fz, 1 gx; 5 n.
Eccleston, Thomas F. 1 ex; 15 n.
Harrison, John, 1 bx, 1 ex, 1 fz; 1 n.
Hanford, John, 2 ax, 1 az, 1 dz, 1 ex.
Laine, William, 1 ax, 1 az, 1 bx, 1 dx, 1 dz, 1 fx, 1 fz; 1 n.
Brierwood, John, 3 ax, 1 az, 1 bx, 1 bz, 1 dx, 1 fz, 1 gx; 5 n.
Mills, Right, 2 ax, 1 az, 1 bz, 1 dx, 1 dz, 1 ez; 1 n.
Hooper, William, 2 bx, 2 cz, 1 ex, 1 fz; 4 n.
Tregor, Nuton, 2 ax, 2 az, 1 bz, 1 dx, 1 ez, 1 fx; 4 n.
Willis, Leavin, 1 ax, 1 az, 1 cx, 1 cz, 1 dz, 1 ez, 1 fx; 2 n.
Woollen, Leavin, 2 ax, 1 az, 1 bz, 1 cz, 1 dx, 1 ez, 1 fx.
Mills, Edward, 1 ax, 1 cz, 1 dx, 1 dz.
Hill, Solomon, 1 ax, 1 az, 1 dx, 1 dz; 1 n.
Keene, Thomas, 2 ax, 2 az, 1 bx, 1 dz, 1 ex.
Whetaker, John, 2 az, 2 cz, 1 dx; 1 n.
Saunders, Thomas, 1 az, 1 bz, 1 fz, 1 gx.
Harrison, Siller, 1 az, 1 cz, 1 dz; 2 n.
Byron, Lamberth, 2 ax, 1 cz, 1 dx, 1 ez; 1 n.
Ennalls, Elizabeth, 10 n.
Beckwith, Emanuel, 3 az, 1 bx, 1 ex, 1 ez.
Gossage, Daniel, 3 ax, 1 ex, 1 fz.
Norman, Thomas, 2 az, 1 cz, 1 dx, 1 dz; 1 n.
Arnett, Ann, 1 ax, 1 bx, 1 bz, 1 fz.
Arnett, James, 1 ax, 1 az, 1 dx, 1 dz.
Martin, Thomas, 7 n.
Porter, James, 1 ax, 1 az, 1 dz, 1 ex.
Muse, Magr. Thomas, 10 n.
Cheshire, Mary, 1 ax, 1 az, 1 bx, 1 dx, 1 dz, 1 ez; 3 n.
Partridge, Jonathan, 1 ax, 1 az, 1 cz, 1 fx, 1 fz; 8 n.
Porter, Arthur, 1 bx, 1 dx, 1 fz, 1 gx; 2 n.
Reed, Rosanna, 2 dx, 1 dz, 1 ex, 1 gz.
Stewart, Henry, 2 ax, 2 az, 1 cz, 1 dz, 1 ez, 1 fx; 5 n.
Manning, John, 1 az, 1 bx, 2 bz, 2 ex, 1 ez, 1 fz; 18 n.
Griffin, William, 3 ax, 1 az, 1 bz, 1 ex; 1 n.
Woolford, Roger, 1 dx, 1 gx, 2 gz; 15 n.
Saunders, Henry, 3 ax, 4 az, 1 bx, 1 bz, 1 cz, 1 dx, 1 dz, 1 ez, 1 gx; 3 n.
Parmer, James, 2 ax, 1 az, 1 bz, 1 dz, 1 ez, 1 gx, 1 gz; 9 n.

Ennalls, Thomas, 2 ax, 3 az, 1 cx, 1 dz, 1 fx, 1 fz, 1 gz; 27 n.
Wheelar, Charles, 1 az, 1 cz, 1 fx.
Button, William, 2 ax, 3 az, 1 bz, 1 cx, 1 dz, 1 ex, 1 ez; 8 n.
Stewart, John T. 3 ax, 2 az, 1 cz, 1 dx, 1 dz, 1 ex; 10 n.
Stewart, Thomas, 2 ax, 1 ez, 1 fx; 2 n.
Cheshire, John, 1 ax, 1 az, 2 bz, 1 cz, 1 ex, 1 fz; 3 n.
Manidier, Mary, 1 bz, 1 cz, 1 dx, 1 fz; 15 n.
Murray, Doctr. James, 5 n.
Pennington, Segar, 7 n.
Daffin, Capt. Joseph, 1 cx, 1 dx, 1 dz, 1 ex; 20 n.
Bluch, William, 1 bx, 1 ez, 1 fx.
Muir, Thomas, 1 ax, 1 bz, 1 dx, 1 dz, 1 ex, 1 ez; 2 n.
Hale, Jene, 2 ax, 1 az, 1 cx, 1 ez, 1 fx; 2 n.
Hughs, Revd. Phillemon, 2 bz, 1 ez, 1 fx, 1 gx, 1 gz; 4 n.
Slee, Joseph, 1 dx; 1 n.
Norris, Moliein, 3 ax, 1 bx, 1 dz, 1 ex.
Cox, Nathaniel, 1 ax, 1 az, 2 bx, 1 bz, 1 cz, 1 ez, 1 gx, 1 gz.
Haile, Elizabeth, 2 ax, 1 bz, 1 dz, 1 fz; 8 n.
Ennalls, Andrew S. 1 cx, 1 ex, 1 ez; 6 n.
Ennalls, Joseph, 1 dz, 1 ex, 1 fx, 1 gz; 29 n.
Mulania, James, 3 az, 1 cx, 1 dz, 1 ex.
Colson, John, 1 ax, 1 bz, 1 dx, 1 dz.
Airey, Thomas H. [H^e?] 1 ax, 1 az, 1 dx, 1 dz; 28 n.
Scott, Charles, 2 az, 1 bx, 2 bz, 1 ex, 1 fx; 6 n.
Dawson, Joseph, 1 ax, 1 az, 1 cx, 1 dx, 1 dz.
Dawson, William, 2 ax, 1 az, 3 bx, 1 bz, 1 cx, 1 ex, 1 ez, 1 fz.
Kees, James, 4 ax, 1 az, 2 bx, 1 cx, 1 cz, 1 ez, 1 fx.
Kees, John, 3 ax, 1 bx, 1 bz, 1 ex, 1 ez; 1 n.
Vincent, William, 1 az, 1 dx, 1 dz.
Muse, Magr. Thomas, 12 n.
Dawson, John, 1 az, 1 bx, 1 cx, 1 cz, 1 dx, 1 dz, 1 fz, 1 gx.
Wheelar, William, 2 az, 1 cz, 1 dx, 1 dz.
McCollister, Nathan, 1 az, 1 dx, 1 dz.
Hayward, Leavin, 1 ax, 1 az, 1 bx, 1 bz, 1 dx, 1 dz, 1 fz.
Cornish, John, 2 n.
Connerway, Dennis, 3 az, 1 bx, 1 bz, 1 ez, 1 fx; 1 n.
Dingle, John, 3 ax, 1 dz, 1 ex; 1 n.
Hanford, Thomas, 1 dx, 1 dz.
Stephens, Edward, 3 ax, 2 bx, 1 cx, 1 dx, 1 dz, 1 fx, 1 fz; 9 n.
West, Loten, 2 ax, 1 az, 1 ex, 1 ez.
Nixon, John, 1 cx, 1 ex.
Blair, John, 1 dx.
Evans, Mary, 1 ez.

Totals, 2897: 313 ax, 281 az, 162 bx, 118 bz, 78 cx, 100 cz, 133 dx, 130 dz, 92 ex, 102 ez, 59 fx, 69 fz, 42 gx, 35 gz; 1175 n.

Dorchester County Ss. Septr. 9th, 1776. Personally Appeared Samuel Hooper, before the Committee of Observation for the County afore said, & made Oath on the Holy Evangels of Almighty God that the aforegoing is a true & perfect List, to the best of his Knowledge of the Number of the Inhabitants of Transquakin Hundred in the County afd, so far forth, as was in his power to obtain.

Signed P order of the af^d. Committee
JOHN C. HARRISON Clk.

HARFORD COUNTY

Harford County, Broad Creek Hundred, Census of 1776

"A list of the Inhabitants both Whites & Blacks in Broad Creek Hundred 1776." "Total 342."

A. *Ages*

Armond, William 32
Elizabeth 28
Thomas 8
Hanna 6
William 4
Isaac 2
Total, 6; taxable, 1.

Anderson, George 40
Jane 49
Mary 13
Jenny 7
Total, 4; taxable, 1.

Allison, William Lame 1

B.

Bodkin, Robert 40
Margrett 36
Rachell 16
John 15
William 14
Thomas 12
Robert 10
Charles 9
James 8
Richard 6
Margrett 6
Molly 5
Nancey 4
Janey 2
Sally 1
Total, 15; taxable, 1.

Ages

[1] Brice, James 25
Alice 20
Barnett 1
Owen Corker 20
Mary Perry 20
Son Thos. 1
Total, 6; taxables, 2.

Barclay, John 30
Elizabeth 20
Negroes
Dick 18
Neale 14
Jenny 60
Total, 5; taxables, 2.

——nington, Henry 51
——ary 20
——niah Benington 21
—— —— 15
——riscilla 12
——enry 10
[T]om 6
Kessia 4
[N]ancey McDaniel 4
Mary Hagerty 23
Total, 10; taxables, 2.

Barnard, Mark 30
Jane 26
James 6
Thomas 4
Saml. 2
Mark 1/12
Total, 6; taxable, 1.

	Ages
Beard, John	19
Total, 1; taxable, 1.	

C.

	Ages
Cuningham, John, Isaac Thos. Scurly	28
Total, 1; taxable, 1.	
Crooks, Henry	28
Jane	23
William	5
Andrew	3
Margrett	½
Elizabeth Kerby	26
Total, 6; taxable, 1.	

D.

	Ages
Daubt, Roger	40
Margrett	26
Saml.	4
—— —— ——	2
Robert	6
Total, 5; taxable, 1.	
Dun——a——, William	28
Wife	34 [?]
Thos.	1
Total, 3; taxable, 1.	
Downing, —— Francis	40
Susanna	37
William	23
Rebecca	18
John	½
John	15
Saml.	13
Molley	12
Puck [?]	10
Frances	5
Ruth	2
Negroes	
York	40
Oliver	30
Jack, —— Lome	30
Abraham	20
Hanna	23
Lucy	16
Ned	2
Nell	4
Total, 19; taxables, 7.	

E.

	Ages
Ekin, Sam[1]	48
Nelly	36
Jusch	13
Jane, Cud [?]	30
Delieca [?]	½
Total, 5; taxable, 1.	

[2] F.

	Ages
Foster, Phidelis	4–
Keatty	3–
Rebecca	–5
Betsey	—
Peggey	6
John	—
Fedelious	—
Keatty	—
Total, 8; taxable, 1.	

G.

	Ages
Gordon, John	3–
Rebecca	33
Henry	13 [?]
Mary	10 [?]
John	8
Sarah	4
Rebecca	2
Total, 7; taxable, 1.	
Glen, Mary	60 [?]
Robert	18
Joseph	16
Total, 3; taxables, 2.	
Guppey, Henry	45
Margrett	40

Ages

John.......................12
Jane.......................10
Henry...................... 7
Mary....................... 3
Margrett...................1/4
Negroes
Hana.......................20
Ned........... ....1/2
Elizabeth alone............21
Total, 10; taxables, 2.

Gillisson, John............40
Jane.......................30
Jane.......................16
John....................... 5
Mary....................... 3
Noble...............20/10 [?]
Total, 6; taxables, —.

Gordon, James..............31
Jane.......................30
John.......................10
Agnis...................... 6
Margrett................... 4
Elizabeth.................. 2
Mary.......................1/12
Aurthur Gilles.............13
Total, 8; taxable, 1.

H.

Howlett, Andrews...........50
Margrett...................49
Mary.......................19
Elizabeth..................17
Ann........................15
John.......................10
Sert. Philip...............20
Total, 7; taxables, 2.

Hood, Andrew...............40
Margrett...................38
Jennett.................... 8

Ages

Robert..................... 4
James......................1 1/2
Total, 5; taxable, 1.

Howlet, James..............22
Margrett...................18
Total, 2; taxable, 1.

Hubard, Ruth, Mulato.......54
Belt.......................13
Joe........................10
Hanna...................... 6
Total, 4; taxable, 1.

Henry, Saml................58
Mary.......................55
Robert.....................23
Elizabeth..................19
John.......................15
Isaac......................13
Total, 6; taxables, —.

Hamilton, Jonathan.........35
Betsey.....................30
Polly......................10
Robin...................... 8
Peggy...................... 6
Alexander.................. 4
Sally...................... 2
Betsey..................... 2
John....................... 1
Total, 9; taxable, 1.

[2] J.

Johnson, Thomas, Jr [?]....26
Total, 1; taxable, 1.

Jones, Aqulia..............27
Total, 1; taxable, —.

James, Jefferry, Negroe....31
Martha.....................20
James...................... 3
Nancey.....................1/2
Total, 4; taxable, 1.

	Ages
Johnson, Thomas	50
Mary	40
James	15
Isaac	13
Thomas	10
Mary	8
Elizabeth	6
Sarah	4

Total, 8; taxable, 1.

K.

Knight, Hanna	36
Sally	17
Thomas	14
Cassandra	12
Aquillia	—
Michael	8
James	6
Abraham	2

Total, 8.

[3] L.

Litten, John	58
Mary	44
Mary	13
Hanah	10
John Lee	11

Total, 5; taxable, 1.

M.

McNabb, James	35
Alice	30
Jim	10
Alice	8
Keatty	6
Elizabeth	4
Rachell	2

Total, 7; taxable, 1.

Mafford, James	4

Morrison, Ann	42
Ann	10
John	13

	Ages
Mary	3
Joseph Morgar	19

Total, 5; taxable, 1.

Mckisson John	32
Jane	30
James	8
——	6
Aurthur	4
Sally	14

Total, 6; taxable, 1.

McClam, James	45
Mary	40
Betsey	19

Total, 4; taxable, 1.

McGeomery, John	37
McGomery, Wm.	37
Rachell Karr	18
John	1/2

Total, 4; taxables, 2.

P.

Penix, John	35
Sarah	33
Sarah Poage	70
Keatty	6
Sarah	4
James	3
Susanna	1/2

Total, 7; taxable, 1.

Pompey Negro	
J. Rigbies	40

Total, 1; taxable, 1.

Phill Negro	35

Total, 1; taxable, 1.

Parks James	63
Jane	52
Martha	15
James	12

Total, 4; taxable, 1.

R. *Ages*

Rumage, Davis 22
Martha 18
Total, 2; taxable, 1.

Rumage, George 61
Mary 45
Geor 14
Tom 15
Total, 4; taxable, 1.

Robinson, Walter 40
Total, 1; taxable, 1.

Robinson, William 35
Mary 30
Jane 6
Mary 4
James 2
Total, 6; taxable, 1.

Reese, William 59
Ann 55
Mary 30
Nancey 19
Hanna 17
Nelly 16
Margrett 14
Alexander 12
William 8
Jese 1/2
Total, 10; taxable, 1.

S.

Sweeny, David 28
Mary 30
Sarah 9 1/2
Henrietta 8 1/2
Richard 6
Olive 2
Ser't. Mary 25
Dinia 1/2
Negro Jeffery 30
Total, 9; taxables, 2.

Ages

Scharbraugh, Euclid 62
Mary 51
Thos. 20
Rebecca 19
Sally 16
Sammy 14
Hanna 15
Jemmy 10
Total, 8; taxables, 2.

Shores, Richard 23
Elizabeth 19
Mary 1/2
Total, 3; taxable, 1.

Sims, Robert 45
Alice 26
Betsey 10
Rol 8
Jane 6
Wm. 4
Margrett 3
Frances 1/2
Total, 8; taxable, 1.

Sims, Realph 36
Ann Boyle 30
Mary 6
Ann 4
Total, 4; taxable, 1.

Sims, James 60

Spain, Beaver 72
Elizabeth 45
Nelly 19
Hana 16
William 13
Jacob 10
Total, 6; taxables, —.

Samuel Negro Husband's 34

T.

	Ages
Taylor William	23
Ruth	20
Thomas, John	30
Mary	47
Nancey	3½
Rachell	1½
Martha	17
——	13
——a	—
Total, 7; taxable, 1.	
Thomas Isaac	23
Total, 1; taxable, 1.	
Tarbert, James	26
Mary	20
Janey	1
Total, 3; taxables, —.	

W.

	Ages
Wilson John Glade	57
Jane	50
Jane	17
Betsey	14
Robert	12
John	21
Total, 6; taxables, 2.	
Winman John	60
Total, 1; taxable, 1.	
West, John	39
Susanna	34
John	13
James	11
William	10
Margrett	6
Lidia	4
Susanna	¼
Sarah	¼
Total, 9; taxable, 1.	
Wilson James, Blind	50
Isable	48
Mulatoes	
George	11
Benjamin	9
Wilson, Archable	48
Margrett	30
Jane	6
Mary	3
Agnis	2
Whyle, Nath'l	40
Kathrine	38
John	18
James	15
Philip	13
Mary	10
Sarah	8
Jane	4
Total, 8; taxables, 2.	

HARFORD COUNTY, BUSH RIVER LOWER HUNDRED

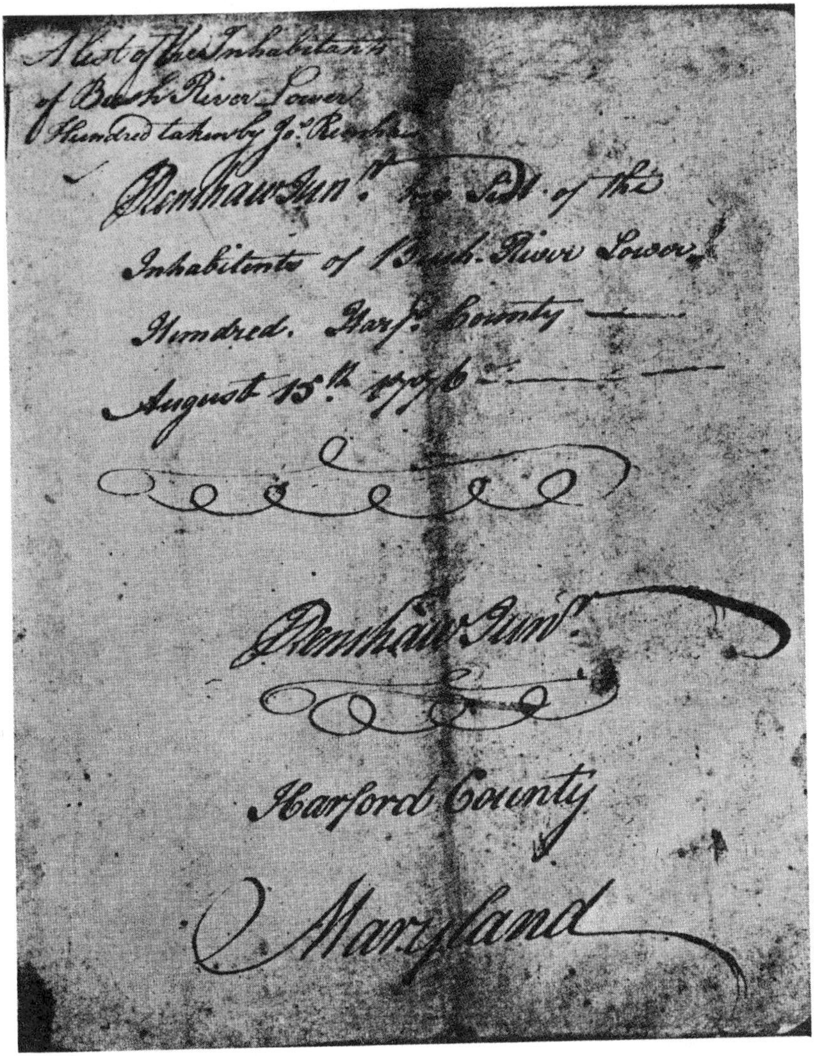
A List of the Inhabitants
of Bush River Lower
Hundred taken by Jos. Renshaw

Jos. Renshaw Junr. his List of the
Inhabitents of Bush River Lower
Hundred. Harfd. County
August 15th 1776

Jos. Renshaw Junr.

Harford County

Maryland

John Latimore	35
Mary Dermott	55
John Dermott	22
James Dermott	14
Caterine Dermott	18
William Bay	20
Jennet Bay Senr	53
Hugh Bay	18
Alexr Bay	12
Jennet Bay Junr	18
Elizabeth Bay	16
Sarah Bay	16
Alexr Frew	67
Rose Frew	67
James Frew	23
Rose Simpson	30
Margaret Simpson	5
Job Spencer	26
Nathaniel West	36
Hannah West	40
Jacob Johnson	16
Phebe West	9
Jonathan West	4
Ruth West	2
Barnard Preston	22
Elizabeth Preston	17
Negro Jude	16
Sarah Preston 3 Weeks	

James Scott of Aquila	14
Negro Patience	38
do Rache	9
do Nell	4
do Roger	1
do Ned	65
Servt William Butler	19
Servt Tom	14
Thomas Thruston	40
Milky Thruston	30
William Thruston	12
Barnet Thruston	6
Unity Thruston	9
Ann Thruston	7
Martha Thruston	2
Aquila Scott of Aquila	25
Mary Scott	22
James Scott	5
Clemmency Scott	3
Elizabeth Scott	1
Negro Jacob	22
do Sam	22
do Esther	6
Alexr Hughston	24
Mary Rhoads	50
Thomas Rhoads	19
Magdeline Rhoads	15
Martha Rhoads	13
Hannah Rhoads	8
Mary Rhoads	6

2 Thomas Thompson	30
Sarah Thomson	30
Andrew Thomson	7
Elizabeth Thomson	5
Ann Thomson	4
Martha Thomson 8 Months	
Mary Thomson	3
Servt John Thomas	49
Richard Robinson	32
Ann Robinson	29
William Robinson	5
Thomas Robinson	3
Elizabeth Robinson 1 Day old	
Servt Richd Burris	35
Negro Phebe	22
do Ned	3
do James 9 Months	
Isaac Whitaker	41
Elizabeth Whitaker	35
John Sweynard Whitaker	15
Joshua Whitaker	14
Samuel Whitaker	12
Elizabeth Whitaker Junr	10
Benjamin Whitaker	6
Martha Whitaker	2
Servt Esau Turk	27
Servt Edmond Evans	40
Negro Hart	40
do Samson	44

Negro Ned	30
do Pegg	42
do Dinah	26
James Scott	48
Margarett Scott	37
Alexr Scott	17
Elizabeth Scott	14
John Scott	10
Ezbel Scott	6
Sarah Scott	5
Mary Scott	2
Bartholomew Savage	30
Servt Mary Bryan	26
John Fulton	50
Hannah Fulton	42
Casandra Fulton	19
William Fulton	17
Alexis Fulton	15
Lalitia Fulton	13
Pricilla Fulton	8
Susannah Fulton	6
James Fulton	11
Rachel Fulton	4
Henry Wilson Senr	55
Pricilla Wilson	62
Casandra Wilson	18
Negro Power	22
do Henry	16
do Sam	11
do Plato	11
do Isaac	11
do Nace	10

3. Negro Stephen	6
do Jacob	6
do Tower	4
do Abrm	4
do Sue	46
do Pris	6
do Charlote	4
Henry Wilson Junr	29
Margaret Wilson	27
Henry Wilson	4
William Wilson	2
Samuel Wilson	1
Negro Tower	39
do Tom	21
do Abrm	15
do Dinah	23
do Linda	13
do Hinney	9
Servt John Wakeland	25
Free Negro Jude	24
do do Harry	1
Doctor Tate	55
Ann Tate	50
Mary Dooley	20
Thomas Barns	50
Mary Barns	25
Joshua Barns	5
Thos Barns Junr	2
James Deal	27
Mary Deal	24
William Deal	1

Limuel Howard	40
Martha Howard	34
Ruth Howard	14
Elizabeth Howard	12
Ann Howard	8
Martha Howard Junr	6
Sarah Howard	4
Susanah Howard	4
Aquila Howard	10
Dorsey Howard	2
Negro Guinea	40
do Samson	36
do Tom	30
do Dick	17
do Pilus	14
do George	10
do Charles	3
do Marere	17
do Hanah	1
do Philis	8
Benjamin Howard	44
Mary Howard	29
Benjamin Howard Junr	15
John Dutton	14
Limuel Howard	7
Hanah Howard	10
Elizabeth Howard	8
Mary Howard	4
Sarah Howard	2
Mary Denton	54
Negro Toney	15
do Joe	10
do Guy	7
do Sam	5

Negro James	16
do Jimmey	16
do Jemmy	6
do Dealea	7
do Rachel	10
Free Negro Harry	44
do do Pegg	30
do Abrm	2
William Smithson	32
Elizabeth Smithson	27
Servt Christopher Semmons	22
Servt Laughron Cooney	23
Negro Jack	56
do Rose	19
do Sall	19
do Sam	10
do Nero	9
do Tower	2
Thomas Smithson	63
Mary Smithson	53
Nathaniel Smithson	21
Arch Smithson	11
Mary Smithson Junr	18
Margaret Smithson	16
Casandra Smithson	13
Negro Floro	40
do Hannah	27
do Hatia	25
do Ceasar	3
Edward Hamilton	37
Margaret Hamilton	35
Edward Hamilton Junr	5

Buckler Bond	30
Charity Bond	32
Martha Bond	3
Sarah Bond	1
Servt Sarah Fox	30
Jesse Hicks	3
Rebeccah Fox 6 Months	
Negro Ned	27
do Joe	20
do Sook	10
Joshua Durham	43
Sarah Durham	43
John Durham	21
Elizabeth Durham	19
Daniel Durham	16
Benjamin Durham	14
Alizanah Durham	11
Climency Durham	7
Pricilla Durham	5
Hannah Durham	3
Servt Richd Jewel	20
Robert Trimble	27
Ann Trimble	27
Robt Trimble Junr	3
William Trimble	2
Esther Trimble 4 Months	
Servt Jude Sillery	30
John Lang	58
John Taylor	62
Sarah Taylor	59
Mary Taylor	20
Elizabeth Taylor	18

Ann Taylor	15
Frederick Taylor	12
Delia Taylor	11
Ann Taylor	7
Daniel Taylor 7 Months	
Thomas Whitting	33
Sarah Whitting	33
Ann Whitting	6
Elizabeth Whitting	3
Hannah Whitting 5 Months	
Elizabeth Mager	64
Thomas Mager	23
Rachel Mager	22
Abigal Williams	15
John Pain	33
Elizabeth Pain	47
Pricilla Pain	10
Elizabeth Pain Junr.	9
John Pain Junr.	6
Isiah Ratcliff	23
Servt. Giles Hodges	25
Jacob Bull	46
Renis Bull	44
Jacob Bull Junr.	18
William Bull	15
Bennet Bull	7
Jorrell Bull 5 Months	
Mary Bull	13
Eli Bull	5
Renis Bull Junr.	11

Jesse Bull	9
Esther Bull	3
Negro Cesar	50
do. Bob	37
do. Oliver	26
do. Hager	20
do. Moses	13
Edward Bull	22
Sarah Bull	20
Jacob Bull	1
Servt. George O'Neill	23
Mary Rigdon	20
Ann Bond	56
Ann Bond Junr.	24
Elizabeth Bond	16
James Bond	19
Negro Pomp	54
do. Dick	35
do. Henry	30
do. Duke	30
do. Knight	13
do. Prussia	7
do. Jim	4
do. Flora	30
do. Rachel	25
do. Doll	19
do. Amie	15
do. Priss	12
do. Hannah	26
do. Richard	13
do. Poll	5

6. William Cuthbert	36
Richard Norris	56
Jane Norris	31
Mary Norris	10
Hannah Norris	6
Margaret Norris	5
Jane Norris Junr. 3 Weeks	
William Bond	30
Sarah Bond	30
Doctor Finley	29
John Taylor	45
Amelia Bond	12
Servt. Michael McKeim	38
Negro Hannah	30
do. Richard	13
Sarah Norris	79
Sarah Norris	51
Sarah Norris	18
Benedict Norris	10
Negro Coffe	70
do. Oliver	68
do. Nanny	65
do. Joan	35
do. Titus	30
John Norris of John	27
Susanah Norris	51
Alexr. Norris	17
Susanah Norris Junr.	22
Sarah Norris	20
Servt. Andrew Jackling	

Patrick Cantling	52
Elizabeth Cantling	48
Mary Cantling	17
Thomas Cantling	14
Patrick Hughs	23
Samuel Wilmott	28
Ann Wilmott	26
Samuel Davis	4
Vincent Gouldsmith	25
Rosannah Gouldsmith	20
Charles Coleman	52
Rose Coleman	44
Margaret Coleman	13
Charles Coleman Junr.	7
Rose Coleman Junr.	5
John Coleman	3
Aquila Standiford	35
Sarah Standiford	32
Hannah Standiford	10
Milkey Standiford	8
Nathan Standiford	7
George Standiford	5
Sarah Standiford Junr.	3
Mary Standiford	1
Servt. Thomas James	22
Negro Abigale	32
do. Rose	26
do. Primus	17
do. Joe	7
do. Pompy	5
do. Peg	2
do. Phillis	6
do. Rachel	4

7. Benjamin Sedgwick	25
Sarah Sedgwick	30
Mary Driskin	18
Ann Driskin 3 Months	
Sarah Bothe	27
David Bothe	9
Rachel Bothe	3
John Wadlow	25
Ruth Wadlow	20
Moses Wadlow	5
Francis Wadlow 6 Months	
Andrew Shell	76
Mary Shell	70
Benjamin Bradford Norris	30
Elizabeth Norris	28
Martha Norris	6
Sarah Norris	2
un-named son 9 Weeks	
Thomas Norris	21
Serv.t John Andrews	21
Negro Adam	25
John Weaks	31
Mary Weaks	37
Zachariah Weaks	10
Elizabeth Weaks	8
Ruth Weaks	6
Rachel Weaks	4
Mary Weaks Jun.r	2
Ann Weaks 2 Months	
Sarah Patee	60
Peter Patee	21
Elizabeth Patee	24
Sarah Patee	1
John Howling Hughs	6
Negro Marere	60
d.o Samson	26
d.o Sam	7
John Hague	43
William Anderson	29
Mary Anderson	29
Robert Anderson	5
Elizabeth Anderson	4
William Anderson Jun.r	2
John Anderson 5 Months	
Serv.t Daniel Calihon	26
James Steal	22
John Lewis	36
Sarah Lewis	32
Mary Lewis	8
Walter Lewis	4
Rebeccah Lewis 5 Months	
James Jervis	36
Esther Jervis	78
Elizabeth Jervis	33
William Jervis	16
Joseph Jervis	4
Thomas Jervise	2
Mary Jervis 6 Months	

8.

William Smith	27
Rachel Smith	26
Isabel Smith	5
Theophilus Smith	2
Ann Wright	46
Christopher Clements	22
Thomas Wright	13
Servt. Dennis Downs	37
Daniel Scott of Jos.	29
Servt. Patrick Magon	30
Servt. Mary Armstrong	34
Servt. Peter Raticard	14
Negro Jack	34
Edward Tredway	26
Rothwick McKinsey	30
Mary McKinsey	24
Elenor McKinsey	1
Mary King	25
Jane Nugen	60
Ann Nugen	30
Sarah Nugen	7
Elizabeth Nugen	5
Rebecah Nugen	3
Hannah Thruston	13
John Buckley	28

Timothy Neave	53
Sarah Neave	50
Mary Neave	21
John Neave	10
William Neave	7
Thomas Prendergast	71
Ellethew Prendergast	23
Servt. Richd. Fitzjerrald	19
Francis Billingslea	33
Avena Billingslea	28
Samuel Billingslea	11
Sarah Billingslea	9
William Billingslea	7
Walter Billingslea	5
Francis Billingslea Jnr.	3
Silas Billingslea 8 Month	
Servt. Joseph Connoly	35
Negro George	13
do. Rachel	12
do. Sarah	8
do. Tower	80
James Holmes	48
Mary Holmes	40
Samuel Holmes	9
Servt. Thomas Shreding	25
Servt. John Tilbrook	22
William Jewcb	13
Ann Griffith	20
Margaret McCown	22

9. William Bennington	50
Servt. Jonathan Cole	26
Servt. Stephen Searlet	25
Negro Valentine	23
Servt. Mary Smith	14
Jacob Norris	23
William Jones	53
Elizabeth Jones	43
Gilbert Jones	23
Elizabeth Jones Junr.	20
Magdeline Jones	20
William Jones Junr.	17
Jacob Jones	14
Isaac Jones	12
Cassandra Jones	11
Stephen Jones	8
Benjamin Jones	6
[illegible] Jones	1
Servt. Jno. May	27
Servt. Christopher Long	23
Negro Cloe	23
John McComas	33
Mary McComas	25
Servt. Thomas Bowey	29
Aquila McComas	2
Negro Suecy	15
do. Sam	1
William Brown	50
Sarah Brown	25
Ann Brown 5 Weeks	

James Monday	35
Joseph Renshaw	53
Elizabeth Renshaw	53
Cassandra Renshaw	28
Jane Renshaw	26
Joseph Renshaw Junr.	25
Elizabeth Renshaw Junr.	23
Thomas Renshaw	21
Philip Renshaw	18
Samuel Renshaw	15
Susanah Renshaw	11
Negro Moll	40
do. Doll	26
do. Jim	11
do. Jack	6
do. [illegible]	5
do. Cate	4
do. Jorey	2
do. Fann	
do. Affe 3 Months	
Daniel Thomson	36
Mary Thomson	39
John Thomson	15
Ann Thomson	13
Mary Thomson Junr.	11
Thomas Thomson	8
Sarah Thomson	6
Margaret Thomson	3
Archd. Thomson	1
Elizabeth Thomson	1
Negro Rachel	14

10 Ann Scott	50
Aquila Scott	20
Martha Scott	17
Ann Scott Junr.	14
Negro Jack	23
do. Phillis	30
do. Isaac	14
do. Sook	12
do. Pris	8
do. Will	70
Samuel Greenlea	24
Rachel Greenlea	23
Susannah Gilbert	18
Negro Nicholas	50
do. Flora	60
do. Harry	28
do. Jerry	20
do. Isaac	21
do. Sue	50
do. Sook	30
do. Esther	24
do. Sarah	10
do. Hanah	25
do. George	13
do. Nan	11
do. Charles	7
do. Amos	7
do. London	5
do. Poll	3
do. Jenny	1
do. Sarah 1 Week old	–
Christopher Hunt	36
Rosannah Hunt	60

William Paris	49
Sabinah Paris	36
Elizabeth Paris	18
Rachel Paris	15
Susannah Paris	12
Keziah Paris	12
William Paris Junr.	10
Mary Paris	7
Sabinah Paris Junr.	5
Moses Paris	3
Rebeccah Paris 6 Months	
John Shinton	54
Sarah Shinton	56
Elizabeth Shinton	20
Ann Shinton	15
William Shinton	1
John Tenewell	34
Jane Davis	24
Isaac Davis	2
Thomas Waters	46
Rebeccah Waters	34
John Waters	13
Martha Waters	11
Sarah Waters	10
Basil Waters	6
Elizabeth Waters	5
Henerittee Waters	4
Ann Waters 4 Months	
William Rotherick	55
Mary Rotherick	40
Elizabeth Rotherick	3
William Hanna	27
Dilliverance Hanna	20

11.

James Matthews	40
John Carr	30
Negro Jim	35
do. Bob	35
do. Billinda	36
do. Will	7
do. Ben	2
Servt. John Russel	38
Daniel Dugless	36
Sarah Dugless	26
Bennet Dugless	4
Linty Dugless	1
Elizabeth Thomson	29
Thomas Thomson	5
Mary Thomson	3
Caterine Thomson 3 Weeks	
Elinor Edleton	23
Samuel Durham	48
Ann Durham	38
Mary Durham	20
Susanah Durham	17
Elinor Durham	15
Samuel Durham Jun.	11
Thomas Durham	8
Aquila Durham	6
Loyd Durham	5
Lee Durham	2
Servt. Mary Mcginley	20
Negro Jane	34
do. Harry	17
do. Sall	17

Negro Jude	16
do. Samson	12
do. Pleasent	10
do. Moll	8
do. Jesse	6
Robert Collins	65
Jiminah Collins	60
Servt. Jos. Bates	21
Negro Dick	50
do. Rachel	17
do. Jack 4 Months	
Jacob Bond	51
Elizabeth Bond	28
Ann Bond	23
Priscilla Bond	17
Dennis Bond	16
Ralph Bond	13
Marha Bond	13
Charlote Bond	9
Negro Tony	17
do. Philis & Ceasar each	50
do. Hannah	47
do. Antoney	35
do. Dinah	35
do. Prudence	22
do. Roger	22
do. Charles	21
do. Phebe	16
do. Honor	18
do. Nell	15
do. Sarah	12
do. Dick	10
do. Joe	8
do. Adam	7
do. Jamer	6
do. Darkey	4
do. Ben	4
do. Phile	[illegible]
do. Ephraim	[illegible]
Servt. John Sadler	[illegible]

12. John Hays	30	John Ewing	10
Negro Hannah	2[illegible]	Jane Ewing Junr	5
do. Tom	2[illegible]	James Carrol Junr	30
do. Sall	5	Mary Carrol	19
do. Jack	3	William Carrol 8 Months	
do. Flora	1	Saml Richard Harvey	25
Joseph Morrison	52	Negro Grace	13
Mary Morrison	29	Jacob Bond Junr	26
Martha Morrison	1	Elizabeth Bond	24
George Burns	28	Ann Dutton	12
Ann Burns	19	Sarah Wheeler	5
Thomas Bond Senr	73	William Ross	21
Elizabeth Bond	71	James Wheeler	19
Martha Bond	29	Negro Samson	50
Charles Goodman	40	do. Dinah	40
Stephen Onion	15	do. London	17
Thomas Onion	14	do. Pugg	14
Christian Roland	60	do. Rachel	8
Negro Honor	60	do. Sall	7
do. Poll	53	do. Doll	6
do. Jenney	40	do. Jim	3
do. Grace	15	do. Diah	2
do. Sam	25	Elinor Ross	47
do. Valentine	25	Mary Ross	18
do. Ben	25	Cavandrew Ross	16
do. Prussia	17	Sarah Ross	12
Alexr Ewing	45	Elinor Ross Junr	7
Jane Ewing	40	Negro Poll	15
Jos. Ewing	18	John McComas	45
James Ewing	11	Salinah McComas	35
		Hannah McComas	12

13. Elizabeth McComas	4
William Joshua McComas	2
Servt Elias Smith	15
Deborick Smith	12
Negro Grace	25
do Samson	24
do Jim	7
do Phillis	2
do Jinn	4
Robert Mitchel	40
Elizabeth Mitchel	28
Sarah Mitchel	6
William Mitchel	2
John Mitchel 2 Weeks	
Peter Comstock	80
James Nower	46
Phebe Nower	45
Mary Cadigin	22
Casandra Jackson	15
Samuel Jackson	13
Jesse Nower	11
Alexr Nower	9
Ann Nower	6
James Cadigin	6
Sarah Cadigin	4
Rachel Nower	4
Margaret Gordin	72
William Gordin	39
Hannah Gordin	37
Elizabeth Gordin	15
Margaret Gordin	11
Philip Gordin	5

Daniel Norris	46
Sarah Norris	47
Elizabeth Beaver	20
Negro Jade	10
Richard Booth	52
Joseph Rose	25
Constant Rose	24
Rebeccah Rose	3
Aquila Rose 6 Months	
Joshua Day	15
Samuel Ingram	10
Thomas Saunders	35
Joseph Saunders	31
William Saunders	25
Elizabeth Saunders	20
Elizabeth Greenley	20
~~Will~~ George Whittow	4
Capt William Bradford	40
Sarah Bradford	30
Martha Bradford	12
Elizabeth Bradford	10
Mary Bradford	8
Sarah Bradford Junr	6
George Bradford	4
Samuel Bradford	2
Servt John Johnson	20
Negro Harry	14
William Williamson	14
Robt Price	30
Hannah Price	25
James Price 4 Months	

14. Caterine England	35
Edward McComas	24
Mary McComas	20
Aquila McComas	3
Alexr. McComas	1
Robt. Waters	27
Mary Waters	25
Deborah Waters	6 Months
Mary Chebin	60
Patrick Campbell	35
Elenor Durham	78
James Durham	40
Mordicai Durham	38
Aquila Durham	30
Hannah Durham	27
Negro Phebe	30
do. Dinah	30
do. Tom	27
do. Fanney	14
do. Phillis	16
do. Hammon	16
do. Tom	5
do. Phebe	2
do. Hammon	00
do. Nanne	00
John Green	50
Ann Green	50
Henry Green	19
John Green Junr.	15
Joshua Green	14
Ann Green Junr.	5
Elizabeth Weekley	15

Negro Jim	1
do. Sarah	4
do. Dee	
do. Hannah	
Robert Rogers	4
Ruth Rogers	4
Ruth Rogers Junr.	1
Sarah Rogers	11
Bilinda Rogers	8
Robert Rogers Junr.	5
Daniel Reardin	3
Elizabeth Williams	24
William Wildon Junr.	26
Negro Adam	50
do. Bristol	50
do. Davy	12
do. Charles	10
do. Leander	5
do. Jacob	2
do. Samson	1
do. Fanney	50
do. Affe	45
do. Jinney	28
do. Poll	20
do. Dinah	11
do. Phebe	4
do. Betty	4
Robt. Callender	65
Jane Callender	25
Robt. Callender Junr.	15
William Calender	12
Ann Callinder	7
Thomas Callinder	1

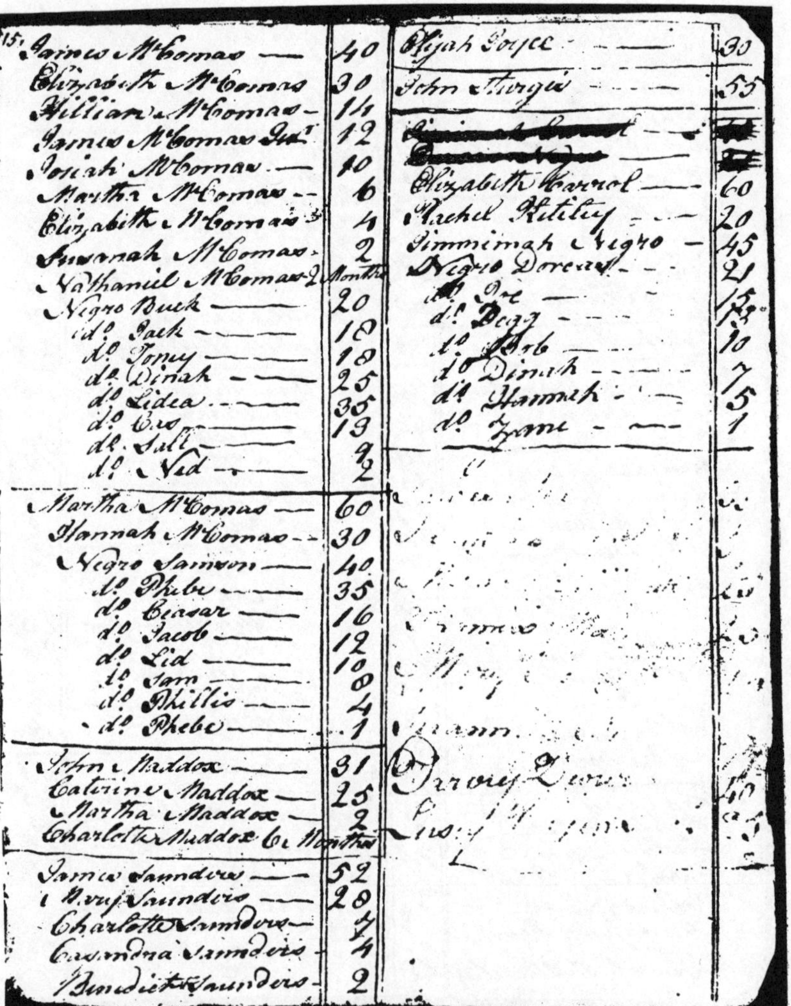

Name	Age
15. James McComas	40
Elizabeth McComas	30
William McComas	14
James McComas Junr	12
Josiah McComas	10
Martha McComas	6
Elizabeth McComas	4
Susanah McComas	2
Nathaniel McComas	2 Months
Negro Buck	20
d^o Jack	18
d^o Tony	18
d^o Dinah	25
d^o Lidea	35
d^o [illegible]	13
d^o Sall	9
d^o Ned	2
Martha McComas	60
Hannah McComas	30
Negro Samson	40
d^o Phebe	35
d^o Ceasar	16
d^o Jacob	12
d^o Lid	10
d^o Sam	8
d^o Phillis	4
d^o Phebe	1
John Maddox	31
Catirine Maddox	25
Martha Maddox	2
Charlotte Maddox	6 Months
James Saunders	52
[illegible] Saunders	28
Charlotte Saunders	4
Casandra Saunders	4
Benedict Saunders	2

Name	Age
Elijah Joyce	30
John Sturgis	55
[illegible]	[illegible]
[illegible]	[illegible]
Elizabeth Carrol	60
Rachel Hitiley	20
Jimminah Negro	45
Negro Doreas	21
d^o Doe	15
d^o Pegg	12
d^o Bob	10
d^o Dinah	7
d^o Hannah	5
d^o Zane	1
[illegible]	[illegible]
[illegible]	[illegible]
[illegible]	[illegible]
[illegible]	[illegible]
[illegible]	[illegible]
[illegible]	[illegible]
Doreas [illegible]	[illegible]
[illegible]	[illegible]

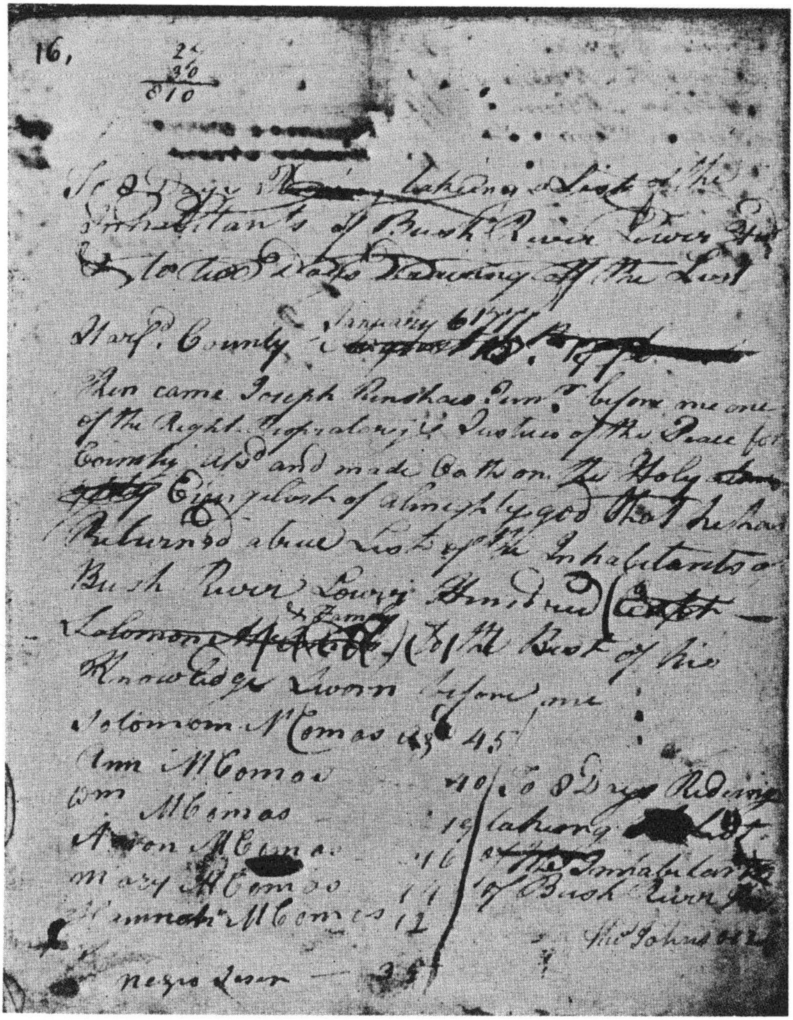
16,

takeing a List of the
Inhabitants of Bush River Lower Hund

Harfd. County January 6 1776

Then came Joseph Renshaw Junr. before me one
of the Right Honourable Justices of the Peace for
County afsd and made Oath on the Holy
Evangelist of Almighty God that he has
Returned a true List of the Inhabitants of
Bush River Lower Hundred
to the Best of his
Knowledge Sworn before me

Solomon McComas 45
Ann McComas 40
Wm McComas 19
Aaron McComas 16
Mary McComas 14
Hannah McComas 12
Negro 35

To 8 Days Rideing
takeing List
of the Inhabitants
of Bush River

HARFORD COUNTY, SPESUTIA LOWER HUNDRED

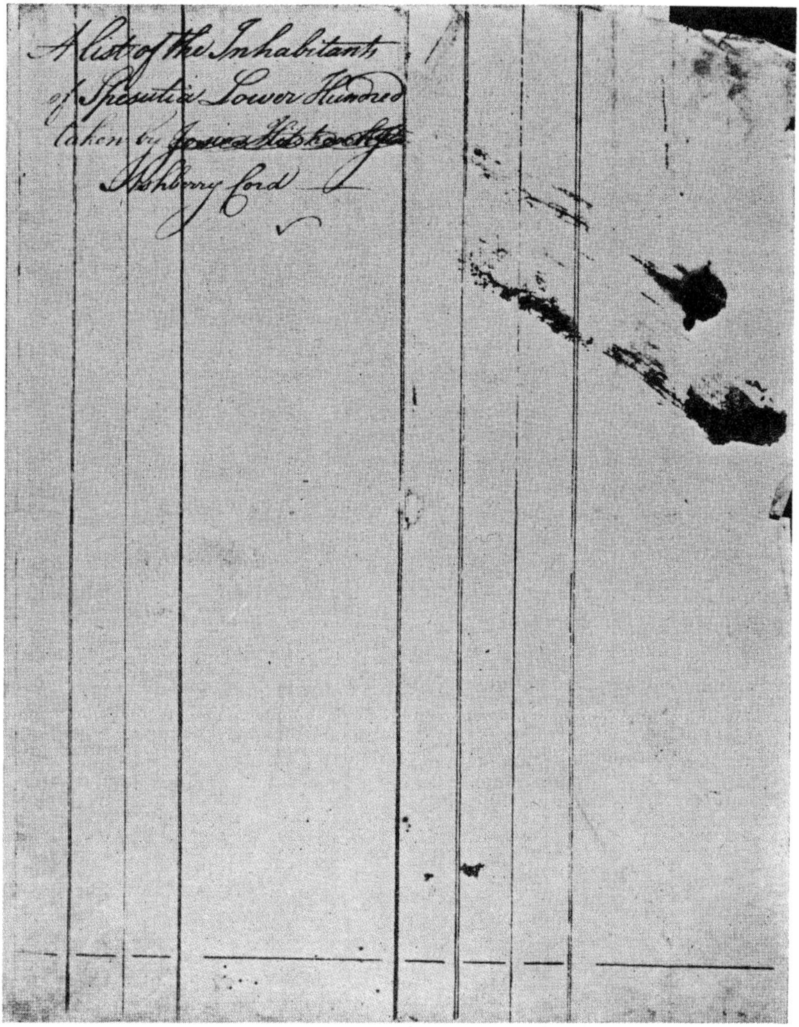

A list of the Inhabitants
of Spesutia Lower Hundred
taken by ~~Josias Hitchcock~~
Ashberry Cord

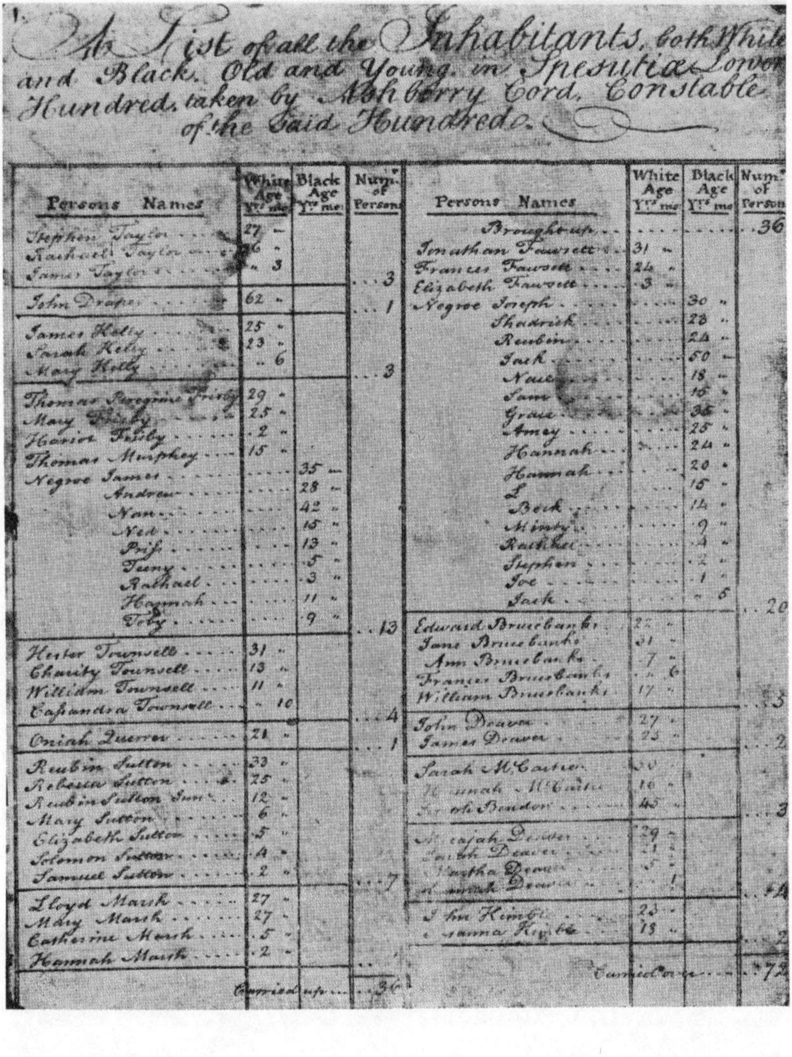

A List of all the Inhabitants, both White and Black, Old and Young, in Spesutia Lower Hundred, taken by Ashberry Cord, Constable of the Said Hundred.

Persons Names	White Age Yrs mo	Black Age Yrs mo	Numr of Persons
Stephen Taylor	27 -		
Rachael Taylor	26 -		
James Taylor	- 3		3
John Draper	62 -		1
James Kelly	25 -		
Sarah Kelly	23 -		
Mary Kelly	- 6		3
Thomas Peregrine Frisby	29 -		
Mary Frisby	25 -		
Hariot Frisby	2 -		
Thomas Murphey	15 -		
Negroe James		35 -	
Andrew		28 -	
Nan		42 -	
Ned		15 -	
Priss		13 -	
Teeny		5 -	
Rathael		3 -	
Hannah		11 -	
Toby		9 -	13
Hester Townsell	31 -		
Charity Townsell	13 -		
William Townsell	11 -		
Cassandra Townsell	- 10		4
Oniah Querrer	21 -		1
Reubin Sutton	33 -		
Rebecca Sutton	25 -		
Reubin Sutton Junr	12 -		
Mary Sutton	6 -		
Elizabeth Sutton	5 -		
Solomon Sutton	4 -		
Samuel Sutton	2 -		7
Lloyd Marsh	27 -		
Mary Marsh	27 -		
Catherine Marsh	5 -		
Hannah Marsh	2 -		
Carried up			36

Persons Names	White Age Yrs mo	Black Age Yrs mo	Numr of Persons
Brought up			36
Jonathan Fawsett	31 -		
Frances Fawsett	24 -		
Elizabeth Fawsett	3 -		
Negroe Joseph		30 -	
Shadrick		28 -	
Reubin		24 -	
Jack		50 -	
Nace		18 -	
Sam		16 -	
Grace		35 -	
Amey		25 -	
Hannah		24 -	
Hannah		20 -	
L		15 -	
Beck		14 -	
Minty		9 -	
Rathael		4 -	
Stephen		2 -	
Joe		1 -	
Jack		- 5	20
Edward Brucebanks	22 -		
Jane Brucebanks	31 -		
Ann Brucebanks	7 -		
Frances Brucebanks	- 6		
William Brucebanks	17 -		5
John Deaver	27 -		
James Deaver	23 -		2
Sarah McCarter	30		
Hannah McCarter	10 -		
Sarah Bendor	45 -		3
Micajah Deaver	29 -		
Sarah Deaver	21 -		
Martha Deaver	5 -		
Hannah Deaver	- 1		4
John Kimble	23 -		
Susanna Kimble	13 -		2
Carried Over			72

2.

Persons Names	White Age Yrs mo	Black Age Yrs mo	Numr of Persons
Brought over			72
Joseph Gordon	50 ..		
James Gordon	16 ..		
Eleanor Gordon	15 ..		
Ofsir Reardon	36 ..		
Mary Reardon	25 ..		
John Reardon	1 ..		6
John Garrettson	24 ..		
Martha Garrettson	21 ..		
Jane Connar	49 ..		
Negroes Dinah		21 ..	
Fan		12 ..	
Nisbet		6 ..	
Joy		5 ..	
Sam		4 ..	
Jim		1 ..	9
John Lee	33 ..		
Ann Lee	22 ..		2
Stephen Kimble	38 ..		
Margaret Kimble	39 ..		
George Kimble	15 ..		
James Kimble	14 ..		
William James Kimble	12 ..		
Stephen Kimble Junr	9 ..		
James Kimble	7 ..		
Frances Kimble	4 ..		
Eleanor Kimble	1 ..		9
Thomas Ayres	38 ..		
Bethiah Ayres	23 ..		
Elizabeth Ayres	6 ..		
Wilbee Ayres	3 ..		
Abraham Ayres	1 6		
George Todd	17 ..		
Guer Kimble	26 ..		7
James Brown	25 ..		
Mary Brown	29 ..		
Thomas Brown	11 ..		
Negroe Peg		12 ..	4
Timothy Murphy	22 ..		
Mary Murphy	31 ..		
John Murphy	19 ..		
Sarah Murphy	10 ..		
Frances Murphy	20 ..		
Mary Yokely	31 ..		
John Yokely	14 ..		
Elizabeth Yokely	3 ..		8
Carried up			117

Persons Names	White Age Yrs mo	Black Age Yrs mo	Numr of Persons
Brought up			117
James Taylor	66 ..		
Sarah Taylor	54 ..		
Asia Taylor	22 ..		
Laama Taylor	15 ..		
Jesse Taylor	14 ..		
Susanna Markman	23 ..		
Negroe Caesar		43 ..	
Alice		30 ..	
Jupiter		5 ..	
Hercules		3 ..	
Ned		.. 1	11
Amos Cord	37 ..		
Susanna Cord	32 ..		
Hannah Cord	12 ..		
Greenbury Cord	10 ..		
Aquila Cord	3 ..		
Sarah Cord	5 ..		
Amos Cord Junr	1 6		
William Hamby	16 ..		
Ann Mathews	15 ..		9
Thomas Horner	24 ..		1
Peter Lovell	33 ..		
Elizabeth Lovell	30 ..		
Elizabeth Lovell Junr	6 ..		
John Lovell	4 ..		
Mary Lovell	2 ..		
Frances Lovell	.. 6		6
Cassandra Cruit	30 ..		
John Cruit	8 ..		
Nathan Cruit	1 ..		
Elizabeth Evans	1 ..		4
Martha Combest	32 ..		
Jacob Combest	27 ..		
Charity Combest	15 ..		
Susanna Combest	14 ..		
Mary Combest	7 ..		
Israel Combest Junr	1 ..		
Israel Combest	32 ..		
Susanna Combest	27 ..		
Aquila Combest	11 ..		9
William Wrain Junr	23 ..		
Ann Wrain	18 ..		
Negroe Will		9 ..	3
James Shaw	31 ..		
Jane Shaw	28 ..		2
Carried up			162

3.

Persons Names	White Age Yrs mo	Black Age Yrs mo	Num. of Persons
Brought up			162
Moses Collins	48		
Patience Collins	48		
Jacob Collins	22		
Patience Collins Junr	15		
Mary Collins	11		
Susanna Collins	8		
Cassandra Collins	2		
Moses Morris	7		8
Ulice Combest	26		
Elizabeth Combest	25		
Thomas Combest	7		
John Combest	5		
Mary Combest	4		
Elizabeth Combest Junr	.. 5		
Mary Combest	74		7
Griffith Jones	26		
Patience Jones	24		
Rice Jones	16		–
William Jones	1		
Catherine Thorn	60		
Alice Thorn	17		
Elizabeth Maddocks	20		7
John Duzan	27		
Rachael Duzan	27		
William Duzan	5		
Elizabeth Duzan	3		
John Duzan	1		
Abraham Duzan	13		6
Peter Duzan	52		
Elizabeth Duzan	16		
Peter Duzan Junr	11		
Ezekiah Duzan	9		
Ezekeal Duzan	6		
Nathaniel Duzan	5		6
Isaac Delany	44		
Ann Delany	33		
Joshua Delany	9		
Elizabeth Delany	7		
Mary Delany	7		
John Delany	5		
Sarah Delany	1		7
Jonathan White	27		
Margaret White	20		
Eleanor White	18		
Oliver Dinney	16		4
William Evans	39		1
Carried up			20

Persons Names	White Age Yrs mo	Black Age Yrs mo	Num. of Persons
Brought up			208
Elizabeth Gallion	40		
Martha Gallion	15		
Rachael Gallion	12		
Mary Gallion	13		
James Gallion	10		
Henerittea Gallion	7		
Elizabeth Gallion Junr	6		
William Gallion	3		
Hannah Presbury	15		
James Crumwell	20		
Trueborn	25		
Ann Truelove	37		
Mary Truelove	8		
William Chambers	7		
Negroe Bett		20	
Dick		2	16
James Hearn	29		
Hannah Hearn	30		
Mary Hearn	.. 1		
Body	2		4
Susanna Garrettson	53		
Elizabeth Garrettson	15		
Sarah Garrettson	13		
Garrett Garrettson	10		
Aquila League	35		
Negroe Jim		15	
Jupiter		13	
Peter		10	
Patience		5	9
James Stewart	30		
Elizabeth Stewart	29		
Mary Stewart	6		
Susanna Stewart	4		
Elizabeth Stewart Junr	.. 6		
Negroe Cato		99	
Mingo		55	
Dido		35	
Sinday		13	
Nann		10	
Pririah		5	
Jim		2	12
Charles White	30		
Mary White	34		
John White	5		
William White	4		
Isaac White	2		5
Carried over			254

4.

Persons Names	White Age Yrs mo	Black Age Yrs mo	Numr of Persons
Brought over			254
Archibald Beaty	30 -		
Jane Beaty	25 -		
William Beaty	4 -		
Hannah Beaty	2 -		
Jane Beaty Junr	- 4		
Thomas Pritchard	30 -		
Jane Jones	17 -		
Thomas Newbon	14 -		
Negroe Esther		11 -	9
Balter Fie	41 -		
Mary Fie	21 -		
John Fie	13 -		
Fie	10 -		
Joseph Jones	23 -		
John Collins	32 -		
James Fitzgarrell	24 -		7
James Wiggins	36 -		
Mary Wiggins	33 -		
Cassandra Wiggins	2 -		
George Groves	10 -		
Eleanor Groves	15 -		5
Elizabeth Toulson	30 -		1
Ann Collins	80 -		
Hannah Boudy	30 -		
Ruth Boudy	16 -		
Sophia Boudy	1 -		
Sarah Young	4 -		
Margaret Young	4 -		6
Richard Morris	64 -		
Jane Morris	30 -		
Giles Morris	8 -		
Susanna Morris	4 -		
Susan Morris	2. 6		5
William Collins	50 -		
Elizabeth Collins	15 -		
Frances Collins	13 -		
William Collins Junr	11 -		
Edward Collins	7 -		
Hannah Collins	4 -		6
Abraham Taylor	26 -		
Martha Taylor	28 -		
Aquila Taylor	1 -		3
Carried up			296

Persons Names	White Age Yrs mo	Black Age Yrs mo	Numr of Persons
Brought up			296
Susanna Carty	25 -		
William Carty	4 -		
Hannah Carty	2 -		
Ann Carty	- 7		4
Patrick Babe	33 -		
Ann Babe	33 -		
Mary Babe	5 -		
Enoch Hall Babe	3 -		4
Isaac McSwaine	20 -		1
Francis Holland	30 -		
Hannah Holland	25 -		
Francis Ulix Holland	5 -		
John Holland	3 -		
Ann Atkinson	21 -		
Roger Corrison	30 -		
Negroe Tom		50 -	
Will		35 -	
Toney		25 -	
Joe		45 -	
Violet		33 -	
David		15 -	
Joe Junr		12 -	
Bill		6 -	14
Negroe Judith		13 -	
Dinah		3 -	
Sall		2 -	
Rachael		30 -	
Violet		2 -	5
Daniel Campbell	38 -		
Catherine Campbell	50 -		
Jeremiah Cullimer	23 -		
Mary Casey	20 -		4
Josias Kimble	33 -		1
James Taylor Junr	42 -		
Hannah Taylor	40 -		
Cordelia Taylor	15 -		
Mary Taylor	14 -		
Ashberry Taylor	8 -		
Charlotte Taylor	5 -		
Hannah Taylor Junr	3 -		
Negroe Ned		33 -	8
Josias Kimble	33 -		1
Carried up			338

5.

Persons Names	White Age Yrs. mo.	Black Age Yrs. mo.	Numr. of Persons
Brought up			338
John Kosier	10 "		
Hannah Murphey	28 "		2
Elizabeth Collins	38 "		
Mary Collins	10 "		
Ann Collins	8 "		
Emilia Collins	2 "		4
James Gorden	53 "		
Catherine Gorden	51 "		
Alexander Gorden	25 "		
Mary Gorden	22 "		4
Mary Atkinson	60 "		
Elizabeth Atkinson	18 "		
Frances Atkinson	14 "		
Greenberry Atkinson	10 "		4
John Beck	35 "		
Ann Beck	26 "		
Martha Beck	6 "		
Caleb Beck	3 "		
Daniel Beck	.. 6		
William Peters	35 "		6
Thomas Lancaster	50 "		
Catherine Lancaster	52 "		
Susanna Lancaster	16 "		3
Samuel Jenkins	26 "		
Martha Jenkins	23 "		
Mary Jenkins	" 1		
Richard Kimble	19 "		4
William Chandley	23 "		
Frances Chandley	17 "		
Negroe Dutchess		18 "	3
Laurence Lary	26 "		
Rachael Tush	40 "		2
Sarah Milbourn	45 "		
Mary Milbourn	14 "		
Negroe Ben Galloway (Free)		6 "	3
Frances Cruit	34 "		1
John Clark	26 "		1
Carried up			374

Persons Names	White Age Yrs. mo.	Black Age Yrs. mo.	Numr. of Persons
Brought up			374
James Kimble	49 "		
Francis Kimble	20 "		
Sarah Kimble	2 "		
Aquila Pike	12 "		
Rebecca Pike	13 "		
Negroe Will		49 "	
Phill		39 "	
Peter		15 "	
Hager		80 "	
Hager Jun.		17 "	
Margaret		39 "	
Judith		30 "	
Jane		17 "	
Margaret Jun.		10 "	
Cass		8 "	
Bill		7 "	
Moll		6 "	
Darkey		3 "	
Ben		1 "	
Sal		" 6	20
Thomas Everett	52 "		
Margaret Everett	42 "		
Benjamin Everett	26 "		
John Everett	21 "		
Cassandra Everett	18 "		
Thomas Everett Jun.	12 "		
Richard Everett	10 "		
James Everett	8 "		
Joseph Everett	6 "		
Nathan Thompson	35 "		
Mary Callahan	20 "		
Negroe Fan		20 "	
Nan		4 "	13
Joseph Fields	36 "		
Sarah Fields	25 "		
Elizabeth Fields	5 "		
William Fields	2 "		
Susanna Fields	" 8		5
Ann Howell	31 "		
John Howell Jun.	6 "		
Mary Howell	7 "		
~~Elizabeth Howell~~	4		
William Howell	" 6		
Abraham Howell	12 "		6
Richard Reaven	40 "		1
Carried over			419

6.

Persons Names	White Age Yrs mo	Black Age Yrs mo	Numr. of Persons
Brought over			419
Joseph Everett	32 „		
Margret Everett	28 „		
Charles Everett	9 „		
Joseph Everett Junr.	7 „		
Eleanor Everett	5 „		
Elizabeth Everett	4 „		
Mary Everett	3 „		
Lydia Everett	1 „		
Susanna Armstrong	32 „		
Negro Basil		32 „	
Rachael		17 „	
Dick		2 „	
Ginn		1 „	13
John Walker	39 „		
Jane Walker	39 „		
John Walker Junr.	5 „		
Margaret Walker	2 „		4
Richard Pierce	28 „		
Rachael Pierce	20 „		
Ann Pierce	2 „		3
Gabriel Swain	30 „		
Bethiah Swain	20 „		
Elizabeth Swain	3 „		
Nathan Swain Junr.	1 6		
Elizabeth Greenfield	9 „		5
Elizabeth Berry	24 „		
Sarah Berry	2 „		
Ann Elizabeth Berry	„ 4		
Margaret Corbet	18 „		4
Jacob Combest	32 „		
Sarah Combest	22 „		
Cassandra Combest	5 „		
Mary Combest	3 „		
Francis Combest	„ 8		5
Henry Warfield	27 „		
Mary Warfield	26 „		
John Gallion	7 „		
Martha Gallion	4 „		
Negroe Hannah		37 „	
William		13 „	
Dinah		13 „	
Jane		13 „	
Esther		9 „	9
Carried up			462

Persons Names	White Age Yrs mo	Black Age Yrs mo	Numr. of Persons
Brought up			462
George Ford	63 „		
Sarah Ford	46 „		
Joseph Ford	30 „		
Benjamin Ford	27 „		
Rachael Warham	25 „		
John Warham	4 „		
Mary Ford	22 „		
Mehabel Ford	20 „		
Alexander Ford	18 „		
Ford	15 „		
Sarah Ford Junr.	13 „		
George Ford Junr.	11 „		
Joshua Ford	8 „		
William Ford	4 „		
Michael Fitzpatrick	30 „		
Michael Plunket	28 „		
Negroe George		40 „	
Caesar		35 „	
Jacob		25 „	
Jupiter		30 „	
Ned		35 „	
Hannah		60 „	
Hercules		60 „	
Jim		18 „	
Jerry		17 „	
Andrew		17 „	
Pompy		22 „	
Isaac		15 „	
Margaret		35 „	
Nan		20 „	
Sall		20 „	
Jenny		32 „	
Bess		24 „	
Hannah		50 „	
Allen		65 „	
Nann		15 „	
Lucy		12 „	
Peter		11 „	
Jean		9 „	
Mint		6 „	
Tom		2 „	
Hannah		11 „	
Dinah		6 „	
Kanor		5 „	
Fanee		3 „	
Esther		3 „	
Poll		2 „	
Violet		1 „	
Jack		10 „	
Dinah		9 „	50
Carried up			512

7.

Persons Names	White Age Yrs mo	Black Age Yrs mo	Num. of Persons
Brought up			512
Negroe [illegible]		6 -	
Herculus		4 -	
Pace		3 -	
Nomi		- 2	4
Amos Garrett	53 -		
Frances Garrett	48 -		
Meleah Garrett	19 -		
Francis Garrett Jun:	13 -		
John Hanson	17 -		
Mary Elder	35 -		
Bethiah Hart	19 -		
Sarah Conaley	45 -		
Sarah Cannon	26 -		
Thomas Newland	70 -		
Daniel Mead	65 -		
Elizabeth Flanagin	19 -		
[illegible] Greenfield	12 -		
Nathan Swain	32 -		
Cassandra Swain	8 -		
Catherine Collins	20 -		
Hester Tracey	28 -		
[illegible] Dennison	30 -		
Negroe Santy		36 -	
Oral		38 -	
Pompy		28 -	
George		52 -	
Cuff		60 -	
Ben		25 -	
Tony		23 -	
[illegible]		38 -	
Jack		42 -	
Jacob		25 -	
Will		50 -	
Limbrick		30 -	
Grace		66 -	
Dutchess		34 -	
Esther		24 -	
Phinah		25 -	
Patience		17 -	
Hannah		13 -	
Nessa		7 -	
Sall		6 -	
Harriett		11 -	
Leander		7 -	
Sampson		2 -	
Duke Jun:		2 -	
Simon		- 6	
Duke		24 -	
Sam		25 -	45
Carried up			571

Persons Names	White Age Yrs mo	Black Age Yrs mo	Num. of Persons
Brought up			561
Negroe Fame		30 -	
Penny		18 -	
Nelson		15 -	
Pell		7 -	
Phill		12 -	
Rachael		2 -	
~~Dinah~~ Lydia		28 5	
Jul		- 1	9
Isaac Penrose	28 -		
Cassandra Penrose	25 -		
Henriet Penrose	- 2		3
Thomas Woodward	28 -		
Ann Woodward	25 -		
William Woodward	6 -		
Mary Woodward	- 4		4
Greenbury Dorsey	46 -		
Frisby Dorsey	17 -		
Sophia Dorsey	28 -		
Mary Dorsey	19 -		
Benedict Dorsey	15 -		
Sally Frisby Dorsey	13 -		
Frances Dorsey	10 -		
John Bell Dorsey	4 -		
Meleah Dorsey	3 -		
Edward Dorsey	1 -		
Nathan Hughes	15 -		
Negroe Hannah		63 -	
Dick		62 -	
Pall		50 -	
Casar		48 -	
Sue		34 -	
Jim		16 -	
Sam		14 -	
Ben		6 -	
Peg		4 -	20
John Wood	40 -		
Sarah Wood	44 -		
Rebecca Wood	16 -		
Mary Wood	14 -		
[illegible] Wood	12 -		
[illegible] Wood	3 -		
[illegible]	5 -		
[illegible] Murphey	15 -		
[illegible] Harris	43 -		
Michael Roche	15 -		
Elizabeth Horton	45 -		
Negroe Sarah		80 -	
Sall		12 -	13
Carried over			610

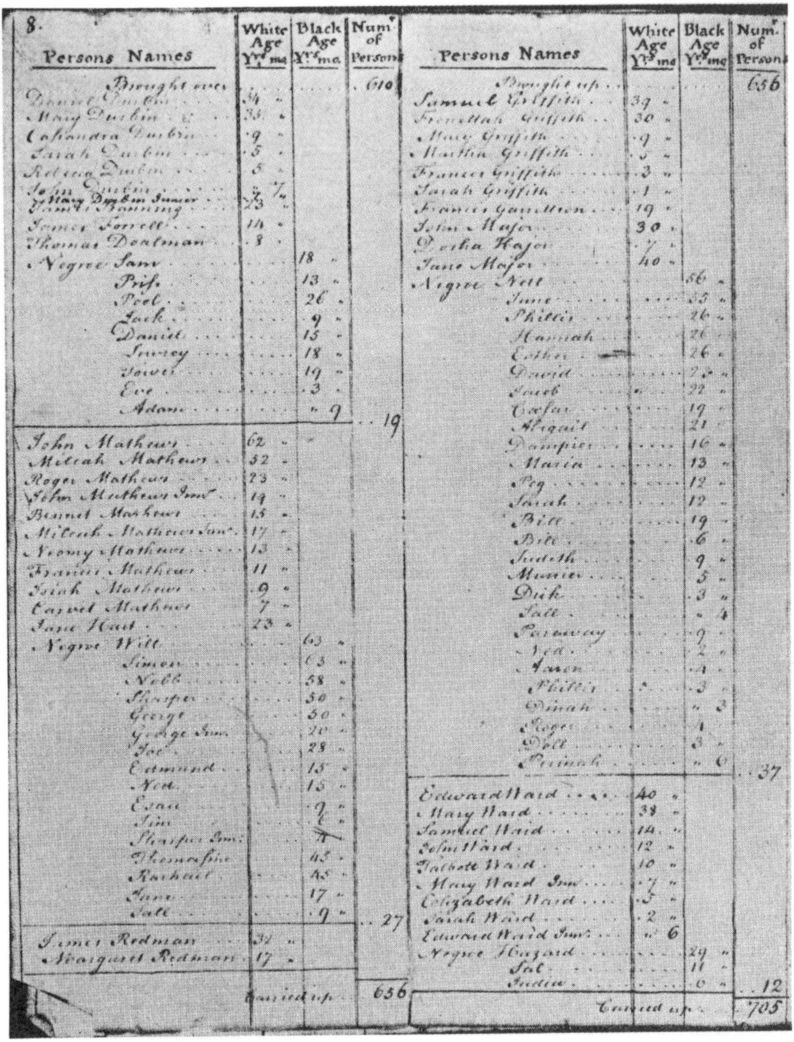

8.

Persons Names	White Age Yrs. mo.	Black Age Yrs. mo.	Numr. of Persons
Brought over			610
Daniel Durbin	34		
Mary Durbin	33		
Cassandra Durbin	9		
Sarah Durbin	5		
Rebecca Durbin	5		
John Durbin	[illegible] 7 mo		
Mary Durbin Junior / James Banning	23		
James Forrell	14		
Thomas Deatman	8		
Negroe Sam		18	
Pris.		13	
Peel		26	
Jack		9	
Daniel		15	
Surrey		18	
Jower		19	
Eve		3	
Adam		9 mo	19
John Mathews	62		
Milcah Mathews	52		
Roger Mathews	23		
John Mathews Junr.	19		
Bennet Mathews	15		
Milcah Mathews Junr.	17		
Neomy Mathews	13		
Francis Mathews	11		
Isiah Mathews	9		
Carvel Mathews	7		
Jane Hart	23		
Negroe Will		63	
Simon		63	
Nobb		58	
Sharper		50	
George		50	
George Junr.		20	
Joe		28	
Edmund		15	
Ned		15	
Esau		9	
Jim		6	
Sharper Junr.		4	
Clemensine		45	
Rachael		45	
Jane		17	
Sall		9	27
James Redman	31		
Margaret Redman	17		
Carried up			656

Persons Names	White Age Yrs. mo.	Black Age Yrs. mo.	Numr. of Persons
Brought up			656
Samuel Griffith	39		
Fronellah Griffith	30		
Mary Griffith	9		
Martha Griffith	5		
Frances Griffith	3		
Sarah Griffith	1		
Francis Gamilton	19		
John Major	30		
Dorha Major	7		
Jane Major	40		
Negroe Nell		56	
Jane		35	
Phillis		26	
Hannah		26	
Esther		26	
David		22	
Jacob		22	
Cæsar		19	
Abigail		21	
Dampier		16	
Maria		13	
Peg		12	
Sarah		12	
Bill		19	
Bill		6	
Judith		9	
Minnie		5	
Dick		3	
Sall		4 mo	
Paraway		9	
Ned		2	
Aaron		4	
Phillis		3	
Dinah		3 mo	
Roger		4	
Doll		3	
Perinah		6 mo	37
Edward Ward	40		
Mary Ward	38		
Samuel Ward	14		
John Ward	12		
Talbott Ward	10		
Mary Ward Junr.	7		
Elizabeth Ward	5		
Sarah Ward	2		
Edward Ward Junr.	6 mo		
Negroe Hazard		29	
Sal		11	
Judia		0	12
Carried up			705

9.

Persons Names	White Age Yrs. mo.	Black Age Yrs. mo.	[illegible]ons
Brought up			705
Hannah Hall	64		
Mary Webster	38		
Negroe Doll		64	
Rachael		50	
Hector		32	
Montross		22	
Leander		27	
Sam		47	
George		47	
Sarah		59	
Chloe		44	
Hannah		45	
Tom		43	
Lynda		35	
Dinah		26	
India		25	
Silence		31	
Amey		21	
Phillis		44	
Lew		21	
Dorcas		21	
Patience		21	
Cynthia		19	
Augustus		20	
Cato		17	
Phill		12	
Oliver		11	
Pompy		10	
Dick		10	
Michael		10	
Joe		10	
Will		7	
Ned		7	
Abner		6	
David		6	
Eudge		6	
Jim		15	
Daphney		17	
Chanie		14	
Ursula		12	
Sall		12	
Violetta		9	
Filot		8	
Lydia		7	
Myrtillo		6	
Deborah		6	
Doll		5	
Rose		4	
Bett		17	
			49
Carried up			754

Persons Names	White Age Yrs. mo.	Black Age Yrs. mo.	Num. of Persons
Brought up			754
Negroe Lucey		13	
Prima		9	
Charles		4	
Jupiter		1	
Bobb		1	
Fanny		4 mo.	
Sam		60	7
William Mooberry	21		
Frances Mooberry	18		2
Ann Kelley	37		1
Josias William Dallam	28		
Sarah Dallam	26		
Elizabeth Smith Dallam	2		
Ann Ruff	25		
Sarah Budd	14		
Elizabeth Webster	14		
John Smith	20		
Charles Cox	32		
Edward Coller	26		
Alexander McBride	15		
John Dunn	26		
Negroe James		80	
Cromwell		38	
Sip		36	
Joiner		27	
Bob		36	
Adam		26	
Caesar		22	
Malborough		27	
Pitt		21	
Sue		24	
Beck		21	
Orange		16	
Pannaway		5	
Tom		5	
Lemmon		3	
Hannah		3	
Jacob		1	
Peg		7	
Nann		7 mo.	30
William Murphey	25		
Susanna Murphey	27		
Joseph Murphey	14		
John Simon	24		
William Hailey	48		5
Carried over			79[illegible]

10.

Persons Names	White Age Yrs	White Age mo	Black Age Yrs	Black Age mo	Num of Persons
Brought over					799
Isaac Truelock	29				
Elizabeth Truelock	20				
Saibot Truelock	12				
Moses Truelock	31				
Mary Dorsey	25				
Negroe Hannah			35		
Cato			7		
Phillis			5		
Affy				3	9
Seven Mathews	40				
Mary Mathews	34				
Seven Mathews Junr.	8				
Ann Mathews	3				
Elizabeth Mathews		3			
Negroe Sip			25		
Phillis			34		
Jacob			28		
Bill			17		
Dinah			15		
Rachael			14		
Pollidore			14		
Jack			3		
Silen			2		
Minary				7	
Hannah a free Mallato			10		16
Cyrus Osbourn	26				
Susanna Osbourn	18				
Ann Osborn		½			
Negroe Jack			13		
Sam			10		
Bill			8		6
George Williamson	44				
Ann Williamson	42				
George Williamson Junr.	8				3
Garrett Garrettson	29				
Mary Garrettson	18				
James Garrettson	14				
Bennett Garrettson	12				
William Green	25				
Negroe Cuff			60		
Silvia			57		
Amey			15		
Bobb			11		9
Elizabeth Roberts	30				
Sarah Roberts	6				2
Carried up					844

Persons Names	White Age Yrs	White Age mo	Black Age Yrs	Black Age mo	Num of Persons
Brought up					844
Cordelia Hall	56				
William Hall	26				
Sarah Hall	17				
Parker Hall	11				
Rebecca Hall	1				
Peter Green	58				
Margaret Spencer	20				
Negroe Jimmy			50		
Abey			40		
Abraham			35		
Williamgynn			28		
Jack			15		
Will			40		
Bill			30		
Dick			[illegible]		
Mike			[illegible]		
George			14		
Bill			12		
Noll			13		
Menney			12		
Isaac			8		
Jake			8		
Ben			6		
Sip			6		
Tom			1		
Dinah			50		
Sarah			55		
Munes			30		
Dinah			40		
Fie			22		
Sarah			50		
Peg			[illegible]		
Rachael			11		
Abigail			10		
Hannah			9		
Hager			4		
Nell			2		
Doll			1		38
Richard China	37				
Thomas China	35				
Elenor Ellis	14				3
Archibald Johnson Junr.	22				1
Daniel Nutterwell	30				1
Mary Owens	30				
Charles Owens	3				
Sarah Owens		6			3
Peter Murphey	30				1
Carried up					891

Persons Names	White Age Yrs. mo	Black Age Yrs. mo	Num. of Persons
Brought up			891
Archibald Johnson	64 "		
Frances Johnson	55 "		
Mary Johnson	19 "		
Ann Johnson	17 "		
Adam Johnson	14 "		
Thomas Johnson	12 "		
Josias Johnson	6 "		7
Edward Bruebanks	27 "		
Susanna Bruebanks	36 "		
Isabella Bruebanks	20 "		
Sam Bennett	11 "		4
Evan Evans	30 "		1
Robert Taylor	25 "		
Isabella Taylor	22 "		
Sarah Taylor	5 "		
James Taylor	3 "		
Joseph Taylor	1 "		5
Patrick McClean	29 "		
Mary McClean	33 "		
Catherine McClean	3 "		3
Mary Cord	70 "		
Ashberry Cord	35 "		
Negroe Jeffery		63 "	
Fortune		60 "	
Margaret		20 "	
Minah		5 "	
Dann		3 "	7
George Daugherty	48 "		
Margaret Daugherty	30 "		
Mary Ann Daugherty	3 "		
John Daugherty	" 3		
Samuel Daugherty	17		
Martha Brown	3 "		
Negroe Sall		18 "	7
Richard Garrettson	55 "		
Freeborn Garrettson	18 "		
Aquila Garrettson	14 "		
Elizabeth Garrettson	12 "		
Catherine Nobel	18 "		
Negroe Moll		30 "	
Combo		18 "	
Cuff		6 "	
Fann		9 "	
Grace		4 "	
Hannah		1 "	
Moll Jun.		" 3	12
Carried up			937

Persons Names	White Age Yrs. mo	Black Age Yrs. mo	Num. of Persons
Brought up			937
Norris Lester	25 "		
Negroe Sass		62 "	2
William Johnson	36 "		
Martha Johnson	35 "		
Aquila Johnson	4 "		
Prissilla Johnson	1 "		4
John Cowen	24 "		
Sarah Cowen	25 "		
Mary Cowen	4 "		
Mark Cowen	" 1		
John Cowen Jun.	2 "		5
John Riddall	46 "		
Eleanor Riddall	33 "		
Mary Riddall	12 "		
Sarah Riddall	8 "		
John Riddall	3 "		
Robert Riddall	" 7		
William Blackbourn	46 "		7
Aquila Hall's Quart[er]			
Negroe Orange		60 "	
Ned		40 "	
Mike		30 "	
George		27 "	
Jacob		26 "	
Lear		56 "	
Moll		16 "	
Jimm		12 "	
Peter		10 "	
Dinah		7 "	10
Moses Loney	27 "		
Frances Loney	20 "		
Ames Loney	2 "		
William Loney	" 8		
Benjamin Burch	7 "		
Ann	12 "		
Robert Gray	15 "		
Sarah Sprott	23 "		
Archibald McMurphey	46 "		9
Thomas Fitzgarrell	60 "		
Mary Fitzgarrell	49 "		2
Joseph Johnson	26 "		
Sophia Johnson	29 "		
Samuel Johnson	1 "		3
Nehemiah Baily	28 "		1
Francis Garland	33 "		1
Carried over			98[illegible]

12.

Persons Names	White Age Yrs. mo	Black Age Yrs. mo	Numr. of Persons
Brought over			988
Abraham Bruebanks	57		
Mary Bruebanks	43		
Blanch Bruebanks	20		
Jane Bruebanks	14		
Jackson Bruebanks	12		
Bennett Bruebanks	10		
Ann Bruebanks	7		
Abraham Bruebanks Jr.	2		8
Jacob Forwards Qua			
William Jeffery	28		
Ormond Lunah	37		
Patrick Fitsimmonds	17		
Negroe Nann		20	
Jim		2	5
Samuel Kimble	50		
Sarah Kimble	32		
James Kimble	23		
Jamima Kimble	16		
Susanna Kimble	9		
Zachariah Kimble	3		
John Monroe	19		
Negroe Abigail		47	
Sampson		21	
Chloe		13	
Santy		11	
Hagar		5	12
Henry Vanricklen	31		
Elizabeth Vanricklen	26		
Catharine Vanricklen	8		
Francis Vanricklen	1		
John Clamman	35		
Mitchell Derby	17		
Mary Coun	20		
Negroe Joe		19	
Aaron		17	9
James McCrackin	36		
Mary McCrackin	18		
Thomas Neulon	26		
Mary Haunce	11		
Elizabeth Vanricklen	4		
Negroe Daniel		4	6
Nehemiah Barns	2		
Rachael Barns	26		
Hannah Hitchcock	16		3
Carried up			1024

Persons Names	White Age Yrs. mo	Black Age Yrs. mo	Numr. of Persons
Brought up			1024
Samuel Dooley	27		
[illegible] Dooley	18		
Negroe Sall		30	
Mora		20	
[illegible]		6	
Poll		2	6
Thomas Browning	32		
Mary Browning	31		
[illegible] Browning	13		
George Browning	11		
Wilcah Browning	7		
Mary Browning	5		
Martha Browning	1		
William Browning	9		8
Thomas Cowley	25		
Sarah Cowley	22		
Elizabeth Cowley	.. 7		3
Thomas Halls Quar.			
Negroe Phill		60	
Peg		50	
Hagar		14	
Ned		13	
Bill		8	5
Luke Griffiths Quar.			
John Castledine	37		
Mary Castledine	45		
Sarah Castledine	11		
Jane Castledine	7		
John Castledine Junr.	3		
Negroe Will		60	
Margaret		25	
Mintah		3	
Darcus		1	9
Norren Bradey	25		
Michael Bradey	.. 1		2
William Daugherty			1
William Murphey	23		
Sarah Murphey	50		
Joab Murphey	20		3
Timothy Bloodworth	67		
Rebecah Bloodworth	40		2
Gabriel Christie	19		1
Carried up			1064

13.

Persons Names	White Age Yrs mo.	Black Age Yrs mo.	Num. of Persons
Brought up			1064
John Lee Webster	41 -		
Elizabeth Webster	33 -		
John Webster	1 -		
Mary Skinner	25 -		
Negroe Dick		35 -	
Will		35 -	
Phill		30 -	
Joe		27 -	
George		19 -	
Milleunn [?]		18 -	
Frank		25 -	
Harry		19 -	
Ben		23 -	
David		20 -	
Mingo		60 -	
Darby [?]		60 -	
Simon [?]		55 -	
Jupiter		18 -	
Dido		28 -	
Sall		26 -	
Esther		28 -	
Dinah		25 -	
Cate		58 -	
Nelly		35 -	
Nann		30 -	
Jane		16 -	
Sarah		100 -	
Coll [?]		65 -	
Margy [?]		70 -	
Nancy		65 -	
Rachael		17 -	
Milcah		4 -	
Abigail		11 -	
Peniah [?]		7 -	
Jacob		5 -	
Bell		3 -	
James		1 -	
London		9 -	
Charles		7 -	
Bill		13 -	
Amey		11 -	
Ben		9 -	
Poll		14 -	
Sall		14 -	
Caesar		10 -	
Tony		11 -	46
Carried up			1110

Persons Names	White Age Yrs mo.	Black Age Yrs mo.	Num. of Persons
Brought up			1110
Negroe Janey		9 -	
Moreau [?]		7 -	
Hagar		5 -	
Abey		3 -	
Dick		1 -	
Doll		7 -	
Harry		5 -	
Sanby [?]		3 -	
Daniel		1 -	
Jack		13 -	
Mingo		11 -	
Nelly		7 -	
Jack		14 -	
Davey		12 -	
James		15 -	
Jack		8 -	
Jerry		7 -	
Ned		5 -	
Charles		15 -	
Minty		4 -	
Tom		2 -	
Alice		- 3	22
J. H. Hughes 2nd			
Negroe Sam		17 -	
Jean		16 -	2
Doct. J. Carvel Hall	29 -		
Caleb Brannan	28 -		
Thomas Ashley	21 -		
Negroe Jacob		60 -	
Stephney		29 -	
Juby		20 -	
Pelse [?]		20 -	
Jeeney [?]		25 -	
Charity		20 -	
[illegible]		6 -	
Blinda		6 -	
Polipus [?]		5 -	
Sam		5 -	
Hannibal		1 -	
Tony		3 -	
Peter		1 -	
Jack		- 3	17
Samuel Hanson	22 -		
Mary Hanson	23 -		2
George Walker	25 -		
Jane Walker	23 -		
Rachael Walker	33 -		
Ruth Walker	1 -		
Jane Connikin	24 -		5
Carried over			1158

14.

Persons Names	White Age Yrs.	White Age mo.	Black Age Yrs.	Black Age mo.	Num. of Persons
Brought over					1158
John Brown	50				
Elizabeth Brown	16				
Martha Brown	13				
Sarah Brown	21				
Sarah Brown Jun	6				
Amelia Brown	11				
Negroe Tony			100		
Mary			100		
Cuff			50		
Combo			45		
Tony Jun			30		
Sam			24		
Fann			29		
Flora			16		
Dinah			15		
Chance			11		
Bob			8		
Dip			7		
Rose			5		
Sampson				5	20
John Carlile	29				
Jeremiah Dally	26				2
Aquila Paca Jun	23				
Negroe Robert			35		
Jack			25		
Bell			30		
Grace			30		
Hagar			14		
Patience			5		
Grace Jun			3		
Phillis			1		9
William Hill	36				
Ann Hill	22				
Moses Hill	3				
Negroe Tom			6		4
Robert Stokes	19				
Negroe Jenny			21		
Poll			20		
David			20		
Daniel			19		
Samuel			17		
Rebecca			14		
Dick			11		
Simon			4		
Mount			3		
Jacob				6	11
Carried up					1204

Persons Names	White Age Yrs.	White Age mo.	Black Age Yrs.	Black Age mo.	Numr. of Persons
Brought up					1204
Samuel Fowler	36				
Frances Fowler	28				
Mary Fowler	10				
Samuel Fowler Jun	8				
Rachael Fowler	6				
Martha Fowler	2				
Sarah Dawson	13				7
Revd. Mr. West Quar					
Negroe Davy			70		
Austin			44		
Mary			46		
Peter			21		
Harry			17		
Jack			10		
Sam			8		
Nann			7		
Peter jun				5	9
Sarah Brown Sen	69				
Elizabeth Bradford	40				
Isabella Arnett	35				
William Arnett	2				
Elizabeth Brown	6				
Negroe Jack			50		
Jack Jun			29		
Murrier			28		
Cupid			33		
Jinnett			26		
Bill			16		
Esther			14		
Simon			8		
Daniel			7		
Lynda			4		
Abigail			3		16
Sarah Brown Jun	33				
Thomas Brown	12				
Amelia Brown	9				
Negroe Murrier			19		
Dutchess			18		
Chaney			4		
Orange				2	7
Hugh Willson	25				
Margaret Willson	27				
Samuel Willson	1	6			3
James Oliver Sen	60				1
Carried up					1247

Persons Names	White Age Yrs. mo.	Black Age Yrs. mo.	Num. of Persons
Brought up			1247
Martha Garrettson	26 -		
Martha Garrettson Junr.	7 -		
Mary Goldsh. Garrettson	6 -		
Elizabeth Garrettson	4 -		
Frances Garrettson	- 7		
Ann Sauder	20 -		
Negroe Duke		26 -	
Tom		17 -	
Menon		67 -	
Dise		28 -	
Jamima		28 -	
Dinah		17 -	
Junas		16 -	
Moses		15 -	
Valentine		12 -	
Alice		13 -	
Aaron		9 -	
Daniel		9 -	
Sanly		5 -	
Nathan		- 4	
Linda		4 -	
Hager		- 6	
Sarah		5 -	
Jane		3 -	
Bill		15 -	
Amos		20 -	
Dinah		27 -	
Doll		9 -	28
Oswin Sutton Senr.	56 -		
Tabitha Sutton	37 -		
Mary Sutten	16 -		
Jonathan Sutton	14 -		
William Sutton	11 -		
Rachael Sutton	9 -		
James Sutton	7 -		
Oswin Sutton Junr.	5 -		
Tabitha Sutton Junr.	5 -		
Susanna Sutton	4 -		
Jacob Sutton	- 6		
Robert Huntly	1 -		
Negroe Chloe		30 -	
Dann		4 -	
Tom		1 -	16
James Ford	22 -		
Hannah Ford	23 -		
Mary Ford	[illegible]		3
Carried up			1293

Persons Names	White Age Yrs. mo.	Black Age Yrs. mo.	Num. of Persons
Brought up			1293
Peregrine Fowler	32 -		
Mary Fowler	52 -		
Mary Fowler Junr.	14 -		
William Fowler	11 -		
William McCartie	10 -		5
Jacob Giles Junr. Quart.			
William Deman	30 -		
Negroe Daniel	30 -		
Cato	35 -		
Dick	65 -		
Joe	25 -		
Jack Bartlett	14 -		6
William Loney	24 -		
Mary Loney	60 -		
Margaret Carlile	28 -		
Michael Coleman	24 -		
Peter Font	35 -		
John Wright	23 -		
Mary Dalley	20 -		
John Dalley	- 7		
Negroe Kate		19 -	
Chloe		12 -	
Dutchess		11 -	
Lemon		7 -	
Will		7 -	
Bell		- 3	14
Thomas Ford	20 -		
Hannah Ford	23 -		
Elizabeth Ford	24 -		
Elizabeth Ford Junr.	1 -		
Mark Noble	15 -		
Samuel Cartie	11 -		6
Aaron Grace	42 -		
Ann Grace	34 -		
Rebecca Grace	14 -		
John Grace	9 -		
Peter Grace	6 -		
Aaron Grace Junr.	4 -		
Ann Grace Junr.	1 -		7
Daniel Williams	27 -		
Williams	19 -		2
Carried over			1333

16,

Persons Names	White Age Yrs mo	Black Age Yrs mo	Num of Persons
Brought over			1333
Thomas Garh	48 "		
Elizabeth Garh	30 "		
Martha Garh	12 "		
Hannah Garh	10 "		
Elizabeth Garh Junr	3 "		
Mary Garh	" 6		
Negroe Dick		65 "	
Davitt		63 "	
Ben		33 "	
Saul		35 "	
Praff		40 "	
Pollidore		14 "	
Farm		9 "	
Nann		6 "	
Dick		3 "	
Peter		3 "	
Nann		70 "	
Agnes		60 "	
Sall		30 "	
Moll		25 "	
Charles		15 "	
Jean		11 "	
Peg		8 "	
Bill		5 "	
Non		3 "	
Phebe		" 6	
Mary		40 "	
Jim		12 "	
Poll		35 "	
David		7 "	
Peter		5 "	
Benn		2 "	
Dinah		60 "	
Kate		30 "	
Jemima		25 "	
Munzes		20 "	
Dick		13 "	
Dinah		9 "	
Abigail		7 "	
Simon		7 "	
Moses		4 "	
Jacey		10 "	
Moll		3 "	
Bob		1 "	
James		2 "	
Sip		10 "	
George		7 "	47
Carried up			1380

Persons Names	White Age Yrs mo	Black Age Yrs mo	Num of Persons
Brought up			1380
Edward Carvel Talley	23 "		
Cordelia Talley	19 "		
Martha Talley	" 7		
William Sheaver	25 "		
Edward Plowman	30 "		
Patrick Corker	50 "		
Negroe Nathan		27 "	
Cato		27 "	
Bell		24 "	
Judy		40 "	
Perinah		17 "	
Shay		27 "	
Jenny		28 "	15
Benedict Edw. Hall	32 "		
Negroe Pollipus		37 "	
Mana		30 "	
Lucey		40 "	
Mora		19 "	
Esther		25 "	
Maud		17 "	
Scipio		14 "	
Pilot		10 "	
Sam		4 "	
Abey		7 "	
Isaac		5 "	
Nann		3 "	
Phill		" 6	14
Susanna Risteau	52 "		
William Smith Junr	28 "		
Susanna Smith	23 "		
Jacob Smith	5 "		
Elizabeth Topping	30 "		
William Paca	3 "		
Negroe Harry		45 "	
Orange		35 "	
Welton		22 "	
Peter		20 "	
Phill		12 "	
Will		14 "	
Dick		14 "	
Marius		3 "	
James		40 "	
Ned		28 "	
Moll		28 "	
Dutchess		35 "	
Rachael 20 Bell 17		37 "	
Kitty	—	20 "	
Sal		10 "	22
Carried up			1437

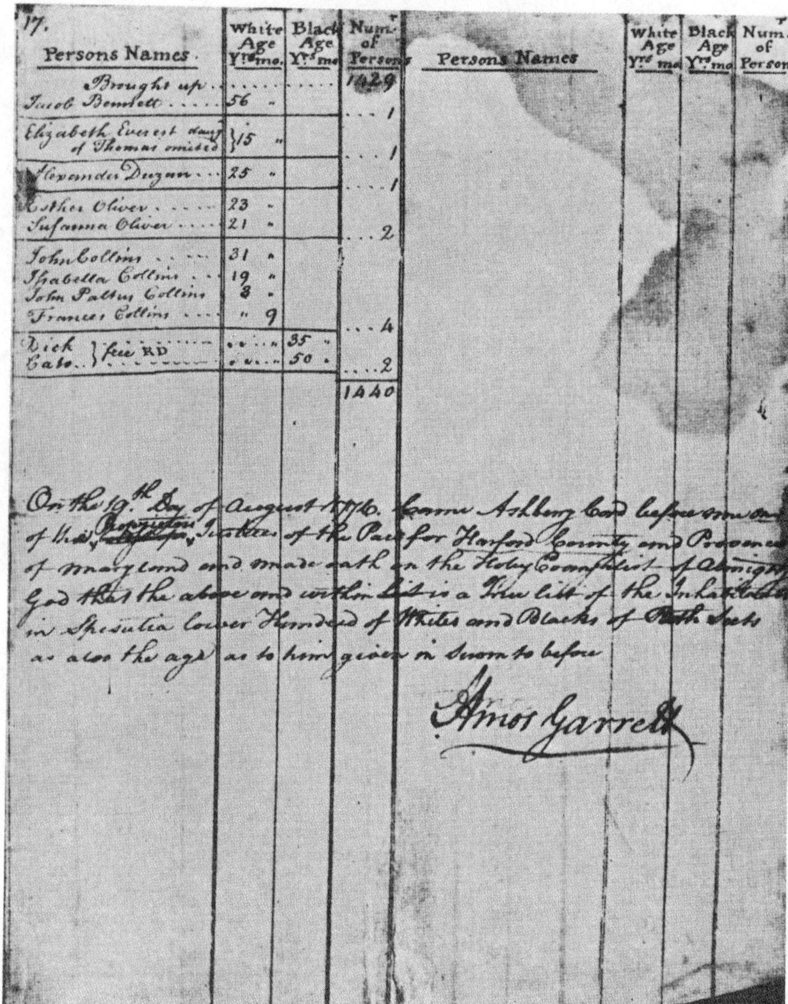

17.

Persons Names	White Age Yrs mo.	Black Age Yrs mo	Num. of Persons	Persons Names	White Age Yrs mo	Black Age Yrs mo	Num. of Persons
Brought up			1429				
Jacob Bennett	56 "		1				
Elizabeth Everest daug of Thomas omitted	15 "		1				
Alexander Dugan	25 "		1				
Esther Oliver	23 "						
Susanna Oliver	21 "		2				
John Collins	31 "						
Isabella Collins	19 "						
John Palter Collins	3 "						
Frances Collins	" 9		4				
Dick } free RD		35 "					
Cato		50 "	2				
			1440				

On the 19th Day of August 1776. [illegible] Ashbery Came before me one of this Proprietary's Justices of the Peace for Harford County and Province of Maryland and made oath on the Holy Evangelist of Almighty God that the above and within List is a true list of the Inhabitants in Spesutia lower Hundred of Whites and Blacks of Both Sexes as also the age as to him given in Sworn to before

Amos Garrett

Census of 1776, Deer Creek Lower Hundred, Harford County,

"A List of Persons In Deer Creek Lower Hundred Taken In By Wm. Fisher Junr. 1776." *

A. *Ages*

Armstrong, Robert . . . 55
  Sarah . . . 54
  David . . . 21
  Mary . . . 19

Armstrong, Robt. Junr. . . . 23
  Mary . . . 19
  David . . . 2

Ammons, Thomas . . . 26
  Margaret . . . 28
  Mary . . . 3
  Ann . . . 1

Arnold, William . . . 29
  Sarah . . . 39
  Ephraim . . . 5
  Sarah . . . 3
  Elizabeth . . . 1 month

B.

Brown, James . . . 22

Bruce, John . . . 53
  Ann . . . 32
  Robert . . . 10 months

Morgan, Hugh . . . 11
  Sarah . . . 9
  Echsah . . . 7
  Druzillah . . . 5
  Rich, John, a servt. . . . 25

Barns, Job . . . 52
  Mary . . . 45
  Job . . . 23
  Rachael . . . 21
  Ezekiel . . . 17
  Mary . . . 14
  Hannah . . . 11
  Ruth . . . 6
  Sarah . . . 3
  Negroes: Charles, 46—Dinah, 48.

C.

Camp, George . . . 45

Cromwell, Joseph . . . 30
  Susannah . . . 18
  Vinisha . . . 54
  Negroes: Sall, 38—Lemas, 6—James, 4—Dinah, 2.

Cook, Robert . . . 43
  Sarah . . . 36
  Danl. . . . 53
  John . . . 14
  Grace . . . 11
  Cassandria . . . 9

* A pamphlet of 23 written pages 8¼ × 6 inches, arranged as herein reproduced, excepting that the Negroes are given in close form, or the number only is mentioned, 834 persons are given.

The "Harford Lower Hundred" list is of the same size and consists of 16 pp.

The members of each family are subordinated to the head of that family, including negroes. Lines indicate the family divisions in the original.

Ages

James . . . 6
Sarah . . . 3
Easter . . . 1/2
John Bowdy . . . 13

Collens, Sarah * . . . 39
Mary Tolston * . . . 21
Sarah Tolston * . . . 1
Casandria Colston * . . . 11

Cumberland Forge:
Negroes: Dundee, 35—Haniball, 30—Marcus, 32—Jack, 38—Andrew, 40—Demitress, 36—Cupit, 40—Black John, 40—Carpenter Tom, 37—Barbadoes Tom, 50—Aaron (Hired), 26—Smith Jam, 35.

Cotsgrave, John . . . 32
W^m. Watkins . . . 3

Coale, Skipwith . . . 38
Sarah . . . 38
Margrett . . . 60
Margret . . . 1
Wallis, Samuel . . . 11
Negroes: Sarah, 50—Frank (Cripple), 43—Sig, 39—Jack, 25—London, 21—George, 20—Ned, 14—Fan, 10—Sesor, 8—Bill, 8—Hannah, 6—Polley, 4—Hector, 3.

Coale, William Senr. . . . 66
Sarah . . . 61
Sarah . . . 30
Ann . . . 26
Skipnith . . . 22
Negroes: Mingo (No Tax) 66—James, 30—Sam, 19—Bett, 25—Jenn, 23—Poll, 4—Lucy, 2—Nanney, 6 mo.—Dick, 12.

Ages

Coale, Philip . . . 40
Ann . . . 36
Cassandria . . . 9
Frances . . . 7
Sarah . . . 5
Richard . . . 3
Ann . . . 1
Sate, Elizabeth . . . 17
Negroes: James, 65—Ned, 7.

Crawford, Mordecai . . . 40
Susannah . . . 39
James . . . 17
Hannah . . . 15
Mordecai . . . 10
Jno. . . . 5
Ruth . . . 3
Negroes: Jane, 27—Cuff, 13—Tom, 8—Ned, 6—Moses, 4.

Chew, Thomas . . . 23
Yates, Sarah . . . 49
Susannah . . . 25
Sarah . . . 19
Negroes: Holiday, 34—Judy, 30—Suck, 25—Rodger, 13—Hannah, 7—Charles, 5—Polley, 3—Levy, 3—George, 1.

Coale, William, Junr. . . . 33
Elizabeth . . . 28
Isaac . . . 12
Susannah . . . 3 mo.
Connaly, Jane . . . 17
Webster, James . . . 15
Lemmons, Marshal . . . 15
Coale, Samuel . . . 23
Negroes: Daniel, 10—Tom, 8.

D.

Dallam, Winston . . . 27
Magrett . . . 26

* Arrangement and spelling identical with original.

	Ages
Francis	4
Elizabeth	2
Coale, William	21
McMath, Matthew	17
Negroes: Limas, 13—Bett, 8.	

Dallam, Richd.	42
Frances	65
Negroes: Doll, 48—Ben, 30—James, 19.	

Dallam, John	32
Samuel	5
Frances	3
Margret	1
Negroes: Tom, 29—Hannah, 7.	

E.

Ely, Thomas, Junr.	24
Hannah	17

Ely, Hugh	22
Sarah	18
Joseph	16
Scott, Sarah	7

Ely, Thomas, Senr.	61
Malin	21
William	18
Ruth	27
Rachael	25
Chapman, Wm.	4

Ellis, Ellis	36

F.

Fisher, James	40
Mary	36
Elizabeth	15
Thomas	13
Isabella	10
Sarah	8
Mary	6
William	3

	Ages
James	1
Linch, John	19
West, Thomas	18
Negroes: Mingo, 46—Jane, 18—Cigas, 1/4.	

Fisher, Wm. Senr.	66
Sarah	61
John	11
Negroes: Dick, 63—Mariah, 64—Jack, 36—Beck, 34—Richard, 13—George, 11—Pegg, 6—Benn, 3—Poll, 1/2.	

G.

Griffith, Evan	33

Gallion, Joseph	44
Sarah	45
John	19
Gregory	22
William	16
Alexr.	13
James	10
Elizbth.	7
Jos.	5

Gover, Elizabeth	50
Cassandria	33
Prissilla	28
Gittings (no Tax)	17
Negroes: Limas, 50—Dinah, 50—Nann, 36—James, 35—Tower, 33—Dinah, 26—Sall, 14—Dampier, 12—Violett, 10—Cesar, 8—Sarah, 6—Cloe, 4—Prince, 3—Affa, 2.	
Gover, Samuel	21
Negro Toney	20

H.

Hawkins, Richd.	27
Lurana	29
John	2
Negro Easter	12

	Ages
Hall, Christopher	27
Heaton, John	33
Rebecca	33
Margrett	11
Sarah	9
Thos.	7
Jno.	4
James	1
Husbands, Wm.	48
Elizabth.	46
Jas.	13
Meleson	12
Mary	7
Hannah	5
Susannah	2
Wm.	6 Weeks
Hill, Wm.	56
Shem	15
Hill, James	45
Sarah	27
Mary	6
Martha	4
James	2
Harris, Margrett	41
Ann	21
Elizbth.	15
George	10
Wm.	9
Benjamin	7
Sarah	5
Thos.	9 mo.

Negroes: Phanney, 35—Tower, 29—Dinah, 16—Tumbah, 14—Venus, 7—Meriah, 7—Lydia, 4—Mary, 4 mo.

	Ages
Hendley, Joseph	70
Hopkins, Jos. Senr.	70
Ann	65
Jos. Junr.	34
Elizbth.	34
Ann	7
John	5
Joseph	4
Elizabeth	1½

Negroes: Sharper, 50—Duke, 40—Pollidore, 30—Sower, 21—Nanney, 35—Hannah (no Tax) 60—Will, 14—Cesar, 13—Hagah, 25—Cumbo, 15—Dafney, 5—George, 4—David, 7—Dinah, 3—Nanny, 6 mo.—Charles, 9.

	Ages
Hawkins, John	60
Samuel	22
Johns, Hosea	7
Tribble, John	79

Negroes: James, 60—Cuff, 55—Moll, 50—Jane, 13—Hager, 11—Jerry, 9—Sall, 7—Pompey, 5.

	Ages
Hawkins, Thomas	31
Sarah	29
Hargrove, Ruth	53
Absalom	11
Richard	6
Lydia	3
Elizabeth	1
Davis, Rachael	23
Hopkins, Saml.	30
Mary	30
Elizabeth	6
Ephrm. Gover Hopkins	5
Phillip	3
Samuel	1

Negroes: Easter, 12—Daniel, 11—Cato, 8.

	Ages
Husbands,* Elizabeth	31
Rachael	11

* May be "Husband" written with a terminal flourish resembling "s."

Ages

Mary.......................9
Susannah...................7
Elizabeth..................4
Ensinger, Susannah Maria, a servant..................23
Negroes: Bob, 15—Ben, 12—Sam, 9—Ned, 5—George, 2.

Hopkins, William..............58
Rachael....................56
Susannah...................27
William, Junr...............25
John.......................23
Leven......................21
Hannah.....................18
Charles....................15
Samuel.....................12
Thompson, Andrew...........18
Negroes: Ned, 70—Pompey, 45—Neptune, 42—Jack, 39—Nanney, 35—James, 32—Will, 29—Hannah, 24—Pegg, 21—Tom, 20—Isaac, 18—Jacob, 13—Nell, 11—George, 5—Abraham, 1—Suck, 15.

Hopkins, Gerrard..............33
Sarah......................29
Wallis, John Hopkins.....8 mo.
Negroes: Benn, 36—Jane, 24—Sall, 13—Will, 7—Susan, 1.

Harris, Daniel................31

J.

Johns, Skipwith...............28
Hannah.....................23
M^c^Clure, Ann (Hired Girl)....26
Negroes: Jacob, 22—Peter, 29—Jupiter, 29—Duke (Cripple), 29—Panoway, 12—Polley, 10—Dinah, 8.

Jolley, John..................42

Ages

Elizabeth..................38
Edward.....................17
Sarah......................15
Ann........................13
Cassandria.................11
W^m^.........................8
John.......................6
Elizabeth..................2½
Smith, John (appren)........16
Chew, Richard (do)..........20
Conry, Margaret (Servt.).....17
Negroes: Dampier, 50—Daniel, 23—Judy, 40—Suck, 28—Will, 12—Joseph, 10—Linty, 5—Hannah, 3—Jane, ½.

James, Robert.................35
Sarah......................26
John.......................9
Thomas.....................7
W^m^.........................5
Robert.....................3
Mary...................4 mo.

Jay, Stephen..................43
Hannah.....................40
Elizabeth..................13
Hannah.....................12
Samuel.....................7
Joseph.....................5
Thomas.....................2
Martha.................1 mo.
Humphreys, Rich^d^. (a Servt.)..40
Lamford, James (do.)........35
Negroes: 18(names here omitted).

Jones, Ruben..................25
Mary.......................27
Joseph................10 mo.

Jones, Joseph.................91
Patience...................81
Rachael....................41

Ages

Johnston, Armstrong..........25

L.

Lilley, William..........45
Linch, William..........21

Laughlin, William..........38
Rachael..........34
Sarah..........11
Mary..........6
Elizabeth..........4
W^{m}..........2

Love, James..........51
Margarett..........44
Thomas..........13

Lee, James, Senr..........72
Elizabeth..........66
Vancleave, Elizbth..........9
Vancleave, Mary..........8
Negroes: 24 (names omitted).

M.

Morgan, William..........32
Cassandria..........32
Elizabeth..........3
Sarah..........$1\frac{1}{2}$
Cassandria..........1
Negroes: 10.

Morgan, Lydia..........46
Mary..........31
Ruth..........18
Robt..........15
Sarah..........12
Margret..........7

McWilliams, Christian..........46
Elizabeth..........14
McKenny, Joseph..........22

Morgan, John..........36
Mary..........28
Rachael..........10

Ages

Thomas..........8
Joel..........6
W^{m}..........4
Elizabeth..........2
John..........3 mo.

Murray, Alexander..........49
Jane..........50
Mary..........18
John..........15
Elizabeth..........14
Archb^{d}..........12
Sarah..........10

"Macklemurray," John..........59
Patrick ("Mackelmurray")..........27
Marg^{t}. ("Mackelmurry")..........25
Starrat..........2
Charity..........5 mo.
Hawkins, John..........8

McBrayerta, Michael..........27

McCullough, Thos..........60
Jane..........53
Williams, W^{m}..........8

McCann, Arthur..........21

Kenny, Easter..........69
Mary..........25

Miller, Mary..........41
John..........20
Martha..........16
Hannah..........14

Miller, Joseph..........31

N.

Nowland, Mary..........25

Norton, Stephen..........26
Sophia..........20
Lambden, Thos..........12

	Ages
Nott, William	33
Jane	28
Mary	6
Sarah	4
W^{m}.	2

P.

Patrick, John	34
Elizabeth	29
Margret	9
John	7
Ann	5
Hugh	3
Elizabeth	$1^1/_4$
Mary	$1^1/_4$
Little, Nathan	17
Amos, John	17
Stephenson, John	25
Stuart, Jane	20
Rees, Margrett	20
Negroes: 3.	
Proctor, Richard	23
Peacock, John	58
Mary	39
Mary	8
Cassandria	5
Jenkins, John	13
Negroes: 13.	

R.

Rigbie, Nathan	54
Sarah	45
Sheridine, Nathan	4
Giles, Nathl's Children:	
Hannah	14
Sarah	9
Elizth.	7
Carolina	4
Low, Deborah	43
Wood, Elizth. (hired girl)	20

	Ages
Servants: Henry Evans a Servt. to Skipth. Johns	35
Harrod, Henry, do	35
Negroes: Suckey (no Tax),70 — and 11 others.	
Rees, Soloman	64
Mary	62
Rees, John	23
Hector	30
Rodgers, Samuel	34
Susannah	25
W^{m}.	14
Rodgers, Mary	26
Rodgers, Elizabeth	32
Cassandra	4
Rodgers, Joseph	28
Rachael	16
Rigbie, James	55
Sarah	42
James, Junr.	19
Susannah	23
Ann	12
Mary	6
Massey, Isaac	19
Negroes: 11.	

S.

Stapleton, Joshua	29
Susan^{h}.	26
David	4
Edward	1
Lydia	2 mo.
Shaw, Armintha	23
Ann	5
Smith, Martha	40
Ann	22
Ralph	20

Ages

Sarah 15
Martha 13
Andrew 11
Ruth 8
Negro: Cesar, 30.

W.

Wells, Susannah 23

Wells, Richard, Junr 20

Wells, Richard, Senr 89
Cassandra 31
Daws, Elisha 20
Negroes: 4.

Wells, Richard, Junr 60
Jane 50
Elizabeth 26
Drusillah 17
Saml 14
Mary 11
Negroes: 7.

Ward, Edward 67
Cassandria 49
Richard 21
Avis 14
Margret 9
Hubbard, Geo. (Servt.) 20
Negroes: 3.

Warner, Cuthbert 23

Warner, Joseph 48
Ruth 46
Jas. J^r^ 21
Hizekiah 15
Aseph 19
Mordecai 12
Silas 10

Wiggons, Joseph 30
Sarah 28
Tarace 7
Bezleel 5

Ages

Hannah 3
Cuthbert 1

Warner, Crosdale 47
Mary 42
Mary, J^r^ 15
Aaron 13
Amos 11
Crosdale 9
Sarah 7
Agnes Crosdel Warner 4
Asa 2

Wilson, Benjamin 33
Eliz^th^ 27
John 4
Sarah 3
Margret 2
Mary . . . . . 1 mo.
John Wilson 80
Knight, Eliz^th^. (Hired Girl) . . . 21
Negroes: 7.

Worthington, John 42
Prissilla 27
Sarah 6
Prissilla 4
Henry 3
John 2
Negroes: Meriah (no Tax), 90—David (do), 87—and 12 others.

Worthington, Samuel 21
Negroes: Cesar (no Tax) 70—and 5 others.

Worthington, Charles 40
Mary 32
Sarah 11
Joseph 9
Charles 4
Ann 2
Margret . . . . . 1 week
Negroes: 9.

	Ages
Wallis, Thomas	24
Wilson, Joseph	74
Hannah	70
Martha	33
Mary	30
Sarah	28
Negroes: 7.	
Wilson, Samuel	40
Negro Tom 28.	
Wilson, Joseph Jun[r].	41
Negro Ned 26.	
Wallis, "Grace"	54
"Phanney"	27
Negroes: 10.	

FREE NEGROES *Ages*

Nathan Rigbie set free: Will, 50—Dafney, 40, and 2 children—Grace, 36, and 3 children—Judy, 30, and 1 son—Parraway, 40.

Philip Coale set free: Benn, 35.

Elizabeth Husbands set free: Sam, 37—Jas. 29—George, 26—Moll, 25 and her baby.

William Coale, Junr. set free: Rachael, 36, and her son Ezekiel.

Jas. Rigbie set free: Hager, 60—Luckey, 27—and 3 others.

W[m]. Coale set free: Betty (42) and Hannah, 2.

Harford County, SS: May 3[d], 1777 Came W[m]. Fisher and made oath on the Holy Evanjelest of almighty God that the within is a true list of all the peopels Names and ages in Deer Creek Lower Hundred as they were give in to him.

Before W[M]. WEBB.

Received of the Committee of Harford County this 1st day of July 1777 Forty Shillings in full for taken the within Habitants of Deer Creek Lower Hundred.

W[M]. FISHER, Jun[r].

Census of 1776, Harford Lower Hundred, Harford County,

"List of Inhabitants in Harford Lower Hundred Taken by Wm. Hollis, August 30, 1776."

	Ages
Osborn, James Junr. (Tax)	31
Osborne, Benjamin (Tax)	20
Semelia	20
Susannah	6 mo.
Cord, Aquila	12
Blacks: 12, of which 3 are taxed.	
Thomas, John (Tax)	49
Martha	36
John, Junr.	9
Joseph	7
Elizabeth	5
William	3
Hollis, Amos (Tax)	40
Martha	30
Amos, Junr.	11
Abirila	13
William	8
James	5
Benjamin	3
Cathrin	11 mo.
Blacks: 3.	
Rhodes, George	35
Chauncey Geo. Senr. (Tax)	68
Benjamin (Tax)	17
Margret	59
Greenfield, Jacob	13
Greenfield, Mary	9
Blacks: 15.	
Little, George (Tax)	35
Cathrin	44
Ann	11
Prewit, James	2
Blacks: 12.	

	Ages
Diction, Morris	43
Drusilla	43
Susan	18
Sarah	16
John	8
Hannah	6
Frances	3
Reason, James (Tax)	18
Beck, Caleb (Tax)	47
Hannah	35
Ann	14
Hannah	10
Joshua	8
Bethsheba	5
Sophia	3
James	1
Jewry (?) Richd. (Tax)	34
Negro: Bett, 55.	
Drew, James (Tax)	22
Sarah	25
Phillip	5 months
Bennet, Joshua, "orphan"	4
Negro: Cass "hirling," 15.	
Mires, John (Tax)	39
Hannah	24
James	3
Leamah	1
Drew, Anthony, Senr. (Tax)	50
Henry	18
Mary	17
Sarah	15
Anthony, Junr.	13
Reason, John	14
Blacks: 15.	

Ages

Drew, Geo. (Tax) 25
Letitisha 25
Ann 4
Anthony 2
Rebecca .... 9 months
Pettlehiser, Lewis (Tax) 20

Kenard, Michael (Tax) 30
Hannah 20
Ann 10
George 7
Mary 6
Michael 4
James 3
Folkner, Ann 43
Folkner, Robt. (Tax) 22
Curry, Brian (Tax) 27
Blacks: 3.

Osborn, William S^{r}. (Tax) 53
Blacks: 5.

Farrell, Thos. (Tax) 35
Phillips, Samuel 60

Hanson, John Senr. (Tax) 55
Keziah 53
John, Junr. (Tax) 30
Hollis (Tax) 28
Elizabeth 18
Phillips, Samuel 12
Phillips, Martha 10
Blacks: 6.

Osborne, W^{m}. Junr. (Tax) 30
Mary 26
Cordelia 8
Abariler 6
Cyrus 4
Cord, John 11
Canfield, Ann 14
Blacks: 4.

Ages

Osborn, James, Senr. 64
Gean 55
Martha 18
Blacks: 4.

Buckley, John 53
Sarah 37
James 11
William 3

Marcum, William (Tax) 45

Blackstone, Thomas (Tax) 29
Elizabeth 28
James 8
Thomas 6
John 4
Elizabeth 2

Cormoway, Mickael (Tax) 33
Elizabeth 19

Brown, John (Tax) 26
Ann 23
Lowman, Elizabeth 52
Crown, Henry (Tax) 45

Jackson, Thomas (Tax) 33
Sarah 18
Beb, John (Tax) 27
Ogg, Stocke (?) 5
Cordelia .... 6 months
Black: Jonas, 14.

Forwood, Jacob (Tax) 39
Faithful 33
Constance 10
Gean 4
Steel, Elizabeth 23
Warner, Ludwick (Tax) 37
Celly, Volintine (Tax) 27
Celly, Mary 27
Fitsimons, Patrick 13
Blacks: 5.

	Ages
Lanagin, James (Tax)	35
Chauncey, Cathrin *	24
Chauncey, Elizabeth	5
Chauncey, Margret	3
Chauncey, Susan	3
Chauncey, Mary	1
Williams, Mary	42
Blacks: 5.	
Evans, Benjamin (Tax)	34
Deaver, Thomas (Tax)	21
Wadkins, John (Tax)	42
Purify	41
John	14
William	13
Amos	9
Ann	2
Hoy, Roger	58
Brown, Thomas (Tax)	32
Mary	26
Jacob	6
Elizabeth	3
Mary	1
Gonins, George (Tax)	40
Jones, Robert (Tax)	27
Thomas, Marget	26
Thomas, John	1
Suttone, Thomas (Tax)	22
Blacks: 6.	
Hughs, John Hall (Tax)	34
Ann Hall Hughs	22
Everitt Hall Hughs	6
John H.	4
Scott H.	2
James H.	3 months
Blacks: 3.	

"To Thos. Henderson, Dr."

	Ages
Stephenson, Jonas (Tax)	25
Stephenson, Rebeca	15
Stephenson, Mary	2
Kady John (Tax)	20
Blacks: 2.	
Garrettson, Garrett † (Tax)	22
Alley	20
Benjamin	15
Blacks: 2.	
Suttone, Samuel (Tax)	37
Sarah	40
Mary	15
Marget	13
Elizabeth	11
Hannah	9
Sarah	7
Robert	7
Ann	4
Azel, Martha	15
Eagle, James (Tax)	30
Herringts, Thos. (Tax)	25
Reed, Elizabeth	90
Dacon, Francis (Tax)	42
Mary	45
Brooks, Thos.	3
Fisher, Amelia	52
William	14
Thos.	12
Asll	9
Johnson, Mary	32
Johnson, Samuel	5
Johnson, Amelian	3
Whitacre, John (Tax)	23
Whitacre, Hezekiah (Tax)	21
Isaac Whitacre, (Tax)	18
McGown, Ann	11
Adams, John (Tax)	38

* There is apparently an "S" following the age "24" in the original.

† In small letters "Short" (?) appears before "Garrett Garretson."

	Ages
Brown, Robert (Tax)	36
Elizabeth	23
John	2
Sarah	1
Abirilah	8 months
Blacks: 2.	
Megay, Robert (Tax)	48
Sarah	38
George (Tax)	17
John	14
Robert, Junr.	12
William	10
Hugh	8
James	6
Alee	4
Richards, John (Tax)	34
Sheridine, Mary	30
Curry, Vionah	18
Oliver, James (Tax)	60
Cathrin	60
James, Junr.	19
Garland, Cathrin	14
Brown, Sarah	2
Burns, Mathew (Tax)	60
Mary	41
Nevel, Ruth	10
Nevel, John	7
Bennet, Benjamin (Tax)	50
Gean	40
Benjamin, Junr.	13
Vensieler, Alener	13
Hanson, Benj. (Tax)	53
Mary	21
Abbrilah	13
Elizabeth	11
Luke	9
Sarah	5

	Ages
Tredway, Elizabeth	11
Pitt, Frances (Tax)	23
Blacks: 10.	
Munroe, William (Tax)	34
Mary	32
John	13
Elizabeth	7
Thomas	5
William F.	1 month
Negro: Sall, 13.	
Macky, George (Tax)	30
Vanhorn, Peter	15
Hall, Edward (Tax)	28
Blacks: 9.	
Hall, John, "Cry." (Tax)	57
Barthia	52
Avarile	20
Orasilla	18
Mary	16
Eliz.	13
Gloglan, Patrick M.* (Tax)	49
Davis, Mary, A Hierlin	59
Timons, Lawrance	45
Scovin, Francis (Tax)	40
Blacks: 26.	
Punteny, Joseph (Tax)	48
Sarah	40
Aquila (Tax)	17
Ann	15
Prisela	12
George H.	9
Nelson	6
Samuel	4
James	2
John	2 months
Blacks: 3.	

* Possibly McGloglan, Patrick.

Name	*Ages*
Giles, James (Tax)	26
Ann	32
Johanna	5
Susanna	1
Jacob W.	2 months
Fell, William	15
Cooper, William (Tax)	35
Caine, Edward (Tax)	25
Duke, Thomas (Tax)	25
Henry, Andrew	15
Coulson, Mary	21
Blacks: 15.	
Henderson, Sarah	39
Chauncey, John (Tax)	26
Nelson, John (Tax)	18
Nelson, Aquila	10
Nelson, Pesilla	7
Henderson, George	2
Blacks: 6.	
Diemer, John (Tax)	30
Johanna	30
Rachel	11
Magee, Sarah	38
Magee, Sarah Junr.	12
Blacks: 13, including Edward, 2 days old.	
Armstrong, John (Tax)	47
Ezebel	42
William	12
John	8
Robert	5
Ezebel	8 Days
Williams, Elizebeth	3
Gawley, William (Tax)	23
Giles, Jacob at Bush Mills	—
Wilkinson, Jno. (Tax)	46
Hyfield, Charles (Tax)	25
Robins, Jno. (Tax)	22
Williams Thos. (Tax)	20
Reese, Sary	27
McComas, Benjamin (Tax)	33
Alexander (Tax)	30
Mary	25
Clark, Patrick	11
Bennet, Peter (Tax)	51
Mary	27
Abram (Tax)	22
Leaven (Tax)	16
Sarah	14
Peter	12
Aquila	7
Benjamin	2
John	11 months
Allham, Dniel (Tax)	25
Negro: Luce, 15.	
Garrettson, Freeborn (Tax)	23
Richard (Tax)	18
Mahon, Thos. hireling (Tax)	25
Blacks: 3.	
Eden, William (Tax)	31
Sarah	26
Jeremiah	8
Elizabeth	6
Benjamin	3
Mary	10 months
Codonia, Peter	15
Boayer, Elizabeth.	
West, William	39
Susanna	39
Geo. Wm.	6
Margt.	4
Sibyl	2
Blacks: "Living at the Glebe," 9—"Living with Wm. West," 8.	
Diemer, Rachael	50

Ages

Hall, Aquila, Senr. (Tax) 49
  Sophia 44
  William 19
  Charlotta 18
  Mary 16
  John 14
  Edward 12
  Sophia 11
  Martha 8
  Benedict 5
  Parker, John (Tax) 21
  Asker, Jane 22
  M^c^laughlin, James 15
  Negroes: 45.

Copeland, George (Tax) 26
  Frances 22
  Mary 2
  Callihan, Mical (Tax) 24
  Negroes: 5.

Copeland, John (Tax) 22
  Blacks: 6.

Phillips, James (Tax) 35
  Martha 32
  James 5
  Elizabeth P. 3
  John P. 1
  Negroes: 28.

Phillips, Susannah 23
  Negroes: 10.

Gallion, Rachael 34
  Prisilla 17
  Sarah 15
  Abariller 12
  Phebe 10
  Martha 7
  George 5
  Mary 3
  Rachael 1

Ages

Edwards, Joseph (Tax) 29
  Finna, Alender 20
  Handley, James (Tax) 25

Garland, Henry 66
  Negro: Jacob, 15.

Moubrey, Mary 29
  James 7
  Robert 5
  Mary 1

Gallion, Phibe 63
  Nathan (Tax) 27
  Christian 27
  Martha 23
  Sarah 3
  Blacks: 11.

Chauncey, George (Tax) 38
  Mary 29
  Sarah 10
  George 8
  Martha 4
  William 1
  Blacks: 14.

Ruff, John (Tax) 27
  Sarah 25
  Dansichlor, Elizabeth 33
  Christian, John (Tax) 21
  Blacks: 9.

Reding, William (Tax) 39
  Ann 38
  Milcah 8
  John 3
  William ....8 months
  Burchfield, Hannah 20
  Prisilla 16
  Adam 13
  Frances 11
  Dunn, Thos. (Tax) 24
  Brown, James (Tax) 26

Name	Ages
Linch, Daniel	35
Mary	24
Carty, Marget	45
Young, William (Tax)	37
Agness	28
Agness, Junr.	2
Jones, Mary	18
Blacks: 5.	
Young, George (Tax)	24
Hollis, William (Tax)	50
Sarah	48
William, Junr. (Tax)	27
Clark	16
Blacks: 8.	
Ore, Mary	19
Rebecca	14
Diction, Peter	54
Marget	42
Johannah	15
William	9
Sarah	5 months
Cambell, Ann	8

Perry, John, Schoolmaster at the Church Denys to Give in his age or be numbered with the inhabitants.

Harford County SS 7th Jany 1777 Came Wm. Hollis and made Oath that the above is a true list of Inhabitants Taken in Harford Lower Hundred and that he was Six Day taking the same list.

J. B. HOWARD.

Census of 1776, Susquehannah Hundred, Harford County

"A List of Inhabitants in Susquehannah Hundred, Taken by Chas. Gilbert." *

Name	Ages
Small, Robert	30
Elizabeth	21
John	9 months
Beacor, George	15
Hare, Patience	11
Small, John	27
Wilson, Andrew	46
Lidiea	36
James	10
Cathron	8
Beniamin	4
Andrew	2
Hallett, John	25
Prigg, Mary	25
Brown, George	14
Hare, Sarah, Widow	39
Mary	17
Sarah	6
Daniel	3

* This Census is written upon 32 pages $9^1/_8'' \times 7^1/_2''$, partly fastened together, and is in excellent preservation.

Name	*Ages*
Rigdon, Charles	27
Molton, Mathew	15
Suilliven, Nathaniel	13
Donovan, Wm.	23
Rachel	19
Anos	6 months
Durbin, Avariller	25
Delila	2
Judd, Daniel	40
Hanah	39
Wiliam	17
Daniel	11
Joshua	9
Rachel	8
Ann	6
Elisabeth	3
James	3 months
Horton, Wm.	53
Elisabeth	32
Wm.	14
Mary	12
James	10
Sarah	8
Elisabeth	5
Ruth	1
Negroes, 2.	
Cummins, Paul	35
Hannah	27
Sammuel	9
James	3
Barns, Joseph	45
Horner, James	29
Mary	28
Elisabeth	7
Thomas	6
Casandrew	4
Mary Gilbert Horner	1
Baker, Jnny Mary	11
Negroes, 2.	
Clarke, ElizaBeth	18
Culver, Bemin	24
Negro, 1.	
Culver, Ann	62
Negro, 1.	
Suillovon, John	27
Margret	18
Coolley, John	21
Rigdon, Sarah	62
Sarah	23
Pritchart, Mary	12
Michael, Belsher	48
Ann	28
John	14
James	13
Bennet	8
Jacob	6
Susannah	4
Daniel	2
Wm.	8 months
horten, John	23
Negroes, 4.	
Macantraus, Hugh	24
Feeby	31
Mary ("Macantrass")	3 mos.
Thomson, Edward	45
Jamime	30
Martha	10
Mallon	6
Mary	3
Wm.	1
Sullavin, James	17
Bedelhall, John	27
Negroes, 5.	

	Ages
Hall, Josias	24
Mecarty, Owing	22
Negroes, 3.	
Choislin, Thomas	41
Young, Thomas	40
Chisholm, Thomas	11
Chisholm, John	7
Hampton, John	85
Ann	84
Mitchel, John	31
Mary	34
Gaberil	19
Elisabeth	6
Rachel	4
Fradrick	1
Purkins, Ritchard	16
Taylor, Ritchard	12
Cortny, Thomas	32
Sarah	27
Jonas	10
John	8
Hollas	6
Semelia	5
Sarah	3
Thomas	2 months
Brown, James	13
Negro, 1.	
Knight, Jonathan	56
Ellender	46
Holliday, Mary	12
West, Thomas	45
Ann	39
Elisabeth	17
James	14
Thomas	12
Samuel	6
Sarah	6

	Ages
Mary	3
ISaac	1
Perry, Wm.	81
Wm.	26
Ely, Hannah	27
Macarty, Jacob	22
Bendal, Joseph	38
Mecarty, Mary	8
Mecarty, Elisabeth	5
Meginis, Mary	2
Fort, Peter	30
Mary	26
Naney	5
Franses	3
Dority	1
Oure, John	20
Hurley, Judy	15
Barns, Zachariah	11
Tayler, Warter	19
Steal, Joseph	25
Elisabeth	23
Elisabeth	50
Rebeca	5
John	3
Abreham	2
Joseph	1 month
Periman, John	43
Martha	38
ISaac	16
John	11
Mary	9
Marth	5
Elisabeth	3
Prise, Mary	27
Prise, Wm.	6
Durben, Thomas	18
Antel, John	59
Blanch	44

	Ages
Ann	15
John	13
Hannah	11
Sarah	9
Thomas	6
West, Susanah	18
Gilbert, Thomas	74
Mary	57
James	19
Fanny	16
Martha	11
Hamby, Samuel	10
Mecarty, Sarah	6
Mecarty, Levy	4
Steal, John	24
Casandra	23
Elisabeth	1
Gallion, James	47
Ruth	45
Thomis	18
Gilbert	14
Betty	13
Cumfort	10
Rachal	3
Gilbert, Michael	31
Sarah	22
Thomas	1
Coal, Jane	56
Elisabeth	18
Thomas	14
Ezecal	10
Carrel, John	27
Coal, James	25
Sofiah	24
John	6
James	4
Samilia	4 months
Phillips, James	13

	Ages
Coal, Ephram	22
Sophra	19
Johnson, Samuel	17
Pearson, Abel	43
Mary	35
Elisabeth	14
Samuel	10
Abel	7
Joseph	5
Orsburn, John	36
Ann	37
Sarah	15
Elisabeth	12
Amous	10
John	8
Bennet	6
Aquillah	4
Josias	1
Hamby, Sarah	35
Fanney	33
Delah	7
James	1
Wm.	1
Wm.	4
Welch, Wm.	24
Cord, Roger	20
Glovver, Mary	26
Boyls, Thomas	40
Mary	34
Ebeth	9
Jane	7
Marthew	3
Thomas	9 months
Cowin, ISabella	15
Smith, Henery	13
Boner, John	12
Cox, Wilm.	58
Mary	53

Ages

Mary Banes Cox 20
Israel 13
Rachel 11
Negroes, 7.

Wright, Charles 30
Blackford, Thomas 66

Evett, Wm. 40
Margret 26
Muckelrath, Sarah 24
Mackfail, Martha 26
Slator, Thomas 18
Glain, Margret 6

Giles, Jacob, Junr. 23
Ame 21
Guist, Amilia 21
Alisabeth 2
Tinlan [?], Mary 40
Lovvel, John 22
Reease, Robart 20
Negroes, 11.

At Rockrun
Smith, Wm. and Jacob Giles, Junr. No ages given.
hampton, David 25
Negroes, 10.

forrage, Crister 50
Page, Mary 49

Virthworth, William 43
Sarah 46
Sarah 8
Negroes, 2.

Mackfiel, Daniel 32
Jaine 20
Ann 2
John . . . . . . 8 months

Mecurdy, Archa 52
Ellender 35

Ages

Margret 6
Lemmon, Elisabeth 63

Marshel, John 30
Feby 26
Henery 2
Camneron, John 14

Shea, Wm. 51
Elisabeth 32
Thomas 11
David 9
Elisabeth 4
Sarah 4
Isabel 2

Fitchgarel, Margret 23
Mary . . . . . . 1 month

Phillips, James 37
Bethia Fillips 29
Sarah Fillips 10
James Fillips 4

Barns, Bethia 71
Closson, Peter 16
Brown, Sarah 17
Hapstone, Mary 7
Negroes, 7.

Deaver, David 29
Mary 33
Rebeccah 6
Ann 4
James 1

Porter, John 63
Deavour, Mary 33
Ellender Porter 14
Sarah Porter 23
Agnis Porter 10
Margret 5

Thompson, Mary 46
John 25

	Ages
Daved	23
Jery	18
James	16
Elisabeth	13
Chappell, Mary	8
Chappell, James	7
Bowlear, Peter	21
Johns, Richard	43
Taylor, Jane	40
Hannah	17
Mary	15
Alryhan	13
Evret (?), Wm., Junr.	4
Johns, Nathaniel	41
Elisabeth	33
Ann	13
Ruth	12
Franses	10
Casandrew	8
Elisabeth	3
William	1
Touchstone, Mary	18
"Fre Negors," 8.	
Edwards, James	34
Margret	30
Thomas	6
Mary	5
Joseph	2
Brown, Elisabeth	46
Cowan, Elisabeth	16
Cowing, Ann	8
Brannon, Mary	4
Howel, Samuel	22
All, Margret	22
All, Hannah	1
Howard, John	18
Negroes, 4.	

	Ages
Giles, Jacob	73
Johannah	57
Johannah Giles Wartes	9
Scot (?), Sukey	38
Smith, Winston	4
littleton, Ann	30
Cannabal, Michael	27
Husterfield, Charles	27
Negroes, 18, of which one is called "Bumbrow."	
Gilbert, Michael	70
Mary	60
Samuel	23
Mary	20
Presbury, Elisabeth	13
Negroes, 9.	
Wamigim, Thomas	50
Ann	48
Boman, Henry	40
Ellener	41
John	16
David	14
Henery	12
Mary	10
MarGret	9
Affnea	7
Elles	4
ChrisTian	2
Smith, Jabish	66
Mary	62
Luis	5
Chesney, Richard	24
Mary	24
Wm.	3 months
Rumsey, John	33
Martha	38
Harritt	4
Mary	2
Negroes, 14.	

	Ages
Scantlin, John	23
Rachel	23
James	1
Haukins, Robart	59
Lidia	56
Richard	23
Ellisabeth	11 months
Averiller	25
Nancy	3
Robert	2
Negroes, 5.	
Haukins, Wm.	27
Sarah	25
Joseph	5
Margret	4
Elisabeth	2
Musgrove, Franses	30
Negro, 1.	
Vanhorn, ESeacall	26
Sary	21
Jessay	6 months
Smith, Cathron	44
Litten, Samuel	39
Ann	35
Clemnency	17
Sarah	15
Alisabeth	13
Mary	11
Susannah	9
Samuel	7
Ruth	5
Ann	2
Fulk, Mary	17
Craford, John	72
Negro, Peter, 70.	
Deven, Hugh	22
Mary	27
Hugh	1

	Ages
Hursbend, Joseph	39
Mary	34
Puesly, Lidia	18
Root, Mary	25
Aldmand, Sarah	18
Slond, Sarah	16
Josua "Husband"	11
Mary "Hursband"	9
Sarah "Husband"	7
Hannah "Husband"	5
Ann "Hursband"	2
Joseph "Husband"	4 months
Negro, 1.	
Root, Daniel	57
Ann	56
Danniel	26
Jean	21
John	19
James	15
Margret	13
Richard	11
Pervail, Gidian	29
Mary	18
Margret	8 months
Gover, Robert	15
harres, James	12
harres, John	15
Scotten, Lucey	20
Negroes, 3.	
Lampper, John	33
Margret	37
Death, James	56
Soffiah	60
Wm.	21
Charity	18
George Simes Death	14
Negroes, 5.	
Farmer, John	34

	Ages
Snodgrass, Wm.	36
Cathroan	36
Roberd	13
Margret	14
James	11
Mary	8
Wings, Arther O	25
Curswell, Wm.	62
Esabeellah	50
Robert	22
Mary	19
James	59
Robert	33
Mary	74
Negroes, 9.	
Knight, Sarah	55
Mary	22
Slone, John	58
Mary	37
Saras	13
Elisabeth	10
Hennery	6
Ramsey, Wm.	53
Mary	40
Andrew	22
Alisabeth	17
Jane	14
James	11
Wm.	7
Thomas	3
Negroes, 2.	
Murfey, James	38
Elisabeth	37
Rosannah	80
Franses	12
John	6
Rosannah	3
Alea	1

	Ages
Bayles, Samuels	40
Elisabeth	26
Samuel	18
Elis	16
John	13
Feaby	11
Mary	9
Mehetabet	6
Sarah	3
Silvers, Mellison	41
Wm.	21
Mary	16
Margret	14
Ammons	12
David	7
Sarah	6
Rachel	5
James	3
Silvers, Benjamin	24
Affey	26
John	10
Gashim	4 months
Smith, Sarah	11
Bayles, "Biamin" (Benj.?)	42
Debbrow	40
Feby	19
Robert	17
Hannah	15
Sarah	12
Samuel	8
Benjaman	2
Debrow	6 months
Augustus	46
Hoges, John	26
Collerage, Wm.	25
Forgerson, Andrew	33
Abigill	35
David	12

Ages

Annah.....10
Samuel Smith..... 6
Elisabeth..... 4
Andrew..... 2
Beniamin.....6 months

Clowes, George.....36
Elisabeth "Clows".....36
Cathron..... 5
Gorge..... 3
John.....9 months

Swarth, Samuel.....37
Catherine.....38
Gorge.....14
Mary.....13
Samuel.....11
Sarah..... 9
Peter..... 7
Christian..... 4
David..... 3
Isaac.....3 months

Steaverson, John.....28

Brown, Freeborn.....32
Crummel, Neger Oliver.....21
Negroes, 4 others.

Steal, Abraham.....25
Sarah.....25
Josua..... 3
Casandra.....3 months

Jimmison, John.....35
Mary.....33
Marthie.....76
Ellexander.....37
Marthie..... 4
Sarah..... 2
William..... 6
Long, Ellender.....21

Ages

Lee, James.....25
Smith, Thomas.....55
Hannah.....46
Hugh.....22
Elisabeth.....16
James.....14
Samuel.....11
Mary and W^m^..... 9
Hannah..... 8
Nathaniel..... 4
Negro Jeff, 40.

Vandigrift, George.....30
Mary.....22
Elisabeth.....5 months

Crues, Nicollous.....80
Mary.....80
Purkins, John.....51
Orusan, Mary.....12

Crues, John *.....48
Elisabeth "Crusan".....33
Michael "Crusan".....11
John "Crusan"..... 9
Mary "Crusan"..... 6
Garret "Crusan".....3 months
Negro, 1.

Wood, George.....37

Wartus, Godfrey.....37
Negroes, 4.

Culver, Robert.....29
Johannah.....31
Mary..... 2
Benjaman..... 1
Trass, Hugh mackan.....24
Negroes, 2.

Marten, Wm......29

* The arrangement seems to confirm the supposition that the head of this family is John Crusan, though written "Crues"—G. M. B.

	Ages
Harthorn, John	52
Margret	37
Jane	15
Robert	13
Agnis	10
Margery "Harthhorn"	9
Margrit "Harthhorn"	7
Mary "Harthhorn"	5
John "Harthhorn"	3
Marthy "Harthhorn"	1
Clarke, John	26
Mecan, Patrick	26
Elisabeth	27
John	4
Charles	2
Daniel	1
Umbel, Isaac	36
Cathran	24
Mary	3
Smith, Patrick	62
Elisabeth	60
Gorge	15
Elisabeth	15
Bayles, Nathaniel	28
Sarah	26
Ann	3
Samuel	1
Sutten, Edward	17
Negro, 1.	
Bayles, "Jamas"	22
Bots, George	45
Margret	37
Mary	17
Charity	15
John	14
Gorge	13
Ruth	11

	Ages
Rachel	6
Sarah	5
Elisabeth	2
Isaac	6 months
Wood, Josua	24
Donnovan, "Donovan," Daniel	58
Hanah	43
Danniel	25
Jacob	21
Thomas	21
John	16
Elisabeth	14
Joseph	9
Martha	7
Ephram	5
Arnold, Wm.	50
Cumfort	56
Brown, Mary	8
Brown, Jacob	4
Croscil (Oroscil?)	22
Arnold, Ephram	24
Marah	40
Wm.	3
Taylor, Elisabeth	15
Mitchel, James	22
Preston, Elisabeth	71
Watkins, Elisabeth	16
Roberson, Sarah	11
Barns, Wm.	41
Margret	41
John	16
Wm.	14
Sarah	13
Ford	9
Rachel	6
Elisabeth	3
Cotten, John	50
Butler, MarGret	16
Negro, 1.	

	Ages
Armstrong, Josua	44
Margret	37
Sollaman	18
Mary	16
Ford	13
Margret	9
Joseph	7
Hannah	4
Alishea	2
Bruer, James	40
Elisabeth	40
Jacob	20
Elisabeth	12
John	11
Marah	8
Sarah	4
James	2
Wm.	4 months
Mitchel, Kent	33
Hannah	33
Shadick	10
Elisabeth	8
Mary	5
Thomas	3
Sarah	1
Rachel	27
Asel	6 months
Rogers, John	47 [?]
Barnes, James	45
Benjamin	18
Sarah	16
Annah	10
Elisabeth	4
Cantler, Wm.	38
Mary	33
Casander	10
Wm.	5
Elisabeth	3
Ellabeller	5 months

	Ages
Mitchel, James	24
Martha	24
Martha	4
Kent	2
Wm.	28
Negro, 1.	
Barns, Ruth	47
Ford	13
Hosea	11
Asyl	9
Beck, Elisabeth	26
Negro, 1.	
Barns, Bennet	23
Hestor	22
Durben, Thomas	16
Mitchel, Wm.	28
Clemmency	27
Barker	7
Shurlotter	4
Elisabeth	3
Negro, 1.	
Barns, Ellisabeth	45
Ruth	16
Margret	14
Williams, John	32
Elisabeth	21
Negroes, 2.	
Kirns, Margret	30
Elisabeth	11
Matthew	7
Mary	3
Power, Wm.	56
Elisabeth	50
Boner, Nathan	25
Boner, Cathran	15
Boner, John	13
"Bouner," David	10

	Ages
Doleman, Sarah	35
Wood, James	43
Elisabeth	40
Posuarus?	15
John	13
Elisabeth	11
Susana	9
Roles, Joseph	29
Mary	20
Matthew	1
Larance, John	30
Margret	30
Elexander	8
John	1
Welch, Thomas	32
Hannah	26
Ruth	6
Griffetth, John	50
Averilla "Griffin"	34
Hannah	14
Elisabeth	12
Fanney	9
Mary	8
James	4
Wm.	2
Negro, 1.	
Standly, Wm.	69
Margret	58
Mitchel, Edward	50
Rachel	37
Aquiller	7
Ann	3
Rachel	1
Negroes, 3.	
Meake, Andrew	28
Martha ("Meeke")	27
Esteher	5

	Ages
John	2
Martha	2
Adam	1 month
Crage, John	30
Thoritan, Elisabeth	22
West, Enock	56
Elisabeth	43
Enock	10
Wm.	7
Williams, James	26
Margret	22
Wm.	3
Susannah	2
Mary	13
Williams, Wm.	52
Sarah	43
Barnet	19
Martha	15
Frances	13
Margret	12
Ephrame	9
Eseakel	7
Sarah	5
John	3
"Coer" "Coon" [?], John (No age) "Tochua, Wood" [?]	25
Porter, Wm.	41
Elisabeth	37
Roberson, Ellender	37
Eseakel	5
Molten, Ann	16
Rees, John	48
Cathron	50
Margret	21
Joseph	20
John	16
James	13

	Ages
Abreham	10
William	6
Miller, Margret	45
Sammuel	21
Agnis	19
"Fhomisdike"	12
Sarah	10
Mary	4
Anderson, Daniel	45
Sarah	39
Mary	18
Sarah	15
Margret	13
Charles	9
Prissiller	2
Negroes, 6.	
Mackfaddin, Joseph	41
Cox, Wm. Junr.	25
Rachel	25
Mary	1
Wm.	3 months
Bonner, John	46
Christan	40
Arther	17
Martha	14
John	11
Ann	8
Barnney	6
Charles	4
Mitchel, Micajah	24
Averrillah	19
Martha	2
Negroes, 2.	
"Jehugh a free Neger, 65," and 5 others.	
Keen, Timmothy	37
Ann	40
Rebekah	18

	Ages
AQuillah	15
Timmothy	10
John	8
Sarah	5
Wm.	3
"Mary a negro, 45" and 14 others.	
Wilson, Wm.	56
Casandra	65
Negroes, 9.	
Wilson, Samuel	22
Mary	24
Negroes, 9.	
Wilson, Rachel	26
Negroes, 7.	
"Cononal At quillah halls quartr."	
Wilson, William	36
Negroes, 27.	
Wilson, Wm.	36
Rooth	23
Mary	3
Sarah	7 months
Negroes, 5.	
Mecendlis, William	25
Elisabeth	25
Sarah	6
John	4
Ester	1 month
Homes, Ann	22
Negroes, 6.	
Logue, Wm.	60
Mary	48
Cathran	19
Wm.	16
Mary	14
Charity	12
Elisabeth	9

Ages

Walker, James 36
Elender 37
Elisabeth 10
Gorge 5
Ann 3
James . . . . . 6 months
Vanhorn, Richard 18
Henson, Jacob 19
Brown, Gustus 16
Negro, 1.

Cruse, Richard 50
Elisabeth 49
Elisabeth "Crues" 19
Catharine "Crues" 19
Richard "Crues" 17
Paydan, Thomas 15
Vandigraft, Richard 8
Stiles, Elisabeth 1

Campton, "Richarg" 19

Marten, Edward 26
Mary 17
Margret 1

Mils, Robert 71
Susannah 62
John 23
Lookket, John 31
Grant, James 29
Donohue, Margret 18
Grooms, Mary 13

medowel, Mary "Marymedowel 60" 60

Daverson, John 37
Sarah 31
Agnis "Deverson" 3
Daniel "Deverson" 4
Elisabeth "Deverson" . 9 months
Negro, 1.

Ages

Nutwell, Daniel 35
Minty 19
Bennet 2
Negro, 1.

Hill, John 50
Margret 40
Harmin 19
John 15
Samiel 8
Elisabeth 6
Aurilla 2

Gover, Phillip 57
Mary 42
Sam 11
Elisabeth 9
Garrat & Robert 7
Phillip & Hennery 5
Prissiller 3
Negroes, 23.

Wilson, John 38
Alianna 32
Christopher 11
Isaac 9
John 7
Sarah 5
James 3
Margret 1
gill, John 74
Roberson, Amelia 13
Negro, 1.

Wilson, Peter 25

Cox, John 30
Sarah 30
Mary 7
John 2
Sarah . . . . . 3 months
Weaver, Casper 16
Negro, 1.

	Ages
Power, Nicoles	50
Grant, Ann	22
Pritchard, James Junr	33
Elisabeth	18
John	14
Sarah	4 months
Pritchard, James	63
Elisabeth	58
Harmon	20
Sammuel	15
Benjamin	13
Daniel Jams	3
Pritchard, Elisabeth	26
Elisabeth	2
Rees, Sollimin	32
Averilla	33
John	8
George	7
Sarah	5
Margret	3
Sarah	2 months
Spenser, Roland	63
"Jame"	63
Ritchard	28
Wilcock, John	76
Wilcock, John	14
Brukes, Susanah	19
Ray, Gorge	37
Cathron	31
Mary	6
Robert	4
Samuel	1
Gallion, James	50
Ruth	57
Thomas	19
Gibert	16
Elisabeth	12

	Ages
Cumfort	9
Rachel	4
Mitchel, Kent	52
Molten, John	13
Negroes, 2.	
Pots, Rynard	51
Cathran	46
Cathran ("potts")	17
Jacob ("potts")	14
John ("potts")	10
Elisabeth ("potts")	2
David, Reed	38
Cord, Elisabeth	55
Susana	24
Neomie	14
Jacob	11
Fowler, Patrick	30
Elisabeth	24
Joseph	6
John	4
Wm.	2
David	6 months
Smith, Mary	80
Gallion, Samuel	30
Sarah	21
Mary	2
Knight, Thomas	30
Margret	25
Wm.	6
Mary	5
Elisabeth	3
"Light"	2
Barns, Grigary	42
Elisabeth	38
Ford	15
Richard	14
Rachel	13

	Ages
Grigory	11
Mary	9
Sarah	6
"Fiariner"	4
John	2
Averilla	1
Negroes, 4.	
Knight, George	42
Martha	31
Debrow	15
Hannah	11
Elisabeth	9
Susannah	5
AQuiller	2
Mitchel, Thomas	33
Ann	32
Elisabeth	8
Sarah	6
Ritchard	5
Barnet	3
Averilla	1
Taylor, Aquiller	13
"Bayles" [Bayley?]	64
Margret "Baley"	46
Charles "Bayley"	23
Aquillea "Bayley"	21
Bennidick "Bayley"	17
Sarah "Bayley"	15
Eseakel "Bayley"	12
Averilla "Bayley"	10
Mitchel, James Weaver	51
Jane	34
Elaxanders	6
James	3
Sarah	3 months
Stuard, Alexander	55
Ann	55
Wm.	13

	Ages
Ann	11
Mary	20
Margret	10
"Boner," Elisabeth Widow	33
Robert	14
Mary "Bonner"	10
Wm. "Bonner"	8
Brise "Bonner"	6
Margret "Bonner"	4
Elisabeth "Bonner"	1
Chandley, James	56
Susannah	49
Mohan, John	42
Judy	38
Edward	13
John	11
Margret	9
James	7
Mary	5
Elisebeth	3
Wm.	1
Deaver, Sarah widow	46
Samuel ("Deavour")	13
David	10
Hughs, "Amea's" Widow	60
Hughs, John	24
Jane	20
James	7 months
Negroes, 2.	
Bayley, Josias	26
Averilla	17
Negro, 1.	
"at Samuel Thomases Quorter." 11 negroes.	
Hughs, Nathaniel	26
West, Robert	39

	Ages
Ann	36
Elisabeth	15
Benjamin	12
Hannah	10
John	8
Mary	7
Martha	4
Michael	3
Ephram	2
Williams, Morras	60
Prissilla	50
Mary	22
Martha	19
John	15
Ann	11
Wm.	9
Ford, James	35
Oleve	20
Mecool, Mary	60
Beale, Thomas	59
Knight, "Jame" or "Jane" [?]	17
Stump, Henary	48
Rachel	40
Mary	16
John	22
Henery	15
Rubin	10
William	8
Elisabeth	6
Hannah	3
Esther	2
Negroes, 8.	
Bots, John	43
Elisabeth	33
Sarah	12
Ann	10
Isaac	7
James	2
Negroes, 3.	

	Ages
Wood, Isaac	85
Elisabeth	70
Martin, Elaxander	40
Martha	34
Isaac	7
Fleetwood, Beniamin	35
Hannah	28
Ann	3
Wilmonton, Joseph	15
Cothlon, John	61
Hannah	50
Mary	18
Roberson, Abraham	27
Elisabeth	23
Sarah	5
John	5 months
Knight, Light	59
Rachel	46
Wm.	20
Mary	26
Rachel	16
Isaac	12
Sarah	9
Hannah	5
Gudding, Margrit	40
Ann ("Goodings")	15
Moses ("Goodings")	11
Hagon, Cathran	60
Gorrel, Issabellah	46
John	24
Wm.	21
Joseph	20
Thomas	19
Esther	15
James	14
Hannah	11

Ages

"Sarah A free Neger" and 2 children.

Durbin, Mary....30
Amos.... 2
Elisabeth....8 months

Rutter, Richard....30
Ann....24
Esther.... 2
Sarah.... 1
Gipson, Robert....15
Whiticer, Mary....18

Durbin, Fransis....28
Ann....26
Mary.... 5

Gilbert, Martin Taylor....35
Martha....31
Mary....11
Charles.... 7
Maren Taylor.... 4
Elisabeth.... 1
Negro, 1.

Brannon, Patrick....62
Darkes....42
Wm....16
Hannah....12
Ellender....11
John.... 8
Joseph.... 4
Jane.... 2

Rees, Joseph....40
Aberam....35
Jane....88
Brown, Sarah....30
Jane.... 7

Cowen, Wm....52
Judy....52
Mary....28
Susannah....18

Ages

Thomas....21
Eddward....15
Stephen....11
Rachel.... 9

White, Richard....30
Sarah....25
Margret.... 3
Ann.... 1

Biars, Ephraim....28

Gilbert, Charles....53
Elisabeth....53
Michael....21
Elisabeth....18
Sarah....16
Hare, Robert....17
Negroes, 12.

Durbin, Averiller....17

Dilling, Larrance....27
Catherene....24

Dilling, Gorge....40
Marther....30
John.... 6
Edward.... 5
Robberd.... 3
Hannah....2 months

Baker, Nicolis....28
Agnes....23
Josaway....14
Hare, James....11
Trame (Frame?) John....19
Stareman, Alisabeth....11

Harbet, Benjamin....53
Grase....58
Benjamin....23

Hall, Rebecah....21
Savage, Gorge....30

	Ages
Burten, Jane	62
Mary	38
Giffeth, Hannah	25
Culber, Levy	3
Gallion, John	25
Mary	56
Mathew	34
Hughs, Elie (Eliel?)	9
Cussans, John	3
Megill, Wm.	42
Elisabeth	26
John	5
Mary	1
Ars, John	22
Negro, 1.	
Cummans, Phillip	66
Sarah ("Cummins")	54
John ("Cummins")	23
Casandra ("Cummins")	20
Benjamin ("Cummins")	19
Sammuel ("Cummins")	17
Andrew ("Cummins")	13
Patterson, Gorge	27
Gardener, Elexander	26
Negroes, 12.	
Goseph, Barns	45
Anderson, Charles	42
Mary	42
Daniel	19
Grase	18
Sarah	16
Charles	13
Richard	11
James	9
Wm.	7
Amous	4
Perry, Thomas	56

	Ages
Margret	32
Sarah	11
Jane	9
Thomas	6
Wm.	4
Peter	1
Donohue, Danniel	33
Judd, Wm.	34
Ann	34
Wm.	6
Daniel	4
Saran and Jane	3
Deaver, Aquillar	15
Gilbert, Parker	36
Elisabeth	37
Sarah	10
Parker	8
Gidian	7
Michael	4
Prissiller	1
Negroes, 2.	
Smith, Benjamin	30
Mary	26
Mary	21
Sarah	1
Greandland, Richard	32
Homes, Merear	21
Gilbert, Michael	42
Mary	36
Aquiller	18
James	16
Sarah	14
Michael	10
Mathew	8
Wm.	5
Amous	2
Negroes, 4.	
Biards, James	33

	Ages
Casander	24
Jane	3
Rachel	8 months

"at Harison Thomases Quorter."

Harris, Joseph	23
Negroes, 20.	
Mohon, Wm.	39
Jane	37
Ann	13
Cathron	11
Martha	9
John	7
Wm.	2
Hadaway, Richard	40
Sarah	26
Hargrove, Richard	35
Rachel	30
Ruth	4
Casandra	4 months
Hambelton, George	9
Knight, David	49
David	21
Mary	13
John	9

	Ages
Ezekel	7
Green, Elisabeth	30
Spenser, Heanary	50
Agnes	46
James	21
John	19
Jare	17
Cathron	15
Heanary	12
Agnes	10
Thomas	8
Wm.	7
Sarah	5
Lenard	4
Mary	3
Elisabeth & Ruth	1
Gorrel, Abraham	50
West, James	40
Ann	33
Mary	14
Heanary	11
Ann	8
James	6
Sarah	1
Pritchard, Obidiah, Sr. Black	30
Stephen	15

The Number of The inhabitance Taken in ye Susquehana Hundred in the year 1776 is 1581—the white People is 1300—the negros is 281—1581.

Harford County S^{t}. 7 Day January 1777 Then Came Charles Gilbert before me the Suscriber one of the Justices of the Peace for the aforesaid County & made Oath on the Holy Evangelist of Allmighty God that the above List is a True account of the Number of Inhabitants of Susquehannah Hundred as Given into me to the Best of his Knowledge Sworn to Before me

J. Beale Howard

NB. He further makes Oath that he was Ten Days taking the above List of Inhabitants, before J. B. Howard.

A List of the Inhabitants of Harford Co^ty^; taken in 1776.

	Whites	Blacks
Spesutia lower Hundred	790	650
Do. upper Do.	767	340
Harford lower Hundred	415	352
Do. upper Do.	548	194
Susquehanna Hundred	1,300	281
Bush River lower Hundred	658	275
Do. upper Do.	623	77
Deer Creek lower Hundred	460	374
Do. upper Do.	960	122
Eden Hundred	1,008	108
Broad Creek Hundred	318	24
Gun Powder lower Hundred	683	331
Do. upper Do.	893	214
Total 12, 765—	9,423	3,342

NB. The List of David Sweeney of Broad Creek Hundred, could not be obtained during the time of the sitting of the Committee, when got, was not proved could not assertain the time he was taking the List, but agreed to take Twenty Shillings for his Trouble which was paid by AG—.

QUEEN ANN'S COUNTY

Queen Anns County, Town Hundred, Census of 1776,

It should be noted that this original enumeration places the *oldest persons first and classes them as "Above 21"* and they are here designated as "a"; "b" means "Between 16 and 21"; "c" means "Between 12 and 16"; "d" means "Under 12," and "e" means "Total." "x" means "White males" and "z" means "White females"; "n" means "Blacks."

"*Heads of Families*":

Anderson, For Doctor James, 34 n.
Anderson, John, 1 ax, 2 az, 1 dx, 2 dz—2 ex, 4 ez;15 n.
Arescott, Richard, 1 ax, 1 az, 1 bx, 1 cx, 1 cz—3 ex, 2 ez; 2 n.
Adkey, Nathan, 1 ax, 1 az, 1 dx—2 ex, 1 ez.
Austin, Absalom, 1 ax, 2 cx, 2 dz—3 ex, 3 ez.
Ashley, Thomas, 1 ax, 1 bz—1 ex, 1 ez; 2 n.
Burrell, Thomas, 1 ax, 1 az—1 ex, 1 ez.
Boots, Nathaniel, 1 ax, 1 az, 1 dz—1 ex, 2 ez.
Brown, W^{m}., Mason, 1 ax, 1 az, 1 cz, 1 dx, 2 dz—2 ex, 4 ez; 7 n.
Boots, Samuel, 1 ax, 1 az—1 ex, 1 ez; 1 n.
Barber, Thomas, 1 ax, 1 az—1 ex, 1 ez.
Betts, Hezekiah, 2 ax, 3 az, 2 bx, 1 cx, 1 dz—5 ex, 4 ez; 9 n.
Blervet, Charles, 1 ax, 1 az, 1 cx, 1 cz, 3 dz—2 ex, 5 ez.
Burchanall, Jeremiah, 1 ax, 3 az, 2 bx, 1 bz, 1 dz—3 ex, 5 ez; 3 n.
Bateman, John, 1 ax, 1 az, 1 dx, 2 dz—1 ex, 3 ez.
Benton, John, 3 ax, 1 az, 1 bx, 2 dx, 3 dz—6 ex, 4 ez; 15 n.
Brown, John, 2 ax, 2 az, 1 cz—2 ex, 3 ez; 38 n.
Byrn, Mary, 2 az, 1 bz, 1 cx, 1 cz, 4 dx—5 ex, 4 ez; 12 n.
Bateman, James, "Taylor," 1 ax, 1 az, 2 cx, 1 dx, 3 dz—4 ex, 4 ez; 2 n.
Boots, Jacob, 1 ax, 1 az, 1 bx, 1 cz, 2 dz—2 ex; 1 ex, 4 ez; 1 n.
Brown, Samuel, 1 ax, 1 az, 1 bz, 1 cx, 1 dx, 1 dz—3 ex, 3 ez; 13 n.
Benton, Ninson, 3 ax, 2 az—3 ex, 2 ez; 13 n.
Benton, Ninson, Junr., 2 ax, 1 az, 2 cx, 3 dx, 2 dz—7 ex, 3 ez.
Benton, William, 1 ax, 1 az, 3 dx, 1 dz—4 ex, 2 ez; 3 n.
Brown, William, 2 ax, 1 az, 2 bz, 1 cx, 4 dx—7 ex, 3 ez; 17 n.
Burk, David, Schoolmaster.
Betts, Solomon, 2 ax, 3 az.
Bolton, George, 1 ax, 1 az, 1 bx, 1 bz, 1 cz, 1 dx, 2 dz—3 ex, 5 ez; 1 n.

Bateman, Michael, 2 ax, 3 az, 2 cx, 1 cz, 1 dz—4 ex, 5 ez.
Bustles, John, 1 ax, 1 az, 2 dx, 2 dz—3 ex, 3 ez.
Butler, Thomas, 1 ax, 1 cx, 1 cz, 1 dx, 1 dz—3 ex, 2 ez.
Benson, Mary, 2 az, 2 dx, 1 dz—2 ex, 3 ez.
Bennett, Jean, 1 az, 1 dz—2 ez.
Colvin, William, 1 ax, 1 az, 1 cx—2 ex, 1 ez.
Corbert, Isaac, 3 ax, 1 az, 1 dz—3 ex, 2 ez.
Certain, William, 1 ax—1 ex; 2 n.
Chatham, Elizabeth, 2 az, 1 bz—3 ez; 9 n.
Cossin, Asel, 1 ax, 1 az, 1 bx, 1 bz, 2 cz, 1 dx, 1 dz—3 ex, 5 ez.
Coleman, Roger, 1 ax, 1 az, 1 bx, 2 cx, 1 cz, 3 dx, 2 dz—7 ex, 4 ez.
Cavillare, Charles, 2 ax—"4 ex, 2 ez"; 1 n.
Carson, Robert, 1 ax, 1 az, 1 dz—1 ex, 2 ez.
Comegys, John, 2 ax, 3 az, 1 bx, 1 bz, 1 cx, 1 cz, 2 dx, 4 dz—6 ex, 9 ez.
Comegys, Sarah, 1 az, 1 cx, 1 dz—1 ex, 2 ez; 1 n.
Coppage, Philemon, 1 ax, 1 az, 1 bx, 1 cz, 2 dx—4 ex, 2 ez; 5 n.
Chavies, Thomas, 2 ax, 1 az, 3 dx, 2 dz—5 ex, 3 ez; 2 n.
Conner, Sech, 8 n.
Carmichael, William, 14 n.
Carmichael, Walter, 3 ax, 1 az, 1 dx, 1 dz—4 ex, 2 ez; 24 n.
Coleman, William, 1 ax, 1 az, 2 bx, 2 cx, 2 dx—7 ex, 1 ez.
Carmon, William, 2 ax, 2 az, 1 dz—2 ex, 3 ez.
Cohee, John, 1 ax, 1 az, 2 dx, 1 dz—3 ex, 2 ez.
Coleman, Derias, 1 ax, 1 bz, 1 dx, 1 dz—2 ex, 2 ez.
Cunningham, Thos., 1 ax, 1 az, 3 bz, 1 dx—2 ex, 4 ez; 1 n.
Cox, John, 1 ax, 2 bx, 1 bz, 1 dx—4 ex, 1 ez; 3 n.
Coursey, Thomas, "For," 5 n.
Cavinder, Nathl., 1 ax, 1 az, 2 dz—1 ex, 3 ez.
Comer, William, 1 ax, 2 az—1 ex, 2 ez.
Carson, Mary, 2 az, 1 bz, 1 dx, 2 dz—1 ex, 5 ez.
Davis, John, 2 ax, 1 az, 1 cx, 1 dz—3 ex, 2 ez.
Dudley, Abner, 2 ax, 3 az, 2 bx, 1 cx, 1 dx—7 ex, 2 ez; 5 n.
Demster, John, 1 ax, 1 bz—1 ex, 1 ez; 1 n.
Dixon, James, 1 ax, 2 az, 2 dx, 2 dz—3 ex, 4 ez; 6 n.
Demster, ——, 1 ax, 1 az, 2 dx, 3 dz—3 ex, 4 ez; 1 n.
Dunkin, Robert, 1 ax, 1 az, 1 bz, 2 dz—1 ex, 4 ez.
Downey, Thomas, Junr., 1 ax, 2 az, 1 cx, 3 dx—5 ex, 2 ez.
Dwericks, Valentine, 2 ax, 2 az, 3 dx, 3 dz—5 ex, 5 ez; 8 n.
Deford, William, 2 ax, 2 az, 1 dx, 1 dz—3 ex, 3 ez; 1 n.
Dawson, Thomas, 1 ax, 1 bz, 1 dz—1 ex, 2 ez.
Duglass, William, 1 ax, 1 az, 1 cx, 1 cz—2 ex, 2 ez.
Downey, Thomas, Sr., 2 ax, 2 az, 1 dz—2 ex, 2 ez.

Dailey, James, 1 ax, 1 az, 1 bx, 1 cz, 1 dx—3 ex, 2 ez.
Dailey, John, 1 ax, 1 az, 3 dx, 2 dz—4 ex, 3 ez.
Dyer, Peter, 1 ax, 1 az, 1 bx, 2 cx, 1 cz, 2 dx, 1 dz—6 ex, 3 ez.
Downey, Valentine, 1 ax, 1 az—1 ex, 1 ez.
Downey, Patrick, 1 ax, 1 az, 1 dx—2 ex, 1 ez.
Dean, Capt. John, 2 ax—2 ex.
Dene, Christopher, 1 ax, 1 az, 1 dz—1 ex, 2 ez.
Deford, James, 1 ax, 1 az, 3 dx—4 ex, 1 ez.
Downey, Tabitha, 2 az, 2 dx, 3 dz—2 ex, 5 ez.
Deavinish, Elizabeth, 1 az, 1 dx, 2 dz—1 ex, 3 ez.
Deford, William, Sr., 1 ax, 2 az, 2 dx, 2 dz—3 ex, 4 ez.
Dempster, Rachel, 1 az, 1 bx, 1 bz, 1 cx, 1 dx—3 ex, 2 ez.
Dodo, Joseph, 1 ax, 1 az, 1 dz—1 ex, 2 ez.
Elliott, Rebeckah, 1 ax, 2 az, 1 dz—1 ex, 3 ez; 10 n.
Ezgate, Valentine, 1 ax, 1 az, 1 bz, 2 dz—1 ex, 4 ez.
Eavins, Jonathan, 1 ax, 1 az, 1 dx, 1 dz—2 ex, 2 ez.
Eareckson, James, 1 ax, 2 az, 1 bx, 1 bz, 1 dx—3 ex, 3 ez; 3 n.
Foreman, Arthur, Junr., 1 ax, 3 az, 3 dx, 1 dz—4 ex, 4 ez; 7 n.
Ford, Daniel, Sr., 1 ax, 2 az, 3 bx, 2 cx—6 ex, 2 ez; 1 n.
Ford, Daniel, Junr., 1 ax, 2 az, 1 bx, 2 dx—4 ex, 2 ez.
Foreman, John, Jr., 1 ax, 1 az, 2 dx, 3 dz—3 ex, 4 ez.
Ford, Isaac, Sr., 1 ax, 1 az, 1 bz, 1 dx, 1 dz—2 ex, 3 ez; 2 n.
Foreman, John, Sr., 2 ax, 3 az, 1 bx, 2 dx, 1 dz—5 ex, 4 ez; 12 n.
Ferrell, Edmond, 1 ax, 1 az, 1 bz, 1 dx, 1 dz—2 ex, 3 ez; 9 n.
Foreman, Arthur, son of Arthur, 1 ax, 1 az, 2 cx, 2 dx, 1 dz—5 ex, 2 ez.
Falconer, William, 1 ax, 1 az, 1 bz—2 ex, 1 ez.
Farbush, Jean, 2 az, 1 dx, 1 dz—1 ex, 3 ez.
Gestes, George, 1 ax, 1 az, 1 cz—1 ex, 2 ez.
George, Bartlett, 1 ax, 1 az, 1 cz, 1 dx, 1 dz—2 ex, 3 ez; 2 n.
Gould, Benjn., Esqr., 1 ax, 1 az, 1 bx, 1 bz, 1 cx, 1 cz, 2 dx, 1 dz—5 ex, 4 ez: 5 n.
Gafford, John, Senr., 4 ax, 1 az, 1 bx, 3 bz, 1 cx, 1 dx, 3 dz—7 ex, 7 ez; 2 n.
Graves, Matthew, 2 ax, 1 az, 1 dz—2 ex, 2 ez.
Gooding, James, 3 ax, 2 az, 1 bx, 1 bz, 1 cz, 2 dx, 1 dz—6 ex, 5 ez; 25 n.
Gafford, John, Junr., 1 ax, 1 az, 3 dx, 1 dz—4 ex, 2 ez.
Glandin, Nathan, 1 ax, 1 az, 2 dx, 1 dz—3 ex, 2 ez.
Gordin, Peter, Junr., 2 az, 1 bx, 1 cx, 2 dx, 2 dz—4 ex, 4 ez.
Gould, Richard, 3 ax, 1 az, 1 dz—3 ex, 2 ez; 11 n.
Gafford, Sarah, 2 ax, 1 az, 1 bz, 2 cx, 1 cz—4 ex, 3 ez; 5 n.
Graves, Thomas, 1 ax, 1 az, 1 bx, 1 bz, 1 cx, 3 dx, 2 dz—6 ex, 4 ez.
Gafford, Valentine, 1 ax, 2 az, 4 dx, 2 dz—5 ex, 4 ez.

Gregory, William, 1 ax, 1 az, 2 cx, 6 dx, 1 dz—9 ex, 2 ez.
Gray, William, 1 ax, 1 az, 1 cz, 1 dx, 2 dz—2 ex, 4 ez.
Gafford, Charles, 1 ax, 1 az, 2 dx, 1 dz—3 ex, 2 ez.
Greenwood, William, 2 ax, 1 az, 1 bz, 1 cz, 1 dz—2 ex, 4 ez.
Garnett, William, 1 ax, 1 bz, 1 dz—2 ex, 1 ez.
Games, Stephen, 3 n.
Graves, Elener, 2 az, 1 cx, 1 dx—2 ex, 2 ez.
Hopkins, Thos. Sawyer, 6 n.
Herring, Edward, 1 ax, 1 az, 1 cx, 3 dx, 2 dz—5 ex, 3 ez.
Hopkins, Thomas, 1 ax, 1 az, 1 bz, 1 dz—1 ex, 3 ez.
Hastings, George, 1 ax, 1 az, 2 bz, 1 cx, 1 dz—2 ex, 4 ez; 6 n.
Harris, Charles, 1 ax, 1 az, 4 dx—5 ex, 1 ez; 1 n.
Holding, Richard, 1 ax, 2 az, 1 bx, 1 dz—2 ex, 3 ez; 3 n.
Hackett, John, 1 ax, 1 az, 2 dx, 2 dz—3 ex, 3 ez; 12 n.
Horsley, Richard, 1 ax, 1 az, 2 dx, 2 dz—3 ex, 3 ez.
Hackett, James, 2 ax, 1 az, 1 bx, 2 bz, 1 cx, 1 cz, 3 dz—4 ex, 7 ez; 16 n.
Holding, John, Junr., 2 ax, 1 az, 1 dx, 3 dz—3 ex, 4 ez.
Hunt, Thomas, 1 ax, 1 az, 1 dz—1 ex, 2 ez.
Hackett, Thomas, 1 ax, 2 az, 1 cx, 2 dx, 4 dz—4 ex, 6 ez; 11 n.
Hammond, Elizabeth, 1 az, 1 bx, 1 bz, 1 cx—2 ex, 2 ez.
Hollingsworth, W^m^., 1 ax, 1 az, 4 dx, 2 dz—5 ex, 3 ez.
Harbitt, Charles, 1 ax, 1 az, 1 dx, 1 dz—2 ex, 2 ez.
Hollingsworth, Jas., 1 ax, 1 az, 1 cx, 2 dz—2 ex, 3 ez.
Hawkins, Matthew, 2 ax—2 ex; 4 n.
Hales, William, 1 ax, 1 az, 1 dx, 2 dz—2 ex, 3 ez.
Hall, Jonathan, 2 ax, 1 az, 1 bz, 1 cx, 1 cz—3 ex, 3 ez; 4 n.
Hudson, Walter, 2 ax, 1 az, 3 dz—2 ex, 4 ez.
Hinds, John, 1 ax, 1 az, 1 dz—1 ex, 2 ez.
Johnson, Hance, 1 ax, 1 az, 1 bx, 1 cx, 1 dx, 1 dz—6 ex, 2 ez.
Johnson, John, 1 ax, 1 az, 1 cx, 1 dx—4 ex, 1 ez.
Johnson, George, 2 ax, 1 az—2 ex, 1 ez.
Jacobs, Henry, 1 ax, 1 az, 1 bx—2 ex, 1 ez.
Jones, Robert, 1 ax, 1 az—1 ex, 1 ez.
Jackson, Stafford, 1 ax, 2 az, 1 dx—2 ex, 2 ez.
Jones, John Taylor, 2 ax, 1 az—2 ex, 1 ez.
Jackson, Samuel, 1 ax, 2 az, 1 bx, 1 cx, 1 dx—4 ex, 2 ez.
Kickman, William, 1 ax, 1 az, 2 dx, 2 dz—3 ex, 3 ez; 1 n.
Kemp, John, 1 ax, 1 az—1 ex, 1 ez.
Kent, Emanuel, 4 ax, 1 az, 1 bz, 1 cx, 1 dx—6 ex, 2 ez; 23 n.
Lamdin, Francis, 1 ax, 1 az, 2 dx—3 ex, 1 ez.
Linzy, Edward, 1 ax, 1 az, 1 cz, 3 dx, 1 dz—4 ex, 3 ez.
Lee, Oinson, 1 ax, 1 az, 2 dx, 2 dz—3 ex, 3 ez.

Lee, William, 1 ax, 2 az, 1 cx, 1 dx—3 ex, 2 ez.
Lary, William, 1 ax, 1 az, 1 cx, 1 dx, 1 dz—3 ex, 2 ez.
Lambert, Robert, 1 az, 1 bx, 1 dx, 2 dz—2 ex, 3 ez.
Lee, Rachel, 2 ax, 1 az, 1 bz, 1 cx, 1 cz, 2 dx—5 ex, 3 ez.
Leek, William, 1 ax, 1 az, 1 dx, 1 dz—2 ex, 2 ez.
Lang, William, 1 ax, 1 az, 1 cx, 1 dx, 2 dz—3 ex, 3 ez.
McClane, John, 1 ax, 1 cx, 1 dx—3 ex.
M.Coy, Alice, 2 ax, 2 az, 2 dx, 2 dz—4 ex, 4 ez; 5 n.
Maxwell, Alexander, 1 ax, 1 az, 1 cx, 2 dx—4 ex, 1 ez; 2 n.
Moreland, Henry, 1 ax, 4 dx—5 ex.
McCskiming, Enen, 1 ax, 1 az, 1 cz, 1 dx, 2 dz—2 ex, 4 ez.
MC gonegill, James, 2 ax, 1 az, 1 bx, 1 dz—3 ex, 2 ez; 1 n.
Marsh, Thomas, 1 ax—1 ex; 24 n.
Mumford, John, 1 ax, 1 az—1 ex, 1 ez; 2 n.
Moaner, Timothy, 3 ax, 1 az, 1 bx, 1 bz—4 ex, 2 ez.
Mountseer, William, 1 ax, 1 az, 3 dz—1 ex, 4 ez.
Mand [?], William, 1 ax, 1 az, 2 cx, 1 dx, 2 dz—4 ex, 3 ez.
More, James, 1 ax, 1 az, 1 dx, 1 dz—2 ex, 2 ez.
M'Clannahan, Samuel, 1 ax, 1 az, 1 dx—2 ex, 1 ez.
Milburn, William, 1 ax, 1 az—1 ex, 1 ez.
Mooney, Patrick, 2 ax, 1 az, 2 bz, 1 cx—3 ex, 3 ez.
Morse, William, 1 ax, 1 az, 1 dx, 1 dz—2 ex, 3 ez; 1 n.
Meridith, Thomas, 1 ax, 1 az, 2 dx, 3 dz—3 ex, 4 ez; 7 n.
Milbey, John, 1 ax, 1 az, 1 bz, 1 dx, 2 dz—2 ex, 4 ez; 5 n.
Meeds, Francis, 1 az, 1 bz, 1 dx—1 ex, 2 ez.
MC ginnis, John, 1 az—1 ez. [Original record places these in female column.]
Merphey, John, 1 ax, 1 az, 1 dx—2 ex, 1 ez.
Mold, Walter, 2 ax, 2 az, 2 dz—2 ex, 4 ez.
M'Clannahan, Elizabeth, 2 az, 1 cx, 2 cz, 3 dx, 1 dz—4 ex, 5 ez; 1 n.
Meeds, Thomas, 1 ax, 1 az, 1 cx, 2 dx, 1 dz—4 ex, 3 ez; 3 n.
Massey, Wm. Clark, 1 ax, 1 az, 2 dz—1 ex, 3 ez; 2 n.
Nabb, Sarah, 1 az, 1 bz, 2 dx, 1 dz—2 ex, 3 ez.
Neronam, Daniel, 2 ax, 3 az, 2 ex, 4 dx—8 ex, 3 ez; 1 n.
Nevil, James, 1 ax, 1 az, 1 cx, 3 dx, 1 dz—5 ex, 2 ez; 3 n.
Neronam, John, 1 ax, 1 az, 2 dx—3 ex, 1 ez.
Neronam, Joseph, 1 ax, 1 az, 1 bx, 1 cx, 1 cz, 1 dx, 2 dz—4 ex, 4 ez.
Nerol, John, 2 ax, 1 az, 1 cx, 1 cz, 2 dx, 2 dz—5 ex, 4 ez.
Nevil, Walter, 1 ax, 2 az, 1 bx, 1 dx, 2 dz—3 ex, 4 ez; 3 n.
Neronam, William, 1 ax, 2 az, 2 cz, 2 dx, 2 dz—3 ex, 6 ez.
Nicholson, For Joseph, Jr., 7 n.
Nevil, Sarah, 1 az, 1 cx, 1 cz, 1 dz—1 ex, 3 ez.

Owings, John, 1 ax, 1 bz—1 ex, 1 ez.
Offley, Vinson, 1 ax, 1 az, 2 dx, 2 dz—3 ex, 3 ez; 1 n.
Offley, Benton, 1 ax, 1 az, 1 dx, 2 dz—2 ex, 3 ez.
Offley, John, 2 ax, 1 bz, 1 cx—3 ex, 1 ez.
Price, Margarett,* 2 az, 1 dx, 1 dz—1 ex, 3 ez.
Purse, Gabriel, 1 az, 1 dx, 2 dz—1 ex, 3 ez.
Plummer, Rizdon, 2 ax, 1 az, 1 dx—3 ex, 1 ez; 3 n.
Preston, Rachel, 1 ax, 3 az, 3 bx, 1 bz, 2 cx, 1 dx, 1 dz—7 ex, 5 ez; 3 n.
Pinder, Edward, 2 ax, 2 az, 1 bx, 1 bz, 1 cx, 2 dx—6 ex, 3 ez; 2 n.
Primrose, George, 1 ax, 1 bx, 1 cz—2 ex, 1 ez; 7 n.
Ponder, John, 1 ax, 2 az, 2 dx—3 ex, 2 ez.
Primrose, John, 1 ax, 1 az, 1 cx, 1 dx, 1 dz—3 ex, 2 ez; 6 n.
Peacock, Robert, 1 ax, 1 az, 1 dx, 1 dz—2 ex, 2 ez.
Peacock, John, 1 ax, 1 az—1 ex, 1 ez.
Price, William, 1 ax, 1 az, 1 cx, 1 dz—2 ex, 2 ez.
Pryor, William, 1 ax, 1 az, 5 dx—6 ex, 1 ez; 7 n.
Perrarone, Thomas, 1 ax, 1 az, 1 bz, 1 dz—1 ex, 3 ez.
Pinder, William, 1 ax, 1 cx—2 ex; 1 n.
Pope, Samuel, 1 ax, 1 az, 1 dx, 1 dz—2 ex, 2 ez.
Perraron, George Hy, 1 ax, 1 az, 1 dx, 2 dz—2 ex, 3 ez; 1 n.
Ponder, William, Jr., 1 ax, 1 az—1 ex, 1 ez.
Price, Margarett, 2 az, 1 bx, 1 bz, 1 cz—1 ex, 4 ez.
Poolley, Sarah, 2 ax, 1 az, 1 dz—2 ex, 2 ez.
Permar, James, 1 ax, 1 bz, 1 dx—2 ex, 1 ez.
Ponder, William, Senr., 1 ax, 1 bz—1 ex, 1 ez; 1 n.
Quimby, John, 2 ax, 1 az, 2 cx, 1 dz—4 ex, 2 ez.
Ricords, William, 1 ax, 1 az, 1 bx, 1 cx, 1 cz—3 ex, 2 ez.
Rigby, John, 1 ax, 1 az, 1 cx, 1 dz—2 ex, 2 ez.
Ruth, Thomas, 1 ax, 1 az, 2 cx, 1 dz—3 ex, 2 ez; 1 n.
Reed, Francis, 1 ax, 1 az, 2 bz, 1 ex, 3 dx, 2 dz—5 ex, 3 ez.
Roberts, David, 1 ax, 1 az, 1 bz, 1 cx, 1 cz, 1 dx, 1 dz—3 ex, 4 ez; 4 n.
Rochester, Elizabeth, 1 ax, 1 az, 2 dx—3 ex, 1 ez; 7 n.
Rippeth, James, 1 ax, 1 az, 1 bx, 3 dz—2 ex, 4 ez.
Roberts, James, 2 ax, 1 az, 1 bx, 1 cx, 1 cz, 2 dx, 2 dz—6 ex, 4 ez; 11 n.
Ruth, John (Smith), 1 ax, 1 az, 2 dz—1 ex, 3 ez; 4 n.
Roseberry, James, 2 ax, 2 az, 2 bz, 1 cx, 3 dx, 1 dz—6 ex, 5 ez.
Ruth, John (of Tho[s]), 2 ax, 1 az—2 ex, 1 ez.
Rochester, Mary, 2 az, 1 bx—1 ex, 2 ez; 2 n.
Rogers, Nathan, 1 ax, 2 az, 2 bx, 1 bz, 1 dx, 4 dz—4 ex, 7 ez.
Reed, Samuel, 1 ax, 1 az, 2 dx—3 ex, 1 ez.

* Following "Margarett" appears to be "R[d] Livr" or "R[d] Sior" or "R[d] Senr."

Ralph, Stephen, 1 ax, 2 bx, 1 cz, 2 dz—3 ex, 3 ez.
Reed, William, 2 ax, 2 az, 1 bx, 1 cx, 1 dx, 1 dz—5 ex, 3 ez; 1 n.
Rouse, John, 2 ax, 3 az, 1 bx, 1 bz, 2 dx, 2 dz—5 ex, 6 ez; 1 n.
Rochester, William, 1 ax, 1 az, 1 bx, 1 dx, 2 dz—3 ex, 3 ez.
Rochester, Francis, Jnr., 1 ax, 1 az, 1 bx, 1 bz, 1 cx, 1 cz, 1 dx—4 ex, 3 ez; 10 n.
Roser, John, 1 ax, 2 az, 2 dx, 1 dz—3 ex, 3 ez.
Rochester, Francis, 3 ax, 2 az, 1 bx, 1 cz—4 ex, 3 ez; 3 n.
Syllavin, Sarah, 1 az, 1 dx, 1 dz—1 ex, 2 ez.
Sparks, Wm. of Jas., 1 ax, 1 az, 1 dx, 1 dz—2 ex, 2 ez.
Sparks, Solomon, 1 ax, 1 az, 1 bz, 1 dx, 1 dz—2 ex, 3 ez.
Smith, Josiah, 1 ax, 1 az, 1 bz, 1 cx, 1 cz, 2 dx, 3 dz—4 ex, 6 ez.
Sparks, Abner, 1 ax, 1 az, 1 bx, 2 cx, 2 dx—6 ex, 1 ez.
Smith, Daniel, 1 ax, 1 az—1 ex, 1 ez.
Smith, Thomas, 1 ax, 1 az, 2 dx, 1 dz—3 ex, 2 ez.
Sparks, Edward, 2 ax, 1 az, 1 bz, 1 cx, 1 cz, 1 dx, 1 dz—4 ex, 4 ez.
Spry, Francis, 2 ax, 3 az, 1 bz, 1 dz—2 ex, 5 ez.
Stephans, George, 1 ax, 1 az, 1 cx, 1 cz, 1 dx, 3 dz—3 ex, 5 ez.
Smith, Henry, 2 ax, 1 az, 1 cx, 1 dz—3 ex, 2 ez; 1 n.
Sutton, John, 2 ax, 1 az, 5 dx, 1 dz—7 ex, 2 ez; 5 n.
Smith, James, 1 ax, 2 az, 1 cx, 2 cz, 1 dx—3 ex, 4 ez; 1 n.
Sudler, Joseph, 2 ax, 1 az, 1 bz, 1 cx, 1 dx, 1 dz—4 ex, 3 ez; 11 n.
Sparks, John, Joynr., 1 ax, 1 az—1 ex, 1 ez.
Sparks, James F.,* 1 ax, 1 az, 3 dx, 1 dz—4 ex, 2 ez.
Sparks, Caleb, Senr., 1 ax, 2 az, 1 bx, 1 cx, 2 cz, 3 dx, 1 dz—6 ex, 5 ez.
Seney, John, Esqr., 1 ax, 1 az, 2 bx, 2 cx, 1 dx—6 ex, 1 ez; 11 n.
Spry, John, 1 ax, 1 az, 1 cz, 3 dx, 1 dz—4 ex, 3 ez.
Sparks, John, Long,† 3 ax, 1 dx—4 ex; 6 n.
Sparks, John, T.,‡ 1 ax, 1 az, 2 bz, 1 cz, 4 dx—5 ex, 4 ez.
Smith, Thomas, Weaver, 1 ax, 1 az—1 ex, 1 ez.
Smith, James, Tayler, 1 ax, 2 az, 1 dz—1 ex, 3 ez; 2 n.
Soott, Edward, 2 ax, 1 az, 1 bx, 1 bz, 1 cx, 1 cz, 2 dx, 3 dz—6 ex, 6 ez; 3 n.
Serrell, William, 1 ax, 1 az, 1 cz, 1 dz—1 ex, 3 ez.
Sparks, Levi, 1 ax—1 ex; 7 n.
Sparks, Millenton, 2 ax, 2 az, 1 bx, 1 cz—3 ex, 3 ez.
Seney, Nevil, 1 ax, 1 az, 1 cx, 1 dz—2 ex, 2 ez; 1 n.
Sparks, Nathan, 1 ax, 1 az, 2 bz, 3 cx, 4 dx, 3 dz—8 ex, 6 ez.
Snail, James, 1 ax, 1 az, 1 dx, 1 dz—2 ex, 2 ez.

* Written "James Sparks, F."
† Written "John Sparks, Long."
‡ Written "John Sparks, T."

Syllavin, Sarah, 1 ax, 1 az, 1 bx, 2 dz—2 ex, 3 ez; 3 n.
Sudler [Seidler?], Thomas, 1 ax, 2 az, 1 bx, 1 bz, 1 dx—3 ex, 3 ez; 15 n.
Seward, Thomas, 2 ax, 1 az, 1 bx, 1 cx, 1 dx—5 ex, 1 ez.
Sparks, Mary, 1 ax, 1 az, 2 bz, 1 cx—2 ex, 3 ez.
Sparks, Wm. of B., 1 ax, 1 az, 1 dx, 4 dz—2 ex, 5 ez.
Smith, Hannah, 3 ax, 2 az, 1 dx, 1 dz—4 ex, 3 ez.
Sparks, Thomas, 1 ax, 2 az, 1 bx, 2 cz, 1 dx, 2 dz—3 ex, 6 ez.
Sparks, Jonas, 1 ax, 1 az, 1 cz, 5 dx, 2 dz—6 ex, 4 ez.
Stoops, David, 1 ax, 1 bx, 1 bz—2 ex, 1 ez; 2 n.
Sparks, Vinson, 1 ax, 1 az, 2 dx—3 ex, 1 ez.
Sudler, John, 3 ax, 1 az, 1 dx, 3 dz—4 ex, 4 ez; 9 n.
Seney, William, 1 ax, 1 az, 1 cz, 1 dx, 3 dz—2 ex, 5 ez.
Smith, Joseph, 1 ax, 1 az, 1 dx—2 ex, 1 ez.
Sharadine, Moses, 1 ax, 1 az, 1 cz, 1 dx, 1 dz—2 ex, 3 ez.
Scott, William, 1 ax, 1 az—1 ex, 1 ez.
Scean [Seean?], Elizabeth, 1 az, 1 bz, 1 cz—3 ez.
Sparks, Julyanna, 1 ax, 1 az, 1 cz, 3 dx, 1 dz—4 ex, 3 ez.
Sparks, William (of Wm.), 1 ax, 1 az, 2 dx, 2 dz—3 ex, 3 ez.
Scott, Absalom, 1 ax, 2 az, 1 bz, 1 cz, 1 dx, 1 dz—2 ex, 5 ez.
Turnier, George, 1 ax, 1 az, 1 cz, 2 dx—3 ex, 2 ez.
Thomas, Edward, 1 ax, 1 az, 1 bx, 1 cx, 2 cz, 1 dx, 2 dz—4 ex, 5 ez.
Tilghman, For Edward, 6 n.
Tittle, John, 1 ax, 1 az, 2 bx, 2 cx—5 ex, 1 ez.
Thompson, Samuel, 1 ax, 2 az, 2 dz—1 ex, 4 ez; 12 n.
Thompson, John, 3 ax, 2 az, 1 bx, 1 cz, 3 dz—4 ex, 6 ez; 29 n.
Thompson, William, 1 ax, 1 az, 3 cx, 2 dx, 3 dz—6 ex, 4 ez.
Tilghman, Richard ye 4th, 3 ax, 2 az, 1 dz—3 ex, 3 ez; 25 n.
Taylor, Thomas, 1 ax, 1 az, 1 bx, 1 dx—3 ex, 1 ez; 1 n.
Taylor, Ninan, 1 bx, 1 bz, 1 dx—2 ex, 1 ez.
Thompson, Richard, 1 ax, 1 az, 1 dz—1 ex, 2 ez.
Taylor, Elizebeth, 1 ax, 2 az, 1 bx, 1 bz, 1 dx—3 ex, 3 ez; 3 n.
Tippins, James, 1 ax, 1 az, 2 dz—1 ex, 3 ez; 3 n.
Turner, William, 1 ax, 1 az, 2 dx, 1 dz—3 ex, 2 ez.
Taylor, Ruth, 1 az, 1 bx, 1 dz—1 ex, 2 ez.
Voice, Ezabela, 1 az, 1 cx—1 ex, 1 ez.
Wright, Edward, 1 ax, 1 az, 1 cx, 1 cz, 2 dx, 1 dz—4 ex, 3 ez; 5 n.
Wells, Benjamin, 1 ax, 1 az, 1 bz, 2 cx, 2 dx, 3 dz—5 ex, 5 ez.
Wiggins, Benjamin, 1 ax, 1 az, 1 bx, 1 cz, 2 dx, 3 dz—4 ex, 5 ez.
Wiggins, Charles, 2 ax, 2 az, 1 bx, 1 cx, 1 dx—5 ex, 2 ez; 5 n.
Willson, George, 1 ax, 1 bz—1 ex, 1 ez.
Williamson, George, 2 ax, 1 az, 1 cz, 1 dx—3 ex, 2 ez.
Wickes, Joseph, 2 ax, 1 az, 1 cx, 1 dx, 2 dz—4 ex, 3 ez; 1 n.

Whittington, John, 1 ax, 1 az, 1 dx—2 ex, 1 ez; 6 n.
Wickes, Matthew, 1 ax, 2 az, 1 bx, 1 bz, 1 cx—3 ex, 3 ez; 2 n.
Williams, Thomas, 1 ax, 1 az, 1 dx, 3 dz—2 ex, 4 ez.
Wilkinson, Thos. (Mast^r.), 1 ax, 1 az, 1 bx—2 ex, 1 ez.
Wiggins, Elizabeth, 2 ax, 2 az, 1 bz, 1 dx—3 ex, 3 ez.
Wiggins, Ebenezer, 1 ax, 1 az, 1 dx, 1 dz—2 ex, 2 ez.
Ware, James, 2 ax, 1 bz, 1 dz—2 ex, 2 ez; 1 n.
Wickes, Simon, 2 ax, 1 az, 1 bz, 1 cx, 1 dx, 4 dz—4 ex, 6 ez; 8 n.
Willson, John, 1 ax, 1 az, 2 dz—1 ex, 3 ez.
White, John, 1 ax, 1 az, 3 dz—1 ex, 4 ez.
Wadkins, Eloner, 1 az, 1 cx—1 ex, 1 ez.
Williss, Mary, 2 az, 2 dz—4 ez.
Wieley, Epheraim, 1 ax, 1 az, 3 dz—1 ex, 4 ez.
Young, William, 3 ax, 3 az, 1 bx—6 ex, 3 ez; 4 n. [2 ex omitted by enumerator.]
Warner, Mary, 1 n.
Straglers, 9 ax, 2 az.
Totals, 388 ax, 377 az, 86 bx, 90 bz, 123 cx, 74 cz, 340 dx, 331 dz—931 ex, 860 ez; 800 n.

Septr. 22^d. 1776 Mark Benton made Oath that according to the Account given by the different House Keepers and from the best Information he has been able to procure the above is a true List of the Number of Persons in Town Hundred except a few Indians.

Sworn before TURBUTT WRIGHT.

Queen Anns County, Upper Hundred, Kent Island, Census of 1776,

"A List of Inhabitants in the uper Hundred Kent Island taken by me the Subscriber by Vertue of a Warrant Granted by the Committee of Observation for Queen Anns County for that Purpose Dated the 22th day of July, 1776."

This Census is written upon one sheet $13^1/_4'' \times 16^1/_2''$. "Above 21 years" is indicated by "a"; "b" means "Between 16 and 21"; "c" means "Between 12 and 16 yrs."; "d" means "Under 12 yrs." "x" means White males; "z" means White females. "n" means "Total Blacks," or "Blacks."

"House Keepers Names":

Emory, Arthur (Black), 3 an, 2 bn, 1 cn, 1 dn—females 2 an, 2 dn; 11 n.

Sneed, Richard, 1 ax, 2 cx, 2 dx, 1 dz.
Wells, Tobias, 1 ax, 3 az, 1 bz, 1 cz; 17 n.
Jeffers, William, 1 ax, 1 az, 1 cz, 1 dx.
Jeffery, Beck (Black), 5 dn—females, 1 an, 1 bn, 2 cn; 9 n.
Waters, Susanh, 3 ax, 1 az, 1 dz; 6 n.
Stevens, James, 1 ax, 1 az, 1 bx, 1 cz, 2 dx, 3 dz; 9 n.
Brion, John, 1 ax, 3 az, 3 dx, 1 dz.
Toyner, Asalum, 1 ax, 1 az, 1 bz, 1 cx, 1 cz, 1 dx.
Toyner, Absalum, Junr., 1 ax, 1 az, 1 bx, 3 dz.
Benton, Franson, 1 ax, 1 az, 1 cx, 1 dx.
Deoachbrume, Lues, 2 ax, 2 az, 1 dz; 9 n.
Wollyhand, Fransis, 1 ax, 3 az, 3 cx, 2 dx, 2 dz.
Osbond, Samuel, 1 ax, 1 az, 1 dx.
Collear, Thomas, 1 ax, 1 az, 1 dz.
Tanner, Phillemon, 2 ax, 1 az, 2 cz—2 n.
Joyner, William, 1 ax, 2 az, 1 cx, 1 dx, 2 dz.
Robson, Elizebeth, 2 az, 1 cx, 1 dz.
Goodhand, James, 2 ax, 1 az, 1 dz—4 n.
Chambers, Richard, 1 ax, 1 az, 1 bx, 1 cx—1 n.
Chambers, Richard, Jnr., 1 ax, 1 az, 3 dz—3 n.
Lanch, Samuel, 1 az—3 n. [No white males enumerated.]
Wilson, Rebecca, 2 az—8 n.
Joyner, Dobs, 2 ax, 2 az, 1 bx, 1 dz—1 n.
Wright, James, 3 ax, 3 az, 1 bz, 1 cx, 1 cz, 3 dx, 2 dz—2 n.
Richardson, Benjamin, 1 ax, 3 az, 1 bx, 1 cx, 2 dx, 1 dz—7 n.
Welch, James, 1 ax, 1 az, 1 dx, 2 dz.
Ringgold, Thomas, 1 ax, 1 az, 2 bx, 1 cx, 3 dx, 2 dz—17 n.
Barnet, Charles, 1 ax, 1 az, 1 bx, 1 bz, 1 cx.
Brown, Edward, 3 ax, 1 az, 1 dx, 1 dz—9 n.
Maradeth, Benjamin, 1 ax, 1 az, 2 dx, 1 dz—1 n.
Greanwhich, Beck (Black), 3 n.
Goodhand, Marmaduke, 1 ax, 2 az, 1 bx, 1 cz, 2 dx, 2 dz—13 n.
Goodhand, Letitia, 1 ax, 2 az—4 n.
Mason, William, 2 ax, 2 az, 1 cx, 1 dz—1 n.
Hampton, Thomas, 1 ax, 1 az, 1 bx, 1 dx—1 n.
Brawn, Aquila, 1 ax, 3 az, 3 dx, 4 dz—8 n.
Blunt, Labin, 1 ax, 1 az, 1 bx, 1 cz, 3 dx, 2 dz.
Shney [?], Sara, 1 ax, 1 az, 1 cz—3 n.
Smyth, William, 2 ax—3 n.
Rouse, Sara, 1 az, 1 dz.
Hutchings, James, 14 ax, 2 az, 1 dx—25 n.
Sinners, Charles, 1 ax, 1 az.

Coger, Samuel (Black), 9 n.
Stevens, William, 2 ax, 2 az, 1 bx, 1 cx, 2 dx, 2 dz—5 n.
Sudler, Emory, 2 ax—12 n.
Downey, William, 1 ax, 1 az, 2 dx, 1 dz.
Molds [Motds?], Dannil, 1 ax, 1 dx.
Grigg, Richard, 2 ax, 1 az.
Jones, Abner, 1 ax, 1 az, 2 dx, 5 dz.
Horn, Elizebeth, 3 az, 1 cx, 1 dz—4 n.
Sinners, James, 1 ax, 1 az, 2 dx.
Totals, 69 ax, 71 az, 12 bx, 4 bz, 15 cx, 11 cz, 45 dx, 49 dz—209 n.

Prise, Thomas, 2 ax, 2 az, 2 cx, 1 dx, 1 dz—1 n.
Sneed, Moses, 1 ax, 1 az, 1 bx, 2 dx, 2 dz—4 n.
Hand, John, 1 ax, 1 az, 1 dx, 1 dz.
Tannar, Benjaman, 1 ax, 1 az, 1 bx, 1 dx.
Faulkner, Gilbert, 1 ax, 1 az, 1 dz.
Wilson, Thomas (Black), 4 n.
Flamer, John (Black), 5 n.
Greanwhich, Sheary (Black), 16 n.
Aleway, Thomas, 1 ax, 1 az—2 n.
Whefing [?], Nath, 1 ax, 1 az, 1 dx, 1 dz.
Webb, Harry, 1 ax, 1 az, 1 dx, 3 dz.
Downey, William, 1 ax.
Tucker, James, 1 ax, 1 az.
Tolson, Alexander, 1 ax, 1 az, 1 bz, 1 cx, 1 cz, 4 dx—3 n.
Bright, Fransis, 1 ax, 1 az, 1 cx, 2 cz, 1 dx—8 n.
Kingsbury, Gabriel, 2 ax, 1 az, 2 bx, 1 bz, 1 cx, 1 dx, 2 dz—10 n.
Bright, Ann, 1 ax, 1 az, 1 bz, 1 dx—4 n.
Watters, John, 1 ax, 1 dx—8 n.
Watters, Benjamin, 1 ax, 1 az, 1 cz, 2 dx, 3 dz—9 n.
Richardson, Benjamin, Junr., 1 ax, 1 az, 2 dz—9 n.
Wilson, Richard (Black), 1 an, 2 cn, 1 dn—females, 1 an, 1 bn, 1 dn—7 n.
Macconikin, Elias, 1 ax, 2 az, 1 bx, 1 cz—13 n.
Kirby, Benjamin, 1 ax, 1 az, 1 bz, 3 dx, 1 dz—7 n.
Wilson, James (Black), 1 ax, 1 az, 2 dx—4 n.
Goodhand, Nathaniel, 1 ax, 1 az, 1 dx, 1 dz—4 n.
Barnes, Thomas, Junr., 2 ax, 1 az, 1 bx, 1 cx, 1 dx, 2 dz—11 n.
Barns, Thomas, 2 ax, 1 az—6 n.
Surcom, Thomas, 3 ax, 3 az.
Grainger, Martin, 1 ax, 2 az, 1 dx, 3 dz.
Weaver, William, 1 ax, 1 az, 1 bz, 1 cx, 2 dx, 2 dz.

Spurry, John, 1 ax, 1 az, 1 bx, 1 bz, 1 cx, 1 cz, 1 dz.
Carter, Richard, 3 ax, 3 az—12 n.
Carter, Arthur, 1 ax, 1 az, 1 cz, 1 dx, 4 dz—7 n.
Baxter, Thomas, 1 ax, 1 az, 3 dx, 2 dz; 2 n.
Harper, Samuel, 1 ax, 1 az, 3 dx, 3 dz.
Lucis, John, 1 ax, 1 az, 2 dx, 3 dz.
Greanwhich, James (Black), 1 an—females, 2 an, 1 bn; 4 n.
Macconichin, William, 1 ax, 1 az, 1 bz, 1 cx, 1 dx; 2 n.
Baxter, William, 1 ax, 1 az, 1 bz, 2 cx, 1 dx; 11 n.
Hoxter, John, 1 ax, 1 az, 1 bx, 1 bz, 1 cz, 1 dx, 3 dz.
Legg, James, 1 ax, 1 az, 1 cx, 1 cz, 2 dx, 1 dz.
Hoxter, Ann, 2 az, 1 dx, 3 dz.
Legg, William, 1 ax, 1 az, 5 dx.
Legg, John, 1 ax, 2 bx, 1 dx.
Legg, Mathew, 1 ax, 1 az, 2 bz, 1 cx, 3 dx, 2 dz; 13 n.
Finnix, Andrew, 1 ax, 1 az, 1 dz; 1 n.
Watters, Robert, 2 ax, 1 az, 3 dz; 7 n.
Wright, Greenbutt, 1 ax; 5 n.
Ringgold, Jacob, 1 ax, 1 bz, 1 dx; 11 n.
Brink [Burk?], James, 1 ax, 1 az, 1 bz, 3 dx, 1 dz; 3 n.
Greanwhich, Rachael (Black), 1 dx—females, 1 an, 1 dn; 3 n.
Crick, Elizabeth, 2 dx, 1 az.
Totals, 52 ax, 48 az, 10 bx, 13 bz, 13 cx, 9 cz, 55 dx, 53 dz; 216 n.

"July 25th 1776 Alexander Waters makes Oath that according to the account given him by the different House-keepers, and from the best Information he has been able to procure, the within is a true list of the Number of persons in the upper hundred of Kent Island.

before J. Bordley."

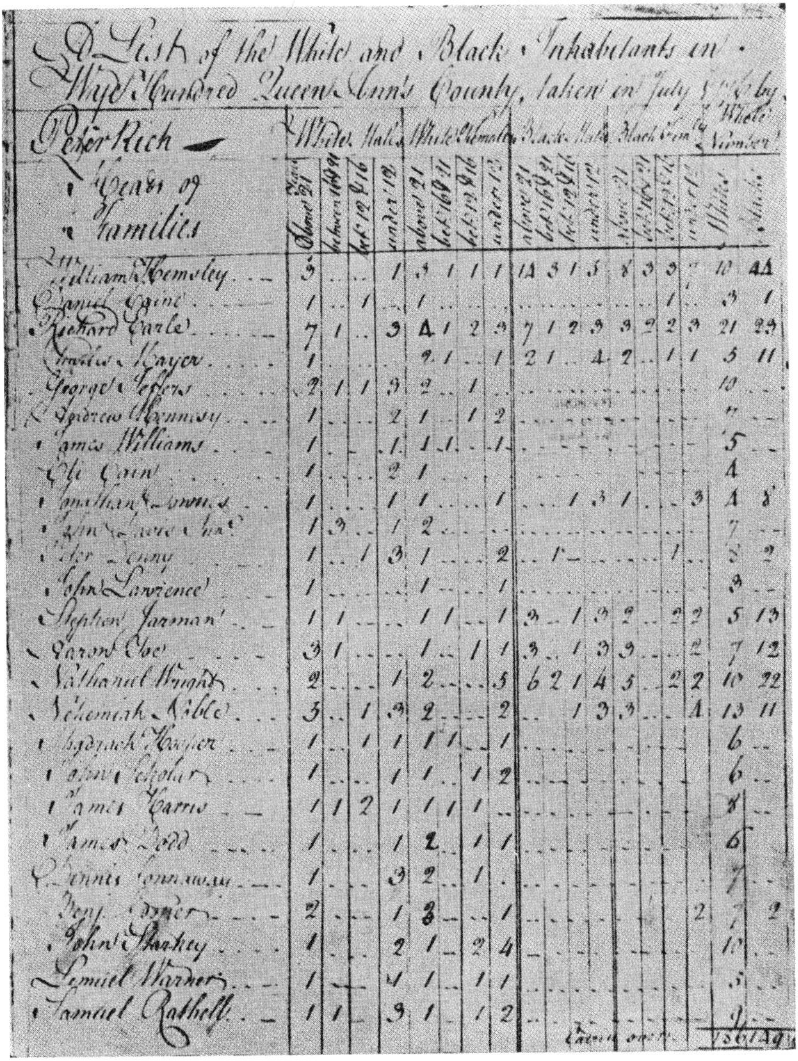

A List of the White and Black Inhabitants in Wye Hundred Queen Ann's County, taken in July 1776 by Peter Rich

Heads of Families	White Males above 21	between 16 & 21	bet. 10 & 16	under 10	White Females above 21	bet. 16 & 21	bet. 10 & 16	under 10	Black Males above 21	bet. 16 & 21	bet. 10 & 16	under 10	Black Females above 21	bet. 16 & 21	bet. 10 & 16	under 10	Whole Number White	Black
Wm. William Hemsley	3	..	..	1	3	1	1	1	14	3	1	5	8	3	3	7	10	44
Daniel Caine	1	..	1	..	1	..	..	..	..	..	..	..	..	..	1	..	3	1
Richard Earle	7	1	..	3	4	1	2	3	7	1	2	3	3	2	2	3	21	23
Charles Mayer	1	..	..	..	2	1	..	1	2	1	..	4	2	..	1	1	5	11
George Jeffers	2	1	1	3	2	..	1	..	..	..	..	..	..	..	..	..	10	..
Andrew Hennesy	1	..	..	2	1	..	1	2	..	..	..	..	..	..	..	..	7	..
James Williams	1	..	..	1	1	1	..	1	..	..	..	..	..	..	..	..	5	..
Eli Cain	1	..	..	2	1												4	
Jonathan Downes	1	..	..	1	1	..	..	1	..	..	1	3	1	..	..	3	4	8
John Lowe Junr.	1	3	..	1	2	..	..	..	..	..	..	..	..	..	..	..	7	..
Peter Denny	1	..	1	3	1	..	..	2	..	1	..	..	..	..	1	..	8	2
John Lawrence	1	..	..	..	1	..	..	1	..	..	..	..	..	..	..	..	3	..
Stephen Jarman	1	1	..	..	1	1	..	1	3	..	1	3	2	..	2	2	5	13
Aaron Cloe	3	1	..	..	1	..	1	1	3	..	1	3	3	..	..	2	7	12
Nathaniel Wright	2	..	..	1	2	..	..	5	6	2	1	4	5	..	2	2	10	22
Nehemiah Noble	3	..	1	3	2	..	..	2	..	..	1	3	3	..	..	4	13	11
Shadrach Harper	1	..	1	1	1	1	..	1	..	..	..	..	..	..	..	..	6	..
John Scholar	1	..	..	1	1	..	1	2	..	..	..	..	..	..	..	..	6	..
James Harris	1	1	2	1	1	1	1	..	..	..	..	..	..	..	..	..	8	..
James Dodd	1	..	..	1	2	..	1	1									6	
Dennis Conaway	1	..	..	3	2	..	1	..	..	..	..	..	..	..	..	..	7	..
Benj. Comer	2	..	..	1	3	..	..	1	..	..	..	..	..	..	..	2	7	2
John Starkey	1	..	..	2	1	..	2	4	..	..	..	..	..	..	..	..	10	..
Lemuel Warner	1	..	..	1	1	..	1	1	..	..	..	..	..	..	..	..	5	..
Samuel Rathell	1	1	..	3	1	..	1	2	..	..	..	..	..	..	..	..	9	..
Carried over																	136	149

Heads of Families	W. Males Above 21	W. Males between 16 & 21	W. Males bet. 12 & 16	W. Males under 12	W. Females Above 21	W. Females bet. 16 & 21	W. Females bet. 12 & 16	W. Females under 12	B. Males Above 21	B. Males bet. 16 & 21	B. Males bet. 12 & 16	B. Males under 12	B. Females Above 21	B. Females bet. 16 & 21	B. Females bet. 12 & 16	B. Females under 12	Whole Number Whites	Whole Number Blacks
																	186	149
Elisabeth Walker	1				1												2	
Hynson Downes Sr.	2	1			2	1			1		1	4	2			4	6	12
James Johnson	1			1	1			2									5	
H. Downes Junr.	1			1	1		1						1				4	1
Jas. Bartlett	1	1	1	3	2			1		1							9	1
Richd. Emerson	1			2	1			3									7	
Phil. Pratt	1		1	3	1	1		1									8	
Zeb. Green	1	1			1			2							1		5	1
John Hargadine	1	1	1		1	1	1	5			1		1				11	2
Edwd. Smith	2				2												4	
Thomas Olson	2			3	1	1			2			2					7	4
Thomas Trezare	2	1	2	4	2	1	1	2									15	
John Trezare	1	2		3	2		2	3		1				1			13	2
James Jones	2	1		3	1		1	2	1			1	1				10	3
John Dodd	1		1		2			1	2								5	2
Risden Hutchings	3				1				1			1	1		1		4	4
Theodore Cox	3	1	1	3	3	1		2	1			2	1				14	4
Vincent Emerson	1				1												2	
John Stark	1			1	1			1									4	
John Jeffers	1					1		1									3	
George Dodd	1		1	2	1		1	2									8	
Thomas Bradley	1			1	2			2									6	
Edwd. Hargadine	2	1	1	3	2	1		2									12	
Carried over																	350	185

Heads of Families	W. Males Above 21	W. Males bet. 16 & 21	W. Males bet. 12 & 16	W. Males under 12	W. Females Above 21	W. Females bet. 16 & 21	W. Females bet. 12 & 16	W. Females under 12	B. Males Above 21	B. Males bet. 16 & 21	B. Males bet. 12 & 16	B. Males under 12	B. Females Above 21	B. Females bet. 16 & 21	B. Females bet. 12 & 16	B. Females under 12	Whole Number Whites	Whole Number Blacks
																	230	185
John Barneclaw	2	1	2	3	2			1						1			11	1
Andw. Barneclaw	1		1	1	1		1	1	1				1				6	2
Will Evans	1			2	1				3	1		1	4			1	4	10
[illegible] McCallister	2			1	1												4	
Will Cooney	1	1		1	1	1		1									6	
Will Emory Capt.	1			1	1	1		2	1		1	1					6	3
John Ross	3		1	1	2			1	1								8	1
Mark Dodd	1	1		2	2			2									8	
Richard Harris	1				1			1									3	
Charles Saunders	1			1	1											1	3	1
James E. St. Tee	1	1		1	2		1	4									10	
John Ireland	3			4	3	1		2				1	2		1	2	13	6
James D. Bennet	1			2	2		1										6	
Geo: Hanson	5			1	2			2						1			10	1
H. Pratt Senr.	1				2			1	2	1	2	2	1		1	2	4	11
Turbut Wright	1		1	2	3		1	1	6		4	2	3	1	1	5	9	24
Abs. Fowler	1			3	1			3									8	
Will Hackett	2		1		1			3	3		1	5	2		1		7	12
Nathan Wilkinson	1			3	1		1	2	1	1			1		2		8	5
Benj. Pratts Overseer																	2	
Jos. Hubbard	1				1													
Revd. Hugh Neal	1	1					1		2		2	3	2	1			3	10
Capt. John Davis	1	1			1	1	1			1		2	3			3	5	9
Sol. Wright	1			1	1	1			1			3	1			2	4	7
Margt. Higgins			1	5	1			1							1		8	1
Carried over																	506	289

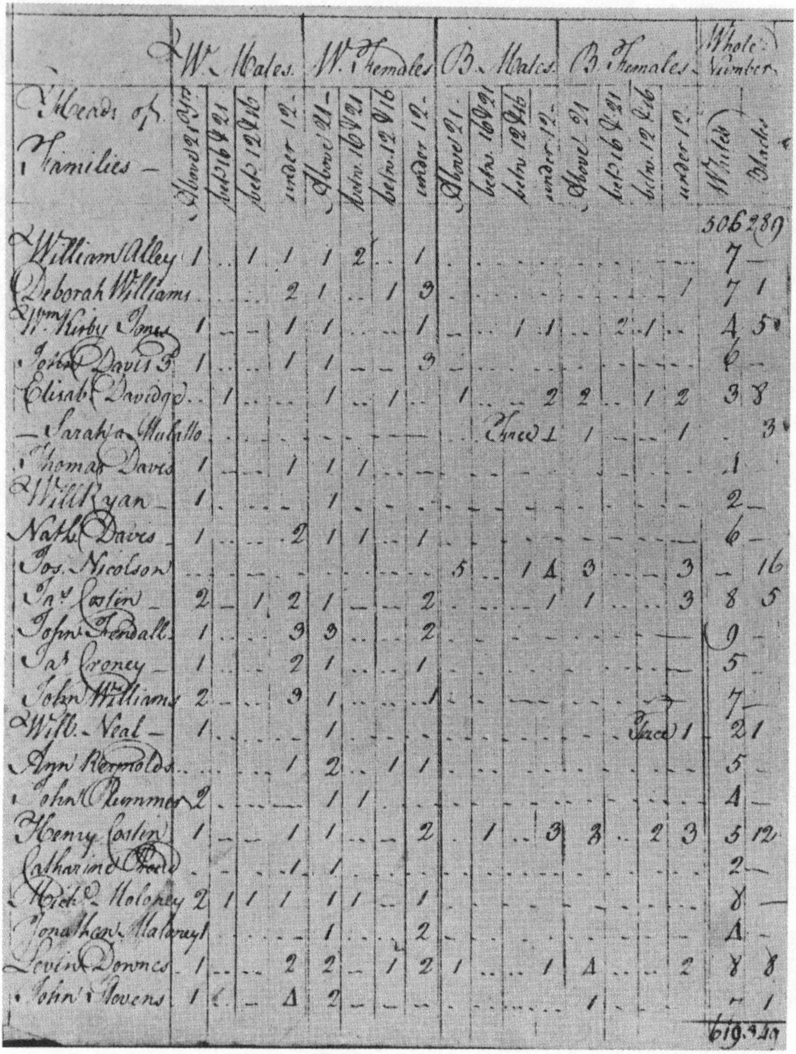

Heads of Families	W. Males: Above 21	W. Males: betw 16 & 21	W. Males: betw 12 & 16	W. Males: under 12	W. Females: Above 21	W. Females: betw 16 & 21	W. Females: betw 12 & 16	W. Females: under 12	B. Males: Above 21	B. Males: betw 16 & 21	B. Males: betw 12 & 16	B. Males: under 12	B. Females: Above 21	B. Females: betw 16 & 21	B. Females: betw 12 & 16	B. Females: under 12	Whole Number: Whites	Whole Number: Blacks
																	506	289
William Alley	1		1	1	1	2		1									7	—
Deborah Williams				2	1		1	3								1	7	1
Wm. Kirby Jones	1			1	1			1			1	1		2	1		4	5
John Davis 3	1			1	1			3									6	—
Elisab. Davidge		1			1		1		1			2	2		1	2	3	8
Sarah a Mulatto										Free		1	1			1	.	3
Thomas Davis	1			1	1	1											4	
Will. Ryan	1				1												2	—
Nathl. Davis	1			2	1	1		1									6	—
Jos. Nicolson									5		1	4	3			3	—	16
Jas. Coslin	2		1	2	1			2				1	1			3	8	5
John Kendall	1			3	3			2									9	—
Jas. Croney	1			2	1			1									5	—
John Williams	2			3	1			1									7	—
Will. Neal	1				1										Free	1	2	1
Ann Reynolds				1	2		1	1									5	—
John Plummer	2				1	1											4	—
Henry Coslin	1			1	1			2		1		3	3		2	3	5	12
Catharine Creed				1	1												2	—
Michl. Moloney	2	1	1	1	1	1		1									8	—
Jonathan Maloney	1				1			2									4	—
Levin Downes	1			2	2		1	2	1			1	4			2	8	8
John Stevens	1			4	2								1				7	1
																	619	349

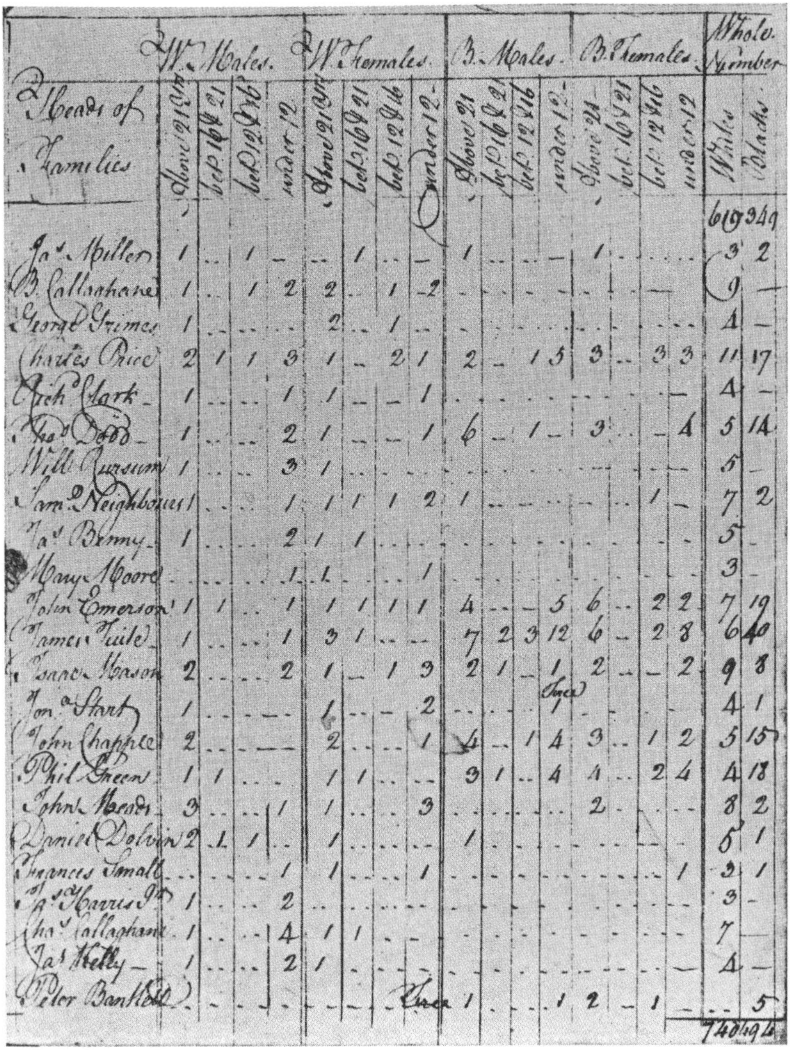

Heads of Families	W. Males: Above 21	bet. 16 & 21	bet. 12 & 16	under 12	W. Females: Above 21	bet. 16 & 21	bet. 12 & 16	under 12	B. Males: Above 21	bet. 16 & 21	bet. 12 & 16	under 12	B. Females: Above 21	bet. 16 & 21	bet. 12 & 16	under 12	Whole Number: Whites	Blacks
																	619	349
Jas. Miller	1		1			1			1				1				3	2
B. Callaghane	1		1	2	2		1	2									9	
George Grimes	1				2		1										4	
Charles Price	2	1	1	3	1		2	1	2		1	5	3		3	3	11	17
Richd. Clark	1			1	1			1									4	
Thos. Dodd	1			2	1			1	6		1		3			4	5	14
Will Pursum	1			3	1												5	
Saml. Neighbours	1			1	1	1	1	2	1						1		7	2
Jas. Benny	1			2	1	1											5	
Mary Moore				1	1			1									3	
John Emerson	1	1		1	1	1	1	1	4			5	6		2	2	7	19
James Tuile	1			1	3	1			7	2	3	12	6		2	8	6	40
Isaac Mason	2			2	1		1	3	2	1		1	2			2	9	8
Jona. Start	1				1			2				Free 1					4	1
John Chapple	2				2			1	4		1	4	3		1	2	5	15
Phil Green	1	1			1	1			3	1		4	4		2	4	4	18
John Meads	3			1	1			3					2				8	2
Daniel Dolvin	2	1	1		1				1								5	1
Frances Small				1	1			1								1	3	1
Jas. Harris Jr.	1			2													3	
Chas. Callaghane	1			4	1	1											7	
Jas. Kelly	1			2	1												4	
Peter Bankhead								Free	1			1	2		1			5
																	740	494

Heads of Families	W. Males				W. Females				B. Males				B. Females				Whole Number	
	Above 21 Years	bet. 16 & 21	bet. 12 & 16	under 12	Above 21	bet. 16 & 21	bet. 12 & 16	under 12	Above 21	betn. 16 & 21	bet. 12 & 16	under 12	Above 21	bet. 16 & 21	bet. 12 & 16	under 12	Whites	Blacks
																	740	494
Thos. Emory	1	2	.	1	1	1	1	.	4	1	2	3	3	1	1	6	7	21
Peter Rich	1	2	..	2	2	..	..	2	..	..	..	1	..	..	1	..	9	2
Mary Mitchell	..	..	..	1	1	..	..	..	..	..	..	..	..	..	..	..	2	—
John Vanderfor	1	..	..	..	..	..	..	..	..	..	..	..	..	..	..	..	1	..
																	759	517

August 12th 1770. Peter Rich makes Oath that according to the Account given him by the different House Keepers and from the best Information he has been able to procure, the within is a true List of the Number of persons in Wye Hundred

Sworn before

J Bordley

TALBOTT COUNTY

Talbott County, Bay Hundred, Census of 1776,

"Talb[t] Co[ty]. Sc[l].

Upon the 3[d]. day of September 1776, James Earl Denny maketh Oath on the holy evangels of Almighty God that this & the following pages beginning with No. 1 and ending No. 4 is a just & true List which contains all the inhabitants in Bay hundred to the best of his knowledge—Except those who were inlisted in the flying Camp.

J. S. GIBSON."

SYMBOLS USED:

"a" means "Above 50 years"; "b" means "Between 16 and 50"; "c" means "Under 16," "x" means "White males," "z" means "White females"; "m" means "Black males," "f" means "Black females." In a few instances "n" is used for "Negro," without specification in combinations.

Thus the third line means 2 white males between 16 and 50, 1 white female between 16 and 50; 3 white males under 16, 1 white female under 16; 1 black female between 16 and 50. Blacks follow the ";" and at end of the line. ["Grace Nathaniel," illustration.]

Woulds, James, 1 bx, 1 bz, 4 cz.
Dodson, Thomas, 1 bx, 1 bz, 4 cx, 3 cz.
Grace, Nathaniel, 2 bx, 1 bz, 3 cx, 1 cz; 1 bf.
Benson, Perry, 1 bx, 1 bz, 7 cx, 3 cz; 1 cf.
Benson, Nicholas, 1 bx, 2 bz, 1 cx, 2 cz.
Chezum, Dan[l]., 1 bx, 1 bz; 1 cm.
Hoithley [Keithley?], James, 1 bx, 1 bz, 1 cx, 1 cz.
Harrington, Rich[d]., 1 bx, 1 bz, 1 cx, 1 cz.
Thomlinson, Thom[s]., 2 bx, 3 bz, 2 cz.
Nuols, Mary, 4 bz; 1 am, 1 bm, 3 bf.
Townsend, Thom[s]., 2 bx, 2 bz, 5 cx, 1 cz.
Vinton, Solomon, 1 az, 2 bx, 2 bz, 1 cx, 1 cz.
Love, Thom[s]., 1 ax, 1 az, 1 bx, 2 bz, 1 cz.
Ashcraft, Thom[s]., 1 bx, 1 bz, 2 cx, 3 cz.
Harrison, James, 1 bx, 1 bz, 2 cx, 1 cz.
Tenant, Mable, 1 az, 1 bz, 3 cx.
Bromwell, Mary, 1 az, 1 bx, 1 bz.
Blades, John, 1 az, 2 bx, 1 bz, 6 cx; 1 af.
Glieve, George, 2 bx, 1 bz.
Hopkins, John Johnnings, 2 bx, 4 cx, 1 cz; 1 bm, 1 bf, 2 cm, 1 cf.

Royal, Joseph, 1 ax, 1 bz, 1 cx.
Brown, Peter, 1 ax, 1 az, 2 cx, 2 cz.
Howes, James, 1 bx, 2 bz, 2 cx, 2 cz.
Wales, Robt., 1 bx, 1 bz, 3 cx, 3 cz.
Bouff, John, 1 af, 1 bx, 1 bz, 3 cx, 1 cz.
Lenard [Lenards?], Jonathan, 1 bx, 1 bz, 2 cx, 1 cz.
Hopkins, W^{m}., 1 bx, 1 bz, 2 cx, 1 cz.
Rolle [Molle?], John, 1 az, 1 bx, 2 bz; 3 bm, 2 bf, 6 cm, 2 cf.
Richardson, Danl., 1 bx, 1 bz, 1 cx, 4 cz; 1 bf.
Hambleton, W^{m}., Junr., 1 bx, 1 bz, 1 cx, 1 cz; 3 bm, 5 bf, 3 cm, 2 cf.
Vickers, Charles, 1 bx, 1 bz, 2 cz.
Applegirth, Robert, 1 bx, 2 bz, 5 cx, 2 cz.
Ledenham, Nathaniel, 2 bx, 2 bz, 1 cx.
Barrow, James, 2 az, 2 bx, 1 bz, 1 cz; 1 bm, 1 cm, 1 cf.
Greenfield, Elizabeth, 1 bz, 2 cx.
Porter, Joseph, 2 bx, 1 bz, 4 cx, 1 cz; 1 bm, 1 cf.
Porter, John, 1 az, 2 bx, 2 bz, 6 cx, 1 cz.
Hall, John, 1 ax, 1 az, 1 bx, 1 bz, 1 cz.
Sherwood, Phillimon, 1 ax, 2 az, 1 cz; 2 af, 1 bf, 2 cm, 1 cf.
Spencer, Phillimon, 2 bx, 3 bz, 3 cx, 1 cz; 1 bm, 1 bf, 1 cf.
Caultz, James, 1 ax, 1 az, 2 bx, 1 bz, 1 cx, 1 cz.
Rimmer (?), James, 1 ax, 1 az, 2 bx, 2 bz, 2 cx, 4 cz.
Porter, Jane, 1 ax, 1 bx, 2 bz, 1 cz.
Cummings, Mary, 3 bz, 1 cx, 3 cz.
Ringrose [Kingrose?], Aaron, 1 bx, 1 bz, 2 cx, 1 cz.
Sinclare, Sawney, 1 ax, 3 bx, 1 bz, 2 cx, 3 cz.
Winters, Jonathan, 1 bx, 1 bz, 1 cx; 1 bf, 2 cf.
Horney, John, 1 ax, 2 bx, 1 bz, 3 cx, 2 cz.
Porter, Hewes, 1 bx, 1 bz, 2 cz.
Lambden, Wrightson, 1 bx, 1 bz; 1 bm, 2 bf, 3 cm, 1 cf.
Spencer, Joseph, 1 bx, 1 bz, 2 cx; 1 bm, 1 bf, 1 cm.
Edgar, Adam, 1 ax, 2 bx, 1 bz, 2 cx, 2 cz.
Hills, Elizabeth, 1 bz, 2 cx, 3 cz.
Daves, Willm., 1 bx, 3 bz, 1 cx; 1 cf.
Daffin, Charles, 1 bx, 3 bz; 1 af, 11 bm, 8 bf, 1 cm, 5 cf.
Dawson, George, 1 bx; 2 bm, 2 bf, 2 cm.
Morsal, James, 1 ax, 3 bz; 3 bm, 2 bf, 4 cm, 2 cf.
Wrightson, James, Junr., 1 bx, 1 bz, 1 cx, 2 cz; 1 bm, 2 bf, 1 cf.
Haddaway, John, 1 bx, 1 bz, 1 cx, 1 cz.
Wrightson, Jonathan, 1 bx, 1 bz, 2 cx, 2 cz.
Cummings, Thomas, Junr., 2 bx, 1 bz, 1 cz.
Cummings, Thomas, 1 ax, 2 bx, 2 bz, 1 cx, 1 cz.

Kersey, John, 2 bx, 2 bz, 1 cx, 2 cz; 5 bm, 2 bf, 2 cm, 2 cf.
Cummings, Elizabeth, 1 az, 3 bx, 1 bz.
Haddaway, Susannah, 1 bx, 2 bz.
Haddaway, Geo., 1 ax, 1 bz, 6 cx, 1 cz; 1 bm.
Porter, John, 1 bx, 2 bz, 3 cx, 2 cz.
Sands, Benjn., 2 bx, 4 bz, 2 cz; 1 bf, 1 cf.
Horney, Thom^{s}., 1 bx, 1 bz, 2 cx; 1 bm.
Haddaway, Willm., 1 bx, 1 bz; 2 bm, 1 cf.
Cooper, Benjn., 1 ax, 1 az, 1 bx, 3 cx, 2 cz.
Kemp, John, 1 bx, 1 bz, 3 cx, 2 cz; 2 bm, 1 bf.
Kemp, Benjn., 1 ax, 1 bx, 2 bz, 2 cx, 5 cz; 3 bm, 2 bf, 1 cm, 4 cf.
Kemp, Magdalain, 1 ax, 1 az, 1 bx, 2 bz, 1 cx; 1 am, 1 af, 1 bm, 2 bf, 2 cm, 2 cf.
Haddaway, Capt., 2 bx, 3 bz, 1 cx, 4 cz; 1 bf, 1 cm, 2 cf.
Lambson, Robert, 7 bx, 3 bz, 3 cx, 2 cz; 2 am, 1 bm, 5 bf, 5 cm, 3 cf.
Haddaway, John, 2 bx, 1 bz, 1 cx, 2 cz; 2 bm, 1 bf, 2 cm, 2 cf.
Sherwood, Thos., 2 bx, 2 bz; 1 am, 1 af, 2 bm, 2 bf, 2 cm, 4 cf.
Fiddaman, Ann, 1 bz, 1 cx, 2 cz; 2 bf, 3 cm, 4 cf.
Hopkins, Joseph, 4 bx, 3 bz, 4 cx, 5 cz; 1 am, 2 bm, 3 bf, 1 cm, 2 cf.
Stains, Moses, 1 bx, 2 bz, 3 cx.
Harrison, Joseph, 1 ax, 1 az, 3 bx, 1 bz, 1 cx; 1 am, 1 af, 3 bm, 4 bf, 3 cm, 1 cf.
Harrison, Robert, 1 bx, 1 bz; 1 cm.
Steddam [?], Elizabeth, 1 bz, 4 cx.
Shanahan, John, 1 az, 2 bx, 1 bz, [3?] cx, 2 cz; 4 bm, 1 bf.
Tuttle, Willm., 2 bx, 2 bz, 1 cz.
Mather, John, 2 bx, 2 bz, 3 cx; 2 bm, 1 cf.
Marshall, Rich^{d}., 1 ax, 2 az, 1 bx, 1 bz, 1 cx, 1 cz.
Kemp, Thom^{s}., 1 bx, 1 bz, 1 cx, 4 cz; 1 bm, 1 cf.
Norwood, Ann, 1 bz, 1 cx, 2 cz.
Lenard, Sarah, 1 bz, 2 cx, 1 cz.
Vinton, Danl., 1 ax, 1 az, 1 bx.
Skinner, Phillimon, 3 bx, 2 bz, 2 cx, 1 cz; 1 bm.
Hopkins, James, 1 bx.
Hopkins, Thom^{s}., 1 ax, 4 bx, 1 bz, 1 cx; 1 af, 1 bm, 2 bz, 1 cm, 3 f.
Harrington, Joseph, 1 ax, 1 bx, 2 bz; 1 af, 2 bm, 1 bf, 2 cm.
Harrington, Alice, 1 az, 1 bz, 1 cz.
Harrington, Mary, 1 bx, 1 bz, 3 cx, 1 cz.
Hull, Danl., 1 ax.
Harrison, James, BC, 1 ax, 1 az, 2 bx, 3 bz, [2?] cx.
Hambleton, W^{m}., 4 bx, 2 bz, 1 cx, 2 cz; 1 af, 1 bm, 2 bf, 2 cm, 2 cf.
Hambleton, Phill^{p}. [?], 1 bx, 2 bz, [3 or 9?] cx; 1 am, 2 bm, 1 bf, 2 cm.

Barney, W^{m}., 1 bx, 1 bz, [2?] cx, 6 cz.
Davisson, Empy, 1 ax, 1 bx, 2 bz; 6 bm, 2 bf, 6 cm, 3 cf.
Dawson, Robert, 1 bx, 1 bz, 2 cx, 1 cz; 1 bm, 1 cf.
Tripp, James, 1 bx, 1 bz; 1 am, 1 af, 3 bm, 3 bf, 2 cm, 3 cf.
Fairbanks, Phill^{m}., 1 ax, 2 az, 1 bx, 2 bz, 1 cx; 1 bm.
Wayman, Thom^{s}., 1 ax, 2 bx, 2 bz, 1 cx, 3 cz; 3 bf, 3 cm, 3 cf.
Dawson, Hugh, 1 bx, 1 bz, 3 cx; 1 af, 2 bm, 1 bf, 2 cm.
Fairbanks, David, 1 bx, 1 bz, 5 cx, 2 cz.
Applegirth, George, 1 bx, 1 bz, 1 cx, 1 cz; 1 cf.
Bridges, Danl., 2 bx, 1 bz, 1 cx, 4 cz.
Ould [Oulds, Auld?], Hugh, 1 az, 1 bx, 1 bz; 1 bm, 1 bf, 3 cm, 1 cf.
Ould [Oulds, Auld?], John, 1 ax, 1 az, 3 bz, 2 cz.
Sewell, Jam^{s}., 1 bx, 1 bz, 1 cx, 2 cz.
Braddsetz, James, 2 bx, 1 cx; 1 bf, 1 cm.
Sherwood, David, 2 bx; 2 bf.
Caulty, John, 3 bx, 2 bz, 4 cx, 1 cz; 1 bm, 2 bf, 4 cm, 2 cf.
Haddaway, W^{m}., 1 ax, 1 az, 2 bx, 1 bz; 2 am, 2 bm, 2 bf, 1 cm, 1 cf.
Applegirth, Geo: 1 ax, 2 bx, 3 bz, 1 cx, 2 cz.
Harrison, Thos., 3 bx, 1 bz, 2 cx, 3 cz; 1 am, 1 bm, 1 bf, 4 cm, 1 cf.
Carrol, Denny, 1 bx, 1 bz, 1 cx, 2 cz; 1 bm, 1 cm, 1 cf.
Richardson, Robert, 2 bx, 1 bz, 1 cx, 2 cz; 1 af, 2 bm, 2 bf, 3 cm, 2 cf.
Haddaway, James, 1 bx, 1 bz.
Ball, Thom^{s}., 2 ax, 1 az, 1 bx, 1 bz, 2 cx, 1 cz.
Ball, W^{m}., 1 bx, 1 bz, 3 cz; 1 bf.
Carrol, James, 1 bx, 1 bz, 3 cx.
Haddaway, Robert, 1 bx, 2 bz, 3 cx, 2 cz.
Wrightson, James, 1 bx, 2 bz, 3 cx, 2 cz.
Harrisson, James, 1 az, 1 bx, 1 bz, 2 cx, 3 cz.
Grace, W^{m}., 1 bx, 3 bz, 2 cx, 3 cz.
Richardson, Peter, 3 bx, 2 bz, 6 cx, 2 cz.
Ould [Oulds?], Danl., 2 bx, 3 bz, 2 cx, 2 cz; 1 bm, 2 cm, 2 cf.
Ball, James, 1 bx, 3 bz, 2 cx, 2 cz; 1 bm.
Denny, Joseph, 1 ax, 1 az; 1 am, 2 bm, 1 bf, 1 cm.
Denny, Joseph, Junr., 1 bx, 1 bz, 1 cx; 1 bf.
Reddish, Joseph, 1 ax, 1 az, 2 cx, 2 cz.
Porter, Sarah, 1 az, 2 bz, 2 cx.
Lawrence [?], [Mar?]y, 2 bz, 2 cx, 2 cz.
Fairbanks, Anna, 1 az, 1 bx, 1 bz, 2 cx.
Sewell, Marty, 1 az, 2 bx, 2 bz, 5 cx, 2 cz.
Fitzjerrel, Rebecca, 1 az, 1 bx, 1 bz.
McQuay, Patrick, 1 ax, 1 az, 1 bx, 3 bz, 1 cx, 1 cz; 1 bf, 2 cm, 2 cf.
Gooves, Thom^{s}., 2 bx, 2 bz.

Fooss, Elizth., 1 az.
Barnes, James, 1 bx, 2 bz, 3 cx; 1 bf, 2 cm, 2 cf.
Jefferson, Thoms., 1 bx, 1 bz, 1 cz.
Camper, Wm., 2 bx, 1 bz, 2 cx, 2 cz; 1 bm.
Haddaway, Thoms., 1 ax, 1 az, 2 bx, 1 cx, 3 cz.
Lowry, Thoms., 2 bx, 1 bz, 2 cx, 4 cz; 1 bm, 1 cm.
Winterbottom, John, 1 ax, 1 az, 2 bx, 1 cx.
Winterbottom, Robt., 1 bx, 1 bz, 1 cx, 1 cz.
Lowry, Joseph, 2 bx, 1 bz, 3 cx, 4 cz.
Cardeff, Robt., 1 ax, 1 az, 1 bx, 1 bz, 1 cx.
Harrison, (torn), 2 bx.
Gardner, Richd., 1 bx.
Fairbanks, Mary, 1 az, 1 bx, 2 bz, 3 cx, 4 cz.
Hunt [?], Peter, 1 ax, 2 bx, 4 bz, 1 cx, 4 cz.
Cooper, John, 1 ax, 1 az, 2 bx, 1 bz, 3 cx, 1 cz.
Dawson, Sarah, 1 az, 2 bx, 1 bz; 1 am, 1 af.
Dawson, Margaret, 1 bx, 1 bz, 1 cx; 1 bf, 2 cm, 2 cf.
Linkom, Richd., 1 bx, 1 bz, 1 cx, 1 cz.
Dawson, Wm., 1 bx, 2 bz, 1 cx.
Ould [Oulds?], Phillip, 2 bx, 1 bz, 2 cx, 3 cz; 1 cm.
Jefferson, Geo: 3 bx, 1 bz, 4 cx, 2 cz.
Jones, Robt., 1 ax, 1 bx, 1 bz, 3 cx, 2 cz.
Haddaway, Wm., 1 bx, 1 bz, 2 cx, 3 cz.
Larramore, Mary, 1 az, 2 bx, 1 bz, 1 cx, 2 cz.
Batsey, Richd., 1 bx, 1 bz, 1 cx, 1 cz.
Jefferson, Francis, 1 bz, 3 cx, 1 cz.
Harrisson, Robt., 1 bx, 1 bz, 1 cx, 1 cz.
Larramoor, Jenney, 2 bx, 2 bz, 1 cx.
Leadnenham, Edwd., 1 bx, 1 bz, 2 cx, 2 cz.
Larramoor, Cathrine, 2 bz, 1 cx, 4 cz.
Mansfield, Richd., 1 az, 3 bx, 2 bz, 1 cx, 2 cz.
Camper [Comper?], Thoms., 2 bx, 2 bz, 2 cx.
Fairbanks, Danl., 3 bx, 4 bz, 2 cx, 2 cz.
Harrisson, Joseph, 1 bx, 1 bz, 2 cx, 3 cz.
Harrisson, Jonothon, 1 bx, 1 bz, 3 cx, 4 cz.
Colleson, Geo: 1 bx, 1 bz, 4 cx; 1 bm, 1 bf, 1 cm, 1 cf.
Low, James, 2 bx, 2 bz, 3 cx, 4 cz; 1 am, 2 bm, 3 bf, 1 cm.
R[?]eaugh, John, 1 bx, 2 bz; 1 bm.
Bridges, Wm., 1 az, 1 bx, 1 bz, 1 cx, 1 cz.
Smith, Thoms., 1 bx, 2 bz, 5 cx; 1 bf, 1 cm, 2 cf.
Dawson, [R]alph, 1 ax, 2 bz, 3 cx, 1 cz; 1 am, 1 af, 2 bm, 1 bf, cf.
Elliot, Edwd., 1 ax, 2 bz, 3 cx, 2 cz; 2 bm, 1 bf, 4 cm, 1 cf.

McNulty, John, 2 bx, 1 bz, 1 cx, 1 cz.
Ploughman, John, 2 bx, 2 bz, 5 cx, 2 cz.
McQuay, Catthrine, 1 az, 1 bx.
[Illegible—creased & torn]ll, ——, 1 bx, 1 bz, 2 cx, 1 cz; 1 bm, 1 bf, 1 cm, 2 cf.
Sherwood, [Illegible, perhaps Napn.?], 2 bx, 2 bz, 1 cx, 3 cz; 1 bf.
Lamden, Elizth., 1 bx, 2 bz, 2 cx, 1 cz; 1 af, 2 bm, 3 bf, 1 cm, 2 cf.
Haddaway, Wm. Webb, 1 ax, 1 az, 1 bx, 1 bz, 2 cz; 3 bm, 2 bf, 3 cm, 1 cf.
Jones, Lurinah, 1 az, 1 bz.
Leeds, John, 1 ax, 6 bm, 6 bf, 5 cm, 4 cf.
Tilghman, Mathew, 2 ax, 1 az, 2 bx, 2 bz; 5 af, 18 bm, 21 bf, 21 cm, 28 cf.
Mahony, Anthony, 1 bx, 1 bz, 1 cx, 2 cz.
West, Wm., 1 bx, 2 bz, 3 cx, 3 cz.
Sears, Wm., 1 bx, 3 bz, 1 cx, 2 cz; 2 am, 7 bm, 11 bf, 5 cm, 5 cf.
Nash, Thoms., 1 bx, 1 bz, 2 cx, 1 cz.

Gossage, Charles, 1 bx, 1 bz, 5 cx, 2 cz.
Cryer [?], John, 2 bx, 1 bz.
Totals, 6 ax, 7 az, 41 bx, 52 bz, 61 cx, 50 cz; 17 am, 7 af, 46 bm, 52 bf, 45 cm, 47 cf.

Free mullotes *

Collwell, Martin, 2 bf, 1 cx.
Auldery, Thomas, 1 ax, 2 bx, 3 cx, 1 cz.
Cornesh, Rebec., 1 bm, 1 cx, 1 cz.

James Earl Denny.

* These enumerations are evidently placed in wrong columns in the original report.

Talbott County, Mill Hundred, Census of 1776,

"A list of the Inhabatents taken In Mill Hundred By Tho[s]. Tibbels in yeare 1776."

This record is literally in shreds and has been carefully matched together, and read by aid of a magnifying glass. Three sheets each 14 × 16½ inches were fastened together, side by side, with sealing wax.

"a" here means "Above 50 years"; "b" means "Between 16 and 50"; "c" means "Under 16," and "e" means "Total," which latter includes the "Blacks." "x" means white "Males"; "z" means white "Females"; "n" means "Blacks." To carry out the partial uniformity with the preceding lists the "n" is placed last (after "e" or "Totals").

Heads of Families:

Levell, William, 2 bx, 1 bz, 1 cx, 1 cz, 8 e; 3 n.
Morgan, Thos. Spery [?], 1 bx, 2 bz, 1 cx, 1 cz, 41 e; 36 n.
Snelling, Sarah, 1 bx, 1 cx, 1 cz, 3 e.
Comberford, Mary, 1 bz, 1 cx, 1 cz, 3 e.
Torresh, William, 1 bx, 1 bz, 1 cx, 2 cz, 6 e; 1 n.
Nobs, Joseph, 1 bx, 1 bz, 1 cx, 2 cz, 5 e.
Carrel, John, 1 bx, 1 bz, 3 e; 1 n.
Nussey, Johanna, 1 bx, 1 bz, 1 cx, 3 e.
M[c]Carnon, Daniel, 1 ax, 1 az, 2 bz, 3 cx, 1 cz, 11 e; 3 n.
Low, Henry, 1 ax, 3 bz, 7 cx, 2 cz, 14 e; 1 n.
Jackson, James, 1 bx, 1 bz, 1 cx, 3 e.
Faulkner, Thos., 1 az, 1 bx, 1 bz, 2 cx, 3 cz, 10 e; 2 n.
Faulkner, Abram, 1 ax, 2 bz, 4 cx, 3 cz, 10 e.
Davis, Jean, 1 az, 1 cx, 2 e.
Davis, ——, 1 bx, 1 bz, 4 cx, 6 e.
Worner, ——, 1 bx, 1 bz, 1 cx, 1 cz, 4 e.
Greenhout, ——, 1 ax, 1 az, 1 cx, 1 cz, 6 e; 2 n.
Stewart, ——, 1 ax, 4 bx, 2 bz, 4 cx, 11 e.
Austin, ——, 1 bx, 2 bz, 1 cx, 1 cz, 5 e.
Mathews, —ew, 2 bx, 1 bz, 2 cz, 5 e.
Chapman, ——, 1 bx, 1 bz, 5 cx, 1 cz, 8 e.
Norress, ——, 1 bx, 1 bz, 1 cx, 2 cz, 5 e.
Wilson, ——, (Free mulatto), 1 e; 1 n.
Austin, ——, 1 ax, 1 bz, 3 cx, 4 cz, 23 e; 14 n.
—wes, ——, 1 bx, 3 bz, 2 cz, 7 e.
Faulkner, [Isaac?], 2 bx, 2 bz, 5 cx, 2 cz, 11 e.
Fouthner, Elizabeth, 1 az, 1 bz, 2 e.
Dixson, John, 1 ax, 2 bz, 3 cx, 3 cz, 13 e; 4 n.

Barrett, Elezebeth, 1 bz, 1 cx, 1 cz, 4 e; 1 n.
Burgess, William, 1 ax, 2 bz, 3 e.
Trice, Vencent, 1 bx, 1 bz, 1 cx, 1 cz, 5 e; 1 n.
Chrisp, John, 1 bx, 1 bz, 2 cx, 1 cz, 5 e.
Atkinson, Aaron, 4 bx, 3 bz, 3 cx, 2 cz, 25 e; 13 n.
Short, Samuel, 1 bx, 1 bz, 1 cz, 5 e; 1 n.
Nicols, Mrs. Henney, 1 bx, 1 bz, 2 cx, 2 cz, 41 e; 35 n.
Woolcott, Methias, 1 bx, 1 bz, 3 cz, 5 e.
Dowling, William, 1 bx, 1 bz, 2 cx, 1 cz, 5 e.
Mathews, Thos., 1 bx, 1 bz, 2 cx, 1 cz, 5 e.
Austin, William, 1 bx, 1 bz, 2 cz, 4 e.
Austin, Ann, 1 az, 1 cx, 1 cz, 3 e.
Terry, Denisha, 1 bx, 2 bz, 1 cx, 2 cz, 6 e.
Acorn, Thos., 1 bx, 1 bz, 2 e.
Dewling, Joseph, 1 ax, 1 az, 1 bx, 1 bz, 1 cx, 1 cz, 6 e.
Ferrell, William, 2 bx, 1 bz, 2 cx, 1 cz, 11 e; 5 n.
Durkins, Ann, 1 bz, 3 cx, 3 cz, 7 e.
Jackson, Isaac, 1 ax, 1 bz, 2 cx, 1 cz, 5 e.
Snelling, William, 1 ax, 2 bz, 3 e.
Walker, Richard, 1 bx, 1 bz, 1 cx, 3 e.
Eubanks, John, 1 bx, 1 bz, 2 cz, 4 e.
Eubanks, Rebecah, 1 az, 2 cz, 3 e.
Norwood, Robert, 3d, 3 bx, 2 cz, 5 e.
Sherwood, Prudence, 1 az, 2 bz, 2 cx, 2 cz, 7 e.
Humes, Susannah, 1 bz, 2 cz, 3 e.
Barrow, James, 1 ax, 2 bx, 3 bz, 4 cx, 1 cz, 15 e; 4 n.
Barrow, Thos., 1 ax, 4 bx, 2 bz, 3 cx, 12 e; 2 n.
Warner, Wilim., 1 ax, 1 bz, 1 cx, 1 cz, 5 e; 1 n.
Neithsmith, John, 1 ax, 1 bx, 2 cx, 5 e; 1 n.
Fleming, David, 1 bx, 2 bz, 3 cx, 2 cz, 8 e.
Coborn, Ann, 1 bz, 2 cz, 3 e.
Evens, Mary, 3 bx, 1 bz, 2 cx, 3 cz, 18 e; 9 n.
Holladay, Heny., 2 ax, 1 bx, 5 bz, 1 cx, 3 cz, 67 e; 55 n.
Bowdel, Willm., 2 bx, 1 bz, 3 cx, 1 cz, 10 e; 3 n.
Caslick, Edward, 1 az, 1 bx, 1 cx, 1 cz, 5 e; 1 n.
Milwood, Willim., 1 bx, 1 bz, 1 cz, 3 e.
Buckley, Henry, 1 bx, 1 bz, 2 cx, 2 cz, 9 e; 3 n.
Corner, Adam, 1 ax, 1 az, 1 bx, 1 bz, 1 cz, 14 e; 9 n.
Harwood, Robert, 1 ax, 1 bx, 2 bz, 4 cx, 1 cz, 30 e; 21 n.
Hopkins, Lambath, 1 bx, 3 bz, 2 cx, 4 cz, 10 e.
Tibbels, John, 2 bx, 1 bz, 1 cx, 3 cz, 7 e.
Smith, Archabald, 3 bx, 1 bz, 2 cx, 6 e.

Hombleton, Wm., 1 ax, 2 bx, 2 bz, 6 e; 1 n.
Botfeild, Zadock, 1 bx, 2 bz, 1 cz, 5 e; 1 n.
Hopkins, Joseph, 2 bx, 1 cx, 3 e.
Hopkins, Dennis, 1 bx, 2[?] bz, 2 cz, [?] e; 2 n.
Hopkins, Francis, 1 ax, 1 bx, 4 bz, 3 cx, 2 cz, 16 e; 5 n.
Isgate, Thos., 1 ax, 1 bz, 3 cx, 1 cz, 9 e; 3 n.
Negros, Free, 7 e; 7 n.
Dixson, William, 1 bx, 2 bz, 1 cx, 2 cz, 7 e; 1 n.
Harwood, Samuel, 1 ax, 1 az, 3 bz, 2 cz, 16 e; 9 n.
Atkinson, Joseph, 1 ax, 1 bx, 1 bz, 2 cz, 18 e; 13 n.
Harwood, Mary, 2 bx, 1 bz, 2 cx, 2 cz, 7 e.
Harwood, Robert, 1 bx, 1 bz, 1 cx, 2 cz, 5 e.
Harwood, Ann, 1 bz, 7 e; 6 n.
Low, Rachel, 1 bz, 4 cz, 5 e.
Hews, Christopher, 1 bx, 1 bz, 1 cx, 2 cz, 5 e.
Stanton, Elezebeth, 1 az, 3 bz, 1 cz, 6 e; 1 n.
Summers, Mary, 1 az, 1 bz, 1 cx, 3 cz, 6 e.
Goldsborough, Robt.,2 bx, 2 bz, 2 cx, 30 e; 24 n.
Goldsborough, Robt., 1 ax, 1 az, 1 bx, 2 bz, 51 e; 46 n.
Condon, James, 1 bx, 1 bz, 1 cx, 1 cz, 4 e.
Meggs, John, 1 bx, 1 bz, 1 cx, 3 e.
Goldsborough, Howse, 1 bx, 2 bz, 1 cx, 1 cz, 28 e; 23 n.
Condon, William, 1 ax, 1 az, 1 bx, 1 bz, 1 cz, 5 e.
Neighbours, Thos., 1 ax, 1 bx, 2 bz, 2 cx, 2 cz, 9 e; 1 n.
Bartlet, Richard, 1 bx, 1 bz, 2 cx, 1 cz, 5 e.
Bartlet, John, 2 bx, 3 bz, 1 cz, 6 e.
Harper, Thos., 1 bx, 4 bz, 2 cx, 1 cz, 21 e; 13 n.
Spry, John, 2 bx, 2 bz, 1 cx, 11 e; 6 n.
Lecount, Anthoney, 1 ax, 1 az, 2 bz, 1 cx, 1 cz, 13 e; 7 n.
Robson, Andrew, 1 bx, 1 bz, 2 cx, 1 cz, 9 e; 4 n.
Rigbey, Jonathon, 1 bx, 1 bz, 1 cx, 3 e.
Stokes, Elijah, 1 bx, 1 bz, 1 cx, 3 e.
Rigbey, Philmon, 2 az, 2 bx, 1 bz, 12 e; 7 n.
Norwood, William, 2 ax, 1 bx, 2 bz, 5 cx, 1 cz, 11 e.
M Neal, Arch. 1 ax, 4 bz, 3 cx, 3 cz, 11 e.
Mathews, David, 1 ax, 1 bx, 2 bz, 2 cx, 4 cz, 10 e.
Farr,* Richard, 1 ax, 1 bx, 1 bz, 4 cx, 1 cz, 9 e; 1 n.
Lennard, Thos., 1 ax, 1 az, 3 bx, 3 cx, 1 cz, 9 e.
Robson, John, 3 bx, 2 bz, 5 cx, 3 cz, 15 e; 2 n.
Maynard, Foster, 1 bx, 1 bz, 3 cx, 1 cz, 8 e; 2 n.
Kirbey, Elezebeth, 1 az, 1 bx, 1 bz, 6 cx, 2 cz, 11 e.

* This may be Farr, Tarr, Garr, etc., being peculiarly and indistinctly written.

West, Mary, 1 az, 2 bx, 2 bz, 1 cx, 1 cz, 7 e.
Ridgaway, William, 1 ax, 1 az, 1 bx, 1 bz, 6 e; 2 n.
Dawson, John, 1 bx, 1 bz, 2 cx, 1 cz, 10 e; 5 n.
Denney, Mary, 1 az, 2 bx, 2 bz, 4 cx, 2 cz, 13 e; 2 n.
Wats, William, 1 bx, 1 bz, 7 cx, 1 cz, 14 e; 4 n.
Norress, William, 1 bx, 1 bz, 1 cx, 1 cz, 8 e; 4 n.
Rigbey, Moses, 1 bx, 1 bz, 2 cx, 3 cz, 15 e; 8 n.
Doughoty, John, 2 bx, 2 bz, 3 cx, 2 cz, 14 e; 5 n.
Gelon [Gelor?], James, 1 bx, 1 bz, 3 cx, 2 cz, 7 e.
Smith, James, 1 bx, 1bz, 4 cx, 2 cz, 15 e; 7n,
Seymour, Joseph, 1 bx, 1 bz, 2 cx, 1 cz, 5e.
Richardson, Henry, 1 bx, 2 bz, 1 cx, [?] e.
Lemon [Lamarr?], James, 1 bx, 2 bz, 3 cx, 3[?] cz, [?] e.
Marchel, John, 1 bx, 1 bz, 2 cz, 4 e.
Marchel, Ather, 1 bx, 1 bz, 2 cz, 4 e.
Coborn, Anney, 1 az, 1 bx, 1 bz, 3 e.
Colston, Henry, 1 az, 3 bx, 2 bz, 2 cx, 2 cz, 13 e; 3 n.
Smith, Elisha, 1 bx, 1 bz, 2 cz, 4 e.
Gossage, John, 1 bx, 2 bz, 3 cx, 4 cz, 11 e; 1 n.
Harress, John, 1 ax, 1 bx, 2 bz, 2 cx, 1 cz, 8 e; 1 n.
Marchel, Joseph, 1 bx, 1 bz, 1 cx, 4 e; 1 n.
Oram, Rachel, 1 az, 2 bx, 2 bz, 3 cx, 4 cz, 12 e.
Vallont, William, 2 bx, 1 bz, 1 cx, 4 cz, 8 e.
Vallont, Bennet, 2 bx, 3 bz, 3 cx, 2 cz, 10 e.
Vallont, Nicolas, 1 az, 1 bx, 1 bz, 1 cx, 4 e.
Vallont, John, 1 ax, 2 bx, 1 bz, 1 cx, 2 cz, 8 e; 1 n.
Eaton, Richard, 3 bx, 1 bz, 1 cx, 2 cz, 7 e.
Nix, Elezebeth, 1 az, 1 bz, 1 cx, 3 e.
Eaton, John, 1 az, 1 bx, 1 bz, 1 cx, 2 cz, 9 e; 3 n.
Oram, William, 1 bx, 1 bz, 1 cx, 1 cz, 5 e; 1 n.
Seymour, Henry, 1 bx, 1 bz, 3 cx, 3 cz, 8 e.
Skinner, Mordica, 1 bx, 1 bz, 7 e; 5 n.
Robson, Thos., 1 bx, 1 bz, 2 e.
Grace, James, 1 bx, 1 bz, 1 cx, 3 cz, 8 e; 2 n.
Colslon, James, 2 bx, 2 bz, 2 cx, 1 cz, 9 e; 2 n.
Grace, Nathaniel, 2 ax, 1 az, 1 bx, 1 cx, 5 e.
Grace, Mary, 1 bz, 1 cx, 4 cz, 8 e; 2 n.
Newcom, Robert, 1 ax, 1 az, 1 bx, 1 bz, 2 cx, 1 cz, 33 e; 26 n.
Sewel, Dianna, 1 az, 5 bx, 1 bz, 1 cx, 1 cz, 9 e.
Barisood, Adeath "whie" [?], 2 bz, 1 cz, 3 e.
Dorter [?], Jonathn, 1 bx, 2 bz, 1 cz, 39 e; 35 n.
Stokes, Susannah, 1 ax, 1 bx, 2 cz, 4 e.

Whorten, Henry, 1 ax, 1 az, 1 bz, 1 cx, 4 e.
Whorten, ——, 1 bz, 2 cx, 3 cz, 6 e.
Harmon, Rachel, 1 ax, 1 cz, 2 e.
Dowel, William, 1 bx, 1 bz, 1 cx, 1 cz, 4 e.
Aldren, Elizebeth, 2 az, 2 bz, 1 cz, 15 e; 10 n.
Rigby, Thos., 1 bx, 3 bz, 1 cx, 1 cz, 12 e; 6 n.
Norwood, Edward, 1 ax, 1 az, 3 bz, 1 cz, 4 e.
Seymour, John, 1 ax, 1 az, 1 bx, 2 cx, 1 cz, 6 e.
Edwards, Ann, 1 az, 1 bz, 1 cx, 3 e.
Colston, John, 1 bx, 1 bz, 1 cx, 4 e; 1 n.
Hindman, Willim., 1 az, 3 bx, 3 bz, 46; 39 n.
Morling, Francis, 1 bx, 2 cx, 13 e; 10 n.
Richardson, ——, 1 ax, 1 bz, 2 cx, 4 e.
Hopkins, ——, 1 bz, 2 cz, 3 e.
Beaten, ——, 1 bz, 1 e.
Spencer, ——, 1 bz, 1 cx, 1 cz, 3 e.
Coborn, —an, 1 bx, 1 bz, 3 cx, 5 cz, 10 e.
Bartlett, ——, 1 ax, 3 bz, 2 cx, 1 cz, 7 e.
Kirbey, ——, 1 ax, 1 az, 1 bx, 1 bz, 2 cx, 1 cz, 7 e.
—orkston, John, 1 bx, 1 bz, 1 cx, 3 e.
Kirby, —ary, 1 bz, 1 cx, 1 cz, 3 e.
Negro Dick, 6 e; 6 n.
Dunn, John, 1 ax, 2 bx, 4 e; 1 n.
Robson, [Rob]ert, 1 ax, 1 bx, 1 bz, 2 cx, 4 cz, 9 e.
Lennard, [J]ohn, 1 ax, 1 az, 1 bx, 2 bz, 1 cx, 1 cz, 7 e.
Gordon, —— (This record is worn away) 1 cz, 3 e.
Hopkins, —ard, 1 ax, 1 az, [?] bx, 5 bz, 3 cx, 1 cz, 14 e; 3 [?] n.
Banning, —imeah, 2 bx, 12 e; 10 n.
Banning, [He]nry, 2 bx, 2 bz, 4 cx, 2 cz, 25 e; 15 n.
Marchel, —es, 1 bx, 2 bz, 15 e; 12 n.
Denney, James Earl, 2 bx, 2 bz, 1 cx, 2 cz, 15 e; 8 n.
Porter, ——, 1 bx, 1 bz, 1 cx, 2 cz, 7 e; 2 n.
Dixson, [Is]aac, 1 ax, 1 bx, 3 bz, 1 cx, 1 cz, 27 e; 20 n.
Chapman, ——, 1 bx, 2 bz, 1 cz, 7 e; 3 n.
Allen, —oses, 2 bx, 3 bz, 1 cx, 2 cz, 29 e; 21 n.
Tibbels, Thos., 3 bx, 2 bz, 3 cx, 1 cz, 15 e; 6 n.
Siddel, John, 1 ax, 1 bz, 2 cx, 2 cz, 6 e.
Brascup, Thos., 2 bx, 2 bz, 5 cx, 1 cz, 10 e.
Marchel, [Ja]mes, 1 ax, 1 az, 2 bz, 1 cz, 5 e.
Floyd, [Jo]seph, 1 ax, 1 bz, 1 cx, 3 e.
Eubanks, [A]dam, 1 bx, 1 bz, 1 cx, 1 cz, 4 e.
Thomas, [Wi]lliam, 2 bx, 3 bz, 4 cz, 23 e; 14 n.

Cardeff, [A]nn, 2 bz, 2 e.
Irvine, [A]lexand., 2 bx, 2 bz, 4 cz, 8 e.
Dawson, James, 1 bx, 1 bz, 1 cx, 2 cz, 11 e; 6 n. "Total 1913."

"Talbot Co. Si. Upon the 3^d day of Septr. 1776. Thom^s. Tibbels maketh Oath that the foregoing and within lists is a just & true Account of the number of inhabitants in Mill Hundred taken by order of the committie of Observation in the Coty afsd. before J^o. S GIBSON."

Upon the back of this record is written in tabular form and in a handwriting different from that of Thomas Tibbels:

"Whites—under 16 years, [c], Males 1450, Females 1259—between 16—50 [b] Males 1227, Females 1361—above 50, [a] Males 193, Females 204—5694. Add 1/6, 949. No Whites 6643."

"Blacks—under 16 years, [c], Males 911, Females 904—between 16—50, [b], Males 692, Females 720—above 50, [a], Males 154, Females 129—3510. Add 1/6, 585. No. Blacks 4095, Free Blacks 149, Total 10,887."

Talbott County, Tuckahoe Hundred, Census of 1776

This yellow and fragile record consisted apparently of sheets 13 1/4 × 12 inches, fastened together by red sealing wax, having a total length of 28 inches, doubled. Of the first half but 7 1/2 × 12 inches remains, and an inch strip 21 inches long, from the left side of the other half, and carrying the Christian, or "given," names is also missing. All decipherable letters, using the magnifying glass, are reproduced for the investigator.

"a" here means "Above 50" years; "b" means "Between 16 & 50"; "c" means "Under 16," and "n" means "Blacks." "x" means white "Males"; "z" means white "Females."

Gibson, John, 1 ax, 3 bx, 2 bz, 3 cz; 30 n.
Baker, Francis, 1 az, 4 bx, 3 bz, 2 cx, 1 cz; 9 n.
Nicholson, Daniel, 1 bx, 1 bz, 1 cx, 1 cz.
Gibson, Wollman, 3^d, 2 bx, 2 bz; 10 n.
Jackson, William, 1 [or 4?] bx, 1 bz, 1 cz; 1 n.
Clayland, John, 1 bx, 2 bz, 1 cx, 1 cz; 6 n.
Collener, John, 1 bx.
Shepard, John, 1 bx, 1 bz, 2 cx.
Middleton, William, 3 bx, 1 bz, 1 cx; 11 n.

Hartt, Chri^{h}., 1 az, 1 bx, 1 bz, 4 cz.
Porter, William, 1 bx, 1 bz, 2 cx, 3 cz; 8 n.
Lloyd, Edward, 6 bx, 4 bz, 3 cz; 15 n.
Ford, Charles, 1 bx, 2 bz, 1 cx, 2 cz.
Hall, George, 1 bx, 3 cz.
Alleway, William, 1 bx, 1 bz, 5 cz.
Webster, William, 1 ax, 1 cx.
Jones, Ann, 1 bz, 1 cx, 1 cz.
Sunksout [?], Mary, 1 bx, 3 bz, 1 cx, 3 cz.
Cheavis [?], John, 1 bx, 1 bz.
Powell, John, 1 bx, 2 bz; 9 n.
Warner, —bert, 1 bx, 2 bz, 1 cx, 2 cz.
Hall, —rbert, 2 bx, 2 bz, 4 cx, 2 cz; 3 n.
Cooper, [Will]iam, 1 bx, 1 bz, 2 cx, 3 cz; 6 n.
Countiee, ——, 1 az, 1 bx, 2 bz [Torn].
Plumer, Yarnall, 1 bx, 1 bz, 1 cx, 2 cz.
Plumer, Thomas, 1 bx, 2 bz, 4 cx, 1 cz; 1 n.
Callahan, Ann, 1 bx, 2 bz, 3 cx; 2 n.
Surat, [Sweat?], Edward, 2 ax, 2 bx, 1 bz, 2 cx, 2 cz.
Dwiging, Robert, 2 bx, 1 bz, 2 cx, 3 cz; 2 n.
Milington, Nickson, 1 ax, 1 az, 1 bx, 1 bz, 1 cx, 1 cz; 3 n.
Morley, Joseph, 1 bx; 10 n.
Millington, ——, 1 bx, 3 cx, 3 cz; 2 n.
—allehorn [?], ——, 1 bx, 3 bz, 4 cx [Torn].
Harris, —ett, 1 ax, 1 bx, 2 bz, 2 cz.
Williams, ——, 6 bx, 1 bz; 3 n.
Stacy, ——, 1 bx, 1 bz, 1 cz.
Rex [?], Rua [?], 1 bx, 1 bz, 2 cz.
Williss, ——, 1 ax, 1 bx, 1 bz, 5 cx, 2 cz.
Nickers, ——, 1 az, 1 bx, 2 bz, 2 cz; 9 n.
Nickers, ——, 1 bx, 1 bz, 1 cx, 2 cz.
Pamer, ——, 1 bx, 1 bz, 2 cx, 4 cz; 2 n.
Roberts, ——, 1 az, 2 bx, 2 bz, 4 cz; 1 n.
—ke, ——, 1 bz, 3 cx, 1 cz.
Forster, ——, 3 bx, 3 bz, 2 cx; 2 n.
Buly or Beely, ——, 1 az, 2 bx, 1 bz, 2 cx, 4 cz; 9 n.
Mattorn [?], ——, 2 bz, 1 cx; 1 n.
Norton, ——, 1 ax, 1 bx, 2 bz, 2 cx, 1 cz.
Pattin, ——, 1 bx, 1 bz, 3 cx.
—np, ——, 1 az, 5 bz, 1 cx, 1 cz; 8 n.
Griffeth, —t, 1 bx, 2 bz, 2 cx, 2 cz.
Norton, ——, 1 ax; 4 n.

Warner, ——, 1 ax, 1 az, 1 bx, 2 bz, 3 cx.
Batey, ——, 1 bx.
Maxwell, ——, 19 n.
Lloyd, —nnet, 58 n.
Dimmond, ——, 2 bx, 2 bz, 1 cx, 1 cz; 9 n.
Renolls, ——, 1 bx, 2 bz, 1 cx, 2 cz.
—k, ——, 1 bx; 7 n.
—ilder, ——, 2 bx, 1 bz, 1 cz; 7 n.
Miller, ——, 1 bx.
—kril, ——, 1 ax, 1 az, 1 bz, 3 cx, 2 cz; 3 n.
Berwick, ——, 1 bx, 1 bz; 1 n.
Cottner, —er, 1 bx, 1 bz, 1 cx.
Blackwell, ——, 2 bx; 6 n.
—arron, ——, 1 bx; 2 n.
Sware, ——, 1 bx, 1 bz, 1 cz.
—iets, ——, 1 bx, 1 bz, 2 cx, 1 cz.
—nes, ——, 1 bx, 1 bz, 4 cx, 1 cz.
Bordly, ——, 3 bx, 3 bz, 2 cx; 16 n.
Cole, ——, 1 bx, 1 bz, 2 cx, 2 cz.
Williams, ——, 1 bx.
Warner, ——, 1 bx.
Foster, ——, 1 bx.
Ozemon, —n, 1 bx.
ᵛRoberts, ——, 1 bx, 3 bz; 4 n.
Sylvester, ——, 1 az, 1 bx, 1 cx, 3 cz.
Wrench, ——, 1 bx, 1 bz, 1 cz; 4 n.
Gannon, ——, 1 bx, 1 bz, 2 cx, 6 cz.
Grace [?], ——, 1 az, 1 bx, 1 bz, 2 cx, 2 cz; 3 n.
Long, ——, 1 ax, 1 bx, 2 cx, 2 cz.
North, ——, 1 bx.
Roberson, ——, 1 bz; 6 n.
Curry, ——, 4 bz; 5 n.
Lane, ——, 1 ax, 1 az, 1 bx, 1 bz, 1 cx, 2 cz.
plummer, —n, 1 az, 1 bx, 1 bz, 1 cx, 2 cz; 1 n.
pickiran, —obert, 2 bx, 4 bz; 10 n.

Totals: 7 ax, 11 az, 64 bx, 75 bz, 76 cx, 70 cz; 254 n, "including 21 Free Mulattoes."

"6" September, 1776, James Wrenst [?] maketh oath to the List of within inhabitants in Tuckahoe Hundred taken by him.

before J°. S [?]. GIBSON."

HARFORD COUNTY

Harford County, Oaths of Fidelity, March Court, 1778

A List of persons in Harford County who have taken the following Oath before the Different magistrates as mentioned below and returned by them to Harford County Court.

Harford County was established 1773, from Baltimore County.

(See Oaths reproduced in Prince George's Co. section)

Taken before the Worshipfull James McComas

Sixteen Returns—1146 men. Recorded Md. Hist. Soc. A copy from a copy of the original.

1. THE WORSHIPFULL JAMES MCCOMAS' RETURNS.
2. Norris, Abraham
3. Rose, Joseph
4. Callender, Robert
5. Booth, Richard
6. Wigings, Samuel
7. Aooistock, Peter
8. Green, Abel
9. Durham, John (Snr.)
10. Norris, Thomas (of John)
11. Mather, Thomas
12. Mather, Michael
13. Rumage, George
14. Smithson, Nathaniel
15. Paris, William
16. Carroll, James (Jnr.)
17. Norris, Daniel
18. Saunders, William
19. McComas, John (of Danl.)
20. Ruth, Joseph
21. Bridge, James
22. Ruff, Henry (Jnr.)
23. Frier, Isaac
24. Dobbins, James
25. Whitaker, Isaac
26. Billingsley, Francis
27. Vance, Samuel
28. Vance, David
29. Henlon, Patrick
30. Multon, Patrick
31. Porter, Charles
32. Baker, Charles
33. Banks, Andrew
34. Bronnwood, John
35. Brown, William
36. Toppey, William
37. Murphy, Archabald M.
38. Callender, Robert (Jnr.)
39. Goodwin, William
40. Finnagon, Patrick
41. Saunders, Thomas (Farmer)
42. Walker, John
43. Norris, James
44. Duley, James
45. McComas, Wm. (of Solm.)
46. White, Stephen
47. Everett, James
48. Bronnley, Arthur
49. Baker, Theophelus

50. Baker, Gedion
51. Freeman, Thomas
52. Norris, Aquila
53. Wild, John
54. Trons, John
55. Spencer, Rowland
56. Howard, Samuel
57. Ewen, Alexander
58. McComas, Solomon
59. McComas, John (of Wm.)
60. Connaway, Lawrence
61. Amoss, Maulden
62. Everett, Samuel
63. Chalk, George
64 Wheeler, James
65. Norris, Richard
66. Cunningham, Thomas
67. Kembol, James
68. Tossett, Jonathan
69. Brown, James
70. Stevenson, Jonas
71. Cain, James
72. St. Clair, William
73. Hanson, Edward
74. Quinnlin, Philip
75. Webster, Samuel (Snr.)
76. Brooks, John
77. Jarnes, John
78. Huggins, James
79. Lewes, Jessee
80. James, Sedwick
81. Beck, Peter
82. Rogers, Thomas
83. Suoit, Alexander
84. Small, Robert
85. Mattocks, John
86. Norris, Joseph
87. McGaw, James
88. White, Graston
89. Steuart, William

The within is a true Copy of the names of those who have taken the Oath of Fidelity and Support to the State of Maryland

Sworn before

JAMES McCOMAS.

1. THE WORSHIPFULL WILLIAM SMITHSON'S RETURNS
2. Waters, Thomas
3. Williams, Francis
4. Jones, Gilbert
5. Smith, James
6. Hutchens, Thomas
7. Thomas, Daniel
8. Norris, Edward (of Edwd.)
9. Norris, Alexander
10. Richardson, Vincent
11. Ruth, Moses (Jnr.)
12. Brandrick, William
13. Rogers, Robert
14. Standerford, Samuel
15. Conn, Robert
16. Richardson, Thomas
17. Cochean, Isaac
18. Bond, Peter
19. Armstrong, Sheperd
20. Morrow, Benjamin
21. Calwell, Samuel
22. Martin, Robert
23. Herbert, Charles
24. Armstrong, John
25. Bay, Hugh
26. Allen, John
27. Bull, William
28. Everett, James
29. Ady, William
30. Todd, Patrick
31. Todd, Andrew
32. Richardson, Henry
33. Norris, James

34. M^c^Cord, James
35. Richardson, William
36. Richardson, Thomas
37. Norris, John (of John)

Harford County. This is to Certify that this is a true Copy of the names of the persons that has taken the Oath of Fidelity according to Laws.

W^m^. SMITHSON.

1. THE WORSHIPFULL THOS. JOHNSON RETURNS
2. Drummond, Thomas
3. Moore, James
4. Sweny, Mathew
5. Hill, Stephen
6. Kyle, William
7. Wilson, Henry, Jnr.
8. Thomas, Henry
9. Seney, Patrick
10. Taes, Andrew
11. Johnson, Thos., Jnr.
12. Denny, Simon
13. Bibb, James
14. Clark, Robert
15. Monroe, William
16. Clark, David
17. Rigdon, James
18. Gavvett, John
19. Stapleton, Edward

Harford Co. State of Maryland. I hereby Certify that the above named Persons did take and Subscribe the above Oath before me

THOS. JOHNSON.

A LIST of THOSE WHO TOOK REPEATED and SUBSCRIBED THE AFORESAID OATH BEFORE WILLIAM WEBB, ESQ DECD.

1. Webb, Samuel
2. Beshang, John
3. Webb, Samuel, Jnr.
4. Jenkins, Samuel
5. Crockett, Gilbert
6. Marmold, James
7. Crockett, Samuel
8. Jrudir, Simon
9. Wells, William
10. Johnson, Isaac
11. Carlan, George
12. Modin, Patrick
13. Allender, William
14. Allender, Thomas
15. Crooks, Henry
16. Clark, Robert, Jnr.
17. Goffey, Henry
18. Steel, James
19. Howlett, Andrew
20. Howlett, James
21. Browne, Joshua
22. Taylor, Thomas
23. Cunningham, Edward
24. Osborn, Benjamin
25. Burr, John
26. Osborn, William (of Benja.)
27. Bailey, Jas. Francis
28. Scarff, Benjamin
29. Baker, Maurice
30. Baker, John
31. Hill, Thomas (Sailor)
32. James, Walter
33. Smith, Zachariah
34. Brown, John (wheelright)
35. Bailey, Groombright
36. Maxwell, James
37. Day, John (of Edward)
38. Waltham, Thomas

39. Waltham, William
40. Day, John, Jnr.
41. Debruler, James
42. Polson, Joseph
43. Woodland, Jonathan
44. Dorsey, Jno. Hammond
45. Hughston, John
46. Woollin, Major
47. Tuder, John
48. Hughs, John
49. Woollin, Richard
50. Debueler, William
51. Hall, Isaac
52. Allinder, John
53. Saunders, Robert
54. Monk, Richard
55. Taylor, John Hodges
56. Smith, Josias
57. Baker, William
58. Baker, John (of Theophilas)
59. Reeves, Josias
60. Wetherall, Henry
61. Dailey, William
62. Bolton, John
63. Wilson, John
64. Sweeney, David
65. Benton, Henry
66. Bennington, Nehemiah
67. Barclay, John
68. Warman, Joseph
69. Lockart, Samuel
70. Barnet, James
71. Gough, Hugh M.
72. Crooks his X mark Robert
73. McElmarey, Patrick
74. Clark, James
75. Crooker, James
76. Wilson, Arsbel
77. Allexander, James
78. Giffin, Robert

A true Copy by Jno. Archer.

1. THE WORSHIPFULL WILLIAM BOND'S RETURNS.
2. Finley, Joseph
3. Clemmons, Christopher
4. Morrison, Joseph
5. Durham, Samuel
6. Durham, Aquila
7. Scott, James (of Aquila)
8. Smith, Bazie
9. Thurston, Thomas
10. Taylor, John (Planter)
11. Dinham, John (of Jesse)
12. Lattimore, John
13. Smithson, Thomas
14. Scott, Aquila (of James)
15. Hambleton, Edward
16. Knight, Thomas
17. Bond, James (of Jos.)
18. Slator, Thomas
19. Shipley, Elijah
20. Stanley, William (Miller)
21. Hunt, Robert
22. Hanna, James
23. Moores, John
24. Jeovis, James
25. Bond, Buckler
26. Joice, Elijah (Carpenter)
27. Calder, John
28. Bamhill, John
29. Deingan, Daniel
30. Taylor, John (son of John)

These are to Certify that the above named persons took and Subscribed their names to the above Oath before me, one of the State of Maryland Justices for Harford County

Wm. BOND.

1. THE WORSHIPFULL WILLIAM WILSON'S RETURNS
2. Giles, Jacob, Jnr.
3. Giles, Jacob
1778, Feb 28 Samuel Hopkins
4. Wilson, Saml. (son of William)
5. Gover, Philip
6. Vandergrift, George
(Signed) WILLIAM WILSON.

1. THE WORSHIPFULL AQUILA PACA'S RETURNS, MARCH 1ST 1778
2. Ellis, John
3. Madford, Wm.
4. Phillips, James
5. Smith, Wm.
6. Chistee, Gabriel
7. McComas, Alexa.
8. Carroll, James, Snr.
9. McComas, Edward Day
10. Jones, John ×
11. Gale, William
12. Smith, Joseph
13. Stevenson, John
14. Dars, Richard Tootill
15. Tare, James
16. Nuth, Moses, Snr.
17. Hanesey, Patrick ×
18. Dixon, Peter ×
19. Cartin, John ×
20. Reardon, James
21. Dooly, Edward
22. Jones, Awbray ×
23. Cunningham, Clothworth
24. Ecksen, Nichas
25. Cunningham, George ×
26. Hamon, John
27. Dunny, Simon, Jnr.
28. Riely, Narmt ×
29. Byfoot, Moses ×
30. Dallam, Richard, Snr.
31. Jones, William
32. Rigdon, Charles
33. Chrisholm, Thos.
34. Ayres, Thos. ×
35. Brown, Edward ×
36. Rhoads, George Lerton ×
37. Nelson, John
38. Giles, Thomas
39. Mubery, William
40. Beck, John
41. Fraulknor, Robert ×
42. Brown, Robert ×
43. Osborn, Cyrus
44. Trickert, Obadiah ×
45. Lerter, Norris
46. Eseldein, John
47. Sutton, Saml. ×
48. Ganetson, Freeborn
49. Ganetson, Richd.
50. Hall, Thos.
51. Deimer, John
52. Dearon, Francis
53. Cord, Abraham

Harford County A true Copy Mch 1st 1778
AQUILLA PACA.

A List of Persons that have taken their Affirmation of Fidelity and Support to this State Agreeable to an Act of Assembly entitled An Act for the better Support of the Government.

Harford County. Before me SAML. GROOME OSBORN.

1. Paul, John
2. Paul, James
3. Birckhead, Samuel
4. Timmons, John

1. The Worshipfull Mordacai Amoss' Returns
2. Morgan, Geo.
3. Bell, John
4. Smith, Nathan
5. Flatt, John
6. Cambell, James
7. Dunnahoe, Dent
8. Brierley, George
9. Brierley, Henry
10. Warwick, John
11. Brierley, Robert
12. Dome, William
13. Stewart, James
14. Slaide, Ezehiel
15. McComas, Danl. (of John)
16. Parsons, John
17. Bull, Cacob
18. Montgomery, Thomas
19. Watkins, Samuel
20. Wright, William
21. Slade, Ezekiel, Jnr.
22. Foster, Samuel
23. Foster, Henry
24. Bassett, John
25. Leonard, Edward
26. Anderson, James
27. Lyon, John
28. Slade, Thomas
29. Mead, James, Jnr.
30. Fox, Richard
31. Slade, Wm.
32. Clark, Robt.
33. Cowan, Edward
34. Amoss, Benja.
35. Tonte, Abram
36. Parsons, Isaac
37. Connolly, John
38. Norris, ——
39. Norris, Jno.
40. Pryne, James
41. Peteel, Thos.
42. Amoss, Wm. (of James)
43. Turner, Robert
44. Pryne, John
45. Long, Daniel
46. Harper, George
47. Spencer, Zachariah
48. Tany, James
49. Doran, Hugh
50. Benfield, David
51. Warwick, William
52. Leakin, James
53. Hawcy, William
54. Hawkins, Robert
55. Richardson, Samuel
56. Roberts, John
57. Alton, John
58. Smith, John
59. Richardson, Benja.
60. Mogan, James
61. Amoss, Joshua
62. Norris, John
63. Chew, Job M.
64. Smith, Vincent
65. Amoss, Aquila
66. Long, Peter
67. Doran, Patrick
68. Doran, John
69. Amoss, George
70. Amoss, Mordicai, Jnr.
71. Amoss, William
72. Thacker, John
73. Gibson, Francis
74. Gibson, John
75. Hughes, "Aram"
76. Poceer, Danl.
77. Ellett, Thos.
78. Price, Benja.
79. Bond, Daniel

A true Copy of the names of all the persons who have taken the Oath of Allegience, as prescribed by the Assembly of the State of Maryland before me Mch. 18", 1778.
Mordicai Amoss.

1. THE WORSHIPFULL SAMUEL G. OSBORNE'S RETURNS.

2. Presbury, George B.
3. Fulton, John
4. Norris, Agl [Aql?] (of Edward)
5. Roberts, Billingsley
6. Waltham, Charlton
7. White, James
8. Turner, Thomas
9. Carlisle, Lancelot
10. Boyce, Roger
11. Owens, Edward
12. Sewell, John
13. Jarrett, Henry
14. Phips, Joseph
15. Hewett, Joseph
16. Morsell, Kidd
17. Clarke, John
18. Owens, James
19. Sutler, Isaac
20. Chew, Richard
21. Barnett, John
22. Dungan, Benjamin

A List of persons that have taken the Oath of Fidelity to Support this State Agreeable to an Act of Assembly Intitled An Act for the Better Support of the Government. Harford County

SAMUEL G. OSBORNE.

1. THE WORSHIPFULL AQUILA HALL'S RETURNS.

2. Stokes, Robert
3. Hall, James White
4. Holliday, Robt.
5. Dallan, Francis
6. Bull, John
7. Brasher, Robert
8. Vancleane, John
9. Giles, Edward
10. Paca, John
11. Hall, Edward
12. Tolley, Edward Caroil
13. Lewis, Clement
14. Ruff, Richard
15. Jones, William ×
16. Lushody, Francis
17. Hall, William, Snr.
18. Mathews, James
19. Hall, Aquila, Jnr.
20. Bevard, Charles
21. Ward, Edward, Jnr.
22. Legoe, Benedict
23. "Wite" Richard
24. Stiles, Joseph
25. Andrews, Abraham
26. Hall, John Beedle
27. Coupland, George
28. Gibson, John Lee
29. Bradford, George
30. Vansukler, Henry
31. Patterson, John
32. Scott, James (son of Jas.)
33. Young, Samuel
34. Conhoway, Michael
35. Hall, Benedt. Edwd.
36. Grace, Aaron
37. Combest, Utey
38. Osbourn, James, Jnr.
39. Little, George
40. Mather, James
41. Griffith, Samuel
42. Brown, Garrett
43. White, Thomas
44. Hall, John (of Cranberry)
45. Henerson, Philip
46. Hughes, John Hall
47. Walkins, John
48. Chaney, John
49. Evans, Benjamin

50. Hanson, John, Jnr.
51. Walcott, John ×
52. Beck, Caleb
53. Osbourn, William
54. Sutton, Thomas
55. Robinson, William
56. Osbourn, William
57. Drew, Henry
58. Smith, William
59. Dixon, Morris ×
60. Cheney, George, Jnr.
61. Garland, Francis ×
62. Hanson, Hollis
63. Combes, Jacob
64. Pentenney, Joseph
65. Kimble, James, Jnr.
66. Chaney, George
67. Reading, William ×
68. Chaney, Benjamin
69. Whiteaker, Isaac ×
70. Hollis, Amos
71. West, William
72. Hall, Josas
73. Hays, John, Jnr.
74. Bennett, Peter
75. Taylor, John
76. Crawford, Alexander
77. Patterson, George
78. Mathews, Roger
79. Standley, John ×
80. Bennett, Levin
81. Johnson, William
82. Try, Paultis
83. Daugherty, Samuel
84. Woolsey, Joseph
85. Beatty, Archabald
86. Jackson, Thomson ×
87. Paca, Aquila, Jnr.
88. Loney, William
89. Drew, James
90. Drew, Anthoney
91. Mash, Loyd
92. Hall, William, Jnr.
93. Drew, George
94. Kennard, Michael
95. Shinton, John
96. Armstrong, John
97. Hollis, Wm., Snr.
98. Hollis, Wm., Jnr.
99. Ruff, John
100. Reason, James ×
101. Coupland, John
102. Nutterwell, Daniel
103. Kimble, Samuel
104. Wood, John
105. Brown, John
106. Garrittson, Garritt
107. Steuart, James
108. Michael, Balsher
109. Gordon, Alexander
110. Crouch, Stephen ×
111. Budd, George
112. Dorsey, Frisby
113. Frisbey, Thomas Peregrine
114. Mobsler, James
115. Gilmore, Charles
116. Debrular, Anthony
117. Taylor, John
118. Pike, Hutchins
119. Gelley, William
120. McCarty, James
121. Buckley, John ×
122. Warfield, Henry
123. Mathews, John, Sen.
124. Mathews, John, Jnr.
125. Eagle, James ×
126. Ashley, Thomas
127. Dallam, John
128. Lenagin, James
129. Mcegay, Robert
130. Whiteaker, John
131. Bennett, Benjamin
132. Caine, Edward

AQUILA HALL.

1. The Worshipfull Robert Amos' Returns
2. Baker, Charles, Capt.
3. Hitchcock, Asael, Jnr.
4. Britton, Wm.
5. Hitchcock, Josiah, Jnr.
6. Miles, Aquila
7. Robinson, Edwd.
8. Talbott, James
9. Carlile, Robert
10. Ashten, Joseph
11. Parker, Aquila
12. James, Wm.
13. Amoss, Joshua (of James)
14. Hitchcock, Asel, Snr.
15. Norris, Wm.
16. McDonald, Cornelius
17. Nelson, Hugh
18. Amoss, James, Snr.
19. Dale, John
20. Hutchins, Richard
21. Peairs, John
22. Parker, Martin
23. Parker, John
24. Amoss, Nicholas
25. Evans, Evan
26. Talbott, Matthew
27. Taylor, Charles
28. Knight, Wm.
29. Creswell, Marthew
30. Harper, Moses
31. Robinson, Richard (of Edw.)
32. Ditto, Wm.
33. Biddle, Benja.
34. Corbet, John
35. McCourtie, James
36. Cambell, John, Snr.
37. Horrod, Wm.
38. Curry, James
39. Harthey, Joseph
40. Barton, James
41. Amoss, James, Jnr.
42. Duncan, James
43. Lyon, Jonathan
44. Coleman, George
45. Turner, John
46. Mekemson, John
47. Cowley, Mathew
48. Mekemson, William
49. Mekemson, Thos.
50. Ayers, Stephen
51. Meegaa, James
52. Brown, John
53. Davidson, John
54. Smith, John
55. Patterson, Wm.
56. McDonald, John
57. Hanna, Hugh
58. Almony, John
59. Kelly, Arthu
60. Roberts, Wm.
61. Giles, James
62. Thomas, John
63. Markham, William
64. Hanna, Caleb
65. Smithson, David
66. Garrison, John
67. Dublin, John Stewart
68. Stewart, John
69. Simpson, Wm.
70. Bently, Joshua
71. Sturgem, Robt.
72. McDonald, Hugh
73. Amoss, Benjn., Capt.
74. Carter, Benjn.
75. Whiteford, Hugh
76. Oldham, Henry
77. Hutchins, Jacob
78. Williams, David
79. Ensor, Thomas
80. Beaven, John I.
81. Robinson, Charles
82. Taylor, John (of Chas.)
83. Butersbo, John

84. Robinson, Wm., Jnr.
85. Hutchins, Wm.
86. Burton, Richard
87. Garrison, Cornelius
88. Guyon, John
89. Chocke, John
90. Clark, Aquila
91. Hitchcock, John
92. Hitchcock, Wm.
93. Rockhold, John, Jnr.
94. Taylor, John
95. Norris, James
96. Jivdon, Richard
97. Carroll, Peter
98. Rockhold, Asael
99. Carman, Andrew
100. Craven, Andrew
101. Rice, Walter
102. Polson, John
103. Eagon, Samson
104. Jarrett, Jesse
105. Day, Samuel
106. Garrott, Wm.
107. Thomas, Thos.
108. Johnson, Moses
109. Beard, Thos.
110. Elder, Robt.
111. Donoley, Jas.
112. Rutledge, John
113. Robins, Job
114. Standiford, Jas.
115. Smith, John
116. Smith, Jas.
117. Carson, John
118. Morris, John
119. Marsh, John
120. Scofield, Wm.
121. Parker, Wm.
122. Appelton, Edwd.
123. Amos, Henry
124. Ditto, Henry
125. Forrisdale, Stanford
126. Reves, Noah
127. Day, Robt.
128. Baldwin, Wm.
129. Scarff, John
130. Shipley, Richard
131. Hitchcock, Josiah, Snr.
132. Hitchcock, Henry
133. Robinson, Wm., Snr.
134. McClelan, Nathan
135. Evans, Griffith
136. Jones, Joseph

Coppy of ye affirmation and affirmers thereto proceeding taken before me

ROBERT AMOSS.

1. THE WORSHIPFULL JOHN ARCHER'S RETURNS
2. Smith, Samuel
3. McClintock, Mathew, Jnr.
4. Monohan, Arthur.
5. Baylis, Daniel
6. Stack, Jacob
7. Smith, David
8. Teats, C. S.
9. Bull, Jacob
10. MClure, William
11. Jameson, Alexander
12. Hart, John
13. Boardsman, William
14. Smith, James
15. Monohan, John
16. Baylis, Samuel
17. Perry, Thos. × Feb. 2d, 1778
18. Slack, John
19. Cretin, John, Feb. 7th, 1778
20. Jervis, John
21. MLaughlin, George

22. Cretin, Patrick
23. Smith, Wm. (son of Wm.)
24. Bromly, Joseph, Feb. 7th 1778
25. Hanna, James
26. Moorn, John
27. Morgan, Edward
28. Hormott, Andrew
29. Kroesen, Richard
30. Pritchard, Thomas ×
31. Millien, Patrick ×
32. Pritchard, Obediah
33. Kennedy, James
34. Bonar, William
35. Jeffry, Robert ×
36. Rowntree, Thomas
37. Armstrong, James
38. Gilbert, Michael, Snr.
39. Baylis, Benjamin
40. Gilbert, Parker
41. Gilbert, Philip
42. Perkins, John
43. Kroesen, John
44. Hagon, Henry
45. Moore, James
46. Holmes, James
47. Horner, James
48. Smith, Thomas
49. Powar, Nicholas
50. Gilbert, Samuel
51. Gilbert, Taylor
52. Smith, Hugh
53. Wamagin, Thomas ×
54. Clark, John
55. Kroesen, Nicholas, Feb. 21, 1778
56. Huff, Abraham
57. Price, Daniel
58. Vanhorn, Ezekiel
59. Kirkpatrick, Hugh
60. Smith, Robert
61. Dever, Hugh
62. Butler, George
63. McLaughlin, Robert, Feb. 21, 1778
64. MClure, Robert
65. Jamison, John
66. MBride, John
67. MDonald Patrick
68. Pritchard, James, Jnr.
69. Dickson, David
70. Caldwell, John
71. Kennedy, Thomas
72. Ramsay, William
73. Chiswell, Robert
74. Creswell, Robert
75. Criswell, Robert
76. Courtney, Thomas
77. Smith, Ralph
78. Sims, George
79. Vanhorn, Richard
80. MClintock, Mathew
81. Langhin, Peter
82. Jibb, John ×
83. Gilbert, Mich.
84. MLaughlin, John
85. Hanson, Jacob ×
86. Baylis, Nache.
87. Silner, Benjamin
88. Wells, James
89. Baylis, Robert
90. Gilbert, Charles (son of Michl.)
91. Baylis, Elias
92. Smith, Benja.
93. Andrews, Thomas
94. Durbin, Daniel
95. Carey, John
96. Pritchard, James, Feb. 26th 1778
97. Dallam, Richard
98. Garrett, Amos
99. Hanna, John
100. Cretin, John, Jnr.
101. Curry, John ×

102. Cuddy, James, Feb. 26″, 1778
103. Jevis, Joseph
104. Jameson, John (Farmer)
105. Monohon, Arthur
106. Hanna, Alexander
107. Esther, James ×
108. Cunningham, John
109. Logne, Wm., Snr. ×
110. Boyle, Thos., Feb. 28th 1778
111. Cultraugh, William
112. Eratt, William
113. Loney, Amos
114. Walker, James
115. Wilmott, Richard
116. Corsly, Richard
117. Breden, Robert
118. Cooley, John
119. Davidson, John
120. Barns, William
121. Mathews, Bennet
122. Gilbert, Michael
123. Taylor, Walter, Feb. 28th 1778
124. Watson, Archibald
125. Clark, Lawrence
126. Smith, Nathe.
127. Gilbert, Charles, Snr.
128. Tilbrook, John
129. Waldron, Richard
130. Britchard, John
131. Sheredine, James
132. Denny, Michael
133. Small, John
134. Hawthorn, John
135. Harrington, Thomas
136. MClure, James
137. Campbell, Daniel
138. Criswell, William
139. Blackburn, Robert
140. MCann, Arthur (Miller)
141. Culver, Benja.
142. Browne, Thomas
143. Ferguson, Andrew
144. Smith, Patrick, Feb. 28th 1778
145. ODonnell, Michael
146. Hays, Archer
147. Gilbert, Aquila
148. Jeffrey, Hugh
149. Hasset, William
150. ODillen, Lawrence
151. Huston, James
152. Sharswood, William
153. Culver, Robert
154. Roney, John ×
155. MCann, Arthur × (Weaver)
156. Wilson, Andrew
157. Townley, John ×
158. Dallam, Josias Wm.
159. Worster, Robert
160. Murphy, Edward ×
161. Byard, James
162. Hays, John
163. MFaddin, Daniel
164. Cunning, Philip

JOHN ARCHER.

1. THE WORSHIPFULL JOHN LOVE'S RETURNS
2. Pennith, Thomas
3. West, William
4. Preston, William
5. Honnoll, William
6. Preston, Daniel
7. Key, Job
8. Bussey, Edward
9. Scott, Nathan
10. Clark, William, Jnr.
11. West, Nathaniel, Jnr.
12. Preston, James
13. Corbet, William
14. West, Jonathan
15. Green, John
16. Goldsmith, Vincent
17. Fulton, William

18. Shepherd, William
19. Clark, William (of Robt.)
20. Preston, Martin
21. Green, Henry
22. Huston, Hugh
23. Stooksbery, William, Jnr.
24. Turner, Andrew
25. Watson, James
26. Stooksbery, William, Snr.
27. Rhodes, Benjamin
28. Tomby, Thomas
29. Casedy, Allen
30. Neal, John (of Charles Co.)
31. Neal, W^m^. Francis (of Chas. Co.)
32. Green, Benjamin
33. Green, Lawrence
34. Wheeler, Bennett
35. Cooper, Henry
36. Billinglia, Walter
37. Worrell, Richard
38. M^c^Guire, Phillip
39. Harriss, James
40. Cretin, James
41. Jeffriss, Thomas
42. Blacklearr, John
43. Hannah, William
44. Strode, Thomas
45. Billinglea, Walter, Jnr.
46. Buckman, John
47. Norris, Joseph (of Edwd.)
48. Bull, Edward (of Jacob)
49. Terrey, Patrick
50. Bull, Jacob (of Jacob)
51. Johnson, Robert
52. West, Jonathan, Jnr.
53. Bezerly, Hugh, Jnr.
54. Scott, Aquila (of Aquila)
55. Smithson, Daniel
56. West, Nathan, Snr.
57. Fye, Godfrey
58. Green, Henry (of John)
59. Johnson, Barnet
60. Murphy, Patrick
61. Erwin, James
62. Johnson, Jacob
63. Grafton, Daniel
64. Grafton, William
65. Preston, Barnard (of Danl.)
66. Moone, James (of John)
67. Cooper, William
68. Green, James
69. Hopkins, William, Jnr. (Quaker)
70. Wilson, Henry (Quaker)
71. Robinson, Joseph (Quaker)

I Certify the above to be a true Coppie given under my hand this 3rd March 1778.

JOHN LOVE.

1. THE WORSHIPFULL ABRM. WHITAKER'S RETURNS, MCH. 24TH, 1778.
2. Renshaw, Joseph
3. Robson, Richard
4. Renshaw, Joseph, Jnr.
5. Vanhorn, G. P.
6. Jewett, Charles
7. Thomson, Andrew
8. Renshaw, Thomas
9. Robinson, Archa.
10. Bleany, Thos.
11. MDaniel, Jos.
12. MColough, Jas.
13. Vanhorn, Aaron
14. Sadler, Jas. Norris
15. M^c^Colough, Jas., Jnr.
16. Smith, Peter
17. Makinson, Andrew

18. Kean, Jos.
19. Meekmoor, Robt.
20. Worsby, Geo. H.
21. Mekeem, Jos.
22. McCord, Arthur
23. Alleson, Alexn.
24. Kelley, Jno.
25. Hendersides, Frn.
26. Vance, Jno.
27. Kirkwood, Robert
28. Tayn, Jno. Dealy
29. Cook, Jno.
30. Hall, Wm.
31. Kerne, Jno.
32. Bush, Jno.
33. Patterson, Samuel
34. Patterson, Saml.
35. Clark, Jno. (Revd.)
36. Prestin, Grafton
37. Durner, Thos.
38. Capbell, Jno.
39. Bell, David
40. Finley, Jno.
41. Finley, Jas.
42. Finley, Jas., Jnr.
43. Amass, William (of Joshua)
44. McCloskey, Jas.
45. Rogers, Owen
46. Cross, Richard
47. Davis, John, Revd.
48. Long, Jno.
49. Harper, Samuel
50. McClosky, Jos.
51. Orr, Jno.
52. Dives, Francis
53. Orr, James
54. Smith, Robert
55. Turner, Danl.
56. Varney, James
57. Curry, James
58. Clemmons, Patrick
59. Gleen, Robert
60. Hopes, Richard
61. Norris, Edward
62. Thomas, Jos.
63. Hannah, Robert
64. Cooper, Calvin
65. Whiteford, John
66. McConner, Daniel
67. McColough, Alexander
68. Smith, William
69. Keeps, Robert
70. Turner, Patrick
71. Evans, Griffith
72. Orr, Jas.
73. James, William
74. Thomas, Thomas
75. Shell, Jno.
76. Skwington, James
77. Everett, James
78. Talbott, Edward
79. Tawlard, Benja.
80. Hopes, Thomas
81. Bankhead, Hugh
82. Henderson, Andw.
83. Mead, James
84. Russel, Thos.
85. Sheanes, Henry
86. Ayers, Thos.
87. Wood, Henry
88. Patterson, Jas.
89. Johnson, William
90. Comeve, Jos.
91. McClure, John
92. Turnell, Thomas
93. Dereale, Michl.
94. Griffith, Thos.
95. Eavs, Nah.
96. Gordon, William
97. Deney, Walter
98. Deney, James
99. Whiterker, ——
100. Bankhead, William
101. Riddle, John

102. Stone, John
103. McClung, Adam
104. Nelson, Robert
105. Bek, John
106. Parsons, John
107. McGruigen, ——
108. Sain, ——
109. Fulfet, John
110. Richardson, Wm.
111. Bull, Jacob (of John)
112. Swann, Frederick
113. Feat, David
114. Durham, David
115. Dunsheath, William
116. Ashmead, Samuel
117. Coale, William
118. Corbitt, Jos.
119. Ware, Thos.
120. Lurk, James
121. Dick, David
122. Crop, James
123. Hicks, Zebedee
124. James, Joshua
125. James, Thomas, Jnr.
126. Watson, William
127. Davis, John
128. Davis, Thomas
129. James, Thomas
130. Long, John, Jnr.
131. McComas, William
132. Collings, Robert
133. Frew, John
134. Creighton, James
135. Hannah, Sam.
136. Guff, James
137. Derrow, Jno.
138. Cooly, Richard
139. Scott, James
140. Brown, David
141. Cooly, William
142. Allin, Jno.
143. Cooly, Richard, Jnr.
144. Roads, Thomas
145. Gladden, Jacob
146. Thompson, Daniel
147. Bay, Hugh
148. Pain, Barnit.
149. Robinson, John
150. Renshaw, John
151. Pillet, Thomas
152. Murphy, Thomas
153. Novinton, John
154. Clar, Thomas, Jnr.
155. Dealy, John
156. Lee, John
157. Beaty, Wm.
158. Henry, Michl.
159. Clark, John
160. Poteet, James
161. Wheeler, Thomas
162. Thompson, Alexander
163. Davis, David
164. Willnoth, Godfray
165. Harpan, Andrew
166. Renshaw, Samuel
167. Scott, Alexander
168. Harmer, Samuel
169. Gibs, Jno.
170. Renshaw, Philip
171. Huff, John
172. McKell, James
173. Ashmead, John
174. Street, Thomas
175. Poteet, Thomas, Jnr.
176. Ware, John
177. James, Henry
178. Street, Thomas, Jnr.
179. Coop, Doratio
180. Thomson, James
181. Whaler, Jacob
182. Sinckler, James
183. West, David
184. Lewis, Thomas
185. Wat, Robert

186. Steel, John
187. Mackalheny, Mathew
188. Evans, David
189. Wakeling, John
190. Ask, Thomas
191. Kidd, John
192. Murphy, William
193. Loyd, Thos.
194. Craftin, Samuel
195. Bosley, William
196. Odoneld, Saml.
197. Bay, W^{m}.
198. Mathews, Ignatius
199. Harris, Robert
200. Gormiley, Owen
201. McKinley, Roger
202. Weain, John
203. McColsgh, David
204. Bryerly, Hugh
205. Huskins, Thomas
206. Kidd, James

Gov. Thos. Johnson, Governor of the State.
Eden Town.

I send you a list of the several Gentlemen who took the Oath of Fidelity before me as under and by Act of the General Assembly

ABM. WHITAKER.

OATHS OF FIDELITY AND SUPPORT
PRINCE GEORGE'S COUNTY, MD.

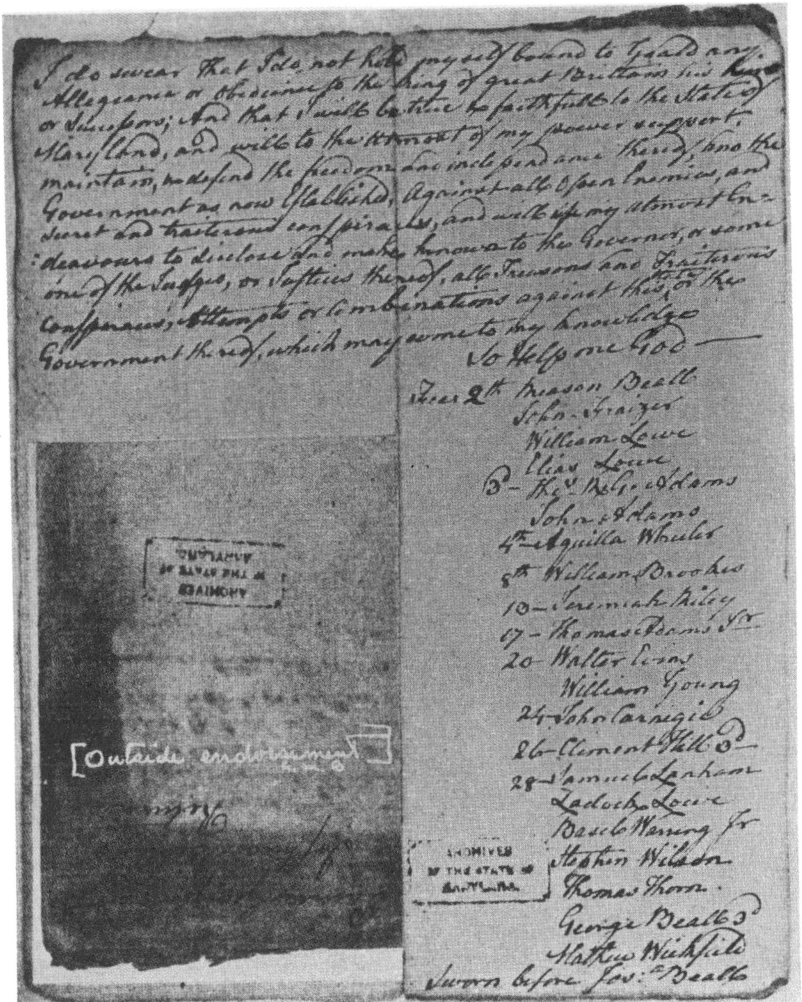
I do swear that I do not hold myself bound to yield any Allegiance or Obedience to the King of great Britain his heirs or Successors; And that I will be true and faithfull to the State of Maryland, and will to the utmost of my power support, maintain, and defend the freedom and independence thereof, and the Government as now Established, Against all Open Enemies, and Secret and traiterous conspiracies, and will use my utmost Endeavours to disclose and make known to the Governor, or some one of the Judges, or Justices thereof, all Treasons and Traiterous Conspiracies, Attempts or Combinations against this State, or the Government thereof, which may come to my knowledge

So Help me God—

Mar 2th Meason Beall
John Fraizer
William Lowe
Elias Lowe
3– Henry Rigs Adams
John Adams
4th Aquilla Wheeler
8th William Brookes
10– Jeremiah Riley
17– Thomas Evans Jr
20 Walter Evans
William Young
24 John Carnegie
26 Clement Hill 3d
28 Samuel Lanham
Zadock Lowe
Basil Waring Jr
Stephen Wilson
Thomas Thorn
George Beall 3d
Matthew Wickfield
Sworn before Jos: Beall

[Outside endorsement]

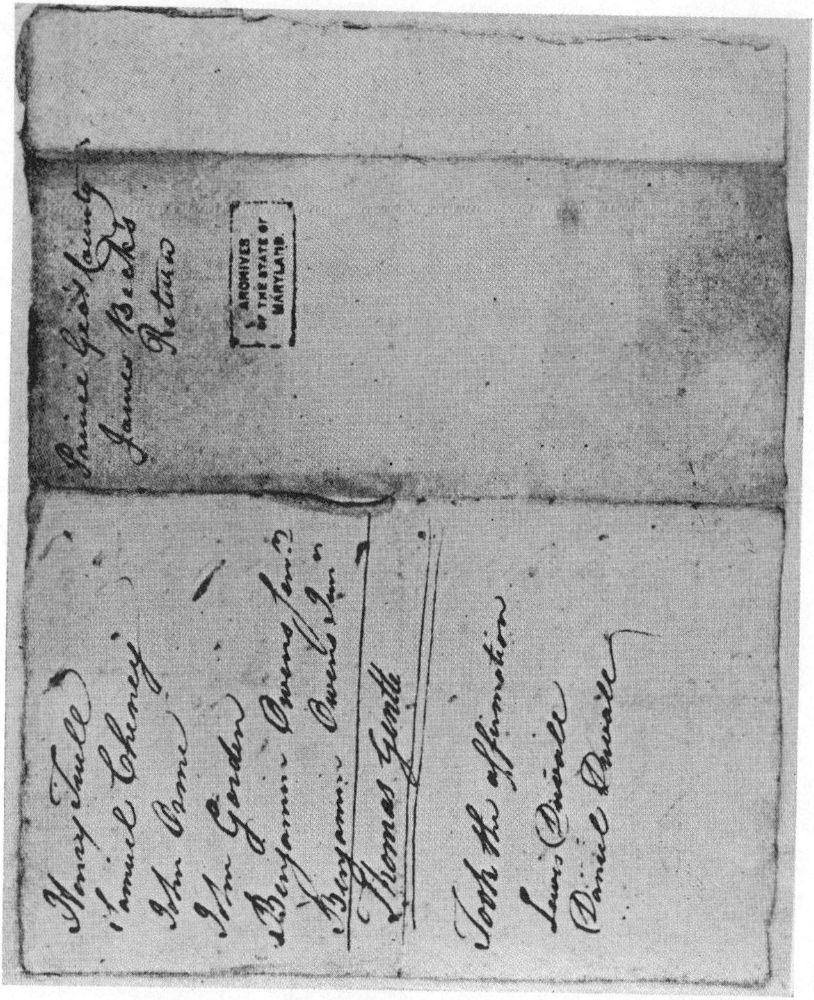
Prince Geo's County
James Becks
Return

ARCHIVES OF THE STATE OF MARYLAND

Henry Truell
Samuel Cheney
Jno Orme
Jno Gordon
Benjamin Owens Senr
Benjamin Owens Junr
Thomas Gantt

Took the affirmation
Lewis Duvall
Daniel Duvall

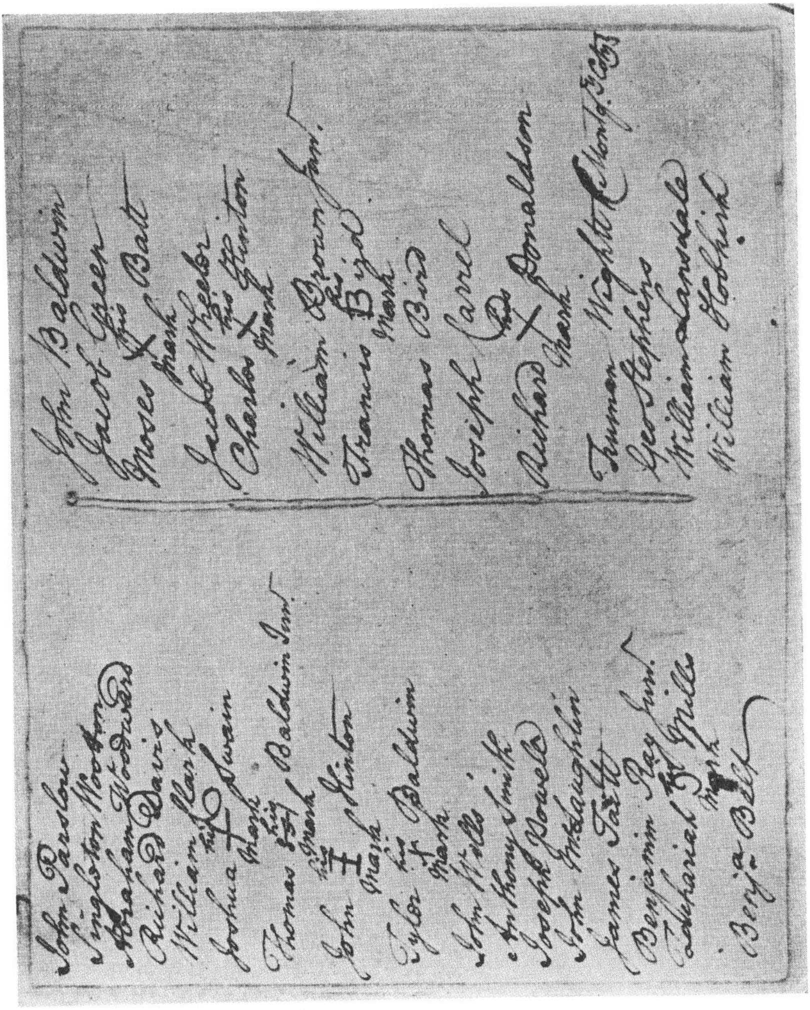

John Parslow
Singleton Wootton
Abraham Woodward
Richard Davis
William his mark Clark
Joshua his mark Swain
Thomas his mark Baldwin Junr.
John his mark Hinton
Tylor his mark Baldwin
John Willis
Anthony Smith
Joseph Powell
John McLaughlin
James Tate
Benjamin Ray Junr.
Zachariah his mark Mills
Benja. Bell

John Baldwin
Jacob Green
Moses his mark Batt
Jacob Wheeler
Charles his mark Hinton
William Brown Junr.
Francis his mark Bird
Thomas Bird
Joseph his mark Carrel
Richard his mark Donaldson
Truman Wight Clerk Montg. Cty.
Geo. Stephens
William Lansdale
William Hobkirk

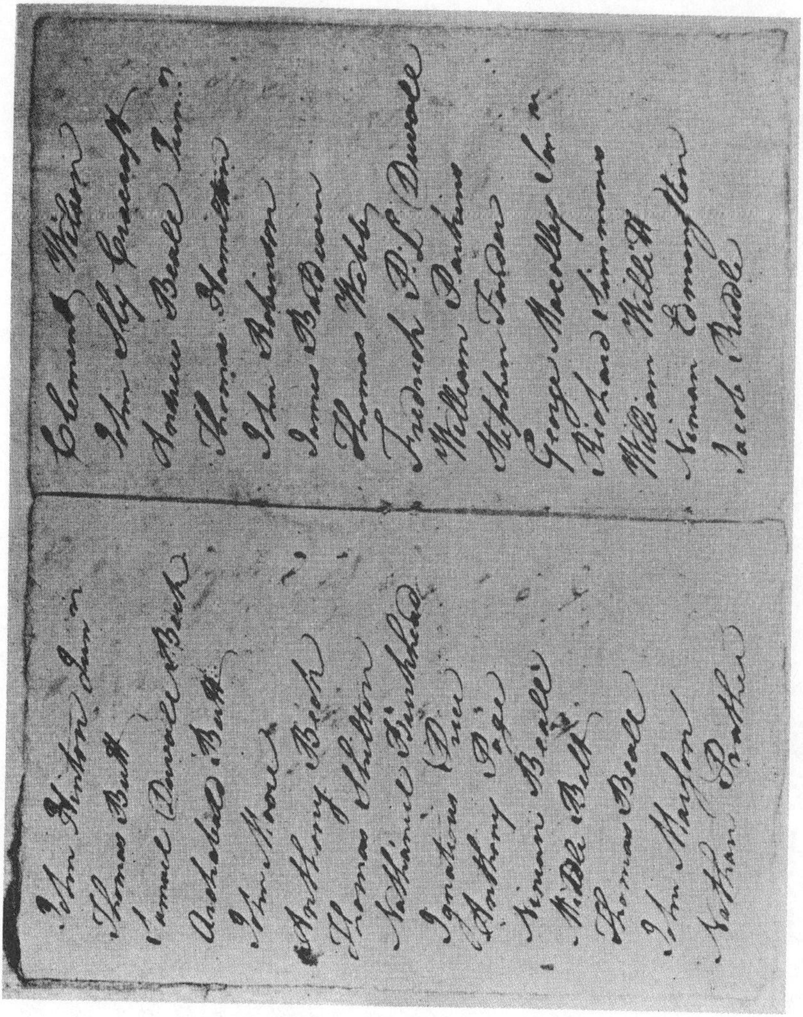

Jno Hinton Junr
Thomas Belt
Samuel Duvall Beck
Archibald Belt
Jno Moore
Anthony Beck
Thomas Shelton
Nathaniel Burkhead
Ignatius Dice
Anthony Page
Ninian Beall
Middle Belt
Thomas Beall
Jno Mayson
Nathan Prather

Clement Wilson
Wm Hy Crawcroft
Andrew Beall Junr
Thomas Hamilton
John Robinson
James B[illegible]
Thomas Webb
Frederick Pl Duvall
William Parker
Stephen Fowler
George [illegible] Senr
Richard Simmons
William Willett
Ninian Edmonston
Jacob Riddle

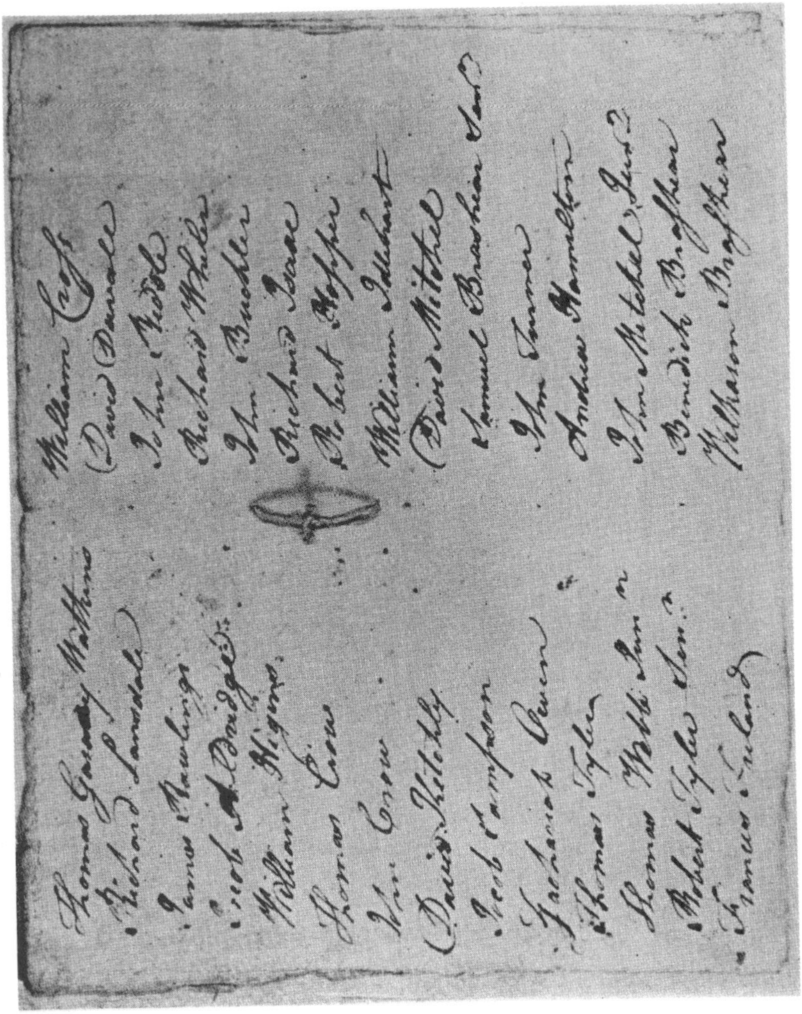

Thomas Garrety Watkins
Richard Lansdale
James Rawlings
Jacob Bridges
William Wiguns
Thomas Crow
John Crow
David Kitchly
Jacob Sampson
Zachariah Owen
Thomas Tyler
Thomas Webb Senr
Robert Tyler Senr
Francis Ireland

William Cross
David Danalee
John Riddle
Richard Wheeler
John Buckler
Richard Isaac
Robert Hopper
William Isdehart
David Mitchell
Samuel Brashear Senr
John Tanner
Andrew Hamilton
John Mitchell Senr
Benedick Brashear
Wilkeson Brashear

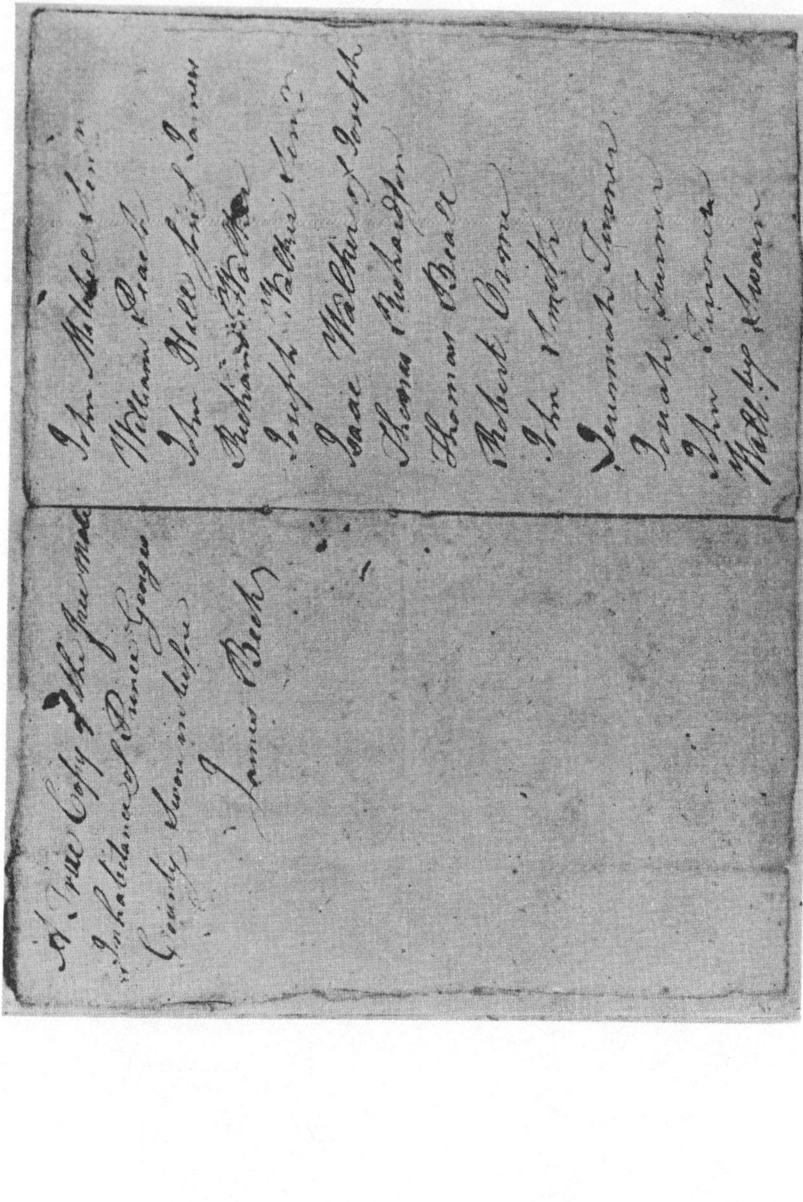

A True Copy of the Free Male
Inhabitants of Prince Georges
County Sworn to before
James Beck

John Wilcoxen Senr
William Pratt
John Hill Son of James
Richard Watkins
Joseph Watkins Senr
Isaac Watkins of Joseph
Thomas Richardson
Thomas Beall
Robert Orme
John Smith
Jeremiah Turner
Josiah Turner
John Turner
[illegible] Swann

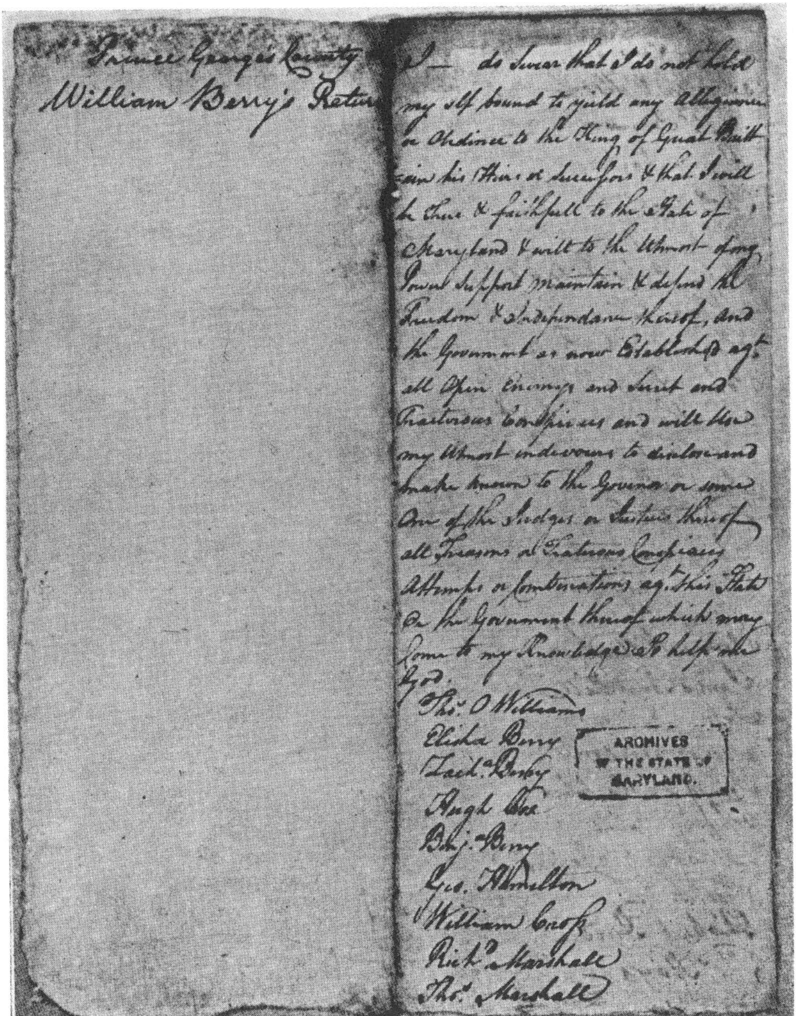
Prince George's County
William Berry's Return

I — do Swear that I do not hold
my self bound to yield any Allegiance
or Obedience to the King of Great Britt-
ain his Heirs or Successors & that I will
be True & faithfull to the State of
Maryland & will to the Utmost of my
Power Support Maintain & defend the
Freedom & Independance thereof, and
the Government as now Established agt.
all Open Enemys and Secret and
Traiterous Conspiracies and will Use
my Utmost endeavours to disclose and
make known to the Governor or some
One of the Judges or Justices thereof
all Treasons or Traiterous Conspiracy
Attempts or Combinations agt. this State
Or the Government thereof which may
Come to my Knowledge So help me
God.

Thos. O Williams
Elisha Berry
Zach^a Berry
Hugh Wee
Benj^a Berry
Geo. Hamilton
William Cross
Richd. Marshall
Thos. Marshall

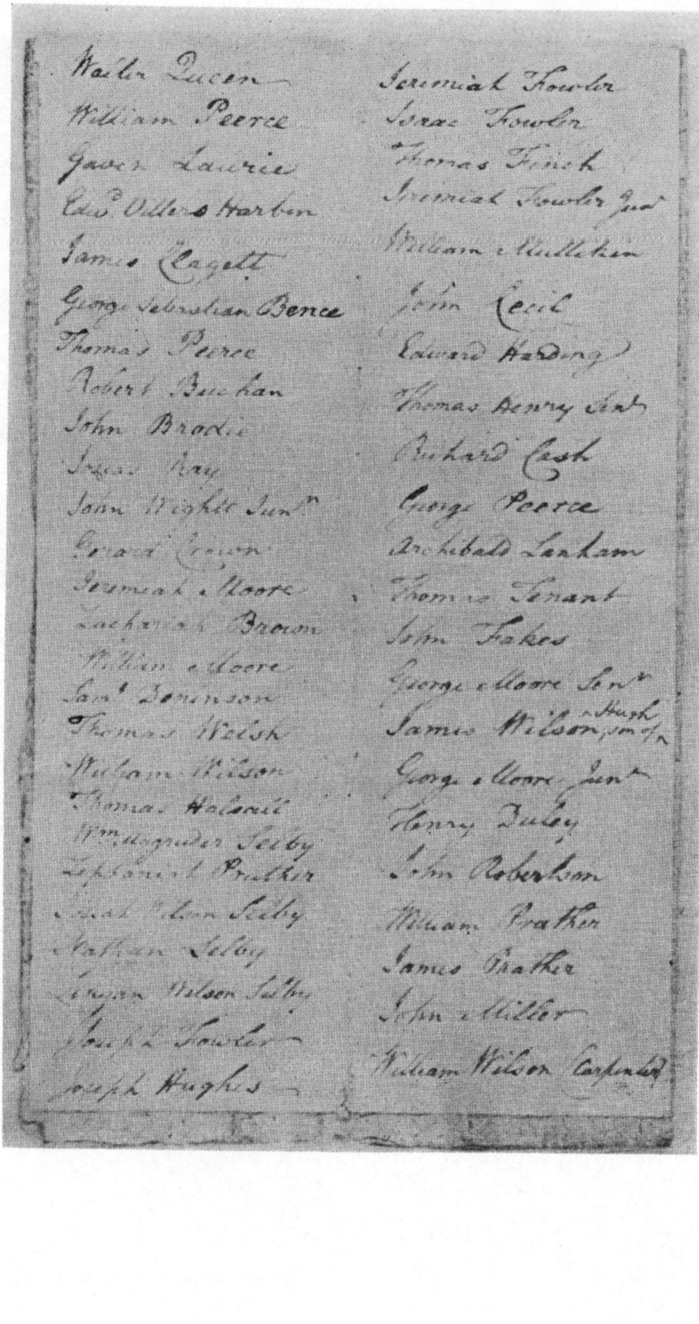

Walter Queen
William Peerce
Gavin Laurie
Edwd. Villers Harbin
James Clagett
George Sebastian Bence
Thomas Peerce
Robert Buchan
John Brodie
Isaac Ray
John Wight Junr.
Gerard Lemon
Jeremiah Moore
Zachariah Brown
William Moore
Saml. Robinson
Thomas Welsh
William Wilson
Thomas Halsall
Wm. Magruder Selby
Zephaniah Prather
Josiah Wilson Selby
Nathan Selby
Lingan Wilson Selby
Joseph Fowler
Joseph Hughes

Jeremiah Fowler
Isaac Fowler
Thomas Finch
Jeremiah Fowler Junr
William Mulliken
John Cecil
Edward Harding
Thomas Henry Senr
Richard Cash
George Peerce
Archibald Lanham
Thomas Tenant
John Fakes
George Moore Senr
James Wilson, son of Hugh
George Moore Junr
Henry Duley
John Robertson
William Prather
James Prather
John Miller
William Wilson Carpenter

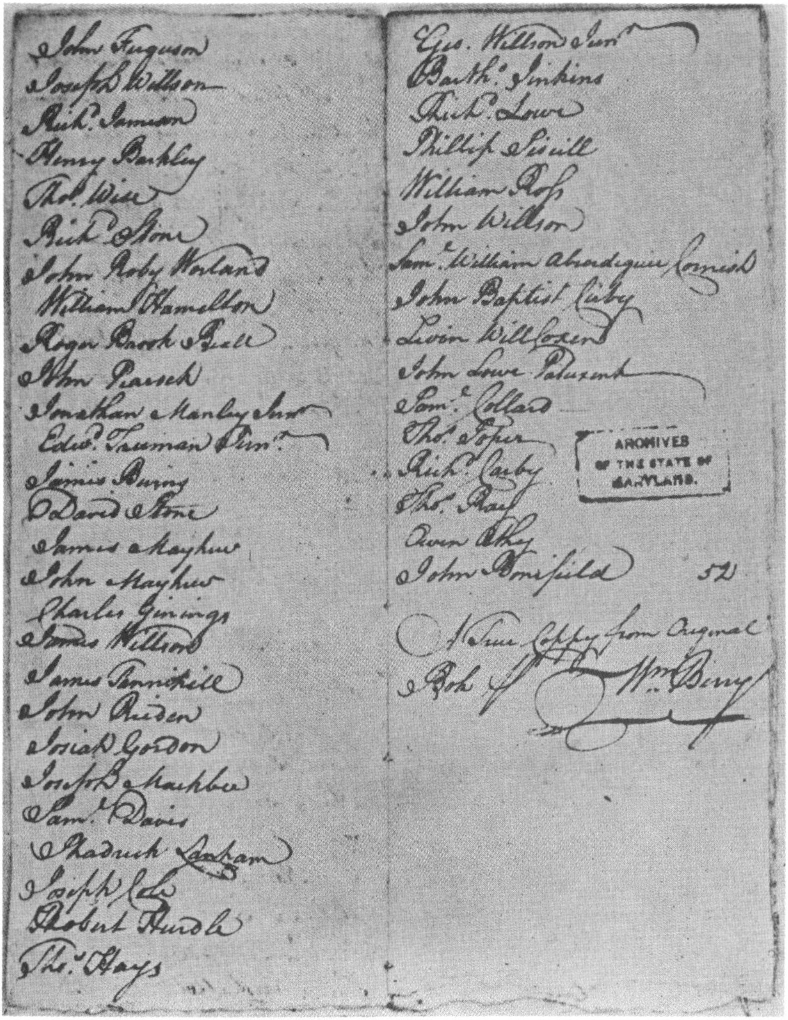

John Fuguson
Joseph Willson
Richd. Jameson
Henry Barkley
Thos. Wise
Richd. Stone
John Roby Worland
William Hamilton
Roger Brook Bell
John Peacock
Jonathan Manley Junr
Edwd. Trueman Senr.
James Berry
David Stone
James Mayhew
John Mayhew
Charles Jinings
Thomas Willson
James Pennikell
John Reeder
Josiah Gordon
Joseph Mackbee
Saml. Davis
Shadrick Lanham
Joseph Cole
Robert Hurdle
Thos. Hays

Geo. Willson Junr
Bartho. Jinkins
Richd. Lowe
Phillip Sissill
William Ross
John Willson
Saml. William Abradiquie Cornish
John Baptist Cuby
Levin Willcoxen
John Lowe Patuxent
Saml. Collard
Thos. Toper
Richd. Cauby
Thos. Ray
Owen Athey
John Brinsfield 52

A True Coppy from Original
Test Wm. Berry

ARCHIVES OF THE STATE OF MARYLAND

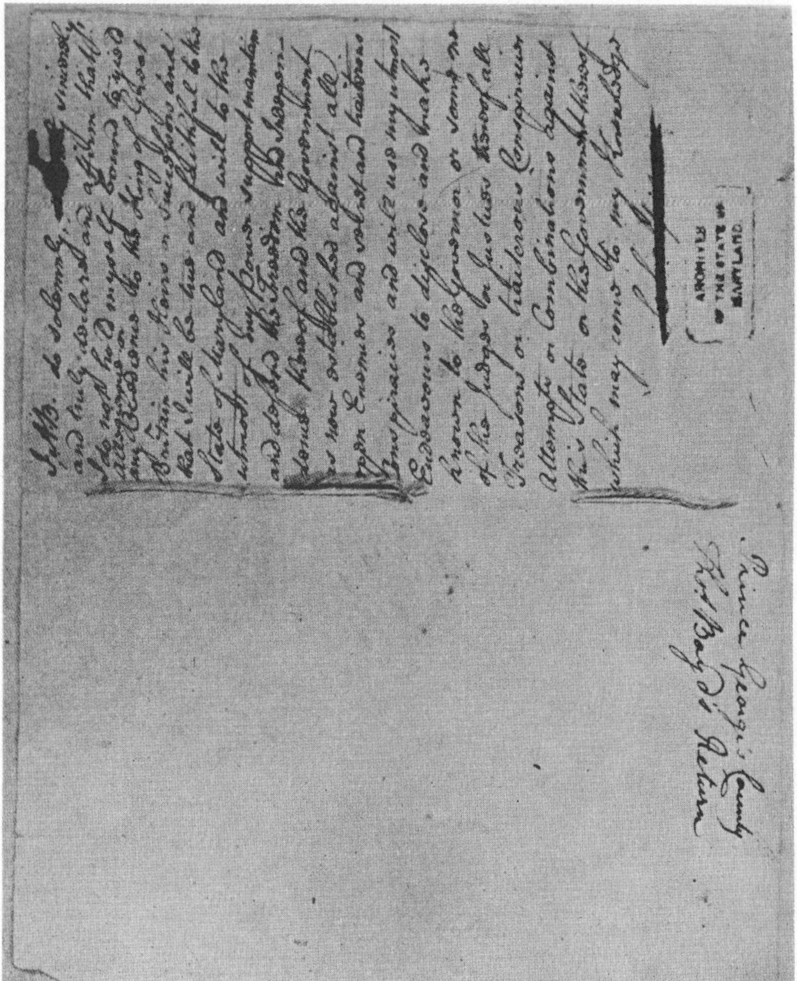
I [illegible] do solemnly [illegible] sincerely
and truly declare and affirm that I
do not hold myself bound to yield
any allegiance or obedience to the King of Great
Britain his Heirs or Successors and
that I will be true and faithful to the
State of Maryland and will to the
utmost of my Power support maintain
and defend the Freedom and Independence
thereof and the Government
as now established against all open
Enemies and secret and traiterous
Conspiracies and will use my utmost
Endeavours to disclose and make
known to the Governor or some one
of the Judges or Justices thereof all
Treasons or traiterous Conspiracies
Attempts or Combinations against
this State or the Government thereof
which may come to my knowledge
Prince George's County

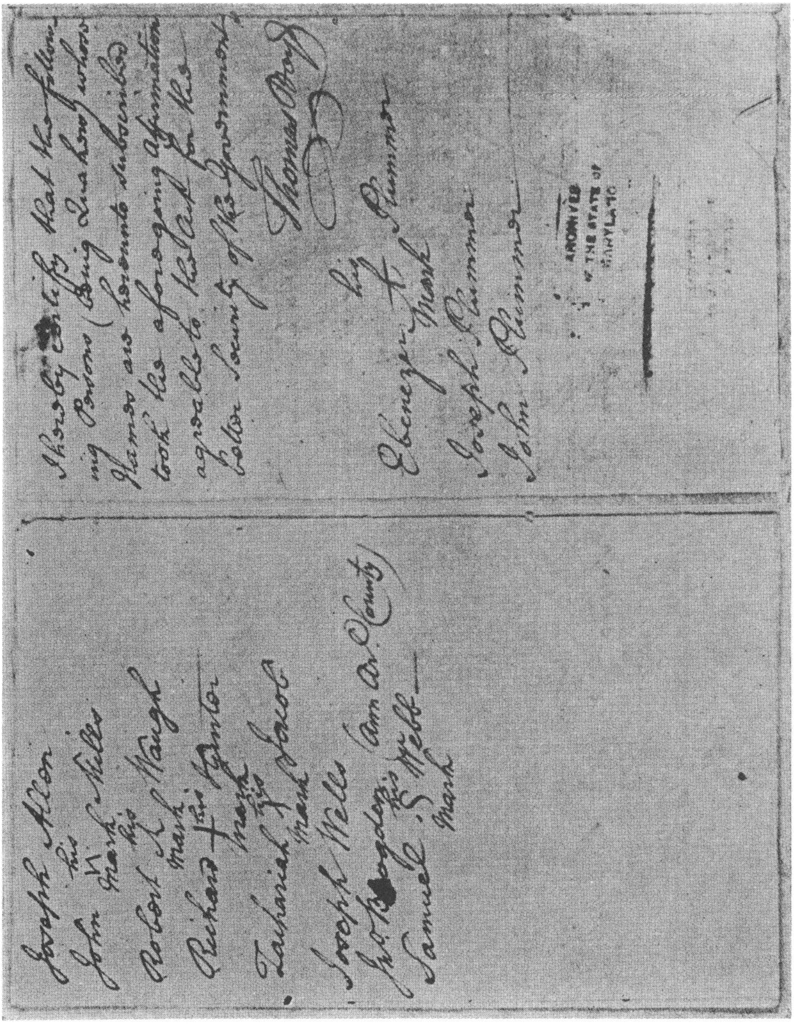

I hereby certify that the following Persons (being Quakers) whose Names are hereunto subscribed took the aforegoing Affirmation agreeable to the Act for the better Security of the Government

Thomas Boyd

Ebenezer his X mark Plummer
Joseph Plummer
John Plummer

Joseph Allen
John his X mark Wells
Robert his X mark Waugh
Richard his X mark Hunter
Zachariah his X mark Jacob
Joseph Wells (Ann Ar. County)
Jno. Ogden
Samuel his S mark Webb

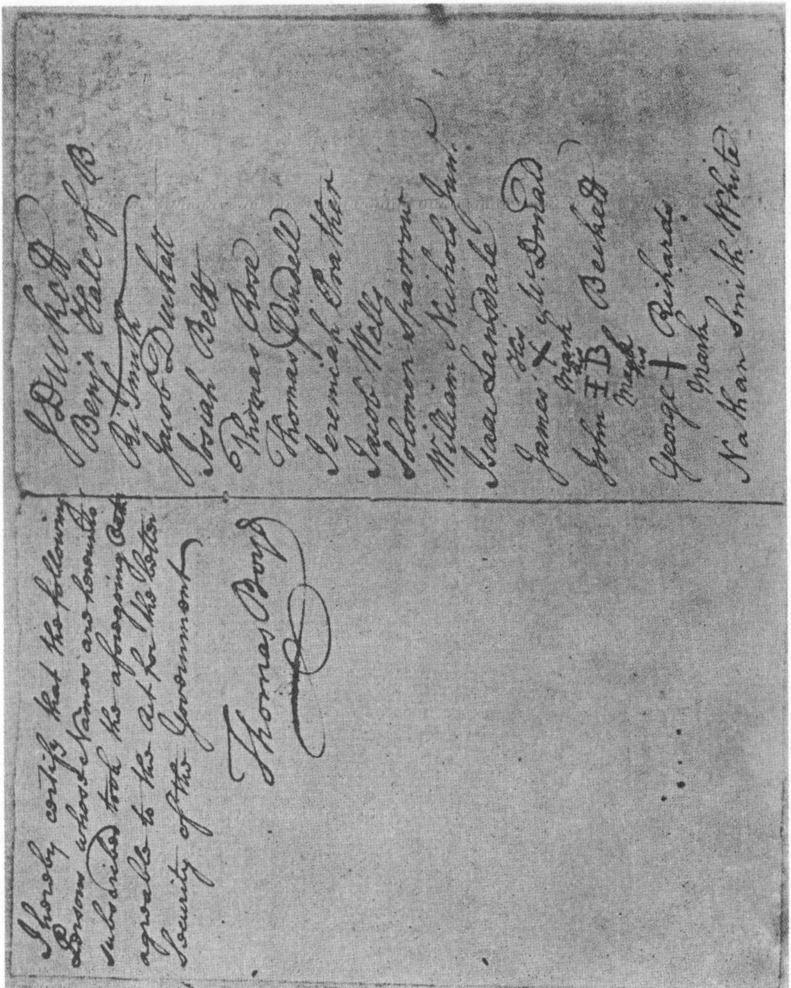

I hereby certify that the following Persons whose Names are hereunto subscribed took the aforegoing Oath agreeable to the Act for the better Security of the Government

Thomas Boyd

J Duckett
Benj Hall of B
Ri Smith
Jacob Duckett
Josiah Belt
Thomas Rose
Thomas Pindell
Jeremiah Crather
Jacob Wells
Solomon Sparrow
William Nichols Junr
Isaac Lansdale
James his X mark McDonald
John his IB mark Beckett
George his + mark Richards
Nathan Smith White

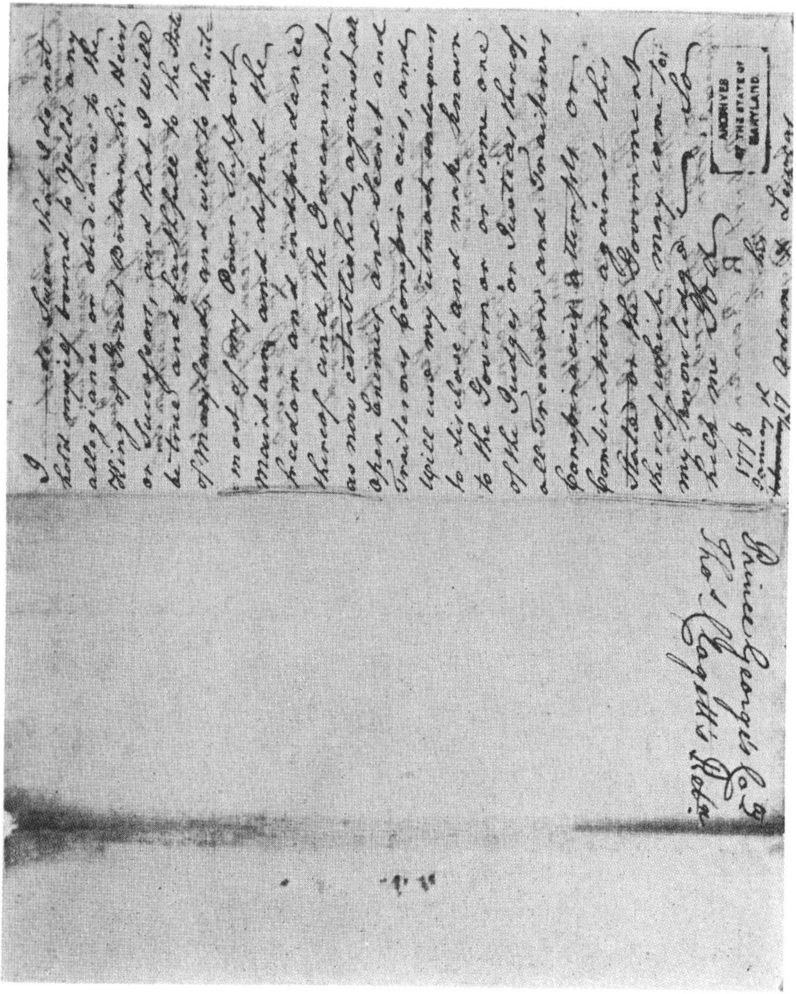

I ______ do swear that I do not hold myself bound to yield any allegiance or obedience to the King of Great Britain, his Heirs or Successors, and that I will be true and faithful to the State of Maryland, and will to the utmost of my Power support maintain and defend the freedom and independence thereof and the Government as now established, against all open Enemies and secret and Traitorous Conspiracies, and will use my utmost endeavours to disclose and make known to the Governor or some one of the Judges or Justices thereof, all Treasons and Traitorous Conspiracies attempts or combinations against this State or the Government thereof

So help me God

ARCHIVES OF THE STATE OF MARYLAND

Prince Georges Co.
Thos Cagett's Retn

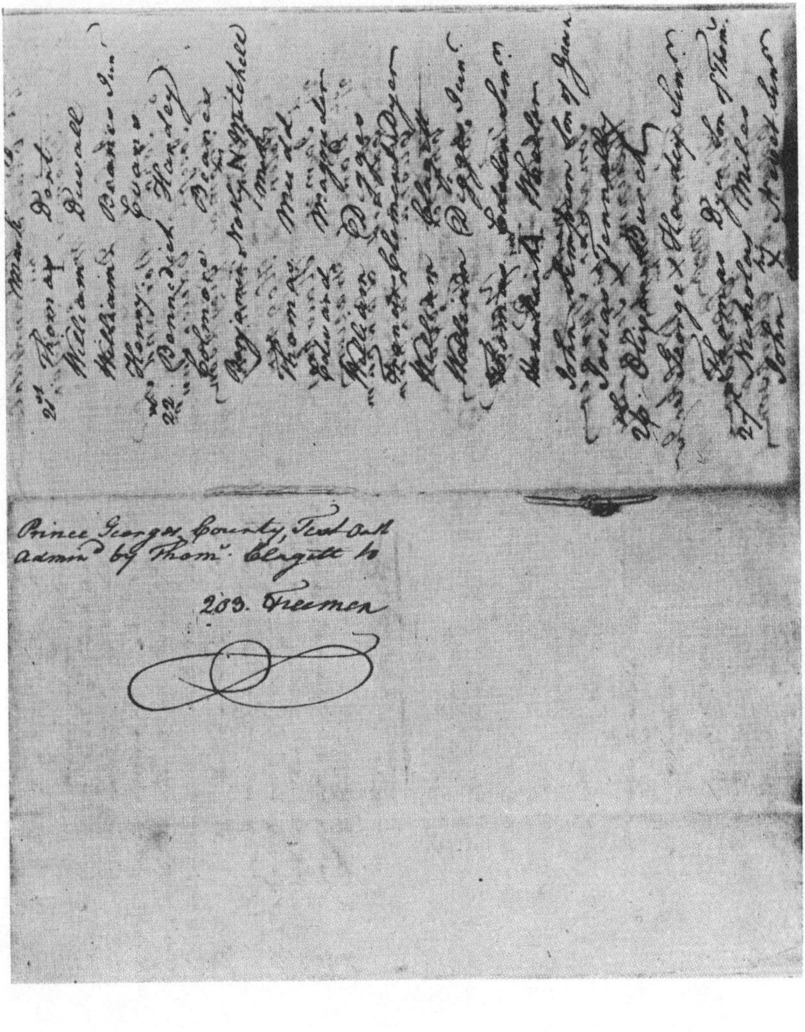

Prince Georges County, Test Oath
admin.d by Thom.s Clagett to
203 Freemen

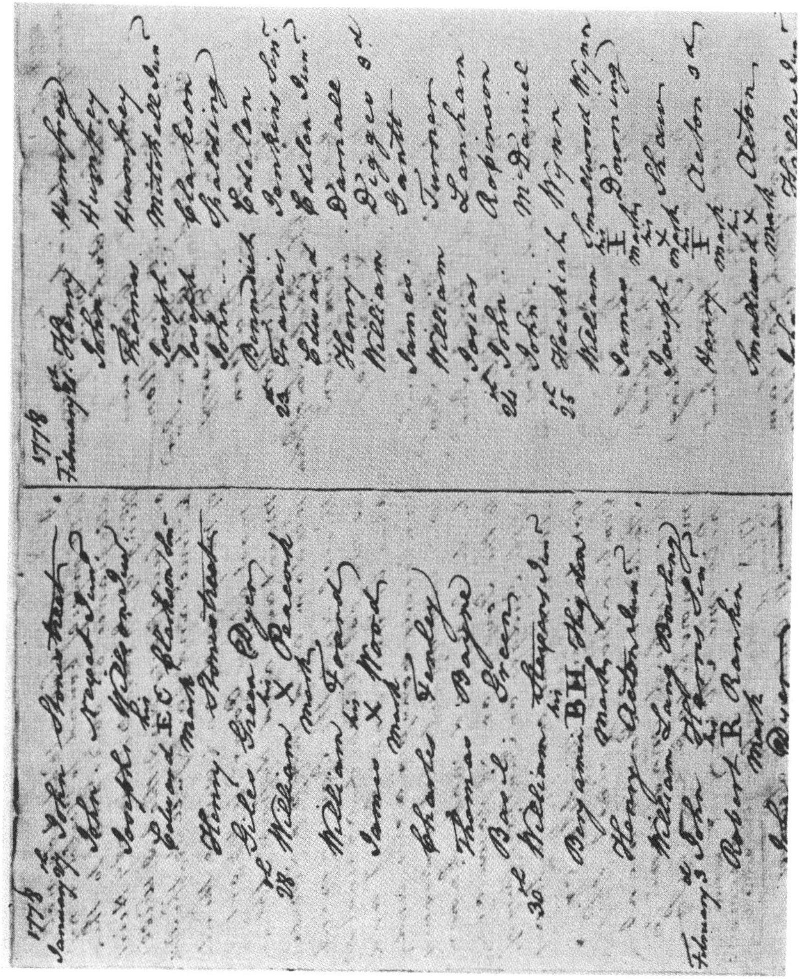
1778
January 27th John Stonestreet
John Neyest Junr.
Joseph Wilkinson Junr.
Edward his EC mark Clarkson Junr.
Henry Stonestreet
Giles Green Dyer
28th William his X mark Peacock
William Foard
James his X mark Wood
Charles Fenley
Thomas Bayne
Basil Green
30th William Stepens Junr.
Benjamin his BH mark Hayden
Henry Acton Junr.
William Lang Bowling
February 3d John Harris Senr.
Robert his R mark Rankin
John Dyer

1778
February 21st Henry Humfrey
John Humfrey
Thomas Humfrey
Joseph Mitchell Junr.
Joseph Clarkson
John Spalding
Bennedict Edelen
23d Francis Jenkins Senr.
Edward Edelen Junr.
Henry Darnall
William Digges 3d
James Gantt
William Turner
Josias Lanham
24th John Robinson
John McDaniel
25th Hezekiah Wynn
William Smallwood Wynn
James his I mark Downing
Joseph his X mark Shaw
Henry his I mark Acton 3d
Smallwood his X mark Acton
John Haller Junr.

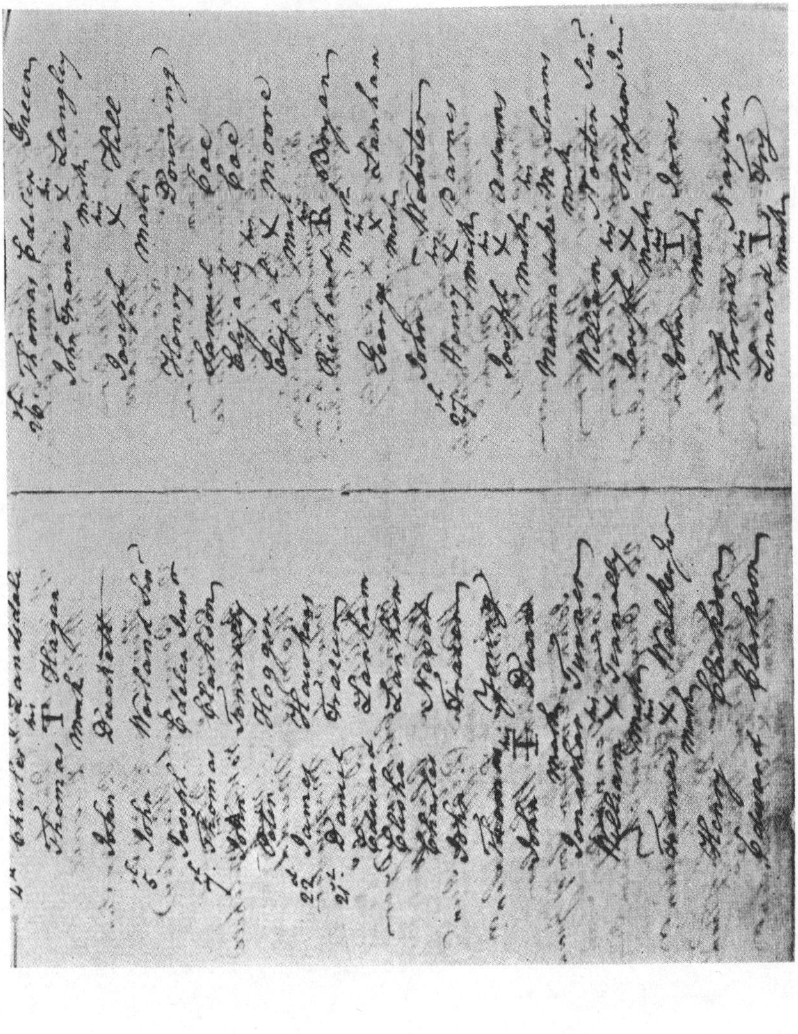
4th Charles Landsdale
Thomas his T mark Hagan
John Duckett
5th John Worland Senr
Joseph Edelen Junr
7th Thomas Clarkson
John Tonnexly
Peter Hogger
22d James Hawkins
21st Daniel Frazier
Edward Lanham
Elisha Lanham
Charles Nepot
John Frazer
Thomas Young
John his I mark Dunn
Jonathan Turner
William his X mark Tranally
Francis his X mark Walker Jr
Henry Clarkson
Edward Clarkson

26th Thomas Edelen Green
John Francis his X mark Langley
Joseph his X mark Hill
Henry Downing
Samuel Coe
Elijah Coe
Elijah his X mark Moore
Richard his R mark Bryan
George his X mark Lanham
John Webster
27th Henry his X mark Barnes
Joseph his X mark Adams
Marmaduke his M mark Simms
William Norton Senr
Joseph his X mark Simpson Junr
John his I mark Jones
Thomas Naydin
Lenard his L mark Fry

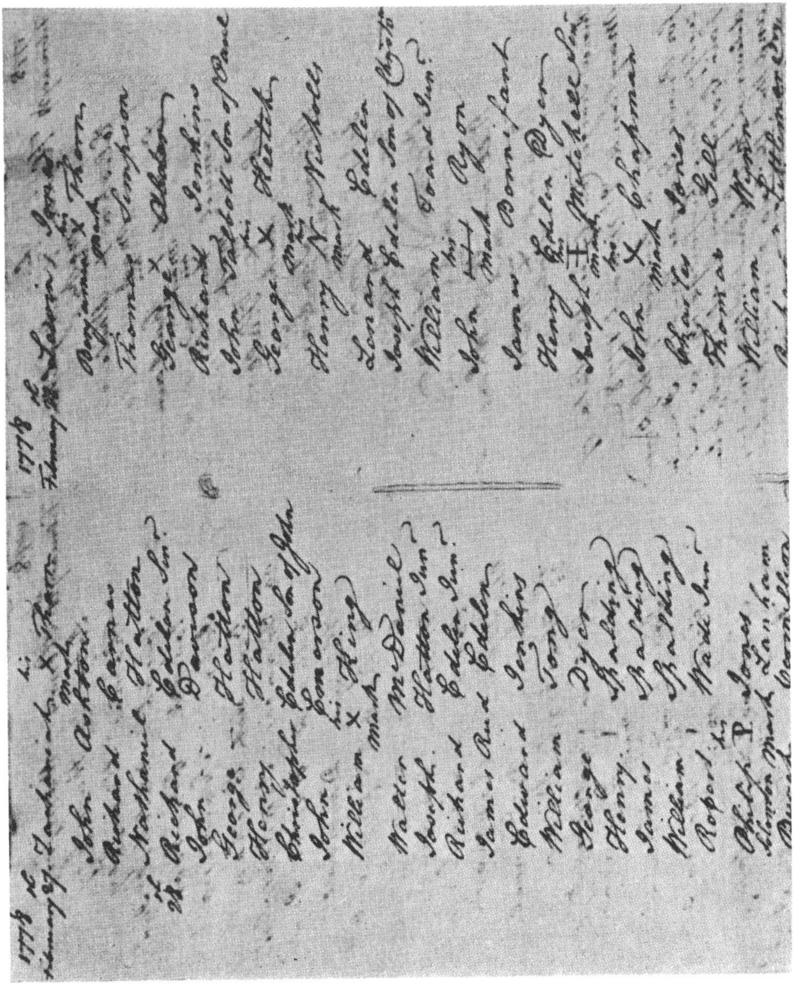

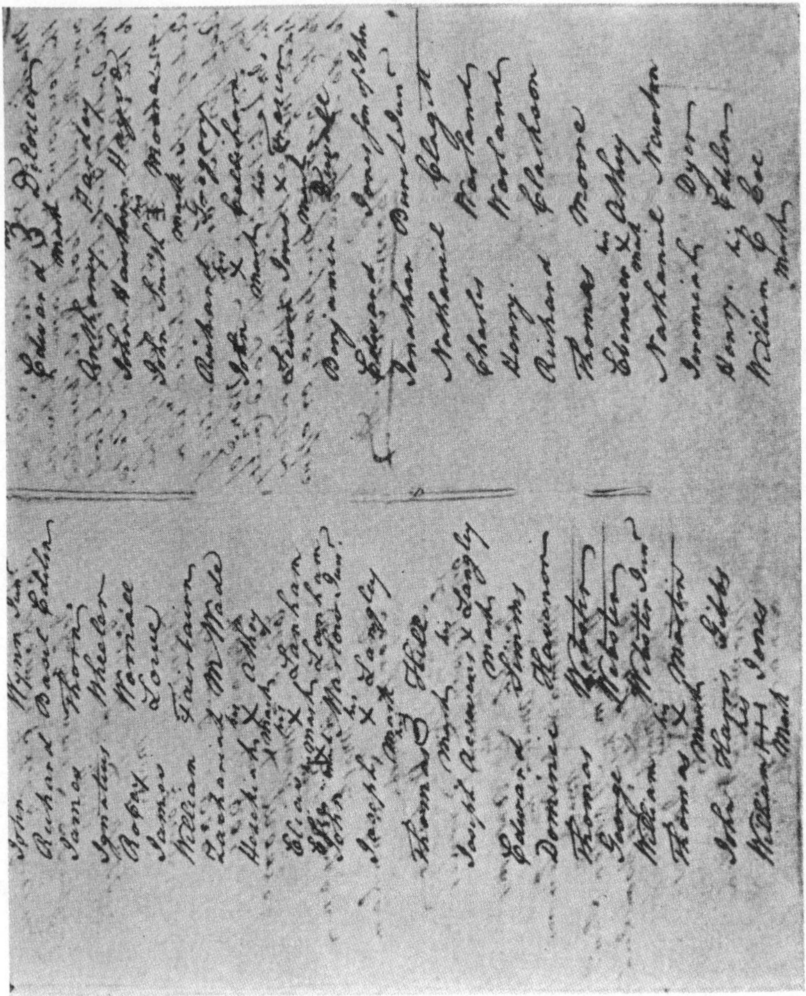

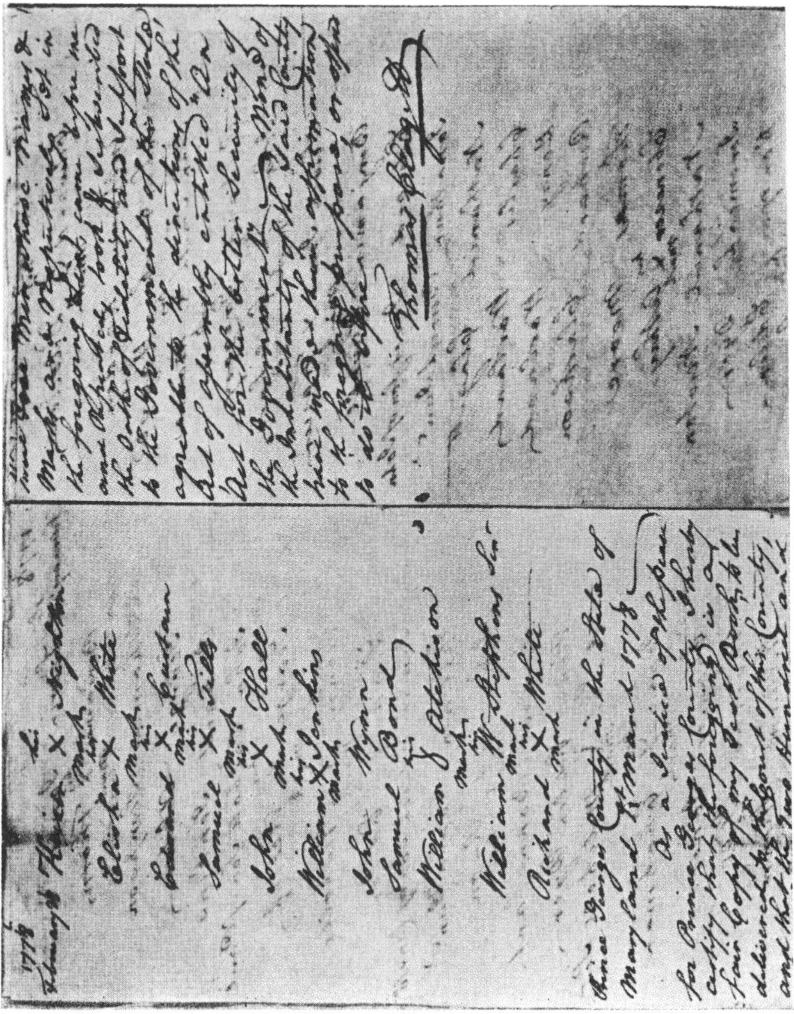

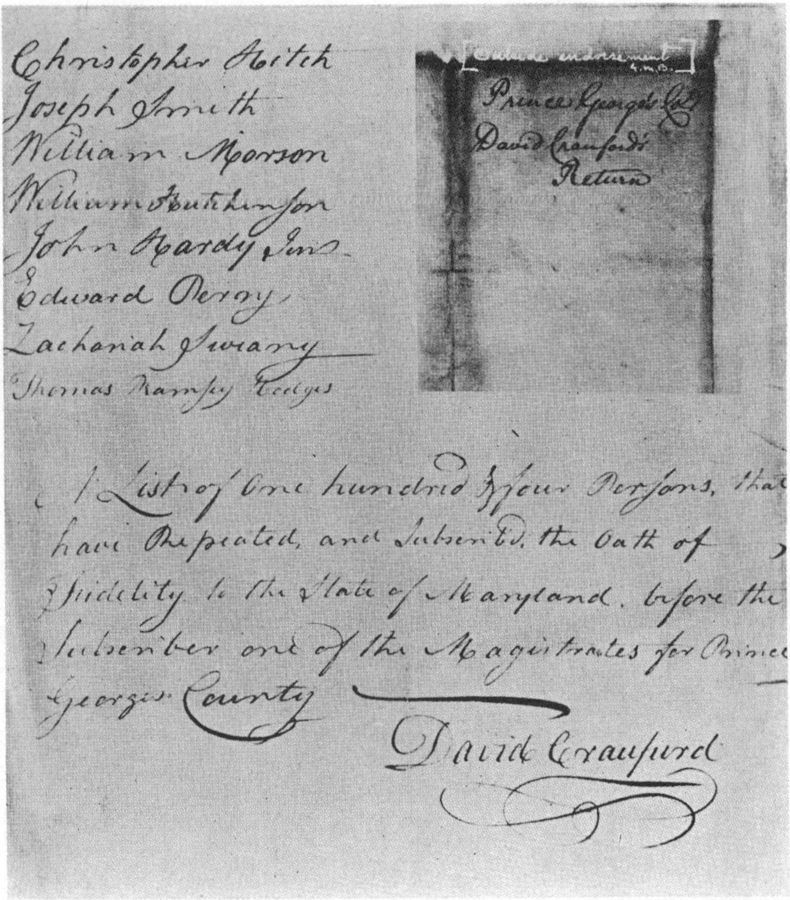

Christopher Hitch
Joseph Smith
William Morson
William Hutchinson
John Hardy Junr.
Edward Perry
Zachariah Sweany
Thomas Ramsey Hedges

[Outside endorsement G.M.B.]
Prince George's Co.
David Craufurd's
Return

A List of One hundred & four Persons, that have Repeated, and Subscribed, the Oath of Fidelity to the State of Maryland, before the Subscriber one of the Magistrates for Prince George's County

David Craufurd

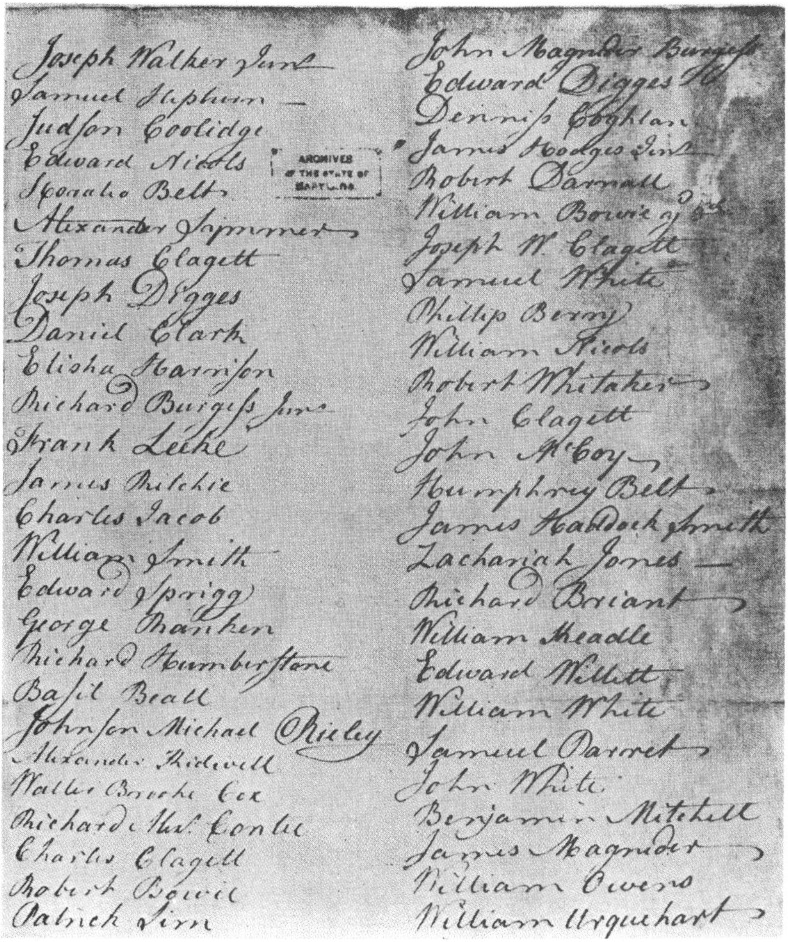
Joseph Walker Junr
Samuel Stephens
Judson Coolidge
Edward Nicols
Jonathan Belt
Alexander Symmer
Thomas Clagett
Joseph Digges
Daniel Clark
Elisha Harrison
Richard Burgess Junr
Frank Leeke
James Ritchie
Charles Jacob
William Smith
Edward Sprigg
George Ranken
Richard Humberstone
Basil Beall
Johnson Michael O'Rieley
Alexander Kidwell
Walter Brooke Cox
Richard Alexr. Contee
Charles Clagett
Robert Bowie
Patrick Sim
John Magruder Burgess
Edward Digges Jr
Dennis Coghlan
James Hodges Junr
Robert Darnall
William Bowie of [illegible]
Joseph W. Clagett
Samuel White
Phillip Berry
William Nicols
Robert Whitaker
John Clagett
John McCoy
Humphrey Belt
James Haddock Smith
Zachariah Jones
Richard Briant
William Headle
Edward Willett
William White
Samuel Parrot
John White
Benjamin Mitchell
James Magruder
William Owens
William Urquehart

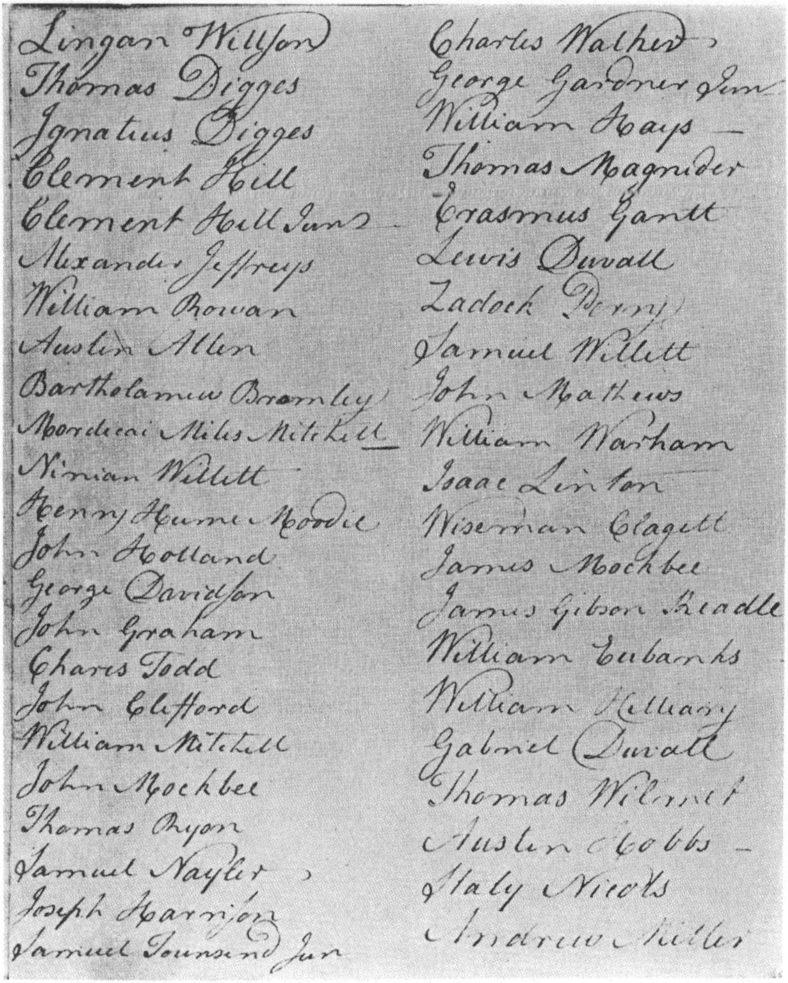

Lingan Willson
Thomas Digges
Ignatius Digges
Clement Hill
Clement Hill Junr
Alexander Jeffreys
William Rowan
Austin Allen
Bartholamew Bramley
Mordecai Miles Mitchell
Ninian Willett
Henry Hume Moodie
John Holland
George Davidson
John Graham
Chares Todd
John Clifford
William Mitchell
John Mockbee
Thomas Ryon
Samuel Naylor
Joseph Harrison
Samuel Townsend Junr

Charles Walker
George Gardner Junr
William Hays
Thomas Magruder
Erasmus Gantt
Lewis Duvall
Zadock Berry
Samuel Willett
John Mathews
William Warham
Isaac Linton
Wiseman Clagett
James Mockbee
James Gibson Beadle
William Eubanks
William Hilleary
Gabriel Duvall
Thomas Wilmot
Austin Hobbs
Italy Nicols
Andrew Miller

To
The Governor & Council
Prince George's County
Benj.a Hall's Return

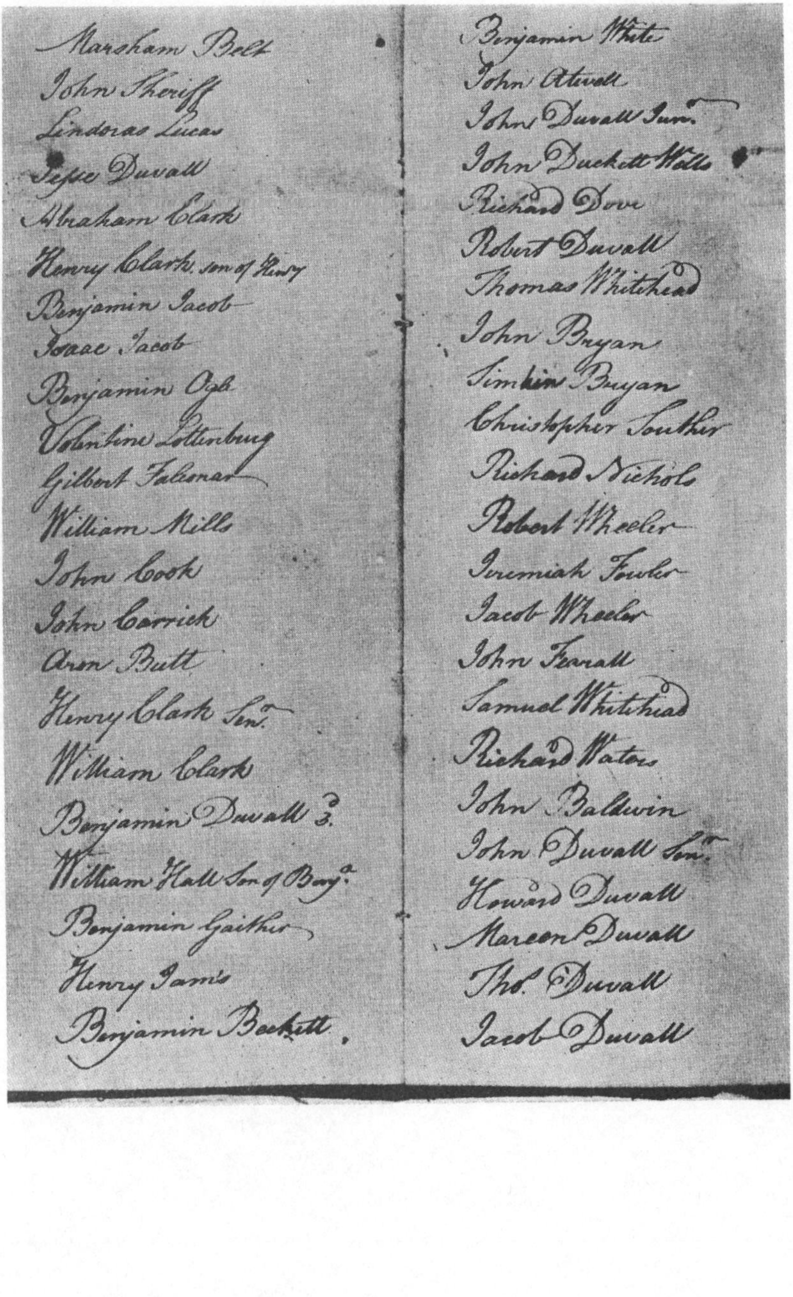
Marsham Belt
John Sheriff
Lindorus Lucas
Jesse Duvall
Abraham Clark
Henry Clark son of Henry
Benjamin Jacob
Isaac Jacob
Benjamin Ogle
Valentine Lottenburg
Gilbert Falconar
William Mills
John Cook
John Carrick
Aron Butt
Henry Clark Senr.
William Clark
Benjamin Duvall 3d.
William Hall Son of Benjn.
Benjamin Gaither
Henry Iam's
Benjamin Beckett.
Benjamin White
John Atwell
John Duvall Junr.
John Duckett Walls
Richard Dove
Robert Duvall
Thomas Whitehead
John Bryan
Simkin Bryan
Christopher Souther
Richard Nichols
Robert Wheeler
Jeremiah Fowler
Jacob Wheeler
John Fearall
Samuel Whitehead
Richard Waters
John Baldwin
John Duvall Senr.
Howard Duvall
Mareen Duvall
Thos. Duvall
Jacob Duvall

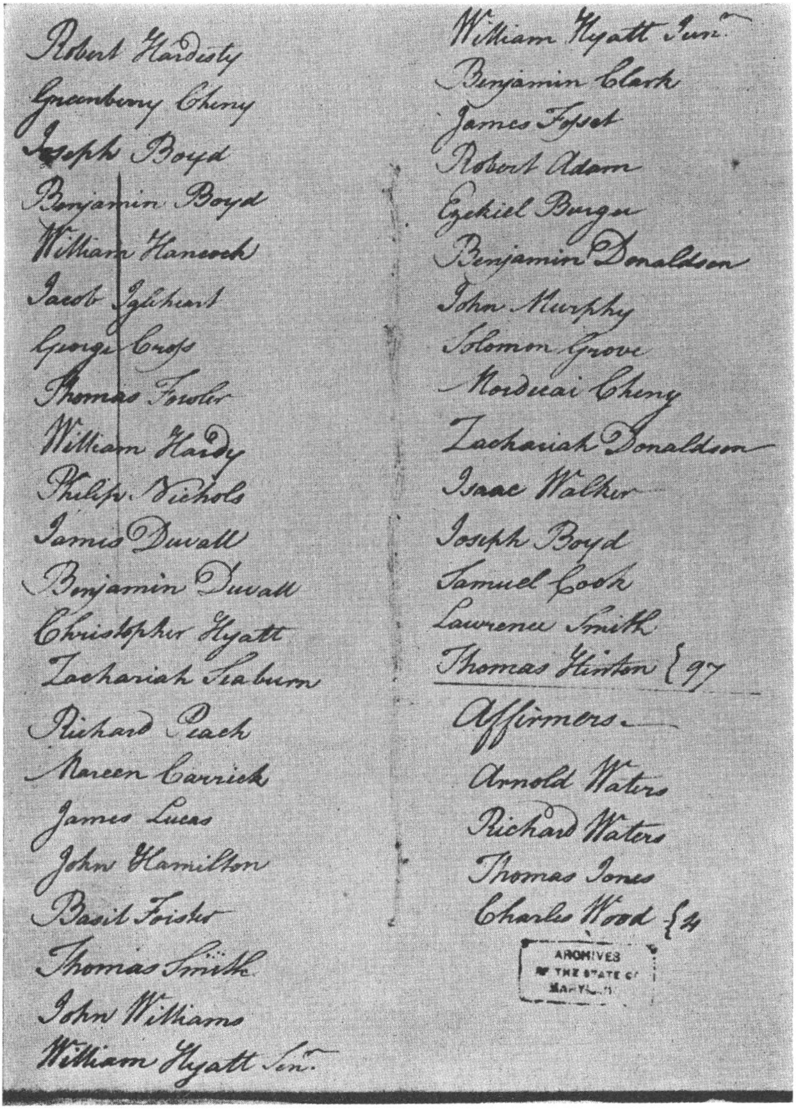

Robert Hardisty
Greenbury Cheny
Joseph Boyd
Benjamin Boyd
William Hancock
Jacob Iglehart
George Cross
Thomas Fowler
William Hardy
Philip Nichols
James Duvall
Benjamin Duvall
Christopher Hyatt
Zachariah Seaburn
Richard Peach
Mareen Carrick
James Lucas
John Hamilton
Basil Foster
Thomas Smith
John Williams
William Hyatt Senr

William Hyatt Junr
Benjamin Clark
James Fosset
Robert Adam
Ezekiel Burgee
Benjamin Donaldson
John Murphy
Solomon Grove
Mordecai Cheny
Zachariah Donaldson
Isaac Walker
Joseph Boyd
Samuel Cook
Lawrence Smith
Thomas Hinton {97

Affirmers

Arnold Waters
Richard Waters
Thomas Jones
Charles Wood {4

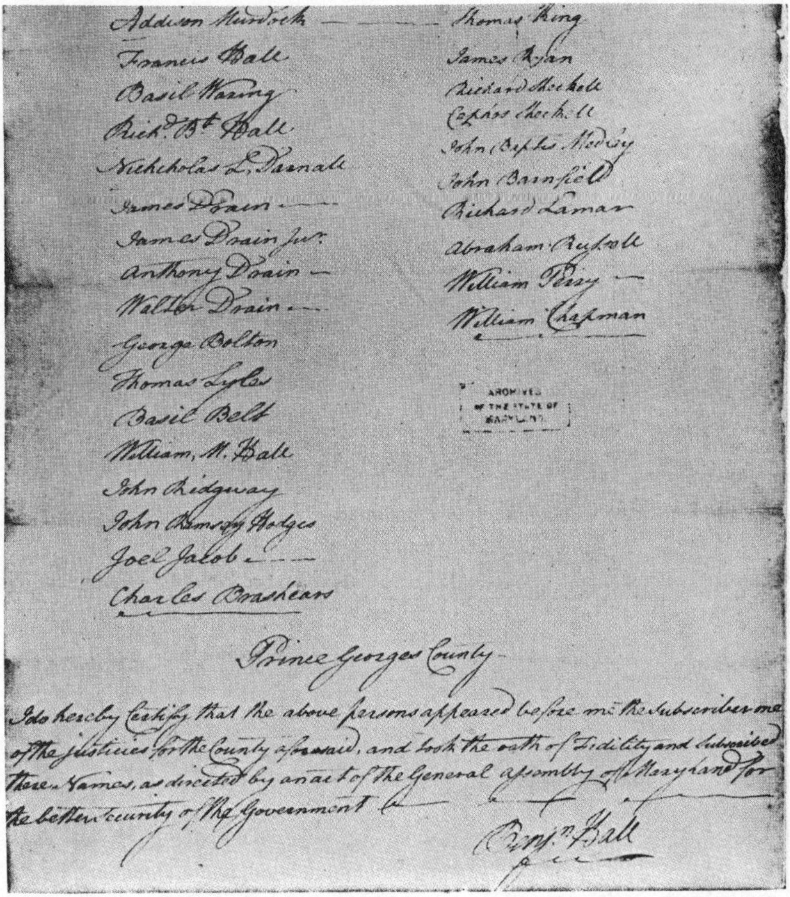

Addison Murdock — Thomas King
Francis Hall — James Ryan
Basil Waring — Richard Meckell
Richd. Bt. Hall — Cephas Meckell
Nicholas L. Darnall — John Bayles Medley
James Drain — John Barnfield
James Drain Jur. — Richard Lamar
Anthony Drain — Abraham Russell
Walter Drain — William Perry
George Bolton — William Chapman
Thomas Lyles
Basil Belt
William M. Hall
John Ridgway
John Hamsley Hodges
Joel Jacob
Charles Brashears

Prince Georges County

I do hereby Certify that the above persons appeared before me the Subscriber one of the justices for the County aforesaid, and took the oath of Fidelity and subscribed there Names, as directed by an act of the General Assembly of Maryland for the better security of the Government

Benjn. Hall

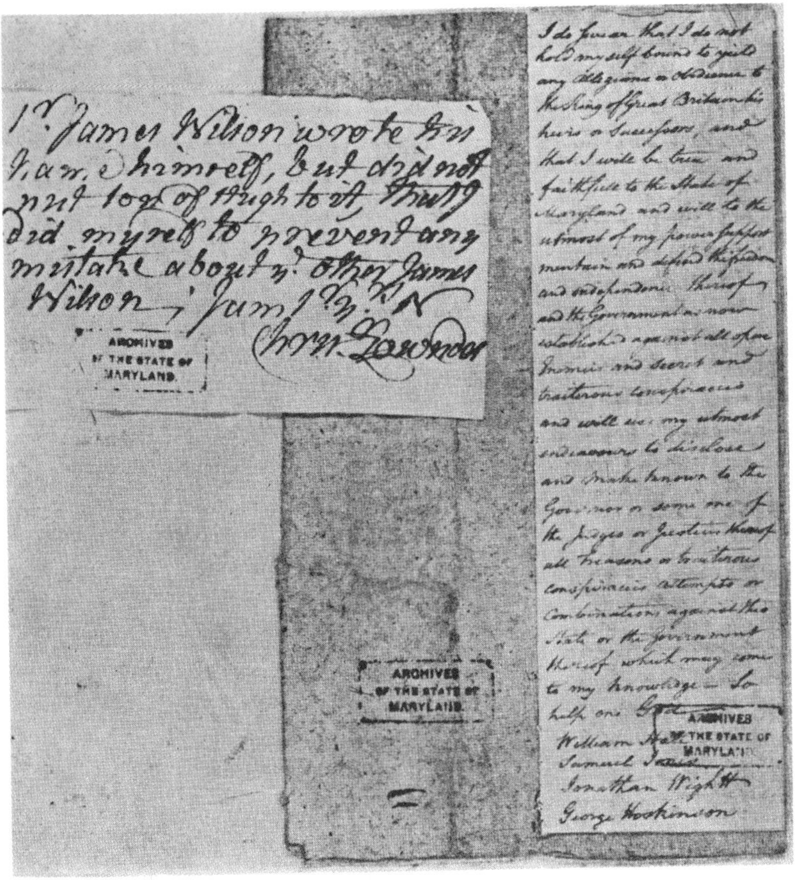
Mr James Wilson wrote his nam: himself, but did not put Senr. to it, therefore I did myself to prevent any mistake about ye other James Wilson, Junr.
Wm. Lowndes

ARCHIVES OF THE STATE OF MARYLAND

I do swear that I do not hold my self bound to yield any Allegiance or Obedience to the King of Great Britain his heirs or Successors, and that I will be true and faithfull to the State of Maryland and will to the utmost of my power Support maintain and defend the freedom and independence thereof and the Government as now established against all open Enemies and secret and traiterous conspiracies and will use my utmost endeavours to disclose and make known to the Governor or some one of the Judges or Justices thereof all Treasons or traiterous conspiracies attempts or Combinations against this State or the Government thereof which may come to my knowledge — So help me God

William Hall
Samuel [illegible]
Jonathan Wright
George Hoskinson

ARCHIVES OF THE STATE OF MARYLAND

ARCHIVES OF THE STATE OF MARYLAND

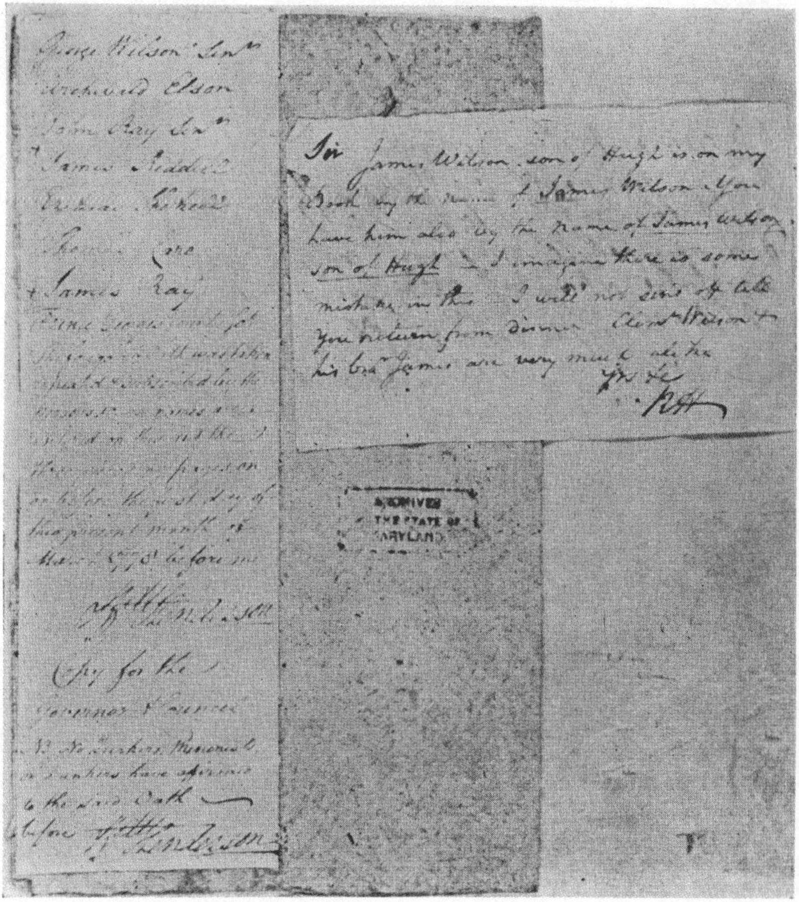

George Wilson Senr
Archibald Elson
John Ray Senr
James Beddle
William Shekell
Thomas Core
James Ray

March 1778 before me

Copy for the Governor & Council

Sir James Wilson son of Hugh is on my Book by the name of James Wilson You have him also by the name of James Wilson son of Hugh — I imagine there is some mistake in this I will not send it till you return from dinner Clem^t Wilson & his bro^r James are very much alike

Yrs &c

RH

Gentlemen. Below you you have Copy of the names of all those who have taken Repeated and subscribed the Oath of Fidelity before

ARCHIVES OF THE STATE OF MARYLAND.

Gentlemen
Your obed.t Servant
[illegible]

Prince Georges County
March 9th 1778

1 John Addison
1 Basil Lowe
1 Thomas Hanson
1 Richard Stonestreet
1 William Bayne
1 John H. Marlow
1 David Boswell
1 H. Rozer
1 John Casey
1 Thomas D. Marlow
1 William Marlow
1 Notley Young
1 Edward Digges Junr
1 John Lowe
1 Henry Lowe
1 Henry Rozer Junr
1 Hebsworth Bayne
1 James Gill
1 Francis Jones
1 William Clarkson
1 Moses Gill
1 Barnard Dedenick
1 Will Willcoxen

23 brot up
1 Samuel McPersh
1 Patrick Beall
1 Josiah Willcoxen
1 Joseph Waters (a Dutchman)
1 Ralph Hodgkins
1 Thomas P. Edelin
1 Thomas Dawson
1 Henry Jones
1 George Lewis
1 Jeremiah Clifford
1 John H. Lowe
1 John James
1 George Bean
1 Basil Hodgkins
1 Thomas Wellmoth
1 Luke Jefferson
1 Smith Middleton
1 Robert St. Clare
1 Robert Norton
1 William O'Neil
1 Saml H. Bayne
1 John Allen Hodgkins
1 Doras Neil
46 Total

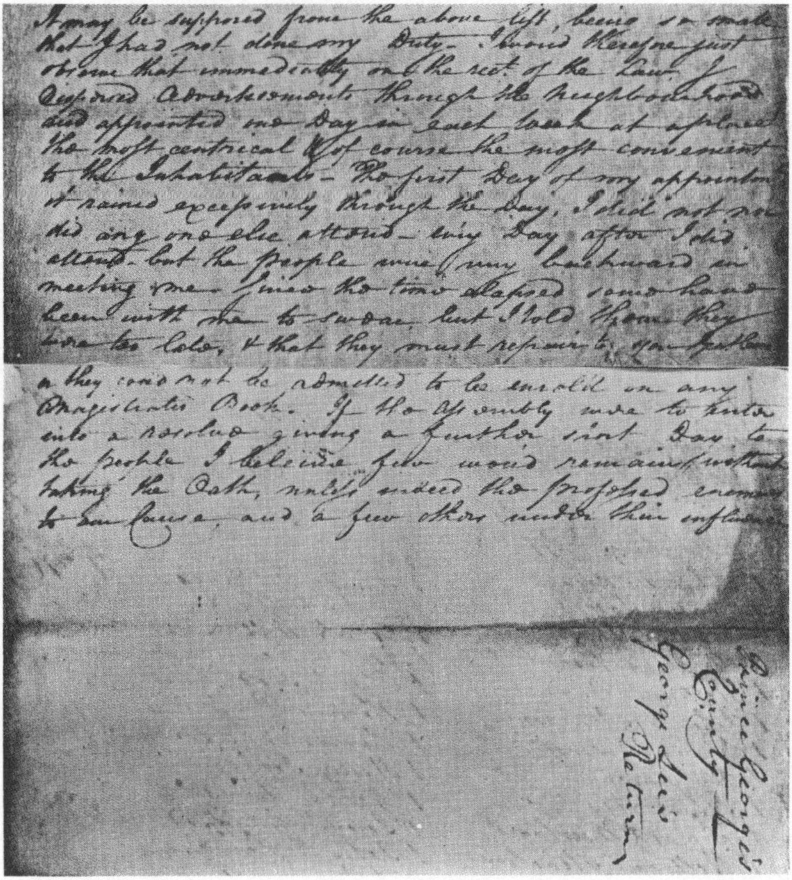

It may be supposed from the above list, being so small
that I had not done my Duty. I would therefore just
observe that immediately on the rec^t of the Law, I
dispersed Advertisements through the Neighbourhood
and appointed one Day in each Week at a place
the most centrical & of course the most convenient
to the Inhabitants. The first Day of my appointm^t
it rained excessively through the Day, I did not nor
did any one else attend. Every Day after I did
attend but the People were very backward in
meeting me. Since the time elapsed some have
been with me to swear, but I told them they
were too late, & that they must repair to your Excellency
as they could not be admitted to be enroll'd on any
Magistrates Book. If the Assembly were to enter
into a resolve giving a further sixt Day to
the people I believe few would remain without
taking the Oath, unless indeed the professed enemies
to our Cause, and a few others under their influence

Prince George's County
George Lee's Return

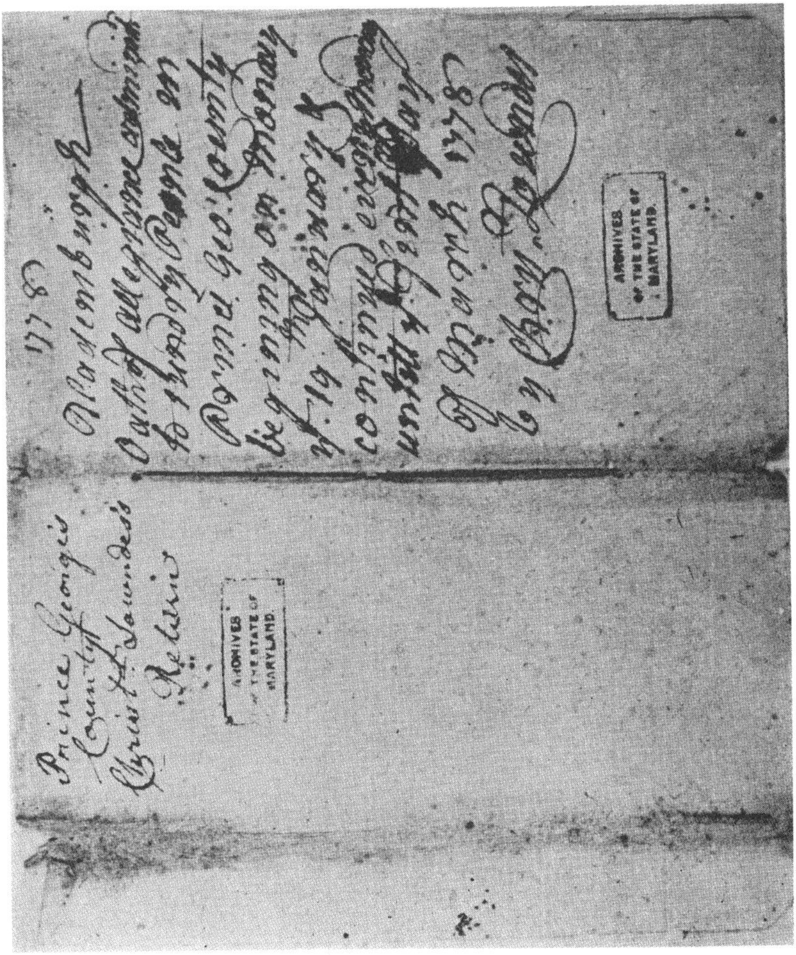
Prince George's
County
Christ. Lowndes's
Return
1778
ARCHIVES OF THE STATE OF MARYLAND

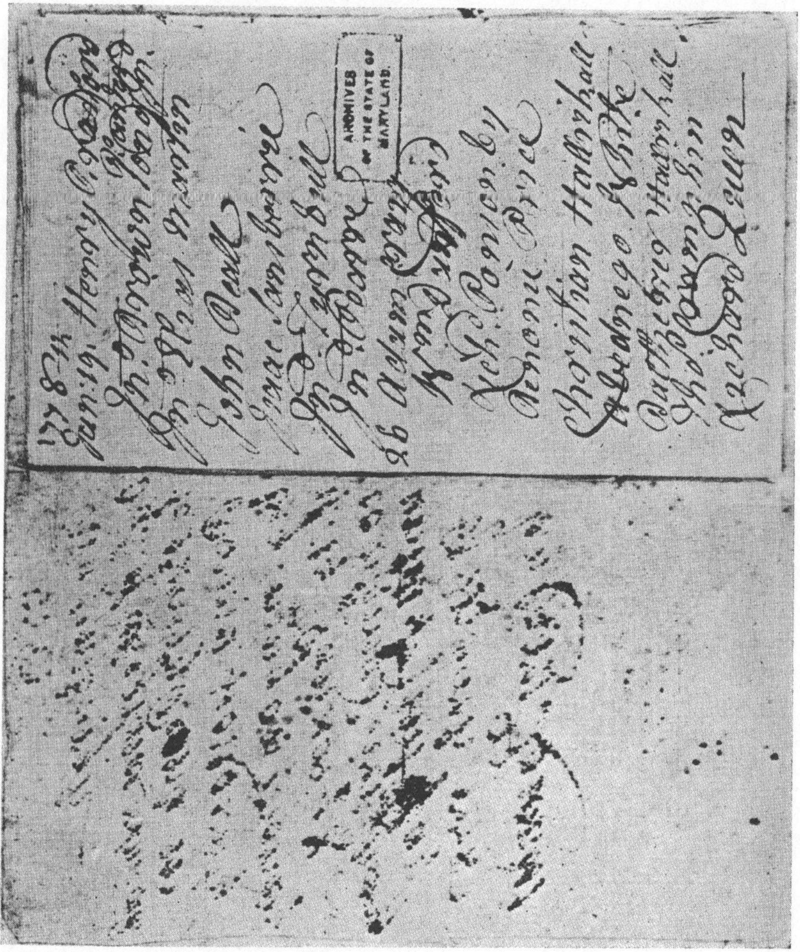
ARCHIVES OF THE STATE OF MARYLAND

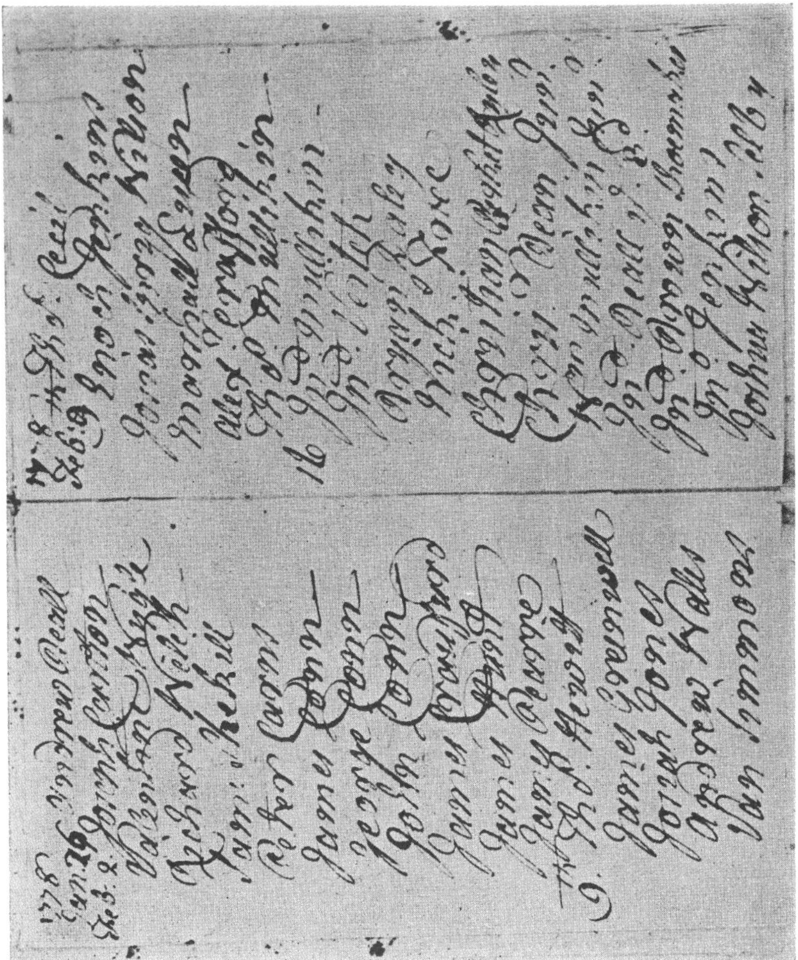

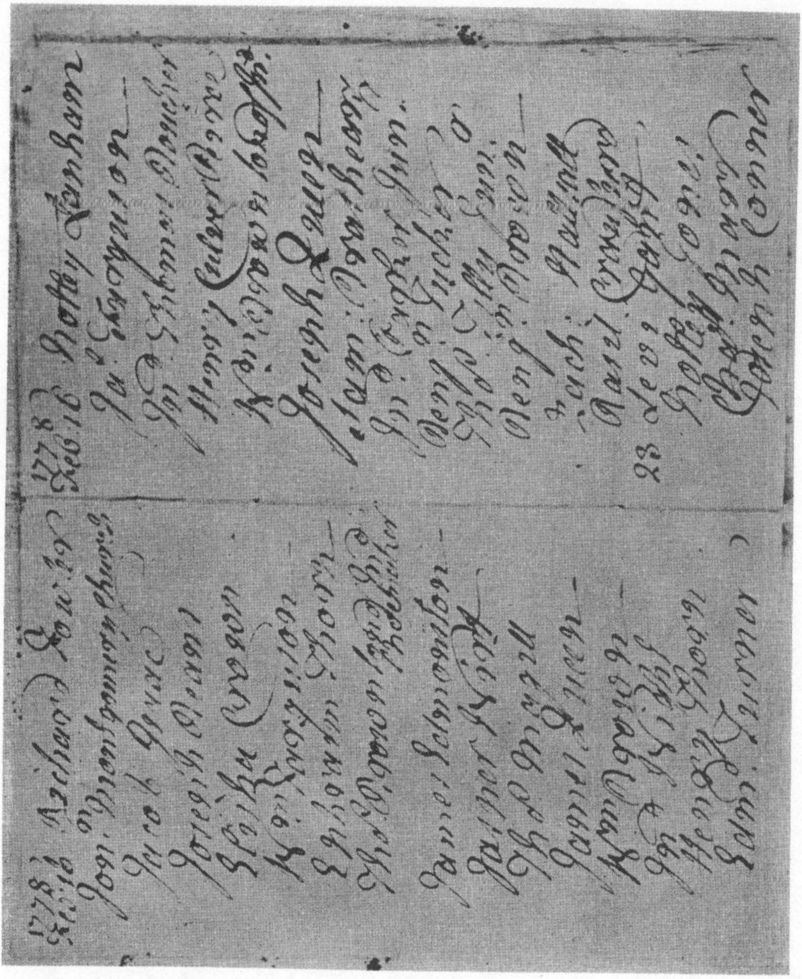

1778 Feb 16 Richard Fowler
Jon.n Montgomery Church
Jacob Grace
Joseph Beans
Elisha Brown
Wm. Ferguson
Ephraim Thorn
Thos. Brown shoemaker
James Edmonston
Jasper Wirt
Thos. Merrill
James Queen
Wm. Brown
Jno. Wight
Henry Thorn
Edmd. Turner

1778 Feb 16 Notley Lanham
Jas. Ferguson
Jno. Thomas Boucher
Henry Culver Pierce
Wm. Brown blacksmith
Joseph Queen
Sam: Bratheard
Jno. Fisher Jun.
Benjn. Tucker
Thos. Tilly Jun.
Benjn. Brown
Zach: Hall
Basil Crawford
23 Levi Gantt
Notley Jones
Chas. Ward
Joseph Conner

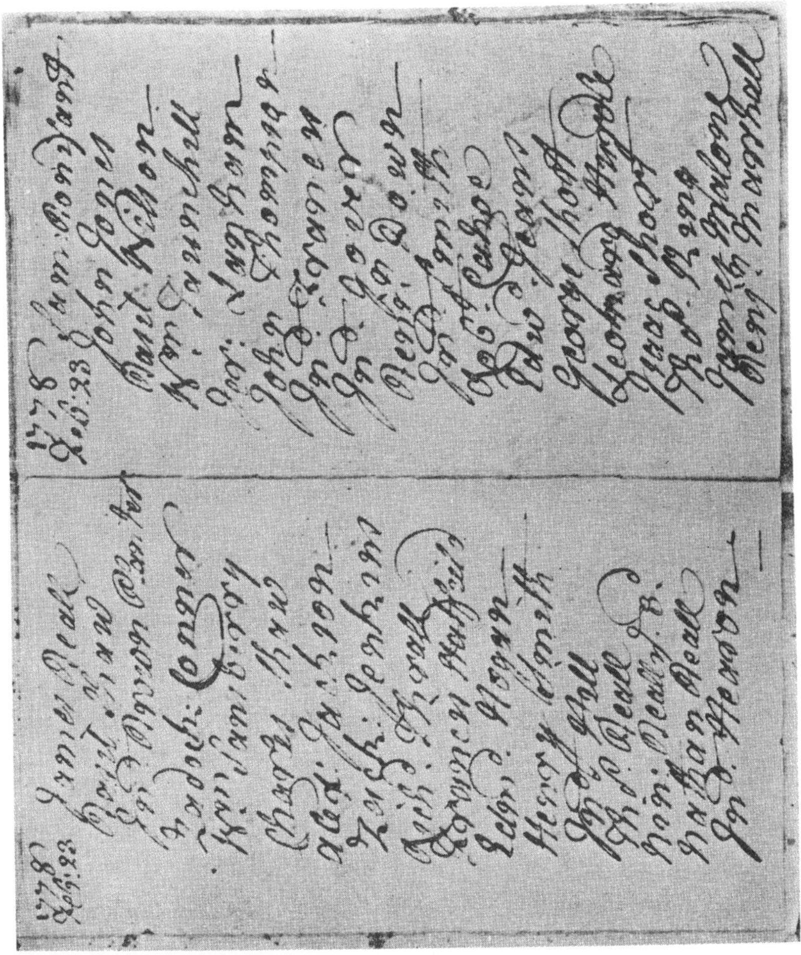

1778 Feb: 23 James Beall
Basil Shaw
Jn.° Brown Painter
Zadock: Conner
Wm. Sansberry
Charles Shaw
Alexr: Jackson
Zach: Jenkins
Richd. Thrall
Frances Hatfield
Edmd. Hogan
Henry Smith
Jno. Hall
Thos. Beall
Nin: Beall of B.
Nathan Beall
Jno. Hearon

1778 Feb: 23 Sam: Constant
John Jones
Basil Wilson
Wm. Saunchell
Jos: Ingham
John Thompson
Jno. Frame
Jno. Gover
Benja. Down
Jno. Smith
Robt. Cahoe
Edw.d Jeans
George Short
Leonard Hurgole
Isaac Short
Thos. King
James Malone
Benja. Marshall

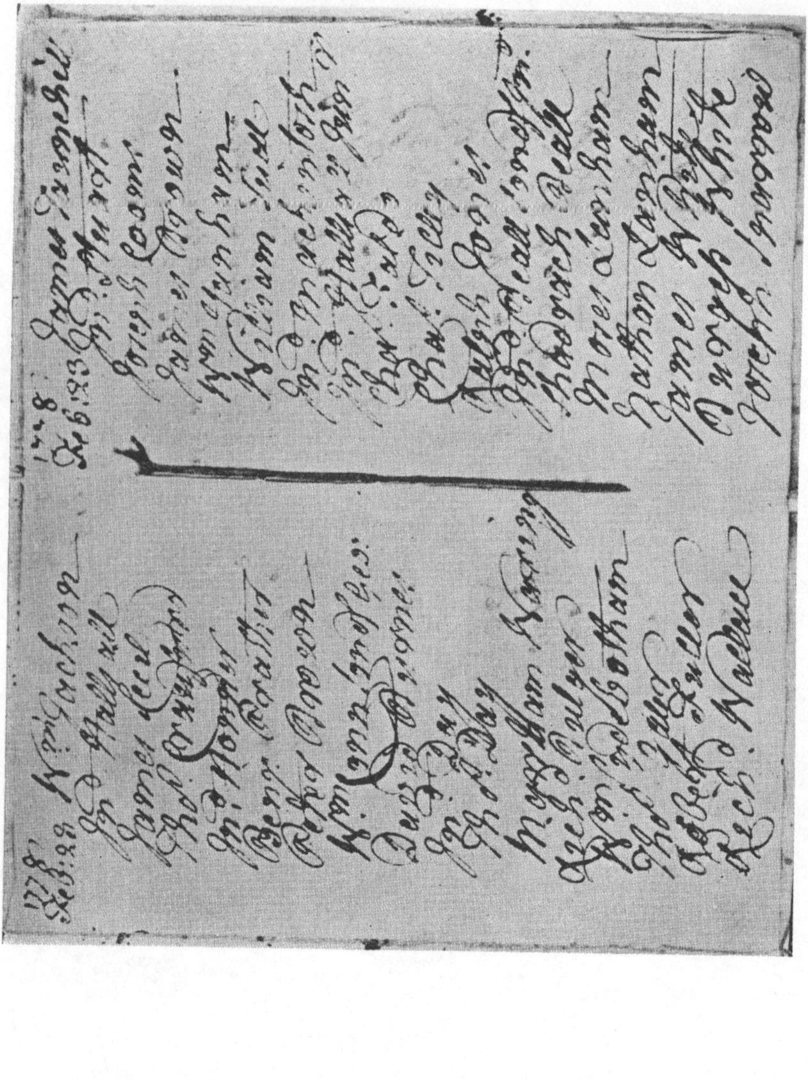

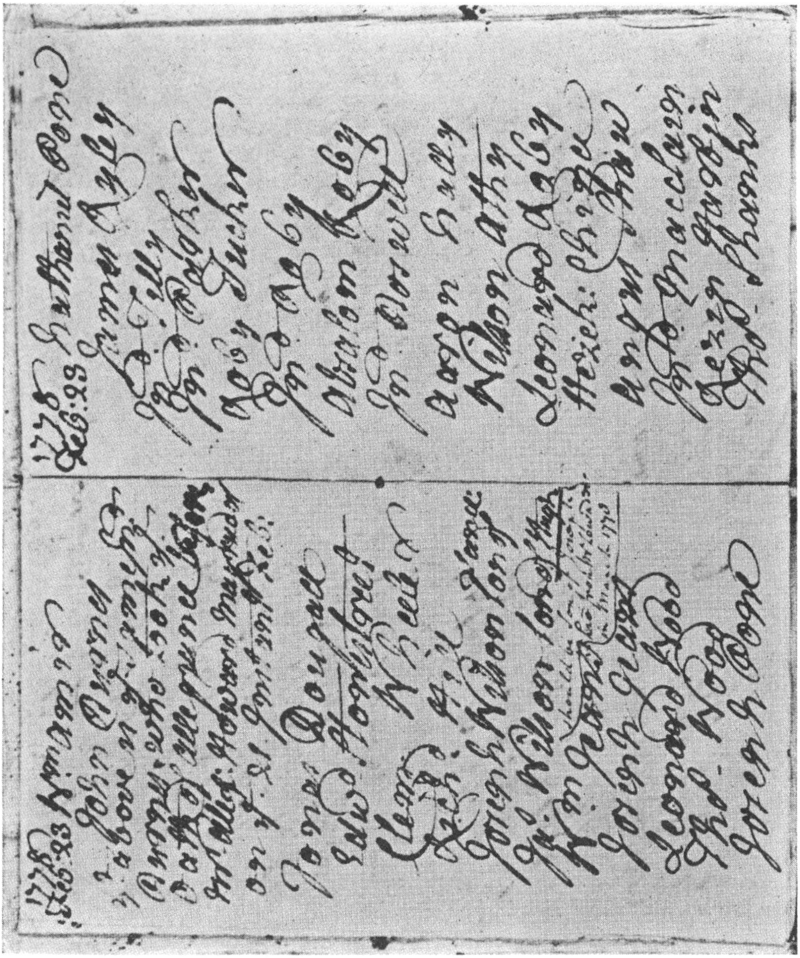

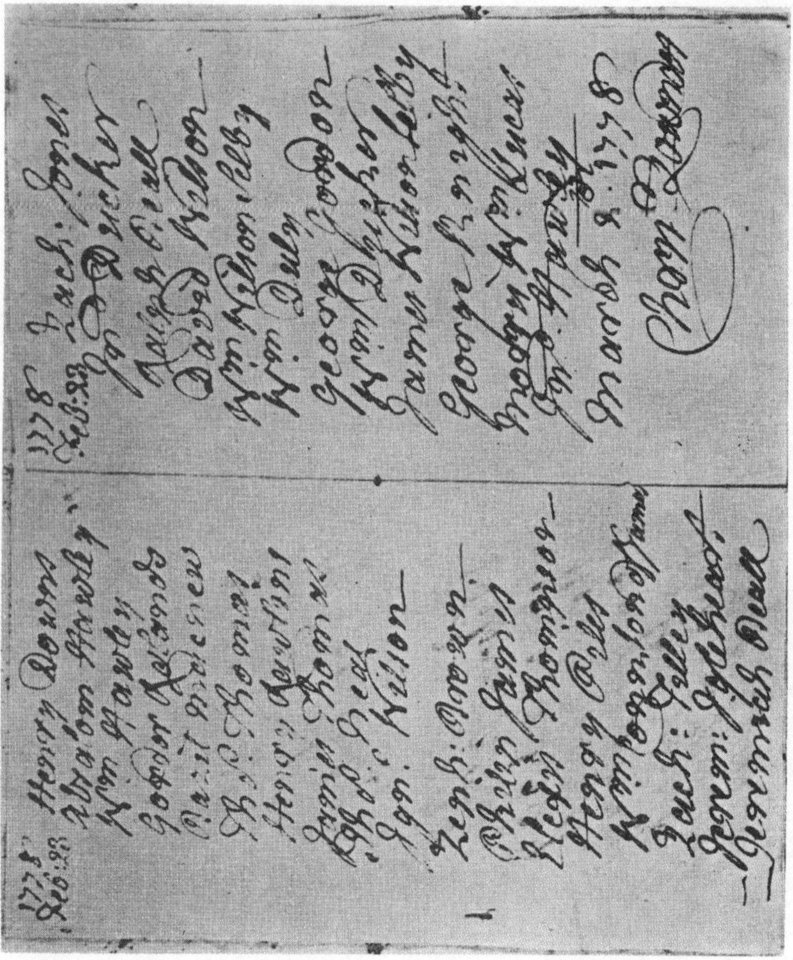

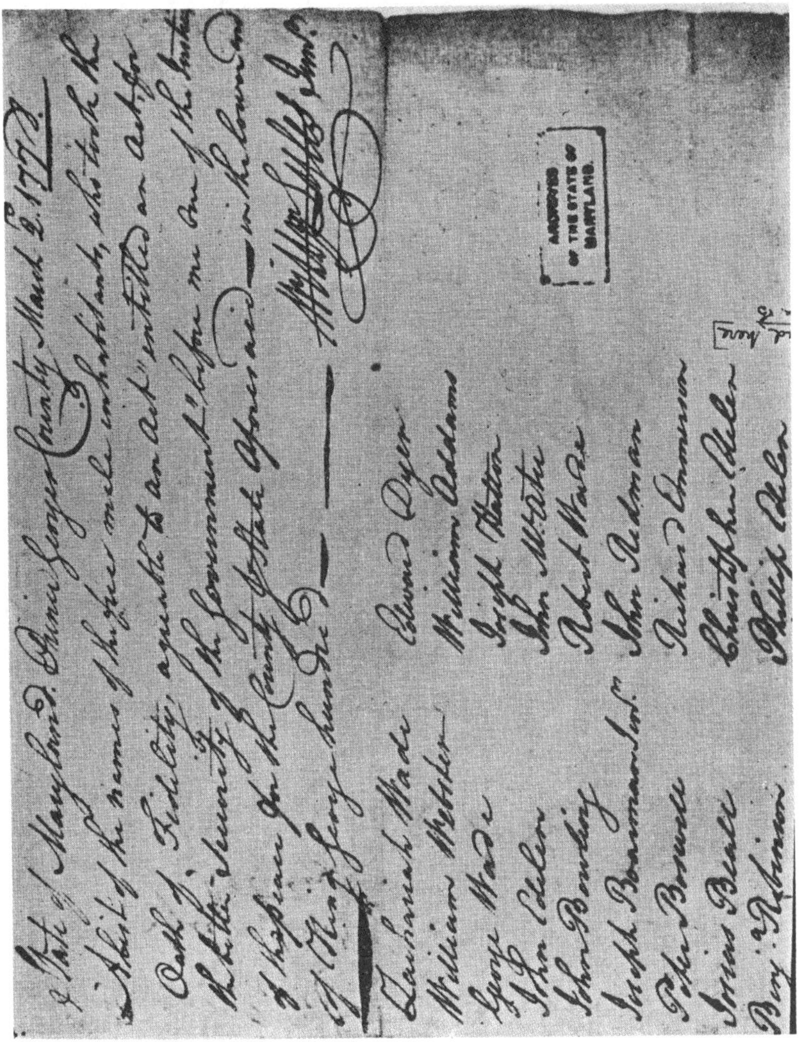

State of Maryland. Prince Georges County March 2. 1778.
A list of the names of the free male inhabitants, who took the Oath of Fidelity, agreeable to an act "entitled an act, for the better Security of the Government" before me One of the Justices of the Peace for the County & State aforesaid — in the lower end of King George hundred — — William Lyles Junr.

Zachariah Wade	Edward Dyer
William Webster	William Addams
George Wade	Joseph Hatton
John Edelen	John McAtee
John Bowling	Robert Wade
Joseph Boarman Senr.	John Redman
Peter Boswell	Richard Emmerson
Josias Beall	Christopher Edelen
Benjn. Robinson	Phillip Edelen

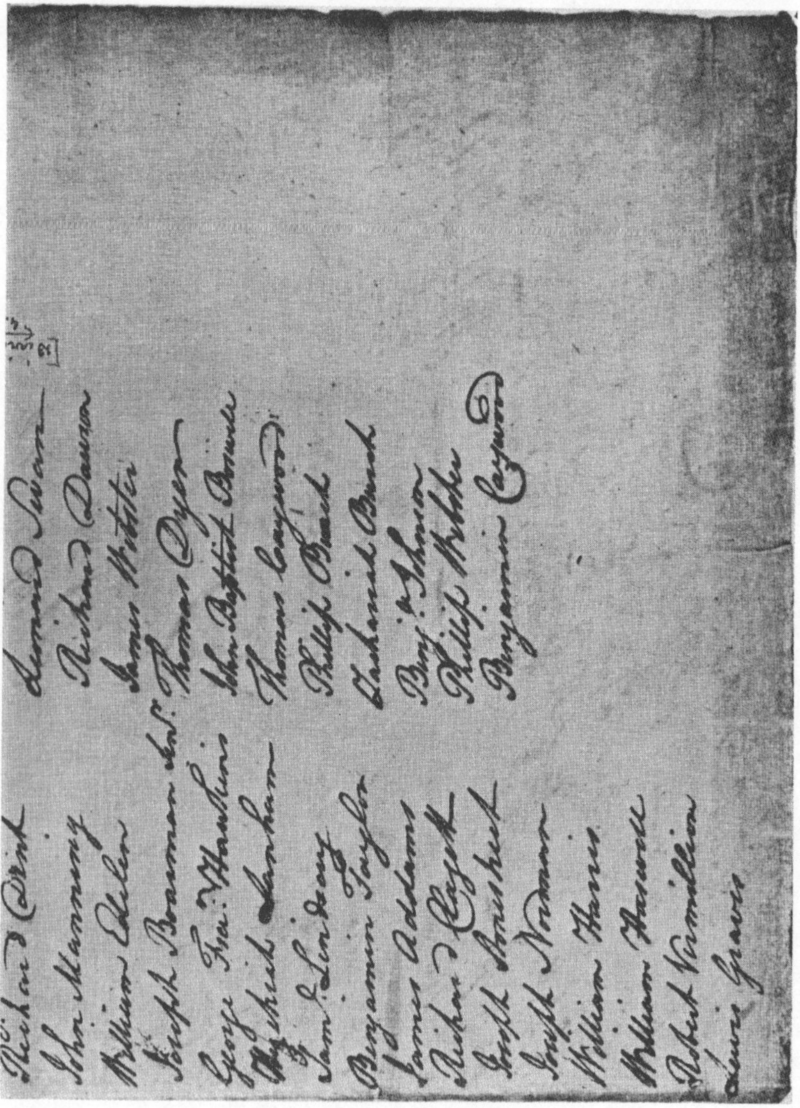

Richard Brent	Leonard Swan
John Manning	Richard Dawson
William Edelen	James Webster
Joseph Boarman Sen.r	Thomas Dyer
George Fra: Hawkins	John Baptist Boswell
Hezekiah Lanham	Thomas Caywood
Sam.l Lindsey	Phillip Beach
Benjamin Taylor	Zachariah Beach
James Addams	Benj.a Johnson
Richard Clagett	Phillip Webster
Joseph Stonestreet	Benjamin Caywood
Joseph Norman	
William Harris	
William Haswell	
Robert Vermillion	
Lewis Graves	

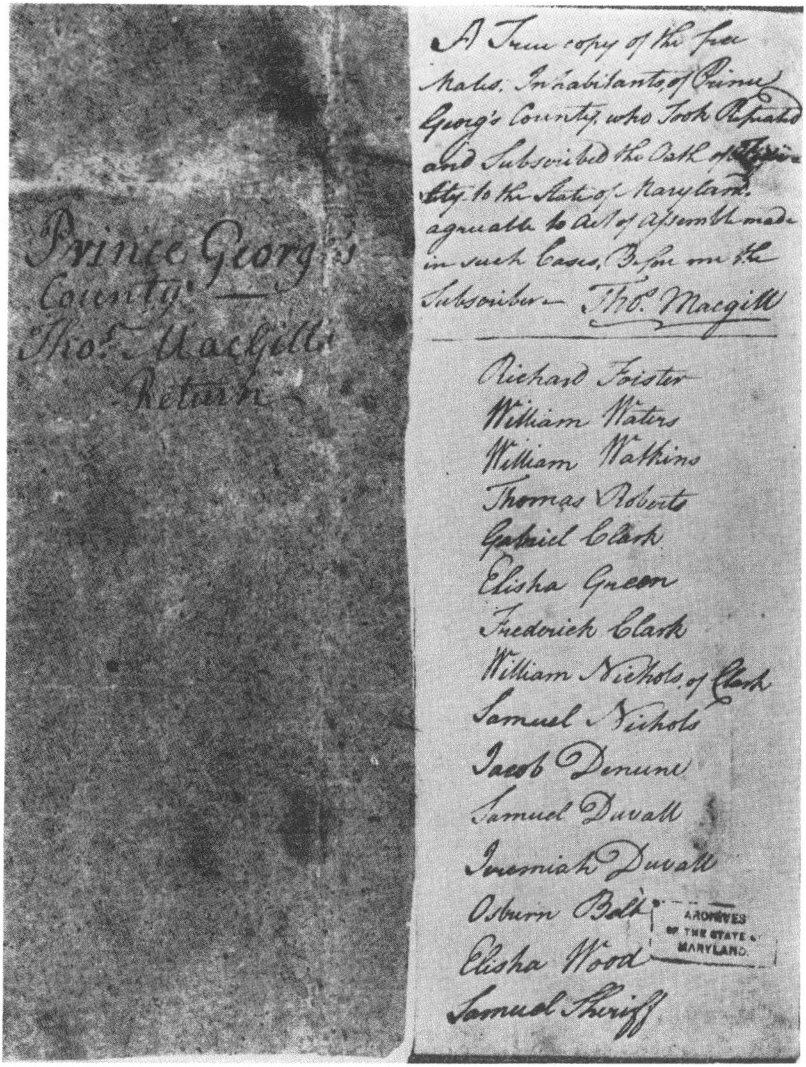
Prince George's County — Thos. Macgill Return

A True copy of the free
Males. Inhabitants of Prince
George's County, who Took Repeated
and Subscribed the Oath of Fidelity to the State of Maryland.
agreeable to Act of Assembly made
in such Cases, Before me the
Subscriber — Thos. Macgill

Richard Foister
William Waters
William Watkins
Thomas Roberts
Gabriel Clark
Elisha Green
Frederick Clark
William Nichols of Clark
Samuel Nichols
Jacob Denune
Samuel Duvall
Jeremiah Duvall
Osburn Belt
Elisha Wood
Samuel Sheriff

ARCHIVES OF THE STATE OF MARYLAND

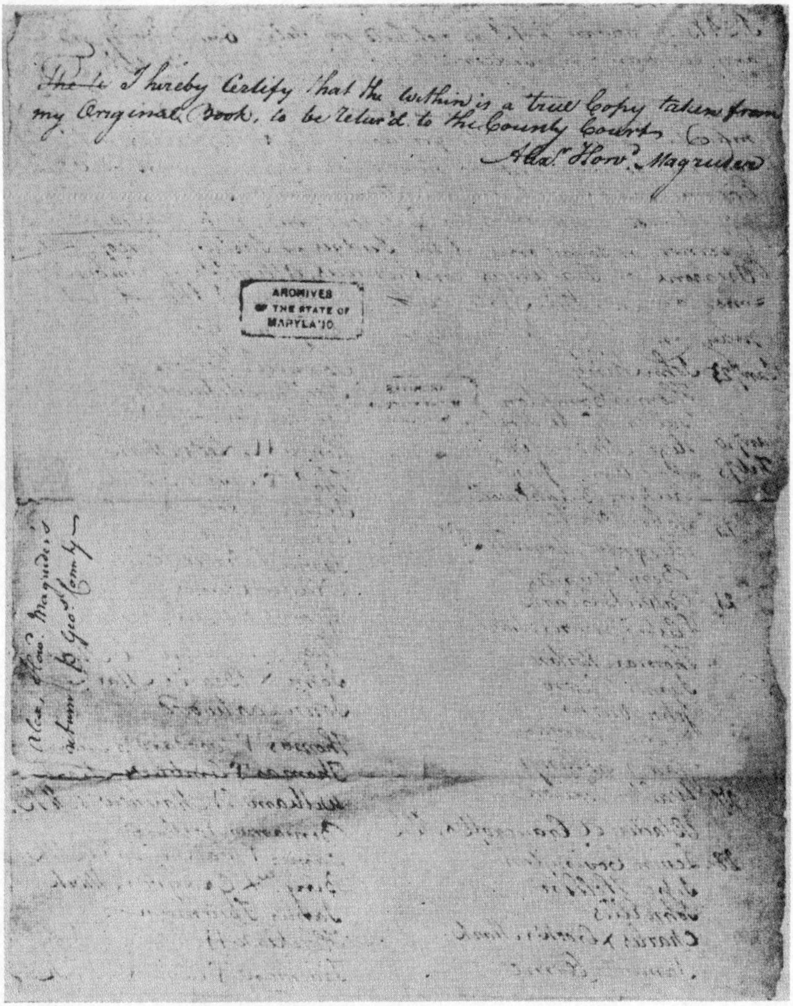

I hereby Certify that the within is a true Copy taken from my Original Book, to be return'd to the County Court.

Alexr. Howd. Magruder

Alex. Howd. Magruder's return P. Geo. County

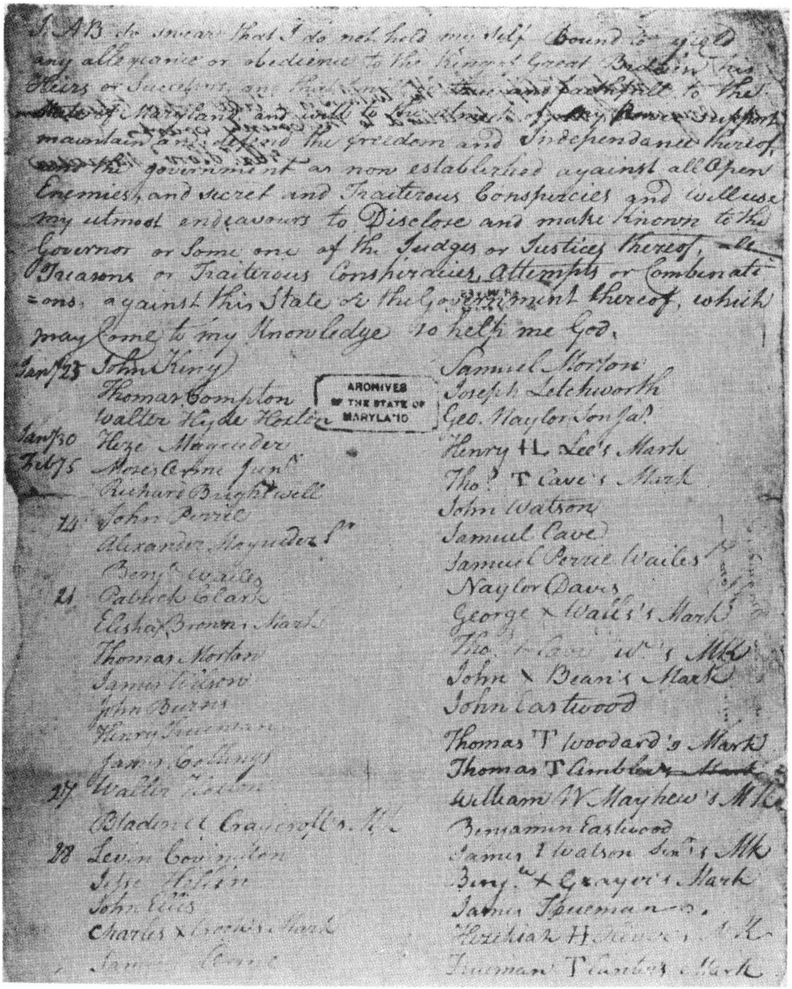

I A B do swear that I do not hold my self bound to yield any allegiance or obedience to the King of Great Britain his Heirs or Successors and that I will be true and faithfull to the State of Maryland and will to the utmost of my power support maintain and defend the freedom and Independance thereof, and the government as now established against all open Enemies, and secret and Traiterous Conspiracies and will use my utmost endeavours to Disclose and make known to the Governor or some one of the Judges or Justices thereof, all Treasons or Traiterous Conspiracies, attempts or Combinations against this State or the Government thereof, which may come to my knowledge so help me God.

Jany 23 John King
Thomas Compton
Walter Hyde Hoxton
Jany 30 Heze Magruder
Feby 5 Moses Orme Junr
Richard Brightwell
14 John Perrie
Alexander Magruder Sr
Benjn Wailes
21 Patrick Clark
Elisha (Brown's Mark
Thomas Norton
James Wilson
John Burns
Henry Trueman
James Collings
27 Walter [illegible]
Bladen C Craycroft's Mk
28 Levin Covington
Jesse Hilton
John Ellis
Charles x Brooke's Mark
Samuel [illegible]

Samuel Norton
Joseph Letchworth
Geo. Naylor Son of Jal
Henry H Lee's Mark
Thos T Cave's Mark
John Watson
Samuel Cave
Samuel Perrie Wailes
Naylor Davis
George x Wall's Mark
Thos [illegible] W's Mk
John x Bean's Mark
John Eastwood
Thomas T Woodard's Mark
Thomas T Ambler's Mark
William W Mayhew's Mk
Benjamin Eastwood
James I Watson Senr's Mk
Benjn + Grayer's Mark
James Trueman
Hezekiah H [illegible]'s Mk
Trueman T [illegible]'s Mark

Prince Georges County March
I hereby Certify the within is a true Copy of all the names subscribed in the Original Book: agreeable to an Act of the General Assembly of Maryland entitled an Act for the better Security of the Government
James Mullikin

Prince Georges County
James Mullikins
Return

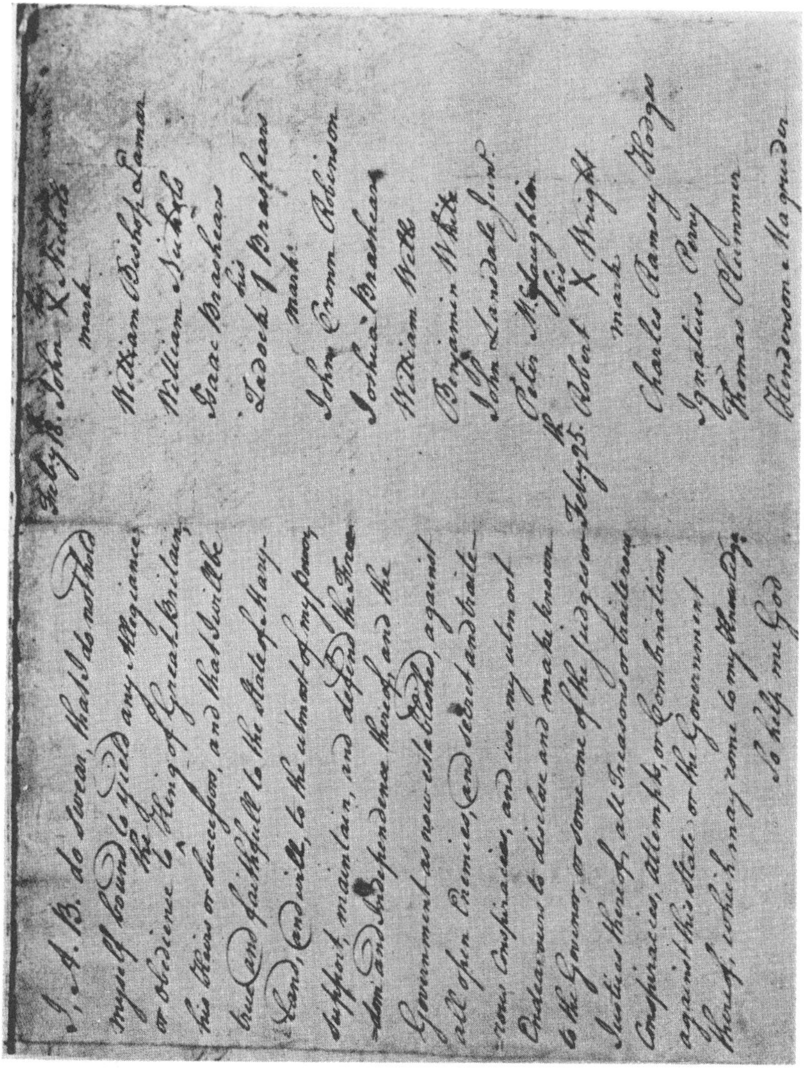
I, A. B. do swear, that I do not hold myself bound to yield any Allegiance or obedience to the King of Great Britain, his Heirs or Successors, and that I will be true and faithful to the State of Maryland, and will, to the utmost of my Power, support, maintain, and defend the Freedom and Independence thereof, and the Government as now established, against all open Enemies, and secret and traiterous Conspiracies; and use my utmost Endeavours to disclose and make known to the Governor, or some one of the Judges or Justices thereof, all Treasons or traiterous Conspiracies, Attempts, or Combinations, against this State, or the Government thereof, which may come to my Knowledge.

So help me God

Feby 18. John X Nichols
mark
William Bishop Lamar
William Sickols
Isaac Brashears
his
Zadock Z Brashears
mark
John Ermin Robinson
Joshua Brashears
William Wells
Benjamin White
John Lansdale Junr
Peter McLaughlin
his
Feby 25. Robert X Wright
mark
Charles Ramsey Hodges
Ignatius Perry
Thomas Plummer
Henderson Magruder

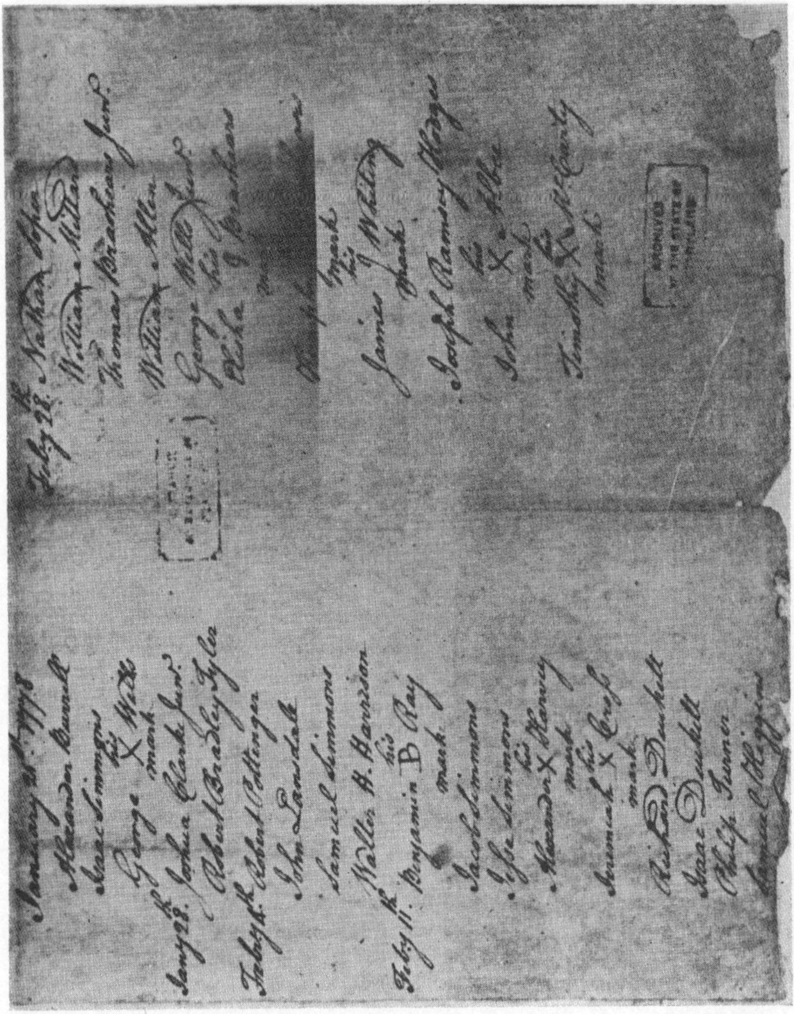
January 28th 1778
Alexander Burrell
Isaac Simmons
George his X Wilk[illegible] mark
Jany 28th Joshua Clark Junr
Robert Bradley Lyles
Febry 4th Robert Pottinger
John Lansdale
Samuel Simmons
Febry 10th Walter H. Harrison
Febry 11. Benjamin his B Ray mark
Jacob Simmons
Jesse Simmons
Alexander his X Henry mark
Emmanuel his X Cross mark
Richard Duckett
Isaac Duckett
Philip Turner
Samuel Higgins
Febry 28th Nathan Soper
William Wilson
Thomas Brashears Junr
William Allen
George Wells Junr
Elisha his Brashears mark
[illegible]
James his Whiting mark
Joseph Ramsey Hodges
John his X Kee mark
Timothy his X [illegible] County mark

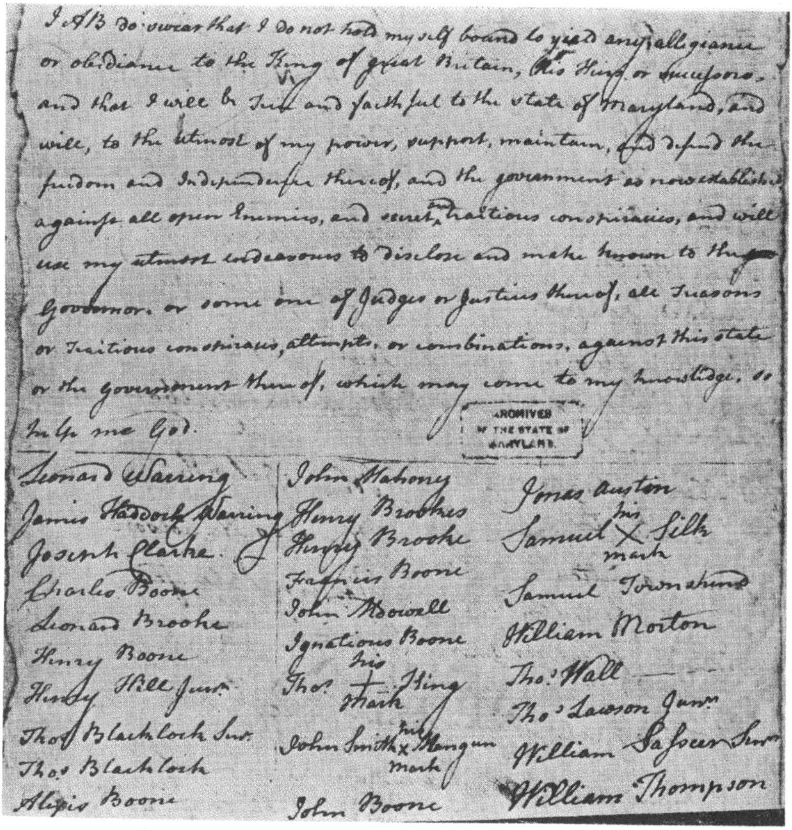

I A B do swear that I do not hold my self bound to yield any allegiance or obedience to the King of Great Britain, his Heirs or Successors, and that I will be true and faithful to the state of Maryland, and will, to the utmost of my power, support, maintain, and defend the freedom and Independence thereof, and the government as now established against all open Enemies, and secret and traitorous conspiracies, and will use my utmost endeavours to disclose and make known to the Governor, or some one of Judges or Justices thereof, all Treasons or traitorous conspiracies, attempts, or combinations, against this state or the government thereof, which may come to my knowledge. So help me God.

Leonard Waring	John Mahony	Jonas Auston
James Haddock Waring	Henry Brookes	Samuel his X mark Silk
Joseph Clarke	Henry Brooke	Samuel Townshend
Charles Boone	Francis Boone	William Morton
Leonard Brooke	John McDowell	Thos. Wall
Henry Boone	Ignatious Boone	Thos. Lawson Junr.
Henry Hill Junr.	Thos. his + mark King	William Safocer Senr.
Thos Blacklock Senr.	John Smith his X mark Mangun	William Thompson
Thos. Blacklock	John Boone	
Alexis Boone		

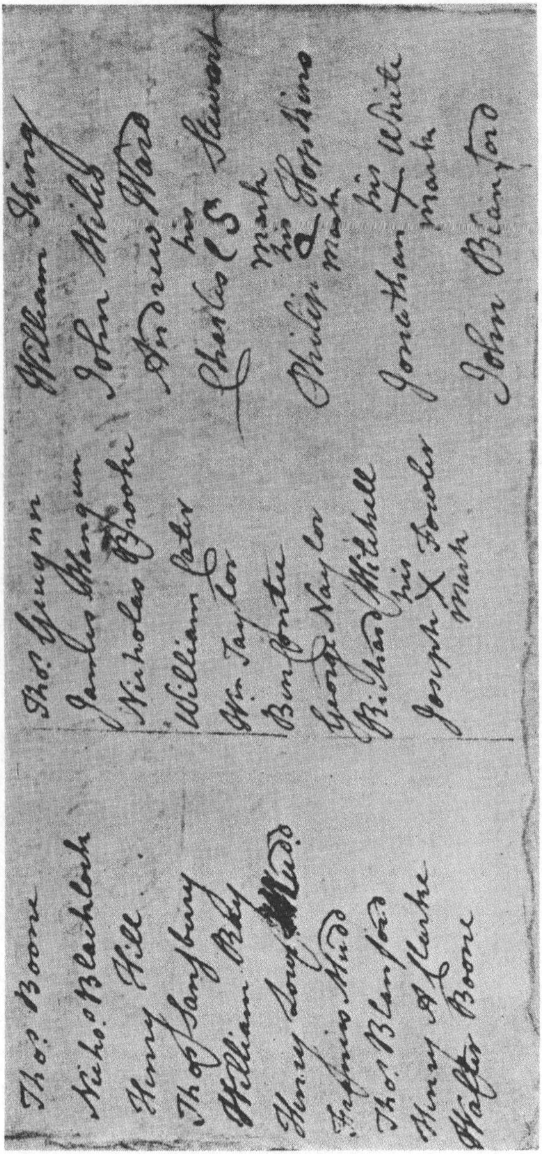

Thos Boone	Thos Gwynn	William King
Nicho. Blacklock	James Mangun	John Wild
Henry Hill	Nicholas Brooke	Andrew Ward
Thos Sansbury	William Cater	Charles (CS) Steward his mark
William Riley	Wm Taylor	Philip Q Hopkins his mark
Henry Long Mudd	Benj Fenticer	Jonathan X White his mark
Francis Mudd	George Naylor	John Blanford
Thos Blanford	Richard Mitchell	
Henry A Clarke	Joseph X Fowler his mark	
Walter Boone		

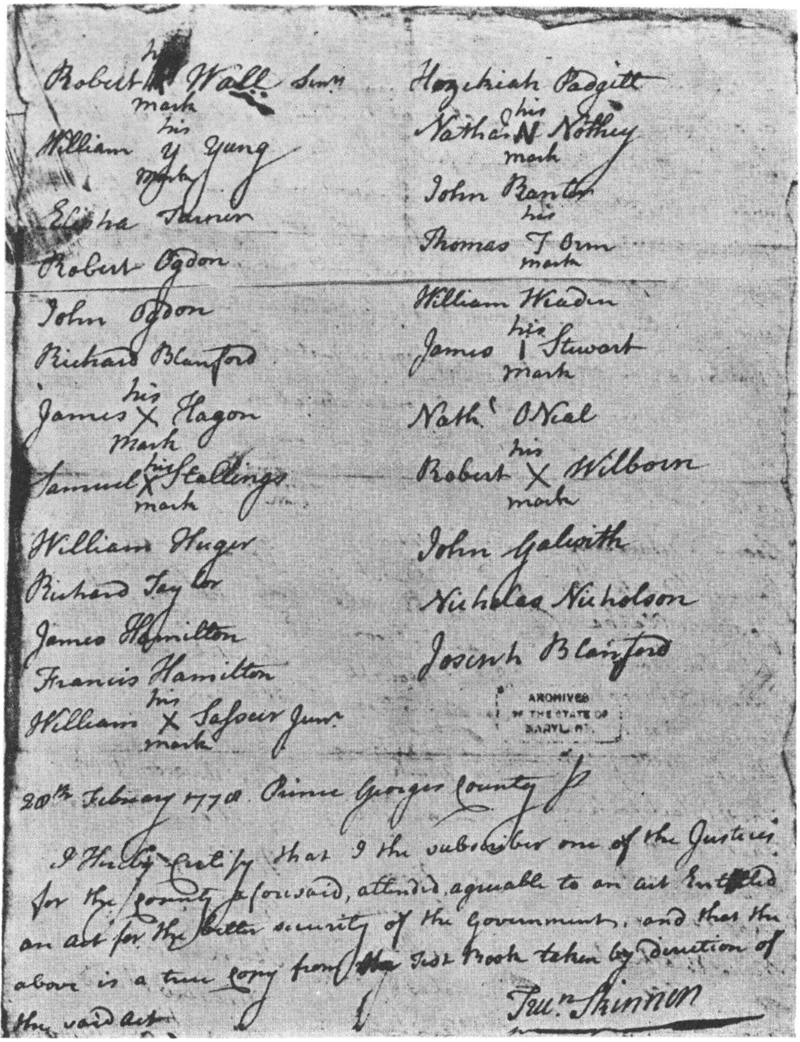

Robert his Wall mark Senr
William his Y Yung mark
Elisha Turner
Robert Ogdon
John Ogdon
Richard Blanford
James his X Hagon mark
Samuel his X Stallings mark
William Huger
Richard Taylor
James Hamilton
Francis Hamilton
William his X Sasseir Junr mark

Hezekiah Padgitt
Nathan his N Nothey mark
John Baxter
Thomas his T Orm mark
William Weaden
James his I Stewart mark
Nathl O'Neal
Robert his X Wilbourn mark
John Galworth
Nicholas Nicholson
Joseph Blanford

20th February 1778. Prince Georges County ss

I Hereby Certify that I the subscriber one of the Justices for the County aforesaid, attended agreeable to an act Entitled an act for the better security of the Government, and that the above is a true Copy from the List book taken by direction of the said act

Thos. Skinner

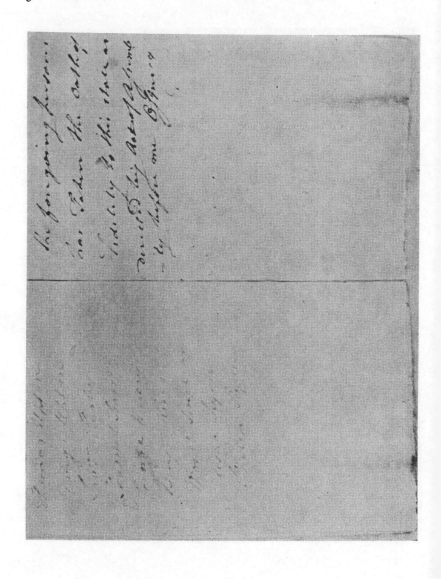

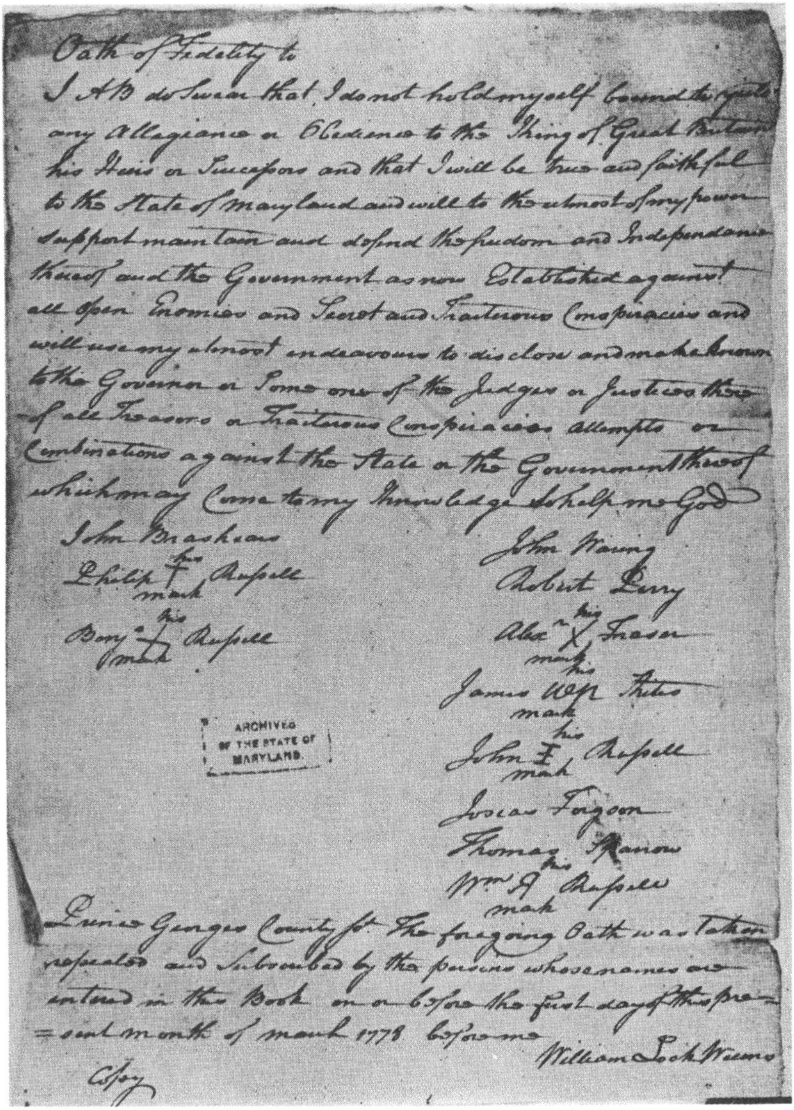

Oath of Fidelity to

I A B do Swear that I do not hold myself bound to yield any Allegiance or Obedience to the King of Great Britain his Heirs or Successors and that I will be true and faithful to the State of Maryland and will to the utmost of my power support maintain and defend the freedom and Independence thereof and the Government as now Established against all open Enemies and Secret and Traiterous Conspiracies and will use my utmost endeavours to disclose and make known to the Governor or some one of the Judges or Justices thereof of all Treasons or Traiterous Conspiracies, attempts or Combinations against the State or the Government thereof which may Come to my knowledge So help me God

John Brashears
Philip his + mark Russell
Benja his + mark Russell

John Waring
Robert Berry
Alexr his X mark Fraser
James his WP mark Stiles
John his I mark Russell
Josias Ferguson
Thomas Sparrow
Wm his R mark Russell

Prince Georges County ss. The foregoing Oath was taken repeated and Subscribed by the persons whose names are entered in the Book on or before the first day of this present month of March 1778 before me

William Lock Weems

Copy

A List of the names of those who hath taken the Oath of Allegiance & Fedelity to the State of Maryland, before Thos. Williams

Benj.a Harwood	James Waring	Richd. Simmons
Walter Williams	Henry Hilleary	Thos. Cross
Walter Williams Jun.r	Walter Hilleary	Jerem.h Brashears
Thos. Boyd Jun.r	Chas. Duvall	John Beck
Abra.m Boyd	Jere.h Cross	Joseph Cross
Jere.h Belt	George Cross	Fran.s Mahon
Josias Shaw	Chas. Soper	John Iglehart
William Matthews	Joseph Brashears	Jacob Duvall of Jno.
Richd. Beall of Wm.	Richd. Higgins	Benj.a Cross
Baruch Duckett	Richd. Lyles	Baruch Butt
Mord.a Jacob	Benj.a Duvall of Sam	Thos. Baldwin
Joseph Duvall	Will.m Mears	Chas. Mitchel
Alex.r Duvall	Nathan Hodge	Thos. Wells (of Red Stone)
Will.m Godphrey	Jonathan Simmons	Hilleary Willson
John Mitchell	Robt. Simmons	Edw.d Butt
James Willson Jun.r	John Tyler	Edmond Willson
Geo. Fras. Magruder	Zach.h Butt	David Beall
John Willson	John Oakley	Joseph Hinton
Elisha Williams	Morris Miles	Fred.k Miles
John Brashears	Nathan Miles	Theodore Mitchel
William Tyler	Wm. Trowell	Joseph Jenkins
Thos. Belt	Edw.d Gantt Jun.r	Zach.h McCotty
Joseph Perry	Josias Beall Jun.r	Gilbert Falconer Jun.r
John McGill	Tilghman Hilleary	Abram Clarke
Regnal Duckett	Nacy Brashears	Saml. Perry
Mark M. Duvall	Saml. Lucass	Caleb Clarke (Constable)
Edw.d Belt	Thos. Lucass.	

Totall 80

Published from Original Returns in the Archives of Maryland, and By Permission of The Historical Society of Maryland.

Pages 25 to 36, Revolutionary Records of Maryland, Brumbaugh and Hodges, contain numerous references to individuals mentioned in the following "Returns" from Prince George's County, Md. and should be consulted.

Revolutionary Records of Maryland, page 30:

"At a County Court held at Upper Marlborough Town, March 23, 1779.

* * * * *

Richard Henderson produces to the Court here his account against the County for an allowance for Administering the Oath of Fidelity and is allowed six pounds current money in the present County Levy for that purpose." (See Return No. 11.)

Fielder Bowie's Return

1. ——, John
2. Baden, Robert
3. Baden, Benj^{a}.
4. Naylor, Geo: Jr.
5. Bowie, Allen, Jr.
6. Hollyday, Leo^{d}., Jr.
7. Baden, John, Senr.
8. Baden, Jeremiah
9. Hollyday, Leonard
10. Harrison, John
11. Haye, Thomas
12. Harriss, George
13. Cox, Thomas
14. Harvey, William G.
15. Sadler, James
16. Boteler, Edward
17. Naylor, John Lawson
18. Haye, Cephas
19. Ryan, Nathaniel
20. Bowie, John Fraser
21. Haye, Sabrit
22. Orme, Richard
23. Piles, Francis
24. Hamilton, Dr. Thomas
25. Roberts, Evan
26. Earley, William, Jr.
27. Hooker, Jonas
28. Warfield, John, Jr.
29. White, Thomas T.
30. M^{c}——, Benjn.
31. Fry, James
32. Ryan, Darby
33. Freeman, Benjn.
34. Boteler, Henry
35. Boteler, Charles, Jr.
36. Boteler, Charles

37. Peter, Jonathan H.
38. Haye, Dorsett
39. Ryan, John of Nat.
40. Turner, Jesse
41. Earley, William, Jr.
42. Selby, Joseph
43. Orme, Hezekiah
44. Hodgken, Thomas, of Philip
45. Cramphin, Damond
46. Johns, William
47. Orme, John
48. Dorsett, William N.
49. Hodgken, Thomas
50. Harvey, James
51. Dorsett, Thomas
52. Hooper, John
53. Orme, William
54. Gray, Thomas
55. Stallions, Thomas
56. Baden, John of Thos.
57. Sadler, William

57 Sworn in before Court

The Following is what I ad[d]. to my list at March Court.

58. Larkin, Elias
59. S——, Tho[s].
60. Moore, Elij[a].
61. Clagett, Edward
62. Harvey, Thomas
63. Jackson (?), Nehemiah
64. Martin, Henry
65. Ridgway, Jonathan
66. Simpson, Gilbert
67. Sullivan, Thomas
68. ——, Nathan
69. Mullikin, Samuel
70. Ridgway, Richard
71. Dorsett, Theodore
72. Curr, John
73. Simmons, Robert
74. Higdon, Truman
75. Standage, Thomas
76. Hickey, Francis
77. Lane, John
78. Talbert, Nathaniel
79. Tannar, Ign[ss]. Nevett
80. Harris, James
81. Sollers, Sabrit
82. Campbell, James
83. Wilson, Nath[a].
84. Moore, John
85. Busey, William
86. M[c]Donald, John
87. Farr, Nicholas
88. Mattingley, Clement
89. Gilpin, Edward
90. Swann, Samuel
91. Grimes, Charles
92. Long, Thomas
93. Grimes, John
94. Soper, Jonathan
95. Hale, ——
96. C——, Matthew "41"
97. Lovejoy, John
98. Gibbons, John
99. Hown, Henry
100. Gibbons, Walter
101. Michell, John
102. Sinclair, Nath[a].
103. Hardey, John, son of Ign[ss].
104. Naylor, George, of Batson
105. Naylor, Batson
106. Sandsbury, Richard

"51 ad[d]. in Court."

March 20th, 1776

Gentlemen:

Inclosd is a true Copy from my Test Book, delivered in the Court. Please to excuse my not sending these sooner & I am

Gentlemen
With Great Respect.
Your Most Hum. St.
FIELDER BOWIE.

"A Return of Persons having taken the Oath by Thomas Gantt jun^r. Prince George's County

[Oath in full]

1. Swann, Edward
2. Thomas, Alexander*
3. Greenfield, William T.
4. Frazier, John*
5. Addams, Luke
6. Swann, James
7. Wear, James
8. Frazier, William
9. Smith, Thomas
10. Gantt, George, Junior
11. Brooke, Richard
12. Gantt, Thomas
13. Greenfield, Thomas Smith
14. Lawson, Thomas*

Thomas Gantt—Return of "Capt. Tapley of the Brig Royal"

1. Hardacre, W^m.
2. Lawson, John*
3. Rutter, Jonathan*
4. Greenfield, Walter Truman
5. Greenfield, Ger^d. Truman
6. Beddoe, James*
7. Roughton, Job
8. Hown [?], Henry, Junior
9. Hill, Job
10. Newhouse, John*
11. Brightwell, John Lawson
12. Gantt, George
13. Weeden, Joseph*
14. Wells, Samuel
15. Smith, Isaac*
16. Gantt, Thos. ye 3^d, of Calvert County

"I hereby Certify that the above is a true Copy taken from the Original Book, to be returned to the County Court;

Thos. Gantt, Junior."

* "His mark."

Osborn Sprigg's Return

1. Sprigg, John
2. Smith, James
3. Belt, Tobias
4. Priestley, Thomas
5. Mitchell, Rich^{d}.
6. Osborn, John
7. Warman, Thomas C.
8. Burgess, Charles
9. Watson, James
10. Sprigg, Phillip
11. Warman, J. H.
12. Moodie, W^{m}.
13. Osborn, Francis
14. Osborn, Dennis
15. Morton, Richard
16. Duvall, Mareen
17. Summers, John
18. Burgess, Mordis
19. Glover, Thomas
20. Miles, Shadrick
21. Bassett, Richard
22. Soaper, Lea^{r}.
23. Clower, John, Junr.
24. Beall, Rich^{d}.
25. Hall, Nathaniel
26. Fraizer [Fraizen?], Henry
27. Week, W^{m}.
28. White, George
29. Page, Daniel
30. White, Thomas
31. Harvin, Clem^{t}.
32. Cox, Abraham
33. Robison, James
34. Wigfield, Thomas
35. Roland, George
36. Losson, W^{m}.
37. Soaper, Abr^{m}.
38. Townshend, Leo^{d}.
39. Hurley, W^{m}.
40. Hobbs, John
41. Cove, George
42. Thomson, John
43. Thomson, W^{m}.
44. Sergant, Benjn.
45. Beall, James
46. Waters, Plimmer
47. Moore, John
48. Grundie, W^{m}.
49. Stone, Joseph
50. Harvey, Henry
51. Harvey, James
52. Taylor, John
53. Ryon, Clement
54. Hosper, Thomas
55. Duce, Deen, Duer [?], Samuel
56. Mocbee, W^{m}.
57. Lowe, Nathan
58. Gale, Peter
59. Vermilion, Howard
60. Stallion, Thomas H.
61. Hall, Phillip
62. Peary, Samuel
63. Wilson, Zach^{r}.
64. Maddooke, James
65. Peary, Howard
66. Robeson, Stephen
67. Perkins, Thomas
68. Chamberlain, Clem^{t}.
69. Hilleary, John
70. Gwynn, Benjn.
71. Macbee, Zadock
72. Soaper, John
73. Cross, W^{m}.
74. Duvall, Jeremiah
75. Jones, Silvester
76. Onion, Henry
77. Howell, John
78. Atkin, Thomas

79. Summers, Nathan
80. Riston, Elisha
81. Riston, Zadock
82. Allby, W^{m}.
83. King, Richard
84. Brown, John
85. Darcey, John
86. Sanders, John
87. Magruder, Samuel
88. Magruder, Robert
89. Mockbee, Booth
90. Magruder, Dennis
91. Mockbee, Barie
92. Mockbee, W^{m}. N.
93. Moore, Benjn.
94. Wood, John
95. Newman, Butler
96. Lintern, Lintem, Linkem [?], John
97. Lowe, Henry
98. Mitchell, Thomas
99. Sandsburry, Thomas
100. Wood, Thomas
101. Weaver, Jacob
102. Sandsburry, Francis
103. Hardey, Ignatious
104. Arnold, Christopher
105. Wilkinson, George
106. Warman, Benjn.
107. Mundley, John
108. Robison, James
109. Moore, James, son Benjn.
110. Cross, John
111. Hutchenson, Samuel
112. Wallingford, George
113. Hinness [Henness, Inness?], John
114. Bidden, Richard
115. Mudd, Hez^{h}.
116. M^{c}lurk, Daniel
117. Jacson, W^{m}.
118. Ryon, James Brown
119. Roberts, Howard
120. Wigfield, Joseph
121. Ray [Kay?], Phillip
122. Cooke, John
123. Jenkins, W^{m}.
124. Moore, James, Senr.
125. Burgess, Richard
126. Addams, Rich^{d}.
127. Tolbert, Paul
128. Summers, Josiah
129. Jenkins, Zadock
130. Harday, Baptist
131. "Lisby," Samuel
132. Turner, Benjn.
133. Lucas [Lewis?], Thomas
134. Ryon, John
135. Stone, Vict^{r}.
136. Biggs, Henry
137. Cox, Josiah
138. Waters, Mord^{i}.
139. Waters, Jacob H.
140. McKensey, James
141. Wells, Samuel
142. Fisher, Abraham
143. Yerling, Thomas
144. Lowe, Zeph^{h}.
145. Sprigg, John Clark
146. Brashears, John
147. "Felphs," Robert
148. Moore, Zadock
149. Emerson, George
150. Keth, James
151. Moore, Joseph
152. Peary, Thomas
153. Moore, James
154. King, James
155. Clarkson, Notley
156. Cooke, Joseph
157. Burch, Thomas
158. Faivale, Daniel
159. Standage [Handage?], Hez^{h}.
160. Ridgaway, Benjn.

161. Davis, Robt.
162. "Marton," Jacob
163. Bird, Thomas
164. Tucker, Thomas
165. Robert, John
166. Clagett, Thomas
167. Bean, Thomas
168. Burch, Edward
169. Evans, John
170. Robison, Benjn.
171. "Morgin," Marmaduke
172. Butler, Thomas
173. "Camble," W^{m}.
174. Smith, John
175. Bean, Benjn.
176. "Buckinham," Richard
177. King, John
178. Sinclear, W^{m}.
179. Adams, George
180. Hutchinson, W^{m}.
181. Nailor, Joshua
182. Davis, Nathl.
183. Adams, George
184. Gibbons, Thomas
185. "Jeffrais," John
186. Phillips, Bedder [Belder?]
187. Martin, John
188. Talburt, Benjn.
189. Canberry, Stephen
190. Firman, John
191. Clubb, Samuel
192. Hopkins, Rich^{d}.
193. Lewis, Thomas
194. Hinniss, John
195. Grimes, George
196. Fraizer, Robert
197. "Cidwell," Hez^{h}.
198. Beckett, John
199. Harvey, Newman
200. Gibbons, W^{m}.
201. King, Henry
202. Upton, Thomas
203. Upton, George
204. Hurley, Sab^{m}.
205. Pearse [?], [Searce?], Shadrick
206. Harday, George
207. King, Benjn.
208. Sinclear, Mord^{i}.
209. Ryon, Elisha
210. Ryon, Philip

The foregoing persons has Taken the Oath of Fidelity to this state as directed by Act of Assembly before me

O. SPRIGG.*

* The writing in this Return is so indistinct that but the last page is reproduced. (See Plate 300).

[Thomas Upton
George Upton
Sab^{n}. Hurley
George Harday
Ben^{m}. King
Mord. Sinclear
Elisha Ryon
Philip Ryon]

EARLY MARYLAND NATURALIZATIONS

Early Maryland Naturalizations, Etc., From Kilty's Laws

Achilles, Peter. Session 1674, Ch. 25.
Allen, Thomas. His two children to be redeemed from Indians. 1650, Ch. 18.
Alward, John. Session 1682, Ch. 11.
Anderson, Mounts. Session 1674, Ch. 12.
Anleton, Peter. Session 1683, Ch. 4.
Annapolis. Erected into a town and port and place of trade, under name of Town Land at Proctor's. Session 1683, Ch. 5.
Arenson, Cornelius. Session 1674, Ch. 12.
Barette, Isaac de, &c. Session 1669, Ch. 4.
Bayard, Peter. Session 1684, Ch. 8.
Beeson, Stephen. Session 1671, Ch. 1.
Berts, Paul, &c. Session 1686, Ch. 6.
Blakemstein, William. Session 1682, Ch. 14.
Blaney, Lewis. Session 1681, Ch. 10.
Boys, Cornelius. Session 1681, Ch. 9.
Brown, Derrick. Session 1686, Ch. 5.
Cadger, Robert. Session 1676, Ch. 10. Real & personal estate, &c.
Cartwright, Matthew. Session 1671, Ch. 10.
Cawood, Ann. Act for relief of her children. Session 1676, Ch. 22.
Christian, Lawrence. Session 1674, Ch. 12.
Cleyborn, Capt. Wm. Compliance, &c. prohibited. Session 1650, Ch. 4.
Colke, Oliver. Session 1674, Ch. 12.
Comegye, Cornelius, &c. Session 1671, Ch. 29.
Cordea, Hester. Session 1674, Ch. 12.
Cordea, Mark. Session 1671, Ch. 10.
Corsins, John. Session 1683, Ch. 1.
Dauntrees, Jaspar. Session 1684, Ch. 8.
Delamaire, John. Session 1674, Ch. 12.
de Costa, Matthias. Session 1671, Ch. 28.
DeLa Grange, Arnoldus. Session 1684, Ch. 8.
DeLa Roche, Charles. Session 1699, Ch. 4.
Demouderer, Anthony. Session 1671, Ch. 10.
Demoisne, Peter Maise. Session 1683, Ch. 1.
Desjardins, John. Session 1674, Ch. 12.
DeYoung, Jacob Clause. Session 1671, Ch. 10.

Dhyniossa, Alexander, &c. Session 1671, Ch. 10.
Duhattoway, Jacob. Session 1674, Ch. 25.
Elexon, John. Session 1671, Ch. 10.
Enloes, Henry. Session 1674, Ch. 12.
Errickson, Mathew, of Kent Co. Session 1682, Ch. 10.
Fountaine, Nichs. Session 1671, Ch. 10.
Fowcate, Peter. Session 1681, Ch. 9.
Freeman, Henry. Session 1674, Ch. 12.
Garrets, Rutgerson. Session 1671, Ch. 10.
Gotes, John, &c. Session 1671, Ch. 1.
Green, Henry. Session 1674, Ch. 14.
Guibert, Joshua. Session 1678, Ch. 12.
Hack, Anna. Session 1666, Ch. 7.
Hanson, Hans. Session 1671, Ch. 29.
Harman, Augustine. Session 1666, Ch. 7.
Henderson, Henry. Session 1674, Ch. 12.
Holdsworth, Samuel, Calvert Co. Act for his benefit confirming title as against Edwd. Husband and his heirs. Session 1681, Ch. 17.
Jacobson, Jeoffrey. Session 1674, Ch. 12.
Jarbo, John. Naturalized, Session 1666, Ch. 7.
Jarboe, John, Lt. Col. Noncupative will confirmed. Session 1676, Ch. 19.
Johnson, Albert. Session 1682, Ch. 10.
Johnson, Bernan. Session 1682, Ch. 10.
Johnson, Cornelises. Session 1674, Ch. 12.
Johnson, John. Session 1674, Ch. 14.
Johnson, Peter. Session 1664, Ch. 9.
Johnson, Simon. Session 1682, Ch. 4.
Jourdain, Jean. Session 1669, Ch. 4.
Lecount, John, &c. Session 1674, Ch. 12.
Lederer, John. Session 1671, Ch. 10.
Lockerman, Jacob. Session 1678, Ch. 13.
Long, John of London, merchant. Lease confirmed to him. Session 1674, Ch. 24.
Looton, Jacob. Session 1682, Ch. 9.
Mans, Rowland. Session 1682, Ch. 15.
Matson, Andrew. Session 1683, Ch. 1.
Matthews, Henry. Session 1674, Ch. 12.
Mills, Peter. Session 1671, Ch. 10.
Moisne-see Peter Maise DeMoisne.
Mugenbrough, Martin. Session 1674, Ch. 12.
Mullock, Andrew-see Poulson. Session 1683, Ch. 4.

Neale, James-His children. Session 1666, Ch. 8.
Nomers, John. Session 1674, Ch. 12.
Oldson, Peter. Session 1681, Ch. 10.
Peane, James, &c. Session 1678, Ch. 13.
Peterson, Cornelius. Session 1674, Ch. 12.
Peterson, Hans. Session?, Ch. 12.
Peterson, Mathias, &c. Naturalized Session 1671, Ch. 10, and 1683, Ch. 4.
Rowlands, Robert. Session 1669, Ch. 4.
Seth, Jacob. Session 1684, Ch. 9.
Stille, Axell. Session 1674, Ch. 12.
Syserson, Marcus. Session 1674, Ch. 12.
Tick, William. Session 1674, Ch. 12.
Toulson, Andrew, Baltimore Co. Session 1671, Ch. 10.
Turner, Thomas. Session 1671, Ch. 10.
Vanheeck, John. Session 1669, Ch. 4.
Vansweringen, Garret, &c. Session 1669, Ch. 4.
Verbrack, Nich. Session 1684, Ch. 7.
Ward, Henry, of Cecil Co. Gent. Act punishing for a certain abuse.) Session 1676, Ch. 21.
Ward, Mary. Executrix of Matthew Ward, decd.-confirmation of 1 late) husband's purchase of plantation on Patuxent River, called "Further) Neck." Session 1678, Ch. 14.
Young, Jacob Clause De-see DeYoung. Naturalization Session 1671, Ch. 10.

Digest of Kilty's Laws[1] Showing Maryland Revolutionary War Pensions; Maryland Revolutionary War Pensions in Report of Secy. of War, 1835; Some Original Commissions

Notes and Abbreviations Used.

The Act of Congress of Sept. 29, 1789, directed the payment of Pensions, which had been granted and paid by the States respectively, to the Invalids who were wounded and disabled during the late war, should be continued and paid by the United States from the 4th of March, 1789—U. S. Laws, vol. 1, p. 118; Pa. Archives, 2d Ser., Vol. XI.

Passed Nov. session, 1799, No. 10. "Resolved, That the payment of the five months pay due the officers and soldiers, the sum due for services on board the barges, the redemption of the emissions of June, 1780, and the payt. of certificates issued by this state, amounting in the whole to 9276£—9s—11d, be and the same are hereby suspended until Jan. 1, 1801; and the said sum shall be liable to the appropriations made for the present year.

[a] List of Invalid Pensioners who have been in receipt of pensions at the Agency of Md., & whose residence cannot be ascertained, in consequence of the destruction of the papers of the War Office in 1801 and 1814.

[b] Pensions granted under Act of Mch. 18, 1818.

* Names of the Revolutionary Pensioners which have been placed on the Roll of Maryland, under the Law of Mch. 18, 1818, from the passage —, thereof, to this day, inclusive, with the Rank they held, and the Lines in which they served, viz:

(X, No. 1, etc.) Maryland Historical Society Original Commissions.

There are numerous Original Commissions (1775–1782) in the extensive collections of the Maryland Historical Society, practically all of which were included in the manuscript for this volume, but only a few with important indorsements have been retained. G. M. B.

† Report of the Secretary of War, Pension Establishment of the U. S., 1835.

Abbott, George. Passed Nov. session, 1812 (Jan. 2, '13)—No. 36. Treas. Western Shore pay to George Abbott, late a soldier in the Md. line, during the rev. war,—half pay of a private, as a further remuneration, &c.

Adams, Adam. Passed Dec. session, 1815—No. 35. Treas. Western Shore pay to Adam Adams, during his life, a sum of money equal to the half pay of a private, annually in quarterly payts.

* *Adams, Adam.* Private, Md. line, (p. 540, Jan. 1820).

* *Albert, Jacob.* Private, Pa. Line (Jan. 1820, p. 540).

[1] The valuable set in the Library of Congress was used in this investigation. G. M. B.

Alcock, Robert. Passed Jan. 30, 1829—No. 7. Treas. Western Shore pay to Robert Alcock, of Anne-Arundel county, during life, half yearly, half pay of a private for his services during the rev. war.

Alexander, Jacob. Passed Feb. 13, 1835—No. 24. Treas. Western Shore pay to Mary Alexander, widow of the late Jacob Alexander, who was a sergeant in the Rev., during widowhood, half pay of a sergeant for the services of her husband.

Allen, Jacob,—see Gerrish, Edward.

Allen, Nathan. Passed Feb. 3, 1834—No. 14. Treas. Western Shore pay to Nathan Allen of Queen Anne's county, during life, quarterly, half pay of a private, for services rendered by him during the Rev. war.

Allen, Steven, recommended for Ensign, Worcester Co., 1782—see Duer, Joshua.

† *Alsop, John,* private, Rev. Army[a]. Pensioned under Act of June 7, 1785, from Mch. 4, 1789, at $40.00 per an. (recd. $640.00). Died in 1805. (U. S. Pens. Roll, 1835, p. 20.)

* *Altigh, Michael,* private, Pa. Line (Jan. 1820, p. 540).

Alvey, Josias. Passed Dec. session, 1815—No. 25. Treas. Western Shore pay to Josias Alvey, of St. Mary's county, late a private in the rev. war, during life, quarterly, half pay of a private, as a further remuneration for those services by which his country has been so essentially benefitted.

* *Alvey, Josias,* private, Md. Line (Jan. 1820, p. 540).

Amos, Elizabeth. Passed Mch. 5, 1834—No. 44. Treas. Western Shore pay to Elizabeth Amos, of Baltimore city, quarterly, half pay of a captain, in consideration of the services rendered by her husband, during the rev. war.

Amos, Elizabeth. Passed Mch. 16, 1840—No. 31. Treas. Western Shore pay to Samuel B. Hugo, of Baltimore, all monies due to Elizabeth Amos, a deceased pensioner of the State of Md., said Hugo being her heir.

Amos, Joshua, of Wm. Ensign of Co. of Harford Co. Militia, 1778—see Corbet, James.

† *Anderson, John,* private, Rev. Army[a]. Pensioned at $40.00 per an. from Mch. 4, 1789 (act June 7, 1785). (U. S. Pens. Roll, 1835, p. 20).

Anderson, John. Passed Dec. session, 1817 (Feb. 13, 1818)—No. 51. Treas. Western Shore pay to John Anderson, quarterly, the half pay of a private, as a further remuneration for his rev. services.

Anderson, Capt. Richard. Passed Nov. 1785, Vol. 11, Chap. XVI. Gen. Assembly granted half pay of a captain to Richard Anderson for disability acquired in the service, late a capt. in the Md. line in the Continental army.

* *Annis, Micajah,* private, Va. Line (Jan. 1820, p. 540).

* *Athey, William,* private Va. Line, died 21 Aug. 1819 (Jan. 1820, p. 540).

Auld, Daniel. Mch. 9, 1826—No. 102, p. 260. Treas. Western Shore pay to Daniel Auld of Talbot Co. half pay of a private for his services during the rev. war.

Auld, Daniel. Passed Feb. 17, 1832—No. 35. Treas. Western Shore pay to Sarah Auld, of Talbot county, widow of Daniel Auld, a soldier of the revolution, such sum as may be due her said husband at time of his death.

Auld, Daniel. Passed Mch. 9, 1832—No. 84. Treas. Western Shore pay to Sarah Auld, of Talbot county, widow of Daniel Auld, a soldier of the rev. war, during widowhood, half yearly, half pay of a private, for services rendered by her husband during said war.

Auld, Daniel. Passed Jan. 19, 1848—No. 10. Treas. of State pay to Philip Pasterfield, of Talbot county, surviving brother & legal representative of Sarah Auld, widow of Daniel Auld, a soldier of the rev. war, bal. of any pension due to Sarah Auld, on June 28, 1847, at time of her death.

Ayres, Thomas. Passed Jan. 26, 1837—No. 13. Treas. Western Shore pay to Elizabeth Ayres, widow of Thomas Ayres, half pay of a private during her life, as a further remuneration for his services, during the rev.

* *Azelip, Richard,* private, German Regt. (p. 540, Jan. 1820).

† *Azelip, Richard,* private Md. line, age 54. Pensioned Sept. 30, 1818 at $96.00 per an. from Apr. 6, 1818. "Died"—rec'd. $279.73; resided in Frederick county[b]. (U. S. Pens. Roll, 1835, p. 36).

* *Badger, Charles,* private, Hazen's regt. (Jan. 1820, p. 541).

* *Bailey, Joseph,* private, Md. Line (Jan. 1820, p. 541).

Bayly, Capt. Mountjoy. Passed Nov. session 1810—No. 2. Whereas it appears to this gen. assembly, that Mountjoy Bayly, a capt. in the late rev. war, and who served to its termination, did not receive the commutation money of five years pay in lieu of the half pay for life promised to the officers and soldiers who continued in service to the end of the war; therefore, Resolved. That the Treas. Western Shore—pay to said Mountjoy Bayly, five years full pay as a captain, free from interest, as a full compensation for his services during, the rev. war.

Bailey, Mountjoy. Feb. 8, 1826—No. 25, p. 239. "Resolved, the register of the land office issue to Mountjoy Bailey, a warrant for 200 a. of land, to be located on any unappropriated land belonging to this state, in Allegany county heretofore unpatented, as a donation granted by this state to the officers of his rank, who served in the Maryland line, during the revolutionary war, and to which they consider him entitled."

† *Bailey, Thomas,* private, Md. Line, age 72, died in 1824; resided in Frederick county[b]. Pensioned Sept. 30, 1818, at $96.00 per an. from Mch. 27, 1818. (Recd. $570.03. U. S. Pens. Roll, 1835, p. 36).

Baily, Thomas. Passed Feb. 19, 1819—No. 78. Treas. Western Shore to pay to Thomas Bailey, late a rev. soldier, half pay of a private.

* *Baily, Thomas*, private, Md. line (Jan. 1820, p. 540).

Baker, Lieut. Henry Cleland. Passed Nov. 1791, No. 1. It appears that Henry C. Baker, late a lieut. in the third Md. reg. is deprived of the use of his limbs, and thereby rendered incapable of maintaking himself, his wife and children; and it also appearing that he probably derived the disorder, under which he now labours, from being exposed in the service of his country, during several campaigns in S. C.—Gov. of Md. grant unto Henry Cleland Baker, half pay which he received in the continental service, quarterly by orders drawn on the treas. of western shore for the same, and that the same be charged to the U. S.

* *Baker, John H.*, private, Pa. Line (Jan. 1820, p. 541).

† *Baker, John H.*, private Pa. line, age 79; died Oct. 30, 1823. Resided in Frederick county[b]. Pensioned Sept. 25, 1818, at $96.00 per an. from Apr. 4, 1818. (Recd. $535, 46, U. S. Pens. Roll, 1835, p. 36).

† *Baker, Thomas*, private, Rev. army[a]. Pensioned at $40.00 per an. (Act of June 7, 1785) from Mch. 4, 1789 (Recd. $920.00—U. S. Pens. Rolls, 1835, p. 20).

Baldwin, Henry, Lieut. Passed Feb. 18, 1830—No. 30. Treas. Western Shore pay to Maria Gambrill, widow of Henry Baldwin, an officer of the revolution, during her widowhood, quarterly, half pay of a lieut, in consideration for the services of her said husband.

Baldwin, Lieut. Henry. Passed Jan. 3, 1835—No. 38. Treas. Western Shore pay to Wm. H. Baldwin, of Anne Arundel county, two months pay, due his mother, Maria Gambrill, deceased, upon the pension list of this State.

Baldwin, Samuel. Passed Feb. 26, 1836—No. 33. Treas. Western Shore pay to Samuel Baldwin, a soldier of the rev. half pay of a private during his life.

* *Ballard, Jonathan*, private, Md. Line (Jan. 1820, p. 541).

† *Ballard, Jonathan*, private, Md. line, age 76, residing in Frederick county[b]. Pensioned Oct. 17, 1818, at $96.00 per an. from May 15, 1818. (Recd. $1,517.33. U. S. Pens. Roll, 1835, p. 36).

* *Balzar, Anthony*, private, Pa. Line (Jan. 1820, p. 541).

Baltzel, Monocacy Manor, Lot 40—patent issued June 21, 1797.

Jacob Baltzel should be *Charles* (No. 3, Nov. session, 1801).

Bantham, Peregrine. Passed Dec. session, 1816—No. 51. Treas. Western Shore pay to Peregrine Bantham, of Kent county, late a private in the rev. war, quarterly, during life, the half pay of a private, as a further remuneration for those services by which his country has been so essentially benefitted.

* *Bantham, Peregrine*, private, Md. line (Jan. 1820, p. 541).

† *Barnet, Robert*, private, Rev. army, of Frederick county. Pensioned at $40.00 per annum, Oct. 30, 1819, under act of June 7, 1785, and dating from Mch. 4, 1789 (recd. $1,085.56)—at $64.00 per an. Apr. 24, 1816 (recd. $151.11). (U. S. Pens. Rolls, 1835, p. 13).

* *Barnheiser, John*, private, Pa. Line (Jan. 1820, p. 541).

† *Barnover, George*, private Rev. army, of Baltimore county, pensioned May 1, 1820 at $96.00 per year from Nov. 13, 1814 (received $381.86). Transferred from Dist. Col. Mch. 4, 1818. Died Nov. 4, 1818. (War Dept. 1835, p. 4).

Barrett, Joshua. Passed Nov. session, 1804—No. 13. Treas. Western Shore pay to Joshua Barrett, a late sergeant in the rev. war, in quarterly payts., half pay of a sergeant during the said war, as a further remuneration to the said Joshua Barrett for services rendered his country, and as a relief from the indigence and misery which attend his decrepitude and old age.

Barrott, Solomon. Passed Dec. session, 1815—No. 15. Treas. Western Shore pay to Solomon Barrott, or order annually in quarterly payts., the half pay of a fifer for life. [Listed amongst rev. war pensioners.]

* *Barrett, Solomon*, musician, Md. Line (Jan. 1820, p. 540).

Bateman, George. Passed Dec. session, 1815—No. 29. Treas. Western Shore pay to Geo. Bateman, a corporal in the rev. war,—half pay of a corporal, as a compensation for those services by which his country has been so essentially benefitted.

* *Bateman, George*, private, Md. Line (Jan. 1820, p. 541).

* *Batterson, Wm.*, private, Md. Line (Jan. 1820, p. 541).

Baynard, Geo. Captain of a Queen Anne Co. Company of Militia in 5th Battn. Jan. 3, 1776.—(See Scrivener, Isaac and Wright, Robert).

* *Beacroft, John*, private, Md. Line (Jan. 1820, p. 540).

* *Beall, Christopher*, private, Md. Line (Jan. 1820, p. 541).

Beall, John, "Gentleman." Comd. 2d Lieut. of a Co. of Militia, Harford Co. Jan. 3, 1776; (Orig. comn. in possession of Mr. John A. Robinson, Clerk of Court, Bel Air, Md.)

Beall, Lawson. Passed Mch. 3, 1840—No. 16. Treas. Western Shore pay Henrietta Beall, widow of Lawson Beall, a soldier of the rev., or order, quarterly, during her life, the half pay of a private, from Jan. 1, 1840, in consideration of the services of her husband.

Beall, Capt. Lloyd. Passed Dec. session, 1815—No. 27. Treas. Western Shore pay to Lloyd Beall, late a capt. in the rev. war, or his order during life, quarterly, half pay of a capt., as a reward for those services which he rendered his country in her struggle for independence.

Beall, Lloyd. Passed Dec. session, 1817—No. 7. Treas. Western Shore pay to Elizabeth Beall, widow of Lloyd Beall, late a captain in the rev. war, or her order, during life, quarterly payts., a sum of money equal to the half pay of a captain.

Beall, Maj. Wm. D. Passed Nov. session, 1808—No. 2. Treas. Western Shore pay to Wm. D. Beall, late a maj. in the Md. line of the rev. war, in quarterly payts. half pay of a major, for his rev. war services.

† *Bean, John*, private, Rev. army[a]. Pensioned, Act June 7, 1785, from Sept. 4, 1800 at $30.00 per an. (Recd. $150.00. U. S. Pens. Roll, 1835, p. 20).

Bean, Leonard. Passed Mch. 2, 1832—No. 99. Treas. Western Shore pay to Leonard Bean, of Mason county, Ky. a soldier of the rev. war, during life, half yearly, half pay of a private, as further remuneration for his services during the rev. war.

Beatty, Lieut. Thomas. Passed Mch. 21, 1833—No. 66. Treas. Western Shore pay to Anne Semmes, of Georgetown, D. C., in consideration of services rendered by her husband, Thomas Beatty, a lieut. in the rev. war, during life, quarterly, the half pay of a lieut.

Beatty, Wm. Passed Mch. 12, 1827—No. 72. Treas. pay to Jane Beatty, of Pittsburgh, Pa. during life, half yearly, half pay of a private, for her husband, Wm. Beatty's services during the rev. war.

Beaven, Lieut. Charles. Passed Dec. session, 1815—No. 26. Treas. Western Shore pay to Chas. Beaven, of Harford county, an old rev. officer, or order, half pay of a lieut. during the remainder of his life, as a remuneration for his meritorious services.

Beckwith, Nehemiah. Passed Mch. 2, 1827—No. 24. Treas. to pay Nehemiah Beckwith, of Dorchester county, during life, half yearly, half pay of a private, for his rev. war services.

Becroft, John. Passed Dec. session, 1816—No. 33. Treas. Western Shore pay to John Becroft, of Baltimore county, an old rev. soldier, quarterly, half pay of a private, as a further remuneration to him for those services by which his country has been so essentially benefitted.

* *Bell, Ning*, private, Md. Line (Jan. 1820, p. 540).

Belt, Capt. John Sprigg—see Halkerstone, Robert (1811). Passed Dec. session, 1815—No. 8. Treas. Western Shore pay unto John Sprigg Belt, late a capt. in the Md. line during the rev. war, or order,—half pay of a capt, during his life, as a further remuneration for his services during that war, in lieu of $125.00 allowed him by resolution passed Nov. session, 1811 (No. 36).

* *Belt, John Sprigg*, captain, Md. Line (Jan. 1820, p. 540).

* *Benjamin, Joseph*, trumpeter, Lee's legion (Jan. 1820, p. 541).

Bennett, Frederick. Passed Nov. session, 1811—No. 54. Treas. Western Shore pay to Frederick Bennett, of Dorchester county, an old rev.

soldier, half pay of a corporal during the remainder of his life, as a remuneration for his meritorious services.

Bennett, James, "Gentleman." Comd. 2d Lieut. of Capt. Chas. Bennetts Co. of Militia, Wicomico Battn. in Worcester Co., Aug. 13, 1777. Thos. Johnson.

May 1, 1778, resigned as 2[d] Lieut. on account of appt. to Quartermaster's Birth to the said Battn. by the Field Officers thereof.

I do hereby certifie that James Bennett, 2[d] Lieut. in Capt. Chas. Bennetts Co. of Militia appeared before me, the subscriber one of the Justice's of the Peace for the county of Worcester & took the Oath of Fidelity &c. to the State. This 3[d] day of Oct. 1777. Pr. Holland, (X, No. 36).

† *Bennet, John,* private, Rev. army[a]. Pensioned Act of June 7, 1785, from Mch. 4, 1789, at $40.00 per an. (recd. $720.00. U. S. Pens. Roll, 1835, p. 20).

Bennett, John. Passed Dec. session, 1816—No. 37. Treas. Western Shore pay to John Bennett, an old soldier, in the rev. war, quarterly, during his life, a sum of money equal to the half pay of a private, as a further compensation for his services in the rev. war.

Benson, Capt. Perry. Passed Nov. 1785, Vol. 11, Chap. XVI. Gen. Assembly granted half pay of a capt., for disability acquired in the service, to Perry Benson, late a capt. in the Md. line in the Continental army.

Benson, Perry, General. Passed Feb. 24, 1830—No. 52. Treas. Western Shore pay to Mary Benson, widow of General Perry Benson, during widowhood, quarterly, the half pay of a captain, in consideration for the services of her late husband during the rev. war.

Berry, Edward. Passed Feb. 17, 1832—No. 38, 52$^{3}/_{4}$ acres in Allegany county were granted to Edward Berry, a soldier of the revolution, who it is stated, died intestate, and without heirs; and said land became escheated to the State &c. Resolution gives relief to Robinson Savage, Jr. of Allegany county for said land, called "Cricket legs."

Berry, Wm. Ensign of a Co. of Militia in Talbot Co., 4th Battn. after Apr. 9, 1778—see Maynadier, Wm.

* *Bevin, Charles,* lieut. Md. Line (Jan. 1820, p. 541).

* *Biddle, Richard,* private, Md. Line—died Jan. 5, 1819 (Jan. 1820, p. 541).

Bidwell, Richard. Passed Dec. session, 1816—No. 38. Treas. Western Shore pay to Richard Bidwell, of Baltimore, an old soldier, quarterly, during his life, half pay of a private, as further compensation for his services during the rev. war.

† *Bishop, Thos.,* private, Rev. army[a]. Pensioned Act June 7, 1785,

from Mch. 4, 1789, at $40.00 per an. (Recd. $140.00. U. S. Pens. Roll, 1835, p. 20).

† *Blair, John*, private, Rev. army[a]. Pensioned at $40.00 per an. from Mch. 4, 1789 (Act June 7, 1785) (recd. $120.00) Died in 1792. (U. S. Pens. Roll, 1835, p. 20).

† *Blair, John*, 2d., private Rev. army[a]. Pensioned at $40.00 per an. from Mch. 4, 1789 (Act June 7, 1785. Recd. $220.00). Died in 1794. (U. S. Pens. Rolls, 1835, p. 20).

* *Blake, Jacob*, private, Md. Line (Jan. 1820, p. 541).

Blake, John. Mch. 1, 1826—No. 58—p. 247. Treas. Western Shore pay to John Blake, of Worcester county, quarterly, during life, the half pay of a private, as a further remuneration for his services during the rev. war.

Blake, Patsy. Passed Mch. 7, 1834—No. 48. Treas. Western Shore pay to Patsy Blake, of Worcester county, during life, quarterly, half pay of a private, for the services rendered by her husband, during the rev. war.

† *Blever, James*, private, Rev. army, of Frederick county, Pensioned Oct. 30, 1819 at $40.00 per an. under act of June 7, 1785, dating from Mch. 4, 1789 (recd. $763.87)—at $60.00 per an. from Apr. 8, 1808, Act of Mch. 3, 1809 (recd. $487.67)—at $96.00 per an. from Apr. 24, 1816 (recd. $1,666.66). (U. S. Pens. Rolls, 1835, p. 13).

Bluer, James. Passed Mch. 10, 1832—No. 77. Treas. Western Shore pay to James Bluer, of Frederick county, during life, quarterly, half pay of a private, in consideration of the services rendered by him during the rev. war.

Bolton, John. Passed Nov. session, 1812—No. 66. Treas. Western Shore pay unto John Bolton, or order, quarterly payts., half pay of a private in the late rev. war.

Bomgardner, Wm. Feb. 16, 1820—No. 50. Treas. is directed to pay William Bomgardner of Washington county, half pay of a private for his rev. war services.

Passed May 2, 1827—No. 29. Treas. Western Shore to pay Margaret Bomgardner, of Washington county, during life, half yearly, half pay of a private for her late husband's rev. services.

Bond, John. Mch. 1, 1826—No. 59, p. 247. Treas. of Western Shore pay to John Bond, of Hampshire Co., Va., during life, quarterly, the half pay of a sergeant, as a further remuneration for his services during the rev. war.

Boone, Lieut. John. Passed Nov. session, 1811—No. 57. Treas. Western Shore pay to John Boone, of Charles county, a lieut. in the late rev. army, $125.00 annually, in quarterly payts.

Boone, Lieut. John. Passed Dec. session, 1815—No. 7. Treas. Western Shore pay to John Boone, an officer in the rev. war, during life—the half pay of a lieut., in lieu of the sum already allowed him, as a further compensation for those services rendered his country during her struggle for independence.

† *Botts, Joseph,* private, Rev. army[a]. Pensioned, Act of June 7, 1785, from Mch. 4, 1789, at $40.00 per an. (rec'd. $480.00—U. S. Pens. Roll, 1835, p. 20). Died in 1801.

Bowen, John. Passed Nov. 1788, Ch. 8, and noted in Vol. 11, Chap. 18. "Gen. Assembly granted a pension to John Bowen, a late officer in the Continental army."

* *Bowen, Stephen Lewis,* private, Md. Line (Jan. 1820, p. 541).

* *Bowen, Wm.,* private, Hazen's regt. (Jan. 1820, p. 541).

Bowers, George. Passed Mch. 2, 1837—No. 28. Treas. Western Shore pay to George Bowers half pay of a private during his life, as a further remuneration for his services during the Rev.

* *Bowling, Wm. I.,* private, Md. Line (Jan. 1820, p. 541).

* *Boxwell, Robert,* private, Va. Line (Jan. 1820, p. 541).

* *Boyd, Benj.,* surgeon's mate, Md. Line (Jan. 1820, p. 541).

Boyer, Capt. Michael. Passed Dec. session, 1816—No. 32. Treas. Western Shore pay to Michael Boyer (late a capt. in the rev. war) quarterly, during his life, a sum of money equal to the half pay of a captain, as a further compensation to him for his services during the rev. war.

Bozman, Ballard. 2d Lieut. in 17th Battn. Militia—see Schoolfield, Wm.

* *Bradshaw, Geo. H.,* private, Pa. Line (Jan. 1820, p. 541).

* *Branson, John,* private, Md. Line (Jan. 1820, p. 541).

Branson, John B. Passed Nov. session, 1812 (Jan. 2, 1813)—No. 34. Treas. Western Shore pay to John B. Branson, late a soldier in the rev. war, belonging to the Md. line, quarterly—half pay of a private, as a provision to him in his indigent situation and advanced in life, for those services by which his country has been so essentially benefitted.

Branson, John B. Passed Mch. 3, 1840—No. 12. Treas. Western Shore pay to Mary Branson, of St. Mary's county, or her order, $12.11, the amt. of arrears due her late husband at time of his death.

Treas. also directed to pay to Mary Branson, widow of John B. Branson, late a soldier of the rev. quarterly, during life, the half pay of a private commencing Jan. 1, 1840, in consideration of the services rendered by her husband during the rev. war.

Brashears, Ignatius. Passed Dec. session, 1817—No. 19. Treas. Western Shore pay to Ignatius Brashears, of Prince George's county, an old soldier, quarterly, during life, half pay of a private, as a further compensation for his services during the rev. war.

* *Brashears, Ignatius*, private, Md. line (Jan. 1820, p. 540).

Brewer, Thos. S. Passed Nov. session, 1812 (Dec. 30)—No. 20. Treas. Western Shore pay to Thos. S. Brewer, of Annapolis, late sergeant in the rev. war, so long as he may live, half pay of a sergeant.

* *Brewer, Thomas S.*, private, Md. Line (Jan. 1820, p. 541).

Brewer, Thomas. Feb. 24, 1824—No. 23. Treas. directed to pay to Susanna Brewer, of Annapolis, during life, quarterly, the half pay of a sergeant, as further remuneration for her husband Thomas Brewer's services during the rev. war.

Brice, Julianna. Passed Mch. 21, 1833—No. 64. Treas. Western Shore pay to Julianna Brice, during life, semi-annually, half pay of a Lieut, in consideration of the services rendered by her husband during the rev. war.

Britton, Joseph, Burgess, Joshua and *Willmot, Robert* Lieutenants, Passed Jan. 29, 1830. Treas. Western Shore pay to George Britton, of Hawkins county, Tenn. ("Joseph" appears in printed title and in indexing of the resolution), Joshua Burgess, of Mason county, Ky. and Robert Willmot, of Bourbon county, Ky. during life, half yearly, a sum of money equal to half pay of lieutenants, as a further remuneration for their services during the rev. war.

Brother, Valentine. Resolutions 7 and 8, Nov. session, 1795, direct that Valentine Brother sell gunpowder, brimstone arms &c. in magazine at Frederick, Md.—compensation &c.

* *Brown, Henry*, private, Pa. Line (Jan., 1820, p. 541).

Brown, John. 2d Lieut. of a Co. of Talbot County Militia, 4th Battn. After Apr. 9, 1778—see Maynadier, Wm.

* *Brown, John*, private, Va. Line (Jan. 1820, p. 541).

* *Brown, Patrick*, corporal, Pa. Line (Jan. 1820, p. 540).

Bruce, Robert. Passed Dec. session, 1816—No. 36. Treas. Western Shore pay to Robert Bruce (an old rev. soldier) during his life, quarterly, the half pay of a private, as a further recompense for his meritorious services during the rev. war.

Passed Dec. session, 1817—No. 17. Treas. Western Shore pay to Robert Bruce, of Charles county, quarterly, a sum of money equal to half pay of a trooper, instead of half pay of a common soldier in the line, as was allowed him by the last legislature, and treasurer pay him, or order, a sum of money equal to half pay of a trooper for fifteen months.

* *Bruce, Robert*, private, Pa. Line, died 21 Aug. 1819 (Jan. 1820, p. 540).

Bruce, Capt. Wm. Passed Nov. session, 1812 (Nov. 30)—No. 19. Treas. Western Shore pay to Wm. Bruce, late a capt. in the Md. line during, the rev. war,—half pay of a capt., as further remuneration, &c.

* *Bruce, Wm.*, captain, Md. Line, (Jan. 1820, p. 540).

Bruff, Capt. James. Passed Nov. 1785, Vol. 11, Chap. XVI. Gen. Assemby granted half pay of a capt. to James Bruff, for disability acquired in the service, late a capt. in the Md. Line in the Continental army.

Bruff, James, Capt. Passed Jan. 20, 1820—No. 8. Treas. pay to Margaret Bruff, of Queen Anne's county, widow of James Bruff, late a captain in the rev. war, during life, quarterly, half pay of a captain.

Bryan, Charles. Passed Mch. 2, 1827—No. 34. Treas. Western Shore pay to Charles Bryan, of Lycoming county, Pa., during life, half yearly, half pay of a private, for his services during the rev. war.

Bryant, James. Passed Mch. 4, 1841—No. 15. Treas. Western Shore pay to James Bryant, of Queen Anne's county, during life, half pay of a private, in consideration of services rendered during the rev. war.

† *Bucklup, Charles*, private, Rev. army[a]. Pensioned, Act June 7, 1785, from Mch. 4, 1789, at $40.00 per an. (recd. $320.00. U. S. Pens. Roll, 1835, p. 20).

Bullock, Jesse—see Williams, Charles.

Burch, Benj. Passed Mch. 11, 1828—No. 42. Treas. Western Shore pay to Benjamin Burch, of the state of Ky. during life, half yearly, half pay of a private, as further remuneration for his services during rev. war.

Burgess, Lieut. Basil. Passed Dec. session, 1816—No. 20. Treas. Western Shore pay to Basil Burgess (an officer in the rev. war), quarterly, during his life, the half pay of a lieut. as a further remuneration for those services rendered his country during her struggle for independence.

Burgess, Joshua, Lieut.—see Britton, Joseph. Passed Feb. 3, 1836—No. 6. Treas. Western Shore pay to Nicholas D. Coleman, atty. for heirs of Joshua Burgess, late a lieut. in Md. line, $46.67 bal. due said Burges, a pensioner of State of Md., at his death.

Burgess, Capt. Vachel. Passed Nov. session, 1810—No. 6. Vachel Burgess, a capt. in the rev. war, did not receive the commutation in lieu of the half pay for life promised to the officers and soldiers; therefore, Resolved that the treas. western shore pay to the said Vachel Burgess four years full pay as a capt., free from interest, as a full compensation for his services during the late rev. war.

* *Burgess, Vachel.* Captain, Md. Line (Jan. 1820, p. 541).

† *Burk, James*, private, Rev. army[a]. Pensioned Act June 7, 1785, from Mch. 4, 1789 at $40.00 per an. Died Dec. 3, 1817. (U. S. Pens. Roll, 1835, p. 20).

Burk, Nathaniel. Passed Mch. 13, 1829—No. 64. Treas. Western Shore pay to Nathaniel Burk, of Baltimore city, during life, quarterly, half pay of a private, for his services during the rev. war.

Passed Mch. 7, 1838—No. 23. Treas. Western Shore pay to Elizabeth

Burk widow of Nathan Burk, of city of Baltimore, half pay of a private, as a further remuneration for the services of her said husband, Nathan Burk, during her life.

* *Burk, Nathan*, private, Md. Line (Jan. 1820, p. 541).

† *Burk, Thomas*, private, Rev. army[a]. Pensioned, act of June 7, 1785, from Mch. 4, 1789 at $40.00 per an. (U. S. Pens. Roll, 1835, p. 20).

Burkett, Christopher. Recommended as 1st. Lieut. of a Company of Militia in Frederick Co. Endorsed on a com'n. dated Oct. 13, 1777—see Manyard, Nathan.

Burkett, George. Recommended as Capt. of a Company of Militia in Frederick County, endorsed on a com'n. dated Oct. 13, 1777—see Manyard Nathan.

Burns, John. Passed Feb. 19, 1819—No. 70. Treas. Western Shore pay to John Burns, late a rev. soldier, quarterly, during life, half pay of a private.

* *Burns, John*, private, Md. Line (Jan. 1820, p. 541).

† *Burns, Luke*, private, Rev. army[a]. Pensioned at $40.00 per an. from Mch. 4, 1789 (Act of June 7, 1785. Recd. $120.00). (U. S. Pens. Roll, 1835, p. 20). Died in 1794.

Burroughs, Norman. Passed Mch. 19, 1839—No. 35. Treas. Western Shore pay to Esther Turner Burroughs, of St. Mary's county, widow of Norman Burroughs, who was a soldier in the Rev. war, or to her order, quarterly, the half pay of a private of the Rev., commencing Jan. 1, 1839, during her life.

Bush, Joseph. Passed Feb. 12, 1820—No. 23. Treas. pay Joseph Bush, of Talbot county, for life, quarterly, half pay of a private, for his services during the rev. war.

† *Butcher, John*, private, Rev. army[a]. Pensioned, Act of June 7, 1785, from Mch. 4, 1789, at $40.00 per an. (recd. $340.00—U. S. Pens. Roll, 1835, p. 20).

Byas, Wm. Passed Feb. 14, 1820—No. 65. Treas. Western Shore pay to Wm. Byas, of Dorchester county quarterly, the half pay of a Boatswain, during life, as a compensation for his services during the rev. war.

Byus, Wm. Feb. 16, 1820—No. 43. Treas. Western Shore is directed to pay to Wm. Byus, of Dorchester county, half pay of a lieut. as a compensation for his services during the rev. war—rescinding resolution of Dec. session 1819, No. 65.

Cahoe, Thos. Passed Nov. session, 1812 (Jan. 2, 1813)—No. 44. Treas. Western Shore pay to Thos. Cahoe, of Charles county, late a private in the rev. war, half pay of a private, as a remuneration for meritorious service, &c.

* *Cahoe, Thos. or Kahoe*, private, Md. Line (Jan. 1820, p. 542).

† *Cain, Edward*, private, Rev. army[a]. Pensioned, Act. June 7, 1785, from Mch. 4, 1789 at $30.00 per an. (Recd. $495.00. U. S. Pens. Roll, 1835, p. 20).

Cain, Patrick. Recommended for 1st Lieut. of a Co. of Militia in Harford Co., Apr. 1778—see Long, John, Jr.

Callahan, Lieut. John. Passed Mch. 18, 1839—No. 36. Treas. Western Shore pay to Sarah Callahan, of Annapolis, widow of John Callahan, a first lieut. in the war of the Rev., or to her order, during her life, quarterly, the half pay of a first lieut. of the Rev. commencing Jan. 1, 1839.

Campbell, George. Passed Nov. session, 1800—No. 1. George Campbell is hereby placed on the pension list of the state, and the treas. of the state is to pay him $50.00 per annum, in quarterly payts.

* *Campbell, James*, private, Va. Line (Jan. 1820, p. 542).

* *Cane, Hugh*, private, Md. Line (Jan. 1820, p. 542).

† *Carbury, Peter*, private, Rev. army[a]. Pensioned, Act June 7, 1785, from Mch. 4, 1789, at $40.00 per an. (U. S. Pens. Roll, 1835, p. 20).

Carier, Abraham. Capt. of a Co. in Elk Battn. of Militia, in Cecil County—see Arrats, Harman, and Arrmie, Harman, June 7, 1781).

Carlin, Wm. Passed Mch. 21, 1837—No. 55. Treas. Western Shore pay to Mary Carlin, widow of Wm. Carlin, a soldier of the rev., the half pay of a private, as a further remuneration for his services, during her life.

Carlisle, Adam, of Eastern shore,—"a British subject" owner of confiscated property called "Tower Hill"—See Resolution No. 1, Nov. session, 1792.

Carney, Thomas. Passed Nov. session, 1812 (Jan. 2, 1813)—No. 33. Treas. Western Shore pay to Thomas Carney quarterly,—half pay of a private, as a further remuneration for his services during the rev. war.

* *Carney, Thomas*, private, Md. Line (Jan. 1820, p. 542).

Carr, Hezekiah. Passed May session, 1813—No. 3. Treas. Western Shore pay to Hezekiah Carr, late a drummer in the Md. line,—half pay of a drummer during his life.

Carr, Ingram. Passed Nov. session, 1812 (Jan. 2, 1813)—No. 51. Treas. Western Shore pay to Ingram Carr, late a soldier in the rev. war,—half pay of a private, as a further remuneration to him for those services by which his country has been so essentially benefitted.

Carr, Lieut. John. Passed Nov. session, 1810—No. 16. Treas. Western Shore pay to John Carr, five yrs. full pay of a lieut. in the rev. war, without interest, as a commutation of half pay.

* *Carr, John.* Lieutenant, Md. Line, (Jan. 1820, p. 542).

Carr, John. Passed Mch. 9, 1846—No. 53. Treas. of Md. pay to "Margaret Loney," formerly Margaret Carr, of Baltimore county, widow of John Carr, a soldier of the rev., half pay of a private, quarterly, in consideration of services rendered by her former husband during the war of the rev.

Carr, John. Passed Jan. 20, 1847—No. 7. Treas. of Md. pay to "Margaret Long," formerly Margaret Carr of Baltimore county, widow of John Carr, a soldier of the Rev., half pay of a private, quarterly, in consideration of services rendered by her husband during the War of the Rev. & that she be placed where res. No. 53. Dec. session 1845, placed her, & that said res., No. 53, is hereby repealed.

† *Carrent, James,* private, Rev. army, of Montgomery county, Pensioned at $40.00 per an. Act of June 7, 1785, from Mch. 4, 1789 (recd. $1,085.16)—at $64.00 per an. from Apr. 24, 1816 (recd. $407.11). Died Sept. 4, 1822. (U. S. Pens. Rolls, 1835, p. 16).

Carroll, Charles of Carrollton. Passed Mch. 11, 1833—No. 90. The Gen. Assembly of Md., apprised of the death of the venerated Charles Carroll, of Carrollton, would at the close of a career of such distinguished patriotism and private worth,—offer every tribute of reverence for those excellencies which have proved themselves to Maryland, in permanent benefits; strengthened the Councils of the Fathers of our Freedom, and mingled in the lustre of our revolutionary renown: * * *

Resolved, That the resolute patriotism of Charles Carroll, when at the hazard of his brilliant private interests he dedicated himself to the cause of American Independence, consecrates his life among the memorials of civil heroism, to adorn and enforce the history of human liberty;—that this patriotic sacrifice, and the continued and cogent efforts of his mind, and all his earnest labours in advancing the consummation of our Independence, in awakening the people of Md. to the sense of their rights, and their power, and in sustaining their ardour in their vindication through the crisis of our revolution, command our admiration and our gratitude.

A full length portrait was directed to be procured and placed in the Senate Chamber, "the scene of his legislative labours; the theatre of that body whose peculiar Constitution he framed, and the site of the sublime surrender of military authority, by the Father of our Country, with whose honour the deserts of Carroll are entwined."

Cato, George. Passed Feb. 19, 1819—No. 73. Treas. to pay to George Cato, late a rev. soldier, half pay of a private.

Chambers, Edward. Feb. 16, 1820—No. 34. Treas. is directed to pay to Edward Chambers, of Anne-Arundel county (a man of colour), during life, half pay of a private, as a further compensation for those services rendered by him during the rev. war.

* *Chambers, Edward,* private, Md. Line (Jan. 1820, p. 542).

* *Chambers, James,* private, Pa. Line (Jan. 1820, p. 542).

Chapman, Henry H. Feb. 16, 1820—No. 38. Treas. of Western Shore is directed to pay to Henry H. Chapman, of Georgetown, D. C. half pay of a lieut., further compensation for his services during rev. war. (*Md. Gazette*, p. 17. Rev. Obituaries, D. A. R., died Dec. 13, 1821, Georgetown, D. C.)

Chapman, Henry H. Passed Mch. 18, 1833—No. 60. Treas. Western Shore pay to Mary Chapman, of Georgetown, D. C. in consideration of services rendered by her deceased husband, Henry H. Chapman, a Lieut. in the rev. war, or to her order, during her widow-hood, quarterly, half pay of a Lieut.

Chapman, Thomas. Feb. 25, 1824—No. 30. Treas. to pay Thomas Chapman, of Dorchester county, half pay of a private, further compensation for his rev. war services.

† *Chatlin, Wm.*, corporal, Rev. army[a]. Pensioned, Act of June 7, 1785, from Mch. 4, 1789, at $44.00 per an. (Rec'd. $88.00. U. S. Pens. Roll, 1835, p. 20).

Chesley, Robert, Capt. Passed Mch. 11, 1828—No. 39. Robert Chesley, a captain in the Md. Line of the rev. war, late of St. Mary's county, was entitled, under the acts relative to grant of military bounty lands westward of Fort Cumberland, to four lots, or 200 a, of sd. land; and whereas it appears that said Chesley has never recd. his portion of sd. bounty lands, and that the lots surveyed for that purpose, under resolution of 1787, have either been distributed amongst the officers and soldiers, or have been thrown into the common mass of vacant land in Allegany county; and also, that the said Chesley is since dead, leaving heirs at law:

Resolved, That reg. of land office for Western Shore issue to said heirs a common warrant for 200 a. of vacant land—in Allegany county, and a patent upon survey—without payment of composition money thereon.

* *Clackner, Adam,* captain, Pa. Line (Jan. 1820, p. 541).

Clagett, Dr. Samuel. Passed Mch. 7, 1834—No. 52. Treas. Western Shore pay to Amie Clagett (widow of Dr. Samuel Clagett) during life, quarterly, half pay of a Surgeon's mate, in consideration of the services rendered by her husband during the rev. war.

Clarke, James. Passed Nov. session, 1812 (Jan. 2, 1813)—No. 53. Treas. Western Shore pay to James Clarke,—half pay of a matross during the rev. war, as a further remuneration to the said James Clarke for the services rendered his country, & as a relief from the indigence & misery which attend his decrepitude & old age.

Clarke, James. Passed Mch. 6, 1850—No. 65. Treas. of State pay to Barbara McMahon formerly wife of James Clarke, a private soldier in the war of the Amer. Rev., half pay of a private, for the rem. of her life, commencing Jan. 1, 1850—also Treas. pay to said Barbara McMahon $21.66, being the amt. due her late husband, James Clarke, at his death.

Clewley, Joseph. Passed Dec. session, 1815—No. 37. Treas. Western Shore pay to Joseph Clewley, of Montgomery county, a soldier in the rev. war, quarterly, the half pay of a private, for those services by which his country has been so essentially benefitted.

Clewly, Joseph. Passed Feb. 2, 1830—No. 14. Treas. Western Shore pay to Henry Harding, for use of Mary Whelan, (legal heir of Joseph Clewly) $11.11, bal. due said Joseph Clewly, late a pensioner of state of Md. who was placed on the pension list by resolution of said state.

Clinton, Thos. Passed Nov. session, 1812 (Jan. 2, 1813)—No. 43. Treas. Western Shore pay to Thos. Clinton, annually during his life,—half pay of a fife—major, as a further remuneration for those services rendered his country during the American war.

* *Clinton, Thomas*, private, Md. Line (Jan. 1820, p. 542).

* *Coburn, Primus*, private, Mass. Line (Jan. 1820, p. 542).

Cochran, Capt. James. Feb. 24, 1823—No. 59. Treas. Western Shore is directed to pay to Capt. James Cochran, of Cecil county, $200.00 as a compensation for his services during the rev. war.

Cochran, James. Passed Feb. 13, 1837—No. 21. Treas Western Shore pay to James Cochran, the half pay of a private during his life, as a further remuneration for his services during the rev. war.

Cockrane, James. Passed Jan. 18, 1847—No. 20. Treas. Western Shore pay to Ann Mary Cockrane, of Frederick county, widow of James Cockrane, who was a private in the Rev. war, or to her order, quarterly, during her life, commencing Jan. 1, 1847, a sum equal to the half pay of a private, as further remuneration for the services of her deceased husband.

† *Coddrington, Benj.*, private Rev. army, pensioned Feb. 24, 1821, at $30. per annum ($120.00 recd.) from Apr. 25, 1812, under Act. of July 5, 1812. Same at $48.00 per annum ($785.33 recd.) from Apr. 24, 1816 (under latter Act). Resides in Alleghanny county, Md.

Coe, Richard. Passed Feb. 20, 1830—No. 33. Treas. Western Shore pay to Richard Coe, of Prince George's county, an old rev. soldier, half pay of a sergeant, quarterly, for his services during the rev. war.

Coe, Richard. Passed Feb. 10, 1832—No. 32. Reg. of land office to issue to Richard Coe, of Prince George's county, a soldier of the revolution, warrant and later patent for 50 acres land in Allegany county, without compensation money.

Coe, Mary. Passed Jan. 12, 1835—No. 2. Treas. Western Shore pay to Alexander Benson Coe $50.00, being the amt. of one year's pension due to Mary Coe at time of her death.

Coe, George. Passed Mar. 2, 1844—No. 30. Treas. Western Shore pay to Geo. C. Coe, son of the late Richard Coe, of Prince George's county, Md. $30.00, if so much was due to said Richd. Coe at time of his death.

Coe, Wm. Passed Feb. 12, 1820—No. 39. Treas. Western Shore pay to Wm. Coe, of Baltimore county, for life, quarterly, half pay of a private, for his services during the rev. war.

* *Coe, William*, corporal, Md. Line (Jan. 1820, p. 542).

Coe, William. Feb. 16, 1821—No. 30. Resolution of Dec. session 1819, No. 39 rescinded. Treas. is directed to pay to Wm. Coe, now of Annapolis, half pay of a private of matross, for services rendered during the rev. war.

Passed Feb. 17, 1834—No. 19. Treas. Western Shore pay to Mary Coe, widow of Wm. Coe, a soldier of the rev. $12.50, being three months pay, due to her husband at time of his death.

Coe, Wm. Passed Mch. 4, 1834—No. 39. Treas. Western Shore pay to Mary Coe, widow of Wm. Coe, during life, quarterly, half pay of a Matross, in consideration of the services rendered by her husband during the rev. war.

† *Coffield, Owen*, private, Rev. army[a]. Pensioned, Act of June 7, 1785, from Mch. 4, 1789 at $40.00 per an. Died in 1792. (Rec'd. $120.00. U. S. Pens. Roll, 1835, p. 20).

Coffroth, Conrad. Mch. 8, 1826—No. 69, p. 250. Treas. of Western Shore pay to Conrad Coffroth, of Franklin county, Pa., half pay of a fifer, as a further remuneration for his services during the rev. war.

Passed Feb. 28, 1832—No. 81. Treas. Western Shore pay to Magdalena Coffroth, of Washington county, widow of Conrod Coffroth, a soldier of the rev. war, during widowhood, half yearly, half pay of a private, for the services rendered by her husband during said war.

* *Coins, Dominick*, private, Md. Line (Jan. 1820, p. 542).

* Cole, George, ensign, German Regt. (Jan. 1820, p. 542).

Colegate, Asaph. Passed Mch. 10, 1842—No. 44. Treas. Western Shore pay to Asaph Colegate, a soldier of the Rev., half pay of a private from and after this date.

† *Collember, Thomas*, private, Rev. army[a]. Pensioned, Act of June 7, 1785, from Mch. 4, 1789, at $40.00 per an. (U. S. Pens. Roll, 1835, p. 20).

† *Collins, James*, sergeant, Rev. army[a]. Pensioned, Act of June 7, 1789, from Mch. 4, 1789, at $60.00 per an. (Rec'd. $390.00. U. S. Pens. Roll, 1835, p. 20). Died in 1795.

Connelly, Hugh, Sr. Passed Dec. session, 1816—No. 15. Treas. Western Shore pay to Hugh Connelly, Sr., of Washington county, late a private in the rev. war, quarterly, during his life, the half pay of a private, as a further remuneration to him for his services during the struggle of his country for her independence.

* *Connelly, Hugh*, private, Hazen's, Reg't. (Jan. 1820, p. 541).

Connelly, William. Passed Feb. 28, 1832—No. 46. Treas. Western Shore pay to Priscilla Connelly, widow of W[m]. Connelly, soldier of the rev.

war, during widowhood, half yearly, half pay of a private, for services rendered by her husband during said war.

Contee, John, Lieut. Passed Jan 28, 1830—No. 10. Resolutions expressive of the sense of the Legislature, of the gallant conduct during the late war, of John Contee, a native of Md., formerly a Lieut. in the Marine corps of the U. S., and directing a sword to be presented to him. (Constitution and Guerrier, and Constitution and Java).

Cooke, Henry. Passed Feb. 19, 1835—No. 4. Treas. Western Shore pay to Henry Cooke, a Rev. soldier, the half pay of a private, quarterly, during his life.

Cooper, Wm. Passed Mch. 12, 1832—No. 95. Treas. Western Shore pay to Wm. Cooper, of Ohio county, Ky. a soldier of the rev. war, during life, half yearly, half pay of a private, for his services during the rev. war.

Same date (No. 98) a warrant, later patent, for 50 acres in Allegany county, was authorized to him without payts. of composition money.

Corbet, James, Gentleman. Com'd. Ensign of Capt. George Voghan's Co. in Deer Creek Battn. Harford Co. Militia, Annapolis, Apr. 9, 1778. "Wm. Amos' son Joshua to be in this place," (X, No. 234).

† *Corbett, John,* private, Rev. army[a]. Pensioned at $60.00 per an. from Jan. 1, 1803. (Recd. $220.67. U. S. Pens. Roll, 1835, p. 20).

Courts, Dr. Richard Hanley. Feb. 16, 1820—No. 42. Treas Western Shore is directed to pay to Eleanor C. Courts, of Prince George's county, half pay of a surgeon's mate, as a compensation for those meritorious services rendered by her deceased husband, Doctor Richard Hanley Courts, during the rev. war.

* *Coyle, Mark,* private, Pa. Line (Jan. 1820, p. 542).

Coyn, Dominick. Feb. 25, 1824—No. 33 (p. 172). Treas. to pay to Mary Coyn, of Harford county, half pay of a private, further remun. for her husband Dominick Coyn's services during the rev. war.

Crampton, Thomas. Passed Mch. 16, 1835—No. 61. Treas. Western Shore pay to Thomas Crampton, a soldier of the rev. half pay of a private, in quarterly payts. during his life.

* *Craven, Andrew,* private, Md. Line (Jan. 1820, p. 542).

† *Crawford, James,* private, Md. Line, age 82, resided in Frederick county[b]. Pensioned Jan. 6, 1819, at $96.00 per an. from May 5, 1818. (Rec'd. $1,520.00. U. S. Pens. Roll, 1835, p. 36).

* *Crawford, James,* private, Md. Line (Jan. 1820, p. 542).

Crawford, Nehemiah. Passed Dec. session, 1816—No. 41. Treas. Western Shore pay to Nehemiah Crawford, a sergeant in the rev. war, quarterly during life, the half pay of a sergeant.

Cresap, Lieut. Joseph. Feb. 19, 1819—No. 41. Treas. of Western Shore is directed to pay to Joseph Cresap, a sum of money equal to the half pay of a lieutenant, during his life, as a further compensation for his services during the rev. war.

Cresap, Joseph. Feb. 23, 1822—No. 62, p. 180. Joseph Cresap of Allegany county, a pensioner is said to be wealthy—living in affluence—resolution of Dec. session 1818. No. 41, be rescinded.

Cresap, Joseph. Mch. 3, 1826—No. 67, p. 250. Resolutions No. 41 (1819) and 62 (1822) are secited, and "whereas, from losses sustained by the said Joseph Cresap in consequence of endorsing for others in the Cumberland bank of Allegany he is now greatly embarassed, and has a large family to support." Treas. of Western Shore is directed to pay to Joseph Cresap, of Allegany county, half pay of a lieut., for life, as a further compensation for his services during the rev. war. (See p. 13, Death Notice, *Maryland Gazette* Jan. 5, 1827).

Croft, W^m^. Passed Mch. 4, 1835—No. 71. Treas. Western Shore pay to Catharine Croft, widow of W^m^. Croft, a soldier of the rev., half pay of a corporal, quarterly, during her life.

Cross, Joseph, Lieut. Passed Mch. 14, 1823—No. 64. Unanimous resolution commending Lieut. Joseph Cross, a native of Md., enumerating his services—authorize Governor to secure and present a suitable sword.

Crouch, Robert. Passed Nov. session, 1812 (Jan. 1, 1813)—No. 32. Treas. Western Shore pay to Robert Crouch, quarterly, a sum of money equal to the half pay of a private, as a further remuneration for his services during the rev. war.

* *Crouch, Robert,* private, Va. Line (Jan. 1820, p. 542).

Crouch, Robert. Passed Feb. 19, 1845—No. 13. Treas. Western Shore pay to Hannah Crouch, of Cecil county, $11.33, due her late husband, Robert Crouch at time of his death; he having been a private in the rev. war, and at time of his death a pensioner of the State; it appearing that said Robert Crouch received his pension regularly up to July 2, 1823, & died Oct. 12, next ensuing, and the arrearages of pension being from time of last payt. until his death.

Croxall, Charles, Capt. Passed Mch. 12, 1827—No. 59. Treas. pay to Charles Croxall, of Baltimore city, during life, half yearly, half pay of a captain of dragoons, for his services during the rev. war.

Croxall, Charles. Passed Mch. 9, 1832—No. 82. Treas. Western Shore pay to Claudius Legrande, $31.67, being the sum due to Charles Croxall, a rev. pensioner at his death.

* *Currin, James,* private, Md. Line (Jan. 1820, p. 542).

Curtis, James. Ensign in 17th Battn. of Militia—see Schoolfield, Wm.

* *Curtiss, John,* private, Md. Line (Jan. 1820, p. 542).

Curtis, John. Passed Feb. 23, 1829—No. 30. Treas. pay to John Curtis, of Baltimore city, during life, half yearly, half pay of a matross in the artillery, in consideration of his services during the rev. war.

Dallam, R. Lieut. of Capt. Vanhorne's Co. in Deer Creek Battn. of Militia, Harford Co., Apr. 1778.

Davidson, James. Passed Dec. session, 1816—No. 28. Treas. Western Shore pay to James Davidson, late a private in the rev. war, quarterly, half pay of a private, as a further remuneration to him for military services.

* *Davidson, James,* 2d., private, Md. Line (Jan. 1820, p. 542).

* *Davis, Anthony,* private, Md. Line (Jan. 1820, p. 543).

† *Davis, John,* private, Rev. army[a]. Pensioned, Act of June 7, 1785, from Mch. 4, 1789 at $40.00 per an. (Recd. $1,085.64. U. S. Pens. Roll, 1835, p. 20).

Davis, John. Passed Nov. session, 1812 (Jan. 2, 1813)—No. 49. Treas. Western Shore pay to John Davis, of Charles county, late a sergeant in the rev. war, or order during his life, quarterly payts., half pay of a sergeant.

Davis, Samuel. Passed Feb. 12, 1820—No. 37. "Resolved, That the treasurer of the Western Shore pay to Samuel Davis, of Kent county, late a fifer in the revolutionary war, or to his order, for life, in quarter annual payments, a sum of money equal to the half pay of a fifer, as a further remuneration for his services during the revolutionary war."

Davis, Samuel, and *Gudgington, William.* Feb. 24, 1823—No. 65, p. 141. "The committee of pensions & rev. claims having received information that Samuel Davis, a drummer, and William Gudgington, a private, both of Kent county, who are on the pension list, and are actually receiving annual pensions, were never in the service of the state, or of the United States. Therefore resolved, That they be stricken off the pension list."

Davis, Samuel. Mch. 9, 1826—No. 104, p. 260. Treas. Western Shore pay to Samuel Davis, of Baltimore, half pay of a sergeant, for his rev. war services.

Davis, Samuel. Passed Mch. 13, 1829—No. 66. Treas. of Western Shore required to pay Samuel Davis of Baltimore city, or order, the pension accruing from Feb. 12, 1823 (when he was stricken from the pension roll) and Mch. 9, 1826, when he was replaced thereon, to which he would have been entitled had he not been stricken therefrom.

Davis, Samuel. Passed Mch. 5, 1835—No. 66. Treas. Western Shore pay to Margaret Davis, widow of Samuel Davis, a soldier of the rev., half pay of a private during life, quarterly.

Davis, Thomas. Passed Feb. 12, 1820—No. 31. Treas. pay to Thomas Davis, of Ohio, late an old soldier in the rev. war, during life, quarterly, half pay of a private, for those services by which his country has been so essentially benefitted.

Davis, Wm. Passed Dec. session, 1816—No. 21. Treas. Western Shore pay to Wm. Davis, late a soldier of the rev. war, quarterly, the half pay of a private, as a further remuneration to him for those services by which his country has been so essentially benefitted.

Dawkins, Charles. Passed Feb. 24, 1830—No. 59. Treas. Western Shore pay to Elizabeth Dawkins, of Calvert county, widow of the late Charles Dawkins, a soldier of the revolution, during widowhood, half pay of a sergeant, for services of her late husband.

Dawson, Capt. Joseph. Passed Nov. session 1791—No. 6, Joseph Dawson, late a soldier in the 5th Md. reg. in the service of the U. S., is disabled from wounds recd. at the battle of Eutaw Spgs., & is at certain times rendered incapable of getting a livelihood;—Gov. of Md. grant Joseph Dawson half pay he recd. in continental service, by orders on Treas. of Western Shore, & same be charged to the U. S.

* *Dawson, Joseph*, private, Md. Line (Jan. 1820, p. 542).

Dawson, Wm. Passed Nov. session 1810—No. 5. Treas. Western Shore pay to Wm. Dawson, of Cecil county, late a meritorious soldier in the rev. war, or order, quarterly payts., a sum of money equal to half pay of a private, as a provision to him in his indigent situation, now advanced in life, and as a further remuneration to him for those services by which his country has been so essentially benefitted.

Deakins, Wm. Jnr. Esq. Com'd. Lieut. Col. of the Lower Batt'n. of Militia in Montgomery Co., Sept. 12, 1777. Thos. Johnson. Resigned May, 1782. (X, No. 53).

Deal, Capt. Geo. Passed Feb. 7, 1843—No. 5. Treas. Western Shore pay to Richard Thomas bal. due Capt. Geo. Deal, a rev. pensioner at time of his death.

* *Dean, Robert*, private, Md. Line (Jan. 1820, p. 543).

* *Deaver, Aquilla*, private, Md. Line (Jan. 1820, p. 543).

Deaver, Aquilla. Passed March 2, 1827—No. 27. Treas. to pay to Aquilla Deaver, of Harford county, during life, half yearly, half pay of a private for his services during the rev. war.

Deaver, Aquilla. Passed Feb. 3, 1836—No. 14. Treas. Western Shore pay to Wm. B. Stephenson, for use of Sarah Deaver, widow of Aquilla Deaver, deceased, $6.66, bal. of pension due her husband at death.

Deaver, Aquilla. Passed Feb. 13, 1836—No. 20. Treas. Western Shore pay to Sarah Deaver, widow of "Aquilla Dean," a soldier of the rev., half pay of a private during life.

* *Deaver, Miscal*, private, Md. Line (Jan. 1820, p. 543).

† *Deaver, Miscal*, private, Md. Line, age 83, from Frederick county[b]. Pensioned Dec. 23, 1819, at $96.00 per an. from Jan. 22, 1819. (Recd. $395.46. U. S. Pens. Roll, 1835, p. 36).

Deaver, Wm. Mch. 7, 1826—No. 84, p. 255. Treas. of Western Shore pay to Wm. Deaver, of Mason county, Ky. half pay of a private, as further remuneration for his services during the rev. war.

De Kalb, Baron. Passed Mch. 3, 1848—No. 57. Preamble & Resolutions in relation to the erection of a monument to the memory of the late Maj. Gen. the Baron De Kalb, in the city of Annapolis.

Congress of U. S. in Oct. 1780, passed a resolution:

"Resolved, That a monument be erected to the memory of the late Maj. Gen., the Baron de Kalb, in Annapolis, Md., with the following inscription: Sacred to the memory of the Baron De Kalb, Knight of the Royal Order of Military Merit, Brigadier of the armies of France, and Maj. Gen. in the service of the U. S. of America, having served with honor and reputation for three years, he gave a last and glorious proof of his attachment to the liberties of mankind, and the cause of America, in the action near Camden, in the State of S. C. on Aug. 16, 1780, when leading on the troops of the Md. & Del. lines, against superior numbers, and animating them by his example to deeds of valor, he was pierced with many wounds and on the 19th following expired, in the 48th year of his age. The Congress of the United States of America, in gratitude to his zeal, services and merit, have erected this monument."

The Governor is requested to transmit a copy of the resolutions to the Md. Senators and Representatives in Congress to, if possible, secure the erection of the said monument.

A similar resolution was passed Feb. 6, 1850—No. 24.

De Kalb, Baron. Passed May 3, 1852—No. 8. "Whereas, it is represented to this Gen. Assembly, that the representatives of the Baron De Kalb, a Major General in the service of the U. S., in the war of the Rev., and who at the action of Camden, on Aug. 16, 1780, when leading on the troops of the Md. & Del. Lines, and animating them by his example, to deeds of valor, lost, his life; Therefore:

Resolved by the Gen. Assembly of Md., That our Senators & Reps. in the Cong. of the U. S. be requested to use their influence in procuring the passage of a law, granting to the heirs of the lamented De Kalb compensation for the services of their illustrious ancestor, as a Maj. Gen. in the service of the U. S. in the war of the Rev." &c.

* *De Ligney, Peter,* private, Pa. Line (Jan. 1820, p. 543).

* *Dempsey, John,* private, Va. Line (Jan. 1820, p. 543).

Dennis, Edward. Passed Mch. 25, 1836—No. 69. Treas. Western Shore pay to Edward Dennis, late a rev. soldier, half pay of a private, in remuneration of his services during the rev. war.

* *Dennis, Enos,* private, N. J. Line (Jan. 1820, p. 543).

* *Dennis, Jacob,* private, Pa. Line (Jan. 1820, p. 543).

Denny, Capt. Robert. Passed Dec. session 1814—No. 20. Treas. Western Shore pay to Augusta Denny, widow of the late Capt. Robert Denny,—half pay of a capt., as a compensation for the valuable services rendered by her late husband during the rev. war.

Denoon, John. Passed Feb. 26, 1829—No. 36. Treas. Western Shore pay to John Denoon, of the state of Ohio, a soldier of the rev. war, during life, half yearly, half pay of a drummer, for his services during the rev. war.

* *Dent, George,* private, Md. Line (Jan. 1820, p. 543).

Dent, George. Passed Jan. 30, 1829—No. 9. Treas. pay to George Dent, of Saint-Mary's county, during life, half yearly, half pay of a private, for his services during the rev. war.

Dent, John, Esq. Com'd. Brig. Gen. of Militia of Md. raised to Compose a part of the Flying Camp, July 4, 1776. Pr. order Mat. Tilghman, Pres. (X, No. 56).

† *Dent, John,* corporal, Rev. army[a]. Pensioned, act of June 7, 1785, at $44.00 per an. from Mch. 4, 1789. Died Mch. 26, 1803 (Recd. $616.00. U. S. Pens. Roll, 1835, p. 20).

Dent, John. Passed Mch. 17, 1835—No. 49. Treas. Western Shore pay to Eleanor Dent, widow of John Dent, a private of the third regiment Maryland Line [Rev.], half pay of a private, during life, quarterly.

* *Dewees, Samuel,* private, Pa. Line (Jan. 1820, p. 543).

* *Dickenson, Edward,* private, Md. Line (Jan. 1820, p. 543).

* *Dicks, Isaac,* private, Va. Line (Jan. 1820, p. 543).

Dixon, Samuel. 2^{d} Lieut. in 17th Battn. Militia—see Schoolfield, W^{m}.

Dixon, W^{m}. Passed Dec. session, 1818 (Feb. 19, 1819)—No. 21. Treas. Western Shore pay to W^{m}. Dixon, late a rev. soldier, quarterly, during life, the half pay of a private.

Donally, Patrick. Passed Dec. session 1815—No. 22. Treas. Western Shore pay to Patrick Donally, of Frederick county,—half pay of a private, as a further remuneration to him for those services by which his country has been so essentially benefitted.

Donnelly, Patrick. Passed Feb. 20, 1829—No. 23. Treas. pay to Elizabeth Donnelly, widow of the late Patrick Donnelly, of Frederick county, whatever sum may have been due to said Patrick Donnelly, from the state of Md. at time of his decease, on account of his rev. services.

Donnel'y, Patrick. Passed Mch. 6, 1832—No. 69. Treas. Western Shore pay to Elizabeth Donnelly, of Frederick county, widow of Patrick Donnelly, a soldier of the rev. war, during widowhood, half yearly, half pay of a private, for services rendered by her husband during said war.

Dooley, Capt. James. (War of 1812), payment for cartouch boxes Feb. 11, 1825.

Dorgan, John. Passed Jan. 25, 1828—No. 2. Treas. of Western Shore pay to John Dorgan, of Talbot county, during life, half yearly, half pay of a private, as further remuneration for his services during rev. war.

Dorsey, Ely. Passed Feb. 19, 1819—No. 61. Treas. Western Shore is directed to pay to Ely Dorsey, of Ely, of Frederick county—$960.00 "in full consideration of his services during the rev. war."

Dorsey, Capt. Richard. Passed Nov. session 1791—No. 6. Richard Dorsey, late a capt. in the Artillery from Md. in the service of the U. S., is disabled from wounds received at the battle of Camden, S. C., which prevent him from following any occupation by which a sustenance may be obtained; Resolved, That—the Gov. Md.—grant unto Richard Dorsey half the monthly pay which he received in the continental service, by orders drawn on the Treas. of Western Shore, and the same be charged to the U. S.

Dotrow, John. Passed Mch. 12, 1828—No. 45. Treas. Western Shore pay to John Dotrow, of Frederick county, during life, half yearly, sum of money equal to half pay of a private, as further remuneration for his services during the rev. war.

† *Dougherty, Barnabas*, private, Rev. army.[a] Pensioned, Act of June 7, 1785, from Mch. 4, 1789 at $40.00 per an. (U. S. Pens. Roll, 1835, p. 20).

* *Douglass, Robert*, private, Pa. Line (Jan. 1820, p. 542).

* *Dowdle, W^m^.*, private, Md. Line (Jan. 1820, p. 543).

Downes, Henry, Jnr. Esq. Com'd. 2[d] Major of 28th Batt'n. of the Militia in this Province. Given in Convention at Annapolis, Jan. 3, Anno Domini, 1776. Pr. order Mat. Tilghman, Pres.

"To the Honorable the Convention or Council of Safety of Md. The 2[d] Major's Birth being a very inactive post & the Battalion in great want of an adjutant; Colo. Fedeman has appointed me in which station I shall from this Day endever to discharge my duty untill otherwise ordered by your Honours, at whose command I am allways at; & beg leave to resign this Commission.

I am Gentlemen your most Obt. Soldier & Servent, Henry Downs, Jr. April 10, 1776." (X, No. 60).

Downing, Butler. Passed Feb. 18, 1833—No. 21. Treas. Western Shore pay to Elizabeth Downing, widow of the late Butler Downing, a rev. soldier who died Nov. 18, 1829, $24.24 the amt. due him at death as a pensioner.

Passed Mch. 5, 1835—No. 29. Treas. Western Shore pay to Elizabeth Downing, widow of Butler Downing, quarterly during her life, half pay of a private, for the services of her husband during the rev. war.

Downing, Nathaniel. Passed Dec. session, 1817—No. 22. Treas. Western Shore pay to Nathaniel Downing, of Prince George's county, an old rev. soldier, half pay of a private, as a further remuneration to him for the services rendered his country in that war.

Due, James. Passed Feb. 19, 1819—No. 71. Treas. Western Shore to pay to James Due, late a rev. soldier, quarterly, during life a sum of money equal to the half pay of a private.

* *Due, James*, private, Md. Line (Jan. 1820, p. 543).

Duer, Joshua, Gentleman, Com'd. Ensign in Capt. Holland's Co. of Militia in the Snow Hill Battalion, in Worcester Co. Given at Baltimore Town, Aug. 30th. Thos. Johnson.

(On the back), Worcester, Aug. 3, 1781. I do hereby resign the within commission. Joshua Duer.

Joshua Duer, Ensign resigned. Steven Allen recom'd. 1782.

Duffee, Thos. Passed Feb. 12, 1820—No. 25. Treas. pay to Thos. Duffee, of Harford county, for life, quarterly, half pay of sergeant, for his services during rev. war.

Passed Mch. 16, 1835—No. 15. Treas. Western Shore pay to Bridget Duffee, widow of Thomas Duffee, a soldier of the rev., the half pay of a sergeant during her life, in quarterly payments.

Duffee, Thomas. Passed Mch. 16, 1835—No. 37. Treas. Western Shore pay to James Moores, for use of Bridget Duffee, widow of Thomas Duffee of Harford county, a rev. soldier, $7.50, the amt. due him at time of his death, as a pensioner.

* *Dunn, Wm.*, private, Pulaski's corps (Jan. 1820, p. 542).

Dunning, Butler. Feb. 16, 1820—No. 40. Treas. Western Shore is directed to pay to Butler Dunning, of Charles county, half pay of a private for his rev. war services.

* *Duppelle, Antoiene*, private, Hazen's Regt. (Jan. 1820, p. 543).

* *Duvall, Benj.* of Elisha, private, Md. Line (Jan. 1820, p. 543).

Duvall, Benjamin. Feb. 18, 1822 (No. 32, p. 177). Treas. of Western shore directed to pay unto Benj. Duvall, of Elisha, an old revolutionary soldier, half pay of a private,—as a further remuneration for the services rendered his country during the rev. war.

Duvall, Benj. Passed Feb. 16, 1830—No. 21. Treas. Western Shore pay to Benj. L. Gantt, for use of Benj. Duvall, Jr. of Prince George's county, executor of Benj. Duvall (of Elisha), of said county, a rev. soldier, who died Jan. 30, 1830, $33.22, the amount due him at death as a pensioner.

Duval, Joseph. Feb. 16, 1820—No. 39. Treas. Western Shore is directed to pay to Joseph Duval, of Montgomery county, an old soldier, for life, half pay of a private, for his services during rev. war.

Dyer, Lieut. Walter. Passed Dec. session, 1816—No. 9. Treas. Western Shore pay to Walter Dyer, a lieut. in the rev. war, quarterly, during life, half pay of a lieut. as a further remuneration for his services during the American war.

† *Eaerl, James*, private, Pa. Line, age 84, from Frederick county, died Apr. 11, 1830[b]. Pensioned Nov. 1, 1821 at $96.00 per an., from Sept. 20, 1821. (Rec'd. $821.86. U. S. Pens. Roll, 1835, p. 36).

Ebbs, Emanuel. Passed Dec. session, 1815—No. 48. Treas. Western Shore pay to Emanuel Ebbs, late a private in the rev. war, quarterly, half pay of a private, as a further remuneration to him for those services by which his country has been so essentially benefitted.

* *Ebbs, Emanuel*, private, Md. Line (Jan. 1820, p. 543).

* *Edgar, James*, private, Pa. Line (Jan. 1820, p. 543).

* *Eikelberger, John*, private, Pa. Line (Jan. 1820, p. 543).

* *Eisell, John*, private, German Reg't. (Jan. 1820, p. 543).

Eisell, John. Passed Mch. 9, 1832—No. 83. Treas. Western Shore pay to John Eisell, of Baltimore, a soldier of the rev. war, during life, half yearly, half pay of a private, for his services during the rev. war.

Ellicott. Passed Feb. 18, 1823, 1822–23, p. 123. Ellicott Jonath, Elias, Geo. Benj. Thos. & Chas. T. Ellicott (inf. son of James decd.), & the ch. of *Andrew Ellicott* decd.—incorp. Avalon Co.—Patapsco Falls.

* *Ellicott, Robert*, private, Md. Line (Jan. 1820, p. 543).

Elliott, John, Gentleman. Com'd. 1 st. Lieut. of Co. of Militia in Dorchester Co. Called The Friendship Co., of which you have been elected 1st. Lieut., persuant to the Resolves of the Last Convention, of the Province. Given in Convention at Annapolis, Jan. 3d., 1776. Pr. order Mat. Tilghman Pres. (X, No. 66).

Spencer Waters, Capt. John Ellet Resigns first Lieut. Isaac Reed, 2d. Lieut. Nehemiah Mezzek, Ensign. John Tedyford, 1st. Sergeant.

† *Elliott, John.* Wagoner, of Baltimore county, in Rev. army, pensioned Dec. 26, 1811, under Act. of July 5, 1812, at $30.00 per annum (received $95.75). (U. S. Pension Roll, 1835, p. 5).

Elliott, Robert. Passed Nov. session 1811—No. 26. Treas. Western Shore pay to Robert Elliott, of Harford county, a wounded rev. soldier, during life, the half pay of a private in the Md. Line.

Elliott, Thomas. Passed Nov. session, 1812 (Jan. 2, 1813)—No. 45. Treas. Western Shore pay unto Thos. Elliott, an old rev. soldier—half pay of a private during the remainder of his life, as a further remuneration for his services.

* *Elliott, Thomas*, private, Md. Line (Jan. 1820, p. 543).

* *Elliott, Thomas*, 2[d]. private, Md. Line (Jan. 1820, p. 543).

Elliott, Thomas. Passed Mch. 2, 1827—No. 30. Treas. to pay to Thomas Elliott, of Baltimore, during life, half yearly, half pay of a private, for his services during the rev. war.

Ellis, Michael. Mch. 9, 1826—No. 112, p. 262. Treas. Western Shore pay to Michael Ellis, of Craven county, N. C. during life, half pay of a fifer, as further remuneration for his services during the rev. war.

Elliss, Thos. Feb. 16, 1820—No. 48. Treas. Western Shore is directed to pay to Thomas Elliss, of Harford county, half pay of a private, as further compensation for his rev. war services.

* *Ellis, Thomas*, private, Md. Line (Jan. 1820, p. 543).

Emory, Charles. Passed Nov. session 1801—No. 9. Treas. Western Shore pay to Charles Emory, or order, 7£; bal. due him, an old bargeman, for his services on board of the barges during the late war, as appears by a voucher under the hand of the auditor.

Ennis, Leonard. Passed Feb. 23, 1838—No. 10. Treas. Western Shore pay to Jane Bishop, who was the widow of Leonard Ennis, a soldier of the rev. the half pay of a private during her life, as a further remuneration for his services.

* *Ervin, James*, private, Md. Line (Jan. 1820, p. 543).

* *Etchberger, W^m^*, private, Md. Line (Jan. 1820, p. 543).

* *Etchberger, Wolfgang*, private, German Reg't. (Jan. 1820, p. 543).

* *Evans, Thomas*, private, Md. Line (Jan. 1820, p. 543).

Evans, Thomas. Passed Mch. 1, 1830—No. 64. Treas. Western Shore pay to Thomas Evans, of Frederick county, during life quarterly, half pay of a private, as further remuneration for his services during the rev. war.

Reg. of land office is also directed to issue to said Thos. Evans, soldier of the rev. warrant and later a patent for 50 acres of vacant land westward of Fort Cumberland, in Allegany county, without composition money.

Evans, Thomas. Passed Mch. 4, 1834—No. 41. Treas. Western Shore pay to Eleann Evans, widow of Thomas Evans of Frederick county, during life, quarterly, half pay of a private, for the services rendered by her husband during the rev. war.

† *Evans, W^m^.*, private, Rev. army[a]. Pensioned, Act of June 7, 1785, at $40.00 per an. from Mch. 4, 1789. (U. S. Pens. Roll, 1835, p. 20).

Ewing, Capt. James. Passed Nov. 1785, Vol. 11, Chap. XVI. Gen. Assembly granted half pay of a capt., for disability acquired in the service, to James Ewing, late a capt. in the Md. Line in the Continental army.

† *Eyen, Frederick*, private, Rev. army[a]. Pensioned, Act of June 7, 1785, at $40.00 per an. from Mch. 4, 1789. (Recd. $480.00. U. S. Pens. Roll, 1835, p. 20).

Fairbrother, Francis. Passed Nov. session, 1806—No. 2. Treas. of Western Shore pay to Francis Fairbrother, of Anne-Arundel county, late a soldier in the rev. war, half yearly payts., the half pay of a private.

Fairbrother, Francis. Passed Mch. 6, 1832—No. 72. Treas. Western Shore pay to Patience Fairbrother, of Anne Arundel county, widow of

Francis Fairbrother, a soldier of the rev. war, half yearly, the half pay of a private, for the services rendered by her husband during said war.

Fearson, Joseph. Passed Dec. session 1815—No. 32. Treas. Western Shore pay to Joseph Fearson, during his life, quarterly, half pay of a private, for his services during the revolution.

Fennell, Stephen. Passed Feb. 13, 1833—No. 36. Treas. Western Shore pay to Stephen Fennell, of Brown county, O., during life, quarterly, half pay of a private, for the services rendered by him during the rev. war.

† *Ferguson, John,* private, Rev. army[a]. Pensioned at $60.00 per an. from Jan. 1, 1803; recd. $670.68. (U. S. Pens. Roll, 1835, p. 21).

† *Ferrara, Emmanuel,* private, Rev. army[a]. Pensioned, Act of June 7, 1785, from Mch. 4, 1789, at $40.00 per an. (U. S. Pens. Roll, 1835, p. 21).

Fickle, Benj. Lieut. Passed Mch. 2, 1827—No. 23. Treas. to pay to Benj. Fickle, of Muskingum county, Ohio, during life, half yearly, half pay of a lieutenant, for his services during the rev. war.

* *Fields, George,* private, Md. Line (Jan. 1820, p. 544).

† *Finleyson, George,* private, Rev. army[a]. Pensioned, Act of June 7, 1785, from Mch. 4, 1789 at $40.00 per an. (U. S. Pens. Roll, 1835, p. 20).

* *Fisher, Joseph,* private, Md. Line (Jan. 1820, p. 544).

* *Fisher, Philip,* private, German Regt. (Jan. 1820, p. 544).

† *Fisher, Philip,* private, Rev. army, of Frederick county. Pensioned Feb. 8, 1828, at $40.00 per an. from Mch. 4, 1789, under Act of June 7, 1785 (recd. $1,085.64)—at $64.00 per an. Apr. 24, 1816 (recd. $133.40). (U. S. Pens. Rolls, 1835, p. 13).

† *Fisher, Philip,* private, Md. Line, age 86, from Frederick county[b]. Pensioned Jan. 26, 1819 at $96.00 per an., from Apr. 8, 1818. (Rec'd. $1,526.93. U. S. Pens. Roll, 1835, p. 36).

Fitzgerald, Benj. Passed Mch. 7, 1834—No. 50. Treas. Western Shore pay to Benj. Fitzgerald, of Ky., during life, quarterly, half pay of a Quarter Master Sergeant, for the services rendered by him during the rev. war.

Fitzgerald, Nicholas. Feb. 16, 1820—No. 36. Treas. is directed to pay to Nicholas Fitzgerald, of Washington county, half pay of a private for his rev. war services.

Fitzhugh, Capt. W^m^. Passed Nov. 1791—No. 10. "Resolved that the half pay of a captain on the British establishment be allowed to W[m]. Fitzhugh, of Calvert county, to be computed by the auditor from Sept. 3, 1783, until Nov. 1, 1791, & that the treas. of the Western Shore be authorized and directed to issue a certificate, bearing legal interest therefor, to the said W[m]. Fitzhugh."

Fitzpatrick, Nathan. Passed Mch. 11, 1840—No. 23. Treas. Western Shore pay to Nathan Fitzpatrick, a soldier of the rev., or order, quarterly, during his life, the half pay of a private, from Jan. 1, 1840.

* *Fletcher, Philip*, private, Md. Line (Jan. 1820, p. 544).

* *Fling, James*, private, Va. Line (Jan. 1820, p. 543).

Fling, James. Feb. 24, 1824—No. 27. Treas. directed to pay to James Fling, of Montgomery county, during life, quarterly the half pay of a sergeant, further comp. for his services during the rev. war.

Passed Jan. 23, 1837—No. 11. Treas. Western Shore pay to Henry Harding for use of James W. Fling, executor of James Fling, $7.00, balance of his pension at time of his death.

† *Flonagan, Dennis*, private, Rev. army[a]. Pensioned, Act of June 7, 1785, from Mch. 4, 1789, at $40.00 per an.; recd. $160.00. (U. S. Pens. Roll, 1835, p. 21).

Foggett, Richard. Passed Feb. 12, 1820—No. 35. Treas. to pay Richard Foggett, of Anne Arundel county, late a soldier in the rev. war, during life, quarterly, half pay of a private, as a further remuneration for those services by which his country has been so essentially benefitted.

Foggett, Richard. Passed Mch. 19, 1835—No. 72. Treas. Western Shore pay to Artridge Foggett, of Anne Arundel county, the amt. due her late husband, Richard Foggett, upon the pension list of this State, at the time of his death.

Passed Mch. 20, 1835—No. 65. Treas. Western Shore pay to Artridge Foggitt, widow of Richard Foggitt, a soldier of the rev. the half pay of a private, quarterly, during life.

Foggett, Richard. Passed Feb. 6, 1850—No. 27. State Treas. pay to order of legal representatives of Arthridge Foggett, the arrears of pension due her on May 20, 1849, dated from Jan. 1, 1849, as per res. No. 65, passed Dec. session, 1834.

Passed Feb. 14, 1850—No. 31. Treas. of Md. pay to Gassaway Owens, legal representative of Arthridge Foggett, arrears of pension due the latter.

† *Fogler, Simon*, private Rev. army[a]. Pensioned, Act of June 7, 1785 from Sept. 4, 1793, at $20.00 per an.; recd. $160.00. (U. S. Pens. Roll, 1835, p. 21).

Ford, Hezekiah. Treas. Western Shore Feb. 9, 1822 (No. 20, p. 176) directed to pay to Hezekiah Ford, of Cecil county, an old Revolutionary officer—the half pay of a Lieutenant during the remainder of his life, as remuneration for his meritorious services.

* *Ford, Joseph*, private, Md. Line (Jan. 1820, p. 544).

† *Ford, Joseph*, captain, Rev. army[a]. Pensioned at $120.00 per an. from Jan. 1, 1803; recd. $1101.33; died in 1812. (U. S. Pens. Roll, 1835, p. 21).

Ford, Joseph. Passed Mch. 4, 1837—No. 33. Treas. Western Shore pay to Mary Ford, widow of Joseph Ford, half pay of a second lieut. during her life, as a further remuneration for his services during the rev. war.

Forrest, Uriah, Gentleman. Com'd. 1 st. Lieut. of the Second Independent Co. of Regular Troops to be raised in this Province for the Defense of the Liberties thereof. Given in Convention at Annapolis, Jan. 6, A.D., 1776. Pr. order Mat. Tilghman, Pres. (X, No. 74).

(Reverse) "I, Uriah Forrest do swear that I will well & truly Execute my Office according to the within Commission and the Trust reposed in me according to the best of my power of ability and that I will disband & lay down my Warlike arms whenever I shall be ordered so to do by the Convention of Maryland for the time being or any Authority dirived under it so help me God." Sworn before me this 22d. Jan. 1776. Richd. Barnes.

Forrest, Mrs. Rebecca. Passed Feb. 12, 1844—No. 17. Treas. Western Shore pay to Ann Green and Maria Bohrer, sole surviving children of Mrs. Rebecca Forrest, bal. due her, up to time of her death, on the pension list of the State.

* *Foster, Thos.*, private, Pa. Line (Jan. 1820, p. 544).

Fowler, Thos. M. [War of 1812], Feb. 17, 1820—No. 52. Gov. and council are directed to pass the acct. of Thos M. Fowler, deceased, commissary to the 6th brigade of Md. militia for rations furnished Col. Athenations Fenwick's reg. from 19 July to 17 Aug. 1814.

Fox, Anthony. Passed Nov. session, 1806—No. 1. Treas. Western Shore pay to Anthony Fox, of Anne-Arundel county, late a soldier in the rev. war, half yearly payts., half pay of a private.

Franklin, Thomas and *Neth, Lewis, Jr.*, [War of 1812]. Furnished cartouch boxes—belts—payment Feb. 26, 1824, p. 172, Res. 35.

* *Franks, John*, private, Conn. Line (Jan. 1820, p. 544).

Frazier, James. Passed Feb. 14, 1820—No. 21. Treas. pay to James Frazier, of Dorchester county, an old soldier in the rev. war, for life, quarterly, half pay of a private, "as a further remuneration for those services by which his country has been so essentially benefitted."

Frazier, James. Passed Mch. 9, 1847—No. 31. Treas. pay to Susan Frazier, or to her order, balance of any pension due to James Frazier, at the time of his death.

Resolved, That the pension heretofore paid by the State to James Frazier be continued and paid to widow Susan Frazier, during her natural life.

Frazier, Lieut. Levin. Passed Feb. 12, 1820—No. 32. Treas. pay to Levin Frazier, of Dorchester county, an old rev. officer, for life, quarterly, half pay of a first Lieut. for his services during the rev. war.

* *Frazier, Levin.* Lieut., Md. Line (Jan. 1820, p. 544).

Frazier, Levin. Passed Jan. 10, 1843—No. 2. Treas. Western Shore pay to Elizabeth Frazier of Dorchester county, widow of Levin Frazier, a lieut. in the war of Rev., half pay of a lieut. during her life, quarterly, commencing July 5, 1842; also pay to said Elizabeth Frazier arrears of pension due to her said husband at time of his death under resolution passed at Dec. session, 1819.

Frazier, Levin. Passed Feb. 18, 1848—No. 28. Treas. pay to Priscilla Jackson, legal representative of Elizabeth Frazier, $8.00, bal. of pension due said Elizabeth Frazier at her death.

Passed Mch. 4, 1850—No. 51. Treas. pay to Saml. Harrington, trustee of the late Elizabeth Frazier, $18.22, the amt. of pension money due her at death.

Frazier, Penelope. Passed Jan. 29, 1850—No. 7. State Treas. pay to Priscilla Frazier, executrix of Penelope Frazier, late of Baltimore county, deceased, or order, whatever sum may be due the estate of the said testator, at her death Dec. 2, 1848, as a pensioner of this State.

Frazier, Samuel. Passed Dec. session, 1816—No. 6. Treas. Western Shore pay to Samuel Frazier, of Harford county, quarterly, half pay of a private soldier, as a further remuneration for those services rendered his country during her struggle for independence.

Frazier, Samuel. Passed Mch. 16, 1836—No. 70. Treas. Western Shore pay to Penelope Frazier, widow of Samuel Frazier, a soldier of the rev., half pay of a private during her life.

Frazer, Capt. Solomon. Passed Feb. 19, 1819—No. 80. Treas. Western Shore required to pay to Solomon Frazier, or to his order, in quarterly payments, during life, the half pay of a captain.

Frazier, Capt. Solomon. Passed Feb. 9, 1822—No. 21, p. 176. Treas. Western Shore directed to pay to Capt. Solomon Frazier $337.50 "balance of rations due him while in the service of the State of Md. during the rev. war."

Frazier, Wm. Passed Feb. 7, 1840—No. 7. Treas. Western Shore pay to Henrietta M. Frazier, of the city of Baltimore, widow of Wm. Frazier, who was a lieut. in the rev. war, or to her order, quarterly, commencing with Jan. 1, 1840, the half pay of a lieut. during her life, as a further remuneration for the services of her deceased husband.

Frisby, James, Gentleman. Com'd. 2d Lieut of Capt. Wm. Frisby's Co. of Militia in Kent County, June 7, 1776. Given at Annapolis by Council of Safety, Danl. of St. Thos. Jenifer, J. Hall, Jas. Tilghman, Wm. Hayward.

Fulford, John. Capt. of a Company of Matrosses, Mch. 1, 1776—see More, Nicholas Ruxton.

Gadd, Thomas. Passed Nov. session, 1811—No. 10. Treas. Western Shore pay to Thomas Gadd, late a private soldier in the rev. war, a sum of money, quarterly payts., equal to half pay of a private.

* *Gadd, Thomas*, private, Md. Line (Jan. 1820, p. 544).

Gaither, Benj., late sheriff of Anne Arundel & *John M. Gaither*—Laws of Md. Dec. Sess. 1825—Res. No. 101, p. 260.

Gaither, Zachariah, Gentleman. Com'd. Ensign of Capt. Basil Burgess' Company (late John Burgess) in the Elk Ridge Battn. of Anne Arundel Co. Militia. Given at Annapolis this 30th Day of Mch. A.D. 1779. Thos. Johnson. (Original comn. in possession of Mr. Otho S. Gaither, Chicago, Ill.)

Gale, Henry. Capt. in Salisbury Batln. of Somerset Co. Militia, Jan. 7, 1777—see Handy, Levin.

Gallaher, John. Passed Nov. 1798—No. 8. Treas. Western Shore pay to John Gallaher, late soldier in the 6th Md. reg. 61£–1s–5d, the amt. of depreciation of pay due him for his services as a soldier aforesaid.

Gallagher, Capt. John, U. S. Navy—see Towson, Nathan [1812].

Galworth, Gabriel. Passed Dec. session, 1816—No. 14. Treas. Western Shore pay to Gabriel Galworth, of Montgomery county, late a private in the rev. war. quarterly, half pay of a private, as a further remuneration to him for those services by which his country has been so essentially benefitted.

* *Galworth, Gabriel*, private, Md. Line (Jan. 1820, p. 544).

† *Gambare, John*, private, Rev. army, of Frederick county. Pensioned Feb. 8, 1828 at $40.00 per an. under Act of June 7, 1785, dating from Mch. 4, 1789 (recd. $1,085.64)—at $64.00 per an. from Apr. 24, 1816 (recd. $983.27). (U. S. Pens. Rolls, 1835, p. 13).

Gambell, Abraham. Passed Nov. 1791—No. 9. Abraham Gambell, late a soldier in the first Md. reg. was wounded through the shoulder at Camden, Apr. 21, 1781—unable to support himself by labour; Gov. grant unto Abraham Gambell, in future, such sum as, with the allowance he receives from the U. S., will equal half monthly pay which he received when in the continental service—drawn on Treas. of Western Shore, and charged to the U. S.

† *Gamble, Abraham*, private, Rev. army[a]. Pensioned, Act of Mch. 3. 1809, from Jan. 18, 1809, at $60.00 per an.; recd. $187.67. (U. S. Pens. Roll, 1835, p. 21).

Gambrel, Gideon. Passed Mch. 2, 1827—No. 25. Treas. to pay to Gideon Gambrel, of Caroline county, during life, half yearly, the half pay of a private for his services during the rev. war.

† *Garth, James*, private, Rev. army[a]. Pensioned, Act of June 7, 1785, at $40.00 per an. from Mch. 4, 1789; recd. $980.00. (U. S. Pens. Roll, 1835, p. 21).

Gassaway, Lieut. Henry. Passed Nov. session 1804—No. 2. Treas, Western Shore pay to Henry Gassaway, of Anne-Arundel county, late a lieut. in the rev. war, half pay of a lieut., quarterly payts., during life, as a further reward to those meritorious services which he rendered his country in establishing her liberty and independence.

Gassaway, Capt. John. Passed Dec. session, 1815—No. 17. Treas. Western Shore pay to John Gassaway, late a capt. of the Md. troops in the rev. war,—during life, half pay of a captain.

* *Gassaway, John,* captain, Md. Line (Jan. 1820, p. 544).

Gassaway, John. Feb. 10, 1820—No. 15. Treas is directed to pay to Elizabeth L. Gassaway, of Annapolis, during her widowhood, half pay of a captain as a further compensation for those services rendered by her late husband, John Gassaway, during rev. war.

Gassaway, General John. Passed Dec. 19, 1821—No. 4, p. 174. Treas. Western Shore pay to Elizabeth L. Gassaway, widow of Gen. John Gassaway, of Annapolis, $38.00 due on rev. pension at his death.

* *Gatchell, Saml. H.,* captain Mass. Line—dead (Jan. 1820, p. 544).

Gates, Wm. Passed Dec. session, 1815—No. 33. Treas. Western Shore pay to Wm. Gates, quarterly, during life, the half pay of a private, as a remuneration for his services during the rev. war.

Gerrish, Edward and Allen, Jacob. Passed Nov. session, 1812—No. 56. Treas. Western Shore pay unto Edwd. Gerrish and Jacob Allen,—half pay of privates, as a further remuneration to them for those services by which their country has been so essentially benefitted.

* *Gerrish, Edward,* private, Md. Line (Jan. 1820, p. 544).

Geissinger, David, Capt. Passed Jan. 28, 1830—No. 9. Gen. Assembly of Md. entertain a high sense of the gallantry of David Geissinger, native of Md. and a Captain in U. S. Navy, (details given).

Governor is authorized to present a sword in approbation of his gallant conduct in the late war.

Gibhart, Peter. Passed Dec. session, 1815—No. 31. Treas. Western Shore pay to Peter Gibhart, $200.00 in full compensation for those services which he rendered during the rev. war.

* *Gilman, Joseph,* private, Conn. Line—died 16th May, 1819 (Jan. 1820, p. 544).

Gilpin, Wm. Passed Mch. 2, 1827—No. 26. Treas. to pay to Wm. Gilpin, of Jefferson county, Va. during life, half yearly, the half pay of a private for his services during the rev. war.

* *Glazier, John,* private, Conn. Line (Jan. 1820, p. 544).

* *Goddard, Edward Barton,* private, Md. Line (Jan. 1820, p. 544).

* *Goddard, John,* private, Md. Line (Jan. 1820, p. 544).

Goddard, John. Passed Feb. 23, 1829—No. 29. Treas. pay to John Goddard, of Prince George's county, during life, half yearly, half pay of a private, as further remuneration for his services during the rev. war.

Goddard, John. Passed Jan. 17, 1833—No. 3. Treas. Western Shore pay to Raphael C. Edelen, for use of Benj. Goddard, of Prince George's county, only child and representative of John Goddard, of said county, a rev. soldier who died Sept. 2, 1832, $16.89, the amt. due him at death, as a pensioner.

Godman, Capt. Saml. Passed Mch. 10, 1856. Comr. land office issue to legal representatives of Capt. Saml. Godman, an officer of the Md. Line during the rev. war, a common warrant for 200 acres of vacant land, lying to the westward of Fort Cumberland, in Allegany county, and to issue a patent, &c.

† *Golden, Walter*, private in Rev. army, of Baltimore county; pensioned Nov. 10, 1814 at $30.00 per annum, commencing May 11, 1814 (received $24.50). (U. S. Pension Roll, 1835, p. 6).

* *Goldsberry, Charles*, private, Md. Line (Jan. 1820, p. 544).

Goldsborough, Chas. Passed Dec. session, 1815—No. 34. Treas. Western Shore pay to Chas. Goldsborough, half pay of a private, as an additional compensation for those services which contributed to the establishment of his country's independence.

Goldsborough, Ann. Passed Mch. 11, 1834—No. 62. Treas. Western Shore pay to Ann Goldsborough, of Saint Mary's county, during life, quarterly, half pay of a private, for the services rendered by her husband during the rev. war.

Goldsmith, Thomas. Passed Feb. 24, 1836—No. 46. Reg. land office issue a warrant for 200 acres soldier's land in Allegany county, westward of Fort Cumberland to James Mills, Thos. Mills, Elizabeth Mills, Sarah Campfield & Harriet Goldsmith, heirs at law of Thos. Goldsmith deceased, and their heirs without any titling, &c.

Gomber, John. Feb. 18, 1825. No. 26, p. 159. Treas. to pay to John Gomber, of Frederick county, during life, half pay of a private, further comp. his rev. war services.

Gordon, Archibald. Passed Nov. session, 1807—No. 2. Treas. Western Shore pay to Archibald Gordon, of Cecil county, late a meritorious soldier in the rev. war, in quarterly payts., half pay of a private, as a provision to him in his indigent situation when advanced in life, and—for those services by which his country has been so essentially benefitted.

* *Gordon, Archibald*, private, Pa. Line (Jan. 1820, p. 544).

Gordon, John. Feb. 16, 1820—No. 41. Treas. Western Shore is directed to pay to Elizabeth Gordon, widow of John Gordon, a rev. soldier, during her life half pay of a private.

Gorrell, Thomas (of Hannah) a minor, of Harford county chgd. to Thomas Jeffery—Jan. 12, 1825, Chap. 19, p. 14.

Gould, W^{m}. Passed Feb. 10, 1830—No. 21. Treas. Western Shore pay to Sarah Gould, of Dorchester county, during life, quarterly, half pay of a private, as further remuneration for the services rendered by her husband William Gould, during the rev. war.

Graves, Richard. Passed Jan. 30, 1822. Treas. Western Shore in favor of Richard Graves, the brigade Major of the 6th brigade,—for services performed during the late war.

Gray, George. Passed Feb. 12, 1820—No. 41. Treas. pay to George Gray, of Charles county, for life, quarterly, half pay of a private, for his services during the rev. war.

Green, Henry. Passed Mch. 6, 1850—No. 61. Treas. of Md. pay to Elizabeth Green, widow of Henry Green, a private in the war of the Amer. Rev., half pay of a private for the remainder of her life, from Jan. 1, 1850.

Green, Capt. Lewis. [War of 1812]. Feb. 15, 1820, No. 22.

† *Green, Wm.*, private, Rev. army, of Charles county. Pensioned from Mch. 4, 1789, under Act of June 7, 1785, at $40.00 per annum (recd. $1,085.64)—at $64.00 per an. Apr. 24, 1816 (recd. $407.27) and died in 1822. (U. S. Pens. Rolls, 1835, p. 12).

Greentree, Benj. Passed Feb. 12, 1820—No. 24. Treas. pay to Benj. Greentree, of Montgomery county, during life, quarterly, half pay of private, for his services during rev. war.

Greentree, Benj. Passed Mch. 3, 1840—No. 15. Treas. Western Shore pay to Mary Greentree, of Frederick county, widow of Benj. Greentree, a soldier of the rev. or order, the sum of $10.00 for one quarter pension due her late husband at the time of his death.

Treas. Western Shore also directed to pay to the said Mary Greentree, during life, quarterly, from Jan. 1, 1840, the half pay of a private, in consideration of the services of her late husband during the rev. war.

Greentree, Benj. Passed Jan. 26, 1848—No. 14. State Treas. pay to Elizabeth Beall, or order, any money due to Mary Greentree at time of her death.

Griffin, Nathan. Passed Dec. session, 1816—No. 35. Treas. Western Shore pay to Nathan Griffin, of Dorchester county, an old soldier, during life, quarterly, half pay of a private, as a compensation for his services in the late rev. war.

Griffith, Maj. Philemon. Passed Feb. 19, 1819—No. 57. Treas. Western Shore pay to Philemon Griffith, an old rev. officer, half pay of a Major, for his services during the rev. war.

Griffith, Capt. Samuel. Passed Feb. 19, 1819—No. 64. Treas. Western Shore pay to Samuel Griffith, an old rev. officer, during life, quarterly, half pay of a captain, for his services during the rev. war.

Passed Feb. 10, 1834—No. 18. Treas. Western Shore pay to Ruth Griffith, widow of Samuel Griffith, of Montgomery county, a rev. soldier, the amt. of pension due to her husband at time of his death.

* *Griffith, Samuel.* Capt. Md. Line (Jan. 1820, p. 544).

Grove, David. Feb. 17, 1820—No. 54. Treas. Western Shore is directed to pay David Grove, of Washington county, half pay of a private for his rev. war service.

Passed Mch. 6, 1832—No. 54. Treas. Western Shore pay to Catharine Grove, widow of David Grove, a soldier of the rev. war, during widowhood, half yearly, half pay of a private for the services rendered by her husband during said war.

Grove, Wm. Passed Mch. 1, 1850—No. 48. Treas. pay to Mary Grove, widow of Wm. Grove, a rev. soldier, late of Allegany county, deceased, such sum of money, commencing Jan. 1, 1850, during her life, as will equal the half pay of a private.

Grover, Wm. Passed Feb. 12, 1820—No. 30. Treas. pay to Wm. Grover, of Allegany county, late a private in the Md. Line, during the rev. war, during life, quarterly, half pay of a private.

* *Groves, Wm.*, private, Md. Line (Jan. 1820, p. 544).

Gudgeon, Wm. Passed Feb. 19, 1819—No. 68. Treas. Western Shore is directed to pay to Wm. Gudgeon, of Kent county, an old rev. soldier—half pay of a private for his service during the rev. war.

Gudgeon, Wm. Feb. 17, 1824—No. 21. Treas. Western Shore pay to Wm. Gudgeon, of Kent county, half pay of a private, as further pay for services during rev. war—also present sum due him.

Gudgeon, Wm. Passed Mch. 11, 1828—No. 11. Treas. West Shore pay to representatives of Wm. Gudgeon, deceased, a rev. soldier, such sum as may appear to have been due him at death.

Passed Feb. 20, 1829—No. 22. Treas. pay to Benj. Gudgeon, one of the heirs of Wm. Gudgeon, late of Kent county, whatever sum may have been due to the said Wm. Gudgeon from the state of Md. at time of his decease, on account of his rev. services.

Gudgington, William—see Davis, Samuel stricken from list.

Gwyn, John. Passed Mch. 21, 1837—No. 54. Treas. Western Shore pay to Julia Gwyn, widow of John Gwyn, the half pay of a sergeant during her life, as a further remuneration for his services during the rev.

Hafley, Stephen. Passed Feb. 18, 1830—No. 31. Treas. Western Shore pay to Stephen Hafley, of Frederick county, during life, quarterly, half pay of a private, for his services during the rev. war.

Halkerstone, Robert and others. Passed Nov. session, 1811 (Jan. 6, 1812)—No. 36. Treas. Western Shore be, and is hereby requested to pay unto Robert Halkerstone (see res. Dec. 1817), of Charles county, Edward Tillard of Montgomery county, John McCoy, John S[prigg] Belt, Gassaway Watkins, Cornelius H. Mills and John J. Jacob, and each and every one of them, or their order, the sum of $125.00, annually, during their lives, in quarterly payments, out of any unappropriated monies in the treasury.

Halkerson, Lieut. Robert. Passed Dec. session, 1817—No. 20. Treas. Western Shore pay to Robert Halkerson, of Charles county, an old rev. officer, quarterly, the half pay of a lieutenant for life, instead of the sum allowed him by a resolution passed Jan. 6th, 1812 [No. 36].

* *Halkerstone, Robert*, lieutenant, Md. Line (Jan. 1820, p. 545).

Hall, Richard. Passed Feb. 2, 1832—No. 17. Treas. Western Shore pay to Richard Hall, of Anne Arundel county, a soldier of the rev. war, during life, half yearly, half pay of a private, for his servces during said war.

Hall, Richard. Passed Jan. 5, 1841—No. 3. Treas. Western Shore pay to Mrs. Ann Cadle, legal representative of Richd. Hall, deceased, a pensioner of State of Md., $17.60, amt. due said Hall at time of his death.

Hamilton, Capt. John A. Feb. 25, 1824—No. 34, p. 172. Treas. to pay to Margaret Hamilton, of Baltimore, the half pay of a Capt., as further remuneration for her husband, Capt. John A. Hamilton's services during the rev. war.

Hammond, Elizabeth. Passed Mch. 5, 1844—No. 33. Treas. pay to Elizabeth Hammond, of Frederick county, during her life, half pay of a private in consideration of services rendered by her husband during the rev. war.

* *Hammond, Peter*, private, Md. Line (Jan. 1820, p. 545).

† *Hammond, Peter*, private, Md. Line, age 79, from Frederick county. Pensioned[b] Apr. 3, 1819 at $96.00 per an. from Apr. 8, 1818. (Recd. $230.40. U. S. Pens. Roll, 1835, p. 36).

* *Han, David*, fifer, Pa. Line (Jan. 1820, p. 545).

† *Han, David*, fifer, Pa. Line, age 78, from Frederick county. Pensioned[b] Feb. 1, 1819, at $96.00 per an. from Jan. 29, 1819. (Recd. $538.66. U. S. Pens. Roll, 1835, p. 36).

* *Handell, John*, private, N. Y. Line (Jan. 1820, p. 545).

Handy, Capt. George. Passed Feb. 9, 1820—No. 13. Treas. Western Shore is directed to pay to Elizabeth Handy, widow of George Handy late a captain in the rev. war, half pay of a captain.

Passed Feb. 19, 1838—No. 14. Treas. Western Shore pay to Anne G. Handy, executrix of Elizabeth Handy, late of Somerset county, $54.00, bal. of pension money due said Eliz. Handy.

Handy, Isaac. Passed Mch. 14, 1838—No. 29. Treas. Western Shore pay to Priscilla Woolford, of Somerset county, the former widow of Isaac Handy, half pay of a private during her life, as a further remuneration for his services during the rev. war.

Handy, Levin, Gentleman. Com'd. Ensign of Capt. Henry Gale's Company in the Salisbury Batt'n. of Militia in Somerset Co. Given at

Annapolis, Jan. 7, 1777. Thos. Johnson. Resigned May 12, 1778. To Col. Day Scott. (X, No. 93). Endorsement: Williams, Thomas (Sept. 22, 1777) says "Capt. Cole's Company"—Levin Handy, Ensign.

Handy, Capt. Levin. Passed Feb. 9, 1822—No. 19, p. 176. Treas. Western Shore pay to Nancy Handy, widow of Levin Handy late a Captain in the rev. war, during life, quarterly, half pay of a captain.

Handy, Thomas. Ensign in Princess Anne Battn. of Militia in Somerset Co. after Jan. 7, 1778—see Williams, Thomas.

Haney, Wm. Passed Apr. 1, 1839—No. 61. Treas. Western Shore pay to Susanna Haney, of city of Baltimore, widow of Wm. Haney, a soldier of the Rev. war, or to her order, half pay of a private of the Rev. during her life, quarterly, commencing Jan. 1, 1839, in consideration of the services of her said husband.

Hanson, Lieut. Isaac. Passed Nov. 1785, Vol. 11, Chap. XVI. Gen. Assembly granted half pay of a lieut. for disability acquired in the service, to Isaac Hanson, a lieut. in the Md. line in the Continental army.

Hanspan, John Codlep. Passed Dec. session, 1817—No. 23. Treas. Western Shore pay to John Codlep Hanspan, of Anne-Arundel county, an old soldier, quarterly, the half pay of a private [Rev. services].

* *Hanspan, Cutlip,* private Md. Line (Jan. 1820, p. 545).

Harman, Lazarus. Passed Apr. Session 1792—No. 1, Governor grant to Lazarus Harman half the monthly pay he received in the continental service, by orders on Treas. Western Shore, chargeable to the U. S.

* *Harman, Lazarus,* private, Md. Line (Jan. 1820, p. 545).

* *Harper, Samuel A.,* private, Md. Line (Jan. 1820, p. 545).

Harper, Samuel. Passed Feb. 28, 1832—No. 47. Treas. Western Shore pay to Elizabeth Harper, widow of Samuel Harper, a soldier of the rev. war, during widowhood, half yearly, half pay of a private, for services rendered by her said husband.

Harper, Wm. Passed Nov. session, 1812—No. 54. Treas. Western Shore pay unto Wm. Harper, late a private in the rev. war,—half pay of a private, as a further remuneration to him for those services by which his country has been so essentially benefitted.

Harper, Wm. Passed Feb. 18, 1846—No. 21. Treas. of State pay Bethula Harper, of Dorchester county, widow of the late Wm. Harper, who was a private in the Rev., during life, quarterly, half pay of a private, in consideration of the services of her husband.

† *Harris, Saml.,* matross, Rev. army, of Montgomery county. Pensioned at $40.00 per an. from Oct. 26, 1810 (recd. $219.99)—at $64.00 from Apr. 24, 1816 (recd. $631.27). Died Sept. 19, 1826. (U. S. Pens. Rolls, 1835, p. 16).

Harris, Solomon. Passed Nov. session, 1812 (Jan. 2, 1813)—No. 42.

Treas. Western Shore pay to Solomon Harris, of Dorchester county, quarterly, during life, half pay of a private,—in further remuneration &c.

Harrison, Kinsey. Passed Dec. session, 1816—No. 12. Treas. Western Shore pay to Kinsey Harrison, of Anne-Arundel county, late a private in the rev. war, quarterly, half pay of a private during his life, as a further remuneration for his services.

* *Harrison, Kinsey*, private, Md. Line (Jan. 1820, p. 545).

Harrison, Robert H. Passed Mch. 11, 1840—No. 28. Treas. Western Shore pay to Sarah Easton and Dorothy Storer, the legal representatives of Robert H. Harrison, or their order, a sum equal to three years half pay as Aid-de-Camp to the Commander-in-Chief, as a compensation for the services of the said Robert H. Harrison, in the war of the revolution, and that sum shall be in full of all claims the representatives of said Robert H. Harrison has against the said State for bounty lands.

* *Hart, Nicholas*, private, R. I. Line (Jan. 1820, p. 545).

Hartshorn, John, Lieut. Passed Feb. 13, 1836—No. 17. Treas. Western Shore pay to Nancy Williams, widow of John Hartshorn, who was a lieut. in the rev., during widowhood, half pay of a lieut., for the services of her late husband.

Harvy, Zadok. Passed Jan. 6, 1812—No. 37. Treas. Western Shore pay to Zadok Harvy, of Dorchester county, an old rev. soldier, the half pay of a private during the remainder of his life, as a remuneration for his meritorious services.

* *Harvey, Zadock*, private, Md. Line (Jan. 1820, p. 545).

Hawkins, Thomas—see Nov. session 1804—No. 1, of Frederick co.

Hawman, Elizabeth. Passed Mch. 1, 1850—No. 48. Treas. pay to Philip & Frederick Hawman, legal heirs and representatives of Elizabeth Hawman, deceased, or order, $10.00, bal. of pension due her at her death.

Hays, John. Passed Mch. 9, 1836—No. 52. Treas. Western Shore pay to John Hays, a soldier of the rev., half pay of a private during life, in consideration of his rev. services.

* *Hayes, John Hawkins*, private, Md. Line (Jan. 1820, p. 545).

Hays, John H. Passed Feb. 3, 1828—No. 9. Treas. Western Shore pay to John H. Hays, of St. Mary's county, during life, half yearly, half pay of a private, further remuneration for his services during the rev. war.

Passed Jan. 18, 1839—No. 6. Treas. Western Shore pay to Joseph F. Shaw, for use of Teresa Hays, widow of John H. Hays, a soldier of the rev., bal. of pension due at his death, Sept. 29, 1838.

Passed Mch. 8, 1850—No. 75. Treas. of State pay to Theresa Hays of Saint Mary's county, widow of John H. Hays, a private in the war of the Amer. Rev., half pay of a private for the remainder of her life, commencing Jan. 1, 1850.

Hayward, Thomas, Esq. Com'd. Col. of Princess Anne Battalion in Somerset Co. Given at Annapolis, Aug. 30, 1777. Th. Johnson. To Thomas Simm Lee. (X, No. 95). Resigned Jan. 19, 1781.

Haywood, Thomas. Passed Mch. 10, 1832—No. 78. Treas. Western Shore pay to Thos. Haywood, of Saint Mary's county, a soldier of the rev. war, during life, yearly, half pay of a private, for his services during the said war.

Hazelip, Richard. Feb. 16, 1820—No. 33. Treas. is directed to pay to Richd. Hazelip, of Washington county, half pay of a private—his services during rev. war.

Head, John—Passed Feb. 19, 1819—No. 58. Treas. Western Shore pay to John Head, an old rev. soldier, the half pay of a private for his services in the rev. war.

* *Head, John*, private, Md. Line (Jan. 1820, p. 545).

Heaton, James. Passed Mch. 9, 1827—No. 41. Treas. Western Shore pay to Elizabeth Heaton, of Berks county, Pa. during life, half yearly, half pay of a private, for her husband, James Heaton's services during the rev. war.

* *Helmer, John Wm.*, private, Pa. Line (Jan. 1820, p. 545).

Hempston, Wm. Passed Feb. 19, 1819—No. 66. Treas. Western Shore pay to Wm. Hempston, of Montgomery county, an old rev. soldier, the half pay of a private soldier.

Hempston, Wm. Passed Mch. 7, 1834—No. 51. Treas. Western Shore pay to Nathan T. Hempston, of Montgomery county, whatever sum of money may appear due his father, Wm. Hempston, deceased, upon the pension list [rev. war, according to Index], at time of his death.

† *Herron, James*, private Rev. army, of Baltimore county; pensioned from Aug. 8, 1814 at $96.00 per annum (received $343.00)—died Sept. 4, 1818. (U. S. Pension Roll, 1835, p. 7).

* *Hewett, Robert*, private, Conn. Line (Jan. 1820, p. 545).

Hewitt, Joseph. Passed Feb. 19, 1819—No. 55. Treas. Western Shore pay to Joseph Hewitt, the half pay of a private, quarterly during life, [Rev. services].

Hill, John. Passed Nov. session, 1812 (Jan. 2, 1813)—No. 39. Treas. Western Shore pay annually to John Hill, during life, in quarterly payts., a sum of money equal to the half pay of a private. [Indexed and carried under, Rev. pensioners—G. M. B.]

* *Hill, John*, private, Pa. Line (Jan. 1820, p. 545).

Hill, John. Passed Mch. 5, 1828—No. 25. Treas. Western Shore pay to George Hill, of Anne Arundel county, lawful heir & representative of John Hill, a rev. soldier (who died Feb. 5, last) whatever sum was due him at decease, from Md., on account of his rev. services.

Hill, Richard. Passed Feb. 10, 1832—No. 31. Reg. of land office issue to Lydia Brown and Ann Hill, of Saint Mary's county, legal representatives of Richard Hill, a soldier of rev. war, a common warrant for 50 acres vacant land in Allegany county and a patent upon survey, without compensation money.

Hillman, Wm. Passed Nov. session, 1812—No. 60. Treas. Western Shore pay to Wm. Hillman—half pay of a soldier, as a remuneration to the said Wm. Hillman for services rendered his country in the rev. war, & as a relief from the indigence and misery which attend his old age.

* *Hilman, Wm.*, private, Md. Line (Jan. 1820, p. 545).

Hillman, Wm. Passed Mch. 1, 1833—No. 42. Treas. Western Shore pay to Sally Hillman, of Somerset county, widow of Wm. Hillman, during life, quarterly, half pay of a private, for services rendered by her husband during the rev. war.

Hilman, Wm. Passed Feb. 5, 1846—No. 13. Treas. pay to Constant D. Stanford for use of Nancy Stanford, Elizabeth Smith & Biddy Hilman, children & heirs at law of Sally Hilman, deceased, at time of her death, on account of a pension of $40.00 per annum granted to her, as the widow of Wm. Hilman, a soldier of the rev., in the Md. Line.

† *Hinnis, Samuel*, private, Rev. army[a]. Pensioned Act of June 7, 1785 at $20.00 per an. from Mch. 4, 1789; recd. $450.00. (U. S. Pens. Roll, 1835, p. 21).

† *Hirley, Wm.*, private, Rev. army[a]. Pensioned, Act June 7, 1785, at $40.00 per an. from Mch. 4, 1789; recd. $660.00. (U. S. Pens. Roll, 1835, p. 21).

Hofley, Stephen. Passed Feb. 9, 1839—No. 13. Treas. Western Shore pay to John B. Boyle, as per order of Mary Magdalene Hofley, widow of Stephen Hofley, a rev. pensioner, $31.22 for 9 months & 11 days pension, due said Stephen Hofley at time of his death.

Passed Feb. 15, 1839—No. 15. Treas. Western Shore pay to Mary Magdalene Hofley, widow of Stephen Hofley, a rev. soldier, or her order, half pay of a soldier of the rev. during her life, commencing Jan. 1, 1839.

Holland, Edward. Passed Jan. 22, 1836—No. 25. Treas, Western Shore pay to Mary Holland, quarterly during life, half pay of a drummer, for the services of her husband, Edward Holland, during the rev. war.

Holland, Jacob. Passed Feb. 19, 1819—No. 81. Treas. Western Shore directed to pay to Jacob Holland, late a revolutionary, now a commissioned officer, or to his order, annually, in quarterly payments during life, a sum of money equal to the half pay of a corporal of dragoons.

Holland, James. Passed Feb. 19, 1819—No. 69. Treas. Western Shore pay to James Holland, late a private in the rev. war half pay of a private.

Holland, John. Passed Mch. 13, 1837—No. 38. Treas. Western Shore pay to John Holland, half pay of a private during his life, as a further remuneration for his services during the rev. war.

* *Holland, John T.*, private, Pulaski's Legion (Jan. 1820, p. 545).

Holland, Joseph. Passed Feb. 19, 1819—No. 69. Treas. Western Shore pay to Joseph Holland, late a rev. soldier, quarterly, during life, a sum of money equal to the half pay of a private.

* *Holland, Joseph*, private, Md. Line (Jan. 1820, p. 545).

† *Holland, Joseph*, private, Md. Line, age 76, from Frederick county[b]. Pensioned Oct. 8, 1818, at $96.00 from Apr. 1, 1818. (Recd. $1,529.06. U. S. Pens. Roll, 1835, p. 36).

Hollydyoak, John. Passed Mch. 9, 1827—No. 43. Treas. Western Shore pay to Ann Hollydyoak, of Annapolis, during life, half yearly, half pay of a private, for her husband, John Hollydyoak's services during the rev. war.

Hood, Edward. Passed Feb. 23, 1822—No. 58, p. 180. Treas. Western Shore pay to Edward Hood, of Anne Arundel county, half pay of a private, for his services during the rev. war.

* *Hood, Edward*, private, Md. Line (Jan. 1820, p. 545).

Hood, James. Passed Dec. session, 1817 (Feb. 6, 1818)—No. 33. Treas. Western Shore pay to James Hood, of Anne-Arundel county, quarterly, during his life, the half pay of asst. commissary, for his services during the rev. war.

Hood, James, Lieut. Passed Mch. 28, 1832—No. 90. Treas. Western Shore pay to Kitty Hood, widow of James Hood, a soldier of the rev. war, during widowhood, half yearly, half pay of a lieut. for the services rendered by her husband during said war.

Passed Feb. 5, 1847—No. 10. Treas pay to Isaiah Hood, bal. of any pension due on books of the treasury to Kitty Hood, at time of her death.

Hook, Joseph. Passed Dec. session 1815—No. 9. Treas. Western Shore pay to Joseph Hook, late a corporal in the rev. war,—a sum of money equal to half pay of a corporal.

* *Hook, Joseph*, private, Md. Line (Jan. 1820, p. 545).

† *Hook, Joseph*, private, Md. Line, age 76, from Frederick county[b]. Pensioned Sept. 22, 1818 at $96.00 per an., from Apr. 15, 1818. Dropped from roll, Act May 1, 1820. (Recd. $181.33. U. S. Pens. Roll, 1835, p. 36).

Hooper, Abraham. Passed Dec. session, 1816—No. 31. Treas. Western Shore pay to Abraham Hooper, of Harford county, an old rev. soldier, quarterly, half pay of a private soldier, as a remuneration for those services rendered his country during her struggle for independence.

* *Hooper, Abraham*, private, Md. Line (Jan. 1820, p. 545).

Hoops, Adam, Capt. Passed Feb. 13, 1833—No. 35. Treas. Western

Shore pay to Adam Hoops, of Waterleit, Albany county, N. Y., during life, quarterly, half pay of a captain, for services rendered by him during the rev. war.

Hopkins, Capt. David. Passed Nov. session 1805—No. 8. David Hopkins, a captain of horse during the late rev. war, whose merits as an officer stand honourably established by letters from the late General Washington and his aids, and by letters from Generals Heath and Maylan, and whose infirmities, occasioned by military fatigues and hardships, render him unable to earn a scanty subsistence for a wife and five children,—is entitled to receive half pay as a capt. of horse in the Md. Line, during life. Treas. Western Shore is directed to pay the same to said David Hopkins, or order, in quarterly payts.

* *Hopkins, David,* major, Md. Line (Jan. 1820, p. 544).

Horner, Dr. Gustavus. Passed Mch. 4, 1834—No. 35. Treas. Western Shore pay to Frances Horner, widow of Dr. Gustavus Horner, during her life, quarterly, half pay of a Surgeon's mate, for the services rendered by her husband during the rev. war.

Horney, Wm. Passed Nov. session 1810—No. 11. Treas. pay annually to Wm. Horney, of Talbot county, an old rev. soldier, a sum of money, quarterly payts., equal to half pay of a soldier during the war aforesaid, as a further remuneration to said Wm. Horney for the services rendered his country, and as a relief from the indigence and misery which attend his decrepitude and old age.

* *Hoshal, Jesse,* private, R. I. Line (Jan. 1820, p. 545).

Hoskins, Randall. Passed Mch. 7, 1829—No. 41. Treas. Western Shore pay to Randall Hoskins, alias Randolph Hoskins, of Washington county, state of Kentucky, during life, half yearly, half pay of a private, for his services during the rev. war.

* *House, Michael,* private, Pa. Line (Jan. 1820, p. 545).

House, Michael. Passed Feb. 23, 1822—No. 56, p. 180. Treas. Western Shore directed to pay Michael House half pay of a private for his rev. war services.

Passed Mch. 12, 1827—No. 75. Treas. Western Shore directed to pay Christiana House, of Washington county, during life, half yearly, half pay of a private, for her husband, Michael House's services during rev. war.

Houston, Isaac, Esq. Com'd. Capt. of a Company of Militia in Wicomoco Batt'n. of Worcester Co. Given at Annapolis, Aug. 13, 1777. Th. Johnson. (X, No. 100). Resigned May 8, 1778.

Howard, Benj. Passed Feb. 17, 1832—No. 37. Reg. land office issue to heirs of Benj. Howard, a soldier of the rev. war, warrant and later patent for 50 acres vacant land in Allegany county.

Howard, Col. John Eager. Passed Mch. 15, 1828—No. 83. Preamble recites death "the past year" Colonel John Eager Howard, a native of Md., "one of the most distinguished officers of the war of the revolution," formerly chief magistrate of this state, afterwards our senator in Congress, &c.—whose courage and conduct raised the Md. Line to that high character which our troops acquired and maintained during the struggle for our national independence.

Portrait provided for House of Delegates.

† *Howard, John,* private, Rev. army[a]. Pensioned Act June 7, 1785, from Mch. 4, 1789, at $40.00 per an.; recd. $20.00. (U. S. Pens. Roll, 1835, p. 21).

Howard, John. Passed Mch. 6, 1839—No. 52. Treas. Western Shore pay to John Howard, of Mason county, Ky. a soldier of the rev., in the Md. Line, or order, quarterly, the half pay of a private of the rev.

† *Huggins, Samuel,* private, Rev. army, of Cecil county. Pensioned Dec. 4, 1815, under Act of June 7, 1785, at $40.00 per an. dating from Mch. 4, 1789 (recd. $1,085.64). Pensioned at $64.00 per an. from Apr. 24, 1816 (recd. $119.27), and Died Aug. 24, 1818. (U. S. Pens. Rolls, 1835, p. 11).

* *Hurdle, Laurence,* private, Md. Line (Jan. 1820, p. 545).

* *Hurdle, Robert,* private, Md. Line (Jan. 1820, p. 545).

* *Hurst, Samuel,* private, Md. Line—not in reduced circumstances; stricken from the roll, (Jan. 1820, p. 545).

Hutson, John. Passed Dec. session, 1817—No. 12. Treas. Western Shore pay to John Hutson, of Caroline county, late a soldier in the rev. war, quarterly, during life, the half pay of a private, as an additional compensation to him for those services by which his country has been so essentially benefitted.

Hudson, John. Passed Mch. 14, 1828—No. 54. Treas. Western Shore pay to Elizabeth Hudson, of Caroline county, during life, half yearly, half pay of a private, as further remuneration for her husband John Hudson's services during the rev. war.

Hurdle, Lawrence. Passed Dec. session 1816—No. 22. Treas. Western Shore pay to Lawrence Hurdle, quarterly, the half pay of a sergeant, as a further remuneration for those services by which his country has been so essentially benefitted.

Hurst, Samuel. Passed Dec. session, 1817—No. 15. Treas. Western Shore pay to Samuel Hurst, of Dorchester county, an old soldier, quarterly, a sum of money equal to the half pay of a private, as a further remuneration to him for those services by which his country has been so essentially benefitted.

Hymon, John, Sr. Gentleman. Com'd. Ensign of the Company in Caroline Co. belonging to the 28th Batt'n. in this Province. Given in

Convention at Annapolis, Jan. 3, 1776. Pr. order Mat. Tilghman, Pres. (X, No. 102).

Imeson, John. Passed Nov. session 1803—No. 6. Treas. Western Shore pay to John Imeson, a soldier in the rev. war, 15£ in current money, annually, during remainder of his life, in quarterly payts.

* *Imeson, John,* private, Md. Line (Jan. 1820, p. 546).

Ireland, George. Passed Mch. 14, 1828—No. 53. Treas. Western Shore pay Mary Ireland, of Calvert county, during life, half yearly, half pay of a lieut., as further remuneration for her husband George Ireland's services during the rev. war.

Ireland, George. Passed Mch. 12, 1829—No. 55. Reg. of land office is directed to issue to legal representatives of George Ireland, a rev. officer of the Md. Line, a common warrant for 200 acres vacant land westward of Fort Cumberland, in Allegany county, and a patent for said acres of land without payt. of any composition money. Res. No. 41, Feb. 13, 1832 repeals requirement for location westward of Fort Cumberland.

Ireland, Geo. Passed Mch. 13, 1839—No. 31. Whereas, by act of 1788, Chap. 44, George Ireland, an officer in the rev. war, or his legal representatives, are entitled to 200 acres of land in Allegany county; and, whereas, a warrant for said land was issued, under a resolution of the General Assembly, and the surveyor of Allegany county returned that there was no vacant land;—Therefore Resolved by the Gen. Assembly of Md., That the Treas. of Western Shore &c.—pay to legal representatives of George Ireland, or their order, $250.00.

Irving, Thos. Ensign in 17th Battn. Militia—see Schoolfield, Wm.

† *Isaacs, James,* private, Rev. army[a]. Pensioned, Act of June 7, 1785, from Mch. 4, 1789 at $40.00 per an.; recd. $600.00. (U. S. Pens. Roll, 1835, p. 21).

Issabell, Elizabeth. Passed Feb. 20, 1822—No. 36, p. 178. Treas. Western Shore pay to Elizabeth Issabell, of Annapolis, half pay of a sergeant, for services rendered by her husband during the rev. war.

Jackson, Ann. Passed Feb. 23, 1822—No. 57, p. 180. Treas. Western Shore pay to Ann Jackson, of Annapolis, half pay of a private, for her husband's services during the rev. war.

Jacobs, John J. Passed Nov. session 1811—No. 36—see Halkerstone, Robert.

Passed Dec. session, 1816—No. 40. Treas. Western Shore pay to John J. Jacobs, an officer of the Md. Line in the rev. war, such a sum of money in addition to what he now receives under a resolution passed Nov. session 1811, as will make his pension amount to a sum equal to the half pay of a first lieut., during life, quarterly payts.

Jacob, John J. Passed Feb. 17, 1830—No. 27. Reg. land office required to issue warrant in name of John J. Jacob (late an officer in the rev. war) for 200 acres of vacant land in Allegany county, westward of Fort Cumberland.

Jacob, John I. Passed Jan. 24, 1832—No. 7. Treas. Western Shore pay to John I. Jacob "a revolutionary soldier," $22.12, being amt. of composition money paid by him into the treasury upon certain lands in Allegany county, which were represented to be liable to escheat, but were afterwards found to have been escheated and patented to Edward Norwood.

Jacob, John I. Passed Feb. 17, 1832—No. 40. Repeal of portion requiring that land to "John J. Jacob," a rev. soldier, passed at Dec. session 1830, number 27 [evidently 7], "be located to westward of Fort Cumberland."

Jacobs, Wm. Passed Mch. 2, 1827—No. 21. Treas. directed to pay to Wm. Jacobs, of Hampshire county, Va. during life, half yearly, a sum of money equal to the *full pay* of a private, as a further remuneration for his services during the rev. war.

Jacobs, William. [War of 1812]. (No. 10, p. 175) passed Jan. 8, 1822, "pass the account of William Jacobs, of Queen Ann's county, for the use of his granary as a place of deposit for public arms, &c.

Jaquet, John D. Passed Dec. session, 1815—No. 36. Treas. Western Shore pay to John D. Jaquet, a sergeant in the rev. war, quarterly, the half pay of a sergeant for life, as a further remuneration for those services by which his country has been so essentially benefitted.

Jeffries, Jacob. Passed Dec. session, 1816—No. 52. Treas. Western Shore pay to Jacob Jeffries, of Queen-Anne's county, late a private in the rev. war, quarterly, during life, the half pay of a private, as a further remuneration to him for those services by which his country has been essentially benefitted.

Jenkins, Philip. Passed Feb. 13, 1837—No. 20. Treas. Western Shore pay to Sarah Jenkins, widow of Philip Jenkins, half pay of a private during her life, as a further remuneration for his services during the rev.

Jenkins, Thomas. Passed Jan. 19, 1830—No. 6. Treas. of Western Shore pay to Thomas Jenkins, of Dist. of Columbia, a rev. soldier, during life, half yearly half pay of a private, as further remuneration for his services during the rev. war.

† *John, Thomas,* private, Md. Line, age 84, from Frederick county. Pensioned[b] Aug. 8, 1821, at $96.00 from July 16, 1821. (Recd. $108.80. U. S. Pens. Roll, 1835, p. 36).

Johnson, Archibald. Passed Nov. session, 1812 (Jan. 2, 1813)—No. 46. Treas. Western Shore pay to Archibald Johnson, of Charles county, a sergeant in the rev. war,—half pay of a sergeant, as a further remuneration for his services in the rev. war.

* *Johnson, Archibald*, sergeant, Md. Line (Jan. 1820, p. 546).

† *Johnson, Benedict*, private, Rev. army[a]. Pensioned, Act of June 7, 1785, from Mch. 4, 1789, at $40.00 per an.; recd. $680.00. (U. S. Pens. Roll, 1835, p. 21).

Johnson, Nicholas. Passed Mch. 4, 1835—No. 48. Treas. Western Shore pay to Rebecca Johnson, of Queen Anne's county, widow of Nicholas Johnson, a soldier of the rev., half pay of a private, quarterly, during her life.

* *Johnston, Nicholas*, private, Md. Line (Jan. 1820, p. 546).

Johnson, Wm. Formerly commanded a Co. of Militia in Lower Battn., Montgomery County, Aug. 4, 1780—see Willcoxen, Jesse.

Johnston, Wm. Passed Mch. 2, 1827—No. 22. Treas. to pay to Wm. Johnston, of Harford county, during life, half yearly, the half pay of a private for his services during the rev. war.

† *Jonas, John*, private in Rev. army, residing in Alleghany county, placed on pension roll Feb. 24, 1821 at $60.00 per year (received $1,230.00) commencing Sept. 4, 1794, under Act. of June 7, 1785.

Jones, Aaron. Passed Dec. session 1815—No. 14. Treas. Western Shore pay unto Aaron Jones, of Dorchester county, late a private in the rev. war—half pay of a private, as a further remuneration to him for those services by which his country has been so essentially benefitted.

* *Jones, Aaron*, private, Md. Line (Jan. 1820, p. 546).

* *Jones, Alexander*, private, Va. Line (Jan. 1820, p. 545).

Jones, Cotter. Passed Mch. 12, 1827—No. 58. Treas. pay to Cotter Jones, of Somerset county, during life, half annually, half pay of a private, for his services during the rev. war.

Jones, Joseph. Ensign of a Militia Co. in Prince George's Co., 25th Battn. Jan. 3, 1776—see Wootters, Richd.

Jones, Nancy. Passed Mch. 4, 1834—No. 40. Treas. Western Shore pay to Nancy Jones, of Worcester county, during life, quarterly, half pay of a Private, in consideration of the services rendered by her husband during the rev. war.

Jones, Neale. Passed Nov. session, 1812—No. 58. Treas. Western Shore pay to Neale Jones, late a private in the rev. war,—half pay of a private, as a further remuneration to him for those services by which his country has been so essentially benefitted.

Jones, Samuel, Capt. Passed Mch. 1828—No. 43. Reg. land office issue to Lillias M. Jones, of Charles county, dau. of Capt. Samuel Jones, officer of Md. Line during rev. war, a common warrant for 200 acres vacant land to westward of Fort Cumberland, in Allegany county, and patent without payt. of composition money therefor.

Jones, Thomas. 1st. Lieut. in 17th Battn. Militia—see Schoolfield, W[m].

* *Jones, Thomas,* private, Md. Line (Jan. 1820, p. 545).

Jones, Thomas. Passed Mch. 11, 1834—No. 63. Treas. Western Shore pay to Thomas Jones, of Anne Arundel county, during life, quarterly, half pay of private, for services rendered by him during the rev. war.

Jones, W[m]. Passed Feb. 12, 1820—No. 22. Treas. pay to W[m]. Jones, formerly of Prince George's county, now residing in the state of Va., quarterly, for life, half pay of a private, for his services during rev. war.

Jones, W[m]. Passed Mch. 3, 1833—No. 51. Treas. Western Shore pay to W[m]. Jones, of Caroline county, during life, quarterly, half pay of a private, in consideration of services rendered by said Jones, during the rev. war.

Jordan, Capt. John. Passed Jan. 27, 1836—No. 26. Treas. Western Shore pay to Sarah Easton, who was the widow of Capt. John Jordan, quarterly, during life, half pay of a Captain, for the services rendered by her husband during the rev. war.

* *Jordan, John,* private, Md. Line (Jan. 1820, p. 546).

Kahoe, see *Cahoe.*

† *Kean, Edward,* soldier, Rev. army, of Harford county. Pensioned Dec. 18, 1819 at $60.00 per an. from Jan. 1, 1803 (recd. $799.08)—at $96.00 per an. from Apr. 24, 1816 (recd. $1,570.86). Died Dec. 10, 1832. (U. S. Pens. Rolls, 1835, p. 15).

† *Kearnes, Robert,* sergeant, Rev. army[a]. Pensioned, Act of June 7, 1785, from Mch. 4, 1789, at $60.00 per an.; recd. $30.00. (U. S. Pens. Roll, 1835, p. 21).

† *Kelley, Hugh,* private, Rev. army[a]. Pensioned, Act June 7, 1785, at $40.00 per an. from Mch. 4, 1789; recd. $60.00. (U. S. Pens. Roll, 1835, p. 21).

Kelly, Capt. W[m]. Passed Feb. 15, 1839—No. 14. Treas. Western Shore pay to Martha Kelly, of Carroll county, widow of Capt. W[m]. Kelly, a rev. soldier, half pay of a capt. of the Rev., during her life, commencing Jan. 1, 1839.

Kennedy, Commodore Edmond P. Passed Mch. 13, 1835. Gov. directed to procure and present a sword to Commodore Edmond P. Kennedy, U. S. Navy, in appreciation of his distinguished and gallant services in the action with the Tripolitan gun boats off Tripoli, in Aug. 1804.

Kent, Isaac. Passed Feb. 12, 1820—No. 28. Treas. pay Isaac Kent, of state of Ohio, an old soldier of the rev. war, and of the Md. Line, annually for life, quarterly payts, half pay of a private, for rev. war services.

† *Keough, W[m].,* private, Rev. army[a]. Pensioned, Act of Mch. 3, 1809, at $60.00 per an.; recd. $187.00. (U. S. Pens. Roll, 1835, p. 21).

Kershner, Michael. Passed Dec. session, 1815—No. 40. Treas. Western Shore pay to Michael Kershner, of Allegany county, a private in the rev. war, quarterly, the half pay of a private, as a further remuneration to him for those services by which his country has been so essentially benefitted.

* *Kerchner, Michael,* private, German Reg't. (Jan. 1820, p. 546).

Kershner, Mary Ann. Passed Mch. 2, 1827—No. 35. Treas. pay to Mary Ann Kershner, of Allegany county, during life, half yearly, half pay of a private, for her late husband's services during the rev. war.

Passed Mch. 6, 1832—No. 63. Treas. Western Shore pay to Jacob Lantz, for the use of Mrs. Mary C. Shryer, of Allegany county, next and near friend of Mrs. Mary A. Kershner, deceased, late a pensioner of the state, $14.55, balance due up to her decease.

Keys, W^{m}. Captain of a Co. of Militia, 1777—see Schoolfield, Benj.

Kilty, John. Captain—Jan. 4, 1822. (No. 8, p. 174). Treas. Western Shore directed to pay Catharine Kilty half pay of her late husband "for those meritorious services rendered by her late husband, John Kilty, during the rev. war."

Kimson, John M. "1st. Lieut. Pa." Apr. 1778—see Steel, James.

Kindle, W^{m}. Passed Dec. session, 1817—No. 13. Treas. Western Shore pay to W^{m}. Kindle, of Washington county, a private in the rev. war, quarterly, the half pay of a private, as a further remuneration to him for those services by which his country has been so essentially benefitted.

King, George. Feb. 19, 1819—No. 67. Treas. Western Shore is directed to pay to George King, late a rev. soldier, half pay of a private during life.

King, Henry. Passed Dec. session, 1817 (Feb. 13, 1818)—No. 50. Treas. Western Shore pay to Henry King, in quarterly payts., a sum of money equal to the half pay of a commissary [Rev. services].

King, Levin. Passed Mch. 6, 1832—No. 74. Treas. Western Shore pay to Margaret King, widow of Levin King, late of Somerset county, during widowhood, half pay of an ensign for the services rendered by her husband during the rev. war.

Passed Apr. 5, 1841—No. 7. Treas. Western Shore pay to legal representatives of Mrs. Margaret King, late of Somerset county, deceased, who was a rev. pensioner of Md., amt. of pension due her at her death, Sept. 12, 1839.

King, Levin. Passed Mch. 1, 1842. Resolution No. 7, Apr. 5, 1841 repealed. Treas. Western Shore pay to administrators of said Margaret King, deceased, amt. of pension due the said deceased at time of her death.

King, Thos. Passed June session, 1809—No. 3. Treas. Western Shore pay to Thos. King, immediately $50.00, and a sum equal to the half pay of a sergeant during his life, quarterly, payments to commence this day. "Thomas King, belonging to the artillery company of the city of Annapolis, and who has been a soldier in the rev. war, and who was wounded therein, in discharging his duty on this 10th day of June, has been so unfortunate as to lose his right hand, by the firing of a cannon, which entitles him to the peculiar care of this state"—"having a family dependent on him for support."

King, Thos. Passed Nov. session 1811—No. 2. Half pay of a sergeant granted by legislature to Thos. King, in June session 1809, for support of his family, be henceforth paid by the treasurer, in quarterly payments, to his wife Mary King.

* *King, Thos.*, private, Md. Line (Jan. 1820, p. 546).

† *Kirkpatrick, John*, private, Rev. army[a]. Pensioned, Act of June 7, 1785, at $48.00 per an.; recd. $408.00. (U. S. Pens. Roll, 1835, p. 21).

* *Kisby, Richard*, private, Flying Camp—not continental; stricken from roll. (Jan. 1820, p. 546).

Kline, John. Passed Mch. 12, 1834—No. 65. Treas. Western Shore pay to Mary M. Kline (widow of John Kline) of Frederick county, during life, quarterly, half pay of a private, for the service rendered by her husband during the rev. war.

Knight, Jacob. Passed Feb. 12, 1820—No. 38. Treas. pay to Jacob Knight, of Ohio, late a soldier in the rev. war, quarterly, during life half pay of a private for those services by which his country has been so essentially benefitted.

Koine, Dominic. Passed Nov. session, 1803—No. 2. Treas. Western Shore pay to Dominic Koine, of Harford county, an old infirm soldier, or to his order, $40.00 annually, during his life, in quarterly payts.

* *Kraft, Wm.*, private, German Reg't. (Jan. 1820, p. 546).

Lafayette, General. Invited by Res. No. 2, Dec. 13, 1824, p. 156.—"are deeply impressed with a grateful remembrance of his voluntary and valuable services, during the rev. war"—visit seat of govt.

Lambert, Christopher. Passed Mch. 21, 1838—No. 47. Treas. Western Shore pay to Christopher Lambert, of Baltimore city, the half pay of a private during his life, as a further remuneration for his services during the rev. war.

* *Lambert, Christopher*, 2d., private, Md. Line (Jan. 1820, p. 546).

† *Lambert, Christopher*, private in Rev. army, of Baltimore county. Pensioned at $40.00 per annum from Mch. 4, 1789, under Act of June 7, 1785 (received $1,085.53).

Pensioned at $64.00 per annum from Apr. 24, 1816, under Act of same date (recd. $119.11). (U. S. Pension Roll, 1835, p. 8).

Langford, Elijah. Passed Nov. session 1812 (Jan. 2, 1813)—No. 47. Treas. Western Shore pay to Elijah Langford, of Somerset county, a rev. soldier, quarterly, during rem. of life, half pay of a private, as a remuneration for his meritorious services.

* *Lankford, Elijah,* private, Md. Line (Jan. 1820, p. 547).

Lansdale, Maj. Thos. Passed Mch. 8, 1850—No. 73. Treas. of Md. pay to Cornelia Lansdale, widow of Thos. Lansdale, a Maj. in the 4th Md. Reg., in the war of the Rev., half pay of a Major, for bal. of her life, commencing Jan. 1, 1850.

Lashley, George. Passed Mch. 12, 1827—No. 64. Treas. pay to George Lashley, of Cecil county, during life, half yearly, half pay of a private, for his services during rev. war.

Lashly, Geo. Passed May 27, 1836—No. 107. Treas. Western Shore pay to Granville S. Townsend $20.44, for benefit of Mary Sproul and Nancy Lashly, heirs and legal representatives of Geo. Lashly, a rev. pensioner, deceased, which bal. was due said Lashly at his death.

Laurentz, Vandel. Passed Mch. 24, 1838—No. 36. Treas. Western Shore pay to Ann Laurentz, of Baltimore city, widow of Vandel Laurentz, a soldier of the rev., half pay of a private during her life, as a further remuneration for the services of her said husband.

* *Lavely, Jacob,* private, Md. Line (Jan. 1820, p. 546).

† *Laverty, Jacob,* private, Md. Line, age 74, from Frederick county. Died Nov. 11, 1830. Pensioned[b] Jan. 4, 1819 at $96.00 per an. from June 9, 1818. (Rec'd. $1,192.80. U. S. Pens. Roll, 1835, p. 36).

Law, Wm. Passed Dec. session, 1816—No. 13. Treas. Western Shore pay to Wm. Law, late a private in the rev. war, quarterly, the half pay of a private, as a further remuneration by which his country has been so essentially benefitted.

* *Lawrentz, Wendell,* private, German Reg't. (Jan. 1820, p. 546).

Layman, Lieut. Wm. Passed Dec. session, 1816—No. 34. Treas. Western Shore pay to Wm. Layman, during life, quarterly, a sum of money equal to the half pay of a lieut., as a further remuneration to him for military services.

* *Layman, Wm.,* ensign, Md. Line (Jan. 1820, p. 547).

Layman, Wm. Passed Mch. 1, 1842—No. 26. Treas. Western Shore pay to Francis Valdenar, executor of Wm. Layman, late of Montgomery county, deceased, who was a rev. pensioner of the State of Md., amt. of pension due him at death Feb. 12, 1842.

* *Lazier, John,* private, Md. Line (Jan. 1820, p. 547).

Leake, Henry. Feb. 16, 1820—No. 32. Treas. is directed to pay to James Brown, of Montgomery county, the sum of ten dollars, which appears to be the bal. due Henry Leake, late of Montgomery county, deceased, who was a pensioner of this state.

Leather, John. Passed Dec. session, 1816—No. 27. Treas. Western Shore pay to John Leather, of Frederick county, an old rev. soldier, quarterly, a sum of money equal to the half pay of a sergeant (or to his order during his life) as a further compensation for those services he rendered his country during the rev. war.

* *Lecke, Nicholas,* sergeant marines, Frigate Virginia (Jan. 1820, p. 546).

Lee, Dudley—Passed Nov. session, 1811—No. 24. Treas. Western Shore pay to Dudley Lee—half payment of a soldier, as a remuneration for services rendered his country in the rev. war, and as a relief from the indigence and misery which attend his old age.

Lee, Dudley. Passed Mch. 21, 1838—No. 44. Treas. Western Shore pay to Margaret Lee, widow of Dudley Lee, half pay of a private during her life, as a further remuneration for his services during the rev. war.

Lee, Lieut. Parker. Passed Mch. 5, 1850—No. 62. State Treas. pay to Mary Lee, widow of Parker Lee, a Lieut. in the 4th Md. Reg., in the war of the Amer. Rev., the half pay of a Lieut. for remainder of her life, said pension commencing Jan. 1, 1850.

Leeke, Henry. Passed Dec. session, 1816—No. 39. Treas. Western Shore pay to Henry Leeke, of Montgomery county, an old rev. soldier, quarterly, during his life, the half pay of a sergeant, as a compensation to him for his services during the rev. war.

* *Leeke, Henry,* private, Md. Line (Jan. 1820, p. 546).

* *Lefevour, or Lefever, Wm.,* private, Md. Line (Jan. 1820, p. 546).

* *Lenox, James,* private, Md. Line (Jan. 1820, p. 546).

Leonard, James. Passed Dec. session, 1817—No. 18. Treas Western Shore pay to James Leonard, of Cecil county, an old soldier, quarterly, the half pay of a private, as a further remuneration for his services during the rev. war.

Leonard, James. Mch. 9, 1826—No. 98, p. 259. Reg. of land office issue to James Leonard, a warrant for 50 a. of land, belonging to this state, in Allegany county, unpatented, "as a donation granted by this state, to the rev. soldiers who served in the Md. line, during the rev. war, and to which he is considered entitled."

Lewis, Wm. Passed Feb. 12, 1820—No. 33. Treas. pay Wm. Lewis, of Washington county, an old soldier in the rev. war, for life, quarterly, half pay of a sergeant for his rev. war services.

* *Lewis, Wm.,* private, Houseger's Regt. (Jan. 1820, p. 546).

Lewis, Capt. Wm. Feb. 25, 1826—No. 48, p. 245. Treas. of Western Shore directed to pay to William Lewis, of Washington county, or order, during life, in quarterly payments in lieu of his present pension, the half pay of a captain, in consideration of his valuable military services, both in the revolutionary war, and in the war against the Indians.

Lewis, Capt. Wm. Passed Mch. 14, 1828—No. 55. Treas. Western Shore pay to Mary Lewis, of Washington county, during life, half yearly, half pay of a captain, as further remuneration for her husband, Captain Wm. Lewis' services during the rev. war.

Lingan, Thamas. Feb. 22, 1823—No. 48. Treas. Western Shore is directed to pay to Thamas Lingan, half pay of a lieut. as further compensation for his meritorious services during the rev. war.

* *Lingan, Thomas*, lieutenant, Md. Line (Jan. 1820, p. 546).

Lingan, Jannett. Passed Feb. 19, 1830—No. 43. Treas. Western Shore pay to Jannett Lingan, of Montgomery county, during widowhood, quarterly, sum of money equal to half pay of a captain, further remuneration for her late husband's services during the rev. war.

† *Lipscomb, James*, private, Rev. army[a]. Pensioned, Act of June 7, 1785, at $40.00 per an. from Mch. 4, 1789; recd. $60.00; died 1790. (U. S. Pens. Roll, 1835, p. 21).

* *Litzinger, Henry*, private, Md. Line (Jan. 1820, p. 547).

Lloyd, Thomas. Passed Feb. 12, 1820—No. 26. Treas. pay to Thomas Lloyd of Philadelphia, Pa. for life, quarterly, half pay of a private, for his services during rev. war.

Passed Mch. 9, 1846—No. 54. Treas. of Md. pay to Mary Lloyd, of Pa., widow of Thos. Lloyd, a soldier of the rev., half pay of a private of the rev., quarterly during her life, & that the Treas. pay to said Mary Lloyd the bal. due her late husband for arrearages of pension granted him during his life time.

* *Lohr, Baltzer*, private, Pa. Line (Jan. 1820, p. 547).

Lomax, John. Passed Feb. 19, 1819—No. 74. Treas. to pay to John Lomax, late a rev. soldier, quarterly during life, half pay of a private.

Long, John, Jr., Gentleman. Com'd. 1st. Lieut. of Capt. Gabriel Vanhorn's Co. in the Deer Creek Batt'n. of Militia in Harford Co. Given at Annapolis, Apr. 9, 1778. Th. Johnson. (X, No. 251). Refused by sd. John Long, Apr. 14, 1778.

John Long being much Disabled by an accident happening while in the Service of the Flying Camp is therefore under the necessity of refusing this Commission. G. R. Vanhorne, Capt.

Patrick Cain Recommended to this Commission. R. Dallam, Lieut.

Long, John. Passed Dec. session, 1817—No. 11. Treas. Western Shore pay to John Long, of Harford county, an old rev. soldier, quarterly, half pay of a private, as a further remuneration for those services rendered his country during her struggle for independence.

Long, Wm. Passed Mch. 20, 1840—No. 54. Treas. Western Shore pay to Wm. Long, of Missouri, a soldier of the rev. war, quarterly, during life, the half pay of a private, from Jan. 1, 1840.

Lorantz, Ferdinand. Passed Apr. 1, 1839—No. 60. Treas. Western Shore pay to Elizabeth Lorantz, of Baltimore city, the widow of Ferdinand Lorantz, who was a soldier in the war of the rev., or to her order, the half pay of a private of the rev. war, during her life, quarterly, commencing Jan. 1, 1839.

Lord, Andrew. Passed Dec. session, 1815—No. 45. Treas. Western Shore pay to Andrew Lord, a soldier in the rev. war, quarterly, during life, half pay of a private, as a remuneration for those services by which his country has been so essentially benefitted.

* *Lord, Andrew*, private, Md. Line (Jan. 1820, p. 546).

Lord, Andrew. Passed Mch. 12, 1828—No. 47. Grant of 50 acres vacant land, west of Fort Cumberland, Allegany county to heirs of Andrew Lord of Baltimore city, a soldier of Md. Line during rev. war—or if no heirs, then to Amelia Lord, widow of Andrew Lord—and patent without composition money.

* *Lord, Henry*, private, Md. Line (Jan. 1820, p. 547).

Lord, Henry. Passed Feb. 16, 1820—No. 35. Treas. is directed to pay to Henry Lord of Dorchester county, half pay of a private for rev. war services.

Passed Jan. 23, 1839—No. 7. Treas. Western Shore pay to Amelia Lord, of Dorchester county, widow of Henry Lord, a Rev. pensioner, $12.44, for 3 mos. & 22 days pension due Henry Lord at time of his death.

Lord, Henry. Passed Feb. 27, 1839—No. 22. Treas. Western Shore pay to Amelia Lord, of Dorchester county, widow of Henry Lord, a soldier of the rev., during her life, quarterly, the half pay of a private of the rev, commencing Jan. 1, 1839.

Lowe, Solomon. Feb. 16, 1819—No. 14. Treas. Western Shore is directed to pay to Solomon Lowe $110.00, in full compensation for rations furnished certain British prisoners taken during the late war, by a detachment of the Dorchester county militia, which said rations were furnished by the said Solomon Lowe, by the order of brig. gen. Benson.

† *Lowry, John*, private, Rev. army[a]. Pensioned, Act of June 7, 1785, at $20.00 per an.; recd. $381.98. Under Act of Mch. 3, 1809 at $40.00 per an. from Apr. 19, 1808; recd. $215.09. (U. S. Pens. Roll, 1835, p. 21).

† *Lowry, John, 2d.*, private, Rev. army[a]. Pensioned, Act of June 7, 1785, at $60.00 per an.; recd. $1,460.00. (U. S. Pens. Roll, 1835, p. 21).

Lucas, Basil. Passed Dec. session, 1815—No. 63. Treas. Western Shore pay to Basil Lucas, an old rev. soldier, annually, a sum equal to the half pay of a sergeant.

* *Lucas, John*, sergeant, Md. Line (Jan. 1820, p. 547).

Lucas, John. Passed Feb. 12, 1820—No. 27. Treas. pay to John Lucas, of Anne Arundel county, an old revolutionary soldier, quarterly.

half pay of a sergeant, as a further remuneration for those services rendered his country during her struggle for independence.

Passed Mch. 6, 1832—No. 73. Treas. Western Shore pay Rachel Lucas, of Anne Arundel county, widow of John Lucas, a soldier of rev. war, during life, half yearly, half pay of a private for her husband's services during said war.

Lynch, Hugh. Passed Nov. session 1812 (Jan. 1, '13)—No. 26. Treas. Western Shore pay to Hugh Lynch, late a private in the Md. Line during the rev. war—half pay of a private, as a further remuneration for those services rendered during the American war.

* *Lynch, Hugh,* private, Md. Line (Jan. 1820, p. 546).

† *Lynch, John,* private, Rev. army[a]. Pensioned, Act of June 7, 1785, at $44.00 per an.; recd. $1,078.00; died in 1813. (U. S. Pens. Roll, 1835, p. 21).

* *Lynch, Thos.,* private, Md. Line (Jan. 1820, p. 546).

Lynch, Thomas. Passed Mch. 12, 1828—No. 38. Treas. Western Shore pay to Thomas Lynch, of St. Mary's county, during life, half yearly, half pay of a private, as further remuneration for his services during the rev. war.

Passed Mch. 8, 1833—No. 50. Treas. Western Shore pay to James M. K. Hammett, admr. of Thomas Lynch, sum due said Lynch, on pension roll of Md., Nov. 13, 1832, date of his death.

Lynn, David, Capt. Passed Feb. 28, 1836—No. 43. Treas. Western Shore pay to Mary Lynn, widow of David Lynn, a capt. in the rev. army, half pay of a capt. during her widowhood.

Lynn, Lieut. John. Passed Nov. 1785, Vol. 11, Chap. XVI. Gen. Assembly granted half pay of a lieut., for disability acquired in the service, to John Lynn, late a lieut. in the Md. Line in the Continental army.

Lynn, Lieut. John. Passed Dec. session, 1817 (Feb. 13, 1818)—No. 52. Treas. Western Shore pay to Eleanor Lynn, widow of John Lynn, late a lieut. in the rev. war, during life, quarterly, the half pay of a lieut.

Lynn, Col. John. Jan. 19, 1825—No. 6, p. 156. Treas to pay whatever bal. remains due the late Eleanor Lynn, (who died Apr. 23, 1824), widow of Col. John Lynn, on the pension list of this state, to David Richardson, who intermarried with Elizabeth, one of the daughters of the deceased & Jane Lynn, another of her daughters, they being the only heirs and representatives of the deceased.

† *Lynn, John,* lieut., Rev. army[a]. Pensioned, Act of June 7, 1785, from Mch. 4, 1789, at $200.00 per an.; "dead" (Amt. recd. not stated—U. S. Pens. Roll, 1835, p. 21).

McBride, Hugh. Capt. of Militia, Dorchester Co., 3d Battn. July 1776—see McCloster, Saml. and Muir, Chas.

Elected 1st. Lieut. of Vienna Co. Dorchester County "and since promoted," Jan. 3, 1776—see Shaw, James.

* *McCallister, James*, private, Md. Line (Jan. 1820, p. 547).

McCallum, Wm., Gentleman. Com'd. 2d Lieut. of Capt. Goldsborough's Co. in 4th Battn. of Militia of Talbot County. Given at Annapolis Apr. 9, 1778. Th. Johnson. (X, No. 117).

McCann, Michael. Passed Dec. session, 1817—No. 31. Treas. Western Shore pay to Michael McCann, of Frederick county, an old rev. soldier, the half pay of a private during the remainder of his life, as a remuneration for his meritorious services.

* *McCann, Michael*, private, Md. Line (Jan. 1820; p. 547).

† *McCam, Michael*, private Md. Line, age 88, from Frederick county. Died May 4, 1827. Pensioned[b] Sept. 25, 1818 at $96.00 per an. from Apr. 11, 1818. (Rec'd. $870.40. U. S. Pens. Roll, 1835, p. 36).

* *McCauley, John*, private, Pa. Line (Jan. 1820, p. 547).

* *McChan, John*, private, Pa. Line (Jan. 1820, p. 547).

† *McChan, John*, private, Pa. Line, age 73, from Frederick county. Died 1821. Pensioned[b] Oct. 8, 1818 at $96.00 per an., from Apr. 3, 1818. (Recd. $280.20. U. S. Pens. Roll, 1835, p. 36).

McCloster, Samuel, Gentleman. Com'd. Ensign of Capt. Hugh McBride's Co. of Militia in Dorchester County belonging to the 3d. Battn. of this Province. Given by Council of Safety at Annapolis July 6, 1776. Danl. of St. Thos. Jenifer, Chas. Carroll, Benj. Rumsey, Ja. Tilghman. (X, No. 118).

Resigned Aug. 30, 1776 as Ensign of the Vienna Militia Co.

McConnell, Saml. Passed Nov. session, 1812—No. 57. Treas. Western Shore pay to Samuel McConnell, of Cecil county,—a sum of money equal to half pay of a sergeant, as a remuneration for his services during the rev. war.

* *McConnell, Saml*, private, Md. Line (Jan. 1820, p. 548).

McCoy, John—see Halkerstone, Robert.

* *McCracken, James*, private, Md. Line (Jan. 1820, p. 547).

McCrackin, James. Mch. 1, 1826—No. 60, p. 247. Treas. Western Shore pay to James McCrackin, of Harford county, the half pay of a private, as further remuneration for his services during the rev. war.

Passed Feb. 12, 1844—No. 18. Treas. Western Shore pay to Mary McCracken, of Harford county, during life, quarterly, half pay of a private, in consideration of services rendered by her husband James McCracken during the war of the rev.

† *McCreary, John*, private in Pa. Line, of Baltimore county. Pensioned Aug. 26, 1830, dating from Jan. 1, 1829, at $96.00 per annum (received $161.06). Died Nov. 23, 1830. (U. S. Pension Roll, 1835, p. 8).

* *McElroy, James*, private, Pa. Line (Jan. 1820, p. 548).

† *McElroy, James*, private Pa. Line, age 60, from Frederick county. Died ——. Pensioned[b] Apr. 27, 1819, at $96.00 per an., from May 21, 1818. (Recd. $219.73. U. S. Pens. Roll, 1835, p. 36).

* *McEntire, David*, private, Pa. Line (Jan. 1820, p. 548).

McGee, Chas. Passed Dec. session, 1815—No. 39. Treas. Western Shore pay to Chas. McGee, or his order, during life, the half pay of a private, annually in quarterly payts., as an additional compensation for his services [revolutionary].

* *McGee, Charles*, private, Md. Line (Jan. 1820, p. 547).

McGee, Wm. Passed Dec. session, 1815—No. 12. Treas. of western shore pay to Wm. McGee, or order, half pay of a private, annually in quarterly payts, as an additional compensation for his services.

* *McGee, Wm.*, private, Md. Line (Jan. 1820, p. 548).

* *McKay, John* (or McCay), private, Md. Line (Jan. 1820, p. 547).

* *McKeel, Thomas*, sergeant, Md. Line (Jan. 1820, p. 547).

McKeown, Samuel, Gentleman. Com'd. 2d Lieut. of Capt. Saml. Moffitt's Co. in the Elk Battalion of Militia in Cecil Co. Given at Annapolis, Apr. 21, 1778. Th. Johnson. (X, No. 121).

McKinsey, Moses. Passed Dec. session, 1815—No. 23. Treas. Western Shore pay to Moses McKinsey, of Allegany county,—a sum of money, annually during life, quarterly, equal to half pay of a drummer in the rev. war.

* *McKinsey, Moses*, drummer, Md. Line (Jan. 1820, p. 548).

McKinsey, Moses. Passed Mch. 9, 1827—No. 44. Treas. pay to Sarah McKinsey, of Allegany county, during life, half yearly, half pay of a private, for her husband, Moses McKinsey's services during the rev. war.

* *McKissick, James*, private, Pa. Line (Jan. 1820, p. 547).

* *McLean, Arthur*, sergeant, Md. Line (Jan. 1820, p. 547).

McLean, Arthur. Passed Jan. 30, 1829—No. 8. Treas. Western Shore pay to Arthur McLean, of Baltimore county, during life, half yearly, half pay of a sergeant, as further remuneration for his services during the rev. war.

* *McMahon, Peter*, private, Va. Line (Jan. 1820, p. 548).

* *McMechen, Chas.*, private, Pa. Line (Jan. 1820, p. 548).

McNamara, Darby. Passed Nov. 1798—No. 3. Treas. Western Shore pay to Darby McNamara, an old infirm & disabled soldier, annual sum of $57.00 during life, in lieu of $399.00, the principal and interest due on three state certificates issued to him for depreciation of his pay, which certificates were lost—quarterly, beginning Dec. 10, 1798.

McNamara, Darby. Passed Nov. session 1799—No. 9. Treas. Western Shore pay to Darby McNamara, a poor and disabled soldier of the 1st. Md.

regt., 25£–6s–11d. with interest from Aug. 1, 1780, for a depreciation certificate issued to him for that amt. & lost.

McNamara, Darby. Passed Nov. session 1802—No. 7. Treas. Western Shore pay annually to Darby McNamara the sum of fifteen pounds current money, in quarterly payts., in consideration of his many services as a soldier in the late revolutionary war, by which he has been rendered entirely unable to obtain a subsistence.

† *McNeal, James,* private, Rev. army, of Baltimore county. Pensioned Dec. 4, 1815 at $60.00 per annum dating from Sept. 13, 1814, act of Mch. 3, 1815 (rec'd. $121.84). Pensioned at $96.00 per annum from Sept. 24, 1816 (rec'd $1,434.93), and died Dec. 22, 1831. (U. S. Pension Roll, 1835, p. 8).

* *McNesh, Benj.,* private, Flying Camp—not continental; stricken from roll (Jan. 1820, p. 547).

McPherson, Lieut. Mark. Passed Dec. session 1815—No. 10. Treas. Western Shore pay to Mark McPherson, or order, annually in quarterly payts., during his life, half pay of a lieut.

McQuinny, Thomas. Passed Feb. 19, 1819—No. 76. Treas. Western Shore pay to Thomas McQuinny, late a rev. soldier, quarterly, during life, the half pay of a private.

* *McQuinny, Thomas,* private, Md. Line (Jan. 1820, p. 548).

McPherson, Mark. Passed Feb. 10, 1848—No. 23. Treas. pay to Christian Keener, atty. for Walter McPherson, executor of Mark McPherson, $80.00, amt. due said McPherson, a rev. pensioner at the time of his death.

* *Mackeon, John,* private, Pa. Line (Jan. 1820, p. 547).

Macky, James, Esq. Com'd. Capt. of a Company in Elk Batt'n. of Militia in Cecil Co. Given at Annapolis, Apr. 21, 1778. Th. Johnson. (X, No. 123).

Magee, Wm. Passed Feb. 15, 1830—No. 36. Treas. Western Shore pay unto Sarah Magee, of Saint Mary's county, amt. of money due Wm. Magee, her deceased husband, a pensioner of this State. (Indexed under "Revolutionary pensions").

Magruder, Henderson. Capt. of a Militia Co. in Prince George's County, 25th Battn. Jan. 3, 1776—see Wootters, Richard.

Magruder, Hezekiah, Gentleman. Com'd. 1st. Lieut. of Capt. Wm. Bayly's Co. of Militia in the 29th. Battn. in Montgomery County. Given at Annapolis, Aug. 29, 1777. Th. Johnson (X, No. 125).

Resigned May 7, 1782.

Magruder, Lieut. Nathaniel B. Passed Dec. session, 1815 (Jan. 23, 1816)—No. 20. Treas. Western Shore, pay to Nathaniel B. Magruder, late a lieut. in the rev. war, or order, a sum of money annually in quarterly payts., equal to the half pay of a lieut., as a further remuneration for those services rendered his country in her struggle for liberty & independence.

* *Magruder*, *Nathaniel B.*, private, Md. Line (Jan. 1820, p. 548).

† *Magruder*, *Nathaniel B.*, private, Md. Line age 62. Pensioned Mch. 9, 1819, from Apr. 4, 1818 at $96.00 per an. Recd. $349.86 and died Nov. 25, 1821. (U. S. Pens. Roll, 1835, p. 26).

Magruder, *Samuel Briscoe*. Capt. of a Co. of Militia in Lower Battalion, Montgomery Co., after Aug. 4, 1780—see Willcoxen, Jesse.

Mahoney, *Clement*. Passed Dec. session, 1815 (Jan. 23, 1816)—No. 5. Treas. Western Shore pay to Clement Mahoney, an old rev. soldier,—during his life, a sum of money equal to the half pay of a private.

Mahooney, *Edward*. Passed Nov. session, 1811—No. 60 (Jan. 4, 1812). Treas. Western Shore pay to Edward Mahooney, late a private in the rev. war, half pay of a private, &c.

* *Mahony*, *Edward*, private, Md. Line (Jan. 1820, p. 547).

Mantz, *Maj*. *Peter*. Passed Feb. 20, 1846—No. 23. Treas. of State pay to Catharine Mantz, widow of Peter Mantz, a Maj. of the Rev., during her life, quarterly, half pay of a Major, in consideration of the services of her husband.

Manyard, *Nathan*, Esq. Com'd. Capt. of a Company of Militia in Frederick Co. Given at Annapolis, Oct. 13, 1777. Th. Johnson, (X, No. 126). (See also Mobberly, Lewis).

Recommended as Officers of the within Company: George Burkett, Jr. Capt., Christopher Burkett, 1st. Lieut., John Woolf, Ensign.

Markland, *Lieut*. *Edward*. Passed Feb. 25, 1824—No. 3, (p. 172). Treas. to pay to Edward Markland, of Baltimore, half pay of a lieut. of the naval service, as further remuneration for his services during the rev. war.

Passed Jan. 30 1839—No. 12. Treas. Western Shore pay to Alice Markland, widow of Edward Markland, during her life, quarterly, from Apr. 1, 1838, an annual pension equal to that which her late husband received from Md. under resolution of Dec. session 1823, the half pay of a Lieut. in the Naval service, during the rev. war.

* *Marr*, *Wm*., private, Md. Line—died July 3, 1819 (Jan. 1820, p. 547).

Marr, *Wm*. Passed Feb. 10, 1836—No. 18. Treas. Western Shore pay to Arra Marr, widow of Wm. Marr, a soldier of the rev., half pay of a private, during her life.

* *Marshall*, *Benjamin*, private, Pa. Line (Jan. 1820, p. 548).

† *Marshall*, *Benj*., private, Pa. Line, age 74, from Frederick county. Pensioned[b] Mch. 6, 1819, at $96.00 per an. from Nov. 13, 1818. (Recd. $1,469.86. U. S. Pens. Roll, 1835, p. 36).

Marshall, *Benj*. Mch. 9, 1826—No. 105, p. 260. Reg. of land office directed to issue warrant for 50 a. unappropriated in Allegany county, unpatented, as a donation for the state to rev. soldiers who served in the Md. Line, & to which they consider him entitled.

Marshall, John. Passed Mch. 22, 1833—No. 80. Treas. Western Shore pay to John Marshall, of Cecil county, during life, quarterly, half pay of a private, in consideration of services rendered by him during the rev. war.

Martin, Ennals, Dr. Passed Jan. 17, 1833—No. 2. Treas. Western Shore pay to Dr. Ennals Martin, of Talbot county, a surgeon's mate during the rev. war, half yearly, half pay of surgeon's mate, for the services rendered by him during said war.

Passed Feb. 11, 1835—No. 9. Treas. Western Shore pay to Sarah Martin, widow of Dr. Ennals Martin, of Talbot county, Surgeon's mate in the army of the revolution, half pay to which her husband was entitled, during her life.

Martin, Henry. Passed Feb. 5, 1828—No. 12. Treas. Western Shore pay to Henry Martin, of Frederick county, during life, half yearly, half pay of a private, as further comp. his services during rev. war.

Martin, Jacob. Passed Mch. 9, 1846—No. 47. Treas. of Md. pay to Margaret Martin, of Westmoreland county, Pa., widow of Jacob Martin, a rev. soldier with the Md. troops, during life, quarterly, half pay of a private, in consideration of services rendered by her husband during the war of the Rev.

* *Martin, Philip*, private, Md. Line (Jan. 1820, p. 547).

* *Massey, Henry*, private, Md. Line (Jan. 1820, p. 547).

* *Massey, Jesse*, private, Del. Line (Jan. 1820, p. 548).

Matthews, Bennett, Esq. Com'd. Capt. of the Row Galley called the Independance. Given by the Delegates of the Freemen of Md. Given in Convention at Annapolis (date and signatures torn off) (X, No. 128).

Maxwell, James. Passed Nov. session, 1811—No. 14. Treas. Western Shore pay to James Maxwell, of Cecil county, late a meritorious soldier in the rev. war, half pay of a corporal, as a provision to him in his indigent situation, now advanced in life, and as a further remuneration to him for those services by which his country has been so essentially benefitted.

* *Maxwell, W^{m}.*, private, Del. Line (Jan. 1820, p. 547).

* *Mayhugh, Jonathan*, private, Md. Line (Jan. 1820, p. 547).

Mayhew, Jonathan. Feb. 19, 1819—No. 77. Treas. Western Shore to pay to Jonathan Mayhew, late a rev. soldier, during life, half pay of a private.

Passed Mch. 4, 1834—No. 32. Treas. Western Shore pay to Eleanor L. Mayhugh, widow of Jonathan Mayhugh, of Washington county, during life, quarterly, half pay of a private, for the services rendered by her husband during the rev. war.

Mayhew, Jonathan. Passed Jan. 24, 1838—No. 2. Treas. Western Shore pay to Adam Houk, son-in-law of the late Eleanor L. Mayhugh,

$8.00 for two months and twelve days pension due thes aid Eleanor L. Mayhugh on Dec. 12, 1837, the day of her death.

Maynadier, Wm., Esq. Com'd. Capt. of a Company in the 4th Battn. of Militia in Talbot Co. Given at Annapolis, Apr. 9, 1778. Th. Johnson (X, No. 129).

(Endorsement) Levin Spedding, Capt.; Edwd. Stevens, 1st. Lieut.; John Brown, 2d Lieut.; Wm. Berry, Ensign; Henry Banning, Com.

Mayo, Lieut. Isaac. War of 1812. Mch. 14, 1828—No. 61. Resolution of Gen. Assembly enumerating service of Lieut. Isaac Mayo, a native of Md., "and was among those officers who received medals from the U. S., as a testimony of their country's approbation."

Governor authorized to draw on Treas. of Western Shore for payment of a suitable sword.

Michael, Jacob. War of 1812. Feb. 19, 1819—No. 22. Treas. Western Shore is directed to pay to Jacob Michael of Harford county, $45.29 cents "for supplying the Militia stationed at Stoney Point, in the county aforesaid, during the late war with powder, lead and flints."

Meddagh, Frederick. Passed Nov. session 1801—No. 15. Several county courts of the Western and Eastern Shore respectively, do, and they are hereby authorized and required, upon the application of Frederick Meddagh, of Frederick county, an old and superannuated soldier of the late American army, to grant him from year to year, during his life, a license to hawk and peddle, without his the said Frederick Meddagh paying anything therefor.

Medlar, Bostian. Passed Dec. session 1815—No. 11. Treas. Western Shore pay to Bostian Medlar, late a drum-major in the rev. war—half pay of a drum-major, as a further remuneration for those services by which his country has been so essentially benefitted.

† *Meek, John,* private, Rev. army[a]. Pensioned, Act of June 7, 1785, from Mch. 4, 1789, at $40.00 per an.; recd. $400.00. (U. S. Pens. Roll, 1835, p. 21).

Merrick, Wm. Feb. 16, 1820—No. 44. Treas. Western Shore is directed to pay to Wm. Merrick, of Dorchester county, half pay of a corporal, for his rev. war services.

Merryman, Luke. Passed Mch. 16, 1836—No. 51. Treas. Western Shore pay to Elizabeth Merryman, widow of Luke Merryman, a soldier of the rev., half pay of a private during life, in consideration of his rev. services.

Mezzeek, Nehemiah. Ensign Friendship Co., Dorchester Militia, Jan. 1776—see Elliott, John.

Middleton, David. War of 1812. Draft to be drawn by Gov. & council of Md. to David Middleton "for riding express during the late war." Jan. 27, 1825—No. 8, p. 157.

Middleton, Gilbert. Jan. 25, 1823—No. 11. Treas. of Western Shore is directed to pay to Gilbert Middleton, of Baltimore, half pay of a captain for his services during rev. war.

Middleton, Sarah, of Baltimore. Feb. 9, 1822. (No. 22, p. 176). Treas. Western Shore directed to pay pension—half pay of a Captain, as a further compensation for services rendered by her husband during the rev. war.

Milburn, Nicholas. Passed Nov. session 1812 (Dec. 30) No. 21. Treas. Western Shore pay to Nicholas Milburn, late a private in the Md. Line during the rev. war,—half pay of a private.

* *Milburn, Nicholas,* private, Md. Line (Jan. 1820, p. 547).

Miles, Capt. Joshua. Passed Apr. 2, 1836—No. 93. Treas. Western Shore pay to Jane Miles, widow of Joshua Miles, an officer of the rev., half pay of a captain, in consideration of the services of her husband.

Amended June 4, 1836—No. 115 by addition of words: "during her natural life."

* *Miller, George,* private, Md. Line (Jan. 1820, p. 548).

Miller, George. Passed Mch. 2, 1827—No. 36. Treas. Western Shore pay to George Miller of city of Baltimore, during life, half yearly, half pay of a private as further remuneration for his services during the rev. war.

Mills, Cornelius H.—see Halkerstone, Robert.

Mills, Zachariah. Passed Feb. 12, 1820—No. 43. Treas. pay to Zachariah Mills, of Anne-Arundel county, an old revolutionary soldier, quarterly, for life, a sum equal to half pay of a private, as a further remuneration for those services rendered his country during her arduous struggle for independence.

* *Mills, Zachariah,* private, Md. Line (Jan. 1820, p. 548).

Minitree, Paul. Passed Feb. 19, 1819—No. 54 Treas. directed to pay Paul Minitree, an old rev. soldier of Charles county, half pay of a private, for his rev. war services.

* *Mitchell, Charles,* private, Flying Camp—not continental; stricken from roll (Jan. 1820, p. 547).

* *Mittag, or Meddack, Frederick,* private, Md. Line (Jan. 1820, p. 548).

Montle, or Mondle, Geo. Passed Dec. session, 1817 (Feb. 10, 1818)—No. 27. Treas. Western Shore pay to George Montle, or Mondle, now of the state of Pa. and late a soldier in the Md. Line during the rev. war, or his order, a sum of money annually, quarterly payts., equal to the half pay of a soldier, as a further remuneration for those meritorious services rendered his country during the American war.

Moore, John. Passed Nov. 1798—No. 17. Treas. Western Shore pay to John Moore, late soldier in the extra Md. reg. the sum of $22.00.

Moore, Capt. John C. (War of 1812?) Mch. 1, 1826—No. 62, p. 248. Governor and council "requested to examine the claim of Capt. John C.

Moore, for the repair of arms and equipment of the accoutrements of his company, and to make such allowance as they may consider him entitled to."

More, Nicholas Ruxton, Gentleman. Com'd. 3[d] Lieut. of a Company of Matrosses to be raised in this Province for the defence of the Liberties thereof Commanded by Capt. John Fulford. Given in Council of Safety at Baltimore Town, Mch. 1, 1776. Daniel of St. Thos. Jenifer, Charles Carroll, Benjamin Rumsey, Th. B. Hands, Thos. Smyth. (X, No. 133).

Moore, Lieut. Nicholas R. Passed Mch. 4, 1834—No. 36. Treas. Western Shore pay to Sarah Moore (widow of Nicholas R. Moore), of Baltimore county, during life, quarterly, half pay of a Lieut., for the services rendered by her husband during the rev. war.

Moore, Capt. Nicholas R. Passed Feb. 7, 1840—No. 6. Treas. Western Shore pay to Sarah Moore, widow of Nicholas R. Moore, of Baltimore city, during life, quarterly, commencing Jan. 1, 1840, a sum equal to the half pay of a captain of cavalry, in lieu of half pay of a lieut, heretofore granted, in consideration of the services rendered by the husband during the rev. war.

Moore, Reuben. Passed Feb. 19, 1819—No. 62. Treas. directed to pay to Reuben Moore, of Dorchester county, late a private in the rev. war, half pay of a private, as a further remuneration for his services during the rev. war.

* *Moore, Reuben*, private, Md. Line (Jan. 1820, p. 548).

Moore, Reuben. Passed Mch. 9, 1827—No. 48. Treas. pay to Mary Moore, of Dorchester county, during life, half yearly, half pay of a private for her husband, Reuben Moore's services during the rev. war.

Moore, W[m]. Passed Mch. 21, 1833—No. 65. Treas. Western Shore pay to W[m]. Moore, of Somerset county, during life, quarterly, half pay of a private, in consideration of services rendered by him during the rev. war.

Passed Feb. 11, 1835—No. 8. Treas. Western Shore pay to Samuel T. Moore, the sum of money due to his father, W[m]. Moore, of Somerset county, at the time of his death, in virtue of a resolution of the Legislature, granting a pension to said Moore.

Morris, John. Passed Apr. session 1792—No. 2. John Morris, of St. Mary's county, late a soldier in the third Md. regt. in the service of the U. S., is disabled from wounds recd. at the battle of the Cowpens, and is thereby incapable of getting a livelihood,—Resolved, That his excellency the governor of Md., for the time being, grant to John Morris, in future, half of the monthly pay which the said Morris received in the continental service, by orders drawn quarterly on the treasurer of the Western Shore for the same, and that the same be charged to the United States.

Morris, Jonathan, Capt. Passed Feb. 2, 1830—No. 13. Treas. pay to Jonathan Morris, a captain in the rev. war, half pay of a captain, quarterly, as further remuneration for his services during the rev. war.

Mudd, Bennett. Passed Feb. 19, 1819—No. 59. Treas. Western Shore pay to Bennett Mudd, of Charles county, an old soldier, during life, half pay of a sergeant.

Passed June 4, 1836—No. 118. Treas. pay to Ann Mudd, widow of Bennett Mudd, late a sergeant in the rev. war, quarterly, during life, half pay of a sergeant, for the services of her said husband, in the said rev.

* *Mudd, Bennett,* private, Md. Line (Jan. 1820, p. 548).

Mudd, Mrs. Barbara. Passed Feb. 1, 1834—No. 13. Treas. Western Shore pay to Mrs. Barbara Mudd, of D. C., during life, quarterly, half pay of a Sergeant, in consideration of the services rendered by her husband, during the rev. war.

Mudd, Ann. Passed Mch. 10, 1835—No. 5. Treas. Western Shore pay to Ann Mudd, $24.17, the bal. of pension due her husband at the time of his death, and which was forfeited to the State by resolution No. 26, of 1823.

Muir, Thomas. Passed Feb. 2, 1832—No. 25. Treas. Western Shore pay to Thomas Muir, a soldier of rev. war, during life, half yearly, half pay of private for his services during said war.

Passed Jan. 24, 1839—No. 9. Treas. Western Shore pay to Levin Ballard, of Jarvis, $9.66, for 2 months and 27 days pension due the late Thomas Muir, of Somerset county, at the time of his death, and said Ballard distribute the same to nearest of kin of said Muir.

Murdock, Lieut. Benj. Passed Dec. session, 1817 (Feb. 6, 1818)—No. 27. Treas. Western Shore pay to Benj. Murdock, a lieut. in the Md. Line during the rev. war, the half pay of a lieut. during life.

Murdock, Lieut. Wm. Passed Mch. 4, 1834—No. 34. Treas. Western Shore pay to Jane Clagett, widow of Wm. Murdock, an officer of the rev., during her widowhood, quarterly, half pay of a Lieut. in consideration for the services of her husband.

Nagle, Richard. Passed Feb. 14, 1828—No. 16. Treas. Western Shore pay to Richard Nagle, of Cambria Co. Pa. during life, half yearly, half pay of a private, for his rev. war services.

Neale, Capt. Henry. Passed Mch. 10, 1837—No. 35. Treas. Western Shore pay to Eleann Neale, widow of Capt. Henry Neale, half pay of a Captain, as a further remuneration for his [rev.] services, during her life.

Neale, James. Passed Nov. session 1803—No. 5. Treas. Western Shore pay to James Neale, on application, fifteen pounds current money, and the further sum of fifteen pounds like money annually, in quarterly payments, as a support to him in his infirm situation, and in consideration of his many services as a soldier in the late rev. war, from the effects of which he has been rendered entirely unable to obtain a subsistence.

Needham, Wm. A. Passed Nov. 1791—No. 8. Petition to Gen. Assembly sets forth that he was a sergeant in the late Amer. army, and received a wound by a musket ball which passed through his body & has rendered him incapable of gaining a subsistence by labour; and this assembly considering it reasonable that the same relief should be extended to said Wm. A. Needham, as to others in similar circumstances—Governor Grant to said Wm. A. Needham half of monthly pay he recd. in the continental service, by orders drawn quarterly on Treas. of Western Shore, & same be charged to the U. S.

† *Needham, Wm. A.* sergeant, Rev. army, of Montgomery county. Pensioned at $60.00 per an. from Sept. 4, 1808 (recd. $390.00). (U. S. Pens. Rolls, 1835, p. 16).

† *Nelson, Roger,* lieut. of cav., Rev. army, of Frederick county. Pensioned at $200.00 per an. on May 31, 1815, under act of Mch. 3, 1803, dating from Sept. 4, 1802 (recd. $2,552.21). Died June 7, 1815. (U. S. Pens. Rolls, 1835, p. 13).

Nelson, Roger. Passed Mch. 4, 1834—No. 37. Treas. Western Shore pay to Eliza Nelson, widow of Roger Nelson, of Frederick county, a rev. officer, half pay during life, to which her husband would have been entitled.

Nelson, Lieut. Roger. Passed Mch. 27, 1839—No. 39. Treas. Western Shore pay to Eliza Nelson, widow of Roger Nelson, of Frederick county, a rev. officer, or to her order, half pay of a lieut. in the rev. army, from July 1, 1815, up to the time she was placed on the pension roll, it being the amount to which she is entitled under the resolution of 1779.

Newman, John. Passed Dec. session, 1816—No. 11. Treas. Western Shore pay to John Newman, quarterly, half pay of a sergeant, as a further remuneration for those services by which his country has been so essentially benefitted.

* *Newman, John,* private, Md. Line (Jan. 1820, p. 548).

Newman, John. Passed Jan. 30, 1830—No. 5. Treas. Western Shore pay to Wm. Ridgely, esq., $15.33, being sum due to John Newman, a rev. soldier, late a pensioner of the state of Md., who was placed on the pension list by a resolution of said state.

Newton, John. Passed Dec. session, 1817 (Feb. 7, 1818)—No. 24. Treas. Western Shore pay to John Newton, an old soldier, during life, quarterly, the half pay of a private, for his services during the rev.

* *Newton, John,* private Md. Line (Jan. 1820, p. 548).

Niblet, Wm. Passed Dec. session, 1816—No. 18. Treas. Western Shore pay to Wm. Niblet, of Worcester county, an old rev. soldier, quarterly, during his life, the half pay of a private, as a further remuneration to him for his services by which his country has been so much benefitted.

* *Niblet, Wm.*, private, Md. Line (Jan. 1820, p. 548).
* *Nickle, John*, private, Md. Line (Jan. 1820, p. 548).
* *Nixon, Isaac*, private, N. J. Line (Jan. 1820, p. 548).

Nowell, James, Tutwiller, Jonathan. Passed Nov. session, 1812 (Jan. 2, 1813)—No. 35. Treas. Western Shore pay to James Nowell and Jonathan Tutwiller, or order, in quarterly payts, a sum of money equal to the half pay of privates during the rev. war.

O'Bryan, Dennis. Passed Feb. 20, 1830—No. 32. Treas. of Western Shore pay to Dennis O'Bryan, of Morgan county, Va., an old rev. soldier, during life, quarterly, half pay of a private, for his services during the rev. war.

O'Conner, Michael. Passed Nov. session, 1812—No. 61. Treas. Western Shore pay to Michael O'Conner, of Harford county,—half pay of a matross, as a further remuneration for those services rendered his country during the rev. war.

* *O'Conner, Michael*, private, Md. Line (Jan. 1820, p. 549).

O'Hara, John. Passed Mch. 3, 1840—No. 14. Treas. Western Shore pay to Susan O'Hara, widow of John O'Hara, a rev. soldier, or order, quarterly, during life, the half pay of a private, from Jan. 1, 1840, in consideration of the services of her husband rendered during the rev. war.

* *Oldwine, Barney*, private, Pa. Line (Jan. 1820, p. 549).
* *Oldwine, Charles*, private, Pa. Line (Jan. 1820, p. 549).

Orem, Spedden—Feb. 18, 1825—No. 23, p. 159. Treas. to pay Spedden Orem, of Talbot co.—half pay of a private further remun. for his services during rev. war.

Orme, Moses. Passed Mch. 8, 1833—No. 49. Treas. Western Shore pay to Moses Orme, of Anne-Arundel county, a soldier of the rev. war, during life, quarterly, half pay of a private, in consideration of the services rendered by him during said war.

Orndorff, Capt. Christian. Passed Feb. 19, 1819—No. 82. Treas. Western Shore directed to pay to Christian Orndorff, late a rev. officer, during life, the half pay of a captain.

* *Orendorf, Christian*, captain, Md. Line (Jan. 1820, p. 548).
* *Ott, Adam*, lieut. Pa. Line (Jan. 1820, p. 549).

Ott, Lieut. Adam. Passed Feb. 22, 1822 (No. 46, p. 179). Treas. Western Shore is directed to pay to Adam Ott, of Washington county,—half pay of a Lieut.—his services Rev. War.

Passed Mch. 12, 1828—No. 44. Treas. Western Shore pay to Julian Ott, of Washington county, during life, half yearly, half pay of a lieut. as further compensation for her husband, Adam Ott's services during rev. war.

Ott, Adam. Passed Feb. 20, 1829—No. 25. Treas. pay to Juliana Ott, widow of Adam Ott, a rev. soldier, such sum as may appear to be due him on the pension list of state of Md. at time of his decease.

Page, John. Capt. of Troop of Horse in Kent Co. May 30, 1781—see Raisin, Thos.

* *Painter, Melcher*, private, Md. Line (Jan. 1820, p. 549).

Painter, Melchior. Passed Apr. 1, 1839—No. 62. Treas. Western Shore pay to Mary Painter, of Washington county, widow of Melchior Painter, a Rev. soldier, or to her order, half pay of a private of the Rev. during her life, quarterly, commencing Jan. 1, 1839.

* *Pamphilion, Thomas*, mariner, Frigate Virginia (Jan. 1820, p. 549).

Parran, Thomas. Passed Mch. 11, 1828—No. 40. Warrant and patent for 200 acres vacant land westward of Fort Cumberland, Alleghany county, to issue to heirs of Thomas Parran without payment or any composition money. (Follows No. 39, Chesley Robt. captain 200 acres) but does not specify service.

Parran, Dr. Thomas. Passed Mch. 14, 1828—No. 52. Treas. Western Shore pay to Mrs. Jane Parran, of Calvert county, during life, half yearly, half pay of a surgeon, as further remuneration for her husband Dr. Thomas Parran's services during the rev. war.

Passed Jan. 14, 1830—No. 4. Treas. pay to legal representatives of Jane Parran (deceased) the balance of pension due her at time of her death.

Parrish, Edward. Passed Mch. 2, 1827—No. 32. Treas. Western Shore pay to Edward Parrish, of Baltimore county, during life, half yearly, half pay of a sergeant, for his services during the rev. war.

Passed Feb. 24, 1836—No. 49. Treas. Western Shore pay to James Nelson, for use of Clemmency Parrish, widow of Edward Parrish, deceased, late of Baltimore county, a soldier of the rev., it being the amt. due said Parrish for rev. services, at time of his decease.

Parrish, Edward. Passed Mch. 16, 1836—No. 53. Treas. Western Shore pay to Clemency Parrish, widow of Edward Parrish, a soldier of the rev., half pay of a "serjant" during her life.

Parrot, Christopher. Passed Dec. session, 1816—No. 29. Treas. Western Shore pay to Christopher Parrot, late a sergeant in the rev. war, during life, quarterly, a sum equal to the half pay of a sergeant.

* *Parsons, Daniel*, private, Del. Line (Jan. 1820, p. 549).

Paul, Thomas. Passed Mch. 7, 1840—No. 22. Treas. Western Shore pay to Catharine Paul, widow of Thomas Paul, a soldier of the rev., or order, quarterly, for life, from Jan. 1, 1840, the half pay of a sergeant, in consideration of the services of her said husband in the rev. war.

Peacock, Neale. Passed Nov. session, 1812 (Jan. 2, 1813)—No. 48. Treas. Western Shore pay to Neale Peacock, quarterly, half pay of a private in the rev. war.

Pearce, George. Passed Mch. 1, 1833—No. 37. Treas. Western Shore pay to George Pearce, of Warren county, Ky., a soldier of the rev. war, during life, quarterly, half pay of a private, for the services rendered by him during the rev. war.

* *Peck, Hiel,* lieut. N. Y. Line (Jan. 1820, p. 549).

Pegegram, W^m^. Passed Nov. session, 1811—No. 23. Treas. Western Shore pay to W^m^. Pegegram, of Anne-Arundel county, an old rev. soldier—the half pay of a common soldier, during his life, as a further remuneration for the services rendered his country.

Pendergast, Lieut. W^m^. Passed Feb. 11, 1835—No. 41. Treas. Western Shore pay to Juliet Onion, widow of W^m^. Pendergast, an officer of the revolution, half pay of a lieut., quarterly, during her life, for the services of her husband.

* *Penefill, Thomas,* private, Md. Line (Jan. 1820, p. 549).

Penefield, Thomas. Passed Mch. 20, 1835—No. 76. Treas. Western Shore pay to Hester Penefield, widow of Thomas Penefield, a soldier of the rev., half pay of a private, quarterly, during her widowhood.

Penn, John. Feb. 16, 1820—No. 46. Treas. Western Shore is directed to pay to John Penn of Charles county, during life, half pay of a private for his rev. war services.

Pensions. Disbursed during year ended Sept. 30, 1855 $3,227.42 and $960.00 unexpended.

* *Peterson, Henry,* private, N. J. Line (Jan. 1820, p. 549).

* *Phelan, John,* captain, Mass. Line (Jan. 1820, p. 549).

Philips, Stephen. Feb. 16, 1820—No. 37. Treas. is directed to pay to Stephen Phillips, of Caroline county, a coloured man, for life, half pay of a private for his rev. war services.

Passed Feb. 15, 1844—No. 21. Treas. Western Shore pay to Jacob Charles $13.33 being amt. advanced by said Charles to Stephen Phillips, a soldier of the rev. war.

Pindell, Nicholas. Passed Feb. 18, 1830—No. 32. Gov. & council directed to ascertain amount due Nicholas Pindell, a rev. soldier, at time of his death; and Treas. Western Shore is required to pay to Gassaway Pindell, admr. of Nicholas Pindell, such sum as shall be found due to said Pindell at death.

Pindell, Dr. Richard. Passed Dec. session, 1816—No. 58. Treas. Western Shore pay to Richard Pindell, of Ky., late a surgeon in the U. S. army during the rev. war, quarterly, during life, a sum of money equal to the *full pay* of a surgeon, as a further remuneration for those services he rendered his country during her struggle for independence.

Plane, Jacob. Passed Feb. 24, 1830—No. 56. Treas. Western Shore pay to Catherine Plane, of Anne-Arundel county (widow of Jacob Plane, who was a soldier in the rev. war), during widowhood, quarterly, the half pay of a private, for the services of her late husband.

Poe, Captain, of Baltimore. Passed Feb. 9, 1822—No. 23, p. 176. Treas. Western Shore pay to Elizabeth Poe, of Baltimore, a sum of money equal to the half pay of a captain of the Md. Line.

* *Pollock, Elias*, private, Va. Line (Jan. 1820, p. 549).

* *Pope, John*, private, Md. Line (Jan. 1820, p. 549).

† *Pope, John*, private, Md. Line, age 68, from Frederick county. Died Mch. 3, 1821, Pensioned at $96.00 per an. on Oct. 8, 1818, from Apr. 10, 1818. (Recd. $278.40. U. S. Pens. Roll, 1835, p. 36).

Popham, Benjamin. Passed Mch. 12, 1827—No. 63. Treas. pay to Benjamin Popham, of Anne-Arundel county, during life, half yearly, half pay of a private, for his services during the rev. war.

Porter, Nathan. Feb. 18, 1825, No. 27, p. 159. Treas. to pay Nathan Porter, of Talbot county, half pay of a private, addl. comp. his rev. war services.

* *Poulson, John*, private, Del. Line (Jan. 1820, p. 549).

Powel, Brittian. Ensign of a Co. in Somerset County, 17th Battn. of Militia, 1777—see Schoolfield, Wm.

Powers, Jesse. Passed Dec. session 1815—No. 13. Treas. Western Shore pay unto Jesse Powers, of St. Mary's county, late a private in the rev. war—half pay of a private, as a further remuneration to him for those services by which his country has been so essentially benefitted.

* *Powers, Jesse*, private, Md. Line (Jan. 1820, p. 549).

Power, Jesse. Passed Feb. 25, 1836—No. 41. Treas. Western Shore pay to Milly Power, widow of Jesse Power, a soldier of the rev., during widowhood half pay of a private, for the services of her late husband.

Power, Jesse. Passed Jan. 13, 1845—No. 6. Treas. pay to Henry Fowler, for use of Clement Thompson, legal representative of Milly Power, bal. due her at time of her death, on the pension list of the State.

Price, George. Passed Mch. 2, 1827—No. 31. Treas. pay to George Price, of Talbot county, during life, half yearly, half pay of a private, as further remuneration for his services during the rev. war. Passed Mch. 13, 1829—No. 61. Treas. pay to legal representatives of George Price, deceased, the balance of pension due the said George Price, at time of his death.

Price, Stephen R. Passed Feb. 24, 1830—No. 47. Treas. Western Shore pay to Stephen R. Price, of Mifflin twp. Franklin county, Ohio, a soldier in the rev. war, during life, quarterly, half pay of a quarter master sergeant, as further remuneration for his services during the rev. war.

* *Price, Walter Lane*, lieutenant, navy. Frigate Alliance (Jan. 1820, p. 549).

* *Primm, James*, private, Va. Line (Jan. 1820, p. 549).

Proctor, Richard. Passed Jan. 6, 1812—No. 40. Treas. Western Shore pay to Richard Proctor, late a private in the rev. war, belonging to the Md. Line, quarterly, the half pay of a private, as a provision to him in his indigent situation and advanced life, and as a further remuneration to him for those services by which his country has been so essentially benefitted.

Pruitt, Walter. Passed Mch. 9, 1827—No. 46. Treas. pay to Walter Pruitt, of Worcester county, during life, half yearly, half pay of a private for his services during the rev. war.

Purnell, Zadock, Esq. Com'd Colonel of the Synnapuxent Battalion of Militia in Worcester Co. Given at Baltimore Town Aug. 30, A.D. 1777. Th. Johnson. (X, No. 152).

Endorsement: Col. Zadock Purnell resigned 1778.

To his Excellency Thomas Johnson, Esq. Sir: Being now advanced in years, and at times much affected, I have thought it Expedient to Resign in favour of a younger man and therefore have Delivered my Commission to the Lieut. of this County.

I have the Honor to be your Obt. Servt. Zadock Purnell.

Queen, Marsham. Passed Mch. 13, 1832—No. 106. Treas. Western Shore pay to Marsham Queen, of Charles county, during life, half yearly, half pay of a private, in consideration of his services during the rev. war.

Quinny, Thomas M. Feb. 19, 1819—No. 76. Treas. Western Shore to pay to Thomas M. Quinny, late a rev. soldier, quarterly during life, the half pay of a private.

Raisin, Thomas, Gentleman. Com'd. Cornet of Capt. John Page's Troop of Horse in Kent Co. raised with Notice of an Act to encourage the raising a Volunteer Troop of light Horse in Baltimore Town and each County of this State. Given at Annapolis, May 30, 1781. Tho. S. Lee. (X, No. 154).

Endorsement: Thos. Raisin resigns as Cornet of Horse Kent Co. May 1782.

* *Ramsay, James*, ensign, Md. Line (Jan. 1820, p. 549).

Rasin, Lieut. W^{m}. B. Passed Nov. session 1804—No. 14. Treas. of Eastern Shore pay to W^{m}. B. Rasin, of Kent county, late a lieut. in the rev. war, or order, the half pay as a lieut., annually, quarterly payts., during his life, as a further reward to those meritorious services which he rendered his country in establishing her liberty & independence.

* *Ratcliff, James*, private, Pa. Line (Jan. 1820, p. 549).

Rawlings, Samuel. Feb. 23, 1822—No. 55, p. 180. Treas. Western Shore is directed to pay to Ann Rawlings, widow of Samuel Rawlings, late of Washington county deceased,—half pay of private—services by her late husband during the Rev. war.

Rawlings, Solomon. Passed Feb. 19, 1819—No. 79. Treas. Western Shore to pay to Solomon Rawlings late a rev. soldier, during life, half pay of a private.

* *Rawlins, Solomon*, private, Md. Line (Jan. 1820, p. 549).

Ray, Joseph. Passed Dec. session, 1817—No. 21. Treas. Western Shore pay to Joseph Ray, an old soldier, of Montgomery county, quarterly, half pay of a private, for his services during the rev. war.

* *Ray, Joseph*, private, Md. Line (Jan. 1820, p. 549).

Reading, Henry. Passed Nov. session, 1811—No. 9. Treas. Western Shore pay to Henry Reading late a soldier in the rev. war belonging to the Md. Line, or order, quarterly, a sum equal to half pay of a private, a as provision, &c.; and further remuneration, &c.

† *Redenour, Jacob*, private, Rev. army, of Frederick county, Pensioned at $60.00 per an. on Nov. 19, 1819, under Act of Mch. 3, 1809, dating from Apr. 10, 1806 (rec'd. $602.33)—at $96.00 fee an. from Apr. 24, 1816 (recd. $1,090.66). (U. S. Pens. Rolls, 1835, p. 13).

Reed, Isaac. 2^d Lieut. Friendship Co., Dorchester Militia, Jan. 1776—see Elliott, John.

* *Reed, John, 2d.*, private, Md. Line (Jan. 1820, p. 550.)

Reid, John. Passed Nov. session, 1812 (Jan. 2, 1813)—No. 40. Treas. Western Shore pay to John Reid, of Allegany county, $125.00, during life, quarterly, as a further remuneration for the services rendered his country during the rev. war.

* *Reeves, W^m.*, private, Mass. Line (Jan. 1820, p. 549).

* *Reewark, James*, private, Md. Line (Jan. 1820, p. 549).

Reily, Capt. W^m. Passed Dec. session 1816—No. 30. Treas. Western Shore pay to W^m. Reily, of the District of Columbia, late a captain in the Md. Line in the rev. war, quarterly, the half pay of a captain, as a further remuneration for the gallant services rendered his country during the American war.

Reily, Maj. W^m. Passed Mch. 1, 1833—No. 40. Treas. Western Shore pay to Barbara Reily, of District of Columbia, widow of the late Maj. W^m. Reily, a soldier of the rev. war, during widowhood, half yearly, half pay of a captain in consideration of the services rendered by her husband during said war.

Rench, Andrew, Gentleman, Com'd. to be Lieut. Col. of the 32^d. Battn. of Militia of this Province, being of Frederick Co. Given in Convention at Annapolis, Jan. 3d., 1776. Signed pr. order Mat. Tilghman, Pres. (X, No. 156).

Reynolds, James. Passed Mch. 16, 1835—No. 50. Treas. Western Shore pay to Ruth Reynolds, widow of James Reynolds, a soldier of the rev., half pay of a private, quarterly, during his life.

Reynolds, Tobias. Passed Dec. session, 1817 (Feb. 7, '18)—No. 26. Treas. Western Shore pay to Tobias Reynolds, of Anne-Arundel county, an old soldier, quarterly, a sum of money equal to the half pay of a private [Rev. war].

* *Reynolds, Tobias,* private, Md. Line (Jan. 1820, p. 549).

* *Richards, Paul,* private, Md. Line (Jan. 1820, p. 550).

Richards, Paul. Passed Mch. 13, 1828—No. 50. Treas. Western Shore pay to representative of Mary Richards, widow of Paul Richards, who was a soldier of the revolution, such sum as may appear to have been due her, at time of her death.

Richardson, Charles. Passed Nov. session, 1812—No. 52. Treas. Western Shore pay to Chas. Richardson, late a soldier in the rev. war,—half pay of a private, as a provision to him in his indigent situation and advanced life, and as a further remuneration to him for those services by which his country has been so essentially benefitted.

Richardson, Charles. Feb. 16, 1820—No. 49. Treas. Western Shore is directed to pay to Nancy Richardson, widow of Charles Richardson, late a private in the rev. war, half pay of a private.

Passed Mch. 9, 1846—No. 49. Treas. of Md. pay to Lydia Ackworth, daughter of Nancy Richardson, whatever arrearages of pension may be found due the said Nancy Richardson at the time of her death.

* *Richardson, Charles,* private, Md. Line (Jan. 1820, p. 550).

Richardson, Daniel. Passed Nov. session, 1811—No. 25. Treas. Western Shore pay to Daniel Richardson—half pay of a private in the rev. war.

* *Richardson, Daniel,* private, Md. Line (Jan. 1820, p. 549).

* *Rickner, Daniel,* private, Pa. Line (Jan. 1820, p. 549).

Ridgely, Nicholas, Gentleman. Com'd. 2[d] Lieut. in Capt. Richard Stringer's Company of 22[d] Battn. of Militia. Given at Annapolis, Aug. 28, 1777. Th. Johnson. (X, No. 158). Endorsement: Resigned Apr. 13, 1781.

Ridgeway, John. 1st. Sergeant of a Co. in Prince George's Co. 25th. Battn., Jan. 3, 1776—see Wootters, Richd.

Rigby, W[m]. Passed Feb. 12, 1820—No. 29. Treas. pay to W[m]. Rigby of Fairfield county, Ohio, for life, quarterly, half pay of quartermaster sergeant, for his services during rev. war.

* *Riston, Zadock,* private, Md. Line (Jan. 1820, p. 550).

Risden, Zaddock (Riston). Passed Feb. 24, 1830—No. 48. Treas. Western Shore pay to Zaddock Risden, alias Riston, who was a soldier of the rev. war, of Prince George's county, during life, quarterly, half pay of a private, for his services during the rev. war.

Riston, Zadock. Passed Mch. 26, 1839—No. 42. Treas. Western Shore of Md. pay to Benj. Riston and Cassandra Ann King, or order, only children of Zadock Riston, late of Prince George's county, deceased, a pensioner, the bal. of pension due him from State of Md., at time of his death, and which he was entitled to under a res. of the Gen. Assembly.

Robbins, John. Passed Dec. session, 1817—No. 16. Treas. Western Shore pay to John Robbins, an old soldier, of Montgomery county, quarterly, the half pay of a private, as a further compensation for his revolutionary services.

* *Robbins, John,* private, Md. Line (Jan. 1820, p. 549).

* *Roberts, James,* private, Md. Line—died Jan. 6, 1810 (Jan. 1820, p. 549).

Roberts, Wm. Passed Dec. session 1815—No. 21. Treas. Western Shore pay to Wm. Roberts, of Allegany county, a private in the rev. war—half pay of a private, as a further remuneration to him for those services by which his country has been so essentially benefitted.

* *Roberts, Wm,* private, Md. Line (Jan. 1820, p. 550).

Roberts, Wm. Passed Mch. 4, 1834—No. 33. Treas Western Shore pay to Jane Roberts, of Allegany county, during life, quarterly, half pay of a private for the services rendered by her husband during the rev. war.

Passed Mch. 9, 1835—No. 24. Treas. Western Shore pay to Jane Roberts, widow of Wm. Roberts, deceased, $1.11, bal. due her deceased husband, as a rev. pensioner, at the time of his death.

Roberts, Wm. Passed Mch. 26, 1839—No. 40. Treas. Western Shore pay to Mary Roberts, of Allegany county, $9.89, for 2 mos. & 29 ds. pension due Jane Roberts, of Allegany county, at the time of her death, as a Rev. pensioner.

Roberts, Zachariah. Feb. 24, 1823—No. 55. Treas. Western Shore is directed to pay to Peter Levering, of Baltimore, or his executors the half pay of a corporal, for the support and maintenance of Zachariah Roberts, during his life as a compensation for services rendered in the rev. war.

Robinson, Standly. Feb. 25, 1824—No. 37, p. 172. Treas. to pay Standly Robinson, of Baltimore, half pay of a private, further remun. for his services as a private on board the Dolphin during the rev. war.

Robosson, Lieut. Charles. Passed Feb. 27, 1839—No. 21. Treas. Western Shore pay to Rebecca Robosson, of city of Baltimore, widow of Charles Robosson, a first lieut. in the rev. army, half pay of a first lieut. of the rev., during her life, quarterly, commencing Jan. 1, 1839.

Roby, John. Passed Dec. session, 1815—No. 6. Treas. Western Shore pay to John Roby, during life,—half pay of a private, for the services rendered his country during the rev. war.

† *Roe, Michael*, private, Rev. army, of Somerset county. Pensioned from Sept. 4, 1797 at $40.00 per annum (recd. $745.56)—at $64.00 per an. from Apr. 24, 1816 (recd. $54.11). (U. S. Pens. Roll, 1835, p. 18).

Rogers, Geo. W., Capt. War of 1812. Passed Jan. 19, 1830—No. 9. Resolution authorizing the Gov. to procure and present to Capt. George W. Rogers, native of Md., & a Capt. in the U. S. Navy, as further evidence of the high sense the Legislature entertain for the services he has rendered his country, during the late war—action between Wasp and the Frolic.

Rogers, Capt. Geo. W. Passed Mch. 15, 1833—No. 59. Resolution recites provisions of No. 9 (1830)—"it appears the said Geo. W. Rogers is now dead." Governor is authorized to present the said sword to Raymond Rogers, the eldest son of the deceased, in consideration for the gallantry of his deceased father, &c.

Rolle, Robert, Lieut. Passed Mch. 13, 1829—No. 65. Treas. pay to Robert Rolle, of Talbot county, during life, quarterly, half pay of a lieut. for his services during the rev. war.

Rowse, Lieut. Thos. Passed Nov. session, 1811—No. 13. Treas. Western Shore pay to Thos. Rowse, late a lieut. in the Md. Line of the rev. war, sum of money equal to half pay of a lieut., as further reward for those services rendered his country during the American war.

Rouark, James. Feb. 24, 1836—No. 42. Treas. Western Shore pay to Julia Rouark, widow of James Rouark, a soldier of the rev., half pay of a private, during her widowhood.

Ruark, James. Passed Mch. 7, 1838—No. 19. Treas. Western Shore pay to Barbara Ruark, the widow of James Ruark, the half pay of a private, during her life, as further remuneration for his services during the rev. war.

Passed Feb. 18, 1848—No. 26. Treas. pay to W[m]. Wells, of Anne Arundel county, the amt. due to Mrs. Barbara Ruark, at her death a pensioner.

* *Russell, Robert*, private, Pa. Line (Jan. 1820, p. 549).

Rutledge, Lieut. Joshua. Passed Nov. session 1812 (Jan. 2, 1813)—No. 41. Treas. Western Shore pay to Joshua Rutledge, of Harford county, late a lieut. in the Md. Line, or order, quarterly, equal to the half pay of a lieut., as a further remuneration for those services rendered his country during the rev. war.

Rutlage, Lieut. Joshua. Feb. 23, 1822—No. 61, p. 180. Whereas, Joshua Rutlage, of Harford county, a pensioner, is said to be wealthy, and the intention of this legislature is to assist such as stand in need, and not those that are living in affluence—Therefore.

Resolved, That the resolution passed at Nov. Session, 1812, directing the treas. of Western Shore to pay to Joshua Rutlage of Harford county, late a lieut. in the Md. Line—half pay of a lieut., as a further remuneration for his services rendered his country during the rev. war, be and the same is hereby rescinded.

Rutledge, Lieut. Joshua. Passed Mch. 3, 1840—No. 13. Treas. Western Shore pay to Elizabeth Brooks, of Harford county, widow of Joshua Rutledge, who was a lieut. in the rev. war, or to her order, quarterly, commencing Jan. 1, 1840, half pay of a lieut., in consideration of the services of her said husband rendered during the war of the rev.

* *Rutledge, Joshua*, lieut., Md. Line (Jan. 1820, p. 550).

Sansbury, John. Passed Feb. 7, 1840—No. 8. Treas. Western Shore pay to Sarah Sansbury, of Baltimore city, widow of John Sansbury, a private marine in the rev. war, or to her order, quarterly, commencing Jan. 1, 1840, the half pay of a private, during her life, in consideration of the services of her said husband.

Sappington, Dr. Richard. Passed Mch. 7, 1844—No. 34. Treas. of Md. pay to Cassandra Sappington, of Harford county, widow of Dr. Richard Sappington, who was a surgeon in the rev. war, quarterly, commencing on Jan. 1, 1844, half pay of Surgeon, during her life, as a further remuneration for the services of her deceased husband.

* *Savoy, Philip*, private, Md. Line (Jan. 1820, p. 550).

Schmuck, Jacob, Capt. Passed Jan. 20, 1835—No. 16. Governor directed to ascertain value of sword, directed under res. of Md. Assembly, last session, No. 98, to be presented to capt. Jacob Schmuck, late of the U. S. Army, and to present the amount thereof to Ellen Schmuck, widow of said Capt. Schmuck for the education of Catharine Schmuck, his daughter and only child.

Schmuck, Capt. Jacob. War of 1812. Resolution No. 98, passed Mch. 20, 1835, requesting the Governor to procure and present a sword to Capt. Jacob Schmuck, U. S. Army for his gallant services on the northwestern frontier, during the late war with Great Britain.

Schoolfield, Benj. Gentleman. Com'd. 2^d^ Lieut. of Capt. John William's Company in Princess Anne Battn. of Militia in Somerset Co. Given at Baltimore Town, Sept. 22, 1777. Th. Johnson. (X, No. 164).

Endorsement: 1st. Lieut. of W^m^. Key's Co. Endorsement on comn. of Schoolfield, W^m^.: Captain in 17th Battn.

Schoolfield, George. 2^d^ Lieut. of a Militia Co. in Somerset County, 17th Battn. 1776—see Schoolfield, W^m^.

Schoolfield, W^m^., Gentleman. Com'd. Ensign of a Co. in Somerset County in the 17th Battn. of Militia. Given in Convention at Annapolis, Jan. 3, 1776. Signed pr. order Mat. Tilghman, Pres. (Original Commission, No. 166).

Endorsement: Wm. Schoolfield, 1st. Lieut.; George Schoolfield, 2d. Lieut.; Brittian Powel, Ensign; M. George Waters, Com'dt, Ballard Bozman, 2d Lieut.; James Curtis, Ensign; Wm. Water, Corporal; Wm. Waller, Ensign in Thos. Irving's; Benj. Schoolfield, Capt.; Thos. Jones, 1st. Lieut.; Saml. Dixon, 2d Lieut. in 17th Battn.

Schrach, Andrew. Passed Mch. 12, 1829—No. 51. Treas. Western Shore pay to Andrew Schrach, of Baltimore city, during life, half yearly, half pay of a private, for his services during the rev. war.

* *Scislar, Philip*, private, Md. Line (Jan. 1820, p. 550).

Scott, Gustavus. Robey's Delight—Allegany Co. Aug. 1824—see Feb. 9, 1825, p. 157, No. 12. Also No. 15, Feb. 9, 1825.

Scott, Samuel. Passed Dec. session, 1816—No. 63. Treas. Western Shore pay to Samuel Scott, quarterly, the half pay of a private during his life, for those services he rendered his country during the rev. war.

* *Scott, Samuel*, private, Md. Line (Jan. 1820, p. 550).

Scott, Samuel. Passed Feb. 21, 1834—No. 23. Treas. Western Shore pay to Benj. L. Gantt, for use of Mrs. Elizabeth Scott, widow of the late Samuel Scott, of Prince George's county, a rev. soldier, $14.44, being amt. due him at death as a pensioner.

Passed Mch. 4, 1834—No. 42. Treas. Western Shore pay to Mrs. Elizabeth Scott, widow of Samuel Scott, of Prince George's county, during life, quarterly, half pay of a private, for the services of her husband during the rev. war.

Scott, Samuel. Passed Jan. 19, 1848—No. 11. State Treas. pay to Order of Wm. Scott, one of the legal representatives of Elizabeth Scott, late of Prince George's county, deceased, bal. of pension money due at her death.

Seaburn, John. Passed Nov. session, 1811—No. 12. Treas. Western Shore pay to John Seaburn, during life, quarterly, half pay of a private in rev. war.

Sears, John. Passed Jan. 26, 1828—No. 4. Treas. Western Shore pay to Mary Sears, of Harford county, during life, half yearly, half pay of a lieut., further remuneration for her husband, John Sears' services during the rev. war.

Second, George. Passed Nov. session, 1803—No. 3. Treas. Eastern Shore pay to George Second, or order, the sum of $54.00 per annum, half yearly payts., out of any money in the treasury not otherwise appropriated. (Indexed amongst rev. pensions).

Semmes, Lieut. James. Passed Nov. session, 1812—No. 59 Treas. Western Shore pay to James Semmes, of Charles county, late a second lieut. in the rev. war, or order, annually in quarterly payts., during his life a sum of money equal to the half pay of a second lieut.

Seney, John, Senr. Esq. Com'd. 1st. Major of 5th Battn. of Militia of Province of Md. Given in Convention at Annapolis, Jan. 3, 1776. Signed pr. order, Mat. Tilghman, Pres. (X, No. 169).

Sewall, Charles. Passed Feb. 12, 1820—No. 42. Treas. pay to Chas. Sewall, of Charles county, for life, quarterly, half pay of a first lieut., as a remuneration for his services during the rev. war.

* *Sewell, Charles*, ensign, Md. Line (Jan. 1820, p. 550).

Sewell, Clement. Feb. 24, 1823—No. 62, p. 147. Treas. Western Shore is directed to pay to Clement Sewell, of the D. C., late an ensign in the Md. Line in the rev. war, half pay of an ensign, as a remuneration for the gallant services rendered his country during the struggle for our glorious independence.

Sewell, James. Passed Dec. session, 1817 (Feb. 6, 1818)—No. 34. Treas. Western Shore pay to James Sewell, an old rev. soldier, quarterly, the half pay of a private, as a further remuneration for his services during the American war.

† *Sewall, James*, private Rev. army, of Anne Arundel county, pensioned May 16, 1817, at $60.00 per month from Mch. 4, 1803, under Act of Jan. 1, 1803 (received $788.33).

Pensioned Apr. 24, 1816 at $96.00 per year (received $178.66).

* *Sewell, John*, private, Md. Line (Jan. 1820, p. 550).

Sewell, Wm. Passed Nov. session, 1811—No. 11. Treas. Western Shore pay to Wm. Sewell, of Annapolis, late a soldier in the rev. war, or order, during life, quarterly payts., half pay of a private.

Sewell, Wm. Passed Feb. 22, 1822—No. 41, p. 178. Treas. Western Shore pay to Wm. Sewell, of Talbot county, half pay of a private, for his rev. war services.

Sewell, Wm. Passed Feb. 6, 1832—No. 16. Treas. Western Shore pay to Rebecca Sewell, widow of Wm. Sewell, a soldier of the rev. war, during life, half yearly, the half pay of a private, for the services rendered by her said husband.

Shean, Henry. Passed Mch. 12, 1828—No. 46. Treas. Western Shore pay Henry Shean, of Baltimore county, during life, half yearly, half pay of a private, as further remuneration for his services during rev. war.

Shane, Henry. Passed Feb. 7, 1830—No. 17. Treas. Western Shore pay to Henry W. Shane money due his father Henry Shane, a rev. soldier, at time of his decease.

Shaw, James, Gentleman. Com'd. 1st. Lieut of the Co. of Militia in Dorchester County called the Vienna Co. to which Hugh McBride was elected 1st. Lieut & since promoted. Given in Convention at Annapolis, Jan. 3, 1776. Signed pr. Order Mat. Tilghman, Pres. (X, No. 172). Resigned June 17, 1776.

Sheets, Jacob. Passed Jan. 26, 1828—No. 3. Treas. Western Shore pay to Hannah Sheets, of Frederick county, during life, in half yearly payments the half pay of a private, as further remuneration for her husband, Jacob Sheets' services during the rev. war.

Shircliff, Lieut. W^{m}. Passed Mch. 29, 1838—No. 55. Treas. Western Shore pay to Melinda Shircliff, widow of W^{m}. Shircliff, a soldier of the rev., the half pay of a lieut., as a further remuneration for his services, during her life.

Shirley, Bennet. Passed Jan. 19, 1837—No. 12. Treas. Western Shore pay to Susanna Shirley, widow of Bennet Shirley, half pay of private during her life, as a further remuneration for his services during the rev.

* *Shirtzer, Caspar*, private, Pa. Line (Jan. 1820, p. 551).

* *Shockley, John*, private, Md. Line (Jan. 1820, p. 551).

* *Shockney,Patrick*, private, Pa. Line (Jan. 1820, p. 551).

Shoebrook, Edward. Feb. 24, 1823—No. 70, p. 148. Treas. Western Shore is directed to pay to Joseph Boon of Caroline county, or his executors, for support and maintenance of Edward Shoebrook, during his life, as a compensation for services rendered in the rev. war.

Shotts, John. Passed Dec. session, 1817 (Feb. 7, 18)—No. 25. Treas. Western Shore pay to John Shotts, of Frederick county, an old soldier, quarterly, the half pay of a private during his life.

* *Shots, John*, private, Houseger's G. Regt. (Jan. 1820, p. 551).

* *Shrupp, Henry*, lieut., German Regt. (Jan. 1820, p. 550).

* *Shryock, John*, private, Md. Line (Jan. 1820, p. 550).

Shryock, John. Passed Mch. 16, 1835—No. 60. Treas. Western Shore pay to John Shryock, a soldier of the rev., half pay of a private, quarterly during his life.

* *Silence, W^{m}.*, private, Va. Line (Jan. 1820, p. 551).

Simmons, Aaron. Passed Feb. 19, 1819—No. 72. Treas. Western Shore to pay to Aaron Simmons, late a rev. soldier, or order, quarterly during life, half pay of a private.

Simmons, Sarah. Passed Mch. 4, 1834—No. 31. Treas. Western Shore pay to Sarah Simmons, of Charles county, during life, quarterly, half pay of a private, for the services rendered by her husband during the rev. war.

* *Simmons, W^{m}.*, private, Md. Line (Jan. 1820, p. 551).

Simpson, Lawrence. Passed Dec. session, 1816—No. 23. Treas. Western Shore pay to Lawrence Simpson, of Charles county (an old rev. soldier), quarterly, the half pay of a private soldier, as a further remuneration for his services in the rev. war.

Simpson, Lawrence. Passed Feb. 27, 1843—No. 24. Treas. Western Shore pay to Peter W. Crain, for the widow of Lawrence Simpson, bal. due said Lawrence Simpson, a rev. pensioner, at his death.

Simpson, Rezin. Passed Nov. session, 1812 (Jan. 2, 1813)—No. 37. Treas. Western Shore pay to Rezin Simpson, late a private in the rev. army, a sum of money annually, in quarterly payts., equal to the half pay of a soldier.

Simpson, Rezin. Passed Dec. session, 1815—No. 52. Treas. Western Shore pay to Rezin Simpson, quarterly, a sum of money equal to the half pay of a sergeant of dragoons, in lieu of the sum allowed him by a resolution of 1811 [1812].

* *Simpson, Rezin,* sergeant, Md. Line (Jan. 1820, p. 551).

Simpson, Rezin. Passed Feb. 18, 1830—No. 29. Treas. Western Shore pay to Robert Swan, for use of Mary Simpson, widow of the late Rezin Simpson, a pensioner of the state of Md., $27.50 balance due said Simpson at time of his decease. (Indexed as Rev. pension).

Simpson, Rezin. Passed Feb. 24, 1830—No. 60. Treas. Western Shore pay to Wm. Shaw, for use of Mary Simpson, of Allegany county, during widowhood, quarterly, half pay of sergeant for the services of her late husband, Rezin Simpson, who was a soldier of the rev. war.

Simpson, Thomas. Passed Nov. session, 1812—No. 62. Treas. Western Shore pay to Thomas Simpson, late a corporal in the rev. war—half pay of a corporal, as a further remuneration for those services rendered his country in her struggle for liberty & independence.

* *Sims, Patrick,* lieut. colonel, Md. Line—died Jan. 7, 1819 (Jan. 1820, p. 550).

Sizler, Philip. Passed Feb. 29, 1829—No. 31. Treas. pay to Philip Sizler, of Baltimore city, a soldier of the rev. war, during life, half yearly, half pay of a sergeant in the artillery, in consideration of his services during the rev. war.

Smith, Capt. Alexander Lawson. Passed Feb. 24, 1836—No. 40. Treas. Western Shore pay to Martha Jay, widow of Alexander Lawson Smith, a soldier of the rev., half pay of a capt. during her widowhood.

Smith, Aquilla. Passed Mch. 7, 1834—No. 49. Treas. Western Shore pay to Aquilla Smith, of Ky., during life, quarterly, half pay of a private, for the services rendered by him during the rev. war.

Smith, Benj. Passed Feb. 7, 1830—No. 16. Treas. Western Shore pay to Benjamin Smith, of Ky., during life, half yearly, half pay of a private, for his services during rev. war.

Smith, Charles and Studer, Philip. Passed Dec. session, 1815—No. 24. Treas. Western Shore pay unto Charles Smith and Philip Studer, late privates in the rev. war or order, quarterly, half pay of privates, as a further remuneration to them for those services by which their country has been so essentially benefitted.

Smith, Charles. Passed Mch. 5, 1835—No. 54. Treas. Western Shore pay to Charles Smith, of Talbot county, quarterly, during his life, half pay of a private, in consideration of his services in the war of the rev.

Passed Mch. 7, 1840—No. 21. Treas. Western Shore pay to Thomas Smith, of Talbot county, $10.00, for one quarters pension due his father, Charles Smith, of said county, at the time of his death, as a rev. pensioner.

Smith, Capt. Charles. Passed Mch. 8, 1834—No. 54. Treas. Western Shore pay to Mary Smith (widow of Capt. Charles Smith), of the D. C., during life, quarterly, half pay of a Capt., in consideration of the services rendered by her husband during the rev. war.

* *Smith, Christian,* private, Md. Line (Jan. 1820, p. 551).

Smith, Elijah. Passed Dec. session 1817 (Feb. 6, '18)—No. 32. Treas. Western Shore pay to Elijah Smith, of Baltimore, an old soldier, during life, quarterly, the half pay of a private for his services during the rev. war.

* *Smith, Elijah,* private, Md. Line (Jan. 1820, p. 550).

Smith, Elijah. Mch. 9, 1826—No. 113, p. 262. Treas. Western Shore pay to Mrs. Priscilla Smith of Baltimore whatever balance may be due to her late husband, Elijah Smith as a pensioner of the state.

Smith, Elijah. Passed Apr. 1, 1839—No. 57. Treas. Western Shore pay to Priscilla Smith, of Baltimore county, widow of Elijah Smith, a soldier of the rev., or her order, half pay of a private of the rev., quarterly, during her life.

Smith, Ephraim. Passed Feb. 4, 1843—No. 8. Treas. Western Shore pay to Ephraim Smith, of Baltimore city, during life, quarterly, half pay of a private, in consideration of services rendered during war of rev.

† *Smith, James,* private, Rev. army, of Frederick county. Pensioned Aug. 1, 1816 under Act of June 7, 1785, at $48.00 per an. commencing Mch. 4, 1789 (recd. $1,224.00). (U. S. Pens. Rolls, 1835, p. 14).

Smith, John. Capt. of a Co. of Militia in Baltimore Town Battn. Baltimore Co. before Mch. 16, 1779—see Merryman, John.

Smith, John. Passed Feb. 19, 1819—No. 60. Treas. Western Shore pay to John Smith, of Charles county, late a rev. soldier, quarterly during life, half pay of a private, for his rev. services.

* *Smith, John 1st,* private, Md. Line (Jan. 1820, p. 550).

* *Smith, John 2d,* private, Md. Line (Jan. 1820, p. 551).

Smith, John. Passed Feb. 19, 1819—No. 75. Treas. Western Shore to pay to John Smith, of Anne Arundel county late a rev. soldier, during life, the half pay of a private.

Smith, John. Feb. 26, 1825—No. 50, p. 162. Treas. to pay John Smith, of Anne Arundel county half pay of a private, further remun. for his services during rev. war.

Passed Mch. 14, 1832—No. 119. Treas. Western Shore pay to Sarah

Smith, of Anne Arundel county, widow of John Smith, a soldier of the rev. war, during widowhood, half yearly, half pay of a private, for the services rendered by her husband during said war.

Smith, John. Feb. 24, 1823—No. 56. Treas. Western Shore is directed to pay to John Smith, of Prince George's county, half pay of a corporal, during life, for his services during rev. war.

Passed Feb. 7, 1843—No. 3. Treas. Western Shore pay to Richard L. Jenkins, of Prince George's county, Md., $6.97, bal. due John Smith a rev. pensioner at time of his death.

Smith, Joseph. Passed Dec. session, 1815—No. 16. Treas. Western Shore pay to Joseph Smith, late a captain in the Md. Line during the rev. war—half pay of a captain, as a further remuneration for those meritorious services rendered his country during the Amer. war.

* *Smith, Michael,* drummer, Md. Line (Jan. 1820, p. 550).

* *Smith, Moses,* private, N. Y. Line (Jan. 1820, p. 550).

Smith, Capt. Nathaniel. Feb. 22, 1823—No. 69. Treas. Western Shore is directed to pay to Sarah Smith, of Baltimore, half pay of a captain, during life, as a further remuneration for her husband Capt. Nathaniel Smith's services during the rev. war.

Smith, Nathaniel, Maj. Passed Mch. 9, 1827—No. 45. Treas. pay to Sarah Smith, of Baltimore city, during life, half yearly, half pay of a major, in lieu of the half pay of a captain which she now receives, as a further remuneration for her late husband, Nathaniel Smith's services during the rev. war.

Smith, Thomas. Passed Feb. 26, 1829—No. 35. Treas. Western Shore pay to Thomas Smith, of state of Ohio, a soldier of the rev. war, during life, half yearly, half pay of a private, in consideration of his services during the rev. war.

Smoot, Joseph, Lieut. War of 1812. Passed Mch. 1, 1830—No. 11. Resolutions expressive of the sense of the Legislature of the gallant conduct during the late war of Joseph Smoot, of Dorchester county, now a Lieut. in the U. S. Navy (Hornet and Peacock, and Hornet and Penguin); and directing a sword to be presented to him.

* *Smyth, Daniel,* private, Md. Line (Jan. 1820, p. 551).

Smyth, Thomas. Passed Feb. 18, 1830—No. 33. Treas. Western Shore pay to Anna M. Smyth, widow of late Thomas Smyth, who was a major in the rev., during widowhood, quarterly, half pay of a lieutenant for services of her late husband.

Smyth, Thomas, Maj. Passed Mch. 25, 1836—No. 81. In lieu of pension granted by res. 33, Feb. 18, 1830, revoked. Treas. Western Shore pay to Anna Maria half pay of a major during her widowhood; provided she file relinquishment of claim for arrears, on acct. of her late husband Thos. Smyth, who was a major in the rev. war.

Somervell, James. Passed Mch. 12, 1828—No. 41. Treas. Western Shore pay to James Somervell, of Prince George's county, son and one of the heirs of Captain James Somervell, an officer of the Md. Line during the rev. war, such sum as may appear to be due to him on the pension list of Md. at time of his decease.

Somerville, Capt. James. Passed Nov. 1785, Vol. 11, Chap. XVI. Gen. Assembly granted half pay of a capt. to James Somerville, for disability acquired in the service, late a capt. in the Md. Line in the Continental army.

* *Sommers, Solomon,* private, Md. Line (Jan. 1820, p. 551).

Spalding, Aaron. Passed Dec. session, 1815—No. 28. Treas. Western Shore pay to Aaron Spalding, during his life, half pay of a sergeant. [Amongst rev. pensioners].

Spalding, Daniel. Mch. 7, 1826—No. 85, p. 255. Treas. Western Shore pay to Daniel Spalding of Baltimore, half pay of a private, for his rev. war services.

Passed Mch. 9, 1848—No. 72. State Treas. pay to Samuel Spalding, of Baltmore, $19.06, being bal. of pension due the late Daniel Spalding, a rev. soldier, at the time of his death; provided the said treasurer is satisfied that the said Saml. Spalding is the only heir entitled to receive the same.

Spalding, Henry. Passed Nov. session, 1811—No. 16. Treas. Western Shore pay to Henry Spalding, late a private in the rev. war,—half pay of a private, as a provision to him in his indigent situation and advanced life.

* *Spalding, Henry,* private, Md. Line (Jan. 1820, p. 550).

Spedden, Edward. Passed Feb. 12, 1820—No. 40. Treas. pay to Edward Spedden, of city of Baltimore, an old rev. soldier, for life, quarterly, half pay of a second lieut. for his services during the rev. war.

Spedden, Edward. Feb. 22, 1823—No. 68. Treas. Western Shore is directed to pay to Ann Spedden, of Baltimore, half pay of a lieutenant, as a remuneration for her late husband Edward Spedden's services during the rev. war.

Spires, Richard. Passed Mch. 7, 1829—No. 42. Treas. Western Shore pay to Richard Spires, of Brown county, Ohio, during life, quarterly, half pay of a private for his services during the rev. war.

Stanton, John. Passed Feb. 23, 1829—No. 32. Treas. Western Shore pay to John Stanton, a soldier of the rev. war, during life, half yearly, the half pay of a private, as further remuneration for his services during the rev. war.

Staples, John. Passed Feb. 12, 1820—No. 20. Treas. pay to John Staples, during life, quarterly, half pay of a private, for his services during rev. war.

Passed Mch. 10, 1845—No. 37. Treas. pay to Margaret Staples, widow of John Staples, a soldier of the Rev., quarterly, half pay of a sergeant, in consideration of her husband's services in the war of the Rev.

* *Starr, James*, private, Pa. Line (Jan. 1820, p. 551).

* *Starr, Wm.*, lieutenant, Conn. Line (Jan. 1820, p. 550).

* *Staunton, John*, private, Md. Line (Jan. 1820, p. 551).

Steel, James, Gentleman. Com'd. Ensign of Capt. Gabriel Vanhorn's Co. in Deer Creek Battn. of Militia in Harford County. Given at Annapolis, Apr. 9, 1778.

John M. Kimson, 1st. Lieut. Pa.

"James Steel being Disabled by long sickness is under the Necesity of refusing the above Commission for the above Reasons. Pr. G. Bl. Vanhorn, Capt. Apr. 14, 1778."

Steuart, Elizabeth. Passed Feb. 28, 1844—No. 25. Treas. Western Shore pay to Elizabeth Steuart, of Queen Anne's county, during life, quarterly, half pay of a captain, in consideration of the services rendered by her husband during the rev. war.

Stevens, Benj. Passed Dec. session, 1816—No. 16. Treas. Western Shore pay to Benj. Stevens, of Somerset county, an old soldier, quarterly, during his life, the half pay of a private, as a further compensation for his services during the rev. war.

* *Stevens, Benj.*, private, Md. Line (Jan. 1820, p. 551).

Stevens, Edward, Gentleman. Com'd. Ensign of Capt. Maynadier's Company in 4th Battn. of Militia in Talbot Co. Given at Annapolis, Apr. 9, 1778. Th. Johnson (X, No. 179). (See Maynadier, Wm.)

Stephens, Levi. Passed Dec. session, 1815—No. 38. Treas. Western Shore pay to Levi Stephens, of Somerset county, quarterly during life, the half pay of a private, as a further remuneration for those services rendered his country during the rev. war.

* *Stevens, Levi*, private, Md. Line (Jan. 1820, p. 550).

Stevens, Levi. Passed Feb. 24, 1836—No. 39. Treas. Western Shore pay to Wm. W. Stevens & David Stevens, executors of Levi Stevens, $28.33, being 8 mos. & 15 days pension due said Levi Stevens at his death, Dec. 15, 1834.

Stephens, Levi. Passed Mch. 11, 1835—No. 27. Treas. Western Shore pay to Polly Stephens, widow of Levi Stephens, a soldier of the rev., half pay of a private during her life, in quarterly payts.

* *Stevens, Richard*, sailing master, Frigate Trumbull (Jan. 1820, p. 550).

Stevenson, John, Gentleman, Comd. Lieut. of Marines of the Row Galley called the Independence. Given in Convention or Council of Safety of this State at Annapolis, Jan. 25, 1777. J. Hall, J. Nicholson, Jr., Brice Worthington, Sam Wilson. (X, No. 254.)

Stone, Col. John. Passed Mch. 21, 1839—No. 38. Treas. Western Shore pay to Dr. N. P. Cousin, for the use of the surviving child of Col. John Stone, a sum of money amounting to the half pay of a colonel in the Md. Line between the periods of 1779 and 1782, for 2 yrs. & 11 mos; provided he shall be satisfied by competent evidence that the sum herein authorized to be paid, which is ordered under Act of 1778, Chap. 14, & resolutions of 1779 & 1780, of this State, to be paid to the said heirs for the period of time intervening between the resignation of said Col. Stone, in Aug. 1779, and the date of the first payt. to him in 1782, has not been paid to Col. Stone, or his heirs, by the gen. govt.

Storer, Dorothy. Passed Mch. 2, 1827—No. 33. Treas. Western Shore pay to Dorothy Storer, of the District of Columbia, during life, half yearly, the half pay of a captain, as a further remuneration for her late husband's services during the rev. war.

Strider, Philip. Passed Apr. 6, 1841—No. 13. Treas. Western Shore pay to M. C. Sprigg, for legal representative of Philip Strider, late of Bedford county, Pa, and pensioner of the State of Md., who died Jan. 6, 1840, $12.93, amount of arrears due him from Sept. 10, 1840 to day of his death.

Stringer, Richard. Capt. in 22^d^ Battalion of Militia Aug. 28, 1777—see Ridgely, Nicholas.

Stuart, Elizabeth. Passed Mch. 8, 1850—No. 71. Treas. pay to Woolman I. Gibson, for use of representatives of Elizabeth Stuart, deceased, $33.33 being amt. due said Elizabeth for pension, per resolution No. 23, of 1843, to Feb. 21, 1849, the day of her death.

Studer, Philip—see Smith, Charles.

* *Studer, Philip,* private, Md. Line (Jan. 1820, p. 551).

* *Sullivan, James,* private, Md. Line (Jan. 1820, p. 551).

Summers, Solomon. Passed Dec. session, 1816—No. 25. Treas. Western Shore pay to Solomon Summers, of Queen-Anne's county, late a drummer in the rev. war, during life, quarterly, the half pay of a drummer, as a further remuneration for his services in the rev. war.

* *Sutton, Jacob,* seaman, Ship Defiance (Jan. 1820, p. 551).

Swann, Leonard. Passed Dec. session, 1817—No. 14. Treas. Western Shore pay to Leonard Swan, an old soldier, quarterly during life, a sum of money equal to the half pay of a private. [Listed amongst Rev. war pensioners].

* *Syphird, Matthias,* private, Md. Line (Jan. 1820, p. 551).

Tannehill, Mrs. Agnes M. Mch. 8, 1826—No. 70, p. 250. Treas. Western Shore pay to Mrs. Agnes M. Tannehill, of Allegany county, in the state of Pa., during life, the half pay of a captain, as a further remuneration for her late husband's services during the rev. war.

Tasker, Richard R. Passed Feb. 12, 1820—No. 34. Treas. pay to Richard R. Tasker, of Allegany county, for life, quarterly, half pay of a private, for his services during rev. war.

* *Tasker, Richard R.*, private, Md. Line (Jan. 1820, p. 551).

* *Taylor, John*, private, Md. Line (Jan. 1820, p. 551).

Taylor, John. Passed Mch. 8, 1834—No. 53. Treas. Western Shore pay to John Taylor, of Anne Arundel county, quarterly, half pay of a private, for the services rendered by him during the rev. war.

Taylor, John. Passed Mch. 8, 1836—No. 58. Treas. Western Shore pay to Sega Taylor, of Anne Arundel county, the amt. due her late husband, John Taylor, upon the pension list of this State, at the time of his death. (Indexed under Rev. Pensions).

Taylor, John. Passed Apr. 1, 1836—No. 82. Treas. Western Shore pay to "Sydney Taylor, widow of John Taylor, a rev. soldier," the half pay of a private for the services of her husband.

* *Taylor, Levin*, private, Va. Line (Jan. 1820, p. 552).

* *Taylor, Matthew*, cornet. Gen. Washington's Guards—Died 27 Aug. 1818 (Jan. 1820, p. 551).

* *Taylor, Nevil*, private, Va. Line (Jan. 1820, p. 552).

Taylor, Richd. Passed Dec. session, 1815—No. 30. Treas. Western Shore pay to Richard Taylor, late a soldier in the rev. war, half pay of a private.

Tedyford, John. 1st. Sgt. Friendship Company, Dorchester Co. Militia, Jan. 1776—see Elliott, John.

* *Thomas, Francis*, private, Pa. Line (Jan. 1820, p. 551).

Thomas, John Allen, Esq. Com'd. Capt. of 5th Independent Co. of Regular Troops. Given in Convention at Annapolis, Jan. 5, 1776. Signed pr. Order Mat. Tilghman, Pres. (X, No. 186).

"I John Allen Thomas do swear that I will well & truly Execute my Office according to the within Commission & the trust reposed on me, according to the best of my power & ability & that I will disband & lay down my arms whenever I shall be ordered so to do by the Convention of Md. for the time being, or any authority derived under it. So help me God. Before Thos. Brooke Hodgkin, Jan. 17, 1776."

Thomas, John Jarman. Passed Mch. 16, 1836—No. 50. Treas. Western Shore pay to John Jarman Thomas, a soldier of the rev. half pay of a private during life.

Thomas, Joseph. Passed Feb. 20, 1822—No. 37, p. 178. Treas. Western Shore pay to Frisby Henderson, Esq. of Cecil county, as trustee for Joseph Thomas an old Rev. soldier, half pay as private, &c.

* *Thomason, Ezekiel*, private, Md. Line (Jan. 1820, p. 551).

* *Thomm, Henry*, private, Md. Line (Jan. 1820, p. 551).

Thompson, Barnard. Passed Mch. 1, 1833—No. 38. Treas. Western Shore pay to Barnard Thompson of Washington county, Ky., a soldier of the rev. war, during life, quarterly, half pay of a private, for his services rendered by him in said war.

Thompson, Chas. Passed Dec. session, 1816—No. 17. Treas. Western Shore pay to Chas. Thompson, of St. Mary's county, late a soldier in the rev. war, quarterly, during his life, the half pay of a private, as an additional compensation to him for those services by which his country has been benefitted.

Thompson, Jesse. Passed Nov. session 1812 (Jan. 1, '13)—No. 25. Treas. Western Shore pay to Jesse Thompson, late a sergeant in the Md. Line during the rev. war—half pay of a sergeant, as a further remuneration, &c.

* *Thompson, Jesse*, private, Md. Line (Jan. 1820, p. 551).

Thompson, John. Passed Nov. session 1812 (Jan. 1, 1813)—No. 28. Treas. Western Shore pay to John Thompson, of Kent county, late a soldier in the rev. war,—half pay of a private, in quarterly payts., during life.

Thompson, Thos. Passed Dec. session, 1816—No. 19. Treas. Western Shore pay to Thomas Thompson, of Dorchester county, an old soldier, during life, quarterly, half pay of a private, as a compensation for his services in the late rev. war.

Thompson, Thomas. Feb. 16, 1820—No. 47. Treas. is directed to pay to Mary Thompson, widow of Thomas Thompson, an old soldier, late of Dorchester county, during life, half pay of a private.

* *Thornton, John*, private, Pa. Line (Jan. 1820, p. 551).

Thruston, Col. Chas. M. Passed Jan. 9, 1841—No. 6. [1839 riots—Treas. of State Mch. 2, 1844].

Tillard, Edward—see Halkerstone, Robert.

Tillard, Thomas, Esq., Comd. Major of South River Battn. of Militia in Anne Arundel Co., being the 31st Battn. in this Province. Given in Council of Safety at Annapolis, Jan. 26, 1776, Danl. of St. Thos. Jenifer, Chas. Carroll, J. Hall, Jas. Tilghman. (X, No. 190.)

Resigned Dec. 18, 1776.

Tillard, Lt. Col. Passed Jan. 22, 1820—No. 10. Treas. pay to Sarah Tillard, widow of Lt. Col. Tillard, of Md. Line (during rev. war) during life, quarterly, "a sum of money equal to half pay of a captain."

Passed Feb. 11, 1835—No. 58. Treas. Western Shore pay to Capt. Otho Thomas, of Frederick county, for benefit of heirs of Sarah Tillard, late a pensioner of this State $57.33 due her at the time of her death.

Tillotson, Thomas, Surgeon. Passed Feb. 19, 1830—No. 42. Treas. Western Shore pay to Dr. Thomas Tillotson, of Rhinebeck county, N. Y.

who was a surgeon in the rev. war, during life, half yearly, half pay of a surgeon, as further remuneration for his services during the rev. war.

Mch. 14, 1832—No. 111. Dr. Thos. Tillotson, of New York, "a surgeon in the Md. Line during the war of the revolution" was granted a warrant, later patent, for 200 acres of vacant land in Allegany county.

† *Tomm, Henry*, private, Rev. army, of Washington county. Pensioned under Act of June 7, 1785 at $20.00 per annum from Mch. 4, 1794 (recd. $664.17)—at $48.00 per an. from Apr. 24, 1816 (recd. $89.33). (U. S. Pens. Roll, 1835, p. 19).

Toomy, John. Feb. 16, 1820—No. 29. Treas. is directed to pay to John Toomy, of Queen Anne's county, half pay of a corporal, as a further compensation for his services during the rev. war.

Topham, Benj. Passed Mch. 29, 1839—No. 50. Treas. Western Shore pay to Ann Busey, the sole legatee of Benj. Topham, deceased, who was a pensioner of this State, or her order, the arrear of pension due to said Topham at time of his death, under resolution, numbered 63, passed at Dec. session 1826.

Townsend, Allen. Passed Dec. session, 1816—No. 24. Treas. Western Shore pay to Allen Townsend, quarterly, the half pay of a private, as a further remuneration for those services by which his country has been so essentially benefitted.

Townsend, Thomas. Feb. 18, 1825—No. 22, p. 158. Treas. to pay to Thos. Townsend, of Talbot county, half pay of a private, addl. remun. for his services during rev. war.

Towson, Col. Nathan and *Gallagher, Capt. John.* Passed Mch. 21, 1833—No. 63. Governor directed to procure and present two swords, one to Col. Nathan Towson, U. S. Army, and the other to Capt. John Gallagher, U. S. Navy, as testimony of the admiration and gratitude of their native state for their distinguished gallantry and highly valuable services during the last war with Great Britain.

Traverse, [*Tranierse, Trarierse* ?], *Levin*, Gentleman, Comd. 1st Lieut. of Capt. Rogers A. Hooper's Co. in Upper Battn. of Militia in Dorchester County. Given at Annapolis, May 20, 1778. Th. Johnson. (X, No. 248.) Endorsement: Edward Scott, 1st. Lieut.; Walter Raughley, 2d. Lieut.

Truck, John. Mch. 1, 1826—No. 61, p. 248. Treasury of Western Shore to pay to John Truck of Frederick county, the half pay of a sergeant, as a further remuneration for his services during the rev. war.

Truck, John Mch. 9, 1826—No. 106, p. 261. Reg. of land office issue to John Truck of Frederick county, unpatented state lands in Allegany county. A warrant for 50 a., as a donation granted by the state to the rev. soldiers who served in the Md. Line during the rev. war, & to which he is entitled.

Trux, John. Passed Mch. 6, 1832—No. 71. Treas. Western Shore pay to Elizabeth Trux, of Frederick county, widow of John Trux, a soldier of the rev. war, during widowhood, half yearly, half pay of a sergeant, for services rendered by her husband during said war.

Trueman, Lieut. John. Passed Nov. 1785, Vol. 11, Chap. XVI. Gen. Assembly granted half pay of a lieut., for disability acquired in the service, to John Trueman, a lieut. in the Md. Line in the Continental army.

* *Tucker, George*, private—dragoon, Armand's Corps (Jan. 1820, p. 551).

Turner, Thomas. Passed Feb. 19, 1819—No. 53. Treas. Western Shore pay to Thomas Turner, of Montgomery county, a rev. soldier, half pay of a private for his services during said war.

Tutwiller, Jonathan—see Nowell, James.

Passed Dec. session, 1815—No. 60. Treas. Western Shore pay to Jonathan Tutwiller, or order, quarterly, a sum equal to the half pay of a sergeant, instead of that of a private.

* *Tutwiller, Jonathan*, private, Md. Line—died July 20, 1819 (Jan. 1820, p. 551).

Tydings, Kealey. Passed Nov. session, 1811—No. 22. Treas. Western Shore pay to Kealey Tydings, late a sergeant in the Md. Line during the rev. war—half pay of a sergeant, as a further remuneration for those services rendered his country during the American war.

Tyler, Robert. Officer elected (presumably 1st. Lieut.) in a Militia Co. in Prince George's County, 25th Battn.—see Wootters, Richard.

Ulricks, Peter. Baltimore county 9th election district, Oct. 1826—vote for or against the change of location. Laws of Md. Session Dec. 1825, passed Mch. 9, 1826. Res. No. 107, p. 261.

* *Uncles, Benj.*, private, Md. Line (Jan. 1820, p. 552).

Uncles, Benj. Passed Feb. 22, 1822—No. 45, p. 178. Treas. Western Shore pay to Benjamin Uncles, of Anne Arundel county half pay of a private, for his rev. war services.

Passed Jan. 28, 1838—No. 4. Treas. Western Shore pay to Rebecca Uncles, widow of Benjamin Uncles, a rev. soldier, the half pay of a private during her life, as a further remuneration for his services.

Uncles, Benj. Passed Mch. 10, 1847—No. 53. Treas. of State pay to Mrs. Sarah Earlougher $6.67, being bal. of pension money due from this State to Rebecca Uncles, deceased, at the time of her death.

Vaine, John, of Caroline county, changed to John Clinton Cooper Jan. 12, 1825, p. 14, Chap. 18.

Vane, John. Passed Mch. 12, 1827—No. 57. Treas. pay Lucretia Vane, of Dorchester county, during life, half yearly, half pay of a private, for her husband, John Vane's services during the rev. war.

Vane, John. Passed Jan. 28, 1837—No. 8. Treas. Western Shore pay to James Vane, one of the legal representatives of Lucretia Vane, $9.77, for two months and twenty-eight days pension due the said Lucretia at her death Sept. 28, 1835.

Vanhorne, Gabriel R. Capt. of Militia in Harford Co. Deer Creek Battalion, Apr. 1778—see Long, John Jr.—"G. Bl." Apr. 14, 1778, see Long, John and Steel, James.

Varlow, Stephen. Passed Feb. 12, 1820—No. 36. Treas. pay to Stephen Varlow, of Cecil county, for life, quarterly, half pay of a private as a remuneration for his services during the rev. war.

* *Vaughan, George,* lieut., Md. Line (Jan. 1820, p. 552).

† *Vaughan, George H.,* lieut. Rev. army, of Baltimore county. Pensioned at $144.00 per annum, dating from Jan. 1, 1803 (recd. $1,012.80)—at $160.00 per annum, from Jan. 12, 1810 (recd. $1,005.28), Apr. 27, 1810—at $181.33 1/4 per annum from Apr. 24, 1816 (recd. $353.05)—at $240.00 per an. from Apr. 4, 1818 (recd. $440.00)—at $181.33 1/4 from Mch. 4, 1820 (recd. $1,631.99), Died Dec. 2, 1820. U. S. Pension Rolls, 1835, p. 10.

* *Vaughan, Wm.,* private, Md. Line (Jan. 1820, p. 552).

Vaughan, Wm. Passed Nov. session, 1812 (Jan. 2, 1813)—No. 55. Treas. Western Shore pay unto Wm. Vaughan, or order, an old rev. soldier, half pay as a private during the remainder of his life, as a remuneration for his meritorious services.

Voghan, George. Capt. of Deer Creek Militia, Harford Co.—see Corbet, James.

* *Walckman, Michael,* private, Md. Line (Jan. 1820, p. 553).

Walker, John. Feb. 16, 1820—No. 31. Treas. is directed to pay to John Walker, of Frederick county, half pay of a corporal, as a further compensation for those services rendered by him during the rev. war.

* *Walker, John,* private, Houseger's Regt. (Jan. 1820, p. 552).

Walker, John. Passed Mch. 8, 1848—No. 35. State Treas. pay to Mary Walker, widow of John Walker, a soldier of the rev. quarterly, beginning Jan. 1, 1848, half pay of a corporal, in consideration of her husband's services in the rev. war.

Wall, William. Feb. 19, 1819—No. 63. Treas. Western Shore is directed to pay to Wm. Wall, of Dorchester county, an old soldier, quarterly payments of half pay of a private—further remuneration for his services during the rev. war.

Passed Feb. 25, 1837—No. 27. Treas. Western Shore pay to Kitturah Wall, widow of Wm. Wall, a soldier of the Rev., $10.78 being for three months and seven days pension due her said husband at the time of his death.

* *Wall, Wm.,* private, Md. Line (Jan. 1820, p. 553).

Wall, W^m^. Passed Mch. 16, 1837—No. 42. Treas. Western Shore pay to Kitturah Wall, widow of W^{m}. Wall, soldier of the rev., the half pay of a private, as a further remuneration for his services, during her life.

Waller, W^{m}. Ensign in 17th Battn. Militia—see Schoolfield, W^{m}.

† *Waltman, Michael*, private, Rev. army, of Frederick county. Pensioned Feb. 8, 1818 under Act of June 7, 1785, at $40.00 per annum, from Mch. 4, 1789 (recd. $1,085.56)—at $64.00 per an. from Apr. 24, 1816 (recd. $118.11). (U. S. Pens. Rolls, 1835, p. 14).

Waltman, Michael. Feb. 18, 1825—No. 24, p. 159. Treas. to pay to Michael Waltman, of Frederick county half pay of a private addl. comp. his services during rev. war.

Waltman Michael. Passed Mch. 16, 1840—No. 33. Treas. Western Shore pay to Mary Waltman, of Frederick county, widow of Michael Waltman, a soldier of the rev., or her order, quarterly, during her life, the half pay of a private, in consideration of the rev. services of her said husband.

* *Wann, John*, private, Pa. Line (Jan. 1820, p. 553).

Ware, Lt. Col. Francis. Passed Nov. session 1800—No. 7. Francis Ware (who heretofore commanded the troops of this state, then the colony of Md., with distinguished bravery and fidelity, and who, during the late rev. war, was lieut-col. of the 1st. reg. raised by this state, from which service he was compelled to retire by the infirmities peculiarly incident to the military life in these climates), has, by reason of his said infirm health, and misfortunes arising from those acts of benevolence which the duties of society often render indespensable, and not by imprudence or want of due economy, became reduced to extreme indigence in his advanced age; and it being unworthy (both in example & principle) of the citizens of a free republic, to desert, in their distress, those of their fellow-citizens who have rendered important services in distinguished stations, whilst high honours and great rewards attend public services in other forms of government; Resolved unanimously, That there be granted to the said Francis Ware half pay as lieut-col. (rated according to the establishment when he retired from the service) from date of this resolution, during the remainder of his life;—treas. Western Shore pay same to said Francis Ware in quarterly payts.

Warring, Lieut. Basil. Passed Mch. 4, 1834—No. 43. Treas. Western Shore pay to Ann Warring, widow of Basil Warring, during life, quarterly, half pay of a lieut., in consideration of the services rendered by her husband during the rev. war.

Washington, General George. Passed Nov. session 1781—No. 1. "Resolved unanimously, That the governor be requested to write to Mr. Peale, of Philadelphia, to procure, as soon as may be, the portrait of his

Excellency General George Washington at full length, to be placed in the house of delegates, in grateful remembrance of that most illustrious character."

Passed Nov. session 1799—No. 5. Members of legislature Governor and all other officers of the state to wear scarfs and hatbands, as a tribute of respect to the memory of "the illustrious Washington—" anxious to pay every tribute of respect to the memory of the departed friend to his country, &c.

Water, Wm. Corporal in 17th Battn. Militia—see Schoolfield, Wm.

Waters, Jonathan. Feb. 19, 1819—No. 52. Treas. of Western Shore directed to pay to Jonathan Waters, a rev. soldier, in quarterly payments during life, the half pay of a private.

Waters, M. George. Commandant of 17th Battn. of Militia, Jan. 3, 1776, see Schoolfield, Wm.

Waters, Capt. Richard. Passed Dec. session, 1815 (Jan. 23, 1816)—No. 19. Treas. Western Shore pay to Richard Waters, late a capt. in the Md. Line,—half pay of a capt., as a further remuneration for the services rendered his country during the rev. war.

* *Waters, Richard,* captain, Md. Line (Jan. 1820, p. 552).

Waters, Richard, Capt. Passed Mch. 12, 1827—No. 62. Treas. pay to Richard Waters, of Baltimore, during life, half yearly, sum equal to pay of a captain, for his services during the rev. war.

Waters, Richard, Capt. Passed Feb. 2, 1830—No. 13. Treas. Western Shore pay to Elizabeth J. Waters, during life, quarterly, half pay of a captain, in consideration of the services of her husband captain Richard Waters, during the rev. war.

Waters, Wilson. Passed Mch. 16, 1836—No. 59. Treas. Western Shore pay to Margaret Waters, widow of Dr. Wilson Waters, quarterly during her life, half pay of a surgeon's mate in consideration of the services of her husband. (Indexed under Rev. Pensions).

Watkins, John, Esq. Com'd. Capt. of the 3d. Independant Co. of Regular Troops to be raised in the Province. Given in Convention at Annapolis, Jan. 5, 1776. Signed pr. order Mat. Tilghman, Pres.

Watkins, Capt. Gassaway—see Halkerstone, Robert.

Passed Dec. session, 1815—No. 64. Treas. Western Shore pay unto Gassaway Walkins, late a capt. in the rev. war, quarterly, a sum equal to the half pay of a captain, in lieu of the sum already allowed him by a resolution passed at Nov. session, 1811, as a further remuneration for those services which so essentially contributed to the independence of his country.

* *Watkins, Gassaway,* captain, Md. Line (Jan. 1820, p. 552).

Watkins, Leonard. Passed Nov. session, 1812 (Jan. 2, 1813)—No. 50.

Treas. Western Shore pay unto Leonard Watkins, a sergeant in the Md. Line, during the rev. war, or order, a sum of money annually in quarterly payts., equal to the half pay of a sergeant, as a further remuneration for those services rendered his country during the American war.

Watkins, Leonard. Passed Feb. 28, 1839—No. 37. Treas. Western Shore pay to Mary Watkins, of Montgomery county, widow of Leonard Watkins, a sergeant of the rev. war, or her order, during life, quarterly, the half pay of a sergeant of the rev., commencing Jan. 1, 1839.

* *Watkins, Leonard,* private, Md. Line (Jan. 1820, p. 552).

Watkins, Nicholas, Gentleman. Com'd. 1st. Lieut. in Capt. John Dorsey's Co. of the 22d Battn. of Militia. Given at Annapolis, Aug. 28, 1777. Th. Johnson. (X, No. 196).

Watkins, Thomas, Esq. Com'd. Capt. of a Co. of Artillery of the Defence of the City of Annapolis. Given in Council of Safety, Oct. 26, 1776. Danl. of St. Thos. Janifer, George Hands, J. Nicholson, Nic. Thomas. (X, No. 197).

Capt. of a Co. in Anne Arundel Co., West River Battn. Mch. 1, 1778—see Stockett, Thos. Noble.

Wats, James. Passed Feb. 5, 1833—No. 10. Treas. Western Shore pay to James Wats, of Dorchester county, during life, quarterly, half pay of a private, for services rendered by him during the rev. war.

† *Watts, James,* corporal, Rev. army, of Dorchester county. Pensioned at $60.00 per annum Jan. 15, 1816, dating from Feb. 20, 1808 (recd. $490.67)—at $96.00 per an. from Apr. 24, 1816 (recd. $1,618.66), and died Jan. 21, 1833. (U. S. Pens. Rolls, 1835, p. 12).

Watson, Lt. Col. Wm. H. Passed Mch. 6, 1850—No. 63. Treas. of Md. pay to Sarah Ann Watson, widow of Lt. Col. Wm. H. Watson, during her widowhood, an annual pension, quarterly, to commence from the time of passage of this resolution, "equal to the half pay proper of her late husband, as a Lieutenant Colonel of the Infantry of the United States"; not to exceed $30.00 per month.

* *Webber, Nathaniel,* private, Pa. Line (Jan. 1820, p. 552).

Webster, Capt. John A. Passed Jan. 26, 1835—No. 3. Governor to procure and present a sword to Capt. John A. Webster, native of Md., for gallantry during attack upon Baltimore Sept. 12, 1814.

Wells, Martha. Passed Mch. 20, 1840—No. 51. Treas. Western Shore pay to Martha Wells, of Prince George's county, the widow of a rev. soldier, or to her order, quarterly, during her life, the half pay of a private, commencing Jan. 1, 1840.

Wells, Richard, Gentleman. Com'd. 2d Lieut. of a Company of Militia in Anne Arundel Co. Given in Convention at Annapolis, Jan. 3, 1776. Mat. Tilghman, Pres. (X, No. 193).

To the Honorable the Council of Safety of Maryland, July 12, 1777. I, Richard Wells to whom the Honor of these presents was directed by the Honorable Council at the time being, Tho. Indisposed of a bad state Health, hath rendered him Impossible to attending duty since Sept. last. Should please God to "restore his health to a Capacity of assisting his Country in proportion of its Rights and Privileges, he will always be ready. Till then Humbly beg Permission to resign this Commission that it may not prevent the fulfilling it by an abler body at this Alarming Season. Honble. Sirs. Your ready Servant. Rich. Wells."

West, Benj. Mch. 9, 1826—No. 103, p. 260. Treas. of Western Shore pay to Benj. West of Baltimore, half pay of a private for his rev. war services.

Wheatley, W^m^. Passed Mch. 13, 1832—No. 105. Treas. Western Shore pay to Rhoda Wheatley, of Dorchester county, widow of W^m^. Wheatley, a soldier of the rev. war, during widowhood, half yearly, half pay of a private, for services rendered by her husband during said war.

Wheatley, W^m^. Passed Feb. 25, 1840—No. 10. Treas. Western Shore pay to "Esther Williss, one of the legal representatives of Rhoda Wheatley," or to her order, $7.12^1/_2$ due to said "Rhoda Wheatley," at the time of her death, June 5, 1839.

Wheeler, Hezekiah. Capt. of Co. of Select Militia in Prince George's Co. May 25, 1781—see Smith, Chas.

† Wheeler, Nathaniel, private, Rev. army, of Somerset county. Pensioned under Act of June 7, 1785 from Mch. 4, 1789, at $60.00 per an. (recd. $1,628.33)—at $96.00 per an. from Apr. 24, 1816 (recd. $898.66). Died Nov. 5, 1825. (U. S. Pens. Roll, 1835, p. 18).

Wheeler, Nathaniel. Passed Feb. 2, 1832—No. 19. Treas. Western Shore pay to Mary Wheeler, widow of Nathaniel Wheeler, a soldier of the rev. war, during her widowhood, half yearly, half pay of a private, in consideration of the services rendered by her said husband.

* *Whipple, W^m^.*, gunner, Mass. Line (Jan. 1820, p. 553).

Whitaker, W^m^. Passed Feb. 27, 1839—No. 24. Treas. Western Shore pay to Sarah Scrivner, of Baltimore city, former widow of William Whitaker, a soldier of the rev., or to her order, half pay of a private of the rev., during her life, quarterly, commencing Jan. 1, 1838.

† *White, James*, private, Rev. army, of Montgomery county. Pensioned under Act of Jan 7, 1785, at $40.00 per an. from Mch. 4, 1789 (recd. $1,049.20)—at $96.00 per an. from May 27, 1815 (recd. $1,370.13). Died Oct. 21, 1829. (U. S. Pens. Rolls, 1835, p. 16).

White, James. Feb. 24, 1823—No. 60. Treas. Western Shore is directed to pay to James White, of Montgomery county, half pay of a private, further compensation for his services during rev. war.

Passed, Feb. 5, 1830—No. 19. Treas. Western Shore pay to Henry Harding, for use of Priscilla White, widow of the late James White, a pensioner of the State of Md. $22.33, being balance due said White at his death.

* *White, Jonathan*, private, Va. Line (Jan. 1820, p. 552).

White, Richard. Passed Feb. 11, 1835—No. 11. Treas. Western Shore pay to Margaret Lamb, widow of Richard White, a soldier of the rev., half pay of a private, quarterly, during her life.

White, Samuel B. Mch. 7, 1826—No. 86, p. 255. Treas. Western Shore pay to Samuel B. White of Montgomery county, half pay of private, for his rev. war services.

† *White, Samuel B.*, private, Rev. army, of Montgomery county. Pensioned at $40.00 per an. under Act of June 7, 1785, from Mch. 4, 1789 (recd. $763.78)—at $60.00 per an. from Apr. 8, 1808 (Act of Mch. 3, 1809) (recd. $482.67)—at $96.00 on Nov. 18, 1819, dating from Apr. 24, 1816 (recd. $1,474.66). Died Jan. 18, 1832. (U. S. Pens. Rolls, 1835, p. 16.)

White, Samuel B. Passed Mch. 6, 1832—No. 70. Treas. Western Shore pay to Sarah White, of Montgomery county, widow of Samuel B. White, a soldier of the rev. war, during widowhood, half yearly, half pay of a private, for the services rendered by her husband during said war.

White, Thomas. Passed Feb. 3, 1828—No. 10. Treas. Western Shore pay to Thomas White, of Baltimore, half yearly, for life, half pay of private, further remuneration for his services during the rev. war.

* *Whitmore, Stephen*, private, Md. Line (Jan. 1820, p. 552).

Wicks, Samuel, Gentleman. Com'd. Capt. of a Co. of Militia in Queen Anne's County in 5th Battn. of Province of Md. Given in Convention at Annapolis, Jan. 3, 1776. Signed pr. order Mat. Tilghman, Pres. (X, No. 199).

Wiery, Michael. Passed Apr. 6, 1841—No. 8. Treas. Western Shore pay to Elizabeth Wiery, widow of Michael Wiery, of York county, Pa., during life, half pay of a private, in consideration of services rendered by her husband during the rev. war.

* *Wilheid, Frederick*, private, Houseger's Reg't. (Jan. 1820, p. 552).

† *Wilkerson, Rich'd.*, private Rev. army, of Anne Arundel county, pensioned May 16, 1817 at $40.00 per month, from Mch. 4, 1789, under Act of June 7, 1785 (received $1,085.56).

Pensioned at $64.00 per month Apr. 24, 1816 (received $119.11). (War Dept., 1835, p. 2).

Wilkerson, Lieut. Young. Passed Nov. session 1810—No. 12. Treas. Western Shore pay half yearly to Young Wilkerson, of Anne-Arundel county, a sum of money equal to half pay of a lieut. during his life.

* *Wilkerson, Young*, lieut., Md. Line (Jan. 1820, p. 553).

Wilkinson, Col. James. Passed Dec. session, 1815—No. 47. Whereas, it appears to this general assembly, that James Wilkinson, an officer of the rev. war, and who served to its termination, did not receive the commutation money of 5 years pay, in lieu of half pay for life, promised to the officers and soldiers, who continued in service to the end of the war; therefore.

Resolved, That the treas. of Western Shore pay to said James Wilkinson, quarterly payments, during life, half pay of a colonel of dragoons, as remuneration for services rendered his country in the revolutionary struggle for liberty.

Willcoxen, Jesse, Esq. Com'd. to be Capt. of a Company formerly commanded by W[m]. Johnson in Lower Battn. of Militia in Montgomery Co. Given at Annapolis Aug. 4, 1780. Thos. S. Lee. (X, No. 200).

Endorsement: Resigned May —, 1782. Samuel Briscoe Magruder succeeded him.

Wilcoxen, Thomas, Gentleman. Com'd. 2[d] Lieut. of a Co. of Light Infantry in Prince George's County, belonging to the 11th. Battn. of Militia in this Province. Given in Convention at Annapolis, Jan. 3, 1776. Signed pr. order Mat. Tilghman, Pres. (X, No. 201).

Williams, Charles, Bullock, Jesse. Passed Nov. session, 1812 (Jan. 1, '13)—No. 27. Treas. Western Shore pay to Charles Williams, likewise Jesse Bullock, late privates in the Md. Line during the rev. war, quarterly, a sum of money equal to half pay of a private, as a further remuneration for their services by which their country has been so essentially benefitted.

* *Williams, Charles,* private, Md. Line (Jan. 1820, p. 553).

Williams, David, Gentleman. Com'd. Capt. in John Williams' Co. in Princess Anne Battn. of Militia in Somerset County. Given at Baltimore Town, Sept. 22, 1777. Th. Johnson. (X, No. 222). Endorsement: Thomas Williams, Ensign.

Williams, Elisha, Capt. Passed Feb. 27, 1832—No. 34. Treas. Western Shore pay to Harriet Williams, of Georgetown, D. C., in consideration of services rendered by her deceased husband, Elisha Williams, a captain in the rev. war, during her life, quarterly, a sum equal to half pay of a captain.

Williams, John. Passed Dec. session, 1815—No. 18. Treas. Western Shore pay to John Williams, of St. Mary's county, a late meritorious soldier in the rev. war—half pay of a corporal, as a provision to him in his indigent situation now advanced in life, & as a further remuneration for those services by which his country has been so essentially benefitted.

Williams, John. Passed Feb. 3, 1828—No. 8. Treas. Western Shore pay to John Williams, of Baltimore, during life, half yearly, half pay of a private, further remuneration for his services during the rev. war.

* *Williams, John, 1st.* private, Md. Line (Jan. 1820, p. 552).

* *Williams, John, 2d,* private, Md. Line (Jan. 1820, p. 552).

Williams, John. Capt. of a Somerset Co. Company of Militia in Princess Anne Battn., Sept. 22, 1777—see Schoolfield, Benj.

On the back: Vacancies in the Salisbury Battalion Ensign to Capt. R. Dashield; 2d Lieut. to Capt. Wm. Turpin; Corp'l. to Edward Kellum.

2d Lieut to Capt. Conway's Co.—John Evans (of Nicho), 1st. Lieut. to Capt. Turpin's Co.—John Phillips. Ensign to Capt. Coole's Co.—Levin Handy. Th. Johnson.

Williams, Joseph. Feb. 25, 1824—No. 32, p. 172. Treas. to pay to Joseph Williams, of Annapolis, half pay of a private, further remun. for his services during rev. war.

Passed Mch. 21, 1833—No. 67. Reg. land office issue to Joseph Williams, of Annapolis, a soldier of the rev. war, a warrant and later patent for 50 acres of vacant land in Allegany county, without any composition money.

Williams, Lieut. Osborn. Passed Feb. 19, 1819—No. 65. Half pay of a lieut. is directed to be paid to Osborne Williams during life. (War service is not specified).

* *Williams, Osborn,* lieutenant, Md. Line (Jan. 1820, p. 552).

Willin, Charles. Passed Feb. 27, 1839—No. 23. Treas. Western Shore pay to Eleanor Robertson, of Somerset county, former widow of Charles Willin, a rev. soldier, the half pay of a seaman and private of the rev., during her life, commencing Jan. 1, 1839.

Willin, Evans. Passed Feb. 23, 1832—No. 44. Treas. Western Shore pay to Mary Easom, of Dorchester county, widow of Evans Willin, a revolutionary soldier, during her widowhood, half yearly, half pay of a private, for services rendered by her husband during said war.

Willin, Levin, Sr. Passed Feb. 12 (?), 1833—No. 12. Treas. Western Shore pay to Levin Willin, Sr., of Somerset county, a soldier of the rev. war, during life, quarterly, half pay of a private, for the services rendered by him during the rev. war.

Willis, Andrew. Passed Dec. session, 1817 (Feb. 6, 1818)—No. 29. Treas. Western Shore pay to Andrew Willis, of Washington county, a private in the rev. war, quarterly, the half pay of a private, as a further remuneration to him for those services by which his country has been so essentially benefitted.

* *Willis, Andrew,* private, Md. Line (Jan. 1820, p. 552).

Willis, Andrew. Feb. 18, 1825—No. 25, p. 159. Treas. to pay Lettie Willis, of Wash. county, half pay of a private as further compensation for her husband Andrew Willis's services during rev. war, beginning from date to which husband's pension has been pd.

Willmot, Robert, Lieut.—see Britton, Joseph.

Passed Feb. 13, 1836—No. 23. Treas. pay to Robert Wilmot, a soldier of the rev., half pay of a lieut. of artillery instead of half pay of lieut. of the line during life.

† *Wills, John*, private, Rev. army, of Baltimore county. Pensioned under Act of June 7, 1785 at $40.00 per annum, dating from Mch. 4, 1789 (recd. $1,085.64). Pensioned at $64.00 per an. from Apr. 24, 1816 (rec'd. $55.11). (U. S. Pension Rolls, 1835, p. 11).

Wilson, David. Feb. 16, 1820—No. 45. Treas. of Western Shore is directed to pay to David Wilson, of Washington county, half pay of a private for his rev. war services.

Passed Feb. 20, 1829—No. 24. Treas. pay to Rachel Wilson, widow of the late David Wilson, whatever sum appears to have been due to her said husband David Wilson, at time of his decease, on account of his services during the rev. war.

* *Wilson, David*, private, Md. Line (Jan. 1820, p. 552).

* *Willson, Richard*, captain, Md. Line—died June 27, 1818 (Jan. 1820, p. 552).

Wimber, Thomas. Passed Feb. 3, 1828—No. 11. Treas. Western Shore pay to Thomas Wimber, of Worcester county, half yearly, half pay of a private, further remuneration for his services during rev. war.

Winbrough, Thos. P. Passed Feb. 2, 1832—No. 23. Treas. Western Shore pay to Leah Winbrough, widow of Thomas P. Winbrough, a soldier of the rev. war, during her widowhood, half yearly, half pay of a private, for services of her husband during said war.

* *Wink, Jacob*, private, Houseger's Reg't. (Jan. 1820, p. 552).

Wolcott, Wm. Passed Feb. 26, 1829—No. 34. Treas. Western Shore pay to Wm. Wolcott, of state of Ohio, a soldier of the rev. war, during life, half yearly, half pay of a private, for his services during the rev. war.

* *Wood, Thomas*, private, Md. Line—died Aug. 2, 1819 (Jan. 1820, p. 552).

* *Woodburn, Jonathan*, private, Md. Line (Jan. 1820, p. 552).

Woolf, John. Recommended as Ensign for a Company of Militia in Frederick Co. Endorsed on a com'n. dated Oct. 13, 1777—see Manyard, Nathan.

Wootters, [*Wootton,*] *Richard*, Gentleman. Com'd. 1st. Lieut. of a Company in Prince George's Co. to which Robert Tyler was elected, belonging to the 25th Battn. of Militia of this Province. Given in Convention at Annapolis, Jan. 3, 1776. Signed pr. order Mat. Tilghman, Pres. (X, No. 214).

Officers for this Co. of Militia: Capt. Henderson Magruder; 1st. Lt. Richard Wootton; 2d. Lt. Singleton Wootton; Ensign, Joseph Jones;

1st. Sergent, John Ridgeway. It is the Unanimous wish of the Company that Mr. John Ridgeway take his —— in order.

Wright, Edward. Passed Feb. 9, 1820—No. 11. Treas. Western Shore is directed to pay to Edward Wright of Kent county a balance of 11£. 5s. due as a lieut. during the rev. war.

Wright, Jesse. Passed Nov. session, 1812 (Jan. 2, 1813)—No. 38. Treas. Western Shore pay to Jesse Wright, an old soldier, during the rev. war,—half pay of a private, as a further remuneration, &c.

Wright, Capt. Samuel T. Passed Jan. 30, 1837—No. 10. Treas. Western Shore pay to Ann Wright, widow of capt. Saml. T. Wright, half pay of a captain, during her life, as a further remuneration for his services during the rev.

Wykall, or Wycall, Adam. Passed Mch., 1833—No. 53. Treas. Western Shore pay to Ann Martin, of Prince George's county, widow of the late Adam Wykall, or Wycall, during her widowhood, quarterly, half pay of a private, for the services rendered by her said deceased husband, during the rev. war.

Wyndham, Sarah. Passed Feb. 22, 1822—(No. 42, p. 178). Treas. Western shore is directed to pay to Sarah Wyndham, of Annapolis, quarterly &c., half pay of a sergeant,—services rendered by her husband during the rev. war.

Passed, Mch. 2, 1842—No. 27. Treas. Western Shore pay to Andrew Slicer, of Annapolis, $20.83, being amt. due Sarah Wyndham for pension per resolution No. 42, 1822, to Aug. 5, 1841, the day of her death.

† *Yoe, Stephen,* sergeant Rev. army, of Queen Ann's county. Pensioned from Mch. 11, 1789 under Act of June 7, 1785, at $60.00 per annum (recd. $1,628.33)—at $96.00 per an. from Apr. 24, 1816 (recd. $466.66). Died in 1823. (U. S. Pens. Roll, 1835, p. 17).

Young, Benj. Passed Dec. session, 1816—No. 26. Treas. Western Shore pay unto Benj. Young, of Baltimore county, late a sergeant in the rev. war, quarterly, during his life, the half pay of a sergeant, as a further remuneration for those services by which his country has been so essentially benefitted.

* *Young, Benj.*, private, Md. Line (Jan. 1820, p. 553).

* *Young, Henry,* private, Pa. Line (Jan. 1820, p. 553).

ANNE ARUNDEL COUNTY MARRIAGES

Anne Arundel County, Marriage Licenses*
5800 Licenses = 11,640

Aaron Adams m. Mary Sappington, Sept. 18, 1804.
George Adams m. Elizabeth Mass, [Marr?] Aug. 1, 1796.
George Adams m. Elizabeth Welch, Dec. 4, 1807.
Hance Adams m. Philis Westlick, Dec. 19, 1777.
John Adams m. Henny Philips, Nov. 17, 1797.
John Adams m. Rebecca Johnson, July 28, 1802.
Joshua Adams m. Ann Kelly, Dec. 24, 1791.
Moses Adams m. Rebecca Sappington, Feb. 4, 1806.
Thomas Adams m. Margaret Coleman, June 26, 1802.
John Addison m. Lucy Watkins, Jan. 24, 1783.
Walter Dulany Addison m. Elizabeth Hasselius, June 5, 1792.
Robert Ailsworth m. Anne Duvall, Sept. 28, 1793.
Charles Aisquith m. Mary Wood, Dec. 5, 1817.
Robert Alcock m. Lydia Musgrove, Nov. 10, 1797.
William Alexander m. Polly Harwood Stockett, May 14, 1799.
Adam Allen m. Barbara Burgess, Oct. 21, 1786.
Azel Allen m. Elizabeth Lowman, Nov. 26, 1818.
Benjamin Allen m. Elizabeth Tongue, Jan. 8, 1790.
George Allen m. Ann Chaney, Jan. 18, 1786.
George Allen m. Ann White, May 25, 1815.
John Allen m. Susannah Philips, Feb. 19, 1783.
Jos. McCubbin Allen m. Mary Kirkland, June 18, 1793.
William Allen m. Dinah Sanders, Dec. 1, 1779.
William Allen m. Mary Philips, Feb. 4, 1780.
William Allan m. Elizabeth Rawlings, Jan. 5, 1789.
James Allison m. Elizabeth Bowers, Jan. 6, 1817.
Nathan Allnutt m. Anne Little, Dec. 10, 1803.
John Alwell m. Anne Larimore, Apr. 21, 1815.
William Allwell m. Sarah Phillips, June 1, 1780.
William Allwell m. Sarah Kelty, Apr. 13, 1790.
Holsey Alsip m. Juliet Brown, Dec. 11, 1807.
John Aman m. Rebecca Jones, Sept. 20, 1788.
John Ambler m. Sarah Lyles, Apr. 26, 1799.
Andrew Anderson m. Ann Belmear, Aug. 10, 1778.
Edward Anderson m. Susanna Cheney, Dec. 12, 1797.

* Transcribed from the County Records, by the late George W. Hodges.

Jacob Anderson m. Eliza Owens, Jan. 2, 1811.
James Anderson m. Jemima Taylor, Feb. 11, 1795.
James Anderson m. Anne Whedon, Dec. 10, 1800.
James Anderson m. Ann Wheeler, Feb. 10, 1813.
Joseph Anderson m. Sarah Coulter, Jan. 27, 1797.
Joshua Anderson m. Sarah Farroll, Dec. 5, 1806.
Samuel Anderson m. Elizabeth Anderson, Mch. 26, 1812.
Thomas Anderson m. Henrietta Paca, Nov. 6, 1794.
Thomas Anderson m. Julianna McCoy, June 22, 1820.
William Anderson m. Sarah Wayman, May 28, 1778.
William Anderson m. Sarah Belmear, May 22, 1781.
William Anderson m. Elizabeth Willett, Jan. 11, 1785.
William Andrews m. Lidia Medcalf, May 4, 1790.
Atlanatious Anglin m. Rachel Philips, Feb. 10, 1812.
Rezin Appleby m. Susanna Davis, Aug. 11, 1779.
Benjamin Armager m. Ann Lambert, Dec. 23, 1793.
Benjamin Armiger m. Sarah Hutton, Dec. 21, 1814.
John Armager m. Williama Whittington, Jan. 29, 1781.
John Armager m. Eleanor Trott, Jan. 10, 1798.
John Armiger m. Mary Sheckells, Feb. 29, 1810.
John Armiger m. Ann Dove, Jan. 14, 1820.
Leonard Armiger m. Frances Brown, Aug. 29, 1794.
Leonard Armager m. Anne Elickson, Jan. 22, 1803.
Samuel Armager m. Elizabeth Scott, Sept. 27, 1788.
Samuel Armager m. Elizabeth Gatwood, Dec. 17, 1793.
Samuel Armiger m. Rachel Sheckels, Mch. 27, 1807.
Samuel Armiger m. Rebecca Little, Oct. 13, 1815.
Thomas Armiger m. Elizabeth Hill, Jan. 2, 1818.
William Armager m. Jane Whittington, Dec. 18, 1783.
William Armiger m. Charlotte Duvall, Jan. 21, 1807.
John Arnold m. Rebecca Redmond, Dec. 1, 1819.
Richard Arnold m. Jane Sherburn, Dec. 21, 1805.
Robert Arnold m. Sarah Wells, Mch. 14, 1814.
Samuel Arnold m. Sarah Wheeler, Apr. 20, 1820.
Greenbury Ashley m. Mary Marsh, Sept. 19, 1797.
John Ashley m. Rebecca Phillips, Nov. 16, 1796.
John Ashley m. Elizabeth Culver, Mch. 18, 1802.
Lyles Askew m. Artridge Pritchard, Jan. 23, 1790.
John Askue m. Frances Poor, Dec. 22, 1809.
Jonathan Asque m. Alse Trott, Oct. 17, 1795.
Nathan Atkinson m. Elizabeth Hunter, Feb. 19, 1795.
Augustine Atwell m. Mary Ann Howard, Nov. 14, 1815.

Benjamin Atwell m. Sarah Kidd, Jan. 11, 1781.
Benjamin Atwell m. Rachel Hopkins, Feb. 15, 1792.
Benjamin Atwell m. Elizabeth Randall, Jan. 15, 1799.
Benjamin Atwell m. Mary Wells, Dec. 17, 1808.
Benjamin Atwell m. Honore Tucker, May 27, 1815.
Benjamin Atwell m. Mary Norman, June 11, 1816.
John Atwell m. Rebecca Dawson, May 26, 1810.
Joseph Atwell m. Rebecca Wells, Aug. 24, 1784.
Joseph Atwell m. Ann Pritchard, Nov. 27, 1802.
Roger Atwell m. Jane Kirby, May 8, 1815.
Samuel Atwell m. Mary Maccoy, Dec. 7, 1778.
Thomas Atwell m. Sarah Randall, Aug. 31, 1801.
Thomas Atwell m. Christiana Kirby, Feb. 7, 1817.
William Atwell m. Elizabeth Rawlings, Jan. 25, 1799.
John Austin m. Ann Beeden, May 11, 1777.
Elie Babbs m. Mary Thrawls, Apr. 22, 1805.
Thomas Babbs m. Rachel Pumphrey, Feb. 9, 1799.
John Babes m. Ann McCubbin, Oct. 10, 1780.
Benjamin Baden m. Elizabeth Whittington, Jan. 25, 1793.
Edward Baldwin m. Mary Marriott, Nov. 30, 1801.
Francis Baldwin m. Sarah Duvall, June 5, 1810.
Francis Baldwin m. Mary Sewell, Dec. 19, 1814.
Henry Baldwin m. Sarah Rawlings, Jan. 31, 1784.
Henry Baldwin m. Maria Woodward, Jan. 25, 1790.
John Baldwin m. Rachel Hopper, Jan. 13, 1791.
John Baldwin m. Charlotte Mitchell, Aug. 26, 1807.
Rezin D. Baldwin m. Charlotte Sullivan, Nov. 14, 1812.
Samuel Baldwin m. Eliz. Hopper, Feb. 7, 1786.
Tyler Baldwin m. Tomsey Davidge, Mch. 12, 1785.
William H. Baldwin m. Jane Maria Woodward, Oct. 6, 1817.
William P. Baldwin m. Caroline Williams, Dec. 22, 1818.
John Ball m. Elizabeth Battee, June 24, 1799.
Richard Ball m. Susan Lee, June 15, 1816.
Thomas Ball m. Elizabeth Williams, Apr. 22, 1778.
Thomas Ball m. Elizabeth Guinn, Mch. 14, 1799.
William Ball m. Sarah Dorsey, Feb. 16, 1788.
David Bangs m. Ruth Phelps, June 18, 1789.
John Banon m. Julia Pendergast, Mch. 26, 1789.
John Thomas Barber m. Catherine Taylor, Feb. 28, 1794.
John Thos. Barber m. Susanna Rowlings, Oct. 29, 1796.
Luke W. Barber m. Susanna Rowles, Apr. 20, 1799.
Jacob Bare m. Elizabeth W. Dorsey, Jan. 7, 1813.

John Barker m. Margaret Atwell, Dec. 20, 1781.
William Barker m. Rachel Franklin, Mch. 25, 1783.
Zachariah Barnes m. Catherine Barnes, Feb. 14, 1794.
Caleb Barry m. Elizabeth Anderson, Nov. 21, 1818.
Elisha Barry m. Rachel Lucas, Jan. 10, 1816.
Isaac Barry m. Martha Allien, Mch. 27, 1805.
Jacob Barry m. Susanna Hall, July 31, 1778.
Jacob Barry m. Mary Disney, May 30, 1788.
John Barry m. Mary Watkins, Aug. 28, 1792.
Joshua Barry m. Mirryam Chaney, Feb. 16, 1803.
Philip Barry m. Rachel King, Mch. 30, 1793.
Philip Barry m. Sarah Disney, July 1, 1795.
William Barry m. Mary Hinson, June 22, 1777.
Benjamin Basford m. Elizabeth Sheckell, Jan. 5, 1782.
Benjamin Basford m. Ann Whittington, Apr. 30, 1788.
Henry Basford m. Mary Watkins, Dec. 12, 1794.
Richard Bassford m. Sarah Taylor, Mch. 27, 1812.
Thomas Bassford m. Elizabeth Lusby, Oct. 3, 1811.
Zachariah Basford m. Anne Plummer, Dec. 4, 1789.
James Basil m. Rebecca Read, Oct. 16, 1790.
John Basil m. Ruth Nicholls, Jan. 27, 1781.
John Basil m. Lilly Anderson, Dec. 22, 1818.
Joseph Basil m. Lettitia [Tims/Iims?], June 23, 1791.
Ralph Basil m. Elizabeth Sanders, Nov. 3, 1780.
Ralph Basil m. Elizabeth Cartle, Dec. 10, 1791.
Robert Basil m. Mary Sheers, Dec. 3, 1802.
John Battee m. Lucy Harwood, Jan. 28, 1785.
Richard Battee m. Susanna Mayo, Dec. 10, 1794.
Richard Battee m. Sarah Smith, Dec. 15, 1797.
Richard H. Battee m. Patty E. Cowman, July 22, 1816.
Samuel Bayly m. Mary Ann Dorsey, Nov. 15, 1795.
Zepheniah Beall m. Lotty Ray, Mch. 18, 1800.
Absolom Bealmear m. Anne Waters, Feb. 2, 1820.
John Beard m. Susannah Chapman, Apr. 7, 1798.
John Beard m. Rhody Wells, Feb. 24, 1816.
Jonathan Beard m. Mary Gray, Nov. 29, 1783.
Jonathan Beard m. Rebecca Stockett, Feb. 24, 1791.
Joseph Beard m. Ann Ray, Dec. 29, 1787.
Joseph Beard m. Ann Beard, Apr. 18, 1808.
Matthew Beard m. Mary Dorsey, Oct. 31, 1786.
Richard Beard m. Sarah Coale, Dec. 21, 1789.
Richard Beard m. Eleanor Philpot, Dec. 4, 1816.

Stephen Beard m. Margaret Rutland, Jan. 28, 1802.
Stephen Beard m. Susanna Rawlings, Feb. 17, 1808.
Thomas Beard m. Ann Chapman, Nov. 25, 1779.
Anthony Beck m. Jamima Baldwin, Feb. 8, 1785.
James Beck m. Rebecca Waters, Dec. 9, 1785.
Joseph Beck m. Mary Stewart, Dec. 18, 1792.
Benjamin Beckett m. Margaret Hyatt, Jan. 21, 1792.
William Levin Beckett m. Mary Clarke, Dec. 28, 1791.
W^{m}. Turner Bedford m. Julia Wysham, June 9, 1805.
Francis Belmere m. Elizabeth Anderson, Oct. 6, 1794.
Francis Belmear m. Sarah Warfield, Oct. 9, 1811.
John Belmear m. Mary Vears, Oct. 16, 1783.
Samuel Belmear m. Juith Venus, Nov. 16, 1793.
John Wright Belt m. Sarah McComkin, July 22, 1797.
Osborn Belt m. Eleanor Macnew, May 18, 1796.
Robert B. Belt m. Rachel G. Deale, Apr. 16, 1805.
John Bennett m. Margaret Ray, Feb. 2, 1793.
Sayers James Bennett m. Mary Jenings, Oct. 27, 1796.
Alexander Benning m. Ann Valiant, Aug. 1, 1785.
William B. Benson m. Susan Taylor, July 25, 1816.
Edmund Benton m. Ann Meek, May 6, 1784.
Edward Berry m. Lucinda Trutten, Mch. 18, 1784.
William C. Betherny m. Susanna Welch, May 18, 1798.
George Bevans m. Mary Ogle, July 21, 1804.
Benjamin S. C. Bickford m. Elizabeth Tydings, Sept. 3, 1812.
William Bigg m. Elizabeth Ferguson, Sept. 2, 1783.
Francis Bird m. Rebecca Tucker, July 29, 1808.
Jacob Bird m. Susanna Lee, Nov. 17, 1808.
John Bird m. Mary Phips, Jan. 6, 1813.
Thomas Bicknell m. Julia Clarke, Jan. 19, 1805.
William Bird m. Ann McCauley, Dec. 11, 1788.
William Bird m. Ann Williams, July 16, 1799.
William Bird m. Susanna Rawlings, Aug. 3, 1816.
Francis Birkhead m. Margaret Simmons, Feb. 28, 1780.
John Birkhead m. Elizabeth Plummer, Nov. 5, 1807.
John G. Birckhead m. Mary Chaney, Oct. 26, 1820.
Nehemiah Birkhead m. Anne Parker, June 7, 1810.
Nehemiah Birkhead m. Mary Drury, Jan. 27, 1813.
Thomas Black m. Fanny Jenkins, Jan. 2, 1808.
John Blackswell m. Sarah Lancaster, Jan. 16, 1780.
Richard Blackerston m. Rebecca Franklin, Sept. 4, 1805.
Gilbert Bland m. Mary Syton, May 23, 1778.

John Bloodworth m. Mary Price, Dec. 17, 1795.
Edward Blunt m. Elizabeth Trott, Aug. 22, 1778.
Edward Blunt m. Anne Scrivener, Feb. 11, 1809.
John Bond m. Mary Burke, June 28, 1792.
Burle Boone m. Elizabeth Moss, Apr. 28, 1779.
Burley G. Boone m. Rebecca W. Fowler, Oct. 2, 1815.
Charles Boone m. Mary Cromwell, Dec. 9, 1817.
James Boone m. Anne Small, Nov. 20, 1799.
John Boone m. Providence Pumphrey, Apr. 15, 1780.
Jno. Boone T. Nichs. m. Eleanor Drain, June 17, 1806.
Richard Boone m. Cordelia Pumphrey, Feb. 5, 1780.
Stephen Boone m. Eliza Merriken, Nov. 29, 1815.
Thomas Boone m. Ann Cooper, Jan. 18, 1779.
Thomas Boone m. Hellen Cromwell, Aug. 7, 1799.
Peter Boose m. Priscilla Boose, Oct. 5, 1819.
James Booth m. Eliza Jones, Jan. 19, 1818.
Henry Bordley m. Ann Ware, Dec. 15, 1798.
John W. Bordley m. Sarah Whittington, Aug. 6, 1818.
James Bordman m. Ruth Shepherd, Mch. 22, 1792.
James Boardman m. Sarah Weedon, Feb. 10, 1795.
Somerset Bowen m. Cassander Childs, Jan. 22, 1817.
John Bowers m. Eliza. Priestley, Dec. 3, 1810.
Allen Bowie m. Sarah Chew, Dec. 18, 1787.
Allen Bowie m. Charlotte Boone, Feb. 4, 1803.
Daniel Bowie m. Frances Rebecca Lane, May 13, 1814.
Thomas H. Bowie m. Elizabeth H. Ray, Feb. 1, 1812.
John Boyd m. Elizabeth Carrick, Dec. 18, 1787.
Joseph Boyd m. Mary Scott, Aug. 18, 1791.
Thomas Boyde m. Margaret Lansdall, Feb. 17, 1784.
James Boyle m. Mary Rooke, Sept. 13, 1781.
James Boyle m. Susan Maccubbin, May 11, 1812.
John Bradenbaugh m. Priscilla Few, Oct. 25, 1803.
George Bradford m. Mary Mallone, Dec. 20, 1819.
William Bradford m. Eleanor Isaacs, Jan. 27, 1817.
Thomas Brant m. Rebecca Trott, Feb. 13, 1806.
Francis Brashears m. Eleanor Knighton, Jan. 22, 1811.
Jas. Brasheres m. Ann Chew, Dec. 1, 1784.
Jesse Brashears m. Anne Lambath, Feb. 16, 1792.
Joshua Brashears m. Ann Chew, Nov. 30, 1784.
Levie Brashars m. Fanny Lambeth, Jan. 9, 1793.
John Bray m. Julia Phillips, Sept. 21, 1803.
Joseph Bray m. Sarah Kelly, Jan. 2, 1797.

Henry Bremont m. Elizabeth Rummells, May 16, 1820.
Brice Brewer m. Frances Williams, Apr. 14, 1814.
Enos Brewer m. Elizabeth Lavey, Aug. 4, 1809.
Henry Brewer m. Mary Yieldhall, Aug. 24, 1813.
John Brewer m. Ann Watkins Smith, May 11, 1784.
John Brewer m. Elizabeth Garston, June 28, 1800.
Jno. Hammond Brewer m. Ann Maria Ball, July 16, 1810.
Joseph Brewer m. Mary Birkhead, Feb. 4, 1802.
Joseph N. N. Brewer m. Elizabeth Wilmot, Dec. 21, 1799.
Lloyd Brewer m. Elizabeth Sappington, July 10, 1813.
Nicholas Brewer m. Frances Davis, Aug, 12, 1794.
Nicholas Brewer m. Sarah McCubbin, June 21, 1800.
Nicholas Brewer Jnr. m. Julia Steuart, Oct. 30, 1817.
Thomas Brewer m. Susannah Lampley, Aug. 22, 1782.
William Brewer m. Alecia Thompson, July 5, 1796.
Edmund Brice m. Harriott Woodward, Sept. 10, 1783.
Edmund Brice m. Charlotte Eliza Ann Moss, July 17, 1818.
James Brice m. Julianna Jennings, May 23, 1781.
Daniel Brigdell m. Ann Foreman, Mch. 8, 1779.
Richard Brigdell m. Eleanor Allen, Mch. 6, 1792.
Richard Brigdell m. Patience Parsons, Sept. 13, 1785.
Thomas Brigdell m. Mary Johnson, Jan. 8, 1795.
Jos. Bright m. Belinda Hammond, July 17, 1787.
James Bright m. Mary Ann Tydings, May 24, 1800.
John Bright m. Elizabeth Gray, Aug. 23, 1810.
Nathan Bright m. Hanna Stinchecum, Oct. 3, 1801.
William Brogden m. Margaret McCulloch, Dec. 19, 1795.
John H. Brookes m. Ann Mahan, Jan. 13, 1819.
William Broughton m. Elizabeth Close, Aug. 27, 1781.
Basil Brown m. Henrietta Hammond, Aug. 10, 1787.
Benjamin Brown m. Dinah Phelps, Feb. 26, 1783.
Dauzy Brown m. Mary Ann Chilton, May 21, 1813.
Francis Brown m. Sarah Lamblin, Feb. 9, 1793.
George Brown m. Rachel Chilton, May 19, 1804.
Gideon Brown m. Mary Flowers, June 17, 1807.
Henry H. Brown m. Mary Ann Cross, Dec. 23, 1816.
John Brown m. Laurania Rawlings, Mch. 3, 1783.
John Brown m. Elizabeth Harrison, Apr. 7, 1792.
John Brown m. Mary Joiner, Aug. 23, 1805.
Joseph Brown m. Henrietta Clarke, June 19, 1783.
Joseph G. Brown m. Anne King, June 12, 1810.
Kensey Brown m. Maria Woodward, Dec. 15, 1817.

Philemon Brown m. Margery Gaither, Dec. 12, 1787.
Rasha Brown m. Elizabeth Pople, July 15, 1814.
Richard Brown m. Elizabeth Childs, Jan. 31, 1791.
Richard Brown Sn^{r}. m. Anne Wood, July 8, 1794.
William Brown m. Mary Hammond, Dec. 6, 1782.
William Brown m. Elizabeth Griffith, Apr. 14, 1786.
William Brown m. Nackey Wilson, Jan. 26, 1791.
William Brown m. Tomsey Thomas, Mch. 21, 1810.
John Bruce Jn^{r}. m. Sarah Lane, Apr. 19, 1794.
Frederick Bryan m. Elizabeth Derry, Dec. 21, 1796.
Frederick Bryan m. Julia Bray, Dec. 23, 1805.
James Bryan m. Anne Love, Feb. 9, 1791.
John Bryan m. Lydia M. Donald, June 28, 1777.
John Bryan m. Lavenia Baldwin, Jan. 13, 1797.
John Bryan m. Elizabeth Randall, Feb. 1, 1808.
Joseph Bryan m. Elizabeth Brewer, Apr. 24, 1804.
Samuel Bryant m. Nacky Wood, Dec. 18, 1799.
Thomas Buchanan m. Reb^{c}. Maria Harriet Anderson, April 11, 1798.
John Buff m. Priscilla Read, Jan. 5, 1790.
William Burdit m. Rachel Mobberly, May 6, 1777.
Elijah Burgee m. Mary M. Danieson, Nov. 27, 1816.
Basil Burgess m. Eleanor Dorsey, Jan. 11, 1785.
Benjamin Burgess m. Agnes Battee, Nov. 2, 1780.
Caleb Burgess m. Susannah Mercer, Apr. 6, 1787.
Enock M. Burgess m. Sarah L. C. Smith, May 1, 1806.
John Burgess m. Eleanor Griffith, July 27, 1785.
John Burgess m. Rachel Thomas, Mch. 14, 1798.
John West Burgess m. Sarah Battee, Feb. 3, 1787.
Jno. West Burgess m. Sarah Simmons, Aug. 29, 1796.
Michael Burgess m. Sarah Warfield, Oct. 22, 1783.
Samuel Burgess m. Henrietta Warfield, Jan. 31, 1805.
Vachel Burgess m. Rebecca Dorsey, Oct. 1, 1782.
William Burgess m. Susannah Coale, Oct. 27, 1800.
John Burnet m. Eleanor Butler, Apr. 16, 1808.
Peter E. Burras m. Kitty Lambeth, Dec. 29, 1806.
Henry Burns m. Priscilla Owens, Mch. 21, 1780.
Thomas Burns m. Eleanor Doudle, May 20, 1777.
Edmund Burton m. Ann Henwood, May 4, 1788.
John Burton m. Rachel Henwood, Nov. 22, 1785.
Benjamin Busey m. Eleanor Trott, June 9, 1804.
Benjamin Busey m. Ann Popham, Nov. 24, 1819.
Henry Busey m. Sarah Powell, May 18, 1795.

Henry Busey m. Elizabeth Carr, Sept. 4, 1806.
Joseph Busey m. Eliza S. Kelly, Mch. 30, 1816.
Samuel Bussey m. Mary Mead, Feb. 1, 1785.
Samuel Busey m. Catherine Carr, Feb. 11, 1793.
George Bush m. Susan Smith, Jan. 2, 1809.
James Butler m. Rebecca Welsh, Nov. 30, 1779.
Richard Butler m. Rebecca Foggett, Aug. 22, 1814.
Benjamin Cadle m. Sarah Tucker, Dec. 13, 1782.
Samuel Cadle m. Elizabeth McCauley, Dec. 24, 1778.
Samuel Cadle m. Elizabeth Short, Dec. 5, 1789.
Thomas Cadle m. Nancy Hall, Feb. 15, 1803.
William Cadle m. Mary Hall, Nov. 26, 1805.
Zachariah Cadle m. Rachel Gaither, Oct. 25, 1786.
Charles Caiter m. Sarah Debricks, Dec. 30, 1812.
William Calder m. Harriet Jackson, Jan. 13, 1802.
William Caldwell m. Mary Culbart, Feb. 15, 1780.
John Callahan m. Sarah Buckland, June 22, 1782.
George Calvert m. Rosalie Stier, June 10, 1799.
John S. Camden m. Anne Smith, Nov. 29, 1808.
James Campbell m. Mary Walker, June 2, 1785.
William Campbell m. Rebecca Carter, Aug. 3, 1777.
Henry Carick m. Darky Clarke, Nov. 25, 1789.
John Carl m. Ann Dudley, Aug. 24, 1781.
William Carman m. Mary McCauley, Oct. 28, 1805.
William Carman m. Ann Johnson, May 8, 1813.
Humphrey Carpenter m. Mary Fly, Apr. 1, 1780.
Benjamin Carr m. Mary Denton, Dec. 29, 1802.
Benjamin Carr m. Catherine Welch, June 15, 1805.
Benjamin P. Carr m. Priscilla Ray, Nov. 30, 1792.
Henry Carr m. Anne Drury, Jan. 23, 1819.
Jacob Carr m. Matilda Lambreth, Jan. 2, 1804.
John Carr m. Rachel Purnell, Feb. 11, 1779.
John Carr m. Elizabeth Pindle, June 29, 1781.
John Carr m. Sarah Warfield, May 8, 1804.
John Carr m. Mary Armiger, Dec. 27, 1806.
Richard Carr m. Airy Busey, Oct. 3, 1804.
Robert Carr m. Susannah Childs, Nov. 7, 1789.
Samuel Carr m. Jane Russell, Jan. 2, 1783.
Walter Carr m. Dolly Parrott, June 2, 1799.
Walter Carr m. Martha Ray, July 23, 1783.
Walter Carr m. Mary Scrivener, Aug. 17, 1812.
William Carr m. Sophia Crosby, Feb. 1, 1814.

Henry Carrick m. Eleanor Shrieve, Feb. 23, 1791.
Charles Carroll m. Eliza. Warfield, Jan. 26, 1795.
Edmund Carrell m. Elizabeth Dixon, Aug. 16, 1791.
Joshua Carroll m. Sarah Godman, July 15, 1800.
Nicholas Carroll m. Ann Jenings, Oct. 30, 1783.
Samuel Carroll m. Eliz. Williams, Oct. 17, 1788.
Charles Carter m. Susan Osborn, Jan. 5, 1815.
Jacob Carter m. Mary Wells, Oct. 31, 1801.
Samuel Carter m. Judah Flood, Oct. 19, 1782.
Samuel Carter m. Ann Curry, Oct. 16, 1786.
Sparrow Carter m. Elizabeth Phelps, Mch. 5, 1791.
Robert Case m. Rachel Basil, Mch. 14, 1789.
Richard Caton m. Mary Carroll, Nov. 24, 1787.
William Caton m. Ann Purdy, Aug. 16, 1788.
John Cattonton m. Nancy Lambeth, Mch. 18, 1813.
William Cawly m. Eleanor Hopkins, Apr. 3, 1801.
John Chain m. Ann Tucker, July 31, 1777.
Josia Chain m. Millie Tucker, Sept. 9, 1779.
James Chalmus m. Lucy Skinner, Sept. 18, 1783.
Joshua Chambers m. Sarah Monroe, Sept. 17, 1819.
Thomas Chambers m. Kitty Ryan, Oct. 21, 1797.
William Chambers m. Elizabeth Blunt, July 29, 1782.
Hugh Champlin m. Elizabeth Hender, Mch. 23, 1789.
Walter S. Chandler m. Margaret Rogers, Sept. 19, 1799.
Benjamin Chaney m. Eleanor Lattin, Dec. 8, 1807.
Dennis Chaney m. Delilah Beckett, Aug. 17, 1818.
Henry Chaney m. Mary Childs, Jan. 21, 1814.
John Chaney m. Eliza Russell, Dec. 24, 1817.
Joseph Chaney m. Elizabeth Fitzgiles, Jan. 10, 1809.
Joseph Chaney m. Susanna Forde, Dec. 26, 1811.
Joseph Chaney m. Anne L. Wood, July 19, 1819.
Levi Chaney m. Henrietta Lee, Apr. 1, 1820.
Rezin Chaney m. Eleanor Baldwin, Mch. 24, 1814.
Richard Chaney m. Ann Cromwell, June 24, 1808.
Richard Chaney m. Henny Ryan, Nov. 29, 1815.
Richard Chaney m. Susan White, Mch. 20, 1818.
Samuel Chaney m. Rebecca Phelps, Feb. 13, 1809.
Thomas Chaney m. Jemima Godman, Oct. 1, 1792.
William Chaney m. Sarah Holton, Feb. 23, 1797.
William Chaney m. Ann Steuart, Feb. 16, 1799.
William W. Chaney m. Sarah Roberts, Aug. 31, 1804.
Henry H. Chapman m. Mary Davidson, Jan. 1, 1799.

John Chapman m. Susannah Jackson, May 18, 1793.
Thomas Chapman m. Clare Taylor, Sept. 4, 1792.
William Chapman m. Ann Sellman, June 22, 1781.
William Chapman m. Susannah Gassaway, Mch. 5, 1791.
Cornelius Chard m. Elizabeth Moale, June 25, 1781.
Oliver Chard m. Rebecca Meeke, Aug. 27, 1792.
Jeremiah T. Chase m. Hesther Baldwin, June 24, 1779.
John Chase m. Penelopy Blunt, July 2, 1785.
John Chase m. Cecelia Johnson, May 27, 1820.
Richard M. Chase m. Matilda Green, Nov. 25, 1806.
Richard M. Chase m. Mary Marriott, Jan. 28, 1819.
Thomas Chase m. Matilda Chase, Oct. 17, 1816.
Abraham Cheney m. Mary Curry, July 21, 1791.
Benjamin Cheney m. Rachel Knighton, Jan. 15, 1820.
Elijah Cheney m. Sarah Groves, Jan. 21, 1788.
James Cheney m. Sarah Thorp, July 16, 1791.
John Cheney m. Rachel Benson, Apr. 11, 1785.
John Cheney m. Priscilla Hooper, Jan. 8, 1808.
Joseph Cheney m. Sarah Cheney, Feb. 26, 1802.
Joseph Cheney m. Elizabeth Conner, Feb. 5, 1803.
Richard Cheney m. Sophia Simpson, Dec. 22, 1786.
Thomas Cheney m. Mary Williams, Dec. 3, 1798.
John Chew m. Mary Wilson, Feb. 1, 1787.
Nathaniel Chew m. Martha Bird, Feb. 16, 1814.
Philemon Chew m. Ann Maria Bowie Brooke, Feb. 15, 1813.
Richard Chew m. Jane Fisher, Oct. 22, 1810.
Samuel Chew m. Mary Cockey, Apr. 20, 1791.
Samuel Lloyd Chew m. Dorothy Harrison, June 28, 1777.
Benjamin Childs m. Mary Roberts, Oct. 17, 1781.
Benjamin Childs m. Susannah Griffith, May 27, 1786.
Benjamin Childs m. Elizabeth Munroe, May 12, 1818.
Cephas Childs m. Ann Welch, June 21, 1785.
Cephas Childs m. Sarah Miles, Jan. 28, 1786.
Cephus Childs m. Pheby Tannihill, Dec. 25, 1794.
Henry Childs m. Sarah Smith, Jan. 24, 1793.
Henry Childs m. Mary Tootell, Jan. 23, 1809.
Henry Childs m. Mary Whittington, June 26, 1820.
Isaac Childs m. Eliz. Deale, Feb. 28, 1810.
John Childs m. Ann Owings, Apr. 30, 1778.
John Childs m. Mary Ann Hyde, Feb. 3, 1812.
John Childs m. Sophia Drury, Jan. 7, 1818.
Lewis Childs m. Sarah Watts, Dec. 23, 1793.

William Childs m. Henrietta Brown, Dec. 26, 1785.
William Childs m. Ann Trott, Oct. 3, 1791.
William Childs m. Elizabeth Fisher, Feb. 5, 1812.
Richard Chilton m. Catherine Brown, Feb. 10, 1809.
Archibald Chisholm m. Elizabeth Waters, Sept. 22, 1777.
Judson M. Clagett m. Caroline Hesselius, Mch. 5, 1795.
William Claggett m. Elizabeth Gibbs, Dec. 11, 1792.
Jonas Clapham m. Catherine Cooke, Dec. 5, 1793.
Abraham Clarke m. Mima Jones, Dec. 18, 1792.
Benjamin Clarke m. Rachel Chaney, Mch. 15, 1788.
Benjamin Clarke m. Elizabeth Gambrill, Feb. 4, 1793.
Benjamin D. Clarke m. Sarah Yieldhall, Mch. 5, 1807.
David Clarke m. Rachel Warfield, May 28, 1800.
Frederick Clarke m. Elizabeth Rankin, Nov. 16, 1784.
Hezekiah Clarke m. Eliz^{a}. Stansbury, Feb. 1, 1820.
Jacob Clarke m. Rebecca Halbertee, Feb. 4, 1809.
Jacob Clarke m. Ashsah McCauley, May 28, 1814.
John Clarke m. Susannah Lucus, July 23, 1787.
Joseph Clarke m. Bell Fergerson, Nov. 3, 1777.
Joseph Clarke m. Anne Nicholls, July 29, 1793.
Robert Clarke m. Cassuck Murrow, June 1, 1780.
Satterlee Clarke m. Frances E. Whitcroft, Sept. 22, 1810.
William Clarke m. Dinah White, Apr. 21, 1778.
William Clarke m. Levena Warfield, Sept. 30, 1780.
William Clarke m. Elizabeth Clarke, May 23, 1798.
William Clarke m. Lydia Wheeler, Dec. 9, 1815.
William T. Clarke m. Juliet Gaither, July 29, 1800.
Abraham Claude m. Elizabeth Quynn, Nov. 28, 1785.
Cornelius Claud m. Rhody Robinson, Feb. 20, 1817.
Dennis Claude m. Anne Jacob, Feb. 13, 1816.
Philip Clayton m. Mary Brewer, Oct. 23, 1809.
Francis T. Clements m. Sarah Wall, Feb. 28, 1795.
Samuel Coe m. Mary Fowler, Apr. 5, 1796.
Samuel Coale m. Anne Winterson, July 6, 1798.
Thomas Coale m. Elizabeth Dorsey, Dec. 18, 1798.
Thomas Coale m. Nancy Burgess, Jan. 5, 1803.
William Coale m. Catherine Laughlin, Mch. 28, 1793.
William Coale m. Margaret Tucker, Nov. 16, 1797.
William Coale m. Thomsee Knighton, Aug. 31, 1807.
John Coats m. Johanna Phelps, Nov. 14, 1783.
William Cobb m. Mary Ann Jackson, July 8, 1816.
Patrick Cockran m. Mary Bland, Aug. 8, 1777.

William Coe m. Eleanor Devonish, July 15, 1780.
William Coe m. Mary Sears, June 29, 1793.
Thomas Colbert m. Mary Colligan, Feb. 9, 1779.
James Cole m. Ann Wilkins, Nov. 28, 1777.
John Cole m. Eleanor Hall, Oct. 27, 1777.
John Cole m. Anne Purdy, Feb. 26, 1802.
Thomas Cole m. Sarah Ridgely, Oct. 1, 1781.
William Cole m. Caroline Norman, Jan. 19, 1819.
Milton Francis Coleman m. Mary Teresa Murdock, Apr. 24, 1819.
Bannister Collins m. Elizabeth Hanshaw, Feb. 13, 1810.
James Collins m. Christian T. Daves, Feb. 17, 1780.
John Babtist Collins m. Elizabeth Hannah, Mch. 16, 1778.
Thomas Collins m. Isabella Bowen, Apr. 25, 1801.
John Collinson m. Ann Tongue, June 22, 1819.
William Collison m. Elizabeth Whittington, Sept. 29, 1808.
William Comrady m. Elizabeth Griffin, Jan. 26, 1807.
Richard Conn m. Sarah Woodward, Aug. 27, 1792.
David Conner m. Durkey Burns, Jan. 22, 1783.
James Conner m. Mary Bevans, Feb. 8, 1816.
Marmaduke W. Conner m. Sarah Ann Vessels, May 12, 1820.
Richard Conner m. Henrietta Gott, Jan. 31, 1786.
William Conner m. Eleanor Wyvell, Oct. 9, 1788.
Addison Connoway m. Mary Welch, Jan. 23, 1788.
George Connoway m. Elizabeth Pettibone, Apr. 11, 1798.
Michael Connoway m. Belinda Jean, July 24, 1792.
Richard A. Contee m. Elizabeth Rawlings, Jan. 22, 1794.
Peter H. Cook m. Lydia Bryan, Nov. 11, 1820.
Charles Cooke m. Agnes Burgess, Nov. 24, 1795.
Charles Cooke m. Elizabeth Long, Aug. 26, 1796.
George Cooke m. Fanny Cox, Apr. 7, 1792.
Henry Cooke m. Anne Allen Pennington, Jan. 21, 1815.
Joseph Cooley m. Eliza Howes, Dec. 5, 1817.
William Cooley m. Ann Harwood, Dec. 22, 1777.
John Cooper m. Margaret Maccoy, Apr. 16, 1783.
Robert Copland m. Hetty Long, June 4, 1798.
William M. Corcard m. Letty Pryse, Nov. 10, 1795.
Henry Corner m. Mary Gott, Nov. 6, 1796.
Joseph G. Corner m. Susanna W. Franklin, Aug. 24, 1819.
Robert Corse m. Eleanor Yieldhall, June 28, 1799.
Henry Coulter m. Anne Clarke, Sept. 23, 1802.
James Coulter m. Eleanor Jones Duvall, June 30, 1808.
John Coulter m. Elizabeth McCubbin, Oct. 4, 1798.

William Court m. Leticia James, Dec. 24, 1804.
James Cowan m. Jane McHurd, Feb. 28, 1789.
Charles Cowley m. Ann Elizabeth Deale, July 24, 1790.
John Cowman m. Mary Plummer, Apr. 16, 1793.
Joseph Cowman m. Eleanor W. Hall, Sept. 18, 1799.
Joseph Cowman m. Elizabeth Watson, June 30, 1806.
Philip Cowman m. Elizabeth Shields, Dec. 16, 1806.
Thomas Cowman m. Henrietta Harwood, Nov. 14, 1798.
John Cox m. Henrietta Maria Minskie, May 12, 1778.
Andrew Coyle m. Elizabeth Chisholm, Dec. 26, 1807.
Richard I. Crabb m. Catherine Chase, Nov. 4, 1813.
William Craig m. Mary Joice, May 13, 1819.
Robert Craigs m. Sarah Barry, Mch. 30, 1782.
Samuel Cram [Crane?] m. Delilah Mass, [Moss?] Mch. 7, 1791.
Caleb Crane m. Margaret Smith, July 4, 1805.
Fredk. Cramblick m. Rebecca Day, Jan. 7, 1797.
Abel Crandell m. Elizabeth Mary Lane, Jan. 10, 1793.
Adam Crandle m. Elizabeth Dove, Feb. 19, 1778.
Francis Cranndall m. Susannah Leach, May 31, 1802.
Francis Crandell m. Anne McKenzie, July 18, 1814.
George Crandell m. Jane Parish, Dec. 22, 1788.
Henry Crandell m. Anne Woodfield, Jan. 5, 1804.
John Crandell m. Susanna Whittington, July 1, 1809.
Joseph Crandell m. Rachel Gardner, Jan. 12, 1792.
Richd. Crandell m. Priscilla Gott, Oct. 26, 1789.
Thomas Crandell m. Pamelia Jackson, Dec. 24, 1812.
Thomas Crandell m. Willy Hinton, Dec. 18, 1813.
William Crandell m. Amelia Carr, Aug. 10, 1791.
Samuel Crane m. Sarah Cromwell, Apr. 30, 1795.
Thomas Crane m. Mary Dare, Dec. 9, 1820.
Basil Crapster m. Harriet Watkins, Sept. 24, 1816.
David Crawford m. Elizabeth Price, Sept. 27, 1785.
Isaac Crayton m. Mary Keene, July 30, 1784.
Charles Creek m. Sophia Wells, May 27, 1814.
Abel Creendell m. Susanna Crutchley, Dec. 22, 1810.
Henry Crist m. Elizabeth Pryse, Sept. 5, 1795.
John Cromwell m. Rhody Ridgely, Jan. 28, 1813.
Michael Cromwell m. Charlotte Williams, Mch. 9, 1816.
Oneal Cromwell m. Sarah Cromwell, June 12, 1817.
Thomas Cromwell m. Elizabeth Miller, Oct. 9, 1812.
Zachariah Cromwell m. Sarah Hall, Mch. 31, 1809.
Burton Crosby m. Ann Childs, Jan. 1, 1785.

John Crosby m. Rachel Brown, Jan. 4, 1786.
Josias Crosby m. Mary Carr, Feb. 10, 1784.
Richard Crosby m. Elizabeth Norman, Feb. 16, 1807.
Richard Crosby m. Juliet Trott, Feb. 25, 1818.
John Cross m. Jemima Selby, Apr. 21, 1810.
Joseph Cross m. Patsey Taylor, Jan. 12, 1785.
Thomas Cross m. Elizabeth Taylor, Feb. 4, 1799.
Thomas Cross m. Harriett Howard, Jan. 21, 1804.
Thomas R. Cross m. Area Rockhold, June 4, 1807.
Joseph Crouch m. Sarah Little, Aug. 29, 1780.
Joseph Crox m. Catharine Seibert, Sept. 8, 1785.
Jesse Crutchley m. Mary Philips, Dec. 21, 1791.
Josh Crutchley m. Mary Phelps, Aug. 2, 1814.
Thomas Crutchley m. Mary Ann Forster, Dec. 6, 1784.
Francis Curen m. Mary Cleverly, Dec. 31, 1791.
Michael Curran m. Mary Maybury, Apr. 26, 1800.
Philip Curran m. Juliana Dunn, Oct. 21, 1805.
Edward Curten m. Ann Davidson, Apr. 29, 1785.
Peter Cuting m. Elizabeth Johnson, Apr. 11, 1780.
Emanuel Dadds m. Mary Pierce, Dec. 31, 1798.
Joseph Bryan Dailey m. Mary Childs, Dec. 10, 1791.
Joseph Daley m. Priscilla Darnall, June 17, 1813.
Thomas Dalzell m. Margaret Williams, June 23, 1790.
Samuel Dames m. Mary Ann Lewis, Jan. 24, 1804.
Aaron Dannison m. Henrietta Burton, Dec. 17, 1803.
Elijah Danison m. Rachel Chaney, Nov. 8, 1808.
Caleb Darby m. Elizabeth Ray, Dec. 9, 1783.
Samuel Darley [Darby?] m. Verlin Carr, Nov. 14, 1781.
Henry Darnall m. Pamelia Dawson, Nov. 26, 1814.
Thomas Darnelson m. Elizabeth Cheney, Oct. 12, 1799.
Azel Davidge m. Tomsey Sewell, Oct. 25, 1779.
Israel Davidson m. Mary Stockett, Sept. 13, 1817.
James Davidson m. Milley Read, Feb. 16, 1787.
James Davidson m. Mary Stewart, Feb. 28, 1792.
John Davidson m. Ann McCauley, Jan. 10, 1788.
John Davidson m. Anna Maria L. Grason, Sept. 22, 1796.
William Davidson m. Rebecca Walker, Oct. 8, 1795.
Richard Davinson m. Milea Frans. Wayman, Apr. 29, 1783.
Cornelius Davis m. Elizabeth Taylor, Aug. 29, 1814.
Daniel Davis m. Mary Whitaker, Apr. 30, 1785.
George Davis m. Catharine Green, Jan. 28, 1785.
James Davis m. Susan Lusby, Oct. 8, 1801.

John Davis m. Sarah Ditty, May 26, 1808.
Robert Davis Jnr. m. Ann Collins, July 6, 1778.
Robert Davis m. Mary Fairborne, June 4, 1803.
Robert Davis m. Rainer Ann Queen, May 1, 1819.
Samuel Davis m. Elizabeth Merriken, Aug. 25, 1800.
Samuel Davis m. Eliza Ann Earle, May 27, 1807.
Thomas Davis m. Catherine Worthington, Apr. 18, 1796.
Thomas Davis m. Rebecca Beard, June 6, 1800.
Thomas Davis m. Elizabeth Kilman, Oct. 15, 1805.
Thomas Davis m. Mary Beard, May 7, 1814.
William Davis m. Anne Stewart, Sept. 4, 1795.
William Davis m. Elizabeth Davis, Jan. 11, 1804.
Richard Daw m. Elizabeth Disney, June 27, 1795.
James Dawson m. Elizabeth Norris, Apr. 5, 1798.
Jonas Dawson m. Ann Johnson, Apr. 11, 1785.
Jonas Dawson m. Mary Sumberlin, Dec. 13, 1814.
Joseph Dawson m. Elizabeth Thompson, June 3, 1779.
William Dawson m. Mary Shepphard, Sept. 30, 1818.
Edward Day m. Sarah Lewis, May 2, 1799.
John Day m. Martha Pennington, Mch. 4, 1811.
Nathaniel Day m. Ann Brashares, Feb. 15, 1803.
James Deale m. Elizabeth Sherbrett, Oct. 19, 1802.
James Deale m. Mary Franklin, Feb. 9, 1805.
Marlin Deale m. Rachel Franklin, Feb. 9, 1808.
Nathaniel Deale m. Rachel Crosby, June 27, 1794.
Samuel Deale m. Elizabeth David, Feb. 19, 1787.
Samuel Deale m. Eleanor Norman, Sept. 23, 1793.
Samuel Deale m. Susanna Miles, July 7, 1818.
William Deale m. Ann Norris, June 2, 1777.
William Deale m. Rachel Gott, Nov. 14, 1797.
John Deaver m. Onner Roth, Aug. 3, 1789.
Moses Deaver m. Elizabeth Disney, Feb. 8, 1794.
William DeBlois m. Catharine Nixon, Dec. 4, 1786.
John Deborough m. Mary Hammond, May 12, 1796.
Benjamin Deford m. Ann Hutton, Dec. 21, 1798.
Daniel Delozier m. Ann Higinbotham, Nov. 3, 1791.
Thomas S. Denny m. Mary Norris, Jan. 15, 1800.
John Dent m. Eleanor Cecil, Apr. 2, 1787.
James Deroachbroom m. Mary Blunt, July 31, 1785.
William Derochbroon m. Elizabeth Joice, July 14, 1797.
Robert Denny m. Augusta Green, Feb. 5, 1789.
Thomas Dew m. Catherine Scrivener, Jan. 31, 1816.

William Didenoven [Dielenoven?]m. Polly Welch, Sept. 30, 1793.
Thomas Diffenderffer m. Elizabeth Sewell, Dec. 7, 1811.
Edward Disney m. Ann Phelps, Nov. 4, 1778.
Edward Disney m. Margaret Watkins, Dec. 1, 1795.
James Disney m. Mary Weems, Mch. 22, 1783.
John T. Disney m. Eliz[a]. Shepherd, Dec. 21, 1820.
Mordecai Disney m. Amelia Porter, Feb. 8, 1785.
Richard Disney m. Ariana Porter, Aug. 21, 1784.
Richard Disney m. Mary Watkins, Feb. 28, 1786.
Richard Disney m. Sarah Lawrence Disney, Nov. 6, 1799.
Richard Disney m. Rachel Disney, July 24, 1802.
Richard Disney m. Priscilla Disney, Nov. 27, 1819.
Snowden Disney m. Rachel Deaver, Oct. 29, 1793.
Thomas Disney m. Deborah Williams, Apr. 24, 1802.
William Disney m. Ruth Spurrier, Feb. 21, 1794.
Roger Ditty m. Sarah Jacob, Mch. 8, 1797.
Archibald Dobbins m. Mary Knapp, Sept. 6, 1794.
Thomas Doane m. Hanna Vineyard, Dec. 12, 1795.
Samuel Done m. Elizabeth Stallings, Feb. 3, 1816.
Henry Dodson m. Henney Ganell, Aug. 10, 1819.
John Dodson m. Eleanor Howard, Feb. 13, 1778.
John M. Donald m. Elizabeth Babington, Dec. 15, 1777.
Aaron Donaldson m. Mary Little, June 29, 1781.
Elijah Donaldson m. Mary Ann Cheney, Dec. 29, 1781.
Levy Donalson m. Eleanor Low, Dec. 5, 1804.
Rezin Donaldson m. Ann Dove, Dec. 7, 1802.
Richard Donaldson m. Rachel Waters, Mch. 3, 1783.
Richard Donaldson m. Margaret Rhodes, Apr. 24, 1798.
Richard Donaldson m. Rebecca Marriott, Nov. 10, 1806.
Thomas Donaldson m. Caroline Waters, Oct. 23, 1819.
Simon Donnely m. Eleanor Maguire, Sept. 15, 1798.
Benedict Dorsey m. Margaret Watkins, Apr. 20, 1789.
Daniel Dorsey m. Eleanor Dorsey, Feb. 17, 1779.
Edward Hill Dorsey m. Eleanor Pue, Oct. 1, 1798.
Ely Dorsey m. Sarah Worthington, Sept. 3, 1778.
Henry H. Dorsey m. Mary Wright, Sept. 21, 1795.
John Dorsey m. Margaret Boone, Mch. 19, 1782.
John W. Dorsey m. Rachel Warfield, Oct. 27, 1779.
John Dorsey m. Mary Ann Hammond, Nov. 20, 1815.
Joshua Dorsey m. Margaret Watkins, Mch. 9, 1787.
Philip Dorsey m. Cassandra Burgess, Sept. 12, 1815.
Reuben N. Dorsey m. Sarah D. Meriweather, Nov. 17, 1820.

Richard Dorsey m. Anne Wayman, Feb. 13, 1796.
Richard Dorsey m. Anne Warfield, Nov. 4, 1797.
Thomas Beale Dorsey m. Sarah Dorcey Merrewether, Nov. 28, 1797.
Thomas H. Dorsey m. Ann Dorsey, May 15, 1811.
Vachel Dorsey—of Vachel m. Sarah Nelson, Apr. 9, 1783.
Vachel Dorsey m. Elizabeth Dorsey, Mch. 19, 1798.
Jo^{s}. Dove m. Elizabeth Gardiner, Sept. 8, 1787.
John Dove m. Dinah Wilmot, Dec. 7, 1781.
John Dove m. Mary Lambeth, Jan. 10, 1798.
John Dove m. Nancy Ford, Dec. 29, 1802.
Samuel Dove m. Anne Carr, Nov. 4, 1801.
Charles Dovel m. Ann Sprall, July 9, 1777.
Richard Dowell m. Lydia Dew, Dec. 20, 1788.
Richard Dowell m. Sarah Sellman, July 23, 1813.
Thomas Draen m. Elizabeth Todd, July 14, 1791.
Richard Drane m. Sarah Gwinn, Feb. 4, 1806.
Charles Drury m. Mary Eversfield, Oct. 17, 1794.
Charles Drury m. Margaret King, June 1, 1797.
Henry C. Drury m. Elizabeth Mills, May 16, 1806.
Henry C. Drury m. Sarah Elson, Nov. 25, 1808.
Henry C. Drury m. Elizabeth Franklin, Dec. 2, 1816.
Irvingham Drury m. Sarah Hill, Apr. 14, 1790.
Jerningham Drury m. Sarah Simmons, Sept. 29, 1801.
Samuel Drury m. Ann Irams, May 29, 1779.
William Drury m. Margaret Miles, Mch. 22, 1806.
William Drury Jn^{r}. m. Maria Smith, Nov. 13, 1816.
Allen Bowie Duckett m. Margaret Howard, Oct. 17, 1799.
Basil Duckett m. Sophia Mulliken, Feb. 13, 1798.
Richard Duckett m. Elizabeth Howard, Dec. 20, 1804.
Thomas Duckett m. Ann Cowman, June 7, 1788.
Edward Dudley m. Sarah Record, May 16, 1791.
John Dudow m. Sarah Susan Dorsett, Apr. 20, 1812.
James Dulshier m. Mary Townshend, Oct. 3, 1812.
Benjamin Dungan m. Eleanor Griffin, May 11, 1812.
Joseph Dungee m. Mary Welch, Sept. 1, 1803.
George Dunn m. Rachel Smith, Sept. 14, 1818.
John Dunn m. Milley Cooper, Mch. 12, 1795.
Patrick Dunn m. Judith Donnovan, June 2, 1786.
Abraham Duvall m. Eleanor Chaney, Dec. 5, 1792.
Colmore Duvall m. Elizabeth Peach, Feb. 5, 1791.
Dennis Duvall m. Rachel Cross, Jan. 6, 1816.
Enus Duvall m. Elizabeth Nicholson, Dec. 23, 1794.

Ephraim Duvall m. Jemima Hazle, July 21, 1793.
Henry Duvall m. Elizabeth Boone, Sept. 16, 1800.
Henry Duvall m. Mary Winchester, Apr. 9, 1810.
Howard Duvall m. Elizabeth Duvall, Nov. 27, 1788.
Howard Duvall m. Susanna Duvall, Dec. 12, 1806.
Jacob Duvall—Son of Jn°. m. Jemima Anne Taylor, July 27, 1791.
John Duvall m. Rebecca Rawlings, Nov. 24, 1798.
John W. Duvall m. Ann Miller, Dec. 21, 1813.
Joseph H. Duvall m. Mable Taylor, Dec. 22, 1808.
Lewis Duvall m. Elizabeth Wheeler, Oct. 3, 1777.
Lewis Duvall m. Sarah Harwood, Nov. 22, 1800.
Mareen H. Duvall m. Dorothy Allen, May 6, 1801.
Nathan Duvall m. Elizabeth Glover, Dec. 30, 1807.
Noah Duvall m. Anne Eaglin, May 1, 1795.
Richard Duvall m. Margaret Duvall, May 1, 1817.
Samuel Duvall m. Mary Duvall, Oct. 24, 1808.
Samuel B. Duvall m. Jemima Jones, Jan. 27, 1796.
William Duvall m. Anne Tucker, Mch. 14, 1807.
Zachariah Duvall m. Susan Welsh, Oct. 27, 1814.
Thomas Dyer m. Anne Miles, July 1, 1790.
Abraham Dykus m. Margaret Mewshaw, June 19, 1784.
Thomas Earle m. Susanna Weedon, Oct. 16, 1787.
Thomas Earle Jnr. m. Susanna Thompson, Dec. 22, 1816.
Samuel Easton m. Sarah Winterson, Jan. 10, 1801.
Charles W. Eaton m. Sarah Phelps, Feb. 10, 1790.
Richard Eaton m. Judith Richardson, Oct. 13, 1784.
Thos. Henderson Edelen m. Care Williams Tuck, Oct. 28, 1813.
Edward Edgerly m. Sarah Parsons, Mch. 6, 1803.
John Edmondson m. Susanna Howard, Mch. 28, 1799.
Benjamin Edwards m. Ann Burton, Apr. 1, 1797.
Cadwallader Edwards m. Sarah Chalmers, Nov. 17, 1786.
John Edwards m. Jane All, Feb. 14, 1778.
Thomas Edwards m. Rachel Beard, Oct. 17, 1796.
William Edwards m. Ann Chalmers, June 20, 1789.
Zedekiah Egell m. Elizabeth Burke, Jan. 3, 1818.
Elijah Elder m. Mary Davidge, July 23, 1778.
Britainham Eldridge m. Achsah Ridgely, Dec. 21, 1801.
James Elixon m. Priscilla Phips, Jan. 27, 1804.
Daniel Elliott m. Jemima Howard, Aug. 14, 1788.
Howard Elliott m. Sarah Johnson, Oct. 23, 1813.
Howard Ellett m. Nancy Jacobs, Aug. 25, 1815.
James Elliott m. Sarah Bash, Jan. 21, 1789.

James Elliott m. Elizabeth Miller, Dec. 23, 1813.
John Elliott m. Sarah Warfield, July 12, 1787.
Richard Elliott m. Mary Purdy, Jan. 31, 1794.
Robert Elliott m. Martha Cadle, Jan. 8, 1779.
Robert Elliott m. Ann Lewis, Jan. 23, 1787.
Samuel Elliott m. Mary Richardson, Sept. 16, 1780.
Samuel Elliott m. Elizabeth Baldwin, Dec. 15, 1783.
Thomas Elliott m. Elizabeth Knighton, Dec. 1, 1784.
John Eltham m. Jane Moore, Feb. 28, 1778.
Caleb Ely m. Elizabeth Duck, July 19, 1780.
William Emmerson m. Mary Reamer, Dec. 29, 1819.
William Ennis m. Sarah Atsuel, May 22, 1802.
William Ennis m. Catherine Iglehart, Jan. 8, 1820.
William Erring m. Rachel Brewer, July 3, 1790.
Mathew Errixson m. Ann Sollars, May 24, 1793.
William Earickson m. Ann Wright, Sept. 3, 1800.
Rezin Estep m. Eleanor Ireland, July 26, 1787.
Benjamin Evans m. Maria Bracher, June 1, 1805.
Daniel Evans m. Eleanor Purdy, Dec. 13, 1805.
Henry Evans m. Catherine Wright, Jan. 26, 1795.
Hugh Williams Evans m. Mary Ann Johnson, Apr. 25, 1815.
Richard Evans m. Judah Price, Apr. 14, 1796.
Richard Evans m. Hannah Evans, Apr. 14, 1796.
Samuel Evans m. Rachel Moore, June 6, 1789.
Thomas Evans m. Sarah Husk, Dec. 15, 1777.
W^{m}. Marshall Eversfield m. Mary Lane, Jan. 28, 1794.
Richard Evison m. Lydia Evans, Mch. 21, 1809.
Jesse Ewell m. Rachel B. Weems, May 23, 1804.
Francis Fairbrother m. Mary Newbury, May 3, 1780.
Benjamin Fairall m. Elizabeth Green, Feb. 20, 1817.
Horatio Fairall m. Mary Warfield, Feb. 15, 1819.
Jason Farall m. Elizabeth Cadle, Feb. 17, 1816.
Levi Fairall m. Comfort Chaney, Nov. 27, 1810.
Thomas Fairall m. Alley Griffith, July 11, 1801.
Cornelius Fanton m. Elizabeth Bryan, Mch. 28, 1778.
Caleb Fennell m. Eleanor Torp, Jan. 18, 1788.
William Fennell m. Anne Joice, Dec. 27, 1792.
Leo Fenwick m. Ann E. Childs, May 4, 1819.
Richard Fenwick m. Ann Welch, June 15, 1784.
Demus Fields m. Elizabeth Robinson, Apr. 24, 1794.
Richard Fish m. Sarah Pumphrey, Mch. 21, 1810.
John Fisher m. Axsah Musgrove, Dec. 18, 1778.

John Fisher m. Margaret Eaglin, May 1, 1795.
Lewis Fisher m. Mary Childs, Mch. 16, 1784.
Marlin Fisher m. Rebecca Chalk, Feb. 1, 1783.
Thomas Fisher m. Mary Richardson, Sept. 25, 1817.
William Fisher m. Elizabeth Ward, Nov. 21, 1806.
William Fisher m. Henrietta Conner, Oct. 16, 1816.
Dan[l]. Dulany Fitzhugh m. Margaret Murray Maynadier, Jan. 4, 1810.
Patrick Flaherty m. Maria Wheland, Oct. 1, 1798.
Benjamin Fleetwood m. Dolly Gwinn, Jan. 3, 1807.
Richard Flemming m. Jane Rurke, Nov. 16, 1782.
William Fleming m. Ann Sewell, June 25, 1796.
Richard Foggell m. Ann Hollyday, Apr. 12, 1784.
Richard Foggett m. Artridge Phips, Jan. 17, 1809.
Casper Foible m. Judah Woodburn, Jan. 13, 1785.
Daniel Ford m. Catherine Atwell, Jan. 19, 1819.
John Ford m. Margaret Cheney, Dec. 17, 1816.
Joseph Ford m. Margaret Wood, Mch. 19, 1779.
Joseph Ford m. Mary Wood, Dec. 24, 1781.
Joseph Ford m. Eleanor Lambeth, July 16, 1817.
William Ford m. Elizabeth Phips, June 16, 1785.
Henry Foreman m. Eleanor Hancock, Aug. 1, 1810.
John Foreman m. Anne Mash, Jan. 17, 1804.
John Forman m. Mary White, Nov. 19, 1807.
Joseph Foreman m. Lucretia Lange, Jan. 24, 1782.
Joseph Foreman m. Ann Robinson, June 5, 1792.
Joseph Foreman m. Mary Chaney, Sept. 25, 1809.
Leonard Foreman m. Ann Cary Thomas, Oct. 23, 1816.
Samuel Foreman m. Rebecca Robinson, Feb. 8, 1804.
William Foreman m. Henrietta Drane, Jan. 2, 1783.
John Forrister m. Sarah Hodges, Jan. 9, 1781.
Basil Forster m. Mary Penn, Apr. 2, 1778.
Benjamin Forster m. Elizabeth Faire, Jan. 30, 1794.
John Forster m. Sarah Innis, Dec. 20, 1783.
Joseph Forster m. Elizabeth Grover, Nov. 25, 1788.
John Forty m. Sarah Price, Oct. 29, 1803.
Balack Fowler m. Sarah Fairall, Dec. 21, 1792.
Daniel Fowler m. Mary Smith, Aug. 4, 1810.
Elie Fowler m. Sarah Elliott, Mch. 25, 1807.
George Fowler m. Thomas Childs, May 23, 1801.
James Fowler m. Mary Woodfield, Aug. 21, 1789.
John Fowler m. Hannah Mayo, Sept. 5, 1789.
Mark Fowler m. Sarah Taylor, Feb. 9, 1796.

Rezin Fowler m. Rachel Sewell, Dec. 18, 1797.
William Fowler m. Elizabeth Craig, Feb. 2, 1780.
George Fox m. Rebecca Holloway, Dec. 21, 1791.
George Fox m. Mary Sambling, Dec. 10, 1799.
James Fox m. Ruth Holland, June 13, 1785.
Samuel Foxcroft m. Susan Brown, Dec. 31, 1817.
William Foxcroft m. Elizabeth Reynolds, Nov. 6, 1790.
John Francis m. Araminta Foreman, July 21, 1785.
Benjamin Franklin m. Harriet Allien, Oct. 30, 1818.
John Franklin m. Mary Hopkins, Mch. 25, 1783.
John Franklin m. Harriet Conner, Oct. 26, 1818.
Richard Franklin m. Ann Duvall, July 30, 1777.
Robert Franklin m. Elizabeth Gott, May 13, 1793.
Thomas Franklin m. Eliza Mackubin, Nov. 26, 1808.
Thomas Franklin m. Eliz^a. Shaw, Nov. 12, 1818.
William Franklin m. Isabella Franklin, Jan. 12, 1779.
William Franklin m. Charity Collison, Apr. 7, 1790.
Daniel Frazier m. Elizabeth Whittington, Jan. 30, 1799.
James Frazier m. Anne Duckett, Dec. 6, 1794.
Richard Frazier m. Mary Duckett, Dec. 29, 1785.
William Frazier m. Sarah Jones, Jan. 27, 1780.
John Freeburgher m. Ann Babbs, Sept. 8, 1810.
William Freeman m. Mary Woodfield, Mch. 10, 1819.
Nicholas French m. Rebecca Chaney, Sept. 22, 1802.
John Fulford m. Mary Smith, June 6, 1785.
Thomas Furlong m. Elizabeth Brown, Aug. 10, 1803.
Dermis Gaither m. Elizabeth Disney, Dec. 14, 1810.
Ephraim Gaither m. Nancy Simpson, Dec. 10, 1792.
Ephraim Gaither m. Sarah Eliz^a. Goldsborough, May 16, 1820.
Jerrard Gaither m. Agnes Gaither, May 16, 1787.
John Gaither m. Sarah Carter, Dec. 31, 1816.
John M. Gaither m. Henrietta Lusby, Nov. 12, 1818.
Joshua Gaither m. Ruth Gaither, Nov. 15, 1817.
Ralph Gaither m. Sarah Rowles, Oct. 9, 1788.
Seth Gaither m. Rebecca Yieldhall, Jan. 24, 1778.
Vachel Gaither m. Ruth Marriott, Oct. 25, 1782.
William Gaither m. Margaret Ann Dorsey, Dec. 26, 1812.
Zachariah Gaither m. Sarah Warfield, Aug. 29, 1781.
James Galloway m. Mary Shepard, Aug. 29, 1818.
Amos Gambrill m. Ann Urguhart, Dec. 8, 1802.
Augustine Gambrill m. Maria Baldwin, July 20, 1795.
Augustine Gambrill m. Rebecca Williams, Oct. 29, 1806.

George Gambrill m. Julia Ann Brown, Feb. 3, 1817.
Rezin Gambrill m. Mary Gaither, Dec. 31, 1777.
Richard Gambrill m. Elizabeth Marriott, May 9, 1798.
Stevens Gambrill m. Eliz^a^. Gambrill, May 9, 1820.
Thomas Gambrill m. Belinda Bright, Apr. 1, 1809.
William Gambrill m. Nelia Williams, Sept. 21, 1802.
William Gambrill m. Martha Peach, Oct. 26, 1803.
Henry Gantt m. Sarah H. Weems, Oct. 17, 1801.
Benjamin Gardiner m. Mary Brashears, Nov. 19, 1796.
Charles Gardiner m. Sarah Iiams, Sept. 20, 1783.
James Gardiner m. Welimena Parker, Nov. 16, 1787.
James Gardiner m. Eleanor McCauley, Feb. 19, 1814.
John Gardiner m. Tomsey Vineyard, Dec. 2, 1807.
John Gardiner m. Rebecca Robinson, Jan. 26, 1819.
John Gardiner m. Providence Russell, Feb. 16, 1819.
Jno. McPherson Gardiner m. Sophia Gassaway, Nov. 1, 1805.
Richard Gardiner m. Ann Merrikin, Nov. 22, 1787.
Samuel Gardiner m. Ann Riston, July 14, 1818.
Thomas Gardiner m. Providence Connaway, Feb. 29, 1780.
Thomas Gardiner m. Susanna Brewer, Mch. 13, 1820.
William Gardiner m. Elizabeth Nicholson, Mch. 26, 1807.
Zachariah Gardiner m. Rebecca Stewart, May (Mch?) 25, 1815.
Abraham Gardner m. Catherine Litchfield, Aug. 26, 1796.
Benjamin Gardner m. Susanna Brashears, Jan. 2, 1805.
Charles Gardner m. Margaret Seward, Jan. 5, 1779.
Edward Gardner m. Sarah Phips, Dec. 17, 1793.
George Gardner m. Martha Parker, July 11, 1786.
George Gardner m. Aimy (?) Owings, Dec. 31, 1791.
George Gardner m. Margaret Hopkins, June 20, 1797.
James Gardner m. Onner Selby, Feb. 13, 1799.
John Gardner m. Elizabeth Greenwell, Nov. 7, 1812.
Obed Gardner m. Elizabeth Goldsmith, Nov. 26, 1794.
Samuel Gardner m. Ann Day, Apr. 18, 1810.
William Gardner m. Catherine Shepherd, May 21, 1795.
William Gardner m. Frances Hemwood, Dec. 12, 1797.
William Gardner m. Ann Due, Aug. 4, 1804.
Benjamin Garner m. Elizabeth Parrott, Dec. 22, 1785.
Benjamin Garner m. Eleanor Pierce, Dec. 15, 1795.
Cornelius Garretson m. Mary Crandel, June 8, 1816.
George Garston m. Ann Drane, Sept. 16, 1779.
Thomas Garston m. Susanna Hansliff, Mch. 26, 1785.
Jehosephat Gartrell m. Rachel Carr, July 23, 1783.

Stephen Gartrell m. Mary Cole, Feb. 15, 1779.
Leonard Gary m. Henrietta Miles, Feb. 2, 1791.
Lloyd Gary m. Ann Jarvis, May 1, 1792.
Elie Gassaway m. Rachel Howard, Feb. 1, 1783.
Henry Gassaway m. Margaret Selman, Feb. 3, 1787.
Henry Gassaway m. Levena Killman, Dec. 6, 1807.
John Gassaway m. Mary Quynn, Jan. 1, 1788.
John Gassaway m. Elizabeth Price, Sept. 27, 1799.
Louis Gassaway m. Rebecca Henry, June 17, 1809.
Nicholas Gassaway m. Amelia Isreal, Jan. 7, 1791.
Denton Geoghegan m. Elizabeth Shipley, Dec. 18, 1802.
Robert Geoghegan m. Henrietta Griffith, Sept. 13, 1782.
Robert Getty m. Margaret Willmot, Dec. 27, 1808.
Reverdy Ghiselin m. Anne Robosson, Feb. 19, 1798.
Reverdy Ghiselin m. Margaret Bowie, Dec. 24, 1804.
Thomas Gibbs m. Mary Chisholm, Jan. 15, 1805.
John Gibson m. Ann Ridout, Oct. 25, 1785.
Robert Gifford m. Hannah Meeke, Mch. 14, 1793.
Stephen Gill m. Hester Kenady, Sept. 21, 1813.
Jacob Gillan m. Lyddy Jackson, Nov. 28, 1782.
John Gillison m. Sarah Smithers, Dec. 26, 1786.
George Gilpin m. Jane Peters, Feb. 19, 1780.
William Glover m. Eleanor McKellen, Sept. 13, 1786.
Frederick Goatee m. Laurra Randall, Feb. 3, 1800.
Archibald Golder m. Sarah Ashmead, Apr. 4, 1782.
Archibald Golder m. Elizabeth Howard, Mch. 28, 1812.
Richard Goldsborough m. Nackey Worthington, July 22, 1793.
Thomas Goldsborough m. Maria Thomas, Sept. 17, 1801.
William Goldsborough m. Sarah Worthington, Nov. 8, 1792.
Edward Godman m. Matilda Grace, July 5, 1786.
Edward Godman m. Margaret Smith, Jan. 8, 1791.
Humphrey Godman m. Rachel Hall, Apr. 23, 1783.
William Goodman m. Sarah Green, Mch. 22, 1796.
William Goodman m. Sarah Goodman, Mch. 7, 1818.
John Goodwin m. Sarah Benton, Aug. 8, 1812.
Richard Goodwin m. Mary Henshaw, Jan. 3, 1786.
Richard Goodwin m. Sarah Rawlings, Feb. 5, 1800.
Nicholas Gorsuch m. Mary Gravishitt, Aug. 22, 1788.
Mordecai Gosnell m. Estha Crandel, Aug. 10, 1819.
Ezekiel Gott m. Mary Childs, Sept. 5, 1783.
Ezekiel Gott m. Ann Allen, Jan. 30, 1790.
John Gott m. Sarah Carter, Mch. 7, 1799.

Richard Gott m. Sarah Collison, Jan. 12, 1802.
Samuel Gott m. Amelia M. OReielly, June 16, 1817.
William Gough m. Mary Anne Abbot, Oct. 2, 1790.
Robert Goves m. Mary Mills, Feb. 24, 1781.
Edward Gownd m. Henrietta Sansbury, Sept. 27, 1788.
Gutloop Grammer m. Kitty Countryman, Oct. 1, 1791.
Charles Gray m. Sarah Laraton, June 16, 1797.
Edward R. Gray m. Ellen Foreman, July 24, 1820.
Elijah Gray m. Mary Lawton, Nov. 10, 1787.
Greenbury Gray m. Susanna Chaney, Aug. 3, 1789.
John Gray m. Ann Jacob, Mch. 10, 1781.
John Gray m. Anne Todd, Oct. 18, 1792.
John Gray m. Rachel Atwell, Nov. 20, 1802.
John Gray m. Charlotte Boone, Nov. 8, 1815.
Matthias Gray m. Rachel Crouder, June 15, 1818.
Reuben Gray m. Rachel Robinson, Apr. 14, 1807.
Richard Gray m. Eleanor Richardson July 9, 1796.
Thomas Gray m. Anna Evans, Apr. 14, 1796.
Jacob Green m. Mary Talbot, Jan. 17, 1809.
Jacob Green m. Elizabeth Bird, Jan. 30, 1812.
John Green m. Fanny Brown, Apr. 14, 1781.
John Green m. Achsah Burgess, Nov. 27, 1781.
Lancelot Green m. Mary Selby, Dec. 22, 1784.
Lancelet Green m. Elizabeth Carr, Oct. 28, 1794.
William Green m. Anne McNear, June 22, 1793.
William Green m. Mary Sands, Dec. 21, 1797.
Wm. Sanders Green m. Mary Harwood, May 28, 1808.
Frederick Greenwood m. Mary Robb, May 5, 1784.
John Gregory m. Elizabeth Godfrey, Aug. 4, 1784.
Nicholas Gremel m. Elizabeth Wright, Mch. 18, 1794.
Charles Griffin m. Rachel Marriott, Feb. 3, 1816.
John Griffin m. Elizabeth Crandell, Mch. 23, 1785.
John Griffin m. Nancy Sprigg, June 8, 1813.
Richard Griffin m. Nancy Kirby, Nov. 8, 1813.
Benjamin Griffith m. Mary Nowell, Dec. 17, 1799.
Dennis Griffith m. Elizabeth Ridgely, Jan. 20, 1785.
Edward Griffith m. Elizabeth Trott, Apr. 15, 1786.
Hugh Griffith m. Elizabeth Lavin, June 24, 1790.
John Griffith m. Mary Barefoot, May 26, 1798.
Joseph Griffith m. Sarah Turner, Dec. 27, 1816.
Joshua Griffith m. Elizabeth Ridgely, May 10, 1798.
Lewis Griffith m. Sarah Steward, Dec. 13, 1789.

Lewis Griffith m. Elizabeth Wyvill, Feb. 1, 1816.
Nicholas Griffith m. Anne Ridgely, Dec. 14, 1791.
Robert Griffith m. Betsey Boone, Apr. 4, 1787.
Samuel Griffith m. Elizabeth Trott, July 27, 1796.
Richard Grimes m. Anne Wood, Nov. 22, 1792.
William Grimes m. Margaret Gibbons, July 22, 1815.
Charles Grist m. Ann Smart, Apr. 10, 1780.
Simon Gross m. Mary Lewis, Aug. 14, 1787.
John Groves m. Jane Ball, May 16, 1791.
Jn°. Constantine Mar'Sollon Groves m. Rosalie Margaret Mury, Apr. 18, 1801.
Joshua Groves m. Sarah Boyd, Feb. 7, 1793.
Solomom Groves m. Sarah King, Feb. 14, 1792.
John Guyer m. Margaret Dixon, Aug. 14, 1790.
Bennett Gwinn m. Mary Belt, Jan. 13, 1795.
John Gwinn m. Louisa Ann Hobbs, Nov. 5, 1817.
Samuel Hackett m. Margaret Bristol, Mch. 4, 1796.
Robert Haddoway m. Jane Randall, Feb. 25, 1813.
Peter Hagner m. Frances Randall, Apr. 22, 1806.
Daniel Hall m. Margaret Macclesh, Jan. 24, 1812.
Daniel Hall m. Susan Fowler, July 25, 1814.
Edward Hall m. Mary Stevenson, Mch. 8, 1790.
Elisha Hall m. Delilah Ricketts, Sept. 14, 1801.
George Hall m. Rebecca Frost, Nov. 23, 1809.
Henry Hall m. Rachel Harwood, June 23, 1787.
Henry Hall m. Arianna Stevenson, Apr. 18, 1797.
Henry Augustus Hall m. Anne Lyles Estep, Nov. 1, 1814.
Henry Sprigg Hall m. Ann Garston, Sept. 29, 1803.
John Hall m. Ann Dawley, Sept. 28, 1785.
John Hall m. Mary Williams, Feb. 22, 1808.
John Hall m. Charlotte Johnson, Aug. 4, 1813.
John Stephen Hall m. Elizabeth D. Boyd, Nov. 5, 1789.
Joseph Hall m. Harriett A. Sellman, Feb. 23, 1802.
Joshua Hall m. Priscilla Woodfield, Feb. 1, 1791.
Nathaniel Hall m. Susanna Phelps, Feb. 28, 1778.
Nathaniel Hall m. Delilah Williams, Nov. 13, 1812.
Richard Hall m. Sarah Cowman, Jan. 14, 1789.
Richard Hall m. Mary Connway, June 5, 1802.
Richard Hall m. Eleanor Cadle, Jan. 26, 1811.
Richard Hall m. Martha Jones, June 11, 1814.
Thomas Hall m. Ann Duckett Anderson, Jan. 26, 1807.
Thomas H. Hall m. Henrietta Cowman, Feb. 5, 1806.

Thomas W. Hall m. Mary Anne Hall, Oct. 24, 1816.
William Hall m. Martha Duckett, Apr. 6, 1782.
William Hall m. Margaret Watkins, Jan. 21, 1788.
William Hall m. Caroline Weedon, Sept. 14, 1820.
William I. Hall m. Margaret Harwood, Nov. 18, 1819.
Denton Hammond m. Sarah Hall Baldwin, Aug. 17, 1805.
Henry Hammond m. Henny Stinchcomb, Dec. 22, 1794.
Hezekiah Hammond m. Margaret Lambeth, Dec. 16, 1801.
Hezekiah Hammond m. Sarah Lambeth, June 7, 1809.
James Hammond m. Else Holmes, Nov. 9, 1786.
John Hammond m. Harriet Dorsey, Mch. 22, 1820.
Lloyd Hammond m. Mary Hammond, Mch. 21, 1795.
Lloyd T. Hammond m. Elizabeth Mereweather, Nov. 7, 1803.
Matthias Hammond m. Eliza Brown, May 7, 1812.
Philip Hammond m. Elizabeth Wright, July 17, 1784.
Philip Hammond Jn[r]. m. Julia Ann Hammond, Mch. 1, 1814.
Edward Hampton m. Mary Ann Bryan, Jan. 13, 1779.
Benjamin Hancock m. Sarah Jenkins, Mch. 31, 1803.
Benjamin Hancock m. Mary Pierce, July 25, 1816.
Francis Hancock m. Jemima Selby, Dec. 5, 1798.
Nathaniel Hancock m. Sophia Gray, May 17, 1788.
Nathaniel Hancock m. Ruth Fox, May 15, 1795.
Stephen Hancock m. Anne Cromwell, Jan. 15, 1801.
David Hanlon m. Harriet Moss, Feb. 27, 1808.
Nicholas Hanna m. Elizabeth Lee, Feb. 18, 1779.
Samuel Hannah m. Mary Marshall, Jan. 19, 1790.
William Hanna m. Sarah Turner, Feb. 3, 1778.
Benjamin Hanshaw m. Eliz[a]. Joice, Dec. 27, 1820.
Charles Hanshaw m. Nancy Hanshaw, June 8, 1814.
John Hanshaw m. Anne Goodwin, Dec. 8, 1785.
Lloyd Hanshaw m. Matilda Clarage, June 11, 1817.
James Hanskan m. Hervine Thompson, Apr. 28, 1781.
Alexander C. Hanson m. Rebecca Howard, June 4, 1778.
Alexander C. Hanson Jn[r]. m. Pricilla Dorsey, June 24, 1805.
John Hanson m. Rebecca Hammond, Feb. 16, 1779.
William Hanson m. Helen Gray, Feb. 2, 1788.
William Hanson m. Deborah Burland, June 29, 1797.
Benjamin D. Hardesty m. Sarah Griffin, Sept. 14, 1818.
Edmund Hardesty m. Ruth Chaney, Dec. 22, 1792.
Frederick Hardesty m. Rachel Watts, July 12, 1791.
Henry Herdesty m. Ann Letman, June 28, 1777.
John Hardesty m. Agnes Nettles, June 29, 1803.

Joshua Hardesty m. Elizabeth Wood, Jan. 25, 1814.
Matthew Hardesty m. Elizabeth Williams, Jan. 2, 1805.
Thomas Hardesty m. Ann Chaney, Jan. 3, 1797.
Thomas Hardesty m. Achsah Simmons, Nov. 24, 1819.
William Hardesty m. Eleanor Whittington, Mch. 3, 1810.
John Harding m. Sarah Graham, Apr. 20, 1809.
George Hardy m. Susanna Phelps, Dec. 24, 1806.
James Harvey m. Artridge Norris, Dec. 13, 1784.
Robert G. Harper m. Catherine Carroll, May 7, 1801.
Samuel Harper m. Else Collister, Nov. 4, 1795.
Joshua Harris m. Lucy Rummells, Feb. 19, 1797.
Samuel Harris m. Clare Legg, Mch. 9, 1778.
Samuel Harris m. Jane Gott, Dec. 7, 1784.
Thomas Harris Jn^{r}. m. Eleanor Davidson, Oct. 31, 1795.
Benjamin Harrison m. Deborah Ghiseline, Dec. 12, 1787.
Elisha Harrison m. Ann Chew, May 14, 1787.
James Harrison m. Elizabeth Walker, Feb. 21, 1811.
James Harrison m. Catherine Miller, Jan. 5, 1813.
John Harrison m. Rachel Deale, Jan. 28, 1780.
Joseph G. Harrison m. Matilda B. Wood, May 22, 1816.
Richard Harrison m. Mary Norris, Apr. 17, 1782.
Samuel Harrison m. Susanna Johns, June 13, 1778.
Samuel Harrison m. Mary Steuart, June 7, 1808.
Daniel Hart m. Harriet Smith, Nov. 18, 1813.
James Harvey m. Martha Boyd Groves, July 29, 1796.
Benjamin Harwood of Rh^{d}. m. Henrietta Battee, Oct. 5, 1811.
Benj^{a} Harwood of Pr^{d}. m. Peggy H. Hall, Nov. 4, 1820.
Henry H. Harwood m. Eliza. Lloyd, Feb. 14, 1805.
John Harwood m. Elizabeth Camden, Dec. 8, 1790.
John Harwood m. Mary Newton Brewer, Apr. 21, 1798.
Joseph Harwood m. Anne Chapman, Sept. 22, 1802.
Noble Harwood m. Mary Harwood, Oct. 28, 1796.
Osborn Harwood m. Elizabeth Ann Harwood, Oct. 31, 1791.
Richard Harwood m. Lucy Battee, May 29, 1806.
Richard Harwood of Thos. m. Sarah Callahan, Mch. 29, 1803.
Richard Harwood m. Elizabeth Sefton, Jan. 24, 1810.
Richard H. Harwood m. Anne C. Green, Oct. 23, 1798.
Robert Harwood m. Mary Goodwin, Dec. 22, 1796.
Thomas Harwood of Benj. m. Charlotte Vallotte, Jan. 12, 1805.
Thomas Harwood m. Mary Stevart, Dec. 26, 1820.
William Harwood m. Naomi Watkins, July 5, 1806.
John Haslup m. Mary Griffith White, Oct. 17, 1800.

John Hathaly m. Sarah Ann Brown, Dec. 21, 1813.
Archibald Hawkins m. Mary Queen, Jan. 10, 1817.
Elias Hayden m. Rachel Hopper, Dec. 23, 1779.
Elias Hayden m. Rachel Carroll, Dec. 24, 1784.
Charles Hayes m. Elizabeth Ennis, Dec. 22, 1818.
William Hays m. Sarah Ryan, Mch. 27, 1780.
Caleb Hazle m. Jemima James, July 8, 1785.
Edward Hazle m. Catherine Connoway, Dec. 23, 1791.
James Heard m. Martha Young, Oct. 11, 1817.
Edward Heath m. Mary Garner, Nov. 13, 1798.
Robert Heath m. Ann Gardner, Feb. 29, 1808.
Robert Heath m. Ann Johnson, May 23, 1812.
William Heath m. Mary Atwell, Aug. 28, 1778.
William Heath m. Wilhelmina Brashears, Sept. 14, 1811.
William Hedes m. Rachel Herren, Feb. 14, 1798.
Robert Hendle m. Catherine Roberts, Aug. 28, 1813.
Thomas Hendry m. Margaret Slicer, Nov. 13, 1819.
Thomas Henry m. Ann Nicholson, Feb. 5, 1788.
John Hinson m. Sarah Morgan, Dec. 10, 1787.
Charles Henwood m. Sarah Burton, May 10, 1794.
Vachel Henwood m. Nancy Price, Jan. 27, 1808.
William Henwood m. Mary Stevens, June 2, 1794.
Edward Herbert m. Ann Middleton, Mch. 13, 1788.
William Hesterly m. Mary Polton, Apr. 15, 1778.
Thomas Hewitt m. Margaret Chalmers, Feb. 5, 1791.
Geo. Washington Higgins m. Ann Luckland, Dec. 24, 1798.
Henry Higgs m. Grace Owens Mch. 1, 1785.
Joshua Clarke Higgins m. Priscilla Laville, Nov. 3, 1792.
James Higley m. Anne Johnson, Apr. 17, 1805.
Abell Hill m. Sarah Childs, Jan. 28, 1794.
Joseph Hill m. Susannah Hill, Feb. 8, 1782.
Morgan Hill m. Mary L. Childs, Apr. 23, 1816.
Morgan Hill m. Althea Brown, Jan. 6, 1818.
Richard Hill m. Margaret Drury, Jan. 23, 1816.
William Hill m. Margaret Hutton, Dec. 10, 1792.
Benjamin Hilton m. Hester Taylor, Feb. 4, 1813.
John Hilton m. Rebecca Gardner, Mch. 28, 1798.
John Hilton m. Eleanor Pearce, Apr. 16, 1802.
Osborn Hinton m. Nancy Wheeler, Nov. 6, 1805.
Thomas Hinton m. Lilly Griffith, Jan. 4, 1795.
William Hinton m. Ann Turner, Feb. 6, 1787.
John Hoberth m. Eliz. Hardesty, Oct. 27, 1791.

Charles R. Hobbs m. Comfort Eliz[a]. Bigford, Oct. 19, 1793.
Noah Hobbs m. Rachel Warfield, Feb. 15, 1780.
William Hobbs m. Lydia Warfield, Oct. 6, 1779.
Henry Hodge m. Sarah McCauley, Apr. 21, 1795.
Benjamin Hodges m. Elizabeth Jenings, Oct. 13, 1808.
Henry Hodges m. Mary Sappington, Aug. 15, 1799.
Thomas Brooke Hodgkin m. Elizabeth Towes, Oct. 6, 1779.
Jacob Hoffman m. Hester Ashmund, June 23, 1790.
Christopher Hohne m. Mary Holland, Jan. 7, 1792.
Charles Holland m. Sarah Gardner, July 20, 1799.
Edward Holland m. Jane Sullivan, June 14, 1777.
Edward Holland m. Mary Simson, Dec. 28, 1793.
Edward Holland m. Eliza Wason, Feb. 24, 1810.
Henry Holland m. Nancy Ray, Nov. 16, 1784.
Henry S. Holland m. Susan Darnall, June 21, 1814.
Isaac Holland m. Jane Steward, Apr. 24, 1790.
Isaac Holland m. Delilah Sands, June 4, 1811.
Isaac Holland Jn[r]. m. Mary Shepheard, Apr. 26, 1820.
James Holland m. Mary Ann McKenzie, Dec. 21, 1789.
James Holland m. Anne Sands, Feb. 13, 1806.
John Holland m. Margaret Griffith, Apr. 13, 1789.
Joseph Holland m. Ann Curr, Dec. 1, 1783.
Nehemiah Holland m. Ann Glover, Aug. 25, 1812.
Hezekiah Holliday m. Hannah Disney, May 24, 1814.
John Hollyday m. Sarah Childs, Dec. 9, 1778.
John Hollyday m. Mary Knighton, May 7, 1787.
John Hollyday m. Mary Chalk, Nov. 28, 1787.
Thomas Holliday m. Sarah Phipps, Sept. 17, 1816.
John Hollydayoke m. Eleanor Parrott, May 31, 1814.
Daniel Holloway m. Sarah Rodwell, Oct. 11, 1791.
Hezekiah Holloway m. Harriet Kimble, Sept. 13, 1803.
Nicholas Holliway m. Elizabeth Atkinson, Feb. 8, 1817.
William Holloway m. Anne Wilson, Aug. 16, 1791.
Westol Meek Holme m. Ann Sophia Cross, Oct. 19, 1820.
William Holmes m. Else Williams, July 3, 1780.
John Holston m. Mary Dow, June 14, 1785.
Benjamin Hood m. Sally Wayman, June 5, 1797.
Joshua Hood m. Ann Pumphrey, Dec. 6, 1819.
Henry Hoodward m. Mary White, June 14, 1791.
John Hooper m. Mary Tucker, Nov. 1, 1798.
John Hooper m. Mary Tucker, Jan. 2, 1806.
Nicholas Hooper m. Mary Ridgely, Mch. 15, 1803.

Gerrard Hopkins m. Patience Hopkins, Sept. 29, 1801.
George Hopkins m. Sarah Henwood, Dec. 8, 1790.
Isaac H. Hopkins m. Rachel Watkins, May 5, 1808.
Jolinger Hopkins m. Martha Stockett, Nov. 16, 1813.
Joseph Hopkins m. Sally Duvall, Mch. 28, 1804.
Joseph Hopkins m. Anne Lusby, June 8, 1810.
Philip Hopkins m. Mary Mabberly, Oct. 30, 1777.
Philip Hopkins m. Mary Blunt, June 26, 1802.
Rezin Hopkins m. Nancy Cooley, Dec. 26, 1810.
Richard Hopkins m. Hannah Hammond, Mch. 2, 1789.
Samuel Hopkins m. Hessy Trott, Dec. 24, 1795.
Samuel G. Hopkins m. Anne S. Hall, Oct. 18, 1814.
William Hopkins m. Eleanor Sunderlin, Dec. 18, 1784.
William Hopkins m. Margaret Pindell, June 20, 1807.
Benjamin Hopper m. Amelia Wright, Feb. 27, 1798.
Beale Howard m. Nancy Carman, Mch. 24, 1810.
Burgess Howard m. Elizabeth Macbridge, May 14, 1778.
Burgess Howard m. Elizabeth OFlaherty, July 6, 1778.
Hezekiah Howard m. Airy Carr, Nov. 7, 1816.
Samuel H. Howard m. Mary Higinbotham, Apr. 24, 1789.
Thomas Howse m. Mary Smith, Dec. 26, 1792.
Thomas Howson m. Elizabeth Flemming, Feb. 9, 1780.
Alexander Hoy m. Fanny Basford, Jan. 15, 1803.
George Hoyle m. Anne Childs, Nov. 23, 1813.
Jeremiah Hughes m. Priscilla Jacob, July 8, 1807.
James Hughes m. Elizabeth Sears, Jan. 22, 1780.
James Humphreys m. Mary Shields, Aug. 21, 1781.
John Humphreys m. Ann Bender, Jan. 1, 1784.
James Hunt m. Matilda Lowney, Nov. 19, 1782.
James Hunter m. Sarah McCubbin, Oct. 21, 1797.
James Hunter m. Elizabeth Glover, May 17, 1810.
James Hunter m. Mary Miller, May 20, 1819.
John Hunter m. Margaret Mahoney, Aug. 11, 1796.
John Hurst m. Elizabeth Broome, Mch. 23, 1793.
Charles Hutton m. Mary Gardner, Apr. 6, 1794.
Henry Hutton m. Elizabeth Gott, July 16, 1783.
James Hutton m. Sarah Shearbert, Mch. 2, 1791.
Jonathan Hutton m. Eliza Plain, July 26, 1814.
Richard G. Hutton m. Mary Armiger, Dec. 1, 1817.
Samuel Hutton m. Margaret Pinkney, Aug. 18, 1782.
William Hutton m. Elizabeth Nowel, Jan. 12, 1802.
William Hutton m. Rachel Crandell, Dec. 10, 1802.

Daniel Thos. Hyde m. Ann Merriken, Sept. 4, 1818.
John Hyde m. Sarah Wells, Feb. 21, 1789.
Thomas Hyde m. Rebecca Mantle, Oct. 27, 1792.
Abednego Hyett m. Mary Elson, Feb. 2, 1788.
Joseph Ice m. Belinda Vernon, July 31, 1781.
Dennis Iglehart m. Catherine Atwell, Dec. 24, 1810.
Jacob Iglehart m. Anne Beall, Jan. 24, 1798.
James Iglehart m. Ann Sellman, Jan. 9, 1788.
John Iglehart m. Rachel Nichols, Feb. 4, 1797.
John Iglehart m. Eleanor Smoot, Apr. 10, 1811.
Leonard Iglehart m. Juliana Watkins, Nov. 28, 1811.
Rezin Iglehart m. Hester Watkins, Dec. 14, 1805.
Richard Iglehart m. Sarah Stockett, Nov. 27, 1797.
William Iglehart m. Anne Smith, Dec. 24, 1802.
Gassaway Ijams m. Ann Pearce, Nov. 14, 1804.
John Ijams m. Susanna Taylor, June 5, 1778.
John Ijams m. Rachel Marriott, Feb. 15, 1794.
Samuel Iiams m. Mary Ratliff, Feb. 1, 1779.
Thomas Iiams m. Ann Neale, Nov. 7, 1780.
William Iimes m. Charity Ryan, Jan. 5, 1782.
Snowden Ingmore m. Margaret Cheney, Dec. 3, 1790.
William Inis m. Margaret Jonis, July 18, 1817.
Richard Isaac m. Ann Williams, July 3, 1784.
Joseph Isaac m. Alle Belt, Oct. 24, 1789.
Sutton Isaacs m. Elizabeth Clarke, Feb. 6, 1795.
Charles Ivery m. Ruth Neale, Jan. 13, 1779.
Thomas Ivory m. Elizabeth Pearce, Jan. 5, 1804.
Thomas Ivory m. Polly Brigdell, Apr. 3, 1807.
James Jackson m. Ann Stewart, Oct. 12, 1786.
John Jackson m. Nancy Powell, Dec. 22, 1795.
John Jackson m. Ruth Meeke, Oct. 5, 1797.
John Jackson m. Mary White, Apr. 2, 1801.
Ezekiel Jacob m. Ann Davis, Mch. 9, 1781.
John Jacob m. Mary Davis, June 16, 1798.
John Jacob m. Frances McCauley, Jan. 9, 1809.
Joseph Jacob m. Elizabeth Gray, Jan. 21, 1790.
Richard Jacob m. Anne Johnson, Apr. 2, 1801.
Robert Jacob m. Anne Welch, Feb. 13, 1801.
James Jacobs m. Ann McCauley, Mch. 5, 1810.
James Jacobs m. Mary Journey, June 11, 1816.
John Jacobs m. Margaret Carroll, Nov. 25, 1779.
John Jacobs m. Margaret Carroll, Dec. 16, 1780.

Joseph Jacobs m. Dalinda Little, June 14, 1794.
Samuel Jacobs m. Elizabeth Gray, July 4, 1780.
William D. Jacobs m. Artridge Journe, Nov. 16, 1806.
Benjamin James m. Christian Disney, Dec. 24, 1804.
Nathan James m. Barbara Joice, Dec. 24, 1807.
William Jeames m. Susanna Lusby, Sept. 19, 1789.
William James m. Frances Ray, Apr. 16, 1804.
William James m. Dinah Warfield, Mch. 10, 1807.
William James m. Sarah Boone, Oct. 29, 1813.
John Jarrett m. Sarah Fisher, Feb. 14, 1811.
John Jarvis m. Ann Yieldell, Jan. 5, 1788.
John Jarvis m. Mary Ross, Nov. 12, 1790.
William Jennings m. Elizabeth Ann Macgill, Oct. 17, 1796.
Baker Johnson m. Catherine Worthington, Dec. 8, 1784.
Charles Johnson m. Anna Burton, Sept. 9, 1783.
Charles Johnson m. Aria Johnson, June 28, 1814.
Christopher Johnson m. Mary Gambrill, May 3, 1802.
Elisha Johnson m. Ann Miles, May 21, 1806.
Henry Johnson m. Polly Stevens, Nov. 25, 1794.
Henry Johnson m. Ruth Johnson, Mch. 31, 1799.
John Johnson m. Delilah Lusby, June 18, 1789.
John Johnson m. Deborah Ghiselin, Jan. 9, 1794.
John Johnson m. Abigail Edwards, July 11, 1795.
John Johnson m. Ary Robertson, July 24, 1798.
Johnsey Johnson m. Anne Burton, Apr. 15, 1797.
Lander Johnson m. Rebecca Robinson, Jan. 2, 1793.
Landa Johnson m. Sarah Williams, Dec. 3, 1798.
Lloyd Johnson m. Cordelia Pumphrey, Dec. 8, 1819.
Nicholas Johnson m. Anne Johnson, Dec. 7, 1803.
Oneal Johnson m. Nancy Henwood, June 7, 1814.
Richard Johnson m. Minah Mobberly, Jan. 17, 1781.
Richard Johnson m. Sarah Henwood, Sept. 28, 1799.
Robert Johnson m. Catherine Ghiselin, Jan. 11, 1792.
Robert Johnson m. Anne Price, May 27, 1793.
Robert Johnson m. Mary Burton, Dec. 1, 1817.
Samuel Johnson m. Anne Smith, Dec. 27, 1807.
Samuel Johnson m. Ann E. Brown, Mch. 3, 1814.
Silas Johnson m. Rebecca Travers, Nov. 22, 1814.
Solomon Johnson m. Rachel Johnson, Apr. 3, 1817.
Thomas Johnson m. Durkey Mabberly, Mch. 3, 1781.
Thomas Johnson m. Charlotte Hasselius, June 5, 1792.
Thomas Johnson m. Alla Meeke, Feb. 21, 1797.

Thomas Johnson m. Sarah Phillips, Feb. 20, 1802.
William Johnson m. Mary Arnold, May 12, 1782.
William Johnson m. Ann Davis, Apr. 12, 1786.
William Johnson m. Mary Davidson, June 29, 1798.
William Johnson m. Ann Luithicum, June 5, 1799.
William Johnson m. Sarah Norman, June 23, 1800.
William Johnson m. Mary Davis, Nov. 5, 1800.
William Johnson m. Mary Thomas, May 18, 1815.
Zachariah Johnson m. Elizabeth Ray, July 21, 1794.
Zachariah Johnson m. Sarah Cromwell, Dec. 6, 1809.
Zachariah Johnson m. Rachel Burton, Dec. 24, 1814.
Zachariah Johnson m. Priscilla Mace, Jan. 10, 1817.
Zachariah Johnson m. Sarah Goodwin, Aug. 29, 1815.
Zachariah Johnson Sn^r^. m. Elizabeth Pumphrey, Dec. 15, 1818.
George Joice m. Mary Ann Johnson, Dec. 16, 1818.
Richard Joice m. Nancy Arnold, Jan. 31, 1811.
Richard Joyce m. Nina Reynolds, Jan. 21, 1815.
Stephen Joice m. Elizabeth Yieldhall, Jan. 15, 1801.
Stephen Joice m. Betsy Thomas, Oct. 13, 1806.
Thomas Joice m. Sarah Watts, Jan. 3, 1795.
William Joice m. Elizabeth Yieldhall, Sept. 9, 1789.
Anthony Jones m. Nancy Brown, Apr. 24, 1787.
Benjamin Jones m. Mary Ann Myers, Dec. 31, 1777.
Benjamin Jones m. Anne Eattry, Feb. 6, 1795.
Charles Jones m. Mary Miller, Apr. 10, 1786.
David Jones m. Jamima Robinson, Jan. 4, 1781.
Ezekiel Jones m. Ruth Warfield, Feb. 21, 1792.
Henry Jones m. Rebecca Knighton, Oct. 4, 1777.
Henry Jones m. Mary Elliott, Jan. 6, 1807.
Henry Jones m. Martha Tillard, Feb. 15, 1814.
Isaac Jones m. Mary Duvall, Nov. 6, 1794.
Isaac Jones m. Sarah Hopkins, Jan. 26, 1807.
Isaac Jones m. Ann Waters, Jan. 11, 1808.
Jason Jones m. Rebecca Griffith, Dec. 23, 1785.
Jason Jones m. Elizabeth Thompson, Nov. 25, 1799.
Jeremiah Jones m. Sarah Waters, Dec. 19, 1800.
John Jones m. Rachel Atkison, May 28, 1792.
John Jones m. Sarah Philips, Oct. 7, 1802.
John O. Jones m. Mary Steuart, Mch. 24, 1804.
Nathan Jones m. Eleanor Waters, Feb. 10, 1819.
Philip Jones m. Deborah McCauley, July 7, 1787.
Richard Jones m. Catharine Fitzgerald, Jan. 18, 1779.

Richard Jones m. Mary Southern, May 11, 1784.
Richard Jones m. Eleanor Elliott, Dec. 25, 1807.
Richard J. Jones m. Margaret B. Chew, May 14, 1816.
Samuel Jones m. Signa Hinton, Jan. 6, 1791.
Samuel Jones m. Mary Ball, Oct. 3, 1814.
Samuel Jones m. Priscilla Hawkins, Jan. 6, 1817.
William Jones m. Elizabeth Bridges, Feb. 19, 1785.
George Jordan m. Prudence Wilson, Sept. 12, 1818.
William Jordon m. Sarah Sansbury, Aug. 6, 1807.
Edward Journey m. Ann Hopkins, Mch. 14, 1787.
Edward Journey m. Elizabeth Carvill, Jan. 4, 1798.
John Journey m. Doratha McDaniel, Feb. 7, 1803.
Sabrit Journey m. Elizabeth Watkins, Dec. 5, 1805.
James Jubb m. Rachel Pumphrey, Dec. 17, 1818.
Richard Jub m. Sarah Neagle, Sept. 19, 1795.
Thomas Karney m. Ann Richardson, Feb. 11, 1812.
Arthur Kearnes m. Mary Davidson, Oct. 7, 1777.
George Keatinge m. Mary Ann Caton, July 12, 1817.
Thomas Keef m. Rachel Barber, Feb. 14, 1780.
Noah B. Keeler m. Elizabeth Taylor, Feb. 22, 1817.
Luke Keerstead m. Elizabeth Simmons, Nov. 8, 1779.
Edmund Kelly m. Mary Tucker, Jan. 11, 1794.
Edmund Kelly m. Ann Tucker, Mch. 6, 1813.
Matthew Kelley m. Curtis Carey, Apr. 27, 1781.
Patrick Kelly m. Ariana Conner, Sept. 30, 1790.
Joseph Kemp m. Frances Richards, Feb. 14, 1807.
Hugh Kennedy m. Susanna Fisher, Oct. 26, 1779.
Daniel M. Kennon m. Maria Wilson, Dec. 9, 1777.
Robert W. Kent m. Mary Ann Machubin, June 7, 1814.
Archibald Kerr m. Abigail Faris, Jan. 21, 1802.
John Kerr m. Elfreda Fiarbrother, Nov. 24, 1789.
John Ker m. Mary Reed, July 30, 1798.
Francis Kerrick m. Mary Dove, Feb. 21, 1797.
John Kerrick m. Mary Isaac, Jan. 12, 1790.
Francis Scott Key m. Mary Taylor Lloyd, Jan. 19, 1802.
Thomas Kilgbar m. Mary Hicks, June 25, 1807.
William Kilty m. Elizabeth Middleton, Aug. 12, 1790.
Rowland Kimble m. Ann Cooper, Feb. 18, 1784.
Francis King m. Ally Griffith, June 15, 1819.
John King m. Mary Kilman, Jan. 11, 1791.
John Peter King m. Elizabeth Stansbury, Jan. 31, 1807.
Josias Wilson King m. Letitia Whetcroft, July 16, 1791.

Thomas King m. Eleanor Groves, Mch. 24, 1796.
Thomas King m. Elizabeth Hopkins, Dec. 20, 1819.
William King m. Mary Fowler, Nov. 3, 1798.
George Kirby m. Anne Randall, Dec. 25, 1798.
George Kirby m. Rebecca Fowler, Oct. 19, 1811.
James Kirby m. Ann Stinchcomb, Jan. 10, 1789.
James Kirby m. Rebecca Young, Nov. 17, 1817.
John Kirby m. Lydia Mace, Nov. 4, 1806.
Richard Kirby m. Crissy Phips, Jan. 1, 1799.
Vachel Kirby m. Temperance Rawles, Feb. 3, 1819.
William Kirby m. Susanna Phips, Apr. 4, 1799.
William Kirby m. Mary Larramore, Feb. 20, 1816.
Edward Kirkland m. Sarah Glover, Feb. 18, 1791.
Frederick Kirtier m. Eliza Plunkett, Nov. 27, 1819.
John Kitty m. Catherine Quynn, May 9, 1792.
William Knight m. Anne Cavey, July 25, 1793.
William Knight m. Anne Linge, Mch. 6, 1798.
William Knight m. Eliza Young, Feb. 26, 1807.
Gassaway Knighton m. Sarah Williams, Jan. 25, 1788.
Gassaway Knighton m. Willie Hardesty, July 28, 1806.
John Knighton m. Mary Tayman, Sept. 18, 1804.
Keesa Knighton m. Rachel Parish, May 4, 1803.
Nicholas Knighton m. Elizabeth Elliott, Dec. 23, 1780.
Nicholas Knighton m. Eleanor Watkins, July 20, 1813.
Richard Knighton m. Mary Rark, Dec. 9, 1805.
Richard Knighton m. Margaret Roberts, Sept. 30, 1815.
Samuel Knighton m. Sarah Clues, July 2, 1800.
Samuel Knighton m. Artridge Atwell, Nov. 15, 1810.
William Knighton m. Ruth Wason, Jan. 6, 1797.
Thomas Knott m. Frances Ray, June 14, 1790.
Thomas Kooney m. Elizabeth Silk, Nov. 17, 1787.
Elisha Kuckland m. Susannah Dorsey, Jan. 4, 1819.
John Lamb m. Mary Dowden, Sept. 4, 1778.
John Lamb m. Margaret White, Feb. 17, 1803.
Daniel Lamdin m. Artridge Harvey, Jan. 26, 1791.
Robert Lambdin m. Sarah Brewer, Oct. 29, 1803.
Benjamin Lambeth m. Mary Dove, Dec. 15, 1787.
Christopher Lambeth m. Lucy Lambeth, Jan. 11, 1799.
Henry Lamberth m. Mary Varnall, Jan. 3, 1786.
John Lambath m. Susanna Dove, Feb. 2, 1788.
Joseph Lambeth m. Sarah Sullivan, Jan. 6, 1802.
Thomas Lumbeth m. Mary Carr, Apr. 26, 1788.

William Lambeth m. Elizabeth Carr, Dec. 15, 1802.
Thomas Lamden m. Susanna Sherwood, June 16, 1785.
Thomas Lamden m. Anne Lowe, Feb. 26, 1788.
John Lanashe m. Ann Howard, Sept. 4, 1781.
Harrison Lane m. Eleanor Crandell, May 21, 1789.
Harrison Lane m. Nancy Day, Aug. 26, 1811.
Joseph Lane m. Barbara Childs, Aug. 28, 1820.
Nathan Lane m. Sarah S. Chew, Jan. 24, 1789.
Richard Lane m. Frances Cowman, Dec. 12, 1803.
Thomas Lane m. Barbara Evensfield [?], June 12, 1787.
Thomas Lane m. Rebecca Hardesty, Dec. 29, 1819.
William Lang m. Lucy Bangs, Apr. 23, 1811.
John Langdon m. Elizabeth Evans, June 14, 1782.
John H. Lansdale m. Nancy Warfield, June 6, 1797.
Richard Lany m. Elizabeth Tayman, Apr. 17, 1802.
William Laramore m. Mary Mitchell, Mch. 15, 1813.
Greenbury Larke m. Amelia Henshaw, Jan. 19, 1804.
Stephen Lark m. Sarah Turner, Dec. 15, 1807.
John P. Larmar m. Martha Smith, Mch. 26, 1808.
Randolph B. Latimer m. Catherine Rutland, Mch. 18, 1790.
Richard Laughlin m. Constarine Gaither, Nov. 9, 1807.
James Laureith m. Martha Haslip, July 7, 1815.
James Laurent m. Mary Owens, May 5, 1810.
James Lawrence m. Jane Smoot, Feb. 18, 1816.
John Lawrence m. Mary Lewis, Sept. 15, 1792.
William Lawrance m. Hamulal Warfield, Nov. 15, 1785.
Thomas Leach m. Mary Franklin, Apr. 20, 1809.
Charles Lee m. Alla Nowell, Sept. 19, 1792.
Edward Lee m. Margaret Mayo, Dec. 9, 1789.
John Lee m. Ann Williams, July 14, 1777.
Joseph Lee m. Susanna Purdy, Jan. 15, 1807.
Philip Lee m. Lucy Waters, May 29, 1802.
Stephen Lee m. Rachel Welch, Feb. 12, 1789.
Stephen Lee m. Elizabeth Plummer, Oct. 13, 1801.
Henry Leeders m. Sarah Small, Apr. 4, 1806.
William Leeders m. Ruth Weedon, Apr. 12, 1814.
Nicholas Leeke m. Mary Farrill, Oct. 22, 1778.
Richard Lefton [Sefton ?] m. Mary Adams, July 14, 1803.
Henry Legross m. Catherine Harrison, June 8, 1784.
George Gray Leiper m. Eliz[a]. Snowden Thomas, May 2, 1810.
Henry Letsinger m. Mary Ann Cypus, May 6, 1778.
Jesse Lewis m. Rebecca Davidge, Jan. 7, 1793.

Job Lewis m. Leah Mason, Nov. 10, 1778.
John Lewis m. Sarah Richardson, Aug. 22, 1801.
Robert Lewis m. Sarah Butler, Apr. 15, 1797.
Samuel Lewis m. Elizabeth Todd, Feb. 8, 1809.
Thos. W. H. Lewis m. Elizabeth Moss, July 2, 1801.
William Lewis m. Mary Gray, Aug. 17, 1781.
William Lilley m. Herebiah Bush, May 18, 1782.
Nicholas Lingan m. Susanna McCubbin, June 14, 1796.
Daniel Linsey m. Sarah Marsh, Oct. 20, 1803.
John Linstead m. Susanna Gray, Apr. 5, 1796.
Joseph Linstead m. Rebecca Reeves, May 22, 1800.
Archibald Linthicum m. Mary Leeke, Jan. 28, 1783.
Assael Linthicum m. Lidia Andrews, Jan. 31, 1810.
Edward Linthicum m. Sarah Griffin, Jan. 27, 1794.
Hezekiah Linthicum m. Sarah Jacob, May 8, 1802.
John Linthicum Snr. m. Elizabeth White, Feb. 2, 1805.
Joseph Linthicum m. Sarah Spedding, May 4, 1787.
Joseph Linthicum m. Rachel Wilson, May 30, 1796.
Joshua Linthicum m. Elizabeth Beard, May 19, 1800.
Thomas Linthicum m. Sarah Lampley, Jan. 19, 1781.
Thomas Linthicum m. Rebecca Tucker, Feb. 6, 1787.
Wesley Linthicum m. Mary Merriweather, Nov. 12, 1811.
Charles Linton m. Elizabeth Proctor, Dec. 15, 1798.
John Litchfield m. Eleanor Polton, July 19, 1786.
Jesse Little m. Anne Hall, May 14, 1793.
Edward Lloyd m. Sarah Scott Murrey, Nov. 30, 1797.
Obediah Lloyd m. Ann Williams, Apr. 27, 1813.
William Lloyd m. Sarah Horseman, Apr. 3, 1789.
Richard Lockerman m. Frances T. Chase, Oct. 1, 1803.
Jonathan Loftlin m. Anne Williams, Dec. 6, 1791.
Robert Long m. Mary Phelps, June 24, 1780.
John Loveday m. Sarah Johnson, Apr. 7, 1780.
James Lowe m. Elizabeth Mulliken, July 10, 1802.
John Lowe m. Lydia Dannison, June 4, 1802.
John Lawler m. Rachel Allen, Sept. 1, 1780.
Richard Lowndes m. Ann Lloyd, Oct. 12, 1785.
Benson Lawton m. Elizabeth Burk, Dec. 20, 1794.
Benson Lawton m. Susanna Maddox, Oct. 28, 1800.
Basil Lucus m. Elizabeth Brashears, Feb. 23, 1786.
James Lucas m. Ruth Lewes, Aug. 17, 1780.
Joshua Luckland m. Delila McCauley, Dec. 29, 1778.
Joshua Luckland m. Lusanna Williams, Dec. 29, 1784.

John Luke m. Ann Worthington, Dec. 3, 1795.
Baldwin Lusby m. Elizabeth Mantle, Dec. 20, 1787.
Benjamin Lusby m. Elizabeth Robertson, Jan. 12, 1797.
Edward Lusby m. Ruth Todd, Dec. 24, 1788.
Edward Lusby m. Mary Allen, Feb. 4, 1792.
Henry L. Lusby m. Mary Welch, May 17, 1820.
James Lusby m. Elizabeth Hazle, July 15, 1802.
John Lusby m. Patience Fennell, June 7, 1794.
Robert Lusby m. Henney Lecompte, Nov. 28, 1789.
Robert Lusby m. Polly Welch, Apr. 15, 1795.
Samuel Lusby m. Elizabeth Watkins, Mch. 1, 1791.
Samuel R. Lusby m. Rebecca Beard, Feb. 4, 1813.
Thomas Lusby m. Henney Johnson, May 21, 1791.
Vincent Lusby m. Rachel Stockett, Jan. 26, 1785.
Vincent Lusby m. Ann Stockett, Oct. 21, 1788.
Vincent Lusby m. Jane Beard, Dec. 23, 1796.
William Lusby m. Ann Robinson, Mch. 2, 1808.
Robert Lux m. Deborah Hobbs, Feb. 12, 1779.
Ignatius P. Lyles m. Amelia Clagett, Nov. 2, 1820.
Richard I. Lyles m. Catherine D. Hall, Dec. 29, 1817.
Thomas H. Lyles m. Sarah A. Carcaud, Oct. 24, 1787.
Danuel Lynn m. Mary Galloway, Apr. 28, 1795.
Archibald McCarty m. Sarah Ann Holland, Apr. 30, 1817.
Eluha McCauly m. Priscilla Cadle, Mch. 16, 1811.
Francis Maccauley m. Eliz. Cadle, Apr. 9, 1785.
John McCauley m. Anne Miller, Nov. 8, 1798.
Thomas McCauley m. Ann Ranken, Feb. 15, 1779.
Thomas Maccauley m. Ann Lusby, Dec. 6, 1782.
William McCauley m. Levina Gambrill, Apr. 7, 1804.
Charles McCay m. Elizabeth Pomphrey, Dec. 21, 1795.
Benjamin McCeney m. Susanna Simmons, June 21, 1802.
Joseph McCeney m. Elizabeth Sollars, Feb. 19, 1798.
Joseph McCeney m. Elizabeth Sollars, Oct. 26, 1816.
William McCeny m. Rachel Reed, Jan. 9, 1799.
John McCloud m. Ann Aidings, May 18, 1782.
Daniel McCoy m. Patsey Cadle, Oct. 28, 1805.
Jasper McCurly m. Ann Little, Aug. 16, 1780.
Henry Macklefresh m. Ariana Hammond, Mch. 6, 1790.
Charles McCubbin m. Sarah Allen, May 10, 1793.
Edward McCubbin m. Elizabeth Holland, Mch. 16, 1793.
Edward Mackubin m. Sarah Seaborn, Apr. 21, 1812.
Frederick Mackubin m. Mary D. Roachbram, Dec. 10, 1808.

George Mackubin m. Eleanor Maccubbin, Oct. 26, 1812.
Henry Maccubbin m. Louisa Burton, Mch. 27, 1818.
James Mackubin m. Mary Ann Merriken, Dec. 1, 1808.
John McCubbin m. Eleanor Warmsley, Mch. 18, 1780.
John H. McCubbin m. Ann Gray, July 10, 1790.
John H. McCubbin m. Ann M. Jacob, Oct. 19, 1802.
Joseph McCubbin, m. Dorcas Fennall, Dec. 28, 1791.
Joseph McCubbin m. Sarah Woodfield, July 1, 1802.
Joseph McCubbin m. Anne Warfield, Jan. 16, 1805.
Moses McCubbin m. Sarah Holland, May 27, 1779.
Moses McCubbin m. Ann Shepherd, May 11, 1797.
Nicholas Z. McCubbin m. Kitty Welch, Apr. 8, 1806.
Richard McKubin m. Catharine Waters, Apr. 19, 1788.
Samuel McCubbin m. Mary Rawlings, Dec. 15, 1788.
William McCubbin m. Charity Collins, Sept. 10, 1799.
Thomas McDaniel m. Elizabeth Stallings, Dec. 24, 1819.
Patrick McDonough m. Eliza. Eliza Hancock, Oct. 5, 1812.
James McGill m. Sarah Higgins, Jan. 10, 1794.
Richard McGill m. Ann Cromwell, Aug. 3, 1815.
Robert McGill m. Helen Stockett, June 20, 1804.
Thomas McGill m. Anna Higgins, Apr. 8, 1799.
Thomas Macgill m. Henrietta Cromwell, Feb. 16, 1813.
Peter McGuire m. Mary Fowler, Apr. 3, 1780.
Hugh McMelan m. Anne Boone, June 17, 1783.
George McNeir m. Elizabeth Thompson, Aug. 31, 1816.
Thomas McNier m. Elizabeth Cobath, Jan. 12, 1788.
Thomas McNier m. Catherine Earle, June 17, 1819.
Peter McNorton m. Sarah Elles, Apr. 18, 1780.
Thomas McPherson m. Mary Tongue, Apr. 20, 1795.
William H. McPherson m. Eliz. Worthington, Aug. 11, 1785.
James McQuilland m. Mary Scrivener, Dec. 26, 1805.
James McQuilling m. Elizabeth Watson, Sept. 22, 1813.
William McQuillen m. Hester Cowman, Dec. 29, 1780.
James Macobuin m. Elizabeth Hammond, Nov. 20, 1815.
Nicholas Z. Maccubbin m. Rachel Rawlings, Jan. 17, 1801.
Joseph Mace m. Sarah Jackson, Jan. 2, 1790.
Richard Macey m. Sarah Parish, May 18, 1799.
Benjamin Mack m. Mary Brannan, Feb. 12, 1803.
Waller Magowan m. Elizabeth Harrison, Oct. 27, 1780.
Loyde Magruder m. Rebecca McCubbin, Dec. 3, 1789.
Florence Mahoney m. Mary Higgins, Mch. 17, 1794.
Leonard Mallenee m. Achsah Sewell, Jan. 18, 1791.

Henry Manadier m. Elizabeth Key, July 25, 1781.
George Mann m. Mary Buckland, June 30, 1779.
Zachariah Mann m. Mary Ann Gordon, Mch. 29, 1784.
Philip Mannaca m. Delilah Scrivener, Dec. 6, 1787.
William Marburg m. Anne Odle Brewer, Feb. 6, 1791.
Thomas Marr m. Burtavia Poole, Feb. 10, 1779.
Caleb Marriott m. Margaret Wheeler, Dec. 11, 1797.
Ephraim Marriott m. Mary Chanea, Feb. 11, 1795.
Ephraim Marriott m. Sarah Nicholls, Sept. 29, 1818.
James Marriott m. Rachel Waters, Nov. 28, 1792.
John Marriott m. Mary Hammond, Apr. 4, 1789.
John Marriott m. Harriet Hall, Apr. 4, 1817.
Joseph Marriott m. Jemima Mockbee, Jan. 25, 1796.
Joseph Marriott m. Rebecca Jiams, Mch. 25, 1796.
Joshua Marriott m. Anne Waters, Dec. 31, 1792.
Richard Marriott m. Sarah Hammond, May 31, 1788.
Richard Marriott m. Jane Ball, May 4, 1802.
Thomas Marriott m. Margaret Sappington, Dec. 11, 1780.
Thomas Marriott m. Mary D. White, Jan. 9, 1796.
Thomas Marriott m. Eleanor White, Feb. 11, 1800.
Thomas Marriott m. Ann Ridgely, Oct. 9, 1809.
William Marriott m. Edith Waters, Jan. 14, 1804.
George Marrow m. Anne Matthews, May 28, 1796.
Richard Marrow m. Cassiah Lindsay, Feb. 10, 1779.
John G. Marsh m. Anne Fisher, Oct. 8, 1799.
Richard Marsh m. Sarah Delemeter, May 19, 1792.
Richard Marsh m. Sarah Little, Jan. 2, 1797.
William Marsh m. Luvany Ashley, June 25, 1783.
William Marsh m. Martha Smith, Apr. 19, 1798.
Edward Marshall m. Eliz. Rodwell, Oct. 21, 1784.
John Marshall m. Eliz. Cuttong, Oct. 14, 1784.
John Marshall m. Mary Thomas, Mch. 29, 1799.
John Marshall m. Lucretia Shields, Jan. 28, 1803.
Robert Marshall m. Mary Fox, Jan. 5, 1804.
Athatius Martin m. Mary Ball, Dec. 26, 1784.
Daniel Martin m. Mary Clare Maccubbin, Feb. 6, 1816.
John Martin m. Elizabeth Keephart, May 23, 1778.
John Martin m. Sarah Litchfield, Dec. 20, 1787.
James Mason m. Elizabeth Strachan, Aug. 7, 1783.
Wm. Temple Thomson Mason m. Ann Carroll, June 16, 1812.
Henry Massey m. Sarah Mitchell, May 17, 1779.
Henry Mayne m. Elizabeth Brooks, Jan. 5, 1778.

Isaac Mayo m. Sarah Thornton, June 10, 1788.
James Mayo m. Susanna Lusby, July 11, 1786.
Joseph Mayo m. Hanna Jacob, Mch. 20, 1781.
Thomas Mayo m. Ann Evans, May 11, 1790.
John Matthews m. Elizabeth Hall, Aug. 16, 1815.
Beriah Maybury m. Mary Moufy, Oct. 12, 1794.
Henry E. Mayer m. Mary Grammer, Aug. 11, 1808.
James P. Maynard m. Elizabeth Wilmot, Jan. 7, 1790.
James P. Maynard m. Juliana Owen, Jan. 25, 1806.
Nathan Maynard m. Mary Reynolds, Oct. 7, 1793.
Samuel Maynard m. Anne Callahan, May 12, 1808.
Moses Meace m. Claressa Eads, June 10, 1813.
Samuel Meade m. Anne Richardson, Dec. 6, 1794.
James Meager m. Elizabeth Price, Dec. 20, 1788.
Samuel Mear m. Elizabeth Dew, Jan. 13, 1792.
George Medcalf m. Ann Anderson, Nov. 1, 1786.
John D. Medcalf m. Catherine Willee, Jan. 5, 1801.
Nathan Medcalf m. Harriet Crow, Jan. 28, 1811.
Richard Medcalf m. Susannah Gwinn, Apr. 3, 1801.
William Medcalf m. Eve Fulk, Sept. 15, 1785.
Aaron Meek m. Eliz. Bourke, Aug. 22, 1786.
David Meek m. Anne Bostick, Mch. 14, 1793.
John Meek m. Martha Walton, Feb. 9, 1782.
John Meek m. Evaline Carter, Feb. 12, 1819
Joseph Meek m. Anne Tyler, June 18, 1785.
John Meekes m. Harriett Darnall, July 3, 1810.
Joseph Shinton Meekins m. Mary Cains, Feb. 13, 1813.
Leo Meloney m. Mary Joice, Jan. 24, 1786.
John Francis Mercer m. Sophia Sprigg, Feb. 3, 1785.
William Merchant m. Elizabeth Jefferson, Sept. 15, 1792.
Thomas Merideth m. Lydia Perkins, May 9, 1820.
John Merriken m. Eliz. Boone, Sept. 7, 1786.
John Merriken m. Elizabeth Moss, Nov. 29, 1798.
Jn°. Rich^{d}. Merriken m. Jemimah Taylor, Jan. 7, 1807.
Joseph Merriken m. Anne Gray, Feb. 1, 1799.
Joshua Merriken m. Ann Day, Mch. 30, 1782.
Richard Merriken m. Mary Duvall, May 9, 1792.
Richard Merriken m. Margaret Stewart, Sept. 28, 1819.
Robert Merriken m. Sarah Welch, Feb. 18, 1806.
William Merriken m. Sarah Talbott, Feb. 17, 1789.
William D. Merriken m. Susannah Wells, Jan. 26, 1813.
Nicholas Merriweather m. Elizabeth Hood, Dec. 12, 1797.

Joseph Mewshaw m. Caroline Ryan, Feb. 16, 1779.
Elisha Middleton m. Christian Wiseman, Jan. 27, 1785.
Joseph Middleton m. Kitty Whetcroft, Mch. 19, 1795.
Benjamin Miles m. Ann Piles, Nov. 30, 1785.
Richard Miles m. Mary Pindle, Apr. 11, 1789.
Robert Miles m. Deborah Green, Nov. 23, 1797.
William Miles m. Fanny Smith, Dec. 20, 1777.
William Miles m. Phebe Roberts, Sept. 16, 1779.
Howard Miller m. Elizabeth Marriott, Jan. 31, 1801.
Jesse Miller m. Elizabeth Lliver [Stiver?], June 13, 1789.
John Miller m. Comfort Benson, May 26, 1787.
John Miller m. Mary Anne Welch, Dec. 4, 1790.
John Miller m. Mary Hinton, June 20, 1800.
John Miller m. Mary Armiger, Dec. 3, 1806.
John Miller m. Mary Glenn, Jan. 18, 1816.
John Miller m. Margaret Schwarar, June 27, 1818.
Joseph Miller m. Susanna Dubs, June 5, 1787.
Nehemiah Miller m. Margaret Downes, Feb. 18, 1791.
Peter Miller m. Mary Hunter, Feb. 26, 1791.
Philip Miller m. Mary Folks, Feb. 15, 1790.
Richard Miller m. Eleanor Hunter, Jan. 29, 1794.
Samuel Miller m. Rachel Marriott, Apr. 2, 1790.
Thomas Miller m. Margaret Sappington, Feb. 18, 1803.
Thomas W. Miller m. Eliz[a]. H. Chaney, Jan. 15, 1820.
William Miller m. Larah Miller, Dec. 11, 1794.
William Miller m. Rachel Pearce, Jan. 4, 1806.
Cornelius Mills m. Anne Wiseham, Jan. 12, 1800.
Frederick Mills m. Ann Thomas Richardson, Dec. 22, 1786.
George Washington Mills m. Sarah Merriken, Dec. 28, 1812.
John Mills m. Ruth Jacobs, Jan. 1, 1778.
Samuel Mills m. Rachel Dew, June 5, 1788.
Samuel Mills m. James Krandle, Apr. 22, 1791.
Thomas Mills m. Martha Warren, Sept. 16, 1800.
Samuel Minskey m. Sophia Fowler, Aug. 18, 1777.
Alexander Mitchell m. Ann Sullivane, Sept. 4, 1797.
Alexander Mitchell m. Anne Price, Jan. 8, 1817.
Edmund Mitchell m. Anne Atwell, Aug. 25, 1795.
George Mitchel m. Hannah Seederss, Feb. 3, 1796.
John Mitchell m. Anne Burgee, Mch. 23, 1796.
Samuel Moale m. Ann Howard, Sept. 22, 1796.
Basil Mobberly m. Margaret Brewer, Feb. 5, 1782.
Rezin Mobberly m. Mary Fowler, Feb. 1, 1779.

Rezin Mobberly m. Mary Fowler, Apr. 2, 1781.
Rizin Mobly m. Eleanor Fennell, Dec. 6, 1784.
James Mock m. Mary McCubbin, Feb. 23, 1804.
Thomas Monroe m. Frances Whitcroft, Aug. 14, 1796.
Burton Moore m. Priscilla Rowlings, Oct. 10, 1787.
John Moore m. Jona Moore, Apr. 24, 1781.
John Moore m. Ann Hillery, July 6, 1781.
Robert Moore m. Mary Smith White, Oct. 19, 1795.
William Moore m. Susanna Saunders, May 27, 1789.
Thomas Morgan m. Henry Wilson, Aug. 22, 1814.
William Morgan m. Sarah Price, Jan. 30, 1780.
William Morgan m. Mary Vineyard, Jan. 4, 1798.
John Morrell m. Elizabeth Wilson, Dec. 21, 1787.
Thomas Morrell m. Ann O. Turner, Jan. 4, 1816.
Martin Morris m. Elizabeth Curr, May 9, 1786.
James Mortimer m. Catherine Davis, Oct. 29, 1783.
John Mortimer m. Rachel Diamond, Jan. 1, 1781.
James Moss m. Monica Moss, Dec. 18, 1787.
John Moss m. Rachel Foreman, Apr. 5, 1810.
Robert Moss m. Elizabeth Kelly, June 19, 1787.
Samuel Moss m. Monica Grimwell, May 29, 1781.
Willoughby Moss m. Elizabeth Atkinson, Feb. 27, 1800.
Joseph Moulsworth m. Rebecca Mollineaux, Mch. 26, 1778.
Jacob Moxley m. Sarah Mockabee, Nov. 26, 1794.
Bell Mullikin m. Mary Duckett, Oct. 28, 1785.
Beal Mulliken m. Susanna Ridgely, Feb. 11, 1806.
James Mulliken m. Ann Hall, Jan. 26, 1796.
Osborn W. Mulliken m. Elizabeth Geither, Feb. 28, 1805.
Thomas Mulliken m. Elizabeth Smith, Nov. 30, 1791.
Daniel Munroe m. Mary Kirby, Dec. 4, 1782.
John Munroe m. Ann Wells, May 14, 1789.
Gilbert Murdock m. Elizabeth Lusby, July 17, 1787.
William Murdock m. Juliet Sheppherd, Oct. 16, 1819.
James Murphey m. Elizabeth Armstrong, Mch. 3, 1785.
John Murphey m. Elizabeth Snyder, July 26, 1815.
Matthew Murphey m. Juliet Callahan, June 15, 1784.
James Murray m. Margaret Linthicum, Dec. 22, 1804.
James Murray m. Charrotte Winder Rackliffe, Aug. 28, 1809.
William Murray m. Harriott Brice, Nov. 5, 1788.
John Mus m. Anna Maria Murray, Feb. 11, 1796.
James Neale m. Ann Shoemaker, Mch. 4, 1794.
Thomas Neale m. Martha Philpot, July 23, 1777.

John Neaves m. Lear Thrift, Aug. 26, 1782.
John Neavy m. Mary Whitehead, June 14, 1783.
Thomas Neavey m. Elizabeth Geoghegan, Aug. 18, 1791.
Benjamin C. Neff m. Harriet Hardesty, Feb. 13, 1819.
Lewis Neth m. Elizabeth Adams, July 4, 1786.
James Nettles m. Tomsey Phips, Jan. 27, 1795.
Jeremiah Nicholas m. Hester Nicholson, Apr. 22, 1794.
Andrew Nicholls m. Elizabeth Higgins, Dec. 9, 1818.
Isaac Nicholls m. Rachel Basford, Dec. 6, 1785.
John B. Nichols m. Anne Bird, Dec. 5, 1812.
Nelson Nicholls m. Rachel Ann Nicholls, May 14, 1820.
Robert Nicholls m. Sarah Robertson, July 21, 1787.
Robert Nichols m. Sarah King, Feb. 4, 1815.
Samuel Nicholls m. Susanna Hardy, Sept. 21, 1815.
William Nicholls m. Elizabeth Bird, Dec. 18, 1780.
William Nichols m. Jenny Nichols, Feb. 11, 1812.
Benjamin Nicholson m. Elizabeth Disney, May 11, 1784.
Benjamin Nicholson m. Ann Lang, Dec. 15, 1803.
John Nicholson Jnr. m. Susan Sheckells, Apr. 8, 1812.
Joseph Nicholson m. Rebecca Harvey, Dec. 18, 1816.
Stephen Nicholson m. Sarah Disney, Oct. 30, 1783.
John Nixon m. Elizabeth Lewis, Oct. 20, 1786.
Anthony Noble m. Sarah Hill, Sept. 24, 1792.
Benjamin Norman m. Sarah Deale, Oct. 26, 1789.
Joseph Norman m. Ruth Randal, Jan. 2, 1792.
Joseph Norman m. Mary Wayson, Aug. 26, 1811.
Richard Norman m. Sarah Kirby, Dec. 24, 1802.
Samuel Norman m. Dorcas Simmons, Aug. 8, 1820.
Theophilus Norman m. Elizabeth Cowman, May 7, 1803.
Walter Norman m. Rachel Carter, Nov. 28, 1795.
William Norman m. Mary Cowman, Oct. 6, 1809.
John Norris m. Elizabeth Ward, Apr. 19, 1790.
John Norris m. Susan Coalter, July 16, 1811.
Joseph Norris m. Ann Traverse, June 13, 1815.
Martin Norris m. Margaret Dorsey, Sept. 27, 1792.
Philip Norris m. Mary Anne Folks, Dec. 9, 1819.
Richard Norris m. Elizabeth Harris, Sept. 30, 1780.
Richard Norris m. Elizabeth Kemp, Oct. 24, 1783.
Thomas Norris m. Henrietta Mayo, June 30, 1789.
William Norris m. Susannah Harper, Aug. 28, 1790.
Zachariah Norris m. Elizabeth Watkins, Oct. 30, 1779.
Bell Norwood m. Sarah Gaither, Oct. 3, 1785.

Gilbert Nowell m. Ann Jones, Feb. 21, 1789.
Gilbert Nowell m. Mary Crutchley, May 20, 1805.
Gilbert Nowell m. Eleanor Stallions, Sept. 30, 1805.
Cornelius ODonald m. Margaret Thompson, Oct. 29, 1778.
Benjamin Ogle m. Anna Maria Cooke, Feb. 25, 1796.
James OHara m. Mary Yeates, Aug. 17, 1779.
William OHara m. Susan Tucker, Dec. 5, 1812.
John F. Oldborn m. Johanna Bright, June 10, 1801.
Isaac Oliver m. Mary Ijams, Nov. 6, 1804.
Jacob Oliver m. Elizabeth Vineyard, Dec. 10, 1816.
Thomas Oliver m. Mary Simmons, Oct. 3, 1791.
John A. OReilley m. Letitia Parrott, Apr. 1, 1812.
Jesse Orme m. Lydia Anderson, Nov. 18, 1801.
Thomas ORoarke m. Elizabeth Linthicum, Jan. 27, 1815.
William Osborn m. Hanna Hanshaw, Sept. 15, 1779.
Benjamin Owens m. Mary Shurbert, Oct. 16, 1789.
Charles Owens m. Susannah Shearbutt, Dec. 13, 1797.
Isaac Owens m. Elizabeth Sheckells, July 3, 1789.
Jacob Owings m. George Fox, Sept. 13, 1779.
Jacob Owings m. Rachel Groves, Oct. 16, 1797.
James Owens m. Anne Franklin, Nov. 11, 1799.
James Owens m. Ann Laughlin, Oct. 29, 1810.
James Owens m. Sally Gardiner, Nov. 25, 1816.
John Owens m. Mary Bird, May 8, 1820.
Joseph Owens m. Mary Warfield, Dec. 12, 1791.
Joseph Owens m. Sarah McCeney, Jan. 22, 1817.
William Owens m. Mary Nowell, May 6, 1783.
Lane Owings of Rd. m. Sarah Ann Hathaly, Sept. 20, 1819.
Nicholas Owings m. Sophia Dorsey, July 7, 1794.
Nicholas Owings m. Susanna Owings, May 19, 1801.
Nicholas Owings m. Rachel Welch, Jan. 6, 1813.
Thomas Owens m. Agnes Gaither, Dec. 26, 1814.
William Owings m. Mary Collison, Aug. 5, 1808.
Aaron Parish m. Sarah Phips, Feb. 21, 1788.
Isaac Parish m. Jane Spencer, Jan. 18, 1785.
John Parish m. Marget Atwell, Aug. 25, 1807.
Matthew Parish m. Eleanor Goodwin, Apr. 19, 1800.
William Parish m. Susannah Atwell, Jan. 29, 1799.
William Parish m. Mary Ann Crutchley, Nov. 7, 1803.
William Parish m. Mary Hollidayoke, July 9, 1807.
William Parish m. Hester Ann Thomas, Aug. 26, 1813.
John Panden m. Sarah Marlin Keene, Sept. 8, 1781.

George Pecker m. Mary Robosson, July 16, 1783.
George Parker m. Jane Busey, Aug. 18, 1810.
John Parker m. Ally Cracroft, May 29, 1817.
Jonathan P. Parker m. Eliz[a]. Ann Owings, July 18, 1795.
Abraham Parkeson m. Dianna Woodfield, Aug. 16, 1777.
Abraham Parkerson m. Jane Norman, Sept. 20, 1783.
Abraham Parkeson m. Sarah Taylor, Oct. 11, 1800.
Richard Parkerson m. Susan Ann Welch, July 4, 1818.
William Parkerson m. Sarah Purdy, Apr. 3, 1809.
John Parrott m. Mary Wason, Dec. 23, 1788.
John Parrot m. Sarah Norman, May 21, 1813.
John Parrott m. Jane Norman, Sept. 27, 1817.
Knighton Parrott m. Mary Stallions, Feb. 7, 1811.
Richard Parrott m. Elizabeth Childs, Sept. 13, 1788.
Richard Parrott m. Anne Wood, Feb. 7, 1792.
Richard Parrott m. Elizabeth Howes, Dec. 2, 1797.
Thomas Parrot m. Letta Brown, Aug. 22, 1778.
Thomas Parrott m. Mary Smith, Mch. 5, 1795.
Thomas Parrott m. Rebecca Hutchens, Jan. 12, 1816.
John Parsons m. Jane Jackson, June 9, 1781.
William Parsons m. Sarah Hardesty, May 20, 1791.
Louis Charles Pascault m. Ann Goldsborough, May 28, 1811.
Benjamin Patmore m. Elizabeth Males, Nov. 29, 1777.
Jacob Pattison m. Elizabeth Ward, June 2, 1795.
Robert Patterson m. Mary Anne Caton, May 1, 1806.
Isaac Paul m. Susannah Brown, January 1, 1798.
William Elson Peach m. Sarah Duvall, Feb. 14, 1797.
Samuel Peaco m. Mary Sands, Dec. 31, 1789.
Benjamin Pearce m. Margaret Phelps, Jan. 12, 1796.
Ezekiel Pearce m. Eleanor Powell, Feb. 20, 1781.
Israel Pearce m. Elizabeth W. Rawlings, Apr. 11, 1804.
James Pearce m. Rebecca Lewis, Jan. 7, 1785.
Joseph Pearce m. Elizabeth Gwinn, Jan. 26, 1795.
Richard Pearce m. Martha T. Jacob, Feb. 27, 1808.
William Pearse m. Mary Gardiner, Apr. 16, 1808.
William Pendergast m. Julia Maybury, Sept. 15, 1784.
Charles Pennington m. Elizabeth Shepherd, Jan. 31, 1780.
Elijah Pennington m. Elizabeth Lewis, Dec. 8, 1801.
Elijah Pennington m. Rebecca Stinchicomb, July 23, 1804.
John Pennington m. Nancy Craine, June 7, 1785.
Nathan Pennington m. Rebecca Hands, Aug. 10, 1787.
Nathaniel Penington m. Mary Ivory, May 29, 1819.

Robert Pennington m. Mary Kerbairn, Oct. 2, 1782.
William Pennington m. Elizabeth Stevens, Sept. 17, 1799.
William Pennington m. Anna Littell, Oct. 20, 1803.
Robert Perry m. Elizabeth Jackson, Dec. 31, 1796.
William Peters m. Rebecca Burgee, Nov. 4, 1820.
Charles Pettibone m. Rebecca Elliott, May 19, 1798.
Charles Pettebone m. Deborah Silby, June 9, 1810.
Absolute Phelps m. Anne Poole, Jan. 31, 1809.
Basil Phelps m. Barbara Davis, Apr. 21, 1791.
Elijah Phelps m. Mary Disney, Jan. 20, 1818.
Ezekiel Phelps m. Margaret Watkins, May 7, 1794.
George Phelps m. Emma Pierce, Jan. 6, 1795.
Joseph Phelps m. Sophia Taylor, Apr. 1, 1791.
Joseph Phelps m. Catherine Thompson, Aug. 8, 1801.
Walter Phelps m. Margaret Chaney, Mch, 10, 1781.
William Phelps m. Sarah Fowler, Dec. 18, 1778.
William Phelps m. Eliz. Morgan, June 18, 1785.
William Phelps m. Ann Dannison, Dec. 15, 1815.
Zachariah Phelps m. Sarah Davis, Oct. 11, 1797.
Zachariah Phelps m. Esther Gwinn, Jan. 20, 1804.
Benjamin Philips m. Thompson Attwell, Sept. 23, 1783.
Humphrey Philips m. Elizabeth Weston, May 29, 1798.
John Philips m. Lydia Wheedon, Oct. 29, 1811.
John Philips m. Mary Robinson, Dec. 18, 1812.
Paul Philips m. Ann Rodwell, Apr. 3, 1780.
Paul Philips m. Henrietta M. Williams, Mch. 26, 1788.
Philip Philips m. Sarah Hopkins, Apr. 14, 1781.
Rubin Philips m. Elizabeth Cromwell, July 8, 1795.
Vachel Philips m. Julia Little, June 24, 1800.
William Philips m. Patience Marsh, Dec. 6, 1780.
William Philps m. Elizabeth Chalmers, Nov. 10, 1787.
George Phinlison m. Margaret Dehay, July 9, 1783.
Benjamin Phips m. Suana Kilman, July 21, 1778.
Benjamin Phips m. Anne Hopkins, Feb. 3, 1789.
John Phips m. Mary Kidd, Dec. 19, 1785.
John Phips m. Larah Busey, Feb. 24, 1800.
John Phipps m. Elizabeth Mace, Dec. 22, 1814.
Nathaniel Phips m. Ann Phips, Mch. 22, 1802.
Roger Phipps m. Artridge Phipps, Feb. 5, 1806.
Roger Phips m. Willy Basford, Jan. 12, 1810.
Roger Phips m. Sarah Ann King, Mch. 24, 1814.
Roger Phipps m. Elizabeth Pearl, Dec. 31, 1816.

Thomas Phips m. Sarah Forster, Mch. 2, 1779.
Thomas Phips m. Anne Foreman, Feb. 26, 1805.
Benjamin Pindle m. Julia Anderson, June 14, 1818.
Gassaway Pindell m. Mary Watkins, May 15, 1783.
Philip Pindle m. Ann Duvall, June 15, 1789.
Philip Pindle m. Sarah Watkins, Feb. 11, 1792.
Philip Pindell m. Anne Hall, Jan. 10, 1794.
Richard Pindell m. Ann Ridgely, Jan. 22, 1811.
Rinaldo Pindell m. Eleanor Pindell, July 6, 1815.
Thomas Pindel m. Eleanor Watkins, Dec. 13, 1791.
Anthony Pinkney m. Margaret Gilliss, June 4, 1791.
Jonthan Pinkney Jnr. m. Elizabeth Munroe, May 7, 1791.
Jonathan Pinkney m. Rebecca Davidson, Oct. 27, 1804.
Ninian Pinkney m. Mary Gassaway, Apr. 13, 1802.
Ninian Pinkney m. Amelia Hobbs, May 1, 1806.
Thomas Piper m. Ann Tucker, Nov. 23, 1779.
Thomas Piper m. Ann Iiams, July 12, 1786.
Thomas Pitt m. Sarah Sewell, June 13, 1782.
William Pitt m. Ann Faris, July 7, 1796.
John Plater m. Elizabeth Tootle, Jan. 2, 1790.
Jacob Playne m. Elizabeth Clarke, Aug. 9, 1783.
Jacob Plum m. Catharine Folks, Apr. 24, 1788.
Ebenezer Plummer m. Eleanor Childs, Sept. 25, 1792.
Gerrard Plummer m. Mary Hopkins, Feb. 18, 1802.
Henry Plummer m. Artridg Frankling, June 3, 1797.
Jerome Plummer m. Henrietta Hopkins, June 24, 1807.
Jerome Plummer m. Elizabeth Hopkins, Dec. 19, 1796.
Richard Plummer m. Margaret Daveson, Feb. 9, 1804.
Samuel Plummer m. Susannah Rhodes, Jan. 1, 1806.
Charles Polton m. Sarah Burdin, Jan. 11, 1791.
Edward Poole m. Jane Higginson, June 4, 1797.
Benjamin Popham m. Margaret Phips, Jan. 1, 1788.
James Pople m. Margaret Brown, Jan. 5, 1819.
Nathaniel Porter m. Pamelia Scott, Jan. 1, 1793.
Henry Powell m. Sarah Purnell, Apr. 19, 1779.
John Powell m. Elizabeth Gardner, Aug. 20, 1793.
John Powell m. Elizabeth Sanders, Dec. 23, 1795.
William Powell m. Elizabeth Mead, Oct. 14, 1780.
Thomas Pownall m. Rachel Deale, Dec. 16, 1780.
John Prather m. Mary Moore, June 18, 1796.
Rezin Prather m. Sarah Ray, Mch. 7, 1799.
Jno. Theophelas Beech Blecker Prentiss m. Nancy Kilman, Dec. 4, 1802.

Leonard Preshell m. Nancy Barker, May 24, 1800.
Bennet Price m. Sarah Lane, May 13, 1780.
Henry Price m. Ann Wilks, June 13, 1816.
James Price m. Mary Busey, Feb. 10, 1801.
James Price m. Ann Armager, Dec. 11, 1804.
John Price m. Sarah Vernall, Aug. 10, 1790.
Lubom Price m. Anne Evans, May 1, 1794.
Walter L. Price m. Lavinia Gassaway, Nov. 5, 1818.
Zachariah Prieston m. Nancy Rockhold, Feb. 26, 1795.
William Pritchard m. Eliza Hutton, Oct. 7, 1806.
Samuel Proctor m. Sarah Dorsey, Aug. 31, 1805.
Williams Proctor m. Rebecca Wootton, Nov. 27, 1781.
Daniel Pryan m. Ann Williams, Dec. 25, 1779.
Aquela Pumphrey m. Ann Catherine Walker, Jan. 2, 1804.
Gabrial Pumphrey m. Rachel Brashears, Feb. 24, 1794.
Isaiah Pumphrey m. Sarah Bell, Dec. 9, 1820.
Walter Pumphrey m. Rachel Angler, Feb. 25, 1786.
Walter Pumphrey m. Rebecca Redmond, May 9, 1820.
Zachriah Pumphrey m. Sarah Atwell, Nov. 11, 1797.
Zachariah Pumphrey m. Elizabeth Boone, May 11, 1802.
Henry Purdy m. Mary Phelps, Sept. 30, 1782.
Henry Purdy m. Mary Gwinn, Jan. 7, 1797.
Henry Purdy m. Sarah Bird, July 6, 1818.
James Purdy m. Elizabeth Purdy, May 30, 1801.
James Purdy m. Mary Kirkland, Jan. 14, 1818.
John Purdy m. Susannah Purdy, Feb. 18, 1802.
Lewis Purdy m. Elizabeth Purdy, Feb. 19, 1811.
Sandy Purdy m. Elizabeth McCubbin, Dec. 7, 1799.
William Purdy m. Sarah Pierce, Apr. 28, 1798.
Anthony Queen m. Mary Queen, Apr. 10, 1816.
Daniel Queen m. Hannah Prout, Feb. 7, 1814.
Paul Queen m. Ann Prout, Oct. 8, 1817.
Samuel Queen m. Nancy Barnett, Jan. 14, 1818.
Augustine Randall m. Mary Busey, Aug. 7, 1779.
Beale Randall m. Martha Robosson, Nov. 9, 1815.
Christopher Randall m. Anne Crandall, Nov. 12, 1788.
Edward Randall m. Charlotte Ford, Apr. 11, 1812.
John Randall m. Deborah Knapp, Jan. 7, 1783.
John Randall m. Sarah Clarke, Aug. 20, 1791.
Lewis Ransel m. Sarah Annes, Sept. 1, 1785.
Charles Ratcliff m. Elizabeth Lybrant, Oct. 7, 1777.
Gilbert Ratlif m. Anne Lambeth, Jan. 22, 1807.

Frederick F. A. Rawlings m. Ann Tydings, Dec. 18, 1811.
John Rawlings m. Sophia Duvall, May 9, 1794.
John Rawlings m. Mary Craten, Dec. 7, 1813.
Jonathan Rawlings m. Rachel Bryan, Apr. 2, 1794.
Joseph Rawlings m. Elizabeth Robinson, Jan. 21, 1802.
Joshua Rawlings m. Elizabeth Lusby, July 13, 1789.
Richard Rawlings m. Sarah Thornton, Apr. 24, 1781.
Richard Rawlings m. Mary Bryan, Dec. 23, 1789.
Richard Rawlings m. Elizabeth Taylor, Feb. 7, 1800.
Richard Rawlings m. Susannah Tayman, Feb. 16, 1811.
Richard G. Rawlings m. Airy Jeamis, Nov. 28, 1803.
Stephen Rawlings m. Eleanor Lusby, Jan. 6, 1779.
Thomas Rawlings m. Tebitha Donaldson, Jan. 12, 1804.
William Rawlings m. Elizabeth Retollick, June 13, 1801.
John Ray m. Catharine Beard, Sept. 27, 1787.
James Reed m. Rachel Williams, Apr. 23, 1779.
John Read m. Mary Welch, Sept. 10, 1783.
John Read m. Sebby Rockhold, Dec. 20, 1786.
Elijah Redman m. Catherine Atkinson, July 23, 1793.
Elijah Redman m. Ann Linthicum, Feb. 6, 1797.
Elijah Redman m. Priscilla Black, Dec. 11, 1794.
Michael Redman m. Rebecca Bright, Nov. 8, 1810.
Thomas Redman m. Rebecca Preston, Mch. 2, 1818.
William Reeves m. Rebecca Hanshaw, Dec. 19, 1791.
John Adam Reigle m. Eliza Ann Lusby, Feb. 8, 1813.
Zachariah Reston m. Hero Robinson, June 25, 1812.
Simon Retalaca m. Elizabeth Miles, June 24, 1782.
Simon Retullick Jn^{r}. m. Sarah Phelps, June 8, 1798.
George Reynolds m. Withemina Crandell, Feb. 22, 1793.
Harrison Pella Reynolds m. Mary Stallins, Dec. 2, 1791.
John Rhodes m. Ann Sweeney, Oct. 30, 1777.
John Rhodes m. Margaret Fowler, Mch. 23, 1786.
Clement Richards m. Elizabeth Brewer, Sept. 2, 1784.
Clement Richards m. Sarah Tucker, May 31, 1806.
Edward Richards m. Sarah Lewis, May 10, 1792.
Paul Richards m. Mary Gordon, July 12, 1783.
Adam Richardson m. Ann Watkins, Oct. 17, 1778.
Amos Richardson m. Eleanor Ingram Carr, Feb. 6, 1807.
John Richardson m. Mima Shekells, Dec. 31, 1789.
Thomas Richardson m. Hero Handshaw, Jan. 3, 1784.
Thomas Richardson m. Margaret Davis, Jan. 21, 1789.
William Richardson m. Sarah Phelps, Jan. 22, 1787.

William Richardson m. Sarah Lampley, Feb. 2, 1796.
William Richardson m. Rachel Plummer, Nov. 2, 1801.
Charles Rickcords m. Delilah Hilton, May 22, 1783.
Edmund Rickcords m. Mary Seaders, June 8, 1793.
John Ricketts m. Sarah Abbott, July 15, 1782.
Nicholas Ricketts m. Mary Warfield, Apr. 19, 1784.
Jacob Riddle m. Mary Hopper, Dec. 15, 1788.
Charles Ridgely m. Sarah Gist, July 10, 1779.
Charles Ridgely m. Elizabeth Fowler, Jan. 30, 1810.
David Ridgely m. Julia Maria Woodfield, Apr. 12, 1814.
John Ridgely m. Harriett Callahan, Nov. 3, 1812.
Mordecai Ridgely m. Mary Cromwell, Apr. 14, 1789.
Nicholas Ridgely m. Jemima Meriken, Jan. 16, 1819.
Peregrine Ridgely m. Mary Lewis, Aug. 3, 1789.
Philemon D. Ridgely m. Elizabeth White, Dec. 28, 1791.
Richard Ridgely m. Elizabeth Dorsey, Oct. 3, 1778.
Richard Ridgely m. Mary Jane Brewer, Dec. 14, 1819.
William Ridgely m. Nancy Woodward, Feb. 8, 1803.
George Ridley m. Mary Tucker, June 4, 1781.
Horatio Ridout m. Ann Weems, Oct. 12, 1812.
John Rigby m. Elizabeth Coulter, Sept. 10, 1799.
James Riggs m. Eliza Burnes, Feb. 9, 1796.
James Ringgold m. Eliza Slemaker, Apr. 4, 1808.
James Riston m. Margaret Spencer, June 3, 1786.
Zachariah Riston m. Ann Kirby, Dec. 11, 1817.
James Roark m. Barbara Taylor, Apr. 25, 1806.
John Roberts m. Margery Brashears, Feb. 7, 1785.
Richard Roberts m. Sarah Owens, Nov. 16, 1789.
Thomas Roberts m. Rebecca Braishears, Jan. 25, 1780.
William Roberts m. Margaret Roberts, Dec. 22, 1784.
William Roberts m. Sarah Lambath, July 25, 1787.
William Roberts m. Elizabeth Hall, Jan. 9, 1798.
William Roberts m. Sarah Mules, Nov. 20, 1819.
Thomas Robertson m. Martha Reaves, Apr. 1, 1786.
Thomas Robertson m. Louisa Fairbrother, Jan. 13, 1803.
John Robins m. Ann Riley, Mch. 25, 1779.
Charles Robinson m. Frances R. Watts, July 22, 1779.
Charles Robinson m. Patience Johnson, Nov. 11, 1807.
David Robinson m. Kitty Johnson, Apr. 8, 1800.
Dennis Robinson m. Ann Cheney, Jan. 29, 1788.
Dennis Robinson m. Mary Atkinson, June 13, 1799.
Hezekiah Roboson m. Ellen Collins, Dec. 19, 1797.

James Robinson m. Eliz. Kirby, Sept. 18, 1784.
John Robinson m. Jane Turner, June 8, 1791.
Jno. Baptist Robinson m. Sarah Steuart, Nov. 24, 1797.
Joseph Robinson m. Nancy Howington, June 4, 1818.
Lawrence Robinson m. Eleanor Potter, May 3, 1800.
Luke Robinson m. Rachel Brigdell, Apr. 21, 1777.
Luke Robinson m. Hero Richardson, May 14, 1791.
Richard Robosson m. Mary Shriver, Sept. 2, 1777.
Richard Robinson m. Mary Henwood, Aug. 16, 1817.
Thomas Robinson m. Milley Foreman, Apr. 5, 1798.
Thomas Robinson m. Mary Gardiner, Feb. 24, 1800.
Thomas Robinson m. Elizabeth Selby, May 16, 1801.
Thomas Robinson m. Elizabeth Jacob, Mch. 8, 1794.
Vachel Robinson m. Dorcus McCubbin, Jan. 15, 1805.
Zachariah Robinson m. Elizabeth Phillips, Nov. 10, 1818.
Charles Rockhold m. Jane McCubbin, Oct. 27, 1779.
Elijah Rockhold m. Charlotte Linstool [Linstod?], Feb. 20, 1816.
Thomas Rockhold m. Sarah Rockhold, May 11, 1787.
Thomas Rockhold m. Ara Conaway, June 23, 1802.
Thomas C. Rockhold m. Mary Young, Mch. 27, 1812.
John Rogers m. Tamasina Farnes, May 18, 1778.
Thomas Roland m. Eleanor Harrison, Feb. 21, 1803.
Richard Rooke m. Mary Roberts, June 18, 1818.
Edward Roper m. Mary Williams, Dec. 19, 1789.
William Rose m. Rachel Allen, June 18, 1783.
John Ross m. Magdalane Pitt, Dec. 2, 1786.
Nathaniel Ross m. Ann Little, Mch. 18, 1784.
Peter Ross m. Hester I. Taylor, Dec. 4, 1815.
James Rourke m. Sophia McCauley, Feb. 6, 1789.
Nehemiah Rowles m. Candace Jenings, Nov. 28, 1792.
John Rowley m. Elizabeth Fowler, July 12, 1785.
James Royson m. Mary Lairy, Sept. 27, 1783.
James Ruark m. Luvana Tucker, July 17, 1784.
Stephen Rummells m. Lucy Harris, Oct. 27, 1799.
William Rummells m. Lydia Whitaker, Oct. 16, 1792.
Richard Rush m. Catherine Eliza. Murray, Aug. 28, 1809.
Thomas Rutland m. Ann Hall, July 26, 1784.
Thomas Rutland m. Catherine Howard, Jan. 6, 1785.
James Ryan m. Henrietta Jackson, Dec. 24, 1811.
John Ryan m. Catherine Lowry, Nov. 6, 1784.
Joshua Saffield m. Ruth McCoy, Jan. 25, 1803.
James Sanders m. Elizabeth Groves, June 6, 1791.

John Sanders m. Mary Dunn, Nov. 7, 1777.
William Sanders m. Elizabeth Rawlings, Feb. 27, 1790.
William Sanders m. Eliza Smith, Jan. 24, 1816.
William Saunders m. Sarah Davis, Dec. 11, 1780.
John Sands m. Mary Wiseman, July 19, 1784.
John Sands m. Delila Philips, July 20, 1799.
John Sands m. Ellen Rawlin, Feb. 22, 1809.
Joseph Sands m. Sarah Rawlings, Feb. 17, 1798.
Samuel Sands m. Mary Smith, Dec. 21, 1793.
Samuel Sands m. Ary Goodwin, Oct. 20, 1796.
George Sank m. Anne Ijams, Jan. 29, 1799.
John Sansbury m. Sarah Wiltshire, July 16, 1779.
Levy Sansbury m. Elizabeth Phips, Oct. 25, 1815.
Caleb Sappington m. Margaret Gambrill, Nov. 30, 1790.
Francis B. Sappington m. Ann Ridgely, Oct. 28, 1783.
John Sappington m. Rachel Drane, Dec. 18, 1790.
Nathanuel Sappington m. Mary Jennings, Feb. 17, 1784.
Nathaniel Sappington m. Mary Taylor, Jan. 31, 1801.
Thomas Sappington m. Mary Ann Jenings, Sept. 8, 1783.
Thomas Sappington m. Elizabeth Lewis, Aug. 16, 1790.
Thomas Sappington m. Susanna Allen, Jan. 22, 1800.
William Sappington m. Rebecca Philips, Feb. 10, 1795.
Samuel Sarjent m. Sarah Fountaine, Apr. 29, 1818.
Abner Schultz m. Henny Basil, May 4, 1814.
George Schwarer m. Ketura Ann Watts, July 8, 1812.
Cato Scott m. Priscilla Wallace, Jan. 19, 1790.
Leonard Scott m. Sarah Wheeler, Nov. 7, 1805.
William Scott m. Eliza Bryan, Dec. 9, 1820.
Benjamin Scrivener m. Mary Powell, June 6, 1817.
Francis Scrivener m. Eleanor Robertson, Nov. 25, 1794.
George Scrivener m. Lurana Childs, Mch. 6, 1805.
George Scrivener m. Mary Childs, Dec. 11, 1807.
John Scrivener m. Eliza Smith Boswell, Sept. 18, 1817.
Lewis Scrivener m. Kessiah Trott, Jan. 14, 1781.
Vincent Scrivener m. Mary Griffith, Dec. 11, 1788.
Walter Scrivener m. Jemima Childs, June 2, 1802.
William Scrivener m. Henrietta Dixon, Oct. 29, 1779.
Philip Scrogin m. Mary Keephart, Aug. 10, 1779.
Benedict Seaborn m. Sarah Linstead, Aug. 30, 1788.
Caleb Sears m. Anne Kersey, Apr. 22, 1793.
Caleb Sears m. Charity Mulliken, Feb. 13, 1802.
James Sears m. Anne Beveridge, Aug. 6, 1790.

William Sears Jnr. m. Artridge Lamden, Nov. 30, 1812.
William Sears Jnr. m. Elizabeth Murdock, Oct. 24, 1816.
Bennett Seeders m. Hannah Weedon, Dec. 28, 1793.
Henry Seaders m. Ruth Seaders, Dec. 23, 1799.
John Sefton m. Mary Harwood, Oct. 13, 1819.
John I. Seibert m. Catharine Minskey, Dec. 24, 1779.
Jonathan Selby m. Susanna Welch, June 9, 1786.
Joseph Selby m. Ann Carter, Sept. 4, 1779.
Joseph Selby m. Elizabeth Sellman, Oct. 28, 1785.
Jonathan Sellman m. Rachel Lucas, Jan. 7, 1783.
Jonathan Sellman m. Anne E. Harwood, May 22, 1794.
Leonard Sellman m. Mary Walker Rankin, June 23, 1804.
Thomas Sellman m. Sarah Wood, Jan. 3, 1783.
Thomas Sellman m. Elizabeth Sellman, Nov. 16, 1798.
Charles Seveir m. Sophia Hardesty, Dec. 2, 1820.
Vachel Severe m. Mary Dadds, Dec. 27, 1816.
Daniel Seward m. Ann Banks, Oct. 26, 1781.
Augustine Sewell m. Mary Pitts, Feb. 21, 1784.
Benjamin Sewel m. Hester Nicholson, Jan. 10, 1806.
Elijah Sewell m. Anne Chaney, Mch. 2, 1809.
John Sewell m. Lydia Baldwin, Feb. 27, 1804.
Vachel Sewell m. Debora Johnson, Dec. 18, 1779.
Vachel Sewell m. Sarah Anglin, Mch. 18, 1796.
William Sewell m. Rebecca Disney, Dec. 27, 1790.
John T. Shaaff m. Mary Stewart, Feb. 6, 1812.
William Sharrett m. Trasa Ireland, Apr. 9, 1779.
Elias Shaw m. Elizabeth Langford, July 24, 1813.
George Shaw m. Eliza Robinson, Apr. 3, 1819.
James Shaw m. Anne Knapp, Dec. 8, 1789.
John Shaw m. Ann Welstead Pratt, July 19, 1777.
John Shaw m. Margaret Steuart, Mch. 3, 1798.
John Shaw m. Jane Telby, Feb. 12, 1807.
Caleb Sheckells m. Keziah Hill, Jan. 15, 1820.
Enoch Sheckells m. Sarah Smith, Jan. 10, 1818.
Francis Shekell m. Rebecca Cheney, Oct. 14, 1783.
Francis Scheckells m. Ann Wells, Nov. 2, 1786.
John Sheckells m. Mary Shearbutt, Apr. 26, 1791.
Richard Sheckell m. Sarah S. Richardson, Oct. 17, 1796.
Richard Sheckells m. Anne Jones, Jan. 31, 1800.
Thomas Sheckells m. Jane Owens, Dec. 31, 1807.
Thomas Sheckells m. Ann Hopkins, Nov. 30, 1813.
Basil Shepherd m. Elizabeth McNier, July 29, 1802.

Charles Shepherd m. Ann Brown, May 9, 1807.
Henry Shepard m. Sarah Dove, Dec. 18, 1795.
James Shepherd m. Lucretia Martindale, Jan. 9, 1808.
James Sheppard m. Susanna Mace, Dec. 6, 1817.
John Shepherd m. Ruth Lewis, Sept. 30, 1780.
John Shepard m. Rebecca Forrest, Dec. 24, 1794.
John Shepherd m. Mary Owens, Apr. 10, 1804.
Nathaniel Shepherd m. Rebecca Murphey, Jan. 26, 1779.
Nathaniel Shepherd m. Mary Owens, Oct. 28, 1783.
Nathaniel Shepherd m. Christian Middleton, July 21, 1788.
Samuel Shepherd m. Margaret Humblert, Oct. 6, 1798.
Benjamin Sherbird m. Lidia Hopkins, July 1, 1807.
Benjamin Sherbert m. Ann Hutton, Jan. 6, 1816.
Edward Sherbert m. Mary Ann King, Feb. 14, 1820.
George Shearbert m. Elizabeth Alvey, Apr. 16, 1793.
Rezin Shurbutt m. Mary Winderson, Sept. 7, 1808.
Richard Shearbutt m. Mary Hardisty, Dec. 29, 1800.
Richard Sherbutt m. Anne Maine, Jan. 17, 1809.
Thomas Sherbutt m. Margaret Hutton, June 8, 1782.
Thomas Sheurbutt m. Mary Welch, May 26, 1797.
Philemon Sherwood m. Sarah Wells, Feb. 2, 1799.
Benjamin Shields m. Sarah Johnson, Oct. 8, 1805.
Caleb Shields m. Jane Brown, May 12, 1777.
Benjamin Shipley m. Catherine Marriott, Sept. 2, 1809.
Henry Shipley m. Sarah Scott, Sept. 19, 1806.
Gideon Shoemaker m. Achsah Ward, Jan. 3, 1787.
Samuel P. Shoemaker m. Elizabeth Hurst, Sept. 24, 1783.
Jacob Short m. Eleanor Wells, Dec. 24, 1801.
John Short m. Anne Hood, Feb. 19, 1794.
John Shorter m. Rhoda Cadle, June 18, 1798.
John Martin Shrimps m. Maria Catharine Thurisia Gross, Oct. 20, 1787.
Cornelius Shriver m. Ann Collins, Apr. 5, 1806.
William Shurlock m. Susan Bassford, Jan. 11, 1813.
Henry Sibell m. Elizabeth Steviderson, May 28, 1777.
Jn°. Henry Sibell m. Mary Stallings, Jan. 31, 1805.
Edward Sifton m. Elizabeth Scogell, May 7, 1778.
William Sifton m. Sarah Watkins, Apr. 25, 1785.
John Silence m. Susannah Andrews, Jan. 14, 1788.
Abraham Simmons m. Eleanor Nowell, Aug. 10, 1787.
Basil Simmons m. Ann Wyvill, Apr. 20, 1801.
Chapman Simmons m. Rebecca Stallings, Jan. 11, 1799.
David Simmons m. Dorcas Dorsey, Feb. 11, 1809.

Ezekiel Simmons m. Ashsah Conner, Dec. 21, 1816.
Isaac Simmons m. Ann Childs, Feb. 14, 1784.
Isane Simmons m. Ann Childs, Jan. 26, 1801.
Isaac Simmons m. Elizabeth Masen, Dec. 3, 1818.
James Simmons m. Mary Drury, Sept. 8, 1794.
Jeremiah C. Simmons m. Aira Nowell, Dec. 23, 1800.
John Simmons m. Sarah Holland, Apr. 17, 1819.
Joseph Simmons m. Elizabeth Thomas, Sept. 13, 1787.
Richard Simmons m. Elizabeth Simmons, Jan. 22, 1795.
Richard Simmons m. Susanna Nowell, Feb. 14, 1795.
Richard Simmons m. Agnes Hardesty, Jan. 27, 1806.
Thomas T. Simmons m. Ann V. Harrison, July 14, 1812.
William Simmons m. Margaret Chaulk, Apr. 21, 1781.
William Simmons m. Mary Hall, Dec. 21, 1805.
William Simmons m. Matilda Hinton, Dec. 17, 1808.
William W. Simmons m. Matilda Tillard, Sept. 20, 1804.
Basil Simpson m. Sarah Worthington, Apr. 29, 1783.
John Simpson m. Mary Phillips, Dec. 31, 1796.
Joshua Simpson m. Rebecca Warfield, Jan. 13, 1801.
Thomas Slaughter m. Elizabeth Bash, May 14, 1779.
Jacob Slemaker m. Elizabeth Elliott, Oct. 13, 1803.
Andrew Slicer m. Elizabeth Selby, Nov. 29, 1797.
Philip Slitchbury m. Mary Robertson, Dec. 23, 1782.
John Small m. Ann Pettiboon, Oct. 1, 1777.
William Smallwood m. Sarah Phelps, Oct. 14, 1792.
Anthony Smith m. Mary Ann Brown, Nov. 8, 1816.
Aquila Smith m. Mary Reeves, Feb. 14, 1795.
Edward Smith m. Ann Warfield, Mch. 12, 1782.
Elijah Smith m. Martha Jenkins, Aug. 23, 1788.
Frederick Smith m. Prudence Clarke, June 23, 1783.
Henry Smith m. Elizabeth Thackrell, Apr. 24, 1788.
Henry Smith m. Elizabeth Weedon, Sept. 11, 1788.
Henry Smith m. Mary Williams, Feb. 1, 1794.
Horatio Smith m. Elizabeth Swain, Oct. 29, 1817.
James Smith m. Christian Annis, Aug. 28, 1782.
James Smith m. Amelia Larmar, Sept. 27, 1817.
John Smith m. Margaret Pindle, July 15, 1779.
John Smith m. Mary Laveale, Jan. 22, 1782.
John Smith m. Rachel Dolly, Apr. 24, 1783.
John Smith m. Clarrissa Vineyard, Apr. 10, 1783.
John Smith m. Sarah Tydings, Sept. 26, 1785.
John Smith m. Eleanor Mullikin, Jan. 20, 1789.

John Smith m. Anne Yieldhall, Aug. 22, 1791.
John Smith m. Rebecca Fuller, May 18, 1793.
John Smith m. Eleanor Brigdell, Jan. 29, 1795.
John Smith m. Ruth Gray, Jan. 11, 1798.
John Smith m. Sarah Hunter, Aug. 6, 1807.
John Smith m. Artadge Randall, Feb. 19, 1808.
John Smith m. Mary Dorsey, Mch. 16, 1815.
John Smith m. Airy Iiams, Aug. 17, 1815.
Joseph Smith m. Pasafy Wiley, June 25, 1811.
Joseph Smith m. Elizabeth Warfield, Dec. 21, 1811.
Joseph Smith m. Ann Sprigg, Sept. 27, 1817.
Nathaniel Smith m. Hannah Randall, Apr. 28, 1794.
Nathaniel Smith m. Elizabeth Leech, July 24, 1794.
Philip Smith m. Margaret Gardner, Nov. 14, 1802.
Richard Smith m. Mary Thackrall, Aug. 15, 1778.
Richard Smith m. Elizabeth Meeke, Feb. 1, 1809.
Thomas Smith m. Mary Deale, June 12, 1779.
Thomas Smith m. Elizabeth Churd, Apr. 1, 1788.
Thomas Smith m. Margaret Clarke, Oct. 21, 1803.
William Smith m. Mary Miles, Jan. 22, 1795.
William Smith m. Eleanor Young, May 29, 1813.
William Smith m. Mary Drury, Apr. 7, 1814.
William Smith m. Ann Johnson, July 15, 1817.
Elisha Smithson m. Alley Alsop, May 1, 1802.
John Snowden m. Rachel Hopkins, Feb. 25, 1783.
Nicholas Snowden m. Elizabeth Thomas, Sept. 30, 1806.
Richard Snowden m. Eliza Warfield, Feb. 2, 1798.
Charles Snyder m. Mary Poulton, Dec. 6, 1808.
James P. Soper m. Anne Mayo, June 3, 1801.
Solomon Soward m. Sophia Fuller, Sept. 26, 1785.
James Sowards m. Mary Fuller, Oct. 10, 1787.
Anthony Sparrow m. Susanna Varnel, Sept. 6, 1804.
Danuel Sparrow m. Deborah Williamson, June 28, 1800.
John Sparrow m. Ann Griffith, Sept. 29, 1815.
Solomon Sparrow m. Rachel S. Sellman, Feb. 14, 1805.
Solomon Sparrow m. Rachel S. Hall, June 23, 1818.
Thomas Sparrow m. Catherine Collins, Mch. 24, 1812.
John Spears m. Sarah Waters, Apr. 19, 1820.
Rob[t]. Traill Spence m. Mary Clare Carroll, June 16, 1812.
James Spencer m. Mary Gott, Nov. 29, 1785.
Philemon Spencer m. Mary Carter, Sept. 15, 1787.
William Spicer m. Hannah Traverse, Apr. 20, 1782.

John Spicknall m. Ann Harris, Apr. 13, 1787.
Jacob Sprigg m. Catherine Wallace, Nov. 3, 1792.
Samuel Spriggs m. Rebecca Weston, Nov. 23, 1786.
Samuel Spriggs m. Ann Cook, May 8, 1813.
Lewis Sprogel m. Susan Nicholson, Aug. 3, 1820.
Samuel Sproston m. Jane Marriott, Mch. 30, 1814.
Edward Spurrier m. Ann Griffith, June 10, 1785.
Rezen Spuruer m. Phebe W. Burgess, Jan. 2, 1790.
James Stallings m. Margaret King, Dec. 29, 1819.
John Stallings m. Elizabeth Parrott, June 13, 1808.
John Stallings m. Mary Howes, June 3, 1809.
John Stallings m. Sarah Farrar, June 22, 1814.
Joseph Stallins m. Anne Smith, Mch. 24, 1789.
Thomas Stallings m. Mary Poole, Dec. 2, 1800.
Thomas Stallings m. Anne Lambeth, Jan. 19, 1816.
Lancelot Stallions m. Mary Simmons, Jan. 5, 1786.
James Steele m. Mary Nevit, Jan. 15, 1789.
John Steibart m. Margaret Brown, Jan. 31, 1782.
Dennis Stevens m. Sarah Gambrill, Mch. 10, 1781.
John Stephens m. Juliana J. Brice, Nov. 1, 1808.
Vachel Stevens m. Jennitta R. Waller, July 26, 1780.
William Stevens m. Elizabeth Crandell, Jan. 27, 1809.
John Stevenson m. Eleanor Harrison, Aug. 2, 1803.
Stephen Steward m. Eleanor Clarke, Jan. 16, 1784.
Caleb Steuart m. Anne Watkins, Nov. 26, 1788.
Charles Stewart m. Mary Watson, Feb. 11, 1784.
Charles Stewart m. Hannah Robinson, June 6, 1786.
Charles Stewart m. Mahala Nicholls, Jan. 9, 1812.
David Steuart m. Mary Hall, Jan. 26, 1788.
David Steuart m. Sarah Gray, Sept. 12, 1806.
Edward Stewart m. Ann Selby, Feb. 7, 1786.
Edward Stewart m. Sarah Warton, Aug. 22, 1799.
Ezekiel Steuart m. Alethia Owens, Aug. 2, 1805.
Ezekiel Stewart m. Eleanor Frizzel, Nov. 11, 1817.
James Stewart m. Catharine Smith, June 24, 1778.
James Steuart m. Rebecca Sprigg, Nov. 4, 1788.
James Steuart m. Margaret Knighton, Jan. 19, 1789.
James Steuart m. Elizabeth Davis, Sept. 30, 1815.
John Steuart m. Ann Yeldell, May 16, 1797.
Mordecai Stewart m. Cassandra Tanyhill, May 27, 1794.
Mordecai Stewart m. Anne Pitts, Dec. 15, 1796.
Mordecai Stewart m. Rhody Hancock, Apr. 30, 1811.

Nicholas Steuart m. Amelia Watkins, May 12, 1818.
Richard Steuart m. Louisa Harwood, Jan. 29, 1817.
Stephen Stewart Jnr. m. Elizabeth Thomas, Nov. 7, 1777.
Stephen Steuart m. Anne Johnson, May 6, 1806.
William Stewart m. Sarah Nicholson, Sept. 15, 1779.
William Stewart m. Mary Scott, Oct. 20, 1792.
Nathan Stinchacomb m. Sarah Moss, May 26, 1814.
Thomas Stinchcomb m. Else Kilman, Aug. 13, 1777.
Thomas Stinchcomb m. Sarah Ross, Mch. 14, 1795.
Thomas Stinchicomb m. Sarah Phipps, Feb. 11, 1804.
William Stinchacomb m. Sarah Adams, Jan. 23, 1815.
John Stocker m. Elizabeth Roberts, Dec. 27, 1810.
John Stockett m. Laurro Beard, Dec. 13, 1791.
John Shaaff Stockett m. Ann Matilda Grason, Apr. 18, 1812.
Joseph Noble Stockett m. Ann Caroline Battee, Nov. 17, 1812.
Joseph N. Stockett m. Anne Sellman, June 24, 1816.
Noble Stockett m. Susannah Beard, Nov. 6, 1794.
Richard G. Stockett m. Margaret Hall, Mch. 28, 1799.
Thomas Stockett m. Lucretia Marsham, Oct. 7, 1816.
Thomas Wm. Stockett m. Susannah Beard, Jan. 27, 1797.
William Stockett m. Mary Hollyday, Feb. 27, 1783.
Wm. Thomas Stockett m. Sarah Beard, July 31, 1793.
William I. Stockett m. Mary Watkins, Nov. 14, 1797.
John T. Stoddert m. Elizabeth Gwinn, May 23, 1815.
John Hoskin Stone m. Mary Couden, Feb. 15, 1781.
Marshall Stone m. Betty Harris, Mch. 30, 1791.
Robert Conden Stone m. Mary Mann, July 23, 1805.
William Straughon m. Patsy Cross, Oct. 25, 1816.
James Stremack m. Helen Ross, Oct. 16, 1778.
Abraham Strong m. Ann Weeks, Sept. 7, 1778.
Abraham Strong m. Ann Weeks, Sept. 8, 1778.
Mark Stubbs m. Mary McDonald, May 13, 1778.
Samuel Sudler m. Sarah Lavin, Apr. 1, 1780.
William Sudler m. Charlotte Mackubin, Apr. 10, 1809.
Jesse Suite m. Sarah Giest, Nov. 20, 1784.
John Sullivane m. Rebecca Widdon, Apr. 12, 1788.
John Sullivane m. Milla Butcher, Apr. 1, 1797.
Lemuel H. Sullivan m. Willy Gardiner, Dec. 9, 1820.
Morgan Sullivan m. Sarah Lambeth, Oct. 26, 1816.
William Sullivan m. Henrietta Wood, Jan. 2, 1782.
William Sullivan m. Matilda Carr, May 10, 1820.
Francis Sumblin m. Mary Cisach, Feb. 6, 1801.

Benjamin Sunderland m. Martha Warfield, Dec. 30, 1809.
Benjamin D. Sunderland m. Ann Childs, Mch. 4, 1816.
Jesse Sunderland m. Elizabeth Sunderland, Dec. 10, 1811.
Zachariah Sunderland m. Anne Wood, Aug. 4, 1804.
Theodore Swain m. Elizabeth Rockhold, Feb. 5, 1810.
Philip Swearer m. Mary Miller, Sept. 10, 1788.
Seth Swetzer m. Anne Valliant, Nov. 9, 1790.
Benjamin Talbott m. Sarah Gaither, Apr. 13, 1785.
Joshua Talbot m. Elizabeth Hill, Oct. 29, 1801.
Thomas Talbott m. Elizabeth Green, Nov. 17, 1788.
Henry Tammon m. Elizabeth Landers, Jan. 23, 1799.
Thomas Tanyhill m. Mary Scrivener, Dec. 19, 1797.
Thomas Taunie m. Mary Hannah, Dec. 10, 1779.
Caleb Taylor m. Ann Ranken, Sept. 3, 1778.
Gamieliel Taylor m. Euphen Bruce, Nov. 4, 1804.
James Taylor m. Elizabeth Gill, May 20, 1778.
James Taylor m. Catherine Barber, Feb. 14, 1785.
James Taylor m. Elizabeth Sullivane, Mch. 12, 1793.
James Taylor m. Alice Thomas, Sept. 21, 1815.
John Taylor m. Mary Smith, Feb. 15, 1791.
John Taylor m. Anne Ogle, Oct. 3, 1792.
John Taylor m. Jemima Wilson, Feb. 11, 1793.
John Taylor m. Phebe Mickens, July 3, 1816.
John Taylor m. Louisa Weedon, July 18, 1818.
Joseph Taylor m. Sarah Bryan, Nov. 28, 1798.
Lemuel Taylor m. Ann Rawlings, Nov. 5, 1817.
Lloyd Taylor m. Mary E. Thornton, Jan. 23, 1802.
Richard Taylor m. Mary Ann Selby, Dec. 26, 1782.
Richard Taylor m. Martha Druse, Dec. 24, 1798.
Richard Taylor m. Anne Boston, Mch. 4, 1807.
Snoden Taylor m. Elizabeth Drane, Sept. 7, 1782.
Solomon Taylor m. Eleanor Chaney, Jan. 17, 1780.
William Taylor m. Rebecca Hines, May 8, 1790.
Henry Tayman m. Elizabeth Talbott, Nov. 2, 1802.
John Tayman m. Mary McCauley, Feb. 13, 1804.
Thomas Tayman m. Margaret Turner, Dec. 31, 1811.
Edward Team m. Susanna Taylor, Mch. 30, 1784.
Hugh Templeton m. Mary Hoover, Aug. 9, 1794.
William Terry Jnr. m. Dorothy Brannock, Jan. 1, 1819.
Zachariah Thackrill m. Elizabeth Cooper, Mch. 13, 1778.
Benjamin Thomas m. Elizabeth James, Sept. 27, 1810.
Benjamin Thomas m. Eliza Boone, Dec. 26, 1815.

Ebenezer Thomas m. Anne Boone, Oct. 1, 1802.
Ebenezer Thomas m. Ann Carey Fowler, Dec. 8, 1808.
Jeremiah Thomas m. Cassey Williams, June 27, 1801.
John Thomas m. Sarah Murray, Aug. 22, 1777.
John Thomas m. Rebecca Bryan, Nov. 2, 1784.
John Thomas m. Eliza Ganson, Dec. 11, 1798.
John R. Thomas m. Ann C. Pumphrey, Feb. 11, 1817.
John W. Thomas m. Anna Webster, Jan. 7, 1813.
Levin Thomas m. Margaret McGuire, Dec. 23, 1786.
Luke Thomas m. Jane Caldclough, Sept. 13, 1785.
Philip Thomas m. Sarah Margt. Weems, Mch. 4, 1782.
Philip Wm. Thomas m. Julia Chisholm, Nov. 7, 1803.
Philip W. Thomas m. Rebecca Waters, Sept. 19, 1806.
Robert Thomas m. Ann Purdy, May 24, 1803.
Samuel Thomas m. Anna Warfield, Sept. 16, 1789.
William Thomas m. Rachel Hutcheson, May 3, 1780.
William Thomas m. Rachel Rhodes, Feb. 5, 1791.
William Thomas m. Charlotte Bratcher, Mch. 6, 1796.
Alexander Thompson m. Jane McNew, Apr. 13, 1789.
Francis Thompson m. Mary Watkins, Mch. 27, 1780.
Francis Thompson m. Mary Wood, May 8, 1780.
George Thompson m. Mary McCabe, Sept. 18, 1789.
Hugh Thompson m. Elizabeth Sprigg, Jan. 18, 1794.
John Thompson m. Elizabeth Connoway, Jan. 3, 1786.
John Thompson m. Mary Rowlings, Oct. 12, 1790.
John Thompson m. Ann Marriott, Dec. 16, 1795.
John Thompson m. Eleanor Johnson, Apr. 5, 1806.
John Thompson m. Susanna Tydings, Dec. 8, 1807.
John Thompson m. Eleanor Glover, Mch. 28, 1818.
Thomas Thompson m. Mary Cracroft, Mch. 23, 1792.
William Thompson m. Elizabeth Weeden, Mch. 7, 1818.
Richard Thorp m. Sarah McCubbin, Apr. 24, 1787.
William Thumbbert m. Eleanor Davidson, Oct. 7, 1811.
William B. Tilden m. Louisa H. Howard, Mch. 21, 1801.
James Tilghman m. Elizabeth Johns, Feb. 7, 1778.
John Tilghman m. Maria E. Gibson, Dec. 22, 1807.
John H. Tillard m. Emmeline Pindell, July 22, 1817.
William Tillard m. Delilah Simmons, Sept. 29, 1813.
Jasper E. Tilley m. Elizabeth Higgins, May 23, 1793.
Edward Timanous Snr. m. Margaret Morris, Dec. 5, 1796.
Edward Timmons m. Sarah Smith, Mch. 14, 1782.
Charles Tinges m. Rebecca Goldsmith, Apr. 7, 1789.

James Titus m. Sarah Iiams, Nov. 14, 1815.
Edward Tobin m. Eleanor Berry, Jan. 13, 1785.
John Todd m. Elizabeth Gray, Feb. 13, 1783.
Nathan Todd m. Sarah Rockhold, Apr. 14, 1787.
Richard Todd m. Ann Merriken, Jan. 31, 1788.
Thomas Todd m. Margaret Gardner, Apr. 16, 1792.
Thomas Todd m. Christian Marshall, June 7, 1799.
John Toft m. Elizabeth Welch, Feb. 13, 1797.
John Toft m. Elizabeth Wheat, Dec. 14, 1803.
Thomas Toft m. Ann Welch, Mch. 25, 1780.
Jacob Tolson m. Ruth Carter, Mch. 29, 1780.
James Tongue m. Anne Cowman, June 9, 1803.
Thomas Tongue Jnr. m. Anne Harrison, Jan. 3, 1809.
Richard Tootle m. Harriet Pryse, Dec. 18, 1799.
Richard Tootle m. Mary Victoria Devenew, Dec. 20, 1799.
Michael Towell m. Mary Flaharty, Jan. 11, 1805.
Thomas Towell m. Comfort Robinson, Nov. 26, 1811.
Thomas Townsend m. Ann Hutton, Dec. 23, 1780.
Thomas Townsend m. Rebecca Caton, Nov. 25, 1783.
Joseph Toy m. Mary Sparrow, Mch. 27, 1788.
William Tracy m. Elizabeth Winterson, Nov. 15, 1804.
Henry Hicks Traverse m. Esther Harding, Mch. 7, 1795.
Thomas Traverse m. Elizabeth Tucker, Oct. 24, 1793.
Greenbury Treakle m. Mary Hobbs, Nov. 24, 1812.
Gabriel Trott m. Anne Beford, Jan. 9, 1797.
Gabriel Trott m. Elizabeth McQuillin, May 7, 1817.
James Trott m. Sarah Griffith, Feb. 18, 1789.
John Trott m. Elizabeth Prout, Nov. 9, 1804.
Richard Trott m. Anne Crutchley, Apr. 7, 1817.
Sabret Trott m. Elizabeth Childs, Jan. 2, 1787.
Sabritt Trott m. Anne Conner, Apr. 4, 1809.
Samuel Trot m. Margaret Nowell, Dec. 14, 1793.
William Trott m. Willey Gibson, Dec. 29, 1802.
William Trott m. Mary Griffin, Dec. 26, 1818.
Alexander Truman m. Margaret Reynolds, May 29, 1781.
Washington G. Tuck m. Elizabeth Lee, Oct. 15, 1808.
Washington G. Tuck m. Rachel S. Whittington, Mch. 16, 1814.
William A. Tuck m. Cave Mulliken, May 25, 1801.
Abel Tucker m. Mary Tydings, July 17, 1804.
James Tucker m. Anne Deale, Mch. 12, 1814.
John Tucker m. Ann Tucker, July 12, 1783.
John Tucker m. Lurana Rawlings, Feb. 25, 1801.

Richard Tucker m. Susannah Cockey, Sept. 3, 1796.
Richard Tucker m. Lurana Tucker, Dec. 15, 1802.
Selea Tucker m. Anne Cockey, Oct. 29, 1796.
Thomas Tucker m. Frances Cockey, Dec. 14, 1787.
Thomas Tucker m. Anna Hooper, Sept. 8, 1796.
Thomas Tucker m. Ouara Wells, Jan. 6, 1807.
William Tucker m. Mary Anne Brewer, Aug. 1, 1801.
William Tucker m. Mary Elliott, Aug. 10, 1805.
Zachariah Tucker m. Catharine Myers, Nov. 19, 1778.
Zachariah Tucker m. Eleanor Rawlings, Sept. 25, 1790.
Zachariah Tucker m. Sarah Steuart, Nov. 9, 1802.
Abraham Turgason m. Anne Parot, June 7, 1810.
Philip Turner m. Margaret Smith, May 13, 1799.
Richard Turner m. Elizabeth Scrivener, Dec. 8, 1808.
Thomas Turner m. Jane Rockhold, Aug. 11, 1788.
Thomas W. Turner m. Maria Gambrell, Dec. 22, 1814.
Thomas W. Turner m. Charlotte Marriott, Sept. 19, 1816.
William Turner m. Susannah Childs, Jan. 16, 1808.
Joseph Tuttell m. Rebecca Howenton, Jan. 19, 1815.
George Twinch m. Mary Watson, Dec. 31, 1781.
Horatio Tydings m. Lydia Kirby, Jan. 11, 1817.
John Tydings m. Nancy Atwell, Dec. 12, 1810.
John Tydings m. Rachel Riston, Sept. 28, 1818.
Joseph Tydings m. Anne Tydings, Dec. 12, 1792.
Joseph Tydings m. Artridge Knighton, Dec. 13, 1816.
Keley Tydings m. Mary Beard, Jan. 30, 1782.
Keeley Tydings m. Frances Attwell, Mch. 20, 1793.
Kensey Tydings m. Mary Johnson, Feb. 16, 1819.
Lewis Tydings m. Mary Atwell, May 27, 1805.
Richard Tydings m. Eliza Stewart, Dec. 24, 1801.
Richard Tydings m. Mary Mullikin, July 23, 1806.
Grafton Tyler m. Catherine T. Macgill, Mch. 11, 1818.
William Urquhart m. Ruth Marriott, Jan. 11, 1781.
William Urguhart m. Maria Deford, Apr. 15, 1808.
William Urquhart m. Elizabeth Childs, Dec. 20, 1816.
James Usher m. Rachel Harrison, Mch. 14, 1797.
Joseph Vallean m. Mary Ann Norman, Jan. 27, 1820.
James Valiant m. Sarah Diamond, Jan. 1, 1781.
John Valliant m. Mary Meek, Mch. 8, 1804.
Charles Vandell m. Elizabeth Just, July 31, 1780.
John Veers m. Deborah Russell, Feb. 13, 1804.
Samuel Vernon m. Ann Griffin, June 10, 1787.

Edward Vidler m. Ann Topping, Oct. 13, 1787.
John Viers m. Catharine Bealmear, Mch. 26, 1787.
William Vinson m. Mary Allen, May 13, 1779.
Henry Waderman m. Mary Miles, Aug. 16, 1813.
William Walham m. Mary Stewart, Sept. 19, 1815.
Charles Walker m. Sarah Ryan, July 30, 1778.
Isaac Walker m. Henrietta Miller, Dec. 15, 1812.
James Walker m. Margaret Owens, Aug. 30, 1782.
John Walker m. Elizabeth Hammond, Jan. 7, 1785.
Thomas Walker m. Elizabeth Brogden, Jan. 22, 1778.
Vachel Walker m. Elizabeth Whitehead, June 27, 1815.
William Walker m. Ann Coale, June 28, 1792.
Thomas Wall m. Thomsin White, Mch. 4, 1784.
Charles Wallace m. Mary Rankin, Apr. 26, 1798.
William Waller m. Jannetta Russell Nelson, June 5, 1778.
John Walmsley m. Mary Records, Feb. 1, 1780.
Benjamin Ward m. Eleanor Ward, May 11, 1807.
Henry Ward m. Sarah Shepherd, Nov. 18, 1788.
James Ward m. Lucy Scott, Sept. 5, 1810.
John Ward m. Eleanor Ward, June 20, 1783.
John Ward m. Elizabeth Whittington, Feb. 7, 1809.
Joseph Ward m. Eleanor Ward, Oct. 21, 1815.
Joseph Ward m. Eliz[a]. Pattison, Mch. 9, 1820.
Josephus Ward m. Anne Tydings, July 18, 1793.
Nathan Ward m. Elizabeth Crosby, June 12, 1809.
Richard Ward m. Althea Brown, Jan. 22, 1796.
Richard Ward m. Sarah Wood, May 25, 1814.
Richard Ward m. Elizabeth Fry, Mch. 7, 1818.
Robert Ward m. Catherine Spicknell, Apr. 28, 1802.
Samuel Ward m. Elizabeth Pickeron, Apr. 20, 1787.
Samuel Ward m. Elizabeth Drury, Nov. 23, 1798.
Samuel Ward m. Rachel Basford, Feb. 20, 1816.
William Ward m. Barbara Phelps, Mch. 20, 1799.
William Ward m. Sarah Scrivener, Dec. 24, 1800.
Zachariah Ward m. Pamelia Dockett, Apr. 18, 1791.
Alexander Warfield m. Elizabeth Woodward, Dec. 5, 1788.
Amos Warfield m. Sarah Warfield, Nov. 8, 1793.
Azel Warfield m. Elizabeth Welling, Dec. 4, 1786.
Bane Warfield m. Arey Dorsey, Apr. 28, 1779.
Basil Warfield m. Ann Cecil, Feb. 15, 1803.
Beale Warfield m. Achsah Dorsey, July 25, 1785.
Benjamin Warfield m. Rebecca Spurrier, Apr. 19, 1796.

Charles Warfield m. Sally Warfield, July 10, 1790.
Edward Warfield m. Polly Warfield, Oct. 7, 1794.
Elisha Warfield m. Ruth Burgess, Aug. 6, 1778.
James Warfield m. Elizabeth Biggs, June 7, 1815.
John Warfield m. Mary Green, Dec. 24, 1779.
John Warfield m. Henrietta Pitt, Mch. 16, 1785.
John Warfield m. Humulal Mewshaw, Feb. 13, 1790.
John Warfield m. Deborah White, Apr. 16, 1808.
Joseph Warfield m. Elizabeth Dorsey, June 26, 1778.
Joshua Warfield m. Rebecca Dorsey, Apr. 25, 1781.
Joshua Warfield m. Elizabeth Dorsey, Oct. 6, 1781.
Joshua Warfield m. Mary Jones, Jan. 13, 1783.
Lancelot Warfield m. Rachel Marriott, Jan. 17, 1783.
Lancelot Warfield m. Polly Warfield, Sept. 29, 1795.
Levin Warfield m. Ann Hobbs, Oct. 6, 1779.
Meshack Warfield m. Rachel Charick, Dec. 23, 1803.
Philemon Warfield m. Anne Wright, Oct. 23, 1819.
Richard Warfield m. Nancy Benson, Aug. 16, 1788.
Richard Warfield m. Elizabeth Lucus, June 22, 1802.
Richard B. Warfield m. Anne Marsh, Feb. 2, 1820.
Samuel Warfield m. Susanna Danison, June 26, 1795.
Thomas Warfield m. Elizabeth Hollyday, Dec. 11, 1778.
Thomas Warfield m. Elizabeth Marriott, July 19, 1798.
Thomas Warfield m. Margerry Brown, Mch. 30, 1803.
Thomas Warfield m. Isabella M. Lucas, Apr. 4, 1818.
Thomas W. Warfield m. Sarah White, Jan. 30, 1813.
Vachel Warfield m. Eleanor Griffith, Sept. 23, 1786.
Vachel H. Warfield m. Achsah H. Marriott, Dec. 17, 1819.
William Warfield m. Frances Hinton, Nov. 13, 1790.
William Warfield m. Mary Tyler Worthington, Sept. 17, 1816.
William Warden m. Elizabeth Clarke, Feb. 18, 1778.
Basil Warring m. Elizabeth Hall, Nov. 26, 1805.
Geo. Washington Waring m. Sarah M. Dorsey, Nov. 27, 1819.
Abraham Wason m. Elizabeth Smith, May 10, 1810.
Edmund Wason m. Anne Woodfield, Dec. 23, 1805.
Joseph Wason m. Elizabeth Mace, Nov. 15, 1817.
Levy Wason m. Mary Smith, Nov. 21, 1808.
Richard Wason m. Sarah Lancaster, Jan. 15, 1784.
Thomas Wason m. Sarah Pargerson, Sept. 20, 1803.
Benjamin Waters m. Hannah Fowler, Feb. 10, 1810.
Charles L. Waters m. Rebecca Fowler, May 23, 1792.
Edward E. Waters m. Rachel Jones, Feb. 1, 1799.

Edward Waters m. Honora Ray, Dec. 8, 1813.
Ephraim Waters m. Ann Law [Low?], Jan. 13, 1797.
Jacob Waters m. Elizabeth Wells, Sept. 29, 1798.
Jacob F. Waters m. Harriott Tongue, Mch. 23, 1809.
Jonathan Waters m. Sarah Armaja, Feb. 17, 1798.
Nathaniel Waters m. Mabel Maccauley, May 23, 1794.
Nacy Waters m. Ann Warfield, June 14, 1790.
Richard Waters m. Sarah Cooke, Oct. 1, 1795.
William Waters m. Jane Woodward, June 10, 1785.
Wilson Waters m. Margaret Davis, June 11, 1800.
Jonathan Wates m. Sarah G. Bateman, Apr. 21, 1818.
Benjamin Watkins m. Elizabeth Sheckells, Dec. 31, 1779.
Benjamin Watkins m. Elizabeth Sheckells, Apr. 11, 1780.
Benjamin Watkins m. Anne Harwood, Apr. 10, 1794.
Charles Watkins m. Ester Ferrill, Sept. 15, 1780.
Gassaway Watkins m. Sarah Jones, Dec. 2, 1785.
Gassaway Watkins m. Ruth Dorsey, Feb. 28, 1788.
Gassaway Watkins m. Rebecca Richardson, May 18, 1793.
Ignatius Watkins m. Elizabeth Gale, May 18, 1793.
John Watkins m. Elizabeth Hall, Jan. 7, 1783.
John Watkins m. Margaret Tydings, Nov. 11, 1790.
John Watkins m. Ann Rutland, Oct. 26, 1791.
John Watkins m. Elizabeth Hall, Nov. 27, 1797.
John Watkins m. Willy Ann Davis, Feb. 7, 1812.
Joseph Watkins m. Anne Gray, Nov. 28, 1789.
Nicholas Watkins m. Sarah Disney, Feb. 1, 1782.
Nicholas Watkins m. Elizabeth Walker, Apr. 3, 1786.
Nicholas Watkins m. Margaret Todd, Aug. 23, 1806.
Nicholas G. Watkins m. Margaret Harwood, Aug. 31, 1798.
Nicholas I. Watkins m. Rachel L. Watkins, May 7, 1801.
Rezin Watkins m. Amey Meads, Jan 11, 1798.
Richard Watkins m. Ruth Beard, Oct. 5, 1778.
Richard Watkins m. Mary Purdy, Feb. 28, 1813.
Sabine Wathen m. Nancy Brewer, Oct. 9, 1813.
Samuel Watkins m. Elizabeth Watkins, Jan. 26, 1795.
Stephen Watkins m. Elcy Woodward, Sept. 9, 1793.
Thomas Watkins m. Sarah Disney, Nov. 4, 1797.
William Watkins m. Eleanor Harwood, Feb. 25, 1805.
Charles Watson m. Elizabeth Hall Rutland, May 21, 1804.
George Watson m. Sarah Gambrill, Jan. 11, 1800.
Hezekiah Watson m. Anne Atwell, Oct. 22, 1796.
Robert Watson m. Ann Cooper, July 4, 1780.

William Watson m. Mary Dawson, Feb. 13, 1779.
George Watts m. Mary Lark, Apr. 20, 1799.
George Watts m. Elizabeth Keith, Jan. 21, 1807.
George Watts m. Rachel Tydings, Jan. 17, 1818.
Henry Watts m. Rebecca Stansbury, Jan. 28, 1804.
Isaac Watts m. Mary Blackingham, Dec. 3, 1795.
John Watts m. Juliana Porter, Oct. 29, 1790.
Philip Watts m. Rebecca Welch, Jan. 17, 1793.
Richard Watts m. Rebecca Beard, Aug. 6, 1778.
Richard Watts m. Mary Packer, Dec. 15, 1789.
Richard Watts m. Ann Watkins, Oct. 3, 1792.
Richard B. Watts m. Elizabeth Rawlings, Feb. 21, 1803.
Richard B. Watts m. Mary R. Watson, Mch. 31, 1812.
Edmund Wayman m. Airy Connaway, July 28, 1781.
Hezekiah Waymun m. Jane Lee, June 15, 1786.
Hezekiah Wayman m. Elizabeth Barry, Feb. 19, 1798.
Thomas Wayman m. Elizabeth Crutchley, Jan. 15, 1820.
Charles Weakley m. Ruth Bryan, July 21, 1785.
Lewis Weaver m. Elizabeth Mifflin, May 12, 1801.
Levi Webb m. Casandra Wood, Dec. 10, 1810.
Michael Webster m. Anne Purdy, Feb. 10, 1807.
Eli Weedon m. Catharine Johnson, July 13, 1815.
Henry Weeden m. Mary Seeders, Dec. 8, 1789.
James Weedon m. Frances Yewell, Apr. 29, 1818.
John Weedon m. Martha Seeders, Dec. 18, 1798.
Jonathan Weedon m. Margaret Hutton, July 29, 1819.
Richard Weedon m. Sarah Weedon, Mch. 22, 1788.
Richard Weedon m. Matilda Thomas, Feb. 3, 1801.
Richard Weedon m. Ruth Yewell, Dec. 21, 1811.
Robert Weeden m. Elizabeth Sands, Aug. 17, 1779.
Robert Weedon m. Hellen Small, Feb. 16, 1793.
Samuel Weedon m. Louisa Vessells, Apr. 15, 1811.
James N. Weems m. Elizabeth Ridgely, Sept. 23, 1802.
John Weems m. Mary Dorsey, Dec. 18, 1781.
John Weems m. Mary Cracroft, Apr. 2, 1795.
John Weems of Rich[d]. m. Rachel Norman, Dec. 26, 1803.
Jn[o] Beal Weems m. Priscilla Harwood, Jan. 2, 1806.
Richard Weems m. Mary Wood, May 27, 1809.
William Weems m. Rachel Morris, June 30, 1784.
William Weems m. Priscilla Sellman, May 8, 1804.
Aaron Welch m. Elizabeth Franklin, Nov. 2, 1778.
Aaron Welch m. Elizabeth Drury, Nov. 10, 1801.

Benjamin Welch m. Margaret Daltzel, May 22, 1792.
Francis Welch m. Margaret Lusby, May 1, 1797.
John Welch m. Mary Hall, Aug. 15, 1782.
John Welch m. Eleanor Warfield, Nov. 1, 1783.
John Welch m. Mary Owens, May 9, 1816.
Mordecai Welsh m. Mary Watts, Dec. 21, 1790.
Robert Welch m. Ann Furguson, Sept. 25, 1777.
Robert Welch m. Eleanor Carr, Nov. 24, 1777.
Robert Welch m. Sarah Merrikin, Oct. 29, 1795.
Robert Welch m. Priscilla Owens, Apr. 17, 1797.
Robert Welch m. Sally Mallonee, Nov. 10, 1806.
John Willey m. Ann Macknew, Mch. 24, 1786.
Benjamin Wells m. Elizabeth Traverse, Jan. 4, 1806.
Benjamin Wells m. Artridge Franklin, Oct. 8, 1815.
Daniel Wells m. Mary Taigger, Nov. 27, 1790.
George Wells m. Augusta Maine, Sept. 8, 1798.
Jeremiah Wells m. Anne Carter, Oct. 9, 1813.
John Wells m. Elizabeth Shewbutt, Sept. 3, 1785.
John Wells m. Henrietta Watkins, Oct. 23, 1799.
John Wells m. Hannah Mayo, Oct. 25, 1810.
John Wells m. Elizabeth Haslip, Oct. 30, 1819.
Nathan Wells m. Ruth Brashears, Oct. 17, 1798.
Richard Wells m. Mary Freeland, Jan. 31, 1783.
Richard Wells m. Eliz^a. Beck, Jan. 31, 1784.
Richard Wells m. Druzilla Brashears, Oct. 23, 1787.
Richard Wells m. Sarah Carr, Nov. 18, 1788.
Richard Wells m. Susanna Phips, Jan. 31, 1805.
Richard Wells m. Rachel Deale, Feb. 14, 1814.
Samuel Wells m. Sarah Phips, Jan. 25, 1785.
William Wells m. Susannah Garston, Jan. 11, 1794.
Zadok Wells m. Elizabeth Wheeler, Dec. 4, 1819.
Benjamin Welsh m. Ruth Drury, Feb. 7, 1804.
Francis Welsh m. Rizpah R. Norman, Dec. 6, 1810.
Thomas Welsh m. Anne S. Iglehart, Jan. 23, 1817.
Cornelius West m. Lewesa Humphreys, June 13, 1787.
James West m. Margaret Whitaker, Dec. 31, 1795.
James West m. Margaret Whitaker, Mch. 31, 1796.
Richard W^m. West m. Maria Lloyd, Oct. 9, 1798.
Lewis Weston m. Margaret Thompson, Dec. 22, 1810.
Jesse Wheat m. Harriet Sappington, Oct. 23, 1804.
Thomas Wheatley m. Crissy Kervan, July 10, 1787.
Jonathan Wheedon m. Rebecca Tayman, Dec. 21, 1810.

Thomas Wheedon m. Anne Yewell, Dec. 30, 1811.
Nathaniel Wheeler m. Sarah Duvall, Dec. 31, 1804.
Odel Wheeler m. Caroline Dorsey, Nov. 11, 1818.
Richard Wheeler Jnr. m. Elizabeth Marriott, Oct. 19, 1797.
Robert Wheeler m. Eleanor Watkins, Jan. 24, 1798.
Thomas Wheeler m. Anne Hutton, Feb. 23, 1805.
William Wheeler m. Susanna G. Clarke, Jan. 17, 1814.
William Wheeler m. Elizabeth Downes, Feb. 23, 1816.
Barton Whetcroft m. Elizabeth Knap, Apr. 20, 1789.
Henry Whetcroft m. Sarah Whetcroft, Aug. 14, 1796.
George Whips m. Elizabeth Pearce, Aug. 6, 1778.
Caleb White m. Eliza Cruse, Dec. 18, 1815.
Edward White m. Ann Wootton, Nov. 5, 1784.
Elias White m. Eliza McDaniel, Oct. 6, 1818.
Gideon White m. Hannah Barber, June 21, 1798.
Griffith White m. Sarah Freeland, Dec. 11, 1788.
James White m. Eleanor Litchfield, Dec. 22, 1777.
John Cole White m. Harriet Lee, Apr. 30, 1800.
Jonas White m. Ruth Marriott, Jan. 15, 1793.
Jonathan White m. Elizabeth Williams, Dec. 13, 1788.
Joseph White m. Elizabeth Ross, May 1, 1820.
Osborn White m. Ann Chaney, May 19, 1817.
Reuben White m. Elizabeth Hall, Jan. 15, 1814.
Richard White m. Margaret Garnes, Dec. 29, 1785.
Richard White m. Margaret Reed, Dec. 7, 1796.
Richard White m. Sarah Cragg, May 13, 1797.
Richard White m. Delila Pierce, Apr. 30, 1800.
Richard White m. Phebe Chaney, Apr. 2, 1817.
Thomas White m. Mary Atkinson, Oct. 14, 1819.
Edward Whitehead m. Anne Kingsbury, Jan. 29, 1793.
Hezekiah Whitehead m. Mary Waters, Nov. 3, 1813.
Richard Whitehead m. Susanna Cheney, Nov. 10, 1792.
Jacob Whitwright m. Mary Carr, Jan. 15, 1820.
Philip Whitwright m. Susannah Phips, May 23, 1792.
Benjamin Whittington m. Cassey Smith, Nov. 17, 1788.
Benjamin Whittington m. Margaret Jones, July 14, 1800.
Benjamin Whittington m. Elizabeth Cowman, Jan. 6, 1804.
Francis Whittington Sen. m. Sarah Hammond, July 26, 1816.
James Whittington m. Mary Wood, Feb. 17, 1787.
John Whittington m. Mary Armager, June 1, 1780.
John Whitington m. Eliza. Scrivener, Apr. 18, 1797.
John A. Whittington m. Sarah C. Brown, Oct. 11, 1813.

John A. Whittington m. Sarah Pattison, Sept. 19, 1815.
Joseph Whittington m. Sarah Russell, Dec. 15, 1791.
Samuel Whittington m. Dorothy Wood, Apr. 16, 1819.
Thomas Whittington m. Eleanor Miles, Nov. 24, 1791.
Thomas Whittington m. Ann Basford, Nov. 7, 1794.
William Whittington m. Susannah Wood, Dec. 24, 1788.
William Whittington m. Sarah Welch, Aug. 18, 1804.
William Whittington m. Lydia Hinton, Jan. 7, 1820.
Richard Whittle m. Elizabeth Baldwin, Dec. 13, 1794.
James Whorfe m. Eleanor Brewer, July 28, 1796.
Joseph Wiett m. Margaret Peacock, Jan. 8, 1795.
Edward Willett m. Eleanor Fisher, Dec. 19, 1785.
Ninian Willet m. Chloe Walker, July 30, 1778.
Abraham Williams m. Frances Cromwell, May 15, 1793.
Andrew Williams m. Jane Cunningham, Dec. 22, 1777.
Andrew Williams m. Sarah Lovely, Aug. 10, 1778.
Eli Williams m. Phebe Coal, July 24, 1815.
Elijah Williams m. Rachel Moss, July 30, 1816.
Henry Williams m. Louisa Wheedon, Apr. 29, 1820.
Jeramiah Williams m. Mary Gaither, Dec. 15, 1784.
John Williams m. Elizabeth Davis, Apr. 10, 1779.
John Williams m. Sarah Hancock, Jan. 18, 1805.
John H. Williams m. Olivia Fokes, Dec. 9, 1820.
Jn°. Wilson Williams m. Rachel Pettibone, Mch. 10, 1819.
Joseph Williams m. Eleanor Mew, Sept. 27, 1780.
Joseph Williams m. Mary Short, Feb. 13, 1792.
Philip Williams m. Rachel Pearce, Apr. 27, 1796.
Thomas Williams m. Eliza Thomas, Feb. 21, 1802.
Thomas Williams m. Elizabeth Lowe, Nov. 14, 1818.
William Williams m. Milcah Fowler, Dec. 15, 1792.
James Williamson m. Maria Tuck, Dec. 20, 1804.
James Williamson m. Sarah Mayo, Sept. 26, 1809.
Charles H. Willigman m. Catherine Jackson, Aug. 30, 1808.
Henry A. Wilins m. Elizabeth Grammer, Oct. 29, 1802.
Daniel Willis m. Jemima Taylor, June 15, 1785.
John Vankirk Williss m. Elizabeth Dowling, Oct. 1, 1782.
Alexander Wilson m. Frances Thomas, Aug. 19, 1791.
Daniel Wilson m. Delilah Johnson, Nov. 28, 1801.
James Wilson m. Margery Duvall, Apr. 8, 1783.
James Wilson m. Ann Sumland, July 28, 1784.
John F. Wilson m. Elizabeth Gott, Jan. 16, 1819.
Robert Wilson m. Prudence Thomas, Apr. 19, 1788.

Samuel Wilson m. Elizabeth Wiltshire, Dec. 12, 1778.
Samuel Wilson m. Eve Jennings, Aug. 6, 1787.
Spedden Wilson m. Mary Terry, Apr. 29, 1815.
Thomas Wilson m. Julianna Stewart, Oct. 9, 1796.
Jonathan Wiltshire m. Elizabeth Cooper, Nov. 25, 1782.
Thomas Windham m. Sarah Lamb, June 21, 1785.
Benjamin Winterson m. Hannah Ditty, Jan. 21, 1799.
Benjamin Winterson m. Anne Tucker, July 7, 1801.
John Wiseham m. Ann Blackwell, Dec. 2, 1784.
Charles Wood m. Mary Handy, Nov. 13, 1793.
Dorsey Wood m. Elizabeth Rodwell, June 9, 1781.
Edward Wood m. Elizabeth Talbott, Feb. 19, 1802.
Henry Wood m. Mary Brown, Nov. 28, 1792.
Henry Wood m. Martha Griffin, June 7, 1794.
Hopewell Wood m. Ann Muse, Feb. 10, 1779.
Hopewell Wood m. Ann Hughes, Sept. 27, 1811.
Jack Wood m. Mary Scrivener, Aug. 3, 1809.
John Wood m. Susannah Mitchell, June 29, 1781.
John Wood m. Henrietta Scrivener, Sept. 16, 1789.
John Wood m. Barbara Allein, Oct. 20, 1792.
John Wood m. Margaret Ames, Aug. 6, 1805.
John Wood m. Ann Deroch, Nov. 14, 1817.
John Wood m. Eleanor L. Simmons, Jan. 21, 1818.
Joseph Wood m. Sarah Ward, July 20, 1802.
Robert Wood m. Lieley Wood, Jan. 7, 1789.
Robert Wood m. Eleanor Whittle, Mch. 2, 1789.
Robert Wood m. Elizabeth Stevens, Dec. 19, 1803.
Robert Wood m. Rachel Simmons, Nov. 7, 1807.
Samuel Wood m. Elizabeth Whittington, Feb. 26, 1802.
Samuel Wood Jn^{r}. m. Ann Boswell, Aug. 28, 1811.
Samuel Wood m. Rachel Stevens, Feb. 19, 1819.
Thomas Wood m. Christian Woodfield, Dec. 1, 1783.
Zachariah Wood m. Rebecca Chapline, Sept. 2, 1790.
Anthony Woodfield m. Eleanor Waters, Feb. 14, 1809.
John Woodfield m. Elizabeth Norman, Feb. 13, 1782.
John Woodfield m. Mary Ann Timmins, Dec. 18, 1802.
John Woodfield m. Marian Foreman, Aug. 3, 1809.
Thomas Woodfield m. Sarah Bicknell, Feb. 1, 1791.
Thomas Woodfield m. Anne Purdy, May 30, 1811.
Thomas Woodfield m. Catherine Plain, Nov. 4, 1813.
Henry Woodward m. Eleanor Turner, Feb. 13, 1797.
Isaac Woodward m. Mary Jane Aisquith, Jan. 23, 1818.
Jo^{s}. Henry Woodward m. Susan Butt, Apr. 7, 1817.

James H. Woodward m. Eliz[a]. Bryan, Nov. 3, 1818.
Nicholas Woodward m. Margaret Mulliken, Dec. 31, 1812.
Thomas Woodward m. Margaret Iiams, May 21, 1778.
William Woodward m. Jamima Jacob, Nov. 17, 1790.
John Woolfit m. Ruth Pearce, July 26, 1787.
Richard Wootton m. Margaret Evans, Dec. 21, 1808.
Richard Wootton m. Araminta Jackson, Dec. 22, 1813.
Thomas Wooton m. Mary Wasteneys, Nov. 14, 1809.
William Wootton m. Ann Gardiner, Feb. 22, 1813.
Beale M. Worthington m. Elizabeth R. Ricketts, Mch. 7, 1811.
Charles G. Worthington m. Mary Ann Dorsey, Jan. 16, 1815.
John Worthington m. Christiana Magruder, Oct. 5, 1781.
John Worthington m. Ann Meriweather, Feb. 4, 1790.
Nicholas Worthington m. Elizabeth Rutland, July 6, 1778.
Nicholas Worthington m. Anne Warfield, Aug. 1, 1814.
Tho[s]. Worthington of Tho[s]. m. Eliza Baldwin, Nov. 29, 1808.
Thomas Worthington m. Julia Sewell, Nov. 20, 1815.
William Worthington m. Ann Wilson, Mch. 1, 1785.
John Wriggel m. Rebecca Nicholson, Apr. 27, 1786.
Henry Wright m. Mary Lusby, Dec. 31, 1803.
James Wright m. Anne Fowler, June 9, 1807.
Joshua Wright m. Anne Gray, Feb. 2, 1795.
Thomas Wyatt m. Clara Fox, Feb. 19, 1806.
Walter Wyvill m. Ann Wood, May 17, 1811.
Walter Wyvell m. Margaret Murdock, Feb. 29, 1820.
William Wyvill m. Sarah Burgess, June 17, 1777.
Henry D. Yates m. Mahala Young, June 8, 1818.
Vachel Yeates m. Elizabeth Harris, May 27, 1779.
Benjamin Yieldhall m. Eleanor Druce, Nov. 9, 1782.
Benjamin Yieldhall m. Darky Fennell, Apr. 17, 1787.
Benjamin Yieldhall m. Susan M[c]Gill, Apr. 7, 1807.
Charles Yieldhall m. Catherine Bourdman, Dec. 11, 1783.
John Yieldhall m. Mary Watson, Dec. 6, 1782.
Samuel Yieldhall m. Lydia Hall, Mch. 2, 1780.
John, Young m. Sarah Griffis, Oct. 2, 1790.
John Young m. Mary Turnbull, Feb. 13, 1798.
John Young m. Humulal Moss, Oct. 29, 1801.
John Young m. Elizabeth Buckney, Oct. 18, 1804.
John Young m. Ruth Allen, Jan. 12, 1813.
Nehemiah Younger m. Trisly Taylor, Nov. 7, 1803.
Peter Young m. Elizabeth Simpson, Aug. 5, 1784.
William Young m. Jane Johnson, Aug. 10, 1811.
Nehemiah Younger m. Hannah Osboon, June 28, 1787.

Charles County, Marriages

By Rev. John Bolton*

Osburn, Henry to Ann Tompson, June 23, 1779.
Tompson, Baptist to Mary Lancaster, Nov. 7, 1779.
Edelin, Francis to Sarah Tompson, Nov. 8, 1779.
Montgomery, Thomas to Rebecca Southwell, Dec. 16, 1781.
Langley, Joseph to Sarah Hill, Jan. 5, 1782.
Wheatly, Bennet to Polly Morris, Jan. 17, 1782.
Edelin, Edward to Eleanor Boarman, Feb. 12, 1782.
Cash, John to Chloe Callicoe, Feb. 8, 1782.
Goodrick, Joseph to Eliza. Nash, Aug. 5, 1782.
Simpson, Joseph to Mary Ann Montgomery, Aug. 19, 1782.
Hill, Fran. Xarerius to Lidia True, Sept. 12, 1782.
Osburn, Walter to Mary Miles, Oct. 8, 1782.
Hagan, Raphael to Rebecca Deviel, Oct. 9, 1782.

By Rev. John C. Brockenborough, Rector of William and Mary Parish

Shaw, Samuel to Mary Parish, June 4, 1799.
Lipscombe, Spotswood to Eliza. Smith Pendleton, July 7, 1799.
Smoot, Horatio to Heathy Smoot, July 7, 1799.
Aderton, Joseph to Ann Latimer, Aug. 1, 1799.
Reeves, Thos. C. to Rebecca Ratcliffe, Aug. 8, 1799.
Gardiner, John Chunn to Esther Cawood, Oct. 1, 1799, (in St. Mary's Co.)
Simpson, George to Margaret Bateman, Dec. 24, 1799.
Smith, Samuel to Mary Dutton, Jan. 1, 1800.
Wiseman, Robert to Eliza. Philips, Jan. 14, 1800.
Shaw, Edward to Cloe Posey, Apr. 15, 1800.
Easley, Kemble to Ann Ratcliffe, July 25, 1800.
Bateman, Richard to Margt. Wakefield, Dec. 23, 1800.
Tompkins, W^{m}. to Mary Farr, Dec. 26, 1800.

* From Maryland Marriages, p. 184; Md. Hist. Soc., courtesy of Mr. Charles Fickus, Acting Librarian.

"The counties covered by our 'Maryland Marriages, 1777–1804' are Allegheny, Anne Arundel, Baltimore, Calvert, Charles, Frederick, Harford, Montgomery, Prince George's, St. Mary's, Talbot and Washington. As there are only a page or two for some counties I doubt that they are complete." Charles Fickus, Acting Librarian, July 27, 1927.

Govrick, Elijah to Eliza. Bateman, Jan. 6, 1801.
Chunn, Charles to Jane T. Bowen, Apr. 28, 1801.
Farr, John B. to Jane Cawood, Aug. 9, 1801.
Hemrican, Matthew to Eliza. Penn, Oct. 15, 1801.

Charles Co., Md., Marriages, By Rev. Henry Fendall (Prot. Episcopal)

King, John to Susa. Lynch (of St. Paul's Parish P. G's Co.), Nov. 1777.
Rowe, John to Mary Ward (King George's Parish), Dec. 23, 1777.
Adams, Samuel to Sarah Nelson (Durham Parish), Dec. 28, 1777.
Penny, Thos. to Amelia Adams (Durham Parish), Jan. 4, 1778.
Davis, Zachariah to Sarah Wright (Durham Parish), Jan. 5, 1778.
Nally, Nathan Barton to Sarah Taylor (Durham Parish), Jan. 6, 1778.
Gray, Benja. to Mary Stewart (Durham Parish), Feb. 15, 1778.
Stewart, James to Cath. Milstead (Durham Parish), Mch. 15, 1778.
Grant, John to Eliza. Greenfield Tyler (King George's Parish, Prince George's Co.), Mch. 16, 1778.
Lomax Zeth to Eleanor Gray (Durham Parish), Mch. 29, 1778.
Ryson, Lancelot to Clare Cash (both of Stafford Co., Va.), Mch. 26, 1778.
Woodward, Samuel to Ann Posey (Durham Parish), Apr. 3, 1778.
Beal, Francis to Penelope Ford (Port Tobacco Parish), Apr. 12, 1778.
Jacobs, —— to Ann Grahame, Apr. 30, 1778.
Wells, Samuel to Martha Oliver (P. G. Co.), Aug. 13, 1778.
Ward, Wm. to Verlinda Harrison (Durham Parish), July 27, 1777.
Fields, Wm. to Clare Poor (Durham Parish), Aug. 11, 1777.
Waters, John to Eliza Carter (Durham Parish), Sept. 20, 1777.
McConchie, Wm. to Eliza Muncaster (Durham Parish), Sept. 25, 1777.
Walker, Richard to Mary Gilpen (P. G. Co.), Aug. 25, 1778.
Moore, John Smith to Margt. Musgrove (P. G. Co.), Sept. 20, 1778.
Cox, John to Margt. Howard (P. G. Co.), Sept. 2, 1778.
Lanyhill, Leonard to Ann Anly (Calvert Co.), Oct. 30, 1778.
Naylor, Batson to Eleanor Austin (P. G. Co.), Nov. 8, 1778.
Gabard, John to Margt. Lucas, Mch., 1778.

Charles County Marriages By Rev. Walter H. Harrison

Wheeler, Benedict to Cath. Travers, Dec. 23, 1779.
Watkins, Thomas to Lucy Belt, Dec. 26, 1779.
Rye, Warren to Sarah Smith, Jan. 23, 1780.
Posey, Uriah to Catharine Skinner, Jan. —, 1780
Deacons, Ambrose to Ann Chatham, Jan. 26, 1780.
Haislip, John to Easter Nelson, Jan. 27, 1780.

Grows, John to Christiana Jenkins, Jan. 30, 1780.
Murdock, James to Phebe Delosien, ——, 1780.
Manning, Joseph to Eliza. Dunnington, Mch. 15, 1780.
Nelson, John to Eliza. Burgess, Apr. 9, 1780.
Turner, Walter to Eliza. Blancet, Apr. 23, 1780.
Simmons, Joseph to Mary Deacons, May 15, 1780.
Braund, Joseph to Emily Maddox, May 23, 1780.
Chapman, John to Sarah Jonke, June 1, 1780.
Elgin, William to Ann Anderson, June 18, 1780.
Maddox, Samuel to Anne Warde, July 9, 1780.
Cookssy, Hezekiah to Eliza Grey, July 13, 1780.
Thatcher, Ignatius to —— Saporly, July 16, 1780.
Fitzgerald, John to Ann Green, Aug. 24, 1780.
Lawler, W^m^. to Mary Sacke, Aug. 31, 1780.
Milstead, Thomas to Eliza. Ratcliffe, Sept. 16, 1780.
Griffin, Rosse to Sarah Ratcliffe, Sept. 21, 1780.
Dunnington, Hezekiah to Aa. Magriger, Oct. 9, 1780.
Smith, John to Rebecca Jewel, Nov. 13, 1780.
Bartly, William to Ann Smoot, Nov. 19, 1780.

Charles Co. Marriages By Rev. Ignatius Matthews (Roman Catholic)

Reeder, John to Chloe Green, Oct. 22, 1779.
Dixon, Jacob to Mary Lancaster, 1781–2.
Higdon, Ignatius to Eliza. Taylor, 1781–2.
Cooms, Richard to Clare Green, 1781–2.
Ally, Shadrack to Eliza. Gates, 1781–2.

Charles County, By Rev. John McPherson of Piccawaxon, or William and Mary Parish

King, Robert to Judith Wood, June 13, 1777.
Syme, Nicholas to Eliza. Johnson, July 25, 1777.
Reeves, Thomas to Mary Scroggan Oakley, Sept. 28, 1777.
Scroggan, John to Ann Mastin, Oct. 29, 1777.
Smith, James to Winnie Rogers, Dec. 23, 1777.
Mastin, Francis to Charity Cooksey, Jan. 10, 1778.
Duley, Thomas to Eliza. Bateman, Feb. 6, 1778.
Rock, William to Charity Adams, Feb. 23, 1778.
Collins, John to Eliza. Scroggan, May 10, 1778.
Pollock, Thomas to Susanna Curd, May 19, 1778.
Ashton, Henry Elexr. to Mary Dent, May 25, 1778.

Edwards, John to Mary Turner, June 4, 1778.
Oakly, John Scroggan to Mary Ann Mahoney, June 5, 1778.
Cleyburn, Wm. Dandridge to Ann Dandridge, June 21, 1778.
Griffy, Benja. to Susanna Modisit, Aug. 26, 1778.
Hungerford, Thos. to Violetta Gwinn, Nov. 17, 1778.
Farr, John to Mary Watts, Nov. 25, 1778.
Tyler, William to Mariamore Trueman Stoddrt, Jan. 10, 1779.
Robison, Willm. to Mary Sims, Apr. 8, 1779.
Smoot, John to Anny Ford, Apr. 8, 1779.
Nelson, Willm. to Sally Smallwood, Apr. 13, 1779.
Carrol, John to Eliza. Hamilton, May 9, 1779.
Wilder, John Brown to Mary Ann Smoot, May 27, 1779.
Jenkins, Philip to Eliza. Hungerford, June 8, 1779.
Maddox, John to Sarah Fernandis, June 20, 1779.
Higgs, Jonathan to Eliza. Ford, June 20, 1779.
Penn, John to Eleanor Dutton, July 20, 1779.
Nettle, Thomas Dutton to Muriel Dutton, July 20, 1779.
Shaw, Dr. Louis Dene to Jenny Clements, Sept. 16, 1779.
Baillie, Andrew to Mary Leftrich, Oct. 1, 1779.
Boswel, Walter to Eleanor Smallwood, Oct. 14, 1779.
Smoot, Isaac to Mary Lock, Oct. 28, 1779.
Halkerstone, John to Eliza. Hanson, Nov. 4, 1779.
Lamond, John Christerson to Eliza. Hall, Nov. 18, 1779.
Franklin, John to Virlinda Cox, Dec. 8, 1779.
Gwinn, John to Jean Ludwell Bruce, Dec. 22, 1779.
Washington, Thornton to Milly Berry (of Va.), Dec. 26, 1779.
Hodgson, George to Nancy Jenkins, Dec. 30, 1779.
Mason, Lot to Sally Haselip, Jan. 12, 1780.
May, Richard to Mary Pitman, Jan. 24, 1780
Mahony, Clement to Sarah Ann Oakley, July 17, 1780.
Clark, Ignatius to Ann Hilton (from St. Mary's), July 6, 1780.
Pasco, William to Ann Flaxion, Oct. 14, 1780.
Linkins, Henry to Chlaeh Alin, Oct. 28, 1780.
Roberts, John to Susannah Mason, Nov. 11, 1780.
Guy, Joseph to Sarah Smith, Dec. 13, 1780.
Robertson, Mitchel to Rose Mastin, Dec. 24, 1780.
Albritton, Charles to Cath. Burridge, Jan. 4, 1781.
Truson, Robert to Esther Ray, Jan. 6, 1781.
Marshall, William to Eliza. Hanson, Jan. 22, 1781.
Howard, Benja. to Mary Ann Buckley, Jan. 30, 1781.
Linkin, Abraham to Eleanor Borden, Jan. 30, 1781.
Ware, Francis, Jnr. to Ann Pickerell, Jan. 31, 1781.

Gambia, Richard to Sarah Gardner, Apr. 4, 1781.
Sims, James to Sarah Key, June 9, 1781.
Dent, —— to Mary Ann Hancock, Dec. 18, 1781.
Smoot, Josiah to Ann Douglass, Dec. 22, 1781.
Smoot, Henry to Eliza. Warren, Dec. 23, 1781.
Hanson, Walter to Sarah Hatch Maddox, Dec. 25, 1781.
Rigg, Charles to Eliza. Andrews, Dec. 28, 1781.
Burridge, Thos. to Joanna Chapman, Jan. 18, 1782.
Price, James to Eliza. St. George, Jan. 31, 1782.
Ghant, George to Eliza —— (Calvert Co.), Jan. 31, 1782.
Scott, John to Agnis Hadden, Feb. 5, 1782.
Minitree, Paul to Eleanor Smoot, Apr. 6, 1782.
Howard, Baker to Ann Philips, Apr. 6, 1782.
Forbes, John to Eliza. Marshall, Apr. 21, 1782.
Gray, Wilson to Eliza. Limms [Simms?], Apr. 26, 1782.
Brady, Thomas Gerard to Susanna Brown, May 11, 1782.
Scott, Thomas to Alice Philpot, July 9, 1782.
Stark, Richard to Eliza. Gatewood, Aug. 23, 1782.
Compton, Alex. to Mary Joy, Oct. 4, 1782.
Bateman, Izreel to Sarah Simkson, Nov. 18, 1782.
King, Townley to Rebeckah King, Dec. 16, 1782.
Wakefield, Abel to Margt. Jenkins, Dec. 30, 1782.
Allen, Bartholomew to Frances Ramsey, Jan. 20, 1783.
Massey, Robert to Sarah Warren, May 3, 1783.
Poslyn, William to Sarah Hammel, Aug. 27, 1783.
Billingsley, John to Charity Ford, Oct. 28, 1783.
Douglas, Benjn. to Sarah Marshall, Oct. 27, 1783.
Hawkins, Smith to Eleanor Laidles, Nov. 5, 1783.
Marshall, Thomas to Sarah Maddox, Dec. 6, 1783.
Bateman, Richd. to Mary Ann Hatton, Dec. 22, 1783.
Bunbery, John to Mary Baltrop, Apr. 30, 1784.
Smith, James to Constania Ford, May 1, 1784.
Lawless, Benja. to Eliza. Samuel, June 28, 1784.
Winter, Charles Bruce to Eliza. Mason, June 26, 1784.
Brook, Mathew to Ann Fearson, Dec. 28, 1784

Charles County, By Rev. Benja. Rolls

Boone, Alesus to Mary Smith, Jan. 8, 1779.
Semmes, Thomas to Mary An Brawney, Feb. 1779.
Scott, Aquila to Henrietta Semmes, Apr. 14, 1779.
Mudd, Ezekiel to Eliza. Edelen, May 12, 1779.
Lancaster, John Jnr. to Aloysia Jerningham, July 31, 1779.

Charles County, By Rev. Henry Pile (Roman Catholic)

"Oliuer", William to Nancy Blackstock (License granted Feb. 16, 1785).
Edelin, George to Sarah Edelin (License granted May 14, 1785).
Riney, James to Anne Semes, Dec. 27, 1785.
Haydon, Clement to Fawney Wakefield, Jan. 13, 1786.
Fenwick, James to Henrietta Mary Lancaster, Feb. 14, 1786.
Brent, Wm. Chandler to Eleanor Neale, May 24, 1786.
Hamersley, Henry to Olivia Jerningham, Oct. 1, 1786.
Simpson, Charles to Sarah Bentels, Nov. 19, 1786.
Hamilton, Edward to Mary Anne Boarman, Nov. 20, 1786.
Reeder, Benjn. to Eleanor Slaughton, Dec. 23, 1786.
Wathen, Martin to Eliza. Anderson, May 23, 1787.
Edelen, Oswald to Mary Thompson Bond, Oct. 25, 1787.
Queen, Joseph to Eddie "Jermingham," Dec. 2, 1787.
Mattingley, Raphael to Winefred Higdon, Dec. 29, 1788.
Middleton, James to Nancy Corry, Apr. 23, 1789.
Burtles, Willm. to Sarah Wathen, June 28, 1789.
Simpson, Thos. to Judith Wathen, Nov. 12, 1789.
Luckett, Benj. to Eliza Semmes, Jan. 10, 1790.
Berien, Walter to Charity Simpson, Jan. 12, 1790.
Wathen, John B. to Rebecca Semmes, June 1, 1791.
Duggin, Robert to Teresa Brady, July 10, 1791.
Semmes, Mark to Catherine Simpson, Aug. 9, 1791.
Hayden, James to Anne Robertson, Sept. 4, 1791.
Dixon, Samuel to Eleanor Scott, Jan. 10, 1792.
Shettleworth, Allen to Anne Witherington, Feb. 9, 1792.
Witherington, James to Mary Miles, Feb. 20, 1792.
Long, Josias to Ann Friend, Jan. 13, 1793.

Charles County, By Rev. Thomas Thornton

McDaniel, Thomas to Ann Chattann, June 14, 1777.
Smithson, Wm. Eaton to Rhoda Robey, Sept. 1, 1777.
Gill, Thomas to Sarah Jones, Sept. 3, 1777.
Smith, John to Eliza. Rawlings, Sept. 3, 1777.
Shively, Bernard to Eleanor Longford, Sept. 22, 1777.
Vermilion, Benja. to Tabatha Burch, Oct. 14, 1777.
Talburt, John to Ann Davis, Oct. 19, 1777.
Carney, Daniel to Alice Lovelace, Nov. 1, 1777.
Hatton, Joseph to Martha Jones, Nov. 5, 1777.

CHARLES COUNTY, BY REV. FRANCIS WALKER, OF Wm. & MARY PARISH

Philpot, Benja. to Eliza Smoot, Aug. 3, 1786.
Minitree, Paul to Nancy Dorset, Aug. 1 1786.
Bateman, John to Ann Oakley, Sept. 13, 1786.
Warren, John to Eliza. Shaw, Sept. 20, 1786.
Billingsley, Clement to Eleanor Warren, Nov. 21, 1786.
Duncan, James to Sarah Leach, Apr. 4, 1787.
Martin, John to Lydia Hickman, May 24, 1787.
Marshall, Robert to Joanna Douglass, May 26, 1787.
Nicholas, John to Sally Raines, June 4, 1787.
Tomkins, John to Nancy Norwood, Sept. 27, 1787.
Fisher, John to Eleanor Robertson, Nov. 24, 1787.
Jenkins, William to Eliza. Simpson, Dec. 23, 1787.
Smith, John to Ann King, Dec. 23, 1787.
Shaw, John to Sarah Vincent, Jan. 3, 1788.
Vincent, Thomas to Eliza. Wilder, Jan. 6, 1788.
Saider, John to Cath. Ann Penn, Jan. 8, 1788.
King, Rt. Rev. Reuben to Mary Ann Vincent, Feb. 3, 1788.
Posey, Thomas to Mary Dutton, Mch. 25, 1788.
Contee, Benja. to Sarah Rt. Lee, Mch. 30, 1788.
Weems, John to Alice Lee, Apr. 8, 1788.
Maddox, John to Martha Harris, Apr. 22, 1788.
Jordon, Saml. to Eliza. Thompson, July 31, 1788.
Bateman, Levin to Ann Simpson, Oct. 28, 1788.

CHARLES COUNTY, BY REV. GEORGE H. WORSLEY, RECTOR OF PORT TOBACCO PARISH*

Bennett, Patrick and Mary Squire, Nov. 3, 1780.
Cromwell, Joseph and Kezia Stansbury, Dec. 11, 1780.
Cochran, George and Eleanor Shaw, Dec. 21, 1780.
Hicks, Abraham and Sarah Gorsuch, May 13, 1781.
Gallaway, Thomas and Cath. Dallis, Feb. 25, 1780.
McComas, Edward D. and Sarah Selby of Harford Co., Nov. 14, 1780.
Dick, David and Mary Wilson, Nov. 14, 1780.
James, Thomas and Mary Eager, Nov. 15, 1780.
Nelson, David and Rachel Baker, Nov. 16, 1780.
Jury, Richard and Nancy Stallion, Nov. 23, 1780.
Baker, Isaac and Ann Stewart, Nov. 23, 1780.
Brown, James and Hannah Hitchcock, Dec. 5, 1780.
Osborne, William and Nancy Lytle, Dec. 19, 1780.

* Page 192.

Weight, John and Cath. Colman, Jan. 4, 1781.
Stricklin, John and Eliza. Simpson, Jan. 8, 1781.
Allen, James and Sarah Williams, Jan. 9, 1781.
White, Granfton and Margt. Denny, Jan. 10, 1781.
Brown, George and Rebecca Denny, Jan. 11, 1781.
Groves, William and Jane Euston, Jan. 14, 1781.
Dockarty, Samuel and Han. Caley, Jan. 23, 1781.
Dawes, Mordecia and Elizabeth Goddard, Feb. 5, 1781.
Anderson, James and Catherine McComas, Widow, Feb. 15, 1781.
Chaney, John and Elizabeth Garretson, Feb. 27, 1781.
Sampson, Richard and Hannah Amoss, Widow, Mch. 7, 1781.
Hutchins, William and Eleanor Miles, Widow, Mch. 11, 1781.
Monk, William and Bathia Hairs, Mch. 18, 1781.
Murphy, Henry and Elizabeth Norris, Apr. 3, 1781.
York, Edward and Letty Doughty, Apr. 5, 1781.
Smith, Bazil and Ann Cunningham, May 3, 1781.
Forward, Jacob and Martha Warren, May 22, 1781.
Harris, Josias and Catharine Marton, Sept. 2, 1781.
Lomax, John and Chloe Posey, Sept. 23, 1781.
Ford, John and Winifred Athey, Oct. 2, 1781.
Orme, Moses and Elizabeth Davis, Oct. 23, 1781.
Harrison, Rev. W. H. and Mary Stoddart, Nanjony Parish, Nov. 16, 1781.
Moreland, Isaac and Elizabeth Stephens, Nov. 20, 1781.
Logan, John N. and Sarah Wedding, Nov. 22, 1781.
Harbin, Thomas and Lucy Roby, Dec. 6, 1781.
Bryan, Benjamin and Frances Massey, Dec. 16, 1781.
Kidwell, Matt. and Pris. Moore, Dec. 25, 1781.
King, William and Ann Ware, Dec. 30, 1781.
Roby, Aquila and Mary Cole, Jan. 8, 1782.
Carrington Saml. and Milly McDonald, Jan. 8, 1782.
Kellow, Thomas and Ann Roswell, Jan. 13, 1782.
Philhers, Joseph and Chloe Griffin, Jan. 24, 1782.
German, John and Ann Cole, Feb. 7, 1782
Tucker, John and Jane Weedon, Feb. 10, 1782.
Cox, William and Selina Lindsey, Feb. 12, 1782.
Martin, H. A. and Elizabeth Boswell, Feb. 12, 1782.
Speak, William and Molly Hanlope, Feb. 16, 1782.
Wilkinson, Joseph and Milly McCasley, Mch. 30, 1782.
Boswell, Elijah and Ann Carrington, Apr. 11, 1782.
Simpson, Thos. and S. M. Kidwell, May 23, 1782.
Cawood, Wm. and Martha Beale, June 6, 1782.
Tuedman, Allen and Sabina Fendall, June 8, 1782.

Welch, Edward and Dorothy Clements, June 11, 1782.
McPherson, John and Elizabeth Readen, June 25, 1782.
Fleury, William and Esther Maddox, July 2, 1782.
Richardson, Wm. and Jane Bramhall, July 16, 1782.
McPherson, Wm. and Mary Smoot, July 16, 1782.
Worry, Samuel and Elizabeth Underwood, Aug. 25, 1782.
Clements, Walter and Nancy Garrett, Aug. 28, 1782.
Chandler, John and Cath. Posey, Sept. 5, 1782.
Long, Jonathan and Eleoner Going, Nov. 10, 1782.
Russell, Henry and Chole Smallwood, Nov. 10, 1782.
Smallwood, Bayne and Chole McCatee, Dec. 3, 1782.
McDonald, Jonathan and Violetta Wedding, Dec. 15, 1782.
Maddox, Benjamin and Bennedicta Fernandis, Dec. 21, 1782.
Carter, George and Gizzel Brawner, Dec. 23, 1782.
Gates, James and Lydia Padgett Jan. 1, 1783.
Lurly, John and Hephsehe Harris, Jan. 2, 1783.
Roby, Zachariah and Elizabeth Pickrell, Jan. 16, 1783.
Simmons, Aaron and Sarah Thompson, Feb. 2, 1783.
Glasgow, William to Eleanor Morland, Feb. 10, 1783.
Lock, Thomas to Catherine Estep, Feb. 16, 1783.
Roland, Geo. to Marta Slater, Feb. 25, 1783.
Berry, John to Elizabeth Willett, Mch. 2, 1783.
Vermillion, Uriah to Susannah Barker, Mch. 16, 1783.
Menace, Robert to Eleanor Young, April 11, 1783.
Henson, Walter to Elizabeth Henson, April 20, 1783.
Fisher, Martin to Mary Daily, April 20, 1783.
Gody, Matthew to Mary Mahony, April 29, 1783.
Magruder, Nathaniel to Mary Billingsley, May 4, 1783.
McPherson, John to Elizabeth Thompson, May 12, 1783.
Berry, Ryon to Ann Owen, June 12, 1783.
Wood, John to Ann Welch, June 20, 1783.
White, John to Eleoner Long, June 27, 1783.
Von, John to Agatha Edington, July 17, 1783.
Miller, Christopher to Wismey McIntosh, July 26, 1783.
Wheeler, Ignatius to Ann Morris, Aug. 19, 1783.
Gardner, Hezekiah to Mary H. McPherson, Sept. 18, 1783.
Dyson, Bennet to Verlinda Chunn (St. Mary's Co.), Oct. 8, 1783.
Southean, Richd. to Catherine Southean, Oct. 15, 1783.
Gray, Zachariah to Susannah Parker, July 22, 1777 (of Charles Co.—m. in Montgomery Co.)
Downs, Wilson to Mary Roland, Dec. 27, 1779 (both of Charles Co.—m. in P. G's Co.)

Thomas, Hezekiah to Jane White June 27, 1780 (Charles Co.—m. in P. G's Co.)
Carpenter, John to Frances Perry, Jan. 28, 1779 (Chas. Co.—m. in P. G's Co.)
Risen, Chandley to Mary Hamilton, May 14, 1779 (Chas. Co.—m. in P. G's Co.)
Garner, W^{m}. to Mary Ann Fimses, Nov. 14, 1779 (Chas. Co.—m. in P. G's Co.)
Suit, Walter to Susanna Davis, Aug. 26, 1777 (Chas. Co.—m. in St. Mary's Co.)
Boone, Alexius to Mary Smith, Jan. 8, 1777.*
Summers, Thomas to Mary Ann Brawney, Feb. 8, 1779.
Scott, Aquilla to Henrietta Semmes, Apr. 17, 1779.
Mudd, Ezekiel to Elizabeth Edelen, May 12, 1779.
Lancaster, John, Jr. to Aloysia Jerningham, July 31, 1779.

Frederick County Marriages (52 persons)†

By Rev. John Chalmers, Jr.

Bennet, Willm. and Mary Scholes, —, 1792.
Bennett, Nathan and Deborah Holland, Mch. 14, 1795.
Birkitt, Joshua and Eliza Nelson, —, 1792.
Perry, James and Sarah Warfiel, —, —, 1792.

By Rev. Jonathan Forrest (Meth.-Episco. Mch. 3, 1791–1802)

Howard, Thomas and Ann Hughs, Apr. 26, 1791.
Leaven, Hays and Millie Forrest, —, —, 1802.
Liday, Henry and Delila Hays, —, —, 1802.
Miller, John and Mary Vanferson, June 19, 1791.
Prather, John Garrot and Mary Ann Sargant, Mch. 3, 1791.
Stoner, Daniel and Mary Deaghee, Feb. 9, 1792.
Teal, Jacob and Elizabeth Lineger (Washington Co.), June 30, 1791.

By Rev. Lenox Martin

Harris, Jesse and Darky Norris, June 28th, 1801.

* Page 245.
† "Maryland Marriages," pp. 195, 196, 1777–1804, Md. Hist. Soc., Courtesy of Mr. Charles Fickus.

By Rev. Burgess Nelson, 1801–1803

Baker, Enoch and Molly Carr, May 5, 1803.
Barnes, John and Rachel Walker, Feb. 27, 1802.
Baxton, John and Lydia Dell, Oct. 6, 1802.
Bennet, Lloyd and Rebecca Evins, Oct. 26, 1803.
Buckenham, John and Rachel Frizzie, Mch. 31, 1803.
Cook, John and Anna Syedes, Aug. 28, 1803.
Dudderas, Benjn. and Rebecca Houlton, Dec. 24, 1801.
Dukes, Jesse and Polly Isenberg, Feb. 25, 1802.
England, Joseph and Mary Lippler, Nov. 3, 1802.
Jarvis, Meade and Nancy Stocksdale, Apr. 7, 1803.
Jinkens, Thomas and Rachel Wilson, Dec. 25, 1802.
Paulson, John and Susanna Knight, Jan. 3, 1802.
Pearce, Joshua and Mary Bisset, Jan. 3, 1802.
Shipley, Willm. and Rachel Arnold, Feb. 10, 1803.
Williams, Jacob and Margaret England, Sept. 29, 1802.

Evangelical Reformed Church, Frederick, Md.

By Rev. John Conrad Steiner; Rev. Charles Reighlee, Dec. 29, 1763 to ——; Rev. John H. Smaltz, Oct. 4, 1829 to 1831 (?).*

Abbott, George and Clementine Burrucker, Feb. 3, 1862.
Able, John and Magdaline Decloe, Jan. 5, 1780.
Abell, John and Sarah Thomas, Oct. 23, 1790.
Abricks, Hermans and Jane Liggat, Jany. 1, 1791.
Acker, George B. and Serena A. Sampson, May 10, 1847.
Adam, John and Margaret Weiss, Feb. 15, 1761.
Adams, Antereus and Cath. Delater, Sept. 26, 1764.
Adams, Henry and Duana McCahan, Aug. 2, 1843.
Adams, James and Lyda Meredith, Apr. 15, 1793.
Adams, Joseph and Biddy Curran, Jan. 19, 1791.
Addison, Frederick and Catherine Ann Fraley, Mch. 2, 1859.
Addlesberger, Francis and Catherine Taney, Aug. 31, 1819.
Adelsperger, George and Susanna Eckes, Dec. 22, 1823.
Addlesperger, Josuha and Elizabeth Koons, Feb. 6, 1810.
Adkin, Charles and Rachel Makeby, Nov. 1758.
Adlum, John and Margaret Adlum, Dec. 13, 1805.

* Copied by Abby Gertrude McCardell from the Index of Marriages. Published through courtesy of the Librarian General, National Society Daughters of the American Revolution.

Adlum, Jr. John and Mary Cooley, June 7, 1806.
Ahalt, Henry and Modelena Beigler, Feb. 22, 1805.
Aider, George and Susannah Albaugh, Sept. 18, 1802.
Alaine, George and Mary M. Klein, Mch. 18, 1818.
Albach, Christian and Cath. Reiner, Aug. 5, 1804.
Albach, David and Sarah Mayer, Mch. 26, 1809.
Albach, Moritz and Cath. Bohmer, June 27, 1786.
Albach, William and Mary Weaver, Mch. 24, 1803.
Albach, William and Susan Rothrock, Mch. 24, 1804.
Albaugh, Edward and Lucy R. Unkefer, Dec. 20, 1862.
Albaugh, Elias V. and Mary E. Fogler, Jan. 12, 1850.
Albaugh, George and Catherine Springer, June 20, 1798.
Albaugh, Issac and Margaret Groshon, Dec. 22, 1813.
Albaugh, Issac and Catherine S. Weller, Mch. 4, 1851.
Albaugh, John and Mary Smith, Jan. 26, 1793.
Albright, Henry and Ann Margaret Swawin, Jan. 8, 1781.
Alder, George W. and Hannah A. Myers, Dec. 17, 1864.
Alder, John and Sarah Anst, Nov. 27, 1783.
Alderdice, Hugh and Catherine Myers, Dec. 2, 1811.
Aldridge, Evan J. and Mary E. Eury, Oct. 13, 1864.
Aldridge, George W. and Ara Gilbert, Dec. 25, 1837.
Aldridge, John and Mary Lakin, Nov. 14, 1783.
Alexander and Beckenbach, June 17, 1804.
Alexander, Ephraim and Nancy Kohlenburg, Apr. 18, 1828.
Alexander, Franklin and Lydia Elizabeth Smith.
Alexander, Fred. and Mary Frazier, Feb. 27, 1837.
Alexander, George W. and Henrietta C. Young, Oct. 17, 1857.
Alexander, Henry and Catherine Ropp, Jan. 3, 1814.
Alexander, Henry and Serena Harrison, Feb. 21, 1854.
Alexander, Joseph and Mary Hargishimer, June 16, 1812.
Alexander, Joseph and Marg. Hargishinier, June 20, 1812.
Alexander, Valentine and Elizah. Dailin, Feb. 23, 1762.
Alfort, John and Margaret Ashman, Aug. 19, 1780.
Alldridge, John and Harriet Beall, Mch. 10, 1806.
Allas, Elias John and Sophia Dadisman, Mch. 27, 1826.
Allen, George and Lovice Roop, Oct. 19, 1822.
Allen, Issac H. and Evelina Titlow, Jan. 13, 1840.
Allen, James and Martha Philpott, Sept. 15, 1802.
Allison, George and Christena Zimmerman, June 15, 1797.
Alison, George and Christina Zimmerman, Dec. 3, 1798.
Allisson, Henry and Elizab. Linton, June 22, 1796.
Allder, John and Polly Goodley, Nov. 18, 1803.

Althoff, Henry and Kitty Diffendal, July 24, 1813.
Altried, Geo. M. and Mary Marg. Messmor, (in Va.), May 24, 1768.
Altwein, Charles and Eliz. Schroeder, Aug. 24, 1803.
Aman, George and Harriet J. Wilhide, Sept. 20, 1842.
Ambers, George W. and Mary Dowell, Sept. 18, 1843.
Ambrose, George and Rebecca Row, Dec. 2, 1828.
Ambrose, George and Sarah Flook, Apr. 3, 1849.
Ambrose, George H. and Matilda Marker, May 16, 1849.
Ambrose, George W. and Mary Ann Ramsburg, Apl. 5, 1853.
Ambrose, Henry W. and Sabina Peacher, Oct. 6, 1848.
Ambrose, John and Catherine Lynn, Aug. 1, 1794.
Ambrosius, Christopher and Cath. Getzendanner, Oct. 9, 1787.
Amelong, Frederick M. and Louisa Sophia Furnival.
Ancrum, Jacob and Elizabeth Clark, Mch. 20, 1779.
Anders, George and Ann Clise, Sept. 23, 1837.
Anders, George J. and Lucretia Hilton, Mch. 18, 1856.
Anders, Henry and Elizabeth Vaughn, May 14, 1817.
Anderson, Dr. Edward H. and Catherine Precilla Morris, July 23, 1810.
Anderson, Evan T. and Mary Ellen Norwood, Dec. 14, 1854.
Anderson, Francis and Susanna Jones, Dec. 18, 1809.
Anderson, Francis and Robina Martin, Apr. 26, 1822.
Anderson, George and Elizabeth Saltkill, Dec. 27, 1814.
Anderson, George H. and Caroline V. Moore, May 7, 1857.
Anderson, George W. and Sarah F. Mount, Oct. 18, 1846.
Anderson, Hugh and Mary Boyd, Jan. 13, 1802.
Anderson, John and Catherine Loney, June 12, 1779.
Anderson, John and Elizabeth Ship, Apr. 10, 1794.
Anderson, Jonathan M. and Ann Eater, Nov. 26, 1810.
Anderson, Robert and Mary Brashears, Mch. 15, 1796.
Andros, Thomas, and Delilah Fisher, Jan. 21, 1800.
Angel, Issac and Catherine Devilbiss, Dec. 12, 1814.
Angleberger, George and Margaret Devilbiss, Aug. 23, 1809.
Angleberger, George David and Elizabeth Wachter, Oct. 20, 1854.
Annan, Issac S. and Julia Landers, Feb. 17, 1864.
Ansherman, David and Amanda L. Remsburg, Mar. 21, 1863.
Antes, Adam and Christina Schmit, Jan. 8, 1793.
Anvard, Thomas L. and Martha Ann Rose, Sept. 13, 1831.
Apolo, Benj. M. and Mary Usher, June 19, 1800.
Applebee, Joseph and Elizabeth Tobery, Mch. 28, 1807.
Appler, Issac and Jude Winter, Mch. 27, 1827.
Armstrong, Jacob, Sept. 3, 1812.
Armstrong, Joseph and Jane Alexander Dec. 19, 1799.

Arndperger, John and Mary Smith, Sept. 14, 1801.
Arnhold, Frederick and Martha Schauer, June 11, 1764.
Arnold, Daniel and Mary Ann Wener, Nov. 8, 1855.
Arnold, Ephriam and Eleanor Ensey, Sept. 27, 1802.
Arnold, Ezra and Louise Boyer, Mch. 14, 1855.
Arnold, John and Catherine Morgan, May 17, 1802.
Arnold, Jonathan and Althea Sellman, Dec. 19, 1801.
Arthur, Hiram and Nancy Hiney, Nov. 6, 1851.
Arthur, John and Catherine Weaver, Nov. 21, 1806.
Artz, Edwin and Mary Helen Dixon, Mch. 13, 1863.
Asgur, John and Sarah Woolverton, Oct. 4, 1779.
Ashman, Henry and Elizabeth Moyer, June 5, 1784.
Athein, Horation and Mary Shower, June 11, 1791.
Athein, Horatio and Mary Schaun, June 12, 1791.
Athey, Joseph and Mariah Wheeling, Jany. 27, 1798.
Atkins, George W. and Ann Cath. Jones, Oct. 8, 1850.
Atwell, John and Anne Lewis, Sept. 4, 1797.
Aubb, John and Margaret Baer, June 2, 1812.
Auman, Andrew and Barb. Lutter, (Fred. Co.) Mch. 29, 1785.
Ausherman, Hanson and Huldah Arnold, Aug. 2, 1843.
Austin, Hilleary and Christmas Price, Feb. 11, 1824.
Axline, David and Ann Maria Mumaw, Dec. 27, 1849.
Bache, George and Elizab. Koblentz, Jan. 30, 1791.
Back, Nicholas and Magd. Gullomann, Aug. 9, 1763.
Baechtly, Martin and Veronica Schnebel, Dec. 2, 1764.
Baer, George and Mary Adams, Jan. 29, 1786.
Baer, George Jr. and Cath. Haner, Apr. 13, 1788.
Baer, John and Mary Thomas, Dec. 25, 1788.
Baer, William and Harriet Mantz, Sept. 1, 1812.
Bager, George Saml. and Catherine Bossert, Apr. 7, 1789.
Baily, Joseph and Susanna Hedges, Sept. 21, 1790.
Baker, Henry and Eliz. Geringer, May 1, 1786.
Ball, Gerret and Eliz. Cecil, Jan. 11, 1787.
Ball, Jos. and Ally Phelps, Dec. 21, 1797.
Ball, Richard and Cath. Clary (published but not married).
Ball, William and Elin. Arnold, Dec. 5, 1797.
Balzell, Charles and Elizab. Fulton, June 10, 1794.
Baltzell, Daniel and Sus. Gittinger, Nov. 24, 1799.
Balzel, Henry and Marg. Alexander, Nov. 2, 1760.
Balzel, Jacob and Charlotte Christ, Jan. 11, 1787.
Balzel, Jacob and Marg. Schley, (Wid.) Nov. 30, 1766.
Balsel, John and Elizab. Pumel, Oct. 18, 1801.

Balzel, Peter and Catherine Ruesel, Feb. 23, 1762.
Bambaugh, George and Christina Thomas, Oct. 4, 1829.
Bambergern, John and Elizabeth Ulmann, Jan. 16, 1763.
Banebach, John Hy. and Eliz. Brady, June 26, 1808.
Bantz, Henry and Cath. Schmidt, Aug. 9, 1787.
Bantz, Nimrod and Margt. M. Harding, July 27, 1830.
Barber, Elijah and Nancy Todd, Dec. 7, 1787.
Barber, William and Mary Dorf, Apr. 8, 1810.
Bard, Jacob and Susan Kern, Sept. 28, 1806.
Barker, John and Elizab. Mugg, Jan. 29, 1793.
Barnee, Thos. and Barb. Neuschwanger, (Fred. Co.) Aug. 21, 1785.
Barnes, Leonard and Nancy Price, Oct. 11, 1790.
Barnet, Robert and Nancy Stor Kallings, May 30, 1786.
Barney, John and Clarissa Perill, Dec. 22, 1801.
Bart, Jacob and Mary Schmit, Aug. 30, 1796.
Bartlett, James and Mary Taylor, Nov. 11, 1806.
Barton, Absalom and Lenah Boroman, Apr. 1, 1830.
Bast, Jacob and Cath. Heckedoon, Oct. 11, 1796.
Battenfeld, Jacob and Eliz. Emmerich, Sept. 18, 1798.
Bauer, Conrad and Eliz. Schmidt, Nov. 14, 1797.
Bauman, Daniel and Cath. Let, Nov. 15, 1791.
Bauman, John Iac. and Elizab. Keller (in Va.) Nov. 25, 1767.
Bausman, Benjamin and Eliz. Baierle, Jan. 18, 1808.
Bayer, Abraham and Eva Beringer, June 20, 1786.
Bayer, David and Sarah Krum (Fred. Co.) Nov. 8, 1785.
Bayer, John and Mary Bookhardt, Dec. 28, 1796.
Bayer, Peter and Anna Mary Mossetter, May 22, 1787.
Bayerle, William and Charlotte Mayer, Dec. 3, 1807.
Bazell, Jacob and Anna Campbell, May 10, 1796.
Beall, George and Elizabeth Turner, Jan. 22, 1757.
Beall, Ninian and Christina Stoll, July 25, 1790.
Beall, William and Isabella Ramsy, Mch. 8, 1796.
Beall, William and Mary Winroad, Mch. 15, 1796.
Bear, John and Cath. Hoffman, Nov. 15, 1808
Beattie, John and Sophia Cannen, Oct. 20, 1811.
Becht, Jacob and Mary Schenk, May 29, 1800.
Bechtel, George and Esther Eller, Mch. 18, 1794.
Beckebach, Geo. and Mary Magd. Baulus, Dec. 24, 1792.
Beckebach, Michael and Mary Barthelma, Aug. 26, 1798.
Becker, Conrad, and Mary Jost, May 25, 1795.
Becker, Conrad and Cath. Froshauer, May 31, 1803.
Becker, John Fredk. and Mary Dorothy Durrman, Aug. 6, 1758.

Becker, Peter and Anna Mary Nicol, Sept. 15, 1761.
Becker, Philip and Elizah Baecker, Apr. 5, 1762.
Beeler, George and Elizab. Molledar, Apr. 15, 1794.
Beer, Henry and Margaret Winter, June 28, 1768.
Behmer, Peter and Eliz. Ehrkardt, Apr. 17, 1804.
Beisser, John and Lydia Geber, (Gaver) Mch. 29, 1804.
Beiser, John and Mary Schlosser, Apr. 15, 1810.
Bell, Jacob and Elizab. Diedeman, Sept. 22, 1807.
Bell, Peter and Magdalene Schmit, Jan. 1, 1789.
Belt, Lloyd and El. Causlet Met. Thomas, Dec. 16, 1790.
Belty, Wm. and Mary Dorothy Crush, Mch. 1, 1757.
Beltz, Peter and Magdalen Moll, Nov. 14, 1787.
Bennet, David and Charlotte Shultz, Sept. 16, 1815.
Bently, Levy and Sarah Harlan, May 4, 1790.
Bentz, Daniel and Elizabeth Shull, Nov. 21, 1833.
Bentz, George and Elizab. Gomber, Apr. 6, 1788.
Bentz, Jacob and Cath. Stecker, Jan. 20, 1799.
Berck, Henry and Cath. Sadler, July 2, 1809.
Berg, George and Marg. Krohmer, Nov. 5, 1805.
Berg, John and Elizabeth Grumm, Oct. 17, 1762.
Berg, Peter and Cath. Berg, Aug. 8, 1786.
Berger, Jacob and Mary Candel, Dec. 3, 1807.
Berutheisel, Christopher and Cath. Grof, Oct. 5, 1794.
Bess, Jacob, and Christina Eberly, Dec. 27, 1811.
Bier, Philip and Eva Cath. Schley, Nov. 30, 1766.
Bins, Simon and Sarah Wildman, Jan. 1790.
Bishop, John and Hannah Cooper, Sept. 17, 1789.
Bittle, Jacob, and Rachel Todd, June 24, 1791.
Bixler, Jacob and Barb. Grevel, Nov. 29, 1795.
Blackford, John and Elizab. Kanode, June 17, 1812.
Blackwood, Thomas O. and Susan Martin, Mch. 26, 1831.
Bley, John and Mary Elizth. Appl. (Apple), Nov. 20, 1757.
Bob, John and Magdalen Heckedorn, Feb. 22, 1761.
Bocklop, Charles and Cath. Lang, (Fred. Co.) Aug. 7, 1785.
Bocklop, Charles and Christina Puhl (Wid.) May 22, 1787.
Bocky, George and Christina Haas, Apr. 22, 1787.
Bocky, John and Susan Hausser, May 8, 1810.
Boden, Samuel and Sus. Mahn, Oct. 7, 1800.
Boehmer, Hy. and An. M. Albach, (Fred. Co.) Aug. 2, 1785.
Boetler, Henry and Ann Rebecca Levy, Feb. 22, 1831.
Bohn, John and Rebecca Collins, Jan. 2, 1810.
Bohn, Michael and Magd. Borger, Oct. 14, 1804.

Bookhardt, George and Hannah Hedge, Sept. 14, 1795.
Bookhardt, Joseph and Mary Hausey, Sept. 1, 1789.
Borer, Peter and Magd. Scheukmayer, Jan. 31, 1768.
Bossert, David and Catherine Schuck, Feb. 21, 1786.
Bost, Henry and Sus. Windpiegler, June 5, 1808.
Boteler, Arthur and Elizabeth Siveringer, Sept. 12, 1797.
Botteler, Elias and Susanna Ebit, Jan. 26, 1806.
Botelor, Thomas and Hannah Garrot, Sept. 3, 1801.
Bottenberg, Michl. and Mary Jendes, May 8, 1800.
Bowen, John and Sarah Surly, July 31, 1806.
Bowens, Thomas and Louisa Barnes, Dec. 15, 1793.
Bowling, Saml. and Mary Ann Plumer, Feb. 20, 1787.
Boyd, Edward and Mary Hoffman, Aug. 10, 1800.
Boyd, John and Hannah Smith, Oct. 31, 1799.
Boyle, James and Rhoda Hughes, Oct. 15, 1807.
Bradock, John and Mary Hilton, Feb. 23, 1809.
Bradock, William and Eliz. Hilton, Aug. 25, 1812.
Bram, John and Cath. Clem, Sept. 18, 1805.
Branderburg, Henry and Eliz. Gebhard, Apr. 15, 1804.
Brandenburg, Wm. and Christina Long, Sept. 17, 1806.
Brandenburger, Jacob and Eliz. Rein, Feb. 13, 1787.
Brandenburger, John and Phoebe Garner, Apr. 13, 1794.
Brandenburger, Math. and Barb. Keller, Dec. 16, 1787.
Brandt, Christian and Rosina Walter, Feb. 7, 1786.
Braum, John and Mary Simon, June 11, 1809.
Braun, Michael and Rosima Lantz, Mch. 26, 1786.
Braun, Stoffel and Magdalen Maen, Sept. 9, 1761.
Brayfield, Saml. and Jane Pancoast, Apr. 4, 1796.
Breisz, Adam and Mary Stoll, Dec. 23, 1800.
Breisz, John and Elizabeth Lafever, Feb. 23, 1796.
Brenckel, John and Elizab. Ziehler, Mch. 27, 1803.
Breugle, Alfred F. and Louisa Breugle, May 16, 1832.
Brengel, Jacob and Gertrude Bell, June 30, 1761.
Brengel, Lohrentz and Cath. Scheffy, June 22, 1787.
Brengel, Peter and Cath. Manns, May 1, 1803.
Brightwell, John and Mary Dodson (Fred. Co.) Jan. 4, 1785.
Brightwell, Richard and Betty Howard, Dec. 6, 1787.
Briggs, Robert and Priscilla Jefferson, Dec. 25, 1788.
Briscoe, Ralph and Sarah Delashmutt, Mch. 8, 1792.
Brookover, Thos. and Mary Thomas, Mch. 9, 1786.
Brown, Fielder and Hannah Heague, Nov. 5, 1801.
Brown, John and Sarah Edwards, July 23, 1804.

Browning, Zadock and Mary Browning, Dec. 25, 1793.
Brubacker, Samuel and Barb. Gomer, May 18, 1809.
Bruder, Jacob and Eva Marg. Huber, Jan. 1, 1759.
Brunner, Elias and Cath. Walf, June 5, 1804.
Bruner, Henry and Eliz. Westenhaven, Aug. 16, 1812.
Brunner, Jacob and Mary Barb. Kaufer, Apr. 1, 1759.
Brunner, Jacob and Margaret Geister, July 5, 1761.
Brunner, Jacob and Magd. Schneider, Aug. 13, 1786.
Brunner, Jacob and Mary Dall, Oct. 4, 1807.
Brunner, John and Sophia Doll, Mch. 23, 1830.
Brunner, Jonathan and Sarah Middekauff, May 10, 1832.
Brunner, Lewis and Ann Rebecca Ramsburg, Mch. 21, 1833.
Brunner, Peter and Catherine Simm, Apr. 26, 1789.
Brunner, Valentine and Eliz. Bohrer, Apr. 11, 1803.
Bryan, Thomas and Massy Plumer, July 25, 1793.
Bucher, Barthol and Sus. Walter (Fred. Co.) Sept. 18, 1785.
Bucky, George and Susanna Krieger, Oct. 8, 1796.
Bucky, Michael and Cath. Pfeifer, Mch. 23, 1806.
Bucky, Valent and Chart. Remsperger, Jan. 29, 1793.
Bucky, Valentine and Eliz. Stricker, Nov. 9, 1790.
Burkhart, Nathan and Margaret Simmons, Apr. 16, 1786.
Burner, Iac Young and Sus. Dickenoor, Aug. 29, 1812.
Burneston, Jos. and Julianna Grof, Aug. 5, 1787.
Burns, Michael and Eliz. Kemp, Oct. 1, 1788.
Bush, George and Eliz. Grall, Oct. 11, 1791.
Butcher, John and Margaret Gehr, June 13, 1833.
Butler, Thomas and Jane Gittings, Dec. 29, 1795.
Butler, William and Delilah Browning, Feb. 24, 1789.
Butler, William and Julia W. Deal, Apr. 22, 1806.
Cain, John and Mary Geber, Jan. 8, 1797.
Caldwire, Joseph and Elizab. Frances, Nov. 21, 1802.
Campbel, Archibel and Sarah McDonald, Jan. 29, 1792.
Camel, John and Eliz. Harlin, Apr. 8, 1788.
Cambel, James and Linny Hyatt (Fred. Co.) Sept. 15, 1785.
Campbell, James and Sarah Sewel, Mch. 30, 1794.
Campble, John and Anne Winegardener, May 10, 1791.
Campbell, John and Anna Holmes, Oct. 29, 1832.
Cann, Thomas and Eliz. Norris, May 16, 1809.
Carl, David and Barbara Grof, Feb. 12, 1792.
Carlton, Thomas and Mary Pittel, Oct. 28, 1806.
Carr, John and Mary Keller, Dec. 7, 1788.
Carr, Thomas and Cath. Gashauer, Jan. 29, 1793.

Carson, John and Hannah Haas, Dec. 31, 1789.
Carson, John and Ann Thomas, Mch. 4, 1790.
Carter, Joshua and Cath. Springer, June 28, 1796.
Carter, Thomas and Nancy Jorden, Dec. 15, 1812.
Castle, Thomas and Eliz. Messerle, May 21, 1797.
Ceastel, Samuel and Elizab. Ceastel, Mch. 22, 1808.
Cecil, Aden and Sarah Tool, Oct. 22, 1805.
Cecil, Henry and Sarah Hinton, Jan. 12, 1789.
Charlesworth, Solomon and Mary McVicker, Sept. 25, 1832.
Childs, Edward and Minty (blacks) Oct. 8, 1792.
Chingan, John F. and Maria Sharer, Mch. 8, 1832.
Christ, John and Cath. Umford, June 9, 1805.
Christ, Michael and Elizab. Shurm, Dec. 29, 1763.
Christ, Peter and Margaret Mang, Apr. 16, 1797.
Christman, John and Elizabeth Weather, Sept. 3, 1805.
Chun, Laucelot and Martha Ridgley, Nov. 4, 1792.
Clary, Ashford Dowden and Elizab. Smith, Dec. 31, 1789.
Clary, Nathaniel and Cassandra Thomas, Dec. 19, 1831.
Coale, Isaac and Sarah Ridgeley, Nov. 21, 1797.
Coale, James and Mary Carter, Mch. 11, 1788.
Coale, Vincent and Eleanor Stewardt, May 26, 1801.
Coblenz, Peter and Susanna Keller, May 6, 1759.
Coblentz, Philip and Elizab. Zimmerman, Mch. 29, 1803.
Collins, Humphry and Sarah Bell (Hunt Co.), Feb. 15, 1785.
Collins, Joshua and Mary Rubey, Jan. 13, 1793.
Collins, Mathew and Sus. Bowlass, Nov. 27, 1785.
Colly, Wm. and Rebecca Braun, Apr. 15, 1799.
Conrad, Jacob and Elizab. Steiner, May 5, 1805.
Conradt, Henry and Mary Leth, Apr. 17, 1787.
Constable, Saml. and Rebecca Dobston, Mch. 27, 1785.
Coomes, Aden and Pamelia Williams, Oct. 2, 1794.
Cooper, Adam and Rebecca Hamilton, Oct. 12, 1786.
Cooper, Robert and Cath. Harlin, Aug. 29, 1791.
Corbman, Christ and Harriet Fannehill, Aug. 30, 1807.
Covell, Jonathan Freust and Catherine Jacobs, Sept. 23, 1830.
Coventry, John and Amelia Phillips, Feb. 21, 1808.
Cox, Samuel and Ann Wilson, Oct. 9, 1806.
Crane, John and Rebecca Crum, Feb. 5, 1793.
Cremer, Solomon and Barb. Cettig, Apr. 10, 1808.
Crentzer, Jacob and Eliz. Beckenbach, Nov. 9, 1803.
Crieger, George and Marg. Salmon, Nov. 3, 1805.
Cromwell, John and Marg. Kephard, Feb. 15, 1803.

Cromwell, Oliver and Harriet Gebhart, Nov. 20, 1806.
Cron, Robert and Christina Schmidt, Apr. 8, 1788.
Croneisz, Jacob and Cath. Fonderburg, Apr. 14, 1806.
Crossby, James and Deborah Runnerl (N. C.) Sept. 5, 1785.
Croweis, Henry and Elizab. Knouff, Oct. 8, 1805.
Crum, Evan and Sarah Hertzog, Aug. 19, 1795.
Crum, Isaac and Catherine Kepler, Sept. 8, 1830.
Crum, John and Mary Miller, Feb. 9, 1806.
Crum, Nathan and Amalia Creager, Mch. 15, 1803.
Crum, William and Eliz. Levy (at the poor house) Dec. 29, 1793.
Crumwell, Wm. and Sarah Groff, Jan. 22, 1799.
Cumberledge, George and Rachel Barber, Mch. 31, 1789.
Cunningham, Hugh and Rebecca Gittinger, Jan. 28, 1830.
Curry, William and Sarah Dean, Nov. 9, 1800.
Dabler, William and Elizab. Jones, Dec. 25, 1800.
Dally, Ebenezer and Mary Philips, May 30, 1794.
Danner, Zacharia and Mary Zayer, Oct. 8, 1799.
Darnal, Ralph and Hanna Kohlenberg, June 30, 1808.
Darrey, Balthasar and Barb. Heinkley, Mch. 27, 1759.
Daub, Jacob and Eliz. Merckel, Mch. 4, 1794.
Daub, Valentine and Esther Koenig, Apr. 17, 1804.
Davidson, John and Sealy Hill, Aug. 24, 1805.
Davis, Ambrose and Bewly White, May 20, 1800.
Davis, Francis and Sarah Eliot, May 2, 1790.
Davis, John and Mary Marschand (Wid.) Sept. 10, 1761.
Davis, John Eberhard and Anna Reitenauer, July 1, 1764.
Davis, Luke and Mary Duall, Oct. 11, 1807.
Davis, Matthias and Rachel Maynard, Dec. 21, 1788.
Davis, Reubin and Ellen Taylor, Nov. 13, 1796.
Davis, Samuel and Rachel Walls, Sept. 2, 1800.
Dawson, John and Anna Hays, Sept. 23, 1806.
Dayle, Ephraim and Catherine Hamilton, Apr. 14, 1831.
Dean, William and Alice Reynolds, Jan. 17, 1805.
Deaver, Levi and Sophia Griffith, Jan. 6, 1805.
Doerner, John and Barbara Dilbus, Apr. 10, 1803.
Degenhardt, Christian and An. M. Miller, Dec. 20, 1784.
Dehaven, Andrew and Esther Kempf, Nov. 11, 1792.
Dehaven, Peter and Mary Cellars, June 26, 1787.
Dehof, Nicholas and Sus. Cath. Vogel, Mch. 6, 1787.
Delaplane, Daniel and Sophia Dern, Dec. 1, 1799.
Delaplain, Joshua and Mary Deru, Nov. 20, 1792.
Delashmutt, Trammel and Marg. W. Moriarty, Aug. 19, 1809.

Delater, Jacob and Cath. Mahn, Feb. 21, 1790.
Delater, Jacob and Elizab. Michael, Apr. 21, 1808.
Delater, Jacob and Sara Ann Brown, Aug. 13, 1816.
Dent, Aquilla and Cath. Thomas, Oct. 17, 1803.
Deru, Isaac and Sus. Berger, Dec. 9, 1792.
Dertzbach, John and Christina Knauff, Oct. 20, 1799
Deiwelbiss, George and Sus. Berg, Apr. 5, 1790.
Dewelbiss, John and Mary Mayer, Sept. 9, 1798.
Devilbiss, Joseph and Caroline Stauffer, Oct. 20, 1831.
Dick, John and Elizab. Schraier, Feb. 28, 1808.
Dick, John and Cath. Feagler, May 2, 1809.
Diel, John and Cath. Beltz, Feb. 8, 1790.
Diel, John and Mary Eckhardt, Nov. 19, 1794.
Diehl, John and Philippina Faut, Jan. 19, 1806.
Differen, William and Elizab. Brown, Oct. 13, 1817.
Dinsmoor, Thomas and Marg. Taylor, Oct. 26, 1809.
Diz. (Dietz) John Adm. and Mary Magd. Thom, Sept. 25, 1757.
Dodoro, Davis and Eliz. Heintz, Jan. 3, 1802.
Dodson, Elijah and Mary Karr, Sept. 1, 1789.
Doerr, Jacob and Marg. Wintz, Feb. 4, 1788.
Doerr, Thomas and Barbara Steiner, Apr. 10, 1803.
Doerry, Peter and Cath. Feldman, May 5, 1761.
Dofler, Geo. and Cath. Spanseiler, June 11, 1798.
Dofler, Peter and Margaret Schley, Dec. 21, 1766.
Doll, Conrad and An. M. Schisler, Sept. 20, 1761.
Doll, George and Cath. Schmit, Mch. 11, 1799.
Doll, Jacob and Mary Myers, May 31, 1812.
Doll, John and Sus. Kortz, Jan. 28, 1800.
Doodel, George and Eleanor Ryan, Jan. 16, 1803.
Doof, George and Mary Weber, Nov. 20, 1808.
Dorsey, Basil and Harriet Harris, Aug. 12, 1792.
Dorsey, Evan and Sus. Lawrence, Jan. 6, 1789.
Dorsey, Joshua and Sarah Hammond, Mch. 9, 1788.
Dorsey, Michael and Elizab. Poole, Sept. 27, 1796.
Dorsey, Vachael and Ann Poole, Mch. 13, 1792.
Dowell, Benj. and Barb. Springer, Apr. 15, 1788.
Dowling, Edward and Mary Gordon, Jan. 1794.
Downey, Alexander and Mary Tucker, Feb. 17, 1795.
Drum, Peter and Sarah Hansey, Dec. 8, 1796.
Druman, James and Sarah Starling, Nov. 19, 1798.
Dultyg, Henry and Cath. Young, Oct. 4, 1812.
Dumming, William and Nancy Harry, Nov. 15, 1805.

Duppel, Benj. and Eliz. Reitenauer, Mch. 22, 1796.
Durbin, James and Ann Elizabeth Stoner, Nov. 29, 1831.
Durst, Henry and Cath. Richter, Sept. 21, 1806.
Dutenhoffer, Michael and Rachel Wilkens, Jan. 31, 1764.
Duwall, Samuel and Mary Allison, Aug. 16, 1807.
Early, John and Sarah Gilborthop, June 10, 1809.
Early, John and Mary Fauble, Feb. 3, 1813.
Easton, John and Rachel Pearsons, Jan. 13, 1795.
Eaton, Leonard and Mary Palmer, Feb. 20, 1804.
Eaton, William and Nancy Bryan, May 19, 1793.
Eberly, Valentine and An. Barb. Schmid (Wid.) Feb. 28, 1767.
Ebbert, Augustus F. and Elizabeth M. Bantz, Oct. 19, 1830.
Ebert, Michael and Mary Clara Kappel, Aug. 6, 1761.
Eberz, Mathew and Cath. Magd. Maus, Apr. 7, 1761.
Eby, John and Anna Mary Bantz, Feb. 12, 1765.
Eckhard, Anthony and Cath. Shickenhelm, Sept. 16, 1806.
Eckman, Michael and Mary Jacob, Jan. 14, 1800.
Eder, Abrah. and Cath. Reich (Fred. Co.) Feb. 22, 1767.
Edmonston, Thomas and Ruth Sheckell, Dec. 3, 1793.
Edwards, Abraham and Ellen Jones, Oct. 4, 1796.
Eg (or Ely) John Henry and Rosina Schmitt, Aug. 18, 1761.
Eisennagel, Thos. and Sus. Spanseiler (Fred. Co.), Sept. 20, 1785.
Ekhart, Adam and Eva Reisz (Rice), Aug. 16, 1757.
Eller, Jacob and Mary Willjard, Oct. 14, 1792.
Elliot, George and Mary Beatty, Aug. 21, 1806.
Emmit, Abe. J. and Jane Moore, May 24, 1810.
Emmit, William and Sus. Shelman, Dec. 6, 1808.
Engel, George and Cath. Jung, Dec. 3, 1789.
Engel, George and Sus. Jung, Sept. 8, 1799.
Ennis, George and Catherine Ramsburg, Dec. 10, 1829.
Ensey, Dennis and Elizab. Crawford, Oct. 10, 1797.
Erter, John and Catharine Weber, Nov. 23, 1806.
Eter, Abraham and Susanna Koenig, Feb. 28, 1804.
Evans, Cabel and Eva Wedel, Mch. 5, 1787.
Evans, John and Miranda Owens, Apr. 1, 1800.
Ewerly, Peter and Julianna Wiszman, June 18, 1797.
Fah, Abraham and Mary A. Steiner, Mch. 28, 1790.
Fahly, Geo. and Mary Wolff (Loudon, Va.) Feb. 23, 1791.
Fanbel, David and Margaret Degrange, Apr. 1, 1832.
Faner, John and Rebecca Klee, June 7, 1803.
Farthing, James and Marg. Ott, Jan. 6, 1801.
Faut, William and Magd. Adams, Aug. 24, 1806.

Favorite, Abrah. and Elizab. Shroyack, Dec. 15, 1807.
Fein, Peter and Cath. Marg. Bennet, May 2, 1786.
Ferguson, Danl. and Charity Austom (Fred. Co.) June 14, 1785.
Ferrel, Wm. and Mary Burns, Aug. 10, 1800.
Filius, John and Eliz. Yates, Aug. 5, 1792.
Filius, Joseph and Eliz. Schlicker, Apr. 15, 1798.
Filson, Samuel and Mary Cooper, Apr. 1, 1800.
Finkbohner, John and Sus. Brucker, Aug. 5, 1788.
Fishback, John and Lydia O. Bonner, July 1809.
Fitzgerald, John and Mary Phelps, Oct. 1800.
Fleming, Caleb and Allen Blummer, Apr. 19, 1809.
Fleming, Samuel and Elizab. Reynolds, Dec. 24, 1801.
Flick, Andrew and An. Magd. Reichardt, June 12, 1768.
Flick, Jacob and Eliz. Koblentz, May 4, 1790.
Flora, David and Mary Ann Lambert, Dec. 23, 1829.
Fluck, John and Eliz. Schreiger, Apr. 5, 1801.
Fluck, Mat. and Cath. Jung, Jan. 15, 1787.
Fluck, Peter and Mary Hans, July 9, 1797.
Fluheart, Stephen and Elizab. Randel, Nov. 22, 1785.
Fluke, Henry and Hannah Castle, Nov. 21, 1801.
Forquhar, Robt. and Esther Dodson, May 19, 1789.
Fortuey, David and Elizab. Lewis, May 6, 1800.
Fox, Uriah and Grace Sedwith, Apr. 18, 1794.
French, Otho and Eliz. Anderson, Feb. 18, 1802.
Frey, Daniel and Elizab. Christ, Nov. 19, 1793.
Frey, Nicholas and Catherine Schmecter, Aug. 20, 1769.
Fridshey, John and Barbara Hauer, May 18, 1806.
Fries, Michael and Cath. Grabiel, June 18, 1799.
Frizzel, Lloyd T. and Seeny Turner, Jan. 30, 1800.
Froehlich, John and Salome Rothrock, Jan. 19, 1792.
Fuchs, Henry and Leah Zimmerman, Jan. 18, 1799.
Fuchs, John and Cath. Fuchs, Jan. 23, 1791.
Fuchs, John and Cath. Simmons, Sept. 18, 1798.
Fuchs, Peter and Bridget Ingen Hall, Sept. 16, 1800.
Fulton, George and Margaret Hedge, June 7, 1794.
Fulton, Robert and Barb. Balzell, Mch. 11, 1794.
Fultz, Philip and Cath. Shafer (or Shoster) Mch. 30, 1812.
Fyers, Joseph and Anna M. Dommer, Aug. 3, 1762.
Gaber, David and Mary Beiser, Feb. 21, 1805.
Gach, John and Eliza Schnoog, Mch. 25, 1806.
Gapes, Thomas and Jane Elizabeth McVicker, Apr. 1, 1833.
Garmnie, Andrew and Anna Elizab. Jan. 15, 1759.

Gaudy, Abraham and Sarah Mannihan, Dec. 24, 1793.
Gaut, Daniel and Lucy Anderson, Oct. 5, 1797.
Gebhard, George and Cath. Doll, May 3, 1803.
Gebhardt, John and Sarah Hiestand, Dec. 27, 1801.
Gebhardt, Peter and Eliz. Haas, Aug. 18, 1796.
Gebler, Gotlieb, and Sus. Madera, Aug. 1, 1804.
Gedon, Daniel and Susannah Butler, Dec. 23, 1800.
Gehret, John and Cath. Grimes, Mch. 24, 1807.
Geiniz, John Wm. and Johanna Weiszman, Apr. 19, 1758.
Geissinger, Frantz, and Sarah Levi, Apr. 3, 1790.
Gelwicks, George C. and Mary Nixdorf, Nov. 12, 1807.
George, John and Elizah Woods, Apr. 10, 1806.
Gerecht, Justiss and Elizab. Drenter.
Gerger, John and Elizah Scheffy (Fred. Co.) Mch. 20, 1785.
Gess, Jonathan and Rebecca Dowel, Aug. 22, 1791.
Getzendanner, Abraham and Mary E. Buckley, May 7, 1833.
Getzendanner, Adam and Mary An. Kuhns, Oct. 14, 1787.
Getzendanner, Balthasar and Philippina Stoll, June 12, 1794.
Getzendanner, Henry and Hannah Becker, Apr. 17, 1800.
Getzendanner, Jacob and Eliz. Getzendanner, Jan. 10, 1797.
Getzendanner, John and Rebecca Faut (Fred. Co.) Sept. 6, 1785.
Getzendanner, John and Cath. Dabler, May 31, 1789.
Geyer, Daniel and Mary Brengel, May 10, 1791.
Geyer, Henry and Elizah Ireland, Feb. 15, 1795.
Giesy, John and Cath. Natlzell (Baltzell ?), May 16, 1809.
Gietzentanner, Balthasar and Anna Steiner, May 11, 1758.
Giezentanner, Jacob and Catherine Kast, Apr. 3, 1757.
Gilbert, David and Margaret Koontz, Jan. 17, 1830.
Gilbert, Peter and Elizab. Larkin, Aug. 16, 1803.
Gills, Eckhardt and Cath. Sulzer, May 13, 1788.
Gittinger, John and Marg. Hauck, Apr. 28, 1795.
Glisson, James and Esther White, Oct. 29, 1800.
Goetzendanner, Thomas and Cath. Bar, Apr. 10, 1808.
Gotzendanner, Christian and Cath. Remsberger, Apr. 2, 1786.
Gomber, Jacob and Susannah Beaty, May 20, 1787.
Gordon, Jos. and Mary Balton, Nov. 1797.
Goslin, Ambrose and Anna Shafer, Aug. 14, 1803.
Gosnell, Peter and Mary Mallahon, Oct. 22, 1793.
Gosnel, Peter and Emma Hill, Nov. 1, 1798.
Graham, August and Martha Cock, Oct. 26, 1806.
Graham, Reuben and Rachel Carter, Apr. 20, 1798.
Gray, Zacharias and Elizab. Hardy, Sept. 13, (1815?)

Green, John and Nancy Miller, Apr. 27, 1806.
Greiner, Michael and Sybilla Jendes, Aug. 19, 1792.
Grieger, George and Mary Epler, Apr. 7, 1807.
Grieger, Lewis and Susanna Hauer, May 10, 1808.
Griffith, Zadock and Sar. Hantel (Georget road) Feb. 17, 1785.
Grim, Daniel and Sarah Staub, Aug. 4, 1803.
Grimes, Basil and Betsy Peiket, Oct. 29, 1793.
Grimes, Frederick and Mary Randal, Mch. 22, 1798.
Gross, George and Cath. Sanders, May 1, (1816?)
Grover, John and Jemimah Fitzgerald, Mch. 3, 1795.
Gruber, David and Sus. Moore, Nov. 22, 1798.
Grund, John Ad. and M. Chr. Hoffman, Feb. 7, 1765.
Gryer, John and Mary Nusz, Apr. 30, 1803.
Gunterman, George and Rachel Milhaues, Apr. 1, 1765.

[*Note: From this point the records are evidently deficient. All which are available are being published. G. M. B.*]

Hansen, William and Sus. Frexund, Oct. 24, 1758.
Heichler, Nicholas and An. Marg. Meyer, Feb. 20, 1759.
Hoffman, Rudolph and Dorothy Weisz, May 8, 1758.
Jung, Peter and Barbara Begard, Aug. 9, 1757.
Keller, Jacb. and Elizabeth Leitert, May 28, 1758.
Klein, John and Anna Barly, Apr. 19, 1759.
Leeman, Jacob and Anna Mary Jung, Aug. 9, 1757.
Leidig, Gabriel and Cath. Delater, Mch. 18, 1759.
Lor Beck, Christoph and Sophia Rosin Urbach, Apr. 12, 1759.
Medari, Chs. Fredk. and Cath. Gerson, Nov. 2, 1756.
Meyerer, John Joshua and Mary Kaempf, Mch. 29, 1757.
Michel, Daniel and Mary Schober, May 15, 1758.
Mittelkauf, John and Mary Elth. Brunner, July 19, 1757.
Muller, John Geo. and Magd. Maderi, April 25, 1758.
Ochs, John Adam and Mary Appol. Hoffman, Feb. 7, 1757.
Ogle, Thomas and Sarah Ogle, Dec. 1756.
Reimssperger, Geo. and Maria Elizah. Bruwner, Dec. 20, 1756.
Runner, Philip and Anna Mary Einck, Apr. 17, 1757.
Scheidegger, John and Eva Mary Manz, May 24, 1757.
Schellenbaum, Christn. and Mary Caselman, May 3, 1757.
Scherer, John and Mary Sus. Deuthinger, Dec. 29, 1757.
Schley, Geo. Thom and Mary Gietzentanner, May 16, 1758.
Schmidt, William and Agnes Mey, Dec. 1, 1757.
Schneebeli, Leonhardt and Marg. Weisz, May 8, 1758.
Schneider, Geo. Michl. and Judith Unsel, Nov. 29, 1757.

Schonefeld, John and Mary Cath. Mezier, Mch. 23, 1757.
Schuemacher, Danl. and Mary Elizab. Hoffman, Feb. 1, 1757.
Schur, Christn. and M. Salome Bargelt, Mch. 28, 1758.
——, —— and Marg. Schweinhard, May 6, 1759.
Sin, Jacob and Mary Magd. Biber, Oct. 31, 1756.
Steiner, Jacob and Mary Anna Schley, May 17, 1758.
Strickler, Wendel and Susanna Sax, Aug. 8, 1758.
Sturno, John and Anna Barb. Hoffman, Dec. 13, 1756.
Thomas, Christopher and Sus. Marg. Weisz, Dec. 13, 1757.
Ulmer, David and Rosinack M. Hirschuan, July 2, 1757.
Weber, John and Maria Elizab. Haas, Dec. 30, 1756.
Weisz, Henry and Cath. Brunner, Jan. 9, 1759.
Weisz, John Valent and Cath. Froschaner, April 18, 1758.
Wurtenbecher, John Beruh and Mary Eva Hein, Mch. 22, 1757.
Yofler, Peter and Anna Mary Sturm, April 17, 1757.

Montgomery County Marriages,* 1777–1804

By Rev. Clement Brooke, 1778–1779

Ashford, Thos. and Jane Taylor, Aug. 29, 1779.
Ball, James and Cassandra Ellis, Nov. 11, 1779.
Barnes, Josias and Elizabeth Trammel, Aug. 1, 1780.
Beall, Basil and Arianna Beall, Oct. 24, 1780.
Beall, George and Elizabeth Beall, Dec. 22, 1779.
Beall, Leven and Esther Campbell, July 14, 1779.
Brown, Coaly and Elizabeth Holly, Aug. 20, 1779.
Callis, Garland and Elianor Addison, Dec. 22, 1779.
Chelton, Mark and Clementia Barn, June 17, 1779.
Chin, Christopher and Ann Bartlet, Dec. 17, 1779.
Conner, Gerrard T. and Amelia T. Donaldson, Mch. 13, 1779.
Cox, Walter B. and Anna B. Holliday (P. G's Co.), Nov. 19, 1779.
Donaldson, Benj'n. and Drucilla Peace (P. G's Co.), Oct. 28, 1779.
Evans, Guy and Christian Swan (P. G's Co.), Sept. 16, 1779.
Evans, Robert and Judith Molds, Oct. 24, 1780.
Fields, Luke and Margaret Balser, Sept. 12, 1779.
Fisher, John and Frances Nelson, April 29, 1780.
Grimes, Wm. and Jane Williams, Sept. 18, 1780.
Hall, Palmer and Amelia Ashford, Dec. 15, 1779.

* Maryland Marriages, pp. 203–213; Md. Hist. Soc., Courtesy of Mr. Charles Fickus, Acting Librarian.

Hood, Samuel and Barbara Wienberger, Mch. 14, 1780.
Holms, John and Mary Turner, Dec. 16, 1779.
Jenninson, Thos. and Eleanor Williamson, May 4, 1779.
Kogenderfor, Leonard and Susannah Crons, Sept. 18, 1780.
Kokendoffer, Fredk. and Susanna Yonst, Dec. 29, 1779.
Margress, Saml. and Anne War (P. G's Co.), Sept. 4, 1779.
Miles, Thomas and Elizabeth King, Feb. 7, 1779.
Mitchell, Willm. and Sar. Ashford, Dec. 2, 1779.
Parker, Thos. and Susanna Cahill, Mch. 4, 1779.
Payne, John and Mary Bever, July 16, 1780.
Pendell, Thos. and Anne Rhoads, Sept. 9, 1779.
Pickerell, Richd. and Amelia Marlow (P. G's Co.), Oct. 31, 1779.
Rigdon, Thos. and Lucy Jennings, May 20, 1779.
Sprigg, Thos. and Elizabeth Belt, Feb. 8, 1780.
Stonestreet, Edward and Margery Weight, May 14, 1780.
Sutton, Robert and Judith Canady, Dec. 1, 1779.
Trevis, John to Mary Lewis, May 23, 1778.
Van Nacruth, John and Ann Andison, Mch. 14, 1779.
Williams, John and Sarah Stewart, July 29, 1779.
Willice, W^m^. and Ann Smith, Feb. 14, 1780.
Wilmot, Thos. and Anne Gill, May 20, 1779.
Woodward, Joseph and Jane Taylor, Mch. 7, 1779.

By Bishop John Carroll (Roman Catholic), 1777–1778

Casey, John and Philodelia Edgworth, Aug. 11, 1778.
Green, Leonard and Anne Brown, Jan. 29, 1778.
Knott, Raphael and Cath. Pearce, June 16, 1778.
McGovron, Thomas and Mary Clark, Aug. 30, 1778.
Madden, James and Rebeccah Harrison, Aug. 4, 1778.
Nicholson, Richard and Bridget Farelong, Oct. 18, 1777.

By Rev. John Chalmers, Jr.

Leach, Joshua and Lydia Pritchett, Feb. 4, 1795.
Miller, John and Martha Leach, May 21, 1795.
Wood, James and Sarah Hobbs (Balto. Co.), Dec. 22, 1794.

By Rev. James Hunt, 1778–1782

Armstrong, Willm. and Levi Anna McMannin, Feb. 11, 1779.
Barrott, Alex. and Eleanor Caecil, Jan. 19, 1779.
Barret, John and Mary Price, Dec. 16, 1781.
Bayne, George and Ann Jones, May 1, 1779.

Beall, Thos. and Catherine Brown, Jan. 14, 1779.
Beggarly, David and Rebecca Belt, May 20, 1782.
Burton, Jacob and Sarah Tucker, Nov. 19, 1779.
Butler, Tobias and Sarah Tool, April 5, 1782.
Butterworth, Willm. and Elizab. Darbyshire, Feb. 3, 1779.
Cave, Stephen and Ruth Earidge, Nov. 24, 1779.
Clark, Thos. and Priscilla Barns, Feb. 11, 1779.
Collins, Joshua and Mary Barrance, May 15, 1779.
Collins, Nathan and Ann Maddin, Feb. 11, 1779.
Conner, John and Eleanor Wallace Tracy, Dec. 5, 1778.
Eastep, Joseph and Lucy Prather, Jan. 28, 1779.
English, King and Rebecca Eades, Aug. 24, 1779.
Fitzgerald, Matthew and Sarah Wilson, Jan. 7, 1779.
Greentre, Benjn. and Sarah Roberts, May 19, 1782.
Harrison, Nathan and Verlinda Browning, Nov. 3, 1779.
Hoskins, Charles and Eleanor Standiford, Aug. 10, 1779.
Jenkins, Willm. and Dorcas Masters, Jan. 5, 1779.
Jenkins, Willm. and Sibby Moxly, July 12, 1782.
Jones, Charles and Mary Jackson, Feb. 24, 1782.
Jones, Samuel and Rebecca Wood, Feb. 12, 1782.
Louthie, Benjn. and Mary Ann Tyler, Dec. 3, 1778.
McKay, Alex. and Ann Campbell, Dec. 17, 1778.
Magruder, Walter and Margaret Orme, June 14, 1782.
Neal, Thos. and Elizab. Whittmore, Aug. 8, 1779.
Nelson, Archibald and Hannah Roberts, Nov. 3, 1782.
Offutt, James and Rebecca Offutt, Feb. 14, 1782.
Pearson, John and Sarah Fallin, Sept. 15, 1782.
Peckinson, Solomon and Mary Reily, July 8, 1779.
Pickrell, Henry and Rebecca Low, April 6, 1779.
Sherwood, Thos. and Elizab. Scott, Feb. 15, 1779.
Simson, Samuel and Mary Saunders, April 4, 1782.
Smith, Thos. and Leah Hill, Aug. 28, 1779.
Sparrow, Joseph and Ann Smith, Dec. 9, 1778.
Summers, John and Jean Hoskinson, Dec. 8, 1781.
Talbot, Zadock and Elizab. Standage, Dec. 31, 1778.
Treasdale, John and Catharine Malone, Dec. 27, 1778.
Tryer, Adam and Frenetta Chany, April 6, 1779.
Vigel, Valentine and Catherine Barron, April 8, 1779.
Waters, Weaver and Margaret Miers, April 3, 1782.
White, Joseph and Jean Bear, Oct. 31, 1782.
Wilcoxen, Josias and Anna Statia Smith, Nov. 19, 1779.
Wood, Thomas and Ann Hall, Aug. 11, 1782.
Woodward, Bennett and Elizabeth Cecil, Dec. 17, 1778.

By Rev. Wilson Lee (Elder in M. E. Ch.)

Atcherson, Ephraim and Ruth Simpson, Sept. 11, 1800.
Cawood, Erasmus and Mary Williams, Dec. 26, 1799.
Stonestreet, Thomas and Polly Nicholls, Dec. 19, 1799.

By Rev. Slingsby Linthicum (M. E. Ch.)

Baggerly, James and Elizab. Smith, Oct. 20, 1798.
Penn, Stephen and Eleanor Scribenor, Oct. 28, 1798.
Walker, Nathan and Nancy Beck, July 21, 1798.

By Rev. Thos. Lucas

Wilson, William and Sarah Clark, License granted, Dec. 9, 1797.

By Rev. Thomas Reed, 1777–1778 *

Alnut, Wm. and Mary Riley, Feb. 12, 1778.
Anchors, Snowden and Deborah Gattrell, Feb. 4, 1778.
Arts, James and Keziah Fryer, June 30, 1778.
Beall, Zephaniah and Ann Gattrell, Feb. 5, 1778.
Bowman, Jacob and Mary Chambers, July 6, 1778.
Burris, Henry and Frances Davis, Jan. 22, 1778.
Busby, Christopher and Sarah Byall, June 1, 1778.
Dailey, Patrick and Mary Doyle, May 1, 1778.
Davis, John and Ann Legg, July 3, 1778.
Gartrell, Charles and Sarah Barnes, Dec. 7, 1777.
Gartrell, Francis Rawlings and Rachel Hamilton, Mch. 19, 1778.
Gray, Zachariah and Susanna Parker (Charles Co.) July 22, 1777.
Hill, John and Eliz. Richards, July 14, 1778.
Johnson, Saml. and Agnes Wilson, Oct. 12, 1777.
Johnson, Thos. and Mary Larure, Mch. 17, 1778.
Jones, Richard and Susy Culver, Mch. 17, 1778.
McDonough, James and Judith Flinn, July 29, 1778.
Murmet, Michael and Mary Thomson, Dec. 23, 1777.
Oneal, John and Mary Smith, Dec. 23, 1777.
Peak, Thomas and Eliz. Keymer, Dec. 23, 1777.
Perry, Erasmus and Eliz. Harding, Jan. 13, 1778.
Pigman, Ignatius and Susanna Lamar, Aug. 3, 1777.
Prather, Zachariah and Ruth Allison, Aug. 25, 1778.
Roberts, Hezekiah and Cloe Coffee, July 7, 1778.
Saffel, Joshua and Virlinda Prather, July 24, 1777.

* See page 557, name there spelled "Thomas Read."

Sibbey, James and Amelia Wiley, Sept. 28, 1777.
Stillings, Richard and Mary Dailey, June 6, 1778.
Stoaks, Francis and Sarah Hodgins March 22, 1778.
Thompson, Wm. and Martha Easton, Feb. 24, 1778.
Warfield, Elisha and Ruth Burgess (A. A. Co.), Aug. 22, 1778.
Wilcoxen, George and Mary Swearingen, Jan. 22, 1778.
Wood, Jepheniah and Mary Lucas, Aug. 14, 1777.

By Rev. Joseph Threlkeld,* Oct. 2, 1777–Nov. 13, 1781

Allison, Thomas and Eliz. Baxter, Sept. 14, 1780.
Ashan, Saml. and Amey Self, June 15, 1780.
Ashwood, Wm. and Mary Small, Oct. 29, 1780.
Ballinger, Saml. and Mary Smoot, Oct. 20, 1779.
Banninger, Francis and Ann Hobson, Sept. 24, 1778.
Barnes, Wever and Eliza Pigman, May 13, 1779.
Bayly, Hezekiah and Jane Evans, Mch. 5, 1778.
Begood, James and Lucy Digney, July 27, 1780.
Bennett, Willm. and Mary Green, Apr. 4, 1779.
Berry, Geo. and Margaret Limbrech, Mch. 6, 1778.
Bowman, Geo. and Elizabeth Gue, Feb. 3, 1779.
Bradly, Dennis and Susanna Fox, Nov. 30, 1779.
Brashears, Wayman and Anne Roberts, July 29, 1779.
Brown, John and Alice Noding, Oct. 1, 1778.
Buchanan, Spence and Eliz. [Wiggendem], May 16, 1780.
Buller, John and Catherine Smith, July 27, 1780.
Burchand, Thos. and Mary Gray, Oct. 18, 1781.
Burn, Adam and Mary McCrea, Apr. 3, 1781.
Burn, Wm. and Mary Wilson, Feb. 27, 1781.
Burress, Charles and Anne Morgan, Apr. 4, 1779.
Burris, Wm. and Lucy Redman, Dec. 28, 1780.
Buxton, Wm. and Sarah McCoy, Nov. 12, 1780.
Campbell, Alexander and Mary Sparrow, Dec. 12, 1779.
Cavenough, Patrick and Mary Eustice, June 1, 1780.
Chambers, John and Rebeccah Winsor, Mch. 5, 1780.
Chilton, James and Cath. Burns, June 25, 1778.
Chissell, Joseph Newton and Eleanor White, Nov. 11, 1779.
Clark, Elijah and Mary Graves, July 28, 1780.
Clayton, John and Virlinda Riggs, Nov. 13, 1781.
Cohen, Joseph and Rachel Bidwell, May 30, 1780.
Collier, Wm. and Aeda Arnold, June 22, 1779.

* Rev. Joseph Threlkeld, Cabin John, 1770 to d. 1782, so I am advised, G. M. B.

Countz, Henry and Ann Bowman, Aug. 4, 1778.
Coy, W^{m}. and Mary Ann Dennis, Nov. 25, 1779.
Craft, Edwd. North and Ann Linthicum, Mch. 11, 1779.
Cramlet, Jacob and Eliza Chambers, Mch. 18, 1779.
Crawford, Robert Beall and Eleanor Owen, Apr. 11, 1780.
Davis, Lodowick and Margaret Jones, Feb. 7, 1779.
Davis, Saml. and Rebecca Bucey, Apr. 21, 1778.
Davonport, Abraham and Frances Williams, Jan. 21, 1778.
Dawson, Robert Doyne and Sarah Newton Chiswell, Oct. 25, 1781.
Deakin, James and Eliza Falconer, Feb. 23, 1779.
Dickeson, Zadock and Sarah Cook, Feb. 4, 1779.
Dixon, James and Mary Conn, Jan. 21, 1779.
Donnaldson, Bayly and Milley Cockaril, Apr. 11, 1778.
Douglass, W^{m}. and Elizab. Gentle, April 26, 1778.
Dow, Michael and Margaret Fardo, Jan. 27, 1780.
Dowden, Thos. and Anne Campbell, Sept. 3, 1778.
Dowdett, John and Esther Williams, Nov. 22, 1778.
Ducker, Nathl. and Sarah Segar, Nov. 25, 1779.
Dyer, Saml. and Eliza. Griffith, Oct. 19, 1779.
Elliott, Mark and Sarah Walter, July 29, 1781.
Ellis, Hezekiah and Ann Briggs, Oct. 6, 1778.
Fagan, Willm. and Eleanor Jones, Oct. 1, 1780.
Fields, Abraham and Johan Peck, Mch. 19, 1778.
Fifer, James and Rebeckah Perry, Jan. 23, 1780.
Flemming, John and Anne Hopkins, Nov. 20, 1777.
Fletchall, Thomas and Eliz. Blackmore, June 15, 1780.
Fryer, Walter and Margery Trail, May 9, 1780.
Gaither, Greenbury and Anne Andison, April 13, 1779.
Gaither, Nicholas and Eleanor Greenfield, Oct. 26, 1779.
Gallen, John and Maomy Downey, July 15, 1781.
Gatton, W^{m}. and Sarah Murphy, May 6, 1781.
Gentle, George and Virlinda Locker, April 21, 1778.
Gohagan, W^{m}. and Darkus Loveless, Feb. 23, 1778.
Goodwin, Jacob and Anne Masey, Mch. 19, 1778.
Griffith, Samuel and Ruth Berry, April 1, 1779.
Gruse, Isaac and Eliz. Ellis, May 28, 1780.
Gue, Henry and Sarah Scribner, Feb. 23, 1779.
Harbin, Joshua and Ruth Hoskinson, July 23, 1778.
Hardage, Willm. and Ann Mitchel, Mch. 22, 1780.
Harding, Edwd. and Ann Butler, May 12, 1778.
Harris, John and Darcus Weyman, Feb. 18, 1781.
Harrison, W^{m}. and Susannah Cash, May 30, 1779.

Hays, Levi and Eleanor Harris, Dec. 9, 1779.
Hays, Solomon, and Mary Ann Wise, Feb. 22, 1781.
Heater, George and Cath. Space, Jan. 31, 1779.
Henderson, Willm. and Margaret Broadwater, Dec. 21, 1780.
Herring, John and Mary Strahan, Oct. 2, 1777.
Hickman, Wm. and Ann Lucas, July 29, 1781.
Holland, Wm. and Ann Weyman, Feb. 26, 1781.
Horon (?), Edwd. and Ann Winsor, Dec. 28, 1779.
Howel, Samuel and Milly Brown, Aug. 3, 1780.
Jackson, James and Charity Baker, Jan. 6, 1780.
Jacobs, Edwd. and Mary Summers, Oct. 28, 1779.
Jacobs, Zacha. and Dorkus Summers, Aug. 5, 1779.
Jarvins (Jawins?), Danl. and Anne Welsh, May 21, 1778.
Jenkins, Danl. and Jemima Andison, Dec. 3, 1778.
Johnson, John and Ann Kimey, Jan. 4, 1781.
Johnson, Jonathan and Mary Summers, Oct. 10, 1779.
Kelly, Thomas and Elizabeth Jones, Feb. 7, 1781.
Kelvart, Wm. and Eliz. Noddy, July 18, 1780.
Key, James and Grace Elean, Jan. 1, 1781.
Legat, Henry and Monica Rawlings, Aug. 1, 1780.
Locker, Patrick and Mary Elligan, May 17, 1778.
Locker, Shadreck and Eleanor Gentle, April 30, 1778.
Loveless, Bartm. and Lucy Watson, June 11, 1778.
Loyd, Joseph and Mary Kelly, July 27, 1780.
McCarty, Danl. and Rebecca Carter, Jan. 18, 1780.
McCartee, Thos. and Eliza Williams, Dec. 1, 1778.
McCray, Zephemiah and Mary Gatton, Oct. 21, 1777.
McElfish, Philip and Lyddia Griffith, Mch. 1, 1781.
Mackee, Willm. and Priscilla Jones, June 13, 1779.
Maddin, John and Dolly Steward, Apr. 11, 1780.
Mading, Jonathan and Anne Patrick, Nov. 4, 1779.
Magruder, Joseph and Cath. Flemming, June 25, 1778.
Malone, Thomas and Mary Harper, Dec. 16, 1777.
Martin, Saml. and Jane Walker, Sept. 5, 1779.
Mason, Burgess and Ann Starks, July 26, 1780.
Mayhew, John Love Wm. and Eliza Self, Feb. 26, 1778.
Minor, Thomas and Elizab. Turley, Oct. 15, 1778.
Modding, Richd. and Susannah Lewis, Jan. 26, 1779.
Moxly, Job. and Mary Buckannan, Nov. 7, 1780.
Moxly, John and Elizab. Buckanan, Nov. 30, 1780.
Moxly, Thomas and Milly Burgess, April 4, 1780.
Mullican, Archd. and Elizab. Vincent, March 19, 1778.

Mullakin, Lewis and Susanna Jarvis, Nov. 9, 1780.
Murphy, James and Mary Craddock, June 8, 1778.
Nally, Richd. and Keziah Tannyhill, April 23, 1778.
Oden, Nathan and Ann Norfut, Sept. 24, 1778.
Offutt, Saml. and Elizab. Ray, Oct. 22, 1778.
Offutt, W^{m}. Mockbee and Alley Thrift, Nov. 26, 1778.
Offutt, Zephaniah and Marg't. Butler, Aug. 24, 1780.
Ogden, Cornelius and Mary Pritchet, March 26, 1780.
Ogden, Joseph and Winfred Simms, Jan. 10, 1781.
Owen, John and Elizab. McCallam, Feb. 2, 1778.
Owen Laurence and Sarah Hardy, June 22, 1780.
Owen, Thomas and Sarah McCauley, Nov. 25, 1780.
Peak, Benjn. and Cassandra Trail, Dec. 14, 1779.
Pearce, W^{m}. Gate and Virlinda Lewis, Dec. 26, 1780.
Pierce, Caleb and Sarah Daws, Feb. 4, 1781.
Petty, James and Mary Hickman, April 2, 1780.
Powell, Willm. and Mary S. Edwards, Jan. 13, 1779.
Price, Richd. and Anne Randall, Feb. 15, 1779.
Queary, Danl. and Eve Wilfree, Nov. 9, 1779.
Ray, Christ^{r}. and Eliza Tucker, April 13, 1779.
Read, Alex. and Rebecca Stevens, Nov. 27, 1777.
Reynolds, W^{m}. and Elizabeth Stevens, Dec. 25, 1780.
Rhoads, James and Mary Garrott, Dec. 18, 1778.
Ricketts, Robert and Ellia^{n}. Allison, Oct. 4, 1778.
Ricketts Thos. and Ruth Adamson, June 7, 1778.
Riggs, Greenbury and Ann Hardy, Jan. 25, 1781.
Riggs, John and Mary Eleaner, Feb. 13, 1781.
Roberts, Richd. and Cath. Clements, Nov. 26, 1778.
Saenghan, James and Jane Ross, Feb. 17, 1780.
Saffle, Charles and Sophia Segar, Oct. 5, 1780.
Scott, Robert and Anne Thrift, March 6, 1778.
Seybert, George and Mary Shepherd, Jan. 21, 1781.
Shortridge, Saml. and Anne Roberts, Jan. 25, 1778.
Sparrow, W^{m}. and Mary Ogden, Nov. 6, 1781.
Speak, Ignatious and Cath. McCloud, Jan. 21, 1779.
Spence, W^{m}. and Mary Campbell, Feb. 20, 1780.
Stallings, John and Eliza Cheshire, Sept. 14, 1779.
Stevens, Richd. and Eliz. Jenings, Sept. 26, 1780.
Stone, John and Sarah Raredon, May 10, 1778.
Suiter, George and Mary Beall, Jan. 7, 1779.
Summers, Caleb and Rachel Crawford, Mch. 2, 1780.
Summers, John and Sarah Howard, Feb. 8, 1780.

Summers, Wm. and Rebecca Jacobs, Oct. 1, 1778.
Talbutt, George and Mary McDaniel, Aug. 6, 1778.
Taylor, John and Ruth Bailey, March 16, 1780.
Taylor, John and Elizabeth Morris, May 3, 1780.
Thrift, Charles and Elizabeth Offutt, Oct. 22, 1778.
Trail, Osborn and Francis Fryer, Oct. 9, 1781.
Trammel, Sampson and Carey Jenkins, Mch. 16, 1780.
Umsladt, Abraham and Mary Howard, Dec. 28, 1780.
Vallandingham, Richd. and Rebecca Andison, July 6, 1779.
Viers, Daniel Bucy and Ann Williamson, Jan. 9, 1781.
Walter, David and Eliz. Allison, July 1, 1781.
Walter, Levy and Priscilla Fletcher, Sept. 14, 1779.
Watkins, Leonard and Mary Higden, Dec. 19, 1780.
Watson, Aleanah and Mary Mooreland, June 11, 1779.
West, Osborn and Dorkus Trail, Nov. 19, 1778.
White, Joseph and Martha Riley, Dec. 22, 1778.
White, Matthew and Ann Felvey, Feb. 27, 1781.
Wigginton, Henry and Ann Vallandingham, Mch. 2, 1778.
Wigginton, Willm. and Allison Evans, Feb. 7, 1778.
Williams, George and Rene Said, Dec. 14, 1780.
Williams, Hazael and Mary Gore Hardy, Oct. 13, 1778.
Wilson, James and Ann Johnston, Oct. 16, 1777.
Wilson, Richd. and Mary Landrum, May 29, 1779.
Windsor, Isaac and Anne Riley, March 2, 1779.
Winrit, James and Ann Maria Ward, April 5, 1781.
Young, John and Sarah Offutt, April 29, 1781.

By Rev. Curtis Williams (M. E. Ch.)

Orme, Patrick (of Montg'y. Co.) and Mary Sewell (of A. A. Co.) Dec. 24, 1801.

By Rev. Alexander Williamson, 1777–1783

Beall, Willm. Dent and Mary Beall, April 3, 1783.
Beeding, John and Dorcas Key, Jan. 28, 1783.
Blunt, Washer and Sarah Jackson, Jan. 29, 1778.
Brown, John Alexander and Elizab. Vineyard, July 27, 1783.
Burgess, Josiah and Virlinda Bean, Nov. 18, 1783.
Clymer, Peter and Eleanor Pile, May 5, 1778.
Cook, Elizab. and Jean McNeer, May 12, 1778.
Duley, Barton and Martha Baker, Mch. 3, 1778.
Edwards, John & Mary Leach, Aug. 22, 1778.
Hall, Henry and Elizab. Board, Aug. 17, 1777.

Harrison, Benjn. and Dorcas Lee, Apr. 27, 1783.
Isaacs, Lazarus and Sarah Fightmaster, Oct. 23, 1777.
Jones, Isaac and Margaret Trott, Jan. 26, 1783.
Lenman, John and Debora Reynolds, Feb. 13, 1783.
Lewis, Daniel and Margery Waters, May 10, 1778.
McCubbin, Thomas and Ann Lingan, Mch. 3, 1778.
Middleton, Thomas and Winnifred Powel, Sept. 13, 1777.
Mockbee, John and Marg't. Robinson, Aug. 21, 1777.
Neal, Willm. and Mary Branham, Jan. 4, 1778.
Prather, Walter and Ann Higgins, April 9, 1778.
Redman, Joseph and Sarah Windsor, April 24, 1778.
Richards, William and Tabitha Litton, Sept. 29, 1778.
Rimel, John and Mary Lewis, Sept. 8, 1777.
Sellman, Jonathan and Rachel Lucas, Jan. 16, 1783.
Singer, George and Jenny Wade, April 19, 1778.
Tracy, Philip and Mary Thrasher, Dec. 12, 1782.

Washington County Marriages,* 1777-1804

By Rev. John Chalmers, Jr.

Cash, John and Elizab. Roberts, 1791–2.
Jacobs, Jeremiah and Sarah Larimond, 1791–2.
Lacy, Amos and Sarah Hudson, 1791–2.
Lowman, James and Rachel Downing, 1791–2.

By Rev. George Mitchell, 1778–1780

Breyley, Simon and Ann Boyle, Aug. 22, 1779.
Campbell, Colin and Mary Leonard, July 27, 1780.
Conover, Willm. and Sophia Fitch, May 16, 1780.
Cox, Abraham and Elizab. Clark, Dec. 8, 1778.
Cumming, Herman and Mary James, Sept. 7, 1779.
Debelly, Jacob and Barbara Leganfelder, Dec. 9, 1779.
Doland, John and Elizab. Jones, March 29, 1779.
Grove, Philip and Mary Ekls, Nov. 22, 1780.
Jacques, Denton and Elizab. Powell, June 6, 1780.
Jones, Michael and Sabina Thomas, Sept. 5, 1780.
Laferer, John and Elizab. Baker, Jan. 6, 1779.

* Maryland Marriages, pp. 226–241; Md. Hist. Soc., courtesy of Mr. Charles Fickus, Acting Librarian.

Lewis, Thomas and Helen Mardee, Sept. 1, 1780.
McKenzie, Danl. and Mary Chapman, Dec. 2, 1779.
Roby, Benjn. and Dolly Frizel, Nov. 18, 1780.
Rogers, John and Mary Tannahill, Jan. 23, 1780.
Swearingen, Benoni and Elizab. Newland, April 1st., 1780.
White, Robert and Katharine Philips, July 25, 1780.

By Rev. Jonathan Rawhouser, 1793–1798

Minister of German Reformed Church, Elizabethtown, [Hagerstown]

Adams, Thomas and Elizab. Greer, Dec. 9, 1794.
Angle, Henry and Barbara Schnelby, June 2, 1794.
Arnold, John and Mary Earhart, May 10, 1794.
Baightle, Jacob and Polly Siegmund, Nov. 2, 1793.
Balitel, Samuel and Christian Christ, Oct. 6, 1795.
Been, Jacob and Fany Rohrer, March 27, 1798.
Belsh, Wm. and Elizab. Kershner, April 19, 1795.
Bens, Adam and Catharine Stonebracker, June 28, 1795.
Boshar, John and Elizab. Gerhart, April 24, 1798.
Boyd, Joseph and Susana Haushalden, April 8, 1798.
Brackonier, Jacob and Elizab. Hedrick, Nov. 16, 1794.
Bragonier, George and Margaret Otto, Jan. 27, 1795.
Brembach, Henry and Rebecca Renst, March 25, 1798.
Breneisen, Joseph and Eleanor Miller, Dec. 18, 1797.
Bruer, Henry and Christina Flick, Dec. 11, 1797.
Bruner, Henry and Elizab. Hayns, Aug. 4, 1795.
Campbell, Devault and Eliza. Hershner, Sept. 8, 1794.
Clark, Walter and Eliza. Gordon, Feb. 22, 1794.
Cordel, George Martin and Ruth Hazlewood, Dec. 8, 1797.
Deets, Christian and Cath. Osborn, April 19, 1784.
Delaten, Joh. and Margaret Streiger, March 29, 1798.
Dillman, Henry and Catharina Busker, May 25, 1795.
Dougherty, James and Margaret Kee, July 8, 1794.
Fore, Valentine and Elizab. Frederick, Oct. 22, 1793.
French, Martin and Mary Stoner, Nov. 19, 1797.
Gelsinger, Mathew and Eve Cradel Dusing, Nov. 14, 1793.
Gray, John and Cath. Hartshoff, Nov. 11, 1793.
Gushwa, Jonathan and Cath. Muselman, Mch. 27, 1798.
Hager, Samuel and Cath. Sackman, Mch. 6, 1798.
Harris, Jacob and Ann Walgamot, Dec. 1, 1793.
Harrison, Daniel and Rebecca Hammit, March 19, 1795.

Heiser, Jacob and Catharine Ott, Jan. 14, 1794.
Helm, Thomas and Mary Knode, Sept. 15, 1795.
Hoffman, Henry and Ann Gilbert, Oct. 25, 1795.
Huffman, John and Lucky Schley, Nov. 16, 1797.
Holmes, Henry and Christina Huckman, July 20, 1795.
Hughes, John and Biddy Purcell, Oct. 3, 1794.
Kay, John and Jennett Lowson, Dec. 7, 1793.
Kershner, John and Mary Tooweiler, April 5, 1795.
Lape, Henry and Catherine Grove, Aug. 9, 1794.
Lockard, Saml. and Rachel McCormick, Mch. 5, 1798.
Long, Christian and Elizab. Baker, April 19, 1794.
Long, Henry and Rachel Lawrence, Dec. 31, 1794.
Martin, John and Magdalen Johnson, Feb. 29, 1798.
Mensor, Michael and Mary Beard, May 31, 1794.
Milloskie, Stephen and Cath. Buckanan, Dec. 22, 1794.
Nesbitt, Nathl. and Elizabeth Seibert, Feb. 4, 1798.
Newcomer, Christian and Catherine Beard, Sept. 8, 1794.
Neyhearck, Abraham and Civil Snyder, Dec. 11, 1794.
Oldwine, Charles and Eliza Lottenbarger, July 5, 1794.
Orendorff, Jacob and Susanna Miller, Feb. 8, 1794.
Ott, Jacob and Mary Alter, April 21, 1794.
Perrin, John and Mary Newson, June 14, 1795.
Renst, Danl. and Elisabeth Rohner, March 25, 1798.
Reudenauer, Henry and Sus. Heinsman [?], Dec. 17, 1797.
Ridenour, Joseph and Ann Troxall, Jan. 18, 1794.
Reudenauer, Saml. and Susanna Ott, March 6, 1798.
Root, Jacob and Cath. Conrad, Dec. 14, 1794.
Schnebly, Henry and Anne Beichtle, Dec. 13, 1793.
Seibert, John and Cath. Shwab, Jan. 21, 1798.
Shaneberger, Peter and Susana Schmit, March 25, 1798.
Sigmund, Wm. and Catharina Deal, April 4, 1798.
Smith, Jacob and Mary Harnish, Jan. 1, 1798.
Simpson, Wm. and Jane Thorn, Nov. 11, 1794.
Small, John and Sarah Reidenauer, Nov. 21, 1794.
Snively, John and Nancy Heegy, Oct. 22, 1794.
Startsman, Martin and Susanna Mostiller, April 25, 1794.
Steward, Solomon and Keziah Bantam, Oct. 15, 1794.
Watt, John and Susana White, Oct. 8, 1795.
Whitenet, Philip and Coly Heckman, Dec. 26, 1797.
Winders, John and Elizab. Shaver, Aug. 18, 1795.
Zook, Jacob and Eliza Hammond, June 12, 1794.

By Rev. George Schmucker, 1794–Nov. 1798

Pastor of the Lutheran Church, Hagerstown

Arnold, Henry and Mary Bauman, Sept. 1798.
Backer, Michel and Mollena Hose, March 17, 1795.
Beard, Michel and Hanah Horse, Aug. 8, 1795.
Beck, John and Cath. Biard, June 23, 1795.
Beorson, John and Mary Miller, May 2, 1795.
Byerly, Joh. and Barbara Brendel, August, 1798.
Caywood, Thos. and Sarah Mastaller, Dec. 1797.
Charls, Andrew and Marg. Fogelgesang, May, 1798.
Clapper, Frid. and Sarah Backer, April, 1798.
Clarck, Allen and Sus. Swals, July, 1798.
Confair, George and Eve Nonse, July 2, 1795.
Coock, Hannry and Mary Schutz, Feb. 1798.
Crisap, Thomas and Mary Briscoe, March 23, 1795.
Cunningham, Francis and Margt. Hughes, Nov. 1797.
Cunninghan, Jams and Fanny Startzman, May, 1798.
Davison, Robert and Sus. Bonket, Feb., 1798.
Dusing, Adam and Cath. Buzzard, Aug., 1798.
Eakenberger, Walter and Susana Snider, Aug. 2, 1794.
Erhart, John and Cath. Brendle, March 29, 1795.
Ferrell, John and Mary Carvy, May 29, 1795.
Firy, Jacob and Sus. Hortzman, April, 1798.
Fogelgesang, Christ. and Sus. Arnold, Dec. 1797.
Frey, John and Eliz. Sley, Aug. 25, 1795.
Funk, Jacob and Susannah Rank, Aug. 20, 1795.
Hadley, Richard and Sarah Jobson, June, 1798.
Hefflich, Jos. and Magd. Alter, April, 1798.
Heysone, Nicolaus and Eliz. Flenner, Nov. 1797.
Hocker, Andrew and Sus. Caw, Jan. 1798.
Haushalter, Adam and Cath. Davis, Mch., 1798.
Hyberger, Conrad and Cath. Wolf, June 25, 1795.
Jabson, Jonadan, and Charity Walter, May 13, 1794.
Kuhn, Leonhard and Eliz. Alter, March 20, 1795.
Lane, Seth and Cath. Waltz, Jan., 1798.
Liter, Abrah. and Elisab. Dusinger, July, 1798.
Littel, David and Eliz. Wolz, April 30, 1795.
McCormick, John and Elizab. McCormick, Aug. 10, 1794.
McDanel, Richd. and Mary Boward, Nov., 1798.
Mongand, George and Katy Haur [Hawe?], June 6, 1795.
Musear, Hennry and Marg. Coon, Mch., 1798.

Myer, Adam and Cath. Fritz, Nov., 1798.
Oyer, Francis and Beggy Coock, Jan., 1798.
Pender, George and Rebecca Alter, May 23, 1795.
Pewagard, Robt. and Beggy Dowlor, June 4, 1795.
Piwin, Isaac and Eliz. Pople, Oct. 1798.
Reed, James and Cath. Ringer, April 17, 1794.
Reynols, John and Mary Wolz, March 12, 1795.
Riedenauer, Adam and Cath. Tice, March, 1798.
Reidenauer, Danl. and Barbara Kershner, Mch. 1798.
Scherch, Joseph and Eliz. Betzman, May 2, 1795.
Scherrick, John and Ann Wayand, Feb., 1798.
Schmelzer, Nedren and Cath. Cau, Dec. 2, 1794.
Schock, Jacob and Eliz. Deal, March 20, 1795.
Schwab, Michel and Polly Braun, Nov. 1797.
Schupp, John and Eliz. Conrad, Nov. 1797.
Sillinger, Andrew and Amelia Roberson (Berkly Co. Va.), May 11, 1795.
Smiser, Henry and Elizab. Weaver, Oct. 10, 1794.
Snell, George and Rebecca Mallott, June 6, 1795.
Spesserd, David and Eva Hoye, June, 1798.
Startzman, Martin and Mally Keller, May, 1798.
Strouse, Henry and Christena Clausbrenner, Oct. 6, 1794.
Swingel, Benjn. and Eve Schmith, Nov. 1, 1794.
Tyse, John and Elizab. Kesecker, Nov. 16, 1794.
Tyson, Benjn. and Margaret Morgan, Aug. 27, 1795.
Waver, Frederick and Eliz. Maggin, Dec. 1797.
Zimerman, Gottlib and Eva Hann, Feb. 1798.

By Rev. Jacob Weimer, Sept. 13, 1777–Oct. 6, 1786

Adair, Wm. and Elisabeth Graham, June 17, 1779.
Ancony, Henry and Susanah Jones, Aug. 19, 1793.
Baher, Morris and Mary Allender, Dec. 15, 1777.
Barid, Wm. and Dorothy Camrey, Oct. 3, 1785.
Boohman, George and Eve Breheri, Nov. 22, 1777.
Brewar, Peter and Mary Brooe, Jan. 5, 1785.
Camror, Donald and Elisabeth Saus, Oct. 27, 1779.
Carty, Michael and Martha Hewston, Aug. 25, 1779.
Chamberlain, Jacob and Margaretha Deal, July 12, 1793.
Chrissey, Jacob and Catharina Paulter, March 18, 1793.
Cinkle, Jacob and Ann Lewis, Aug. 5, 1778.
Coldwell, Joseph and Elizabeth Patterson, Dec. 17, 1784.
Crabiel, Jacob and Mary Link, Jan. 3, 1778.
Creichbaum, Philip and Catharina Jolly, June 3, 1780.

Cross, Peter and Susannah Cammerson, Sept. 8, 1778.
Cross, Samuel and Ann Lewis, June 8, 1778.
Curten, Peter and Mary Ward, April 3, 1778.
Dougherty, Neal and Rachel Cross, March 3, 1778.
Duml, Jacob and Elisabeth Hefleigh, Aug. 23, 1784.
Elliss, Nicolous and Rebecca Karrick, Sept. 28, 1786.
Ester, Peter and Elisabeth Kebber, July 31, 1779.
Evans, Isaac and Mary Sboiwd, Sept. 13, 1777.
Fervott, Peter and Dorathy Wales, June 15, 1779.
Fields, George and Sarah Wade, Aug. 31, 1786.
Finly, Willm. and Magdalena Borey, June 5, 1779.
Gemtz, Willm. and Susannah Ross, March 16, 1778.
Gole, Baker and Catharine Garehart, June 1, 1784.
Gripe, Saml. and Catharine Nesbitt, Nov. 22, 1782.
Guin, Nicholas and Margaret Shoup, April 2, 1779.
Hamilton, Robert and Mary Renwicks, Aug. 15, 1793.
Hanch, James and Margareth McCarty, Sept. 27, 1784.
Hartle, Peter and Elisabeth Reiter, Feb. 25, 1778.
Hauser, Jacob and Mary Wernerson, April 20, 1778.
Haynes, John and Babera Baum, July 20, 1779.
Hayse, Mosses and Sarah Daniel, Nov. 14, 1777.
Hermitags, James and Elisabeth Lewis, July 6, 1780.
Howher, Fridrick and Mary Tanner, April 17, 1786.
Hyner, Henry and Catharine Divily, Sept. 27, 1784.
Jamison, James and Sarah Ireland, May 3, 1784.
Jolley, Thomas and Mary Deacock, Mch. 3, 1785.
Kelly, William and Elisab. Wallace, Dec. 9, 1785.
Kisinger, Devault and Catharine Weshenbaugh, Feb. 26, 1785.
Lackland, Joseph and Ann McKoy, May 7, 1778.
Lieter, Philip and Christinah Bower, Nov. 25, 1780.
Lochman, Jacob and Magdalena Shneider, June 5, 1779.
Long, Johnn. and Ann Bune, May 4, 1778.
Long, Johnn. and Elisab. Shaver, March 18, 1780.
Long, Johnn. and Jane Helms, Nov. 19, 1782.
Lower, David and Susannah Wiseheart, July 15, 1785.
Lower, Johan and Catharina Shank, July 10, 1779.
Lowrey, Andrew and Sarah Rippa, April 14, 1786.
Lydey, Johan and Elisabeth Fortny, May 22, 1779.
McCray, George and Elisab. Brown, Dec. 3, 1793.
McCroroly, Daniel and Sarah Reece, June 21, 1793.
McDenal, Agness and Elisabeth Larr, Sept. 7, 1779.
McDeneld, Alexander and Elisabeth Sinclair, June 6, 1779.

McDonald, Kenith and Marg't. Davis, March 20, 1780.
McLane, Hector and Mary Collins, March 6, 1778.
McMulty, James and Sarah Garrard, Aug. 27, 1779.
Mantle, Christopher and Elisab. Sogston, July 20, 1784.
Marks, Johnn. and Mary Mitchell, Jan. 18, 1780.
Meck, Thos. and Martha Davis, Jan. 15, 1780.
Menach, Isaac and Elisabeth Scott, March 11, 1780.
Meridith, James and Isbell Hardesty, March 3, 1779.
Miller, Abraham and Elisabeth Clapper, April 28, 1793.
Miller, Adam and Rosanah Kershner, Jan. 24, 1780.
Miller, James and Margaret Lowrey, Aug. 21, 1780.
Miller, Philix and Mary Brie, Dec. 7, 1784.
Miller, William and Frances Hyner, April 4, 1780.
Mires, Mattes and Mary Webster, Sept. 18, 1780.
Moolespaugh, Philip and Mary Swank, June 4, 1779.
Neighbous, Johnn. and Mary Deninson, Aug. 2[7?], 1793.
Nellson, Moses and Margaretha Thornton, July 8, 1784.
Nicolson, William and Ann Nicolson, Feb. 21, 1785.
Nox, William and Ann Casterlin, March 5, 1778.
Oldwine, Charles and Mary Wyand, Oct. 16, 1784.
Owe, Johan and Susannah Windless, Oct. 24, 1777.
Patterson, W^{m}. and Phebe Daniel, Nov. 13, 1777.
Pennybaher, W^{m}. and Mary Verdie, Sept. 9, 1785.
Phumener, Johnn. and Elisabeth Clarke, Feb. 24, 1784.
Powett, Michael and Elisabeth Wise, April 12, 1793.
Prutsman, John and Mary Heflish, Aug. 19, 1780.
Rafenrider, Henry and Margaretha Chilling, Aug. 12, 1780.
Raymer, Frederick and Elisa^{b}. Jones, Jan. 30, 1778.
Rellare, Jacob and Elisab. Rentch, June 2, 1786.
Renner, Philip and Christina Hinesifer, April 16, 1780.
Resley, George and Christina Bowman, Aug. 21, 1780.
Robinson, W^{m}. and Margt. Russell, June 3, 1779.
Ross, James and Rachel Davis, April 13, 1779.
Ross, Samuel and Ann Trainer, June 28, 1780.
Shauh, Jacob and Mary Sailor, March 12, 1778.
Shank, Michael and Christina Gross, May 19, 1780.
Sharpe, Joseph and Ann Nicoleson, Oct. 3, 1793.
Sheets, Jacob and Elisab. Ruler, Aug. 23, 1785.
Shimer, John and Sarah Walling, Nov. 17, 1793.
Shipley, Richard and Eve Christine Crechbaum, Jan. 27, 1785.
Shipton, John and Ann Cahace, Jan. 22, 1785.
Shnebly, Henry and Catharine Fackler, April 2, 1793.

Shutt, Jacob and Elisabeth Miller, Jan. 4, 1793.
Simpkins, Wm. and Ruth Wolling, March 20, 1780.
Skinner, Wm. and Mary Montgomery, Feb. 20, 1778.
Spears, Willm. and Sarah Miller, Sept. 10, 1778.
Squire, George and Rebecca Queen, June 8, 1778.
Stall, Henry and Rosanah Stample, April 14, 1780.
Tizor, Wm. and Elisab. Marten, Feb. 8, 1785.
Traxler, Emanuel and Catharine Camerer, May 7, 1785.
Tutwiler, Jacob and Cath. Cheney, Feb. 1, 1780.
Valentine, George and Mary Grove, May 15, 1786.
Waggoner, John and Elisab. Litch, July 18, 1785.
Walker, Peter and Elisab. Proce, Sept. 5, 1785.
Wallace, John and Mary Alexander, June 7, 1779.
Waters, George and Dorothy Bunn, May 4, 1778.
Weis, George and Catharine Heiser, Sept. 25, 1779.
Welch, James and Agness Lamson [Tamson?], July 11, 1779.
Welty, Christy and Catharina Yost, Sept. 8, 1778.
Welty, Jacob and Elisabeth Sheller, Sept. 23, 1778.
Werner, Henry and Susana Pragunier, May 28, 1779.
Wharry, John and Jane Hanah, Oct. 9, 1780.
Whitehair, Christian and Margretta Troy, Aug. 12, 1780.
Wiler, Jacob and Elisab. Summer, Sept. 23, 1778.
Williams, Alexr. and Deborah Cahles, May 4, 1780.
Wise, John and Sarah Roberson, June 3, 1793.
Wisnor, Jacob and Susannah Jolly, July 1, 1780.
Wotring, Abraham and Cath. Shnebly, Oct. 6, 1786.
Wyond, Christian and Ann Mary Putnam, Mch. 12, 1778.
Wyond, Youst and Mary Crebs, Dec. 7, 1778.

By Rev. George Young, Aug. 15, 1777–Dec. 27, 1785

Allison, Hughe and Sarah Scott, Sept. 24, 1778.
Archibald, Willm. and Margaret Thomson, Feb. 13, 1778.
Armstrong, David and Sarah Harris, June 30, 1779.
Armstrong, Robert and Mary Starret, March 16, 1779.
Baird, Michael and Catharina Walhem, Sept. 30, 1784.
Bare, Conrad and Mary Whilhair, June 18, 1783.
Barnes, Silvanus and Sarah Phelps, June 21, 1779.
Basford, John and Elizabeth Taylor, Oct. 21, 1779.
Beard, Wm. and Margaret Reynolds, Sept. 22, 1785.
Berand, Jacob and Elisabeth Snevely, Sept. 17, 1778.
Biddle, Thomas and Sarah Watson, May 14, 1778.
Blare, James and Barbara Ellot, Dec. 3, 1778.

Boumgartner, Adam and Cath. Kershman, Oct. 11, 1779.
Bower, Mosies and Catharine Pretter, April 18, 1778.
Boyd, Wm. and Cath. Creamer, Apr. 15, 1779.
Brees, Wm. and Mary McAllen, June 27, 1778.
Bridenbach, John and Mary Eliz. Frey, Sept. 13, 1779.
Broden, Elder and Margareth Accony, April 9, 1783.
Brond, Richard and Kezeeah Wells, Dec. 12, 1785.
Brooner, John and Susa. Delaughter (Frederick Co.), Oct. 9, 1779.
Brown, James and Margaret Echols, June 12, 1778.
Bryant, Joseph and Mary Brantner, Jan. 24, 1779.
Cain, Hugh and Ann Reynolds, Aug. 15, 1777.
Caldwell, Henry and Jean McKesson, June 23, 1784.
Callie, Michael and Mary Parker, Nov. 25, 1779.
Campbell, Willm. and Mary Scott, Oct. 14, 1778.
Cannady, James and Jane Ganniel, Oct. 19, 1784.
Carlisle, James and Lucy Bond, July 23, 1785.
Carson, Richard and Margt. Colliflower, Oct. 14, 1778.
Carter, Robert and Jane Lee, Oct. 19, 1785.
Charles, George and Elizab. Linder, Feb. 14, 1783.
Church, Abraham and Hannah Wilson, May 12, 1778.
Clare, Thomas and Jane Brown, May 13, 1783.
Clarke, James and Margahrett Tumble [Jumble?], Apr. 20, 1783.
Clarke, Joseph and Elizabeth Irvin, Mch. 27, 1779.
Clarke, Robert and Rebeccah Beal, Nov. 29, 1785.
Cochran, Robert and Mary Allen, May 28, 1778.
Cochran, Samuel and Sarah Stuart, July 10, 1778.
Counce, Henry and Cath. Ramback, Sept. 3, 1779.
Cox, Charles and Judy Welch, June 18, 1778.
Craig, Andrew and Margaret Hughes, Oct. 27, 1779.
Cresop, Danl. and Elizab. Swearngen, Dec. 10, 1778.
Crumley, Henry and Margaret Knepper, Sept. 25, 1779.
Cunning, Alexr. and Ruth Mercer, Sept. 25, 1779.
Custer, Jacob and Charity Boyer, April 29, 1785.
Demsy, John and Ellenor Harrington, Mch. 18, 1779.
Doherthy, Patrick and Mary Maley, June 10, 1778.
Dorr, Michael and Mary Frey, Nov. 14, 1778.
Dorsey, Lacon and Ann Shmid, April 23, 1783.
Dowsy, Lakan and Elizab. Ingraham, Sept. 7, 1779.
Dreyton, Samuel and Martha Carswell, Oct. 13, 1778.
Eakle, Harman and Regina Salady, May 26, 1784.
Eaton, Joseph and Jane Ramsey, Nov. 30, 1779.
Ebert, Theador and Elisab. Crabor, May 15, 1778.

Eckels, Wm. and Mary Armstrong, July 6, 1779.
Edmundson, Archibald and Blandey Sheen, Dec. 11, 1777.
Edmundson, Archibald and Linda Barnes, Nov. 23, 1784.
Ekel, Henry and Cath. Pavenberger, Nov. 22, 1779.
Ekenberger, Jacob and Eve Croft, Nov. 26, 1778.
Elder, Wm. and Sarah Abraham, June 14, 1785.
Emmerson, Thomas and Mary Downey, Nov. 12, 1779.
Everet, John and Hannah Knockell, Oct. 27, 1778.
Farmer, Henry and Jean McClan, April 17, 1778.
Farrell, Thomas and Mary Nielly, Nov. 19, 1779.
Fas, Joseph and Catharine Hargan, Nov. 3, 1778.
Feichtner, Martin and Cath. Craft, May 25, 1779.
Feigele, Peter and Cath. Flowd, May 23, 1779.
Finney, John and Margaret Black, April 26, 1779.
Foy, John and Rachel Fight, April 29, 1785.
Frame, William and Elizab. Johnson, Nov. 24, 1779.
Friend, Tobias and Margaret Harshberg, Nov. 2, 1778.
Garvin, John and Jane Noble, Nov. 19, 1779.
George, Joseph and Froney Miller, Jan. 10, 1778.
Goodard, Valentine and Mary Basem Sneider, Oct. 6, 1779.
Gordon, George and Mary Prathor, March 11, 1778.
Grumm, Adam and Catharina Fleeger, Nov. 9, 1779.
Hack, Jacob and Ann Mary Cramer, Nov. 10, 1778.
Hammeslay, Garret and Comfort Simkins, Aug. 27, 1778.
Handerson, Samuel and Jean Jordan, Oct. 30, 1778.
Harre, John and Eliz. Saylor, July 4, 1783.
Harriss, Nehemiah and Sarah Fletcher, Aug. 25, 1777.
Harriss, Richard and Mary Ann Strong, Nov. 24, 1785.
Harvey, David and Margaret Bishop, June 8, 1778.
Harvy, Henderson and Martha McConnell, Feb. 10, 1779.
Harvey, Jacob and Mary Elizab. Saylor, Nov. 13, 1779.
Harvey, Martin, Jr. and Susanna Saylor, Oct. 2, 1778.
Hayes, Thomas and Rosannah Ransom, Jan. 12, 1778.
Hefflich, Valentine and Mary Ruker, Dec. 24, 1778.
Heffner, Valentine and Barbara Miller, April 30, 1783.
Hess, Henry and Mary Shaffer, Dec. 29, 1778.
Hicks, Joshua and Jean Chambers, July 18, 1778.
Hipsley, George and Margaret Allender, Mch. 21, 1785.
Hoeflich, Peter and Margaret Geiger, June 25, 1785.
Hogg, David and Mary Gibb, Mch. 4, 1778.
Hogg, Michael and Elizabeth Woods, Dec. 2, 1778.
Houser, Michael and Susannah Fritchie, Aug. 23, 1783.

Hornish, Philip and Ann Matkins, Oct. 29, 1779.
Huston, John and Sarah Morris, Mch. 10, 1779.
Hyshel, Adam and Margaret Upp, Jan. 30, 1778.
Iliot, Elisha and Mary Gaither, April 18, 1778.
James, Thomas and Elizab. McFall, April 18, 1778.
Karn, Philip and Mary Heflebower, May 22, 1779.
Kegg, Henry and Catharine Miller, May 24, 1783.
King, Peter and Elizabeth Mantle, Nov. 8, 1778.
Kinkead, Thomas and Mary Mackey, Oct. 27, 1778.
Kirkpatrick, Samuel and Elizab. Tomson, April 2, 1779.
Kirkpatrick, Willm. and Mary Reed, April 27, 1785.
Kenegam, Richard and Sarah Flemon, Oct. 1, 1778.
Klinsmith, Andrew and Barbary Wead, Feb. 6, 1778.
Lackland, Elisha and Martha Swearingin, June 11, 1785.
Lahm, Michael and Cath. Clinger, Oct. 29, 1779.
Levenstone, Christian and Ann Spangler, July 19, 1778.
Light, Peter and Elizab. Friend, March 31, 1783.
Linn, John and Jane Fisher, May 3, 1779.
Linn, Robert and Elisabeth London, Sept. 15, 1778.
Little, Joseph and Ester Beard, June 29, 1785.
Long, William and Mary Hughen, Oct. 22, 1778.
McCaine, Willm. and Ann Fugate, July 31, 1779.
McCartney, Willm. and Ann Wallace, Jan. 28, 1785.
McClachey, Robert and Mary Wilkison, Feb. 14, 1778.
McClennen, Joseph and Sarah McCulloe, Nov. 21, 1778.
McCletch, Robert and Mary Disson, Aug. 4, 1778.
McCormicke, Patricke and Margaret Nelson, July 15, 1784.
McCoy, John and Rebecca Malown, Aug. 28, 1779.
McCoy, John and Sarah Clarck, Dec. 16, 1782.
McConagy, James and Isabel Kersy, Feb. 4, 1779.
McCray, John and Peggy Connelly, Sept. 28, 1778.
McCudle, Patrick and Peggy Hale, July 1, 1778.
McGran [McGraw?], Morris and Bridget Magrun, July 2, 1778.
McKenly, John and Mary Bryan, Feb. 18, 1779.
McKibbins, Joseph and Sarah Graham, June 24, 1783.
McKurdy, Alexander and Elizab. Henderson, Oct. 20, 1778.
Maritze, Metsker and Sophia Ropp, Feb. 17, 1784.
Marshall, James and Elizab. Paul, Sept. 25, 1779.
Martin, Joseph and Ann Cullins, Oct. 29, 1778.
Martin, Peter and Elizab. Stanfort, Nov. 18, 1779.
Marvel, Samuel and Margaret Kelly, Oct. 13, 1779.
Meyer, Peter and Catherine Schwazell, Dec. 3, 1778.

Miller, Henry and Mary Brady, March 8, 1779.
Millican, Mark and Jane Campbell, Feb. 6, 1779.
Minsher, Robert and Christina Hooper, Mch. 31, 1783.
Moore, John and Ellener Moore, Nov. 3, 1778.
Moore, Willm. and Mary Gafrey, Sept. 19, 1778.
Moorhead, Alexander and Prudence Morrow, Nov. 20, 1779.
Morgan, Nathal and Judith Leither, Sept. 27, 1785.
Neeshton, James and Sara Steel, Feb. 9, 1779.
Neigh, George and Mary Sailor, Nov. 15, 1777.
Nisbett, Nathl and Elizab. Streight, Apr. 25, 1783.
Nixon, Samuel and Catharine Bramann, Nov. 3, 1778.
Oburn, William and Bethiah Cunningham, Jan. 13, 1778.
Ott, Adam and Juliana Hidinger, Nov. 3, 1778.
Pearce, John and Mary Bentley, Mch. 3, 1778.
Persell, Abraham and Ann Ford, May 7, 1784.
Points, John and Jean Slover, Aug. 27, 1777.
Potter, John and Barbara Doreward, June 5, 1784.
Potts, Richard and Elizab. Hugher, Apr. 15, 1779.
Powel, George and Mary McCoy, Jan. 19, 1779.
Prather, James and Ruth Crownover, Aug. 24, 1784.
Prober, William and Mary Dyal, April 1, 1779.
Ray, Daniel and Elizab. Nicholson, March 25, 1778.
Real, Joseph and Elizab. Newcomer, Feb. 4, 1785.
Reece, Adam and Ann Margt. Neffe, Aug. 14, 1784.
Reidenauer, Henry and Eve Ekenberger, Sept. 22, 1778.
Reidenour, Nicholas and Catherine Tackler, Nov. 14, 1778.
Rentch, John and Elizab. Caler, April 1, 1784.
Ricard, Peter and Mary Creamer, Sept. 2, 1779.
Rice, John and Mary Johnson, June 7, 1784.
Richard, George and Cath. Feltner, June 26, 1778.
Richtels, Philip and Mary Cath Winyard, May 22, 1779.
Rippa, Elisle and Elizab. Thomson, Feb. 20, 1784.
Roach, Morris and Sidney Mackingty, Aug. 5, 1779.
Roads, William and Elizabeth Fowler, July 3, 1778.
Rodrock, Daniel and Elizab. Heflegh, Sept. 13, 1784.
Rodrock, Daniel and Mary Norris, Dec. 27, 1785.
Rorer, Samuel and Cath. Cooper, May 17, 1784.
Rutter, William and Anna Crumb, March 24, 1779.
Ryan, Andrew and Elizabeth McCoy, Dec. 24, 1782.
Salady, Melcher and Barbara Palmer, March 27, 1778.
Salady, Philip and Christine Flikin, April 28, 1779.
Savage, John and Mary Jackson, Jan. 29, 1778.

* Schmid, Michael and Regina Fruit, May 2, 1783.
Schyler, Ephraim and Mary Guttery, Dec. 17, 1777.
Schyler, Willm. and Ann Murphy, Nov. 16, 1778.
Scott, Henry and Mary Jones, Nov. 24, 1779.
Shall, George and Barbara Waggoner, May 15, 1779.
Shawl, George and Mary Creps, Nov. 11, 1782.
* Smith, Charles and Mary Ringer, April 21, 1779.
Shoeman, Thomas and Susannah Bowman, Apr. 19, 1783.
Shrader, Henry and Catharine Knote, Nov. 25, 1779.
Smortz, Abraham and Mary Rorer, July 1, 1784.
Snyder, Daniel and Cath. Sukwald, April 30, 1785.
Speedy, Allen and Margaret McAmish, Mch. 16, 1785.
Stumph, Charles and Elizab. Beall, Sept. 6, 1779.
Swales, Robert and Mary Lyton, Oct. 29, 1785.
Sweny, William and Christina Horbach, May 4, 1779.
Swingle, George and Pristine Houesholder, Apr. 23, 1778.
Syster, Daniel and Hannah Camrer, Aug. 6, 1778.
Teeter, Peter and Margaret Kister, March 24, 1779.
Thomson, Alexander and Mary Craber, May 28, 1778.
Thomson, Allexander and Ruhamah Chapline, Sept. 12, 1785.
Thomson, John and Deborah Chapline, April 3, 1783.
Wadd, Henry and Ruth Mellott, March 5, 1779.
Waggoner, Christopher and Elisabeth Rue, March 18, 1779.
Waggoner, John and Sarah White, Dec. 29, 1783.
Wallace, Samuel and Mary Duffee, June 11, 1778.
Walwert, Frederic August and Susa. Secrest, Feb. 15, 1778.
Weave, George and Mary Elizab. Ichelberger, Jan. 15, 1779.
Wells, Enoch and Elizab. Watt, Mch. 19, 1778.
Wells, Robert and Mary Downing, Jan. 5, 1778.
White, Samuel and Mary Diven, Feb. 28, 1779.
Willson, John and Rachel Magee, Feb. 27, 1783.
Willson, Robert and Jean Elliott, Nov. 4, 1777.
Wise, William and Ellenor Perry, May 17, 1785.
Woster, Robert and Mary Gorman, July 19, 1778.
Young, Jacob and Attila Mony, Oct. 23, 1784.
Zinn, Peter and Jane McKall, Nov. 22, 1779.

St. Mary's County Marriages*

By Rev. William Allen, of Georgetown, D. C.

Davis, Alexander and Elizabeth Sedgwick, of Montgomery Co., July 7, 1802.

By Rev. John Bolton (Probably Roman Catholic)

Mattingly, Edward and Martha Sym, Sept. 17, 1779.

By Rev. George Goldie

Barber, Elias and Elizab: Wainwright, Dec. 14, 1777.
Bond, Willm. and Mary Nevison, Feb. 28, 1777.
Brown, Robt. and Mary Ireland, Dec. 26, 1777.
Buckler, Robert and Anna Bullock, Jan. 10, 1778.
Carpenter, George and Catharine Maddox, July 14, 1777.
Cook, Robert and Susannah Watson, Jan. 7, 1778.
Evans, William and —— Bull, Nov. 16, 1778.
Gardiner, Thomas and Henrietta Goodrum, Sept. 27, 1777.
Gibson, Joshua and Mary Ann Anderson, Feb. 10, 1778.
Lang, John and Dorothy Williams, Feb. 14, 1778.
Long, Peregrine and Rebecca Williams, Nov. 12, 1778.
Murphey, Zekhaniah and Elianor Gray, Jan. 6, 1778.
Watson, Hezekiah and Susannah Pratt, Feb. 11, 1778.

By Rev. Joseph Messenger, Rector of St. Andrews Parish

Sissill, John and Eleanor Combs, Aug. 26, 1777.

By Rev. John Stephen, Rector of All Faith's Parish

Barnes, James and Anne Grimes, Jan. 18, 1784.
Booker, Joseph and Eleanor Plummer, Jan. 3, 1778.
Brawdy, John and Elizab: Davis, April 8, 1778.
Burroughs Richard and Barbara Wilson, Nov. 9, 1783.
Burroughs, Wm. and Susanna Dent, Feb. 9, 1783.
Compton, Stephen and Abigail French Moore, Apr. 1, 1784.
Ewing, Nathl. and Catharine Reeder, Feb. 24, 1784.
Gates, Joseph and Elizab: Jones, Aug. 31, 1778.
Glover, William and Phebe Hutchinson, Dec. 16, 1783.

* From "Maryland Marriages, 1777–1804," pp. 223–225, Md. Historical Society, Courtesy of Mr. Charles Fickus.

Harrison, George and Sarah Dent, Dec. 16, 1777.
Harrison, Robert and Elizab: Douglas, Feb. 17, 1778.
Herbert, James and Mary Marshall, Jan. 2, 1778.
Hill, —— and Elizab: Miller, Sept. 2, 1778.
Hill, Richard and Sarah King, Jan. 7, 1783.
Key, Philip and Rebecca Sothoron, Mch. 4, 1778.
Leach, Nehemiah and Elizab: Lyon, May 1, 1783.
Lippet, Notley and Ann Wood (Banns pub.), Dec. 2, 1783.
Lyon, John and Sarah Thompson, Jan. 19, 1783.
Mills, Charles Nathl. and Eliz^{b}. Ryal, Jan. 17, 1778.
Moran, Hezekiah and Rachel Lyon, Feb. 11, 1778.
Moran, Peregrine and Eleanor Barber, Jan. 8, 1784.
More, Thomas and Mary Burroughs, Feb. 23, 1783.
Moreton, Joseph and Cath. Billingsley, Jan. 3, 1778.
Murphy, Hezekiah and Mary Robinson, Feb. 13, 1778.
Phillips, Henry and Elizab: Walker, Feb. 23, 1784.
St. Clare, Bernard and Dorcas King, Dec. 24, 1778.
Scott, James and Peggy Edwards, Nov. 18, 1783.
Shamwell, Joseph and Nancy Billingsly, Nov. 20, 1783.
Sothon, Samuel and Henrietta Bruce, Jan. 9, 1783.
Suit, Walter and Susanna Davis (Charles Co.), Aug. 26, 1777.
Swan, Henry and Ann Dyson, Dec. 29, 1777.
Wood, Nathan and Elizab: W^{m}. (Bann pub.), Feb. 23, 1783.
Wyndham, George and Mary Cord, Dec. 11, 1783.

MINISTERIAL RECORDS OF PRINCE GEORGE'S PARISH*

* Rock Creek, pp. 370–409.

"Register of Baptism 1792–1845. Prince George's Parish, Montgomery Co., Md.—with other Records—Mutilated Condition"

Rev. Ch. M. Parkman wrote from Spottswood, N. J., Apr. 5, 1883, that he found this mutilated record, in 1883, in the garret of the Rectory. "My predecessor here was Rev. Lorenzo S. Russell and I believe he was once Rector of the Parish." "If you have examined it at all, you will see how valuable it really is, and also that in 'early days' there was a large work being done."

The first 98 pp. are missing. *Funerals*, commencing on p. 99, Jan. 14, 1796, extend to Oct. 8, 1814, and p. 103.

Rev. *Thos. G. Allen* moved from Va., July 30, 1820, and took charge of the Parish. His entries for funerals extend from p. 104 to 108, and for baptisms begin on p. 196. This record extends to p. 211, ending with Nov. 13, 1852.

Rev. *Levin I. Gilliss*, Rector of P. G. Parish, gives his record of Funerals on p. 111, extending from Apr. 7, 1830, to Aug. 26, 1832.

Between p. 111 and p. 112 a sheet of Marriages beginning Jan. 2, 1806, and ending 1813 has been inserted. These appear from an original record in the Md. Hist. Soc. to be residents of Anne Arundel Co.

"Rockville, March 10, 1828. I hereby resign my charge of Prince George's Parish after having endeavoured faithfully to discharge the duties of Rector for seven and two third years. And may the richest blessings of Heaven descend upon the dear people:—May they thus be rewarded for all their kindness and affection towards me:—May they be led to select that faithful minister of the word who shall be the happy instrument of leading them in the way everlasting; and after all our wanderings and trials here, may I be crowned with the great joy of meeting them all in that land of pure delight where Saints immortal reign. Amen. Amen.

Thos. G. Allen."

(Original Record, 1792–1845.)

Prince George's Record, p. 416, contains this entry: "The first person baptized in the New Church at Rockville, Apr. 7, 1822.

"Robert Henry Allen, son of Henry and Sarah.

"Rachel, dau. of Jerry and Charity belonging to Dr. Bowie and Mrs. Middleton." (Orig. Rec., p. 199.)

"In July following the above the *Rev. Henry C. Knight* of the Diocese of Mass. was elected to the rectorship which he held for one year."

1828

"Account of Baptisms by the Revd. Henry Cogswell Knight, late of the Diocese of Mass., now Rector of Christ Church, Rockville, Prince George's Parish; and of St. Bartholomew's Church on Holland's River, Montgomery Co., Md." These records are upon pp. 212–214, Orig. Record.

Knight, Henry Cogswell. This certifies that the subscriber, from the Diocese of Mass., came to Rockville about the middle of July, 1828, and was nominally appointed Rector of Christ Church, in Prince George's parish; and also of St. Bartholomew's parish, Montgomery county, Md.; but that the choice of a Vestry having been neglected on the last Easter Monday, in both parishes, the election of the Rector could not be legally confirmed, in either parish, until some weeks afterwards, when, previous notification being given, the Vestry were chosen, qualified and confirmed the same according to law. Henry C. Knight."

"I was ordained a Deacon in the Protestant Episcopal Church, by the Right Rev. Alexander Vietts Griswold, D.D., of the Eastern Diocese, May 6, 1827.

I was ordained a Priest in the Protestant Episcopal Church, by the Right Rev. Henry Ustick Onderdonk, D.D., Philadelphia, Diocese of Pennsylvania, Dec. 20, 1828, Orig. record, p. 136. Henry C. Knight.

June 15, 1829. At the end of the Annual Convention in Baltimore, which is to meet on the 17th of this month, I shall resign the Rectorship of Prince George's and St. Bartholomew's Parishes, into the hands of the Vestries, affectionately committing the people of my late charge, both in temporal and spiritual concerns, to the mercy and love of God, through our Lord Jesus Christ. Henry C. Knight."

(Orig. Rec., p. 213.)

"On the 24th of July, 1829, the *Rev. Levin Irving Gilliss* succeeded Mr. Knight and served the parish until April, 1844.

The *Rev. Edward Waylen* of the Diocese of Pennsylvania was next elected rector of Prince George's parish and entered on his duties June 1, 1844.

In the same month the *Rev. Orlando Hutton*, late rector of Westminster parish, near Annapolis, took charge of the adjoining parish of St. Barthotomew's hitherto held conjointly with Prince George's."

(Orig. Rec., 1792–1845.)

Edward Waylen was Rector June 1, 1844, and *Geo. F. Worthington* took charge of the Parish Oct. 6, 1845.

Baptisms

1792

June 10, Spalding, John, of Elias and Agnes, b. Mch. 31, 1792.
10, Berynes, Eleanor, of Josiah and Rachel, b. Jan. 28, 1792.
10, Austin, James, of James and Nancy, b. Feb. 10, 1792.
10, Collyer, Ann, of Jno. and Mary, b. Apr. 19, 1792.
10, Soper, James, of John and Rebecca, b. May 16, 1792.
20, Brown, Eliz., of James and Ann, b. Mch. 31, 1792.
30, Herbert, Anna, of Elisha and Margaret, b. May 17, 1790.
30, Hall, Eliz., of Henry and Margaret, b. Aug. 23, 1790.
July 1, Brown, Airy, of Thos. and Sarah, b. May 4, 1792.
8, Davis, Ann., of Jno. and Easter, b. Oct. 19, 1789.
8, Do, Thos, of Do, b. Apr. 5, 1786.
15, Chappell, John, of Thos. and Eleanor, b. Mch. 3, 1792.
22, Long, Mary, of Saml. and Eliz., b. June 15, 1792.
29, Dickerson, Ann, of Serratt and Eliz., b. Dec. 13, 1791.
29, Warfield, Deborah, of Brice and Susanna, b. Feb. 18, 1792.
Aug. 5, Beans, Noble Beall, of Jno. and Catherine, b. June 19, 1792.
19, Summers, Mary, of Zadok and Ann, b. June 23, 1792.
23, Ray, Lydia, of Joseph and Mary, b. May 27, 1792.
23, Barrot, Joseph, of Edward and Sarah, b. June 17, 1786.
30, Dowden, Zachariah, of Zachariah and Sarah, b. May 2, 1792.
30, Swearingen, Benjamin, of Wm. and Sarah, b. Aug. 16, 1792.
30, Harwood, Levin, of Jno. and Mary, b. July 3, 1792.
30, Judy, Martha, of Geo. Jacob and Priscilla, b. Mch. 30, 1792.
30, Lyles, Kitty, of Richd. and Eliz., b. June 8, 1792.
30, Clagget, Ruth, of Ninian and Euphem, b. July 14, 1792.
30, White, Nancy, of Walter and Susanna, b. —, 1790.
30, White, John, of do and do, b. Oct. 1791.
Sept. 12, Page, Rachel, of Jesse and Mary, b. Sept. 30, 1791.
12, Warfield, Eliz., of Azel and Eliz., b. July 19, 1791.
26, Magruder, Othello, of Walter and Margaret, b. —, 1792.
26, Richards, Michael Letton, of Wm. and Tabitha, b. —, 1792.
26, Wootton, Richd., of Richd. and Martha, b. June 22, 1792.
15, Hardesty, Saml., of Robert and Eleanor, b. Aug. 12, 1792.
20, Nicholls, Tomsey, of Henry and Nancy, b. Aug. 9, 1792.
20, Greentree, Eliz., of Benj. and Mary, b. Aug. 11, 1792.
Oct. 7, Orme, Eleanor, of Elly and Susanna, b. Jan. 1, 1792.
10, Lyles, Emma, of John and Cassandra, b. Aug. 24, 1792.

Oct. 10, Thompson, Jas., of Jas. and Ann, b. Aug. 28, 1792.
10, Iglaheart, Mary, of Jereh. and Mary, b. Apr. 23, 1792.
10, Gaither, Henry, of Daniel and Henrietta, b. July 17, 1792.
24, Thompson, Eliz., of Jno. and Rachel, b. Aug. 27, 1792.
24, West, Ann, of Richard and Cassandra, b. Mch. 23, 1792.
27, Selby, Richard, of James and Sarah, b. July 15, 1792.
27, Nickson, Anny (Amy?), of Jonathan and Eliz., b. Sept. 18, 1792.
27, Waters, Margaret, of Cephas and Margaret, b. Feb. 1, 1792.
27, Orme, Ann, of Elly and Susanna, b. Apr. 26, 1789.
27, Shaw, Osbourn, of Charles and Keziah, b. Apr. 21, 1792.
27, Evans, Priscilla, of Samuel and Rachel, b. Mch. 10, 1792.
Nov. 4, Letton, Martha, of Caleb and Mary, b. Oct. 3, 1792.
4, Wilcoxen, Lloyd, of John and Ruth, b. Oct. 4, 1792.
4, Lowrey, Edward, of Wm. and Lucy, b. Sept. 10, 1792.
11, Lucas, Barton, of James and Mary, b. Oct. 3, 1792.
11, Duvall, James, of Samuel and Ann, b. Oct. 28, 1792.
11, Lanham, Jesse, of Thos. and Mary, b. Oct. 14, 1792.
16, Collyer, Charlotte, of Jas. and Eleanor, b. Oct. 19, 1792.
23, Turnbull, James, of John and Rebecca, b. Aug. 28, 1792.

1793

Jan. 6, Mullican, John, of Thos. and Leatha, b. Nov. 9, 1792.
Feb. 1, Hinton, Leatha, of John and Susanna, b. Sept. 26, 1791.
9, Gaither, Greenburg, of Zachh. and Sarah, b. Dec. 3, 1792.
9, Ray, Rachel, of Jno. S. and Catherine, b. Jan. 9, 1793.
16, Armsey, Benj. Burch, of Jno. and Easter, b. Feb. 6, 1793.
28, Burgess, Nancy, of Michael and Sally, b. Mch. 31, 1792.
Mch. 6, Walker, Mary, of Richard and Mary, b. Nov. 7, 1792.
6, Anchors, Edward, of Snowden and Deborah, b. Oct. 21, 1792.
6, Thompson, Eleanor, of Samuel and Ann, b. Jan. 20, 1793.
6, Scrivinor, "Henna," of Philemon and Amelia, b. May 11, 1792.
9, Fulks, Solomon, of Wm. and Mary, b. May 27, 1792.
9, Linginfelder, David, of Valentine and Peggy, b. Sept. 3, 1792.
10, "Janes," Elizabeth, of Edward and Martha, b. Jan. 29, 1793.
19, Saffield, Cassandra, of Chas. and Sophia, b. Jan. 24, 1793.
24, Claghorn, James Maxwell, of Robt. and Eliz., b. Dec. 5, 1792.
24, Veach, Wm., of John and Nancy, b. Feb. 26, 1793.
24, Fife, Eliz., of John and Rebecca, b. Feb. 19, 1793.
24, Read, Levinna, of Geo. and Rosanna, b. Dec. 22, 1792.
24, Smith, Wm. Morris Veach, of Geo. and Eliz., b. Jan. 1, 1793.
29, Day, Polly, of John and Lilly, b. Feb. 7, 1793.
Apr. 3, Tylor, Eliz., of James and Eliz., b. June 24, 1792.
3, Mobley, Archibald Johnson, of Wm. and "Chanty" (Charity?) b. Jan. 21, 1793.

Apr. 3, Wilson, Greenburg, of Ephraim and Mary, b. Oct. 23, 1793.
3, Brown, Robert, of Frederick and Sarah, b. Feb. 26, 1793.
3, Ellis, Joseph, of John and Mary, b. Sept. 29, 1792.
4, Dickerson, Sarah, of Serratt and Eliz., b. Mch. 1, 1793.
4, Collins, Rebecca, of Elijah and Ann, b. Nov. 9, 1792.
4, Burgess, John, of Richd. and Eliz., b. Dec. 1792.
7, Prather, Ann, of Walter and Ann, b. Jan. 19, 1793.
12, Ricketts, Sarah, of Richd. and Eliz., b. Dec. 18, 1792.
12, Helt Eliz., of Nicholas and Sarah, b. Oct. 19, 1792.
14, Pierce, Walter, of James and Henrietta, b. Jan. 17, 1793.
May 3, Magruder, Mary Ann, of Jeffery and Susanna, b. Apr. 20, 1793.
5, Magruder, Susanna Talbot, of Geo. and Charity, b. Nov. 15, 1792.
19, Boyd, Eliz., of John and Ann, b. Mch. 14, 1793.
June 20, Belt, Wm. Joseph, of Joseph and Sarah, b. Apr. 7, 1793.
23, Rawlings, Robt. Gordon, of Geo. and Martha, b. Apr. 30, 1793.
July 19, Jones, Eliz., of Edwd. and Eliz., b. May 17, 1792.
19, Beall, Thos. N., of Perry and Eliz., b. June 1, 1793.
19, Nicholls, Cassandra, of Daniel and Amelia, b. June 5, 1793.
24, Beckwith, Eliz., of Geo. and "Leean," b. Jan. 31, 1793.
28, Burns, Zadok, of Chas. and Ruth, b. May 4, 1793.
Nov. 3, Anderson, Juliet, of Richard and Ann, b. Aug. 24, 1793.
3, Martin, Juliet, of Honore and Sarah, b. —, 1792.
17, Hawkins, Eliz. of John and Eliz., b. Oct. 5, 1793.
17, Rawlins, John, of Thos. and Eliz., b. July 9, 1793.
17, Rawlins, John Hambleton, of John and Anna, b. July 4, 1793.

1794

Jan. 5, Holmead, James Beanry, of Anthony and Sarah, b. Sept. 12, 1793.
Feb. 2, Magruder, Jonathan Willson, of Zadok and Martha, b. Oct. 7, 1793.
Apr. 21, Howard, Lucy, of Thos. and Eleanor, b. Nov. 15, 1793.
May 25, Lucas, Martin and Luther, of James and Mary, b. Jan. 12, 1794.
June 29, Letton, Fielder, of Caleb and Mary, b. May 1, 1794.
29, Swearingen, Benome Ray, of Wm. and Sarah, b. May 28, 1794.
July 20, Greentree, Mary, of Benj. and Mary, b. June 5, 1794.
20, Beans, Dawson, of Josias and Rachel, b. Oct. 12, 1793.
Oct. 5, Boyd, Reubin Tylor, of Benj. and Eleanor, b. July 3, 1794.

1795

Mch. 8, Dixon, Howel, of James and Jane, b. Jan. 25, 1795.
Apr. 9, Bowie, Allen, of Thos. and Margaret, b. —, 1795.
19, Summers, Mary Letton, of John L. and Anna Maria, b. Jan. 24, 1795.

19, Nicholls, Ann, of Simon and Barbary, b. Mch. 11, 1795.
May 3, Higgins, Mary, of Benj. and Matilda, b. Jan. 25, 1795.
17, Wootton, Mary, of Richd. and Martha, b. Mch. 7, 1795.
June 28, Redman, Aquila, of W^{m}. and Milly, b. Apr. 31, 1795.
28, Butt, Azil Swearingen, of Proverbs and Rebecca, b. Apr. 24, 1795.
28, Beckwith, Martha, of John and Martha, b. Feb. 27, 1795.
28, Glaze, Anna, of W^{m}. and Mary, b. Feb. 18, 1794.
28, Glaze, Ruth, of W^{m}. and Mary, b. May 17, 1795.
28, Lanham, Cloe, of Hansy and Eleanor, b. Apr. 8, 1795.
July 5, Shaw, James Pratt, of Robt. and Lucy, b. Apr. 12, 1795.
5, Hardy, Sophia, of Baptist and Hester, b. Sept. 3, 1794.
5, Magruder, Helin, of Walter and Margaret, b. —, 1795.
Aug. 9, Rawlins, Benj. Ray (Roy?), of John and Ann, b. June 30, 1795.
30, Webb, Benj. Young, of Thos. and Mary, b. July 28, 1794.
31, Wayman, Rebecca Ann, of Jno. and Cassandra, b. —, 1795.
Sept. 20, Hawkins, Nathaniel, of Jno. and Eliz., b. Aug. 10, 1795.
Nov. 1, Pollard, Margaret, of Thos. and Rebecca, b. Sept. 28, 1795.
15, Fish, Harriet, of Robt. and Elizth., b. Oct. 7, 1795.
15, Beall, Cassandra and Talbot, of Perry and Eliz., b. —, 1795.

1796

Mch. 20, Beckwith, William, of Geo. and Anna, b. Jan. 22, 1796.
20, Nicholls, Sarah, of Daniel and Amelia, b. Sept. 26, 1795.
27, Holmead, Anthony, of Anthony, Junr. and Sarah, b. Dec. 25, 1795.
31, Martin, Sophia, of Honore and Sarah, b. Dec. 6, 1793.
Apr. 22, Walker, Jonathan, of Thos. and Hester, b. Mch. 29, 1795.
May 1, Anderson, Richard, of Richd. and Ann, b. Jan. 11, 1796.
8, Lucas, Mahala, of James and Mary, b. Jan. 21, 1796.
29, White, Harriet, of Joseph and Lucy, b. Jan. 11, 1796.
Oct. 8, Long, Eliz. of Saml. and Eliz., b. Aug. 24, 1796.

1797

Mch. 30, Willson, Eleanor, of William and Ann, b. Jan. 21, 1797.
Apr. 2, Glaze, Mary Magruder, of W^{m}. and Mary, b. Dec. 14, 1796.
2, Pollard, Eliza, of Thos. and Rebecca, b. Mch. 5, 1796.
30, Ray, Macia, of Benj. and Eleanor, b. Dec. 6, 1796.
30, Summers, Caleb Letton, of John and Anna, b. Feb. 27, 1797.
June 25, Clagget, Samuel, of Samuel and Anna, b. Feb. 8, 1797.
25, Allison, Elisha Offutt, of Joshua and Priscilla, b. Apr. 21, 1797.
25, Magruder, Townsend, of Ninian and Grace, b. Mch. 18, 1797.
25, Smith, Charles, of Benj. and Eliz., b. Dec. 27, 1796.
25, Duley, Thomas, of Barton and Martha, b. Apr. 11, 1797.
25, Lansdal, Charles Gates, of Henry and Minta, b. May 27, 1797.

June 25, Harry, William, of Richard and Rachel, b. May 10, 1797.
25, Burress, Charles Wesley, of Thos. and Ann, b. Apr. 21, 1797.
July 9, Beall, Alphe, of Basil M. and Eleanor Beall, b. May 21, 1797.
9, Groom, Rebecca, of Wm. and Anna, b. Dec. 27, 1796.
16, Ferrell, Delilah, of Zephemiah and Martha, b. June 13, 1797.
23, Collyer, Othey Hambleton, of James and Eleanor, b. May 24, 1797.
30, Yates, David, of Samuel and Maryann, b. June 11, 1797.
30, Lovejoy, Wm. Alexander, of Alexr. and Amelia, b. May 15, 1797.
30, Lovejoy, Thos. Anderson, of Alexr. and Amelia, b. May 15, 1797.
30, Barber, Edward, of Edward and Sarah, b. June 16, 1797.
Aug. 20, Prather, Virlinder, of Walter and Ann, b. June 21, 1797.
20, Mills, Joseph, of Jesse and Ann, b. Apr. 20, 1797.
27, Trundle, Lethe, of Thos. and Leah, b. July 16, 1797.
27, Cathoon, Wm., of Chas. and Ann, b. July 9, 1797.
28, Beans, Henrietta, of John and Catherine, b. July 18, 1797.
Sept. 24, Lucas, Mary, of James and Mary, b. Aug. 20, 1797.
30, Selby, Wesley, of Thos. and Sarah, b. July 31, 1797.
Oct. 29, Burrast, Aquila, of Peter and Mary, b. July 22, 1797.
29, Dixon, Jesse Downs, of James and Jane, b. Aug. 6, 1797.
29, Oneal, Mary, of William and Eliz., b. May 17, 1797.
Dec. 12, Madden, Martha, of Hezekiah and Anney, b. Oct. 14, 1797.
27, Dowden, Juliet, of Massey Dowden and Archibal Dunn, b. Oct. 20, 1797.
27, Dowden, Lucy, of Zachariah and Sarah, b. Nov. 4, 1797.
27, Lodge, Harriet Porter, of Wm. and Frances, b. Oct. 16, 1797.
31, Deakins, Eliza, of Leonard and Deborah, b. Nov. 7, 1797.

1798

Mar. 18, Taylor, Washington, of John and Ruth, b. Jan. 23, 1798.
18, Nicholls, Dennis, of Thos. and Cassandra, b. Sept. 16, 1797.
18, Gatton, Saml. Franklin, of Zachariah and Ann, b. Mch. 14, 1798.
18, Rawlins, Mary Ray (Roy?), of John and Ann, b. Nov. 30, 1797.
Apr. 1, Allison, Lucinda Higgins, of John and Eliz., b. Jan. 22, 1798.
1, Lanham, Thomas, of Henry and Eleanor, b. Nov. 14, 1797.
1, Austin, Zachariah Offutt, of Zach. and Marg., b. Nov. 30, 1797.
1, Fisher, Thos. Lyles, of Benj. and Matilda, b. Jan. 14, 1795.
1, Fish, Mary Jeanes, of Robt. and Eliz., b. —, 1798.
15, Yost, Charity, of Philip and Melander, b. Aug. 17, 1797.
May 9, Swearingen, Sarah, of Elemalech and Susanna, b. —, 1798.
9, Clagett, Magruder, of John and Mary, b. Mch. 14, 1798.
24, Magruder, Wm. Willson, of Geo. and Charity, b. Aug. 25, 1797.
24, Hawkins, James, of John and Eliz., b. Dec. 31, 1797.

June 10, Swearingen, Obed, of Obed and Rachel, b. May 5, 1798.
10, Hardy, W^{m}. West, of Henry and Frances, b. Dec. 23, 1797.
July 7, Higgins, Ruth Wilcoxon, of James and Virlinder, b. June 12, 1798.
8, Beckwith, Ann, of Geo. and Leean, b. Mch. 24, 1798.
Aug. 26, Sparrow, Harriet, of Henry and Anna, b. Apr. 12, 1798.
Sept. 17, Jones, Henry, of Benj. and Margaret, b. —, 1798.
Oct. 28, Anderson, Susanna, of Richd. and Ann, b. July 5, 1798.
Nov. 18, West, Erasmus, of Thos. and Eleanor, b. July 27, 1798.
1799
Jan. 11, Wade, Hilleary, of W^{m}. and Cassandra, b. Jan. 15, 1798.
Feb. 12, West, Garey Davis, of Norman and Eliz., b. Sept. 25, 1798.
26, Wade, Ann, of John and Elizabeth, b. Jan. 10, 1796.
26, Wade, Jane, of John and Elizabeth, b. Feb. 12, 1797.
26, Wade, Martha, of John and Elizabeth, b. Mch. 8, 1798.
Mch. 13, Allison, Nancy Mancaster, of Joshua and Priscilla, b. Oct. 14, 1798.
17, Barrott, Ruth, of Alexander and Eleanor, b. Nov. 19, 1798.
22, Linthecum, Sally, of Thos. and Ann, b. Sept. 13, 1798.
24, Thompson, Robert, of Thos. and Margaret, b. Jan. 8, 1799.
24, Robinson, Polly, of W^{m}. and Sally, b. Jan. 1, 1799.
31, Traill, Sarah, Perry, of W^{m}. and Priscilla, b. Nov. 6, 1798.
Apr. 1, Waymann, Perry, of John and Cassandra, b. Nov. 23, 1790.
1, Waymann, Rebecca Ann, of John and Cassandra, b. Apr. 17, 1794.
1, Waymann, John Warfield, of John and Cassandra, b. May 25, 1796.
1, Waymann, Francis Deakins, of John and Cassandra, b. May 14, 1798.
7, Holmead, John Buckhannon, of Anthony and Sarah, b. Oct. 14, 1798.
7, Willson, Kitty Harris, of W^{m}. Alex. and Sally, b. Mch. 1799.
7, Parker, Augustin, of David and Ann, b. Feb. 7, 1799.
7, Allison, George, of Greenburg and Joannah, b. Nov. 28, 1798.
7, Collins, Harriot, of Joshua and Mary, b. Jan. 18, 1799.
10, Willett, Ann, of Edward and Eleanor, b. Aug. 31, 1798.
14, Ray, Alexander, of Benj. and Eleanor, b. Feb. 1, 1799.
14, Wilcoxon, Eleanor, of Jesse Junr. and Ruth, b. Dec. 27, 1798.
14, Soper, Martha, of John and Rebecca, b. Feb. 20, 1799.
14, Landale, Eleanor, of Henry and Minta, b. Apr. 14, 1799.
14, Summers, Anna Maria, of John L. and Anna Maria, b. Feb. 8, 1799.

Apr. 21, Kelley, John Duke, of Thos. and Mary, b. Nov. 28, 1798.
21, Hays, Eleanor, of John and Susanna, b. Feb. 4, 1799.
21, Selby, Virlinder, of Thos. and Kezia, b. Jan. 12, 1799.
21, Steward, Eliz. of Wm. and Margaret, b. Jan. 8, 1799.
28, Culver, Samuel, of Henry and Mary, b. Nov. 15, 1798.
28, Beall, Virlinder Susanna, of James and Mary, b. Mch. 21, 1799.
May 5, Anderson, Robert, of James and Eliz., b. Sept. 10, 1798.
5, Summers, Sarah Garner, of Paul and Sarah, b. Apr. 12, 1798.
5, Holt, Lawrence Owen, of Lawrence and Mary, b. Mch. 17, 1799.
5, Hardy, Mary, of Noah and Mary, b. Aug. 6, 1798.
12, Fryer, Horace, of Walter and Margery, b. Nov. 24, 1798.
12, Owens, John Candler, of Joshua and Mary, b. Mch. 20, 1799.
13, Davis, Richd. Wootton, of Ignatius and Margaret, b. Mch. 18, 1799.
14, Lee, Amos, of James and Ruth, b. Mch. 31, 1799.
14, Richards, Eleanor, of Jacob and Mary, b. June 25, 1795.
14, Richards, Christiana, of Jacob and Mary, b. May 25, 1797.
14, Richards, Mary Ann, of Jacob and Mary, b. Dec. 24, 1798.
17, Magruder, John Willson, of Zadok and Martha, b. —, 1799.
19, "Ran" (McRan?), Eliz. Cartright M. of Wm. and Mary, b. Apr. 24, 1798.
19, Williams, Matilda, of James and Jane, b. Oct. 25, 1798.
19, Crager, John, of Michael and Rebecca, b. Oct. 18, 1798.
26, Higgins, Martin Fisher, of John and Eliz., b. Nov. 24, 1798.
26, Shook, Peter, of John and Arrana, b. Apr. 10, 1798.
26, Mills, Eliz. of Elias and Ann, b. —, 1799.
26, Allison, Noah, of John and Eliz., b. Mch. 21, 1799.
26, Oneal, Eliz., of John and Mary, b. —, 1799.
26, Summers, Mahala, of Walter and Ursula, b. July 28, 1798.
26, Prather, Walter, of Walter and Ann, b. Mch. 29, 1799.
29, Israel, Rachel, of Robert and Mary, b. Mch. 28, 1798.
29, Dorsey, Richard, of Lloyd and Ann, b. Apr. 18, 1799.
29, Leeke, Cassandra, of John and Cassandra, b. Sept. 26, 1798.
29, Holland, Eliz. of Joseph and Morana, b. Jan. 4, 1799.
29, Warfield, Henry, of Basil and Maryann, b. Feb. 22, 1799.
29, Young, Julian, of Nathaniel and Priscilla, b. Nov. 15, 1798.
29, Boswell, Geo., of Nicholas and Rachel, b. Mch. 29, 1799.
29, Sipe, David, of Christopher and Eliz., b. Jan. 3, 1799.
29, Nicholson, John, of John and Mary, b. May 17, 1798.
29, Johnson, Sarah, of Thos. and Dasky, b. Nov. 10, 1798.
29, Lanham, Margaret, of Notley and Mariana, b. Feb. 27, 1799.
29, Burgess, Ann, of Richd. and Eliz., b. Nov. 28, 1798.

May 29, Walker, John, of Elisha and Eliz., b. Nov. 15, 1798.
29, Grymes, Peggy, of Charles and Nancyann, b. June 9, 1798.
June 2, Riddle, Matilda, of John and Susanna, b. Jan. 12, 1798.
2, LoveJoy, Edward Horatio, of George and Rebecca, b. Dec. 30, 1798.
2, Wellen, Mary, of Amos and Linney, b. Feb. 9, 1799.
16, Lodge, Lavellin, of Wm. O., and Frances, b. Jan. 4, 1799.
16, Fish, Matilda, of Robert and Eliz., b. Apr. 29, 1799.
16, Castor, James Shelton, of Vinsant and Hannah, b. May 6, 1799.
16, Williams, Barbary, of Walter and Christiana, b. Mch. 27, 1799.
16, Fields, John Riley, of John and Mary, b. July 1, 1798.
16, Fish, Ruth, of Francis and Eliz., b. Sept. 27, 1797.
23, Traill, Frances, of James and Maryann, b. Dec. 11, 1798.
23, Harper, Lloyd, of John and Phebe, b. Feb. 21, 1799.
23, Buxton, Juliet, of Wm. and Eleanor, b. Mch. 21, 1799.
23, Griffith, Eleanor Ann, of Henry and Mary, b. Nov. 17, 1798.
23, Crocket, Charles, of Henry and Ann, b. Jan. 1, 1798.
July 1, Shoals, Kitty, of Joshua and Nancy, b. Nov. 1796.
1, Duvall, Rector, of Wm. and Sarah, b. Oct. 20, 1798.
3, Vigal, Polly, of Adam and Nancy, b. Jan. 14, 1799.
7, Veirs, Saml. Clarke, of Hezekiah and Ann, b. Aug. 1, 1798.
7, Beard, John, of Anthony Beard and Ann Moore, b. July 24, 1798.
7, Groomes, Sarah, of James and Sarah, b. Mch. 15, 1799.
14, Trail, Wesley, of Osbourn and Frances, b. May 9, 1799.
14, Cashill, Polly, of James and Jane, b. May 9, 1799.
21, Williams, Nancy, of Richard and Eliz., b. Jan. 7, 1799.
24, Clagett, Thos., and Maryann, of Saml. and Anna, b. Apr. 18, 1799.
28, Cox, Eleanor, of Walter and Eliz., b. Sept. 21, 1798.
28, Cool, Thomas, of Christopher and Sarah, b. June 8, 1799.
28, Whalen, James, of John and Sarah, b. Oct. 27, 1798.
28, Prather, Nancy O., of Wm. and Eliz., b. May 31, 1799.
31, Hows, Clarissa, of Benj. and Mary, b. Dec. 15, 1798.
31, Thompson, Milly, of John and Eleanor, b. June 18, 1799.
31, Price, Hester, of Henry and Sarah, b. June 8, 1799.
Aug. 11, Gray, John, of Barney and Cassandra, b. June 5, 1799.
11, Moore, Alexander, of Alexr. and Eliz., b. May 26, 1799.
11, Stokes, Marsham, of John and Ruth, b. Mch. 1, 1799.
11, Willson, Thomas, "of Lancelot of Henry and Rachel," b. July 14, 1799.
11, Lucas, James, of James and Mary, b. July 1, 1799.
11, Williams, Harriot, of Zadok and Sarah, b. —, 1799.

Aug. 18, Scott, Walter, of Amos and Ann, b. June 7, 1799.
18, Richards, Ann, of Wm. and Tabitha, b. July 29, 1799.
18, West, Susanna, of Richd. and Cassandra, b. Mch. 10, 1799.
18, Thompson, Patsey, "of William and his wife," b. Apr. 17, 1799.
18, Groom, Benjamin, of Wm. and Maryann, b. Jan. 8, 1799.
18. Wootton, William, of Richard and Martha, b. —, 1799.
25, Gardner, Mary, of John and Cassandra, b. Sept. 24, 1798.
25, Catro, Rebecca, of Joseph and Mary, b. June 20, 1799.
Sept. 6, Selby, Peter, of Zachariah and Polly, b. June 16, 1799.
8, Windham, Sarah, of Wm. and Eleanor, b. Mch. 3, 1799.
8, Young, Charlotte, of Adam and Rosenna, b. May 10, 1794.
8, Young, Jacob, of Adam and Rosenna, b. Nov. 29, 1795.
8, Young, John, of Adam and Rosenna, b. Dec. 28, 1798.
22, Farrell, John Dent, of Zepheniah and Martha, b. July 18, 1799.
29, Cooke, John, of Nathan and Rachel, b. June 2, 1799.
29, Bealmear, Susanna, of Lewis and Eliz., b. July 27, 1799.
29, Ridgway, John, of Richard and Henrietta, b. July 8, 1799.
29, Magruder, John Willson, of Geo. and Charity, b. June 14, 1799.
29, Tewill, Rachel Offutt, of Horatio and Grace, b. June 20, 1799.
29, Lewis, Maryann, of Absalom and Susanna, b. June 30, 1799.
29, Machall, Margaretta, of Leonard and Catherine, b. Apr. 2, 1799.
Oct. 6, Hardisty, Johnson, of Robert and Eleanor, b. Jan. 20, 1799.
13, Beall, Polly, of Robert and Ann, b. Jan. 9, 1799.
13, Free, Sophia, of Charles and Ann, b. Feb. 13, 1786.
13, Free, John Read, of Charles and Ann, b. Feb. 4, 1790.
13, Wells, Richard, of Nathan and Sophia, b. Aug. 28, 1799.
20, Groome, James, of Richard and Rosanna, b. Oct. 20, 1799.
20, Anderson, Eleanor, of John and Mary, b. Jan. 5, 1799.
20, Fisher, Mary, of Wm. and Drusilla, b. Aug. 21, 1799.
20, Wade, Mordicai Burgess, of John and Eliz., b. May 28, 1799.
20, Ricketts, Mary, of Zadok and Ann, b. Aug. 6, 1799.
20, Maddin, John Baker, of Benj. and Eliz., b. Apr. 13, 1799.
20, Ricketts, William, of Nathan and Mary, b. Aug. 15, 1799.
20, Smith, Susanna Kelley, of Aquila and Eleanor, b. Apr. 14, 1799.
20, Baker, Lucy Edminson, of James and Eliz., b. Apr. 8, 1799.
20, Hurdle, John Valentine, of Robert and Sarah, b. Apr. 6, 1799.
24, Smith, Sarah, of Isaac and Deborah, b. Mch. 4, 1799.
24, Dickerson, Susanna, of Serratt and Eliz., b. July 27, 1799.
24, Smith, Nathan H., of Daniel and Anna, b. Sept. 29, 1798.
Nov. 5, Linthicum, Maryann Magruder, of John and Priscilla, b. Aug. 28, 1799.
10, Culp, Christiana, of George and Eleanor, b. May 10, 1799.

Nov. 10, Stiles, Horatio, of Thos. and Jane, b. July 9, 1799.
10, Perry, Priscilla Maria, of Erasmus and Eliz., b. July 23, 1799.
10, Shoals, Agatha, of Solomon Shoals and Ann Robinson, b. Feb. 1, 1799.
10, Oneale, Hannah, of Wm. Junr. and Eliz., b. July 16, 1799.
10, Glaze, Wm. Turner, of Wm. and Mary, b. May 30, 1799.
17, Roby, Nancy, of Zadok and Eleanor, b. Aug. 26, 1799.
17, Case, Eliz. of Israel and Margaret, b. Aug. 26, 1799.
21, Mackal, John Dawson, of John and Eliz., b. Oct. 29, 1799.
24, Cecil, Mary Maria Ramsay, of Wm. and Virlinder, b. Aug. 15, 1799.
Dec. 5, Watson, Ann, of James and Ann, b. May 31, 1799.
5, Dorsey, Mortimer, of Richard and Ann, b. Jan. 24, 1797.
5, Dorsey, Eliz. Ann, of Richard and Ann, b. May 24, 1798.
5, Dorsey, Caroline, of Richard and Ann, b. Dec. 3, 1799.

1800

Jan. 3, Plater, Thomas, of Wm. and Sarah, b. Sept. 23, 1799.
3, Nicholls, Keren Happuch Burgess, of Archibal and Sarah, b. July 12, 1799.
21, Roberts, Geo., of John and Eliz., b. June 13, 1799.
21, Riddle, Sophia Porter, of John and Susanna, b. —, 15, 1799.
Mch. 16, Redman, Sandy, of Wm. and Amelia, b. Sept. 9, 1799.
25, Ricketts, Margery, of Robert and Kezia, b. Feb. 18, 1800.
30, Collins, William, of James and Ann, b. Feb. 1, 1800.
30, Tucker, Sarah, of Levi and Susanna, b. Feb. 2, 1800.
Apr. 6, West, Roger Nellson, of Wm. and Ann, b. Nov. 2, 1799.
6, Swamley, Sarah, of Jacob and Eleanor, b. Oct. 21, 1799.
6, Fish, Francis, of Francis and Eliz., b. —, 1800.
10, Austin, Baruch Odle, of John and Cassandra, b. Nov. 17, 1799.
10, Austin, Enoch, of Zachariah and Margaret, b. Nov. 18, 1799.
13, Culp, Geo., of John and Ann, b. Mch. 8, 1799.
13, Fulks, Margaret, of Wm. and Mary, b. Oct. 8, 1799.
13, Thompson, Wm., of Clement and Sarah, b. Nov. 21, 1799.
13, Selby, Rebecca, of Thos. and Keziah, b. Feb. 28, 1800.
14, Dixon, Eliz. Moore, of James and Jane, b. Oct. 27, 1799.
14, Thompson, Anna, of Basil and Mary, b. Feb. 5, 1800.
14, Maddin, Wm. Davis, of Hezekiah and Anna, b. Oct. 12, 1799.
14, Deakins, Wm. Francis, of Leonard and Deborah, b. Dec. 11, 1799.
20, Drane, Anthony, of Anthony and Ann, b. Dec. 19, 1799.
20, Willson, Mehala, of Lancelot and Amelia, b. Aug. 4, 1799.
20, Davis, Thomas Truman Cecil, of James and Anna, b. Mch. 10, 1800.

Apr. 21, Osborn, Eliz., of Archibald and Eliz., b. Feb. 14, 1800.
27, Leach, Eliz. L., of Jesse and Mary, b. Feb. 15, 1800.
27, Hardy, Rachel T. B. T., of Henry and Frances, b. Oct. 6, 1799.
May 4, Pelly, John, of Benjn. and Ann, b. Mch. 31, 1799.
4, Carey, Benedick, of James and Lotty, b. Apr. 15, 1800.
June 2, Austin, Margaret, of Hezekiah and Eliz., b. Nov. 17, 1799.
2, Magruder, Eleanor, of Ninian and Eleanor, b. Dec. 14, 1799.
2, Connell, John, of Philip and Eliz., b. Jan. 10, 1800.
2, Swearengen, Elizabeth, of Elemelech and Eliz., b. Feb. 15, 1800.
15, Rawlins, Franklin, of John and Ann, b. Mch. 18, 1800.
15, Waters, Wm., of Basil and Ann, b. Dec. 28, 1799.
15, Buxton, Britania, of Brooke and Sally, b. Feb. 18, 1800.
15, Ward—"Children of John Ward and Mary his wife baptized 25 Jany. 1800, Viz:"
Eliz. Harriot Ward born 19 May 1777.
Susanna Ward born 4 Feby. 1780.
John Ward born 15 Mch. 1783.
Edward Ward born 27 Augt. 1785.
Daniel Morris Ward born 23 March 1788.
Ulisses Ward born 3 Apl. 1792.
22, Trundle, Sarah Shaw, of Thomas and Leah, b. Mch. 10, 1800.
22, Trundle, Thomas Wood, of Thomas and Leah, b. Mch. 10, 1800.
22, Willson, Margaret, of Nathaniel and Eliz., b. May 3, 1800.
22, Sparrow, Eliz., of Henry and Ann, b. Feb. 6, 1800.
22, Free, Harriot, of John and "Turicia," b. Apr. 22, 1800.
22, Moore, Juliet and Jason, of Barton and Priscilla, b. June 16, 1800.
29, Burress, Mary Prather, of Zadok and Ruth, b. Jan. 3, 1800.
29, Fray, Jerrard, of Joseph and Eliz., b. Nov. 26, 1799.
29, Wilcoxon, Jesse, of John and Ruth, b. Jan. 3, 1800.
29, Wilcoxon, Ely, of Thos. and Sarah, b. Feb. 15, 1800.
29, Higgins, Barbara Lyles, of Benj. and Matilda, b. Mch. 30, 1800.
29, Biggs, Eliz., "of Ninian Mitchel and Sarah Biggs," b. Sept. 10, 1798.
29, Burress, James, of Thos. and Virlinder, b. Feb. 2, 1800.
29, Lanham, Mary, of Hansy and Eleanor, b. Mch. 8, 1800.
29, Wilcoxon, Ursula, of Jesse and Ruth, b. May 2, 1800.
29, China, Eliza, of Shadrick and Sarah, b. Sept. 25, 1796.
29, China, "Caty," of Shadrick and Sarah, b. Feb. 22, 1799.
July 13, Selby, Eliz., of James and Sarah, b. Apr. 29, 1800.
13, Benton, James, of Wm. and Sarah, b. Apr. 2, 1800.
13, Ford, Eleanor, of John and Eliz., b. May 2, 1800.
17, Austin, Warren Burgess, of Thos. and Eliz., b. Mch. 7, 1800.

July 17, Morgan, Harriet Ridgway, of Richd. and Eleanor, b. Mch. 27, 1798.
17, Morgan, Aquila Ridgway Duval, of Richd. and Eleanor, b. June 14, 1800.
17, "MCoy," Thomas, of James and Eliz., b. Nov. 1799.
17, Steel, Wm., of Wm. and Mary, b. Nov. 28, 1799.
17, Cox, Caty Catroe, of Walter and Eliz., b. Mch. 25, 1800.
17, Crown, Saml., of Gerrard and Dolly, b. Mch. 13, 1800.
17, Higgins, Matilda, of John and Eliz., b. May 17, 1800.
17, Adams, Sally, of John and Eleanor, b. Mch. 7, 1800.
27, Fife, John, of John and Rebecca, b. May 12, 1800.
Aug. 3, Swan, Wm., of Henry and Lementer, b. May 18, 1800.
3, Brown, Sarah, of Nehemiah and Mary, b. July 1800.
3, Beall, Washington, of Robt. B. and Eliz., b. Mch. 1, 1800.
10, Speats, Benj. Allison, of Wm. and Priscilla, b. June 26, 1800.
10, Harry, George, of Richard and Rachel, b. June 15, 1800.
10, Mills, Benj., of Elias and Ann, b. June 12, 1800.
31, Willson, Wm. Murdock Beall, of Thos. and Rebecca, b. Apr. 17, 1800.
31, Groomes, Thos. Selby, of Richd. and Rosetta, b. May 6, 1800.
Sept. 7, Saffield, John Scager, of Charles and Sophia, b. Jan. 23, 1800.
7, Hartlove, Mary, of John and Eliz., b. Sept. 5, 1799.
7, Bryan, Ezekiel Orrick, of James and Ann, b. Aug. 16, 1799.
14, Talbot, Anna, of Charles and Mary, b. July 1800.
14, Ridgway, James, of James and Rebecca, b. June 4, 1800.
14, Osbourn, Harriot, of Leonard P. and Sarah, b. Feb. 12, 1800.
Oct. 9, Harbin, Wm., of Elias and Darcus, b. June 7, 1799.
31, Martin, Mary, of Honore and Sarah, b. July 23, 1799.
Nov. 2, Golden, Susanna, of Saml. and Sarah, b. Apr. 11, 1800.
2, West, Caroline, of Ignatius and Ann, b. Sept. 18, 1800.
2, Linch, Patrick, of Patrick and Eliz. b. June 21, 1800.
2, Swearingen, Levy, of Thos. and Eliz., b. July 8, 1800.
2, Bolton, John Bailey, of James and Abnea, b. Aug. 28, 1800.
2, Grymes, Mary Eleanor, of George and Eliz., b. Oct. 12, 1799.
2, Steel, Mary, of Joseph and Ann, b. Oct. 9, 1799.
2, Right, Jane, of John and Eliz. b. June 15, 1800.
2, Right, Lurana, of John and Eliz., b. June 15, 1800.
2, Hurley, Obed, of John and Eliz., b. Aug. 24, 1800.
9, Summers, Aletha, of Alexr. and Mary, b. Feb. 1, 1799.
9, Lord, Samuel, of Thos. and Rebecca, b. July 4, 1800.
9, Summers, Turesa, of Zadok and Ann, b. June 27, 1800.
9, Hempston, Nathaniel Thompson, of Wm. and Susanna, b. July 24, 1800.

Nov. 9, Windle, Wm., of Caleb and Martha, b. Sept. 7, 1800.
9, McEllwaine, Joseph, of John Sampson and Frances, b. July 4, 1800.
23, Hardy, Essea, of Baptist and Essea, b. Oct. 30, 1800.
23, Swearingen, Martha, of Obed and Rachel, b. Sept. 22, 1800.
23, James, Henry and Eliza, of James and Ann, b. Nov. 9, 1800.
27, Hardy, Eleanor, of Noah and Mary, b. July 25, 1800.
30, Robinson, Benj., of Benj. and Sarah, b. Oct. 11, 1800.
Dec. 7, Tracy, Thomas, of Philip and Mary, b. Aug. 12, 1800.
7, Lloyd, Samuel, of Saml. and Jane, b. Oct. 25, 1800.
7, Vermillion, Robert, of Wm. and Eliz., b. Sept. 4, 1800.
7, Ramsay, Eliz., of Wm. and Margaret, b. Nov. 7, 1800.
7, Welling, Nelly, of Amasa and Virlinder, b. July 2, 1800.
16, Porter, Caty Heiter, of Edwd. and Mary, b. Nov. 2, 1800.
16, Offutt, Rezin Ray (Roy?), of Saml. and Eliz., b. Sept. 2, 1800.
21, Chambers, Singleton, of John and Mary, b. May 23, 1800.
21, Traill, Wm. Tomson, of Osbourn and Frances, b. Sept. 7, 1800.
30, Gardner, James, of John and Cassandra, b. Sept. 24, 1800.

1801

Jan. 1, Lowry, James, of Wm. and Rebecca, b. June 20, 1800.
18, Collings, Thomas, of Zachariah and Darky, b. Nov. 2, 1800.
Feb. 5, Lodge, Caroline, of Wm. Junr. and Frances, b. June 27, 1800.
5, Porter, Washington, of Nathan and Pamelia, b. May 8, 1800.
8, Holmead, Geo., of Anthony and Sarah, b. Jan. 3, 1801.
8, Hughes, Harriot, of Henry and Rebecca, b. Dec. 3, 1800.
17, Offutt, Mordicai Burgess, of Baruch and Virlinder, b. Nov. 29, 1799.
17, Offutt, Wm. Magruder, of Baruch and Virlinder, b. Jan. 7, 1801.
17, Wade, Eliza, of John and Eliz., b. June 8, 1800.
24, Beckwith, "Oratio," of George and Lean, b. Jany. 18, 1801.
Mch. 1, Chamberlan, Matthias, of Josias and Susanna, b. Dec. 12, 1800.
1, Cecil, Maryann, of Thomas and Deborah, b. Dec. 7, 1800.
15, Stewart, Wm., of Wm. and Margaret, b. Oct. 27, 1800.
15, Linthicum, Ruth, of Thos. and Ann, b. Oct. 27, 1800.
22, Talbot, Thos., of Levin and Minna, b. Oct. 25, 1800.
22, Collins, Isaac, of Joshua and Mary, b. Jan. 25, 1801.
Apr. 5, Magruder, Rebecca, of James and Eliz., b. Dec. 26, 1800.
11, Gatton, Carleton Ray, of Thos. and Ruth, b. Jan. 24, 1801.
12, Godfrey, Francis Deakins, of Wm. and Eliz., b. Feb. 7, 1801.
May 3, Belt, Thos. Jefferson, of Benj. and Keziah, b. July 5, 1793.
3, Belt, Eliz., of Benj. and Keziah, b. May 30, 1796.
3, Lashly, Margaret, of John Jaquet and Eleanor, b. Sept. 25, 1800.

May 10, Prather, Washington Swearingen, of Baruch and Cassandra, b. Mch. 2, 1801.
10, Cool, Mary, of Christopher and Sarah, b. Jan. 17, 1801.
10, Greentree, Asa, of Benj. and Mary, b. Feb. 8, 1801.
10, Allison, Luraner, of John and Eliz., b. Dec. 4, 1800.
10, Willett, Carleton, of Edwd. and Eleanor, b. Jan. 12, 1801.
10, Smith, Gerrard, of Aquila and Eleanor, b. Dec. 18, 1800.
10, Allison, Christian, of Joshua and Priscilla, b. Oct. 29, 1800.
10, Soper, Luraner, of John and Rebecca, b. Feb. 21, 1801.
17, Rawlins, Harriot, of Thos. and Eliz., b. Feb. 2, 1801.
17, Jones, Sarah Tompson, of Nathan and Britania, b. Nov. 7, 1800.
24, Mullican, Basil, of Basil and Hannah, b. Feb. 21, 1800.
24, Martling, Geo. Wash., of Jas. (L?) and Mary, b. Apr. 9, 1801.
24, Waggoner, Kitty, of Jacob Dawson and Susanna Waggoner, b. Dec. 1800.
24, Williams, Nancy, of Zadok and Sally, b. Oct. 25, 1800.
24, Ball, Maryann, of Richd. and Eleanor, b. Mch. 25, 1801.
24, Barner, Trase Ann, of Greenburg and Joanna, b. Feb. 12, 1801.
31, Perry, Caroline, of Erasmus and Eliza, b. Jan. 23, 1801.
31, Pollard, Priscilla Johns, of Thos. and Rebecca, b. Dec. 24, 1800.
31, Garrot, Wm., of Thos. and Eliz., b. Mch. 11, 1801.
31, Oneal, Burgess Evins, of John and Mary, b. Dec. 26, 1800.
31, Griffith, Eliz. Ridgely, of Joshua and Eliz., b. Sept. 7, 1799.
31, Gaither, Maria, of Frederick and Jane, b. Feb. 27, 1801.
31, Carr, John, of Benj. and Priscilla, b. Sept. 20, 1800.
31, Gaither, Saml. Riggs, of Danl. and Henrietta, b. Jan. 2, 1800.
31, Gne (Gue?), Ruth, of Joseph and Anna, b. Jan. 5, 1800.
31, Dorsey, Anna, of Aquila and Nancy, b. Dec. 10, 1797.
31, Riggs, Saml., of Thos. and Mary, b. Aug. 20, 1800.
31, Gne (Gue?), Hezekiah, of Saml. and Rachel, b. Oct. 22, 1800.
31, Anderson, Mary, of David and Mary, b. Sept. 15, 1800.
31, Corcoran, Sarah, of Joshua and Sarah, b. May 15, 1799.
31, Summers, Samuel, of Paul and Sarah, b. Oct. 15, 1800.
31, Brown, John, of Jacob and Mary, b. Oct. 12, 1800.
31, Merich, Rachel Purnal, of Michael and Virlinder, b. Mch. 14, 1800.
31, Shekels, John, of John and Ruth, b. Oct. 4, 1800.
31, Griffith, Israel, of Samuel and Ruth, b. Aug. 17, 1799.
31, Griffith, Jefferson, of Samuel and Ruth, b. Mch. 16, 1801.
31, Dorsey, Richd. Stringer, of John and Eliz., b. Oct. 13, 1800.
June 14, Willson, Susanna Maria, of Lancelot and Rachel, b. Dec. 19, 1800.

June 14, Summers, Maryann, of John and Cloe, b. Feb. 5, 1801.
14, Johnson, Reubin, of Thos. and Darcus, b. Apr. 27, 1801.
14, Thompson, Mahala, of Thos. and Margaret, b. Mch. 18, 1801.
14, Castor, Vinson Warren, of Vinson and Hannah, b. Mch. 12, 1801.
14, Yost, Mary, of Philip and Melander, b. Feb. 20, 1801.
14, West, Henry, of Thos. and Eleanor, b. Mch. 29, 1801.
14, Hoskinson, Alfred, of Elisha and Rebecca, b. Jan. 9, 1801.
14, Lanham, Tabitha Wheat, of John and Lucy, b. Feb. 8, 1801.
14, Miers, Lawson, of Solomon and Charlotte, b. Aug. 20, 1800.
14, Mullican, John, of Walter and Eliza, b. Sept. 23, 1800.
14, Wright, Ann, of James and Eliz., b. Jan. 18, 1799.
14, Cecil, James, of Richard and Charlotte, b. Feb. 3, 1801.
July 5, Deblois, Lewis, of Lewis and Ruth Hooper Deblois, b. May 22, 1801.
5, Garey, Amos, of Everard and Ann, b. Feb. 22, 1801.
9, Davis, Frances Rebecca, of Ignatius and Margaret, b. Dec. 14, 1800.
12, Anderson, Alfred, of Richd. and Ann, b. Sept. 2, 1801.
12, Darnall, Eleanor, of Thos. and Henrietta, b. May 31, 1801.
12, Orme, Bennet Brooke, of Nathan and Polly, b. Jan. 13, 1801.
12, Thompson, Eliz. Bain, of Wm. and Patsy, b. Feb. 18, 1801.
12, Williams, John Hugh, of Walter and Christianna, b. Apr. 27, 1801.
12, Lee, Wm., of David and Anna, b. May 27, 1801.
12, Williams, Maria, of James and Jane, b. Apr. 23, 1801.
Aug. 2, Fisher, Barbara, of Wm. and Drucilla, b. Apr. 24, 1801.
2, Austin, Helen, of John and Cassandra, b. Feb. 26, 1801.
9, Stewart, Thos. Hanson, of James and Grace, b. Oct. 6, 1799.
9, Roberts, Mahala, of John and Eliz., b. Feb. 7, 1801.
23, Easton, Polly, of Augustine and Sally, b. Mch. 29, 1801.
30, Downes, Alfred, of Wm. and Cassandra, b. May 1, 1801.
30, Carey, John, of James and Charlotte, b. Apr. 28, 1801.
Sept. 5, Belt, William, of James and Eleanor, b. May 19, 1801.
5, Arnold, Cassandra, of Thos. and Mary, b. May 22, 1801.
5, Shaw, Harriot, of Rezin and Amma, b. July 2, 1801.
6, Meran, Susanna Edwards, of Wm. and Mary, b. Dec. 26, 1800.
13, Maddin, Zedekiah, of Hezekiah and Ammy, b. —, 1801.
20, Traill, Wm., of Wm. and Priscilla, b. July 7, 1801.
27, Beall, Robert Berry, of Robert B. and Eliz., b. June 10, 1801.
Oct. 10, Richards, Anna Maria, of Wm. and Tabitha, b. Aug. 16, 1801.
10, Osbourn, Wm. Thrasher, of Leonard and Sarah, b. Aug. 15, 1801.
10, Cooke, Zadok Magruder, of Nathan and Rachel, b. July 1, 1801.

Oct. 10, Summers, Reubin, of John L. and Anna Maria, b. Aug. 11, 1801.
10, Cahell (Carhell?), Geo., of James and Jane, b. Apr. 24, 1801.
10, Magruder, Anna Eleanora, of Geo. and Charity, b. July 7, 1801.
10, Bealmeer, Caroline, of Lewis and Eliz., b. —, 1801.
10, Beall, James Wash., of James and Mary, b. Aug. 11, 1801.
10, Parker, Anna, of Thos. and Mary, b. Mch. 3, 1801.
10, Page, Alexander, of Francis and Cassandra, b. Dec. 23, 1800.
10, Deakins, Leonard Marbury, of Leonard and Deborah, b. July 5, 1801.
10, Davis, John, of John and Ann, b. Sept. 18, 1801.
10, Janes, Masham, of Edwd. and Martha, b. July 21, 1801.
10, Moran, Wm., of Peregrine and Eleanor, b. Oct. 3, 1801.
27, Belt, Sarah Ann, of Cartlon and Eliz., b. June 3, 1801.
Nov. 1, Nicholls, Wm. Mackay, of Thos. and Priscilla, b. Jan. 28, 1801.
15, West, Maria, of Wm. and Ann, b. Aug. 10, 1801.
15, Henderson, Richd., of John and Lydia, b. July 3, 1801.
15, Grainger, Wm., of Jonathan and Ann, b. Aug. 9, 1801.
15, Maddin, Eliza, of Benj. and Eliz., b. May 15, 1801.
15, Anderson, Harriot, of John and Mary, b. May 4, 1801.
15, Wilcoxon, Ruth, of Thos. H. and Sarah, b. July 31, 1801.
15, "MCoy," Turner, of James and Eliz., b. May 2, 1801.
15, Beall, Edward Brooke, of Upton and Matilda, b. Mch. 19, 1801.
Dec. 16, Walker, James Warren, of Elisha and Sarah, b. Sept. 30, 1799.
16, Shekells, Susanna, of John and Ruth, b. Oct. 19, 1798.
16, Cecil, Sabret Henry Willson, of Wm. and Virlinder, b. Sept. 27, 1801.
16, Thompson, Eliza, of Richd. and Eliz. b. May 28, 1801.

Record of Marriages and Funerals—Rev. Thomas Read, 1796–1808*

"One of the most historical of the early parishes is *Prince George*, commonly known as *Rock Creek Parish.* It was erected in 1726, and embraced within its limits all the territory lying between the Potomac and Patuxent Rivers, and the eastern branch and a line drawn from thence to the Patuxent and extending westward to the westerly bounds of the Province; thus including not only a part of the District of Columbia, but Georgetown and all the Counties of Western Maryland; and from it all the parishes now within that domain were originally carved, or are the result of subdivisions."

"The first Rector of the parish was the *Rev. George Murdock*, who was commissioned by Gov. Charles Calvert, in Dec., 1726, and who officiated for thirty-four years, and until his death, in 1761. He was followed by *Rev. Alexander Williamson*, who served fourteen years, and was succeeded by the *Rev. Thomas Read*, who had previously been Curate of the parish, and also Rector of St. Anne's, Annapolis. He was inducted in 1777, and continued to be Rector of the parish thirty-four years, when he resigned. During Mr. Read's pastorate of Rock Creek Parish, he kept a record of the marriages performed by him within the parish, and as well also a necrology covering the same period. A part of this record has been preserved—from 1796 to 1808 inclusive. After the death of Mr. Read it came into possession of his son, the late Robert Read, of Cumberland, after whose demise it was presented by his widow, Sarah Johns Read [through James Walter Thomas] to the Md. Hist. Soc. This old record is singularly valuable, not only because of the large area covered by the parish, embracing, even at that date, nearly the whole of Montgomery County, but more especially by reason of the fact that the Montgomery records do not begin until 1798, and the necrology of the County being exceedingly meagre and limited. —— this marriage record is somewhat more comprehensive than the Montgomery records even after the latter were started, as it is not confined to marriges performed by license issued in that county, as are its records."

* Quoted from "*Chronicles of Colonial Maryland; Thomas*, pp. 208–217." The source of the marriage and funeral record of Rev. Thos. Read is the original volume from which Mr. Richard Henry Spencer, Cor. Secy. Md. Historical Society, kindly caused the entire records to be transcribed and compared.

Marriages—Montgomery County, 1796.*

Jan. 12, Buxton, John to Macoy, Eleanor.
Feb. 2, Roby, Theophilus to Willett, Ann.
9, Stewart, James to Clarke, Grace.
11, Medcalf, Edw. to Butt, Cloe.
18, Bowman, George to Howse, Sarah.
22, Dorsey, Richd. to Wayman, Anne.
28, Cordingly, Wm. Welsh to Moore, Ann.
Mar. 3, Campbell, Jno. to Cratton, Polly.
6, Thompson, Rich. to Pelly, Eliz.
10, Nicholson, Jeremiah to Nicholson, Hester.
22, Wilcoxen, Jesse to Wilcoxen, Ruth.
24, Moody, Thomas to Berry, Mary.
28, Henry Jones' Geo. to Charles Jones' Polly (Negroes).
Apr. 21, Wilson, Wm. to White, Anne.
21, Davis, Thomas to Worthington, Catherine.
May 15, Mr. Crabb's James and Clary (Negroes).
15, Mrs. Johns' Jerry and Mollie (Negroes).
June 16, Lane, Rev. Nicholas to Selby, Esther.
17, Sparrow, Jonathan to Smith, Priscilla.
July 24, Groom, Wm. to Kelly, Maryann.
Aug. 2, Williams, Walter C. to Heugh, Christiana.
15, Downes, Richd. to Rose, Eliz.
30, Nicholls, Benj. to Culver, Drusilla.
Sept. 22, Lowry, William to Groome, Rebecca.
18, Lowe, Henry to Macbee, Ann.
27, Windel, Caleb to Parker, Martha.
Nov. 17, Riggs, Thomas to Riggs, Mary.
24, Buxton, Thomas to Macbeey, Fanney.
Dec. 1, Riddle, Jno. to Porter, Susanna.
8, Ray, James to Warfield, Eliz.
15, Austin, Hezekiah to Odle, Eliz.
22, Fish, Robert to Jeans, Eliz.
25, Leach, John to Bowmen, Rachel.
29, Hardey, Henry to West, Frances.
1797
Jan. 17, Mudd, Andrew to Green, Eleanor.
17, Lodge, William O. to Porter, Frances.

* *Chronicles of Colonial Maryland;* Thomas, pp. 208–217, compared with originals owned by Md. Hist. Soc.

Jan. 4, Roberts, Jno. to Heater, Eliz.
26, Dorsey, Lloyd to Green, Anna.
31, Riggs, Erasmus to Wilcoxen, Eleanor.
Feb. 5, Denoon, Ely to Sanders, Henny.
9, McCoy, James to Brown, Eliz.
21, Higgins, Clark to Thomas, Margaret.
26, Ridgeway, James to Hurdle, Rebecca.
28, Minstalled, Nicholas to Allison, Mary.
28, Warfield, Beale to Ridgely, Amelia.
Apr. 17, Fuburiere, Nicholas to Tucker, Susan.
18, Warfield, Brice to Collins, Sarah.
20, Allison, Jno. B. to Higgins, Eliz.
May 4, Fields, Jno. to Madden, Mary.
21, Wight, Jno. to Boyd, Cary.
28, Hurley, Jno. to Benton, Eliz.
June 1, Ricketts, Robt. to Ricketts, Kezia.
July 20, Ricketts, Zadoc to Groome Ann.
Aug. 3, Higgins, James to Wilcoxen, Virlinda.
5, Sullivan, Sylvester to Hawse, Rosanna.
8, Lyon, Samuel to Davis, Linny.
Sept. 14, Bean, Richd. to Kelly, Prudence.
Oct. 14, Reeder, Benj. to Hungerford, Anne.
26, Benson, William to Hensley, Rachel.
Nov. 23, Archey, Edw. to Allison, Eliz.
Dec. 21, Merriweather, Nicholas to Hood, Eliz.
26, Gardner, John to Dowden, Cassandra.

1798

Jan. 4, Higgins Jno. to Fisher, Eliz.
9, Culver, Henry to Patterson, Mary.
11, Bird, Charles to Barton, Margaret.
16, Wellin, Amasa to Trundle, Linney.
25, Hutchison Francis to Ball, Sarah.
25, Trundle, Evan to Key, Anna.
Feb. 6, Love, Saml. to Jones, Sarah.
13, Snowden, Richd. to Warfield, Eliza.
24, Davis, Benj. to Thrasher, Eliz.
Apr. 1, Coal, Christopher A. to Claton, Sarah.
9, David Crafford's Edward and Linny (Negroes).
May 3, Wilcoxon, Thos. H. to Prather, Sarah.
22, Davis, Ignatius to Wooten, Margaret.
Sept. 11, Scott, Amos to West, Annoe.
Oct. 7, Cash, Dawson to Beens, Jemima.

Oct. 12, Summers, Benjamin to Beckwith, Virlinder.
15, O'Neal, David to Lane, Rebecca.
30, Willoson, Robt. to Shekells, Eleanor.
Nov. 15, Wells, Nathan to Duley, Sophia.
Dec. 8, Crecraft, Benj. to Prather, Nelly.
18, Cox, Jno. M. to Gray, Eleanor.
20, Ward, Geo. to Redman, Ann.
23, Cox, Wm. to Kelly, Liley.
30, Camobell, John to Oden, Priscilla.

1799

Jan. 3, Davis, Charles to Howse, Laurady.
3, Penn, Roby to Howse, Lucreta.
10, Turner, Richd. to Beall, Eliz.
10, Carroll, Daniel to Maccubbin, Ann.
19, Swavaley, Jacob to Fulks, Eleanor.
22, Adams, John to Collyer, Eleanor.
22, Gratton, Thomas to Ray, Ruth.
24, Jones, Charles Offutt to Offutt, Rebecca.
26, Thompson, Benjamin to Haney, Eliz.
27, Parnnion, Henry to Sanders, Eliz.*
Feb. 5, Groomes, James to King, Sarah.
14, Garrott, Thos. and Fee, Elizabeth.
15, Austin, John and Odle, Cassandra.
26, Ofutt, Barak and Offutt, Virlinder.
Mch. 14, Crafford, James B. and Allison, Ann.
19, Waters, Basil and Magruder, Ann P.
Apr. 11, Nicholson, John and Oden, Tabitha.
18, Leatch, Jesse and Letten, Mary.
May 23, Riggs, Edmund to Willson, Jane.
Aug. 8, Pelly, Solomon and Holland, Massy.
29, Kirkman, Jacob and Hall, Susanna.
Nov. 9, Magruder, Jno. and Linthicum, Mary.
24, Frey, Jno. and Lucas, Turecia.
Dec. 5, Hood, Thos. and Wayman, Rachel.
10, Magruder, James and Linthicum, Eliz.
Nov. 30, Parsley, Jonas and Clayton, Eleanor.

* "License, Ann Arundel granted."

"Mr. Wm. H. Talbott is correct in his opinion that the words "License Granted—Anne Arundel County" [Chronicles of Colonial Md., Thomas, 1913, p. 212] were intended to be and should have been printed as a footnote to the Parnnion-Sanders marriage, and not as a caption to those marriages which follow. This footnote occurs at the bottom of p. 5, in the original entry made by Rev. Thomas Read in the following words: 'License, Ann Arundel granted.' Richard H. Spencer, Cor. Secy. Md. Hist. Soc."

Dec. 12, Prather, Baruck and Swearingen, Casandra.
19, Perry, Jno. and Alnutt, Jane.
26, Stewart, Richd. and Renneton, Eliz.

1800

Jan. 2, Ramsey, William and Herren, Margaret.
14, Lanham, Jno. and Ray, Lucy.
16, Riley, Camden and Ray, Anna.
21, Jones, Nathan and Buxton, Anna.
21, Porter, Edward and Heiter, Hary.
21, Orme, Nathan and Beall, Polly.
23, Holland, Solomon and Galton, Margaret.
25, Redman, Jno. and Ward, Harriot.
30, Beckwith, Benedict and White, Eliz.
Apr. 15, Harper, Edw. and Boswell, Sarah Ann.
15, Nicholls, Thos. and Mackey, Priscilla.
May 22, Merrick, Michael and Bowman, Virlinder.
22, Gary, Everrard and Cloud, Ann.
June 26, Riggs, John H. and Howard, Rebecca.
July 17, Offutt, Thos. Odle and Benton, Charity.
Nov. 18, Orme, Doct. Richd. J. and Crabb, Ann.
20, Daniel, Elias M. and Golden, Margaret.
27, Inlose, Samuel and Stone, Eliz.
Dec. 4, Williams, Edwd. O. and Clagett, Eliz.
16, Porter, David and Ray, Mary.
20, Reintzel, Daniel and Robertson, Ann.
23, Lashley, Arnold and Lee, Eliz.
25, Lanham, Notley and Hopkins, Eliz.
25, Kelley, Benj. and Moore, Eliz.
28, Wallace, William and Brookes, Margaret.
30, Mullican, W^{m}. and Dowden, Eliz.

1801

Feb. 1, Moore, Nathan and Hantz, Eliz.
10, Johns, Leonard H. and Williams, Margaret.
17, Clagett, David and Odle, Salley.
24, Fish, Hatton and Benton, Sarah.
27, Easton, Levin and Ricketts, Druzilla.
Mch. 3, Davis, Leonard Young and Worthington, Achsah.
12, Magruder, Samuel and Hawkins, Eliz.
31, Magruder, Geo. and Turner, Anna.
Apr. 5, Wiest, Jno. and Shuck, Lydia.
14, Getty, John and Carey, Eleanor.
May 24, Langford, Richd. and Soper, Amelia.

July 9, Beall, Lewis and Wootton, Eliza.
Oct. 8, Garrett, William and Higgins, Eleanor.
8, Walker, Willson and Prather, Deborah.
8, Selby, Brice and Marker, Cathrine.
25, Bean, Josiah and Wilson, Eleanor.
27, Linthicum, Ezekiah and Hickman, Mary.
Nov. 19, Madden, Joseph and Sparrow, Susanna.
Dec. 1, Linthicum, Fredrick and Macklefresh, Rachel.
8, Dickerson, Nathan and Turnbull, Margaret.
10, Owings, Jesse and Hood, Hannah.
17, Orr, William and Macklewain, Eliz.
22, Trail, Nathan and Buxton, Susanna.
22, Heater, George and Porter, Charlotte.
31, Jones, Wm. R. and Richardson, Eliz. L.
31, Fowler, Henry to Lewis Beall's Mulatto Woman Nelly.

1802

Jan. 7, Jones, Benj. W. and Willson, Margaret.
12, Holt, Lawrence O. and Oden, Sarah.
12, Clagett, Thos. and Offutt, Rachel.
21, Davis, Thos. and Bowie, Eliza.
28, Northcraft, James and Fryer, Rachel.
30, Cooke, James and Beeding, Patsey.
Feb. 9, Harriss, Barton and Griffith, Mary.
Mch. 21, Sparrow, Wm. and Campbell, Eliza.
Apr. 20, Offutt, Andrew and Warfield, Eliz.
Aug. 3, Astlin, Joseph and Beard, Mary.
Sept. 2, Madden, Walter and Mudd, Eliz.
12, Groome, James and Fish, Eleanor.
21, Cox, Joseph and Hogan, Susanna.
Nov. 9, Read, Dr. Jno. M. and Clark, Maryann.
25, Bealmear, Saml. and Williams, Priscilla.
Dec. 7, Buxton, George and Trail, Maryann.
14, Kindle, Azariah and Nicholson, Amelia.
21, Elfresh, Wm. M. [McElfresh?] and Linthicum, Sarah.
30, Klay, Adam and Summers, Sabina.

1803

Jan. 18, Riggs, Geo. W. and Robertson, Eliza.
20, Brown, James and Leek, Ann.
Mch. 10, Jarvis, James and Linch, Eliz.
31, Summers, Archibald and Pain, Margaret.
Apr. 10, Porter, Charles and Fry, Polly.
May 5, Browning, Jeremiah and Summers, Eliz.

June 19, Forsythe, Isaac and Letton, Anna.
28, Candler, William and Ray, Rebecca.
Aug. 7, Magruder, Edward and Ayton Jane.
28, Lyon, Benjamine and Davis, Rachel.
Sept. 11, Smith, Richd. Brooke and Letton, Sarah.
15, Haney, Nicholas, and Golden, Sarah.
22, Letton, Brice and Moore, Hariot.
Oct. 20, Elville, Elias and Burress, Elizabeth.
27, Linsted, Thos. and Summers, Anna Maria.
Nov. 1, Linthicum, Zachariah and Clagett, Ann.
3, Magruder, Warren and Holmes, Harriott.
17, Hammon, Lloyd and Merriweather, Elizabeth.
24, Hilleary, Thos. and Wheeler, Sarah.
Dec. 1, Crown, John and Ball, Eliz.
29, Trail, Ashford and Sanders, Anne.
31, Butt, Hazil and Richards, Sarah.
1804
Jan. 5, Beall, James Alex. and Culver, Eleanor.
Feb. 2, Perry, Benj. and Magruder, Eliz.
11, Ketchen, Joel and Hurst, Sarah.
12, Horner, Samuel and McFarland, Mary.
16, Burditt, William and Fitzgerald, Ruth.
Mch. 27, Dorsey, Joshua W. and Plummer, Lucetta.
Apr. 8, Moore, Peter Dent and Stanger, Louisa.
May 6, O'Neal, William and Bell, Anna.
June 9, Wheatley, Wm. and Cashell, Mary.
17, Cashell, George and Edmonstone, Eliz. B.
19, Rawlings, James and Richardson, Sarah.
Sept. 6, Golden, Saml. and Haney, Dollie.
6, Clagett, Ninian and Burgess, Margret.
8, Saffell, Hezekiah and Davis, Lydia.
25, Muncaster, Zachariah and Magruder, Harriott.
Nov. 29, Bailey, Walter and Ball, Sarah.
Dec. 7, Wade, Jesse and Fleming, Mary.
20, Gatton, Aquila and Owen, Mary.
23, Garlon, Philip and Willson, Sarah.
1805
Jan. 8, Langville, Wm. and Current, Naney.
31, Sparrow, Thos. and Sparrow, Sarah.
Feb. 12, Riggs, Reubin and Thomas, Mary.
27, Shook, Charles and Ball, Priscilla.
Apr. 18, Leemar, William and Roberson, Sarah.

Apr. 23, Mullican, Archibald and Mathews, Anna.
25, Summers, Walter and Swearingen, Sarah.
30, Gray, Abishai and Miller, Eleanor.
May 9, Windsor, Robert and Thompson, Eliz.
June 6, Rabbett, Henry and Wilburn, Anne.
Oct. 15, Waters, Azel and Williams, Cassandra.
Dec. 29, Beall, James and Benson, Margaret Smith.
1806
Jan. 2, Deselem, James and Fulks, Catherine.
Feb. 4, Perry, Elbert and Magruder, Rebecca.
11, Robertson, Daniel and Greenfield, Sarah.
13, Heater, Jno. and Shook, Frances.
Mch. 4, Porter, Denton and Heater, Kitty.
Apr. 3, Gettings, Thos. and Perry, Christiana.
May 13, Warfield, Dr. Peregrine and Sappington, Harriot.
June 17, Wootton, Dr. John and Magruder, Betsy Lynn.
Aug. 28, O'Neal, Lawrence and Galworth, Nancy.
Sept. 18, Dickerson, John and Turnbull, Eliz.
Dec. 4, Davis, Thos. S. and Swearingen, Creece.
25, Williams, Jno. and Neritt, Sarah.
1807
Jan. 1, Miller, Jacob and Ricketts, Naney.
13, Ward, John Wesley to Greentree, Eleanor.
Feb. 26, Case, James and Bowman, Eliz.
Mch. 5, Ray, George and Robertson, Sarah.
8, Grymer, Benj. and Lowery, Sarah.
26, Howard, Thos. W. and Crabb, Elizabeth.
June 16, Dorsey, Henry Woodward and Cooke, Rachel.
Oct. 13, Gassaway, Henry and Griffith, Rachel.
20, Sedgwick, Benj. and White, Eleanor.
Nov. 12, Wilson, Wm. Elson and Swearingen, Eleanor.
Dec. 1, Hammelton, David and Preston, Ann.
1808
Jan. 3, Hurley, John to Offutt, Milly.
Feb. 11, Jenkins, John to Sparrow, Charlotte.
Apr. 18, Golding, Daniel and Harris, Eliz.
June 5, Edmonson, Hosea and Orme, Mary.
Oct. 8, Warfield, Allen and Dugan, Mary.
Dec. 27, Fish, Wm. and Joy, Hellen.
1809
Jan. 12, Stewart, Walter and Gray, Eleanor.
Feb. 12, Gittings, Joseph and Beans, Tabitha.

Funerals—Montgomery County, 1796 *

			£	s	d
Jan[ry].	14.	Eliz. Welch	5	5	0
	16.	Susanna Allison	2	5	0
	28.	Mrs. Wilcoxen of Jn°. [Senr.]	2	5	0
Feb.	9.	Thomas Johnson	1	17	6
	11.	Mrs. Anderson	3	0	0
Mar.	31.	James Brown	1	17	6
May	12.	Eliz. Butt	2	5	0
	19.	Jn°. Oden	2	—	—
June	14.	Andrew Heugh	2	5	0
July	12.	Zadok Clagett	2	5	0
Aug.	23.	William West	2	5	0
Sept.	1.	Catherine Heiter	2	5	0
	6.	M[rs]. Cecil of James	2	5	0
	11.	Wilford Cusick	—	—	—
	11.	Thomas Johnson	—	—	—
	27.	Walter Worthington's child	2	0	10
Oct.	8.	M[rs]. Macneugh of Basil	2	5	—
Nov.	1.	Mrs. Darby of Sam[l].	2	5	—
Nov.	3.	Sarah Linthicum of Zach[h].	2	5	0
	15.	Charity Fortnar	2	6	6
	29.	Eliz. Tucker	2	5	—
Dec.	3.	Polly Mackneugh of Basil	2	5	—
	13.	Mary Windsor	—	—	—

Funerals, 1797

March	12.	Mrs. Garey	1	10	—
	30.	Cassandra Magruder	—	—	—
April	18.	Cloe Pointer	1	10	—
May	4.	Jn°. Prather	2	5	—
June	5.	Mrs. Howard of Leonard	3	15	0
	6.	M[r]. Beans, son of Josiah Beans	1	10	0
	6.	Norman Beall & Sister	2	5	0
July	15.	W[m]. Worthington of W[m].	1	17	6
	18.	A child of Baptist Hardy's	1	2	6

* These consecutive records are thus given, although in many instances the deaths appear in the alphabetically arranged data, as given in another record. The £–s–d entries doubtless refer to the sums given to the Rector and to the sexton.

			£	s	d
Aug.	2.	M^{rs}. ONeal of David	2	5	—
	28.	M^{r}. Beans, P. George's	2	5	—
Oct.	5.	Joseph Perry	3	—	—
	19.	Mrs. Redman of Joseph	2	5	—
Nov.	9.	Vernecia & Margaret Spurrier	1	17	6
Dec.	12.	A Son & Daughter of Saml. Offutt's	2	5	—
	23.	Sarah Beall of Rich^{d}	2	5	—
			31	17	6

Funerals, 1798

			£	s	d
Jan^{ry}.	6.	Ann Ricketts of Capt. Benjamin	2	5	0
	17.	M^{rs}. Sprigg at M^{r}. Wootton's	2	5	0
Mar.	5.	Col. William Deakins	4	10	—
	8.	Charles Jones, Clean Drinking	—	—	—
March	18.	Mrs. Thompson	9	0	—
	23.	Elisha Allison	2	5	0
April	10.	Samuel White, Senr.	2	5	—
	18.	Linny Beckwith	2	5	—
May	15.	Robert Briscoe	2	5	—
	24.	Nathaniel Magruder	2	5	—
	29.	Anna Collins	—	—	—
June	14.	Richard Stevens	—	—	—
July	7.	Virlinder Higgins, wife of James Junr.	1	17	6
	17.	Lucy Whebber	2	5	—
Aug.	7.	Ann Willson, wife of W^{m}.	2	0	3½
	9.	M^{rs}. Waters of Nathan	2	11	9
Oct.	11.	Benj. Machael's Son	2	5	—
	15.	Shadrick Beall's Son	2	5	—
Nov.	22.	M^{rs}. Bulger	2	0	3
			26	9	9½
			9		
			35	9	9½

Funerals, 1799

			£	s	d
Feb^{y}.	12.	John Hawkins	2	5	0
March	16.	Sarah Groome, wife of Ja^{s}. Groome	2	5	0
May	2.	James Traill Senr.	2	1	3
	5.	Charles Beckwith	—	—	—
	14.	Mrs. Perry Mother of Erasmus	2	5	—

			£	s	d
May	16.	Catherine Luell [Tuell?]	—	—	—
June	30.	Mrs. Lowe	2	12	6
July	3.	Jno. Swamly	2	5	—
			13	11	9
July	5.	Susanna Anderson, a child of Col. Anderson	—	—	—
Aug.	6.	Wm. Lowry & Zadok Case	—	—	—
	11.	Matilda Duncanson & Saml. Lenman	—	—	—
	22.	Mrs. Fletcher of Thos.	3	15	0
	27.	Mrs. Traill of Jas., Senr.	2	5	—
Sept.	5.	Wm. Stewart's child	—	—	—
	30.	Jno. Wilcoxin	2	5	—
Oct.	1.	Mrs. Magruder of Edward	2	5	—
Oct.	21.	Adam Vigal	—	—	—
	24.	Sarah Holland, wife of Arnold	2	5	0
Nov.	21.	Mrs. Machael, wife of Benj., St. Pet.	2	5	0
Dec.	18.	Mrs. Briscoe, wife of Robt.	2	5	—
	26.	Daniel Richards, son of Jacob	2	5	—
			19	10	—
			13	13	9
			33	3	9

Funerals, 1800

March	16.	Horatio Thompson, son of William	—	—	—
	30.	David Smith, R. C. Ch.	—	—	—
April	8.	Mrs. Smith	2	0	0
	10.	Hanah Elder	2	0	3½
	15.	Mrs. Beall of Basil	1	2	6
	17.	Wm. Collyar, St. Peter's	3	15	0
	21.	Joseph Crown	—	15	—
	24.	Mrs. Oden	1	17	6
May	8.	Sarah Gatton	2	0	6
			13	10	9
May	26.	Mrs. Howlt of Lawrence, O.	2	5	0
June	4.	Polly Bowie	2	5	0
Aug.	28.	Eleanor Magruder, daughter of Allen of Ninian	2	5	—
Sept.	7.	Rebecca Fife, wife of James Fife	1	10	—
	11.	Sarah Dorsey of Thos. Beale Dorsey	3	—	—

			£	s	d
Oct.	9.	Sarah Willson, Sister of Robt., St. Peter's...	2	5	—
	23.	Mrs. Bealmear of Saml..................	2	5	—
	23.	Samuel Clagett, who died Oct. 21st..........	2	5	—
	31.	Mrs. Sarah Heugh, who died 29th. Oct......	2	9	6
Nov.	8.	Anna Jones, wife of Benj., died Nov. 7.....	2	5	—
	16.	Jno. & Michael Crager, children of Michael Crager..............................	—	—	—
	22.	Wm. Deakins, died 20 Nov., aged 81.......	3	—	—
Dec.	6.	Ninian Magruder's Frank..................	2	5	—
	11.	Ruth Watkins, wife of Gassaway..........	3	15	—
	26.	William Thresher..........................	1	10	—
			33	4	6
			13	10	9
			46	15	3

Funerals, 1801

			£	s	d
Janry.	27.	Mr. Littlemore..........................	1	8	0
Febry.	5.	Mrs. Porter.............................	2	5	—
	9.	Mary Osbourn...........................	1	10	—
Mar.	31.	Richd. Bowie, son of Allen................	2	5	—
April	6.	Mrs. Sarah Collyar.......................	2	5	0
May	26.	George Ward's wife.......................	2	5	—
			11	18	—
May	27.	John Evely..............................	2	5	0
Oct.	17.	James Cecil.............................	2	5	—
	25.	Genl. Thos. B. Beall......................	2	1	3
Nov.	18.	A Child of Jacob Swamley's, Eleanor......	—	—	—
Dec.	5.	Mrs. Ruth Glaze.........................	2	5	—
	16.	Sarah Walker, wife of Elisha..............	2	5	—
	26.	Levin Magruder..........................	2	5	—
			13	6	3
			11	18	
			25	4	3

Funerals, 1802

			£	s	d
Janry.	5.	Solomon Holland's Child..................	2	5	0
	28.	Virlinder Williams........................	2	5	—
Feb.	2.	Nathan Clagett...........................	2	5	—

			£	s	d
March	11.	Aaron Gartrell	3	—	—
	30.	Susanna Ward	—	—	—
April	20.	Mrs. Howard at J. Lewis	2	5	—
June	8.	Mrs. Baily of Leonard at J. Lewis	—	10	—
	11.	Polly Wootton	1	17	6
	14.	Robt. Fish, Senr.	—	—	—
	17.	Mrs. Beckwith of Charles	2	5	0
	17.	John L. Summers	2	5	0
	25.	Caroline Bealmear, daur. of Lewis	—	—	—
			19	17	6
July	4.	Thos. Darnall's & Basil Thompson's Children	—	—	—
Oct.	16.	Mrs. Welch of Richd.	2	12	6
	22.	George Cashly	2	5	0
	29.	Mrs. Clagett of Richd.	2	5	0
Nov.	2.	Mrs. Wilson of Lancelot	2	5	—
	4.	Mrs. Northcraft of James	2	5	—
	18.	Mrs. Summers, wife of Dent Summers	2	5	—
	25.	Harrison Pelly	2	5	—
	30.	Daniel Veirs Jr.	3	—	—
			19	2	6
			19	17	6
			39	0	0

Funerals, 1803

			£	s	d
Janry.	25.	Joshua Owen	2	5	0
Mar.	3.	Edward Penn	2	5	0
	5.	Samuel Jones	4	2	6
	17.	Mrs. Crow	2	12	6
April	2.	Mrs. Dorsey of Henry W.	3	—	—
	12.	A child of Jacob Swamley's	—	—	—
	16.	Jno. Dent	3	7	6
	24.	Miss Pollard, Virginia	7	10	—
May	22.	Allen Bowie	3	—	—
June	1.	Mrs. Sarah Griffith	3	—	—
	28.	Thos. Nicholls	2	5	—
July	3.	Nancy Linthicum	2	5	0
	5.	Philip Cecil	3	—	—
	17.	George Heater's Child	2	5	—
	28.	Mr. Swain at Doctr. Warfield's	3	—	—
Aug.	11.	James Cooke	—	—	—
			43	17	6

			£	s	d
	31.	Thos. Kelly, Sen[r].	2	5	0
Sept.	10.	James Pierce	2	5	—
Nov.	17.	Philip Jenkins	2	5	0
Dec.	8.	Mrs. Dorsey, Mother of Col. Rich[d]. Dorsey	7	10	—
	16.	Nathaniel Magruder	2	5	—
			16	10	—
			43	17	6
			60	7	6

Funerals, 1804

			£	s	d
May	22.	Mrs. Price	1	2	6
	27.	Alex[r]. Mason	2	5	—
June	5.	James Rawlings	3	15	—
July	5.	Lewis Alexander Pichon, son of the French Embassador	2	5	—
Aug.	24.	Margaret Davis, wife of Ignatius	2	5	—
Oct.	11.	Eleanor Riggs, Daughter of Sam[l].	3	—	—
	14.	John Holsey	1	2	6
	24.	Cassandra Gatton	2	1	3
Dec.	18.	Mrs. Magruder, Mother of Jn[o]. Bowie, Maj.	2	5	—
			20	1	3

Funerals, 1805

			£	s	d
March	21.	Thos. Clagett, son of Jn[o].	2	5	0
April	15.	Mrs. Selby of Thomas	—	—	—
	26.	Ninian Magruder, Died 25 Ap[l].	2	5	0
May	12.	Joseph Tucker, R. C. Ch.	4	10	0
	16.	Mrs. Ricketts at Rich[d]. Rickett's	—	—	—
		Mrs. Trundle, June 3, 1805, wife Tho[s]., Sen[r].	2	5	0
		Kelem Gray, June 20, 1805	2	5	0
		A. Child of Glzendanna's, July 25	2	5	0
		Mrs. Harper of Edward, Aug[t]. 19	2	5	0
		Rich[d]. Lurner, Oct. 4th	2	5	—
		Nathan Cooke, Oct. 9	2	5	—
		D[r]. Jeffery Magruder, Oct. 31, 1805	2	4	2
		Elias M[c]Daniel, Dec[r]. 21, 1805	—	—	—
		A Daughter of Benj. Gray's, Dec[r]. 26, 1805	—	—	—
			15	14	2
			4	10	—
			20	4	2

Funerals, 1806

			£	s	d
Feb^{ry}.	11.	Benjamin Becraft	2	5	0
Mar.	6.	Eliz. Magruder, wife of James	2	5	0
	16.	Hugh Riley, died 14th. March	2	5	0
	21.	Zachariah Gatton, died 19th. March	2	5	0
April	12.	Ruth Suter	2	5	0
June	3.	Charles Greenfield	—	—	—
	10.	Mrs. Gray of Benjamin	—	—	—
July	30.	Jno. Wightt, died 29 July	2	5	0
Aug.	12.	Ann Linthicum, wife of Zech^{h}.	2	5	—
	21.	Mrs. Browning at Paul Summers	2	5	—
	26.	Francis Gartrell	2	5	—
Sept.	10.	William Magruder, son of Saml. B.	2	5	—
Oct.	23.	W^{m}., Nancy & Nelly Jones	2	5	—
	27.	Hezekiah Magruder	2	17	9
Dec.	17.	Eleanor Riley	2	5	—
	27.	Rebecca Magruder, wife of Saml. B.	1	17	6
			31	15	2

Funerals, 1807

			£	s	d
March	30.	Rachel Gue	2	5	0
April	6.	James Norrod	2	5	—
	14.	Henry Brookes, died 4 Ap^{l}., 79 years old	2	12	6
	27.	John Suter, son of James	2	5	—
June	25.	John Busey, Senr.	2	5	0
July	2.	Zadok Robey, a child of Zadok	—	—	—
	9.	Mrs. Middleton, wife of Saml.	2	5	0
	21.	Rich^{d}. Ball	—	—	—
Aug.	15.	Jno. Cooke, son of Nathan	2	5	0
	26.	Elijah Collins	—	—	—
Oct.	22.	Priscilla Fish, wife of Robt., died 3 Oct.	2	5	—
Nov.	15.	Barbara Boyd, without sermon	—	—	—
	19.	Mareen Duvall	3	—	—
Dec.	3.	William Richards	—	—	—
		Funl.	21	7	6
		Mar.	26	12	6
			48	0	0

Funerals, 1808

			£	s	d
Febry.	2.	Kitty Gatton	2	5	—
March	24.	Wm. Dennis & wife	3	15	—
	25.	John Fletcher	3	—	—
April	5.	John Candler of Wm., a Child	2	5	—
	7.	Widow Cooke	—	—	—
	24.	Widow Jenkins at Jas. Traills	—	—	—
May	31.	Greenbury Ridgley	3	15	—
Aug.	8.	Rezin Ferguson, died Aug. 6th	2	5	—
	22.	Ninian, a son of Elbert Perry	2	5	—
Sept.	10.	Eliz. Warfield of Dr. Charles	7	10	—
			27	0	—

Tombstone Records, Trinity Church, St. Mary's City, St. Mary's River*

Ashcome:

In memory of/Nancy Brome Ashcome/Born/March 25, 1793/Died/October 19, 1885.

Bayne:

William C. Bayne/Departed this life/March 9th, 1882/aged 70 years/1 month & 4 days.

Mary Julia L. Bayne/Departed this life/Jan'y. 2d. 1880/aged 17 years/2 months & 24/days.

Bean:

A. H. Bean/died/March 11th, 1888/in the 63rd. year of his age.

Jane L. Bean/wife of/A. H. Bean/Feb. 7, 1830/Feb. 17, 1896.

Bennett:

Elizabeth L. Bennett/1809–1888.
John White Bennett/1796–1875.
Susan E. Bennett/1837–1864.
Mary Bennett/1840–1897.
Thomas J. Bennett/1843–1917.

In Memory of/John White/son of John W. &/Elizabeth Bennett/who departed this life/Octr. 4th. 1836 aged 10 mo.

* Near the mouth of the Potomac River, site of the first State House of Md. there is a large monument to Lord Calvert. Copied in 1923 by Mrs. Carrie White Avery (1873–1925) and furnished for this publication by Mr. Herbert P. Gerald, Washington, D. C.

Richard Mitchell/son of/John W. & Elizabeth Bennett/who departed this life/Sept. 30th. 1836/aged 2 years/10 mo. & 25 days.

William Loker/son of/John W. & Elizabeth Bennett/who departed this life/Oct. 15th, 1835/aged 4 yrs. 6 mo. & 13 days.

An infant/son of John W. and/Elizabeth Bennett/Nov. 4th. 1832.

Binny:

Sacred/to the memory of/Archibald Binny/who departed this life/ April 25th. 1838/in the 75th. year of his age.

Bohanan:

Charles Milburn/June 5, 1853/Sept. 12, 1917/His wife/Laura Pursel/ March 26, 1855/April 20, 1917.

Lucy Woodland/daughter of/Charles M. & Laura P./Bohanan/Born Feb. 15, 1895/Died Oct. 9, 1895.

Sallie Anne Fish/wife of/J. Frank Bohanan/Born March 25, 1848/Died Oct. 20, 1917.

J. Frank Bohanan/July 6, 1840–Feb. 17, 1922/

Johnathan/Born 1765/Died 1839/Mary Richardson/His wife.

To/my husband/Dr. William T. Bohanan/Born/March 7th, 1843/ Died/Nov. 22d. 1882.

Sacred/To/The Memory of/Permelia Bohanan/Born/March 3, 1819, Died/May 16, 1891.

Sacred/To/The Memory of/John Bohanan/Born Octr. 20, 1811/died/ June 16, 1871.

Olive Bohanan/wife of S. West Russell/Oct. 18, 1873/June 20, 1920.

Briscoe:

Walter L. Briscoe/Born/Aug. 14, 1824/died/April 19, 1888.

Ann M. P. Briscoe/who departed this life/Oct. 31, 1848/In the 28th year of her age.

Sarah Blanch/daughter of John O. &/Mary J. Lilburn/Died June 17th, 1852/aged 5 mos.

In memory of/Sarah D. Briscoe/Born October 16, 1790/Died/April 16, 1880/aged 89 years & 6 mos.

Brome:

James Thomas Brome/Aug. 13, 1847/June 11, 1910/

Margaret Somervill/daughter of/J. Thomas & Emma/Brome/died March 8, 1882/aged 2 yrs. & 5 mos.

Emma Thomas/infant daughter of/J. T. & E. T. Brome/Died March 27, 1884/aged 6 wks.

In memory of/Dr. John M. Brome/March 7, 1818/July 28, 1887.

In memory of/Susan M. Brome/wife of/John M. Brome/Born Jan'y. 3, 1820/Died April 16, 1881.

In memory of/Sarah Ann Brome/Born Jan. 18, 1843/Died May 26, 1890.

Burroughs:

S. G. M. Burroughs/Born July 24th, 1846/Died July 16th, 1863.

Clocker:

Jennette E. T. Clocker/Born Nov. 17, 1811/Died Jan. 8, 1898.

William Clocker/Born/March 15, 1807/Died/March 4, 1883.

Copley:

Here Lyeth the Body/of/Lionel Copley of Wadworth Co. York, England/Born 1648 died Sept. 27, 1693/and of Anne Boteler, His wife, of Watton/Woodhull Co. Herts, England/Died March 5, 1692/He was sometime/Lieutenant Governor of Kingston upon Hull/1689–1690/ Lieutenant Governor—Governor in chief and/Chief Admiral of Maryland in America/1691–1693/His short tenure of life in this province/was marked by singular Fidelity/in troublous times to/His God, His King and Country /To Him, the First Royal Governor of Maryland/the/Maryland Society of Colonial Dames of America/has erected this memorial/September 27, 1922.

Craddock:

Rosa E./Beloved wife of/Joseph C. Craddock/died August 26, 1895.

Crane:

Sacred/To the memory of R. Kearney Crane/who died Feb. 17th, 1849, aged 24 years.

George Crane/Born/July 28, 1798/died/Aug. 18, 1849.

Sallie A./wife of/John A. Crane/Born March 10, 1833/Died Sept. 30, 1854.

Crookshank:

John Crookshank/Born/Sept. 11th, 1802/Died Nov. 16th, 1886.

Rhoda L./wife of/John Crookshank/who departed this life/Jany. 21st. 1864/aged 57 years.

Davis:

In memory of/Thomas S. Davis/who departed this life/Feby. 22d. 1816/ aged 25 years.

In memory of/John Davis/who departed this life/April 28th, 1803/ aged 3 years.

Dent:

In memory of/Our Mother/Emma R. Dent/Born/May 23rd. 1837/ died/Nov. 12th, 1895.

Joseph Dent/Died March 17, 1881/aged 46 years/& 4 days.

Dunbar:

B. M. Dunbar/Born Oct. 15, 1849/Died July 27, 1905.

Edwards:

Sacred to the memory of/Jane R./Beloved wife of/George W. Edwards/ Born Dec. 31, 1833/Died May 26, 1910.

In memory of/George W. Edwards/Born Dec'r. 12, 1837/Died July 18, 1900.

Fish:

To our sister/Aggie E. Fish/Born Nov'r. 14, 1870/Died/March 12, 1887.

To my Husband/George F. Fish/Born/Oct. 24th, 1854/Died/March 29th, 1880.

To/our boy/George Fish/son of/J. Frank & Sallie A./Bohanan/Born Nov. 16th, 1875/Died Jan. 12th, 1883.

Ford:

Mark S. D. Ford/who died/Dec. 30th, 1816/aged 23 years.

Mary Ford/who died/Dec. 30th, 1841/aged 46 years.

William H. Ford/aged 58 years (No dates).

Freeman:

To my husband/F. V. Freeman/Born Aug. 18, 1849/Died May 4, 1877.

Hilton:

In memory of/Our dear mother/Catherine M. Hilton/Born/October 4, 1837/died Sept. 3, 1901.

Carrie M. Hilton/Oct. 24, 1862/Mar. 7, 1915.

In memory of/my husband/William M. Hilton/born/October 6, 1832/died April 9, 1888.

Holmes:

John H. Holmes/born August 16, 1817/died Nov'r. 26, 1871/aged 54 years 3 mo's./& 10 days.

Maria Holmes/born/January 19, 1819/died/Aug. 23, 1884.

Charles B. Holmes/born May 12, 1851/died Octr. 25, 1871/aged 20 yrs. 5 mos./& 13 days.

Hunter:

Catherine Hammond Hunter/Feb. 27, 1817–May 17, 1876.

Jones:

Caleb Morris Jones/died February 17, 1878.

Elvira A./wife of James F. Ellicott/died Feby. 20, 1892.

Emily Regina Jones/died/March 14, 1901.

Alex. Jones, M.D./who died/Jan'y. 22nd. 1841 aged 23 years.

Rebecca Jones/Consort of/O. M. Jones/died Mar. 5th, 1853/aged 59 years.

J. Kemp Jones/born March 2, 1824/died Feby. 10, 1868.

Kirk:

In memory/of Henry N. Kirk/born July 31st. 1805/died July 17th, 1849.

Langley:

William Alexander, son of/Walter & Rebecca Langley/born Jan. 4, 1823/died June 3, 1904.

Alexander Beauregard/son of/James R. & Indiana/Langley/died May 15, 1885/aged 24 years.

James Clarence/son of/James R. & Indiana/Langley/died July 27, 1898/aged 27 years.

James R. Langley/died Feb'y. 28, 1886/aged 62 years.

Indiana/wife of James R. Langley/died October 19th, 1911 in the 78th year of her age.

Lilburn:

John Gray Hopkins Lilburn/son of R. F. & E. V. H. Lilburn/Nov. 9, 1855–Aug. 29, 1918.

Emeline V. Lilburn/wife of/Robert F. Lilburn/born Octr. 2, 1828/died July 26, 1889.

Robert F. Lilburn/born/Feby. 14th, 1820/died/Sept. 7th, 1864.

Sarah Blanch/daughter of John O. &/Mary J. Lilburn/died June 17th, 1852/aged 5 months.

In memory of/Robert Lilburn/who died April 10th, 1831/In the 68th year of his age.

In memory of Mrs. Jane Lilburn/who departed this life/Decr. 1st, 1814/aged 56 years.

William M. Lilburn/who departed this life/March 20th, 1845/In the 27th year of his age.

McKay:

Laurel Ann McKay/Dec. 29, 1844/April 10, 1918.

Martin:

Alexander Martin/born/March 27, 1822/died June 20, 1886.

Bettie/wife of Alexander Martin/born March 26, 1831/and died March 11th, 1856.

Milburn:

In memory of Mortimer Milburn/who departed this life/March 30th, 1832/aged 9 years.

In memory of/Clara Milburn/who departed this life/Dec. 3rd, 1879.

In memory of/Stephen Milburn/who departed this life/July 30th, 1829/aged 30 years and/3 months.

Adeline/wife of/Alexander Milburn/who departed this life/Novr. 12, 1857/aged 41 yrs. 3 mos./& 1 day.

In memory of/Susan A. Milburn/who departed this life/July 27th, 1835, aged/39 years, 2 months/& 22 days.

In memory of Eliz^{h}. Milburn/who departed this/life October 31/1831/aged 52 years 9/months and 13 days.

My Mother/Permelia Milburn/died Dec'r. 2, 1863/aged 72 years.

Catherine A. H. Abell/Milburn/born Dec. 8, 1823/died April 4, 1895.

James C. Milburn/born/Oct. 8th, 1811/died/Jan. 1st, 1887.

Mary E. Milburn/died/July 31, 1854/aged 21 years, 6 mo./and 6 days.

Jane Milburn/died/June 28, 1854/aged 39 years, 5 mo./and 22 days.

Sacred/to the memory of/William P. Milburn/who departed this life/Sept. 16th, 1837/aged 28 years, 2 mos./& 23 days.

Robert N. Milburn/departed this life/Aug. 14th, 1861/aged 54 years & 7 days.

Susanna/widow of/Robert N. Milburn/died April 13, 1887/aged 81 years.

Augusta Lavina/daughter of Robert N. & Susanna/Milburn/died Nov. 26, 1893/in the 51st year of her age.

Virginia/daughter of/Robert N. & Susanna/Milburn/died Feb. 20, 1907/in the 72d. year of her age.

In memory of/Sue G. daughter/of John and Susan A. Milburn/who departed this life/August 20, 1856/aged 21 years 2 mos. and/21 days.

To the memory of/John Milburn/who departed this life/Dec. 22, 1841/aged 68 years 3 mos./and 3 days.

In memory of/Thomas H./son of John H./and Caroline Milburn/who departed this life/April 3rd, 1830/aged 2 years and 30 days.

In memory of/Caroline E. B. Milburn/who departed this life/Feby. 22nd./1831/aged 1 year 3 months/and 22 days.

In memory of/Catherine H. Milburn/who departed this life/March 9th, 1832/aged 39 years, 7 months and 24 days.

In memory of/John A. H. Milburn/who departed this life/October 2d, 1854/aged 5 months/and 5 days.

James T. Milburn/April 3, 1838/Feby. 19, 1916.

Eliza Susanna/Milburn/born Jany. 5, 1841/died August 28, 1914.

Ann Glovener/Milburn/born June 12, 1841/died Sept. 23, 1913.

Rebecca A. Milburn daughter of/John H. & Caroline/Milburn/born July 1, 1839/died Dec. 3, 1909.

Pembroke:

Evalina A. Pembroke/who departed this life March 8, 1871.

Benjamin Pembroke/who departed this life/Feby. 3, 1882/aged 68 years.

Pursel:

In memory of/Ida R./Beloved wife of/Chester F. Pursel/born April 6, 1856/died May 14, 1896.

Willie F./son of/Chester F. & Ida R./Pursel/born July 22, 1889/died Sept. 27, 1890.

Furman B./son of/Chester F. & Ida R./born Aug. 22, 1886/died Nov. 29, 1888.

Sanner:

In memory of/Samuel A. Sanner/born Nov. 8th, 1819/died Feb. 22, 1854.

In memory of/Mary Ann Sanner/who departed this life/June 8th, 1816/aged 76 years.

Smith:

Sacred/to the memory of/Oscar H. Smith/who departed this life/Oct. 9th, 1842/in the 19th year of his age.

Sacred/to the memory of/Mary Smith/who departed this life/December 1st, 1844/aged 58 years.

Clement Briscoe/beloved husband of Leatha A. Smith/died Nov. 24, 1903/in his 83d. year.

In memory of/Ruth Smith/born/May 8th, 1856/died Nov. 17th, 1858.

Peter P. Smith/born/May 12, 1809/died/May 25, 1864.

Margaret Smith/beloved Consort of/P. P. Smith/who departed this life/Decr. 11th, 1856/aged 32 years 9 months/and 7 days.

Leatha A./Beloved wife of/C. Briscoe Smith/born May 10, 1836/died May 12, 1913/Mortimer/Beloved Grandson of/C. Briscoe & Leatha A. Smith/born Nov. 25, 1885/died June 24, 1896.

In memory/of/Mortimer Smith/died/April 6th, 1885 aged 27 years/4 months and 21 days.

Clement F./Smith/born/Oct. 12, 1880/died/July 5, 1882.

Dudley M. Smith/Died/August 2nd, 1885/aged 2 years/2 months 2 weeks.

Smoot:

Sacred to the memory of Mrs. Ann/Relict of the/Rev. Charles Smoot/late rector of this Pa/rish who died in the Spring of 1810/in the 39th year of his age.

Stephenson:

Rev. James Stephenson, S. T. D./For 17 years/Rector of St. Mary's Parish/Dean of the Convocation/of Cumberland/Rector of Linganore/Parish, P. E. Church/born in Co. Longford, Ireland/died Jan. 11, 1892/in New Market/In the/68th year of his age.

Mary Clare Stephenson/wife of/Rev. James Stephenson, S. T. D./for sixteen years/Rector of this Parish/Died/March 20th, 1867.

Mary Denniston, (Daughter of) Rev. James Stephenson S. T. D./and Mary Clare Stephenson/born March 8th, 1865/died May 3rd. 1867.

Stone:

Ida M. Stone/July 8, 1852/April 4, 1921.

William F. Stone/Sept. 4, 1840/Dec. 28, 1917.

Templeman:

In memory of/Susanna Templeman/who departed this life/September 9th, 1848/in the 74th year of her age.

Thomas:

George Thomas/August 6, 1835/May 14, 1903.

Ellen Ogle Thomas/wife of/Captain George Thomas/Oct. 21, 1841–Oct. 30, 1906.

On a window in the Chapel:
"To the Glory of God/and in Loving Memory of/George Thomas, and/Ellen Ogle, His Wife."
In memory of/Mrs. Henrietta Thomas/who departed this life/Sept[r]. 13th, 1829/aged 67 years.

Thompson:
Robert Thompson/April 19, 1807/October 12, 1865.
Mary/consort of/Robert Thompson/died/Jan'y. 4th, 1850/aged/32 years 10 mos. &/2 days.

Wallace:
In memory of Sarah Wallace/who departed this/life January 3, 1833/aged 77 years.

White:
Samuel White/1814–1880.

Zackery:
Zacheriah Zackery/died/Feb'y. 4, 1842/aged 27 years, 9 mo./and 27 days.

St. Martin's Protestant Episcopal Church Records, Worcester Parish, Worcester Co., Md.*

The following men were under 25 years of age, 1756:

John Ratliff.
Andrew Irons.
Thomas Robeson.
James Dole.
George Glasco.
Robert M. Gray.
John Farrell.
John Fasset.
James Andrews.
Solloman Hudson.
Erasmus Harris.
Armel Showell.

The following men under 25 years of age, July 13, 1762:

William Ironshire.
Ebenezer Campbell.
Sollomon Timmons.
John Postly.
Ananias Hudson.
Beley Wolter.
John Miller.
Samuel Deal.
William Robeson (or Roberson)
Moses Halloway.
Charles Collins.
John Bratten.

* Near Showell, Md. Records are preserved in the Exchange and Savings Bank, Berlin, Md. Sept. 17, 1886, from the latter place, Rev. John R. Joyner, Rector Worcester Parish, wrote an historical letter which is published with later newspaper records in *Md. Orig. Research Soc. of Baltimore*, No. 3, pp. 20–21.

Records here published were copied by the late George W. Hodges.

Vincen Crapper.
Laban Kismet.
Obed Gault.
William Collier.
Thomas Milbourn.
Joseph Smith.
Zedekiah Whalley.
Rubing Crapper.
William Smith.
John Larrance.
John Bravard.
Elisha Gray.
John Massey.
Joshua Roberson.
Levin Dirickson.

Sally Grumby, dau. Stoutten and Shady *Adams*, b. 1805, 5, 30.

John *Aydlot*, m. Hannah, 1761, 12, 2.

Issue:

Tabitha, b. 1763, 3, 19.

Morrison *Ayres*, m. Rachel Ironshear, 1753, 8, 13.

Issue:

Isaac, b. 1754, 8, 20.
Mary, b. 1756, 10, 15.
Comfort, b. 1758, 10, 20.

Absalom, son of Archibald and Anna *Baker*, b. 1806, 5, 7.

Leven, son of John and Polly *Baker*, b. 1803, 11, 13.

Solomon, son of Jonathan and Polly *Baker*, b. 1805, 4, 18.

William, son of Belitha and Nancy *Baker*, b. 1806, 8, 31.

Solomon *Baker*, m. Mary Dale (1st. wife), 1741, 6, 4.

Issue:

Ann, b. 1741, 2, 3–5.
Betty Mills, b. 1746, 10, 21.
Jon, b. 1749, 9, 11.
Elisha, b. 1752, 12, 7.

Solomon *Baker* and Rachel Evans (2d wife), m. 1754, 12, 12.

Issue:

Leaven, b. 1755, 8, 35.
Esther, b. 1758, 12, 31.

Solomon, son of Solomon and Rachel *Baker*, b. 1761, 2, 12.

Zadock, son of William *Baker*, b. 1750, 9, 6.

Richard *Barker* and Mary Wharton, m. 1761, 9, 24.

Issue:

Benjamin, b. 1762, 6, 15.
Burton, b. 1764, 6, 24.
Bailey, b. 1766, 7, 29.

John, son of Elisha and Mary *Baynum*, b. 1800, 2, 21.

Mary, daughter of James and Ann *Bell*, b. 1803, 8, 21.

Isaac Bell and Anne, m. ——.

Issue:

Abigail, b. 1743, 5, 23.
William, b. 1745, 7, 17.
Isaac, b. 1751, 5, 13.
Stephen, b. 1753, 2, 18.

William *Bell*, m. Polly, ——.

Issue:

Hetty, b. —, —, —.
James, b. —, —, —.
Molley, b. 1803, 2, 20.
Nancy, b. 1807, 5, 10.
Betsy, b. 1808, 4, 29.
Sally, b. 1814, 6, 6.

Matilda, daughter of John and Leah *Benson*, b. 1800, 8, 2.

John, son of Absalom and Comfort *Bessex*, b. 1740, 9, 23.

Elizabeth, daughter of Absalom and Comfort *Bessex*, b. 1748, 9, 20.

—ariah [Zachariah?] *Bold*, m. Rachel Worren 1750, 11, 30.

Issue:
—— 1751, 8, 8.
—— 1754, 12, 26.
—— 1758, 5, 17.
—— 1760, 8, 18.

John *Bradford*, m. Esther Smith 174–, 11, 3.
Issue:
Matthew, b. 174–, 10, 21.
Mary, b. 1750, 12, 4.

Leah *Breaddard*, b. 173–, 9, 25.

Jerusha *Breaddard*, b. 173–, 10, 27.

James *Brittingham*, m. Elizabeth ——.
Issue:
Sally, b. 1799, 10, 20.
Seth Harrison, b. 1801, 7, 23.
Martha, b. 1803, 11, 11.
Isaac, b. 1806, 2, 8.
Daniel Williams, b. 1808, 5, 12.

James S. son of Thomas and Charlotte *Buckmaster*, b. 1805, 11, 18.

McKinney Smith, son of Thomas and Charlotte *Buckmaster*, b. 1807, 9, 25.

Children of John and Martha *Campbell:*
Mary, b. 1746, 11, 2.
John Simson, b. 1748, 4, 28.

William *Collier*, m. Nancy ——.
Issue:
John, b. 1805, 10, 8.
William, b. 1808, 1, 3.
Matilda Richards, b. 1810, 5, 23.

Kendell, son of Potter and Elizabeth *Collins*, m. Sarah, daughter of John and Mary Fassit, 1768, 4, 6.
Issue:
Potter, b. 1760, 11, 7.
Kendall, b. 1763, 4, 1.
James, b. 1765, 6, 10.

Molly T. daughter of Belitha and Comfort *Collins*, b. 1805, 1, 26.

Peter Collins, son of Ebenezer and Elizabeth *Powell*, b. 1805, 12, 26.

——, son of William and —— Collings, b. 1740, 1, 8.

——ias, son of William and —— Collings, b. 1743, 1, 21.

——, son of William and —— Collings, b. 1745, 11, 12.

John Cornell, m. Eda Holland 1751, 12, 7.

Ananias, son of Thomas *Covell*, b. 1755, 10, 26.

Jesse, son of Thomas *Covell*, b. 1757, 7, 6.

Isaac Covington died 1762, 4, 27.

John, son of John and Sarah Covington, b. 1800, 3, 20.

Milly Cropper, b. 1802, 3, 15.

Benjamin *Davis* and Mary, 173–, 12, 26.

Benjamin Davis died 1760, 1, 26.
Issue:
Ann, b. 173–, 12, 15.
Matthias, b. 174–, 10, 25.
Leah, b. 174–, 4, 10.
Mary, b. 174–, 3, 21.
Abijah, b. 1752, 3, 8.
Zipporah, b. 1753, 9, 12.
Esther, b. 175–, 3, 12.
Sophia, b. 17—, 2, 28.

Jesse, son of Elisha and Sally *Davis*, b. 1807, 4, 18.

Elisha H., son of Elisha and Sally *Davis*, b. 1811, 3, 11.

Eli, son of George and Sally *Davis*, b. 1804, 1, 25.

Joseph Miller, son of George and Sally *Davis*, b. 1807, 3(?), 12.

Jesse *Davis*, m. Polly ——.
Issue:

Gatty, b. 1806, 3, 28.
Rachel, b. 1808, 4, 24.
Julia Ann, b. 1812, 9, 13.
John Powell, b. 1813, 11, 1.

Matthias *Davis*, m. Martha Powell 1764, 12, 16.
Issue:
Benjamin, b. 1765, 11, 27.
Mordecai, b. 1767, 10, 21.

John *Deal*, m. Hannah Stevenson 17—, 2, 25.
Issue:
Josiah, b. 17—, 11, 29.
Joshua, b. ——, 2, 9.
James, b. ——, 11, 1.
Comfort, b. ——, 12, 16.
William, b. ——, 9, 16.
Matthew, b. 17—, 10, 17.

Benjamin *Derickson*, m. Lishe Whorton 1730, 2, 13.
Issue:
Sarah, b. 1730, 2, 13.
George, b. 1732, 6, 4.
Solomon, b. 1734, 4, 4.
——dwrease, b. 1736, 4, 11.
Rhoda, b. 1737/8, 1, 20.
John, b. 1740, 9, 15.
Benjamin, b. 1742/3, 1, 10.
——, b. 1744/5, 2, 11.
Hannah, b. 174-, 2, 1.
——, b. 17—, 4, 25.

Joseph *Derickson*, m. Mary Waples, 1730, 10, 27.
Issue:
Levin, b. 173-, —, —.
Betty, b. ——.
——ichell, b. ——.
Joseph, b. ——.

Joseph *Dirickson*, m. Comfort Tunnell, 1768, 2, 7.
Issue:
James, b. 1768, 12, 13.
Mitchell, b. 1770, 3, 27.
Levin, b. 1771, 10, 3.

William *Derickson*, m. Arcada Hazzard, 1754, 4, 7.
Issue:
Mary, b. 1755, 2, 18.
Elizabeth, b. 1757, 8, 15.

Rev. Edward *Dingle*, Rector of Worcester Parish, departed this life, 1763, 7, 1.

Sally, daughter of James and Rachel *Downs*, b. 1802, 7, 5.

Ann, daughter of Nathaniel *Duitt* [Dewitt?], b. 1739, 6, 18.

Hannah, daughter of William and Catron *Dunlap*, b. 1755, 10, —.

William, son of Edward and Polly *Dymock*, b. 1804, 3, 21.

Elizabeth Ann, daughter of Stephen and Martha *Ennis*, b. 1815, 6, 10.

Sarah Margaret, daughter of Stephen and Martha *Ennis*, b. 1824, 8, 10.

—— *Evans*, m. Elizabeth ——, 17—, 2, —.
Issue:
——, b. 17—, 3, 6.
——, b. 17—, 3, 6.

Gammay *Evans*, m. Rachel Lockwood, 17—, 10, 6. He died 1754.
Issue:
Moley, b. 17—, 7, 12.
Zelah, b. ——, 2, 25.
Jussin (Jussier?), b. ——, 1, 4.
Elizabeth, b. ——, 6, 23.
Rachel, b. ——, 6, 24.
Gammay (Gammag?), b. ——, —, 27.

John *Evans*, m. Sarah Campbell, 1727, 2, 22.
Issue:
Elisha.

John.
Ebinezer.
Sophia.
Elizabeth.
Edward.
——oe (daughter).
David.

John *Evans* Jr., m. Mary Collens, 1756, 11, 16.
Issue:
Rhoda, b. 1757, 9, 23.
Elizabeth, b. 1759, 8, 4.
Elisha, b. 1762, 4, 13.
Edward, b. 1765, 7, 27.

Rufus, son of Nathaniel and Mary *Evans*, b. 1799, 9, 30.

Jesse, son of Nathaniel and Mary *Evans*, b. 1802, 4, 14.

Nathaniel, son of Nathaniel and Mary *Evans*, b. 1807, 4, 25.

—— *Evans*, m. Sarah Stock (or Hook), 17—, 11, 4.
Issue:
Hanner Stook (or Hook), b. ——, 4, 8.
Herpowell, b. ——, 6, 28.
(Mar)y, b. 1742, 7, 22.
Gammay (Gammag), b. 1744, 11, 22.

Walter *Evans*, m. Ann Truitt, 1748, 8, 9.
Issue:
William, b. 1749, 5, 12.
Leah, b. 1752, 11, 6.
Ann, b. 1754, 2, 19.
Rodah, b. 1756, 6, 29.

William *Fortner*, m. Nelly Boming, 1759, 11, 26.

Francis, son of Thomas and Charlotte *Franklin*, b. 1800, 5, 4.

Moses *Freeman*, m. Luraner Evans, 17—, 6, 18.
Issue:
John, b. ——, 11, 9.

Sally, daughter of Archibald and Rachel *Gault*, b. 1800, 1, —.

Err Truitt, son of Betesha and Pearcy *Gray*, b. 1799, 3, 28.

Hillary Pitts, son of John and Elizabeth *Gray*, b. 1803, 7, 10.

Sally Parker, daughter of John and Elizabeth *Gray*, b. 1805, 1, 18.

Johnson *Gray*, m. Martha ——.
Issue:
Thomas Simson, b. 1795, 11, 21.
Martha, b. 1800, 1, 28.

Robert Gray, son of Rouse and Catharine *Hanson*, b. 1807, 6, 22.

Mary Ann Charlotte Catharine, dau. of Rouse and Catharine *Hanson*, b. 1810, 5, 28.

David *Hazzard*, m. Sarah ——.
Issue:
Neomy, b. 1734, 3, 2.
Sarah, b. 1738, 4, 26.
Neriah, b. 1740, 5, 14.
Elihu, b. 1744, 9, 15.

John *Hill*, m. Margaret ——.
Issue:
Mary, b. 1803, 9, 29.
William, b. 1807, 1, 25.
Sally Pitts, b. 1817, 11, 5.

William, Stephen and Rebeckah *Hill*, m. Elizabeth, daughter of Josiah and Sophia Mitchell, 1768, 9, 14.

Nehemiah *Hodder*, m. Cade ——, 17—, 6, 26.
Issue:
Worron, b. 17—, 12, 8.
John, b. ——, 2, 26.
Elizabeth, b. ——, 6, 7.

Samuel *Holland*, m. Tabitha Campbell, 1744.

Issue:
John, b. 1746, 4, 26.
Elizabeth, b. 1747/8, 1, 12.
Mary, b. 1749/50, 3, 13.
Samuel, b. 1752, 2, 21.

John *Holloway*, m. Frances Bradford, 173–, 1, 27.
Issue:
Esther, b. 1734, 3, 13.
John, b. 1736, 8, 8.
Hasy, b. 1739/40, 1, 12.
Solomon, b. 1744, 3, 30.
Rebecah, b. 1747, 1, 1.
Elijah, b. 1754, 3, 11.

Benjamin Schofield, son of Eli and Patty *Hoshes*, b. 1803, 2, 24.

Nehemiah *Howard*, m. Sarah Collingwood, 17—, 10, 28.
Issue:
Arlanta, b. 17—, 8, 28.
Sarah, b. ——, 1, 3.
Tabitha, b. ——, 2, 1.
George, b. ——, 10, 12.
Elizabeth, b. ——, 3, 6.
Nehemiah, b. ——, 12, 22.

Mahala, daughter of Ananias and Lunetta *Hudson*, b. 1801, 6, 3.

John *Hudson*, m. Rhoda Tingle, 1751, 5, 26.
Issue:
Leah, b. 1754, 12, 29.
John, b. 1756, 8, 22.

John *Hudson*, m. Rachel ——.
Issue:
John, b. 1761, 7, 14.
Catron, b. 1764, 2, 2.
Caleb, b. 1766, 11, 8.

Joseph *Ironshare*, m. Esther Collins.
Issue:
Mary, b. 1754, 7, 1.
Elizabeth, b. 1756, 5, 25.

Catty, daughter of Arcanias (Ananias?) and Rachel *Jarman*, b. 1803, 3, 31.

Martha, daughter of George and Comfort *Jarman*, b. 1746, 12, 28.

Molla, daughter of George and Comfort *Jarman*, b. 1750, 7, 30.

Rachel, daughter of William and Rehodah *Justis*, b. 1806, 2, 20.

William *Kershaw*, m. Betty Derickson, 1756, 11, 24. He d. 1758, 1, 11.
Issue:
Mitchell, b. 1757, 12, 24.

Betty *Kershaw* (widow), m. Levin Vaughan 1760, 5, 23.

William *Killom*, m. Rachel Hankock, 1741, 12, 1.
Issue:
Thomas, b. 1742, 10, 15.
Tabitha, b. 1743, 4, 28.

Maryland Rec.—33176 Gal. 173

Mary, b. 1747, 9, 4.
Leah, b. 1750, 4, 22.
John, b. 1758, 4, 14.
Jesse, b. 1756, 7, 29.
Eada, b. 1758, 5, 23.

Nancy, daughter of Ezehal and Rhoda *King*, b. 1801, 1, 7.

Ebenezer Cannon, son of Ezehal and Rhoda *King*, b. 1804, 8, 22.

James, son of Thomas and Martha *King*, b. 1804, 10, 30.

Sarah, daughter of Thomas and Martha *King*, b. 1817, 11, 18.

Presgrave, daughter of William and Sarah *Kinnett*, b. 1800, 5, 22.

Dunken Farrell, son of Rebekah Farrell and Luke *Lamb*, b. 1755, 10, 21.

Thomas Gray, son of John and Sally *Lane*, b. 1804, 10, 26.

Francis, son of John and Sally *Lane*, b. 1806, 12, 15.
Thomas, son of John Kendal and Mary *Latchem*, b. 1804, 3, 9.
Rebekah, daughter of John Kendal and Mary *Latchem*, b. 1806, 10, 30.
Benjamin *Lockwood*, m. Rebekah Morris, 1746, 3, 24.

Issue:

——, b. 1746, 12, 6.
——, b. 1748, 8, 25.
——ry [Mary?], b. 1750, 7, 20.
——nah [Hannah?], b. 1752, 4, 18.

John *Lockwood*, m. Sarah Holland, 1748, 1, 2.

Issue:

Mary, b. 1750, 8, 17.
Elizabeth, b. 175–, 4, 15.

Samuel *Lockwood*, m. Leah ——, 17—, 12, 16.

Issue:

Elisha, b. 17—, 1, 17.

David *Louge*, m. Ann Lockwood, 173–, 5, 20.

Issue:

——ry, b. 173–, 2, 18.
——, b. 173–, 5, 29.
David, b. 1740, 12, 16.
——na, b. 1742, 1, 12.
Jesse, b. 1744, 12, 1.
——chel, b. 1747, 6, 17.
——n, b. 1749, 2, 9.
Mariam, b. 1750, 1, 2.
Purnell, b. 1754, 2, 17.
——ne, daughter, b. 1756, 5, 19.

Rev. [Wm.] *Macclenachen*, Rector of Worcester Parish, died 1766, 8, 3. [Became Rector Octr., 1765].

John Edward Henry *Marshall*, son of John and ——, b. 1807, —, —.
Rachel Francher, daughter of John and Sary *Massey*, b. 1806, 5, 3.
Louisa, daughter of John and Sary *Massey*, b. 1809, 3, 23.
William *Merrill*, m. Susanne ——.

Issue:

Peter, b. 1772, 3, 1.
John, b. 1774, 6, 21.
Kendell, b. 1777, 2, 21.
Nancy, b. 1780, 6, 15.
Zeno, b. 1782, 9, 8.
Elizabeth Pitts, b. 1785, 1, 28.
Betsy Pitts, b. 1786, 10, 9.

John, son of John and Sarah *Miller*, m. Nanny the daughter of Joseph and Mary Dirickson, 1762, 9, 2.
Peggy Patey, daughter of Claray *Mills*, b. 1804, 11, 30.
John Pope *Mitchell*, m. Polly Purnall, 1773, 5, 3.

Issue:

Robert, b. 1774, 1, 10.

Josiah *Mitchell*, m. Sophia Hill, 1753, 3, 7.

Issue:

Elizabeth [see Hill, Wm.], b. 1754, 5, 22.
Mitchell, b. 1755, 9, 4.
Isaac, b. 1757, 9, 7.
Robert, b. 1759, 7, 27.
Levin, b. 1761, 6, 20.
Mary, b. 1763, 4, 28.
Sarah, b. 1766, 9, 7.
Sophia, b. 1768, 12, 14.
Ann, b. 1770, 10, 13.

Levin *Mitchell*, m. Mary Murray, 1792, 8, 29.

Issue:

Robert, b. 1793, 9, 20.
Josiah, b. 1795, 8, 16.

Peggy, b. 1797, 3, 17.
William Murrah, b. 1799, 3, 20.
Joshua, b. 1801, 12, —.

Sarah, wife of Robert *Mitchell*, died 1788, 9, 9.

Bevins *Morris*, m. Elizabeth Truitt, 1722, 9, 8. [See Rodney's Diary p. 52].

Issue:
——ah, b. 1723, 5, 1.
——, b. 1724/5, 2, 9.
——kah, b. 1726, 4, 22.
——, b. 1729, 2, 7.
——ah, b. 1732/3, 3, 17.
——ans, b. 1734, 6, 18.
——, b. 1736, 10, 23.
——, b. 1739, 9, 2.
——ey, b. 1741, 9, 5.

Jared *Mumford*, m. Elizabeth Freeman, 1782, 7, 11.

Issue:
James, b. 1784, 12, 8.

Isaac Murray, son of Robert and Sarah *Mitchell* was b. 1788, 3, 18, and died 1791, 11, 21.

William *Mumford*, m. —moredy ——, 174–, 8, 27.

Issue:
——son, b. 1751, 12, 16.

Robert *Nelson*, m. Elizabeth Milburn, 1746, 12, 29.

Issue:
Zeruiah, b. 1749, 3, 22.
William, b. 1752, 4, 2.
Thomas, b. 1754, 3, 20.

John *Onion*, m. Susannah Person, 174–, 6, 18.

Issue:
Selby, b. 1742, 5, 27.
Betty, b. 1745, 1, 23.
Selby, b. 1745, 12, 8.
John, b. 1747, 9, 2.
Ayres, b. 1749, 2, 1.
Mary, b. 1753, 8, 23.

Fanny, daughter of Kendall and Fanny *Patty*, b. 1805, 2, 27.

Sally Richards, daughter of Kendall and Fanny *Patty*, b. 1807, 10, 9.

John Franklin, son of Powell *Pattey*, b. 1741, 9, 16.

Mary, daughter of Powell *Pattey*, b. 1744, 10, 11.

Susannah, daughter of Powell *Pattey*, b. 1746, 10, 20.

Zeno, son of Powell *Pattey*, b. 1748, 2, 26.

Kendel, son of Powell *Pattey*, b. 1753, 2, 24.

Anna, daughter of Isaac E. and Rhody *Penawell*, b. 1804, 12, 7.

Wm. Johnson, son of Wm. Johnson *Penewell* and Haner, his wife, b. 1804, 10, 4.

Ann High, daughter of Jesse and Polly *Petty*, b. 1806, 9, 26.

Hillary *Pitts*, m. Easther Powell, (1 wife, died 1780, 8, 29), 1776, 1, 5.

Issue:
Thomas Powell, b. 1777, 3, 8.
Mary, b. 1778, 10, 21.
William, b. 1780, 8, 16.

Hillary *Pitts*, m. Sally Parker, (2d wife, died 1787, 6, 13), 1781, 7, 5.

Issue:
James, b. 1782, 4, 14.
Ann Postley, b. 1784, 4, 14.
Elizabeth, b. 1785, 11, 2.

Hillary *Pitts*, m. Zipporah Hill, (3d wife, died 1790, 4, 24), 1788, 12, 15.

No Issue.

Hillary Pitts, m. Catherine Purnell, (4 wife), 1790, 12, 21.

Issue:

John, b. 1793, 5, 14.
Hillary, b. 1795, 10, 7.
Catherine, b. 1798, 11, 13.
Robert, b. 1801, 7, 10.

Hillary Pitts and Catharine Pitts were confirmed by Bishop Claggett, at St. Martin's, 1795, 7, 6.

Polly Bratton, daughter of James and Margaret *Pitts*, b. 1803, 11, 14.

Leah Davis, daughter of Calleb and Patty *Powell*, b. 1806, 9, 21.

Elisha, daughter Elisha and Martha *Powell*, b. 1799, 7, 27.

Littleton, son of Handy and Hetty *Powell*, b. 1805, 6, 22.

Martha, daughter of Jesse and Elizabeth *Powell*, b. 1788, 6, 4.

Samuel *Powell*, m. Rachel Peary, 1746, 9, 3.
Issue:
Samuel, b. 1747, 12, 14.
James, b. 1748, 10, 28.
Sarah, b. 1750, 11, 19.
Belisha, b. 1755, 1, 24.
Esther, b. 1757, 4, 7.
John, b. 1761, 3, 27.

Joseph *Quillen*, m. Elizabeth Lacham, 1735, 11, 9.
Issue:
Mary, b. 1738/9, 2, 18.
——oz, b. 1740, 9, 19.
——nah, b. 1742, 12, 1.
Benjamin, b. 1745, 9, 5.
John, b. 1748/9, 1, 29.
Samuel, b. 1750, 2, 17.
——urse, b. 1752, 2, 14.
Martha, b. 1754, 10, 15.

William, son of Benjamin and Easter *Quillen*, b. 1744, 8, 10.

Obadiah *Quilling*, m. Mutual ——.
Issue:
William, b. 1805, 8, 30.
James, b. 1807, 11, 5.
John Henry, b. 1810, 5, 7.

Peter Whaley, son of Edward and Hannah *Revel*, b. 1804, 2, 27.

Elizabeth Aralanta [Asalanta?], daughter of James B. and Elizabeth *Robins*, b. 1806, 5, 16.

Littleton *Robins*, m. Martha ——.
Issue:
John Littleton Bowden, b. 1802, 6, 14.
James Bowden, b. 1806, 1, 13.

Ritta Benson, daughter of Joseph and Margaret *Seals*, b. 1800, 10, —.

Martha Mitchell, daughter of Joseph and Margaret *Seals*, b. 18—, —, —.

Molly Davis, daughter of Ebze and Holland *Smith*, b. 1806, 9, 15.

Samuel *Steal*, m. Elizabeth ——, 17—, 4, 28.
Issue:
Nanne, b. 17—, 5, 26.
Elizabeth, b. ——, 12, 13.
Nathaniel, b. ——, 2, 18.
Barshaba, b. ——, 3, 18.
Daniel, b. ——, 4, 21.

John Washington, son of John and Polly *Stuart*, b. 1806, 12, 23.

Elijah and Elisha, sons of William and Athellia *Taylor*, b. 1806, 3, 17.

William Hazzard *Taylor*, m. Sarah ——.
Issue:
Peggy Hannanson, b. 1800, 11, 23.
Ann, b. 1803, 4, 5.
Elizabeth Johnson, b. 1805, 4, 19.
James Madison, b. 1807, 11, 20.

Joseph *Timmons*, m. Elizabeth Hammon, 1728, 5, 30.
Issue:
Solomon, b. 1729, 5, 23.
James, b. 1732, 5, 13.
Elijah, b. 1736, 7, 19.
Nathaniel, b. 1738, 1, 15.
David, b. 1740, 8, 18.
Joseph, b. 1743, 3, 22.
Samuel, b. 1745, 9, 9.
Caleb *Tingle*, m. Elizabeth ——.
Issue:
Hannah, b. 1759, 4, 1.
Daniel, b. 1761, 8, 5.
James, b. 1764, 2, 27.
Elizabeth, b. 1766, 2, 25.
Caleb, b. 1768, 3, 7.
Elijah, b. 1777, 12, 5.
John, b. 1780, 4, 13.
Caleb *Tingle*, m. Elizabeth Fosset (Fasset?), 17—, 12, 11.
Issue:
Mary, b. 17—, 12, 31.
John, b. 17—, 1, 15.
Daniel *Tingle*, m. Katy ——.
Issue:
——, b. 1799, 10, 30.
Elizabeth Racliff, b. 1803, 1, 10.
Mariah, b. 1804, 3, 22.
—— Truitt, m. ——.
Issue:
——, b. 1745, 2, 13.
——, b. 1747, 11, 28.
——, b. 1750, 4, 21.
—— b. 1754, 3, 17.
Nehemiah, b. 1757, 2, 13.
James *Tubes*, m. Sarah Diricksen, (died 1753, 6, 26), 1752, 10, 9.
James *Tubes*, m. Levinah Farwell, 1754, 2, 17.
Issue:
Sarah, b. 1755, 4, 14.
John, b. 1757, 2, 1.
Elizabeth, b. 1759, 10, 20.
Joseph, b. 1762, 9, 27.
Rebecca, b. 1766, 6, 25.
Comfort, b. 1769, 1, 4.
William *Tunnell*, m. Arlanter Howard, 1750, 1, 13.
Issue:
Elizabeth, b. 1756, 10, 9.
Scharbury, b. 1758, 11, 1.
Nehemiah, b. 1760, 12, 27.
Levin *Vaughan*, m. Betty Kershaw (widow), 1760, 5, 23.
Elizabeth, daughter of William *Walton*, Jr. b. 1745, 10, 20.
Molle, daughter of William *Walton*, Jr. b. 1749, 6, 2.
Isaac *Warren*, m. Sarah ——.
Issue:
Littleton Riley, b. 1805, 4, 2.
Nancy Elizabeth Dale, b. 1807, 2, 22.
Thomas Nathaniel Williams, b. 1809, 2, 2.
Phillip Marsh, son of Selby and Sarah *Warren*, b. 1805, 10, 7.
George *Warrenton*, m. Agnes Truitt 1739, 9, 29.
Issue:
Alexander, b. 1741, 4, 5.
Anne, b. 1743, 9, 5.
Agnes, b. 1747, 11, 3.
George, b. 1750, 7, 19.
Esther, b. 1753, 7, 15.
Francis *Wharton*, m. Ann Harne, 173-, 4, 4.
Issue:
Joseph, b. 173-, 5, 30.
John, b. 173-, 3, 16.
Frances, b. 17—, 12, 27.
Harney, b. 174-, 2, 25.
Ann, b. 174-, 10, 11.

Sarah, b. 175–, 3, 24.
Caleb *Williams*, m. Hetty ——.
Issue:
Isaac, b. 1803, 4, 1.
Lambert Ishmael, b. 1805, 4, 22.
Betsy, b. 1807, 1, 9.
Julian (daughter), b. 1808, 5, 15.
Ephriam, b. 1810, 2, 25.
John Edward, b. 1814, 10, 15.
Peter William, b. 1816, 9, 25.
Catharine Purnall, daughter of Price and Neheomy *Williams*, b. 1803, 10, 30.
Esau *Williams*, m. Mary Jones, 1767, 4, 15.
Issue:
Rachel, b. 1768, 9, 8.
Nathaniel, b. 1770, 6, 11.
Comfort, b. 1772, 4, 2.
Elizabeth, b. 1774, 12, 17.
John Jones, b. 1777, 1, 4.
Martha, b. 1779, 8, 28.
Essau, son of Esau and Mary Williams, b. 1781, 9, 4.
Mary, daughter of Esau and Mary Williams, b. 1787, 1, 3.
Jane, daughter of Esau and Mary Williams, b. 1790, 7, 1.
Samuel Williams, m. Rachel ——, 17—, 2, 3.
Issue:
Tamer, b. 17—, 7, 31.
Esau, b. ——, 1, 3.
Ishmael, b. ——, 8, 14.
David, b. ——, 1, 24.
Ann, b. ——, 11, 25.
Rachel, b. ——, —, —.
Samuel Williams, m. Eby ——.
Issue:
Gertrude, b. 1793, 3, 3.
Peter, b. 1796, 3, 10.
Janet, b. 1799, 6, 23.
Zillah Smith, b. 1802, 6, 6.
Joel Hemans Mills, b. 1805, 11, 20.
Nucessa Ball (daughter), b. 1807, 2, 4.
Nuaron Bell (son), b. 1810, 11, 18.
Samuel Hillary, b. 1815, 12, 5.
Nanny Elizabeth, b. 1812, 6, 5.
Jane, daughter of Thomas N. and Nancy *Williams*, b. 1806, 4, 18.
Moses *Wilson*, m. Anne Wildgoose, 17—, 3, 10.
Issue:
John, b. 17—, 1, 29.
Mary, b. ——, 1, 22.
Isaac, b. ——, 6, 17.
Moses, b. 17—, 12, 1.
Mary Ann, daughter of George and Hetty *Woors* (Moors?), b. 1806, 1, 15.

Worcester County (Md.) Marriage Licenses, 1795 to 1799 (208)

David Adkins m. Mary Waller, 1798, 2, 19.
John Allen m. Lucretia Brumbly, 1796, 11, 30.
Angela Atkinson m. Sarah Hudson, 1795, 11, 30.
William Baker m. Martha Evans, 1795, 12, 19.
William Baynum m. Betsy Carey, 1795, 11, 30.
William Bell m. Polly Pitts, 1797, 2, 1.
Barnaby Bernard m. Mary R. Dickerson, 1797, 6, 14.
Thomas Bird m. Anna Flemming, 1797, 12, 20.
Nathaniel Bishop m. Nancy Freshwater, 1798, 5, 16.
Samuel Bishop m. Mary Smith, 1796, 10, 18.
John Bitts (or Betts) m. Sally Truitt, 1797, 9, 28.
James Blades m. Sarah McIvin, 1798, 6, 9.
Samuel Blades m. Tabitha Jones, 1796, 8, 26.
John Bosten m. Piercy Gray, 1795, 12, 1.
John Botham m. Polly Layfield, 1798, 1, 5.
John Bourn m. Polly Coudry, 1798, 1, 23.
Ananias Bradford m. Nancy Richards, 1796, 4, 18.
John L. Bratten m. Polly Quinton, 1798, 1, 31.
Isaac Breathards m. Sally Richards, 1797, 12, 26.
Hanson Brian m. Nancy Holland, 1797, 2, 22.
Isaac Brittingham m. Betsy Townsend, 1796, 9, 29.
William Brittingham m. Polly Gostes, 1796, 7, 30.
William C. Brown m. Leah Wilson, 1797, 1, 23.
Jabez Brumby m. Martha Farr, 1796, 10, 25.
Edward Burbage m. Mary Smock, 1796, 7, 3.
Thomas Calhoon m. Nancy Taylor, 1795, —, —.
John Cathell m. Priscilla Ward, 1796, 12, 9.
William Caudry m. Sally Bowen, 1797, 11, 8.
Eli Christopher m. Litle Driskale, 1796, 5, 3.
Layfield Collier m. Sally White, 1797, 8, 22.
Isaac Collins m. Tabitha Stevenson, 1798, 1, 3.
James Collins m. Polly White, 1797, 2, 8.
Walter Collins m. Martha Townsend, 1797, 7, 18.
William Cordy m. Betsy Mitchell, 1797, 12, 8.
Daniel Cottingham m. Polly Tilghman, 1796, 3, 18.
Isaac Cottingham m. Susanna Lambdon, 1799, 1, 29.
Thomas Cottingham m. Rhoda Townsend, 1796, 6, 23.

Lazarus Cottman m. Betsy Bishop, 1797, 1, 7.
Abijah Davis m. Catherine Pointer, 1796, 1, 4.
Handy Davis m. Rhoda Burbage, 1797, 7, 6.
James Davis m. Hannah Jenkins Adkins, 1797, 2, 21.
James Davis m. Hannah Birch, 1797, 4, 17.
Matthias Davis m. Betsy Handy, 1797, 6, 21.
William Dixon m. Leah Dikes, 1797, 2, 17.
Teague Donohoe m. Elizabeth Handy, 1797, 5, 19.
Turner Dorris Jr. m. Mary Boun, 1796, 12, 21.
Isaac Dreacken m. Mary Alexander, 1797, 9, 15.
Elgate Drishale m. Anna Dykes, 1796, 4, 15.
Stephen Dryden m. Catherine Dryden, 1796, 1, 29.
Josiah Duncan m. Martha M. Dale, 1795, 10, 20.
Levi Duncan m. Leah Purnell, 1797, 5, 26.
William Duncan m. Esther Holland, 1798, 3, 27.
Cutten Ennis m. Polly Gladden, 1798, 1, 12.
Edmund Evans m. Rachel P. Milburn, 1797, 11, 4.
Joshua Evans m. Betsy Nelson, 1797, 5, 27.
Peter Evans m. Nancy Hudson, 1796, 7, 26.
Jesse Farlow m. Sarah Laws, 1797, 3, 7.
William Ferguson m. Eunice Davis, 1797, 8, 3.
Alexander Franklin m. Rachel Riley, 1797, 3, 1.
Thomas Franklin m. Charlotte Kirby, 1796, 6, 30.
William Franklin m. Anna Riley, 1797, 7, 18.
James Givans m. Betsy Lindzey, 1797, 3, 22.
Robert Givans m. Rosanna Butler, 1795, 10, 22.
Robert Givans m. Ruth Robertson, 1797, 10, 17.
Levi Godfrey m. Ann T. Truitt, 1796, 5, 11.
Henry Gornnell m. Mary P. Stevenson, 1798, 1, 19.
John Gowtes m. Polly Disharoon, 1796, 8, 17.
Rouse Gray m. Bridgett Cathell, 1796, 1, —.
John Green m. Betsy Townsend, 1797, 3, 8.
John Gunby (Grenby?) m. Amelia Chaille, 1798, 1, 23.
Benjamin Gurley m. Esther Sturgis, 1796, 7, 12.
George Hall m. Hesse Bowen, 1796, 2, —.
Benjamin Hammond m. Janet Cottingham, 1796, 7, 26.
Bowden Hammond m. Amelia Jones, 1798, 5, 25.
Edward Hammond m. Nancy Howard, 1796, 5, 19.
William Hammond m. Betsy Gibbs, 1797, 1, 11.
Charles Harris m. Esther Noble, 1796, 7, 15.
Thomas Harris m. Sarah Mills, 1796, 3, 8.
Ebenezer Hearn m. Betsy Roach, 1798, 2, 21.

Barneby Henderson m. Margaret Knox, 1797, 10, 23.
Ezekiel Henderson m. Hannah Timmons, 1795, 12, 20.
Isaac Henderson m. Sally Davis, 1797, 2, 22.
Joseph Hercourt m. Polly Williams, 1798, 6, 21.
Josiah Hill m. Polly Franklin, 1798, 2, 28.
Levin Hill, Jr. m. Catherine Johnson, 1798, 4, 17.
James Hinman m. Sarah Scarborough, 1798, 1, 3.
Nehemiah Holland m. Martha Richardson, 1796, 2, 12.
William Hoskin m. Nancy Trader, 1797, 8, 29.
Caleb Houston m. Betsy Mills, 1797, 12, 14.
George Houston m. Rhoda Bratten, 1796, 12, 16.
Warren Hudder m. Polly Johnson, 1796, 12, 21.
Arthur Hudson m. Nancy Taylor, 1797, 2, 22.
Benjamin Hudson m. Elizabeth Williams, 1796, 3, 25.
McKimmey Hudson m. Hannah Dymock, 1795, 12, 26.
Robert Hudson m. Mary Atkinson, 1796, 5, 31.
William Hudson m. Comfort Knox, 1798, 3, 7.
William Hughes m. Mary Houston, 1796, 12, 24.
Timothy Irons m. Sarah Dorman, 1798, 6, 22.
John Jackson m. Elizabeth Burbage, 1796, 10, 18.
Benjamin Jarmin m. Elizabeth Timmons, 1796, 12, 13.
Jacob Johnson m. Nancy Armstrong, 1798, 2, 17.
James Johnson m. Patty Baker, 1797, 1, 31.
John Johnson m. Sally Crapper, 1796, 12, 21.
Leonard Johnson m. Aralanta Brittingham, 1795, —, —.
James Hall Jones m. Margaret Dale, 1797, 6, 6.
Lewis Jones m. Rachel Long, 1795, 12, 20.
Matthew Jones m. Joanna Johnson, 1798, 2, 16.
William Jones m. Catherine Hodder, 1798, 1, 9.
James King m. Mary Kennett, 1797, 5, 10.
Gray Knox m. Hetty Merrill, 1798, 4, 7.
Edward Lambdin m. Polly Merrill, 1797, 12, 22.
William Law m. Polly Miller, 1796, 4, 25.
Levin Layfield m. Nancy Brittingham, 1798, 1, 16.
Isaac Long m. Charlotte Griffin, 1797, 12, 13.
Zadock Long m. Leah Whittington, 1796, 10, 13.
Alexander Low m. Nancy Brewington, 1797, 7, 10.
Daniel McDaniel m. Elizabeth Carey, 1797, 1, 10.
Phillip Marsh m. Polly Selby, 1797, 5, 12.
Israel Marshall m. Polly Collyer, 1798, 2, 5.
Zadok Marshall m. Peggy Costen, 1796, 11, 25.
Levi Merrill m. Elizabeth Stevenson, 1798, 1, 23.

Jesse Mifford m. Betsy Richardson, 1797, 2, 10.
Jonathan Miles m. Leah Tull, 1796, 12, 16.
Robert Mitchell m. Elizabeth Mumford, 1797, 8, 18.
Phillip Morris m. Nancy Mumford, 1795, 9, 18.
Elijah Nelson m. Sophia Melvin, 1798, 1, 4.
Josiah Nelson m. Margaret Smith, 1796, 3, 15.
Levi Nelson m. Hannah Mills, 1797, 12, 5.
William Nelson m. Sally Sturgis, 1797, 1, 31.
William Nelson m. Sarah Brothery, 1797, 12, 20.
Thomas Newbold m. Polly Taylor, 1798, 5, 22.
Charles Parker m. Talitha Johnson, 1797, 1, 10.
John Parker m. Nancy Parker, 1796, 8, 4.
John Pernell m. Patty Pernell, 1797, 11, 8.
McKenny Porter m. Nancy Parker, 1797, 7, 18.
William Porter m. Naomi Sturges, 1796, 1, 4.
Caleb Powell m. Elizabeth Bethards, 1796, 2, —.
Solomon K. Price m. Elizabeth Harris, 1797, 10, 10.
Elijah Pruitt m. Betsy Bishop, 1797, 11, 24.
Severn Pruitt m. Polly Merrill, 1797, 2, 16.
John Purnell m. Dolly Bennett, 1797, 1, 10.
Milby Purnell m. Amelia Parker, 1795, 12, 8.
John Readen m. Hesse Taylor, 1797, 11, 29.
James Redden m. Sarah Bristor, 1798, 5, 21.
James Reed m. Betsy Davis, 1797, 11, 24.
Thomas Reynolds m. Dolly Boun, 1796, 12, 9.
Jacob Richards m. Sarah Riggan, 1797, 6, 13.
Benjamin Richardson m. Catharine Bratten, 1798, 6, 26.
Littleton Riley m. Sally Townsend, 1796, 4, 23.
Stephen Roach m. Mary Lambden, 1797, 8, 17.
Sylvester Uriah Roberts m. Sarah Gillett, 1796, 10, 1.
John Rock m. Polly Mitchell, 1797, 6, 14.
Edward Scarborough m. Nancy Selby, 1797, 5, 2.
John Scarborough m. Elizabeth Smullen, 1796, 7, 8.
Joseph Schoolfield m. Esther Grenby (Gunby?), 1797, 2, 28.
William Schoolfield m. Rosanna Merrill, 1797, 9, 8.
George Selby m. Betsy Curtis Sturges, 1797, 12, 20.
Eli Shockley m. Betsy Coleburn, 1798, 4, 27.
Thomas Shockley m. Nancy Coleburn, 1798, 4, 27.
Andrew Simpson m. Patty Holland, 1797, 2, 28.
John Slocomb m. Polly McCreddy, 1796, 10, 25.
Archibald Smith m. Mary Hammond, 1795, 12, 18.
John Smith m. Anna Smith, 1798, 2, 9.

Robert Smith m. Sarah Martin, 1798, 1, 2.
Holland Smock m. Betsy Williams, 1798, 1, 2.
Jesse Smock m. Sally Truitt, 1797, 12, 19.
George Staten m. Rachel Turner, 1797, 4, 17.
Southey Sterling m. Rachel Dryden, 1797, 11, 24.
Joseph Stevenson m. Elizabeth Stevenson, 1797, 11, 30.
John Sturges m. Tabitha Brumbly, 1797, 1, 24.
John Sturgis m. Nancy Bishop, 1797, 1, 25.
John Tarr m. Peggy Allen, 1797, 1, 31.
William Tarr m. Hannah Guthry, 1797, 9, 22.
George Taylor m. Polly Timmons, 1796, 9, 5.
James Taylor m. Peggy Aydlott, 1795, 12, 11.
John Taylor m. Polly Powell, 1796, 5, 10.
John Gibbs Taylor, Jr. m. Hannah Aydlott, 1797, 10, 12.
Samuel Taylor m. Sally Taylor, 1797, 4, 24.
Jacob Teague m. Zipporah Rounds, 1796, 12, 21.
Henry Thornton m. Euphame Townsend, 1798, 3, 16.
Ephraim Timmons m. Patty Holliday, 1796, 12, 16.
Thomas Tindale m. Agnes Melvin, 1796, 12, 29.
William Tingle m. Sarah Long, 1796, 2, 4.
Stephen Townsend m. Esther Benson, 1796, 6, 20.
James Tripp m. Jane Purnell, 1795, 12, 18.
Benjamin Truitt m. Elener Johnson, 1798, 3, 26.
George Truitt m. Sally Bishop, 1797, 10, 30.
John K. Truitt m. Mary Teague, 1796, 3, 1.
John Tunnell m. Mary Selby, 1796, 10, 6.
Lemuel Turner m. Sally Parker, 1797, 12, 19.
——— Turpin m. Betsy Radcliffe, 1796, 5, 27.
George Twilley m. Rosetta Taylor, 1796, 7, 3.
Ephriam Townsend m. Rachel Custer (or Cutler?), 1796, 10, 20.
John Walker m. Sebrina Crapper, 1798, 6, 25.
Esom Waller m. Polly Elzey, 1797, 12, 18.
David Walston m. Polly Moor, 1797, 11, 22.
John Webb m. Mary Hancock, 1797, 1, 4.
Zadok Wheeler m. Martha B. Dickerson, 1796, 11, 28.
Henry White m. Sally Lister, 1797, 1, 30.
Thomas White m. Sarah Nuton, 1796, 8, 20.
William S. White, Jr. m. Betsy S. Waggaman, 1796, 4, 11.
Eli Williams m. Euphamy Jones, 1798, 5, 22.
Thomas Williams m. Nancy Parker, 1797, 2, 27.
John Willson m. Sarah Ennis, 1796, 7, 25.
Thomas Wilson m. Elizabeth Fisher, 1796, 11, 30.

Hezekiah Wright m. Elizabeth Riley, 1796, 7, 11.
Lot Wright m. Esther Evans, 1798, 2, 6.
Absalom Wyatt m. Nancy Pennewill, 1795, 12, 11.

Record of Marriages in Maryland and Delaware, By Rev. George Moore, 1789–1810*
(202 persons)

Barniby, Richard and Mary Allen, July 12, 1796.
Beard, John and Rachel Mansfield, June 5, 1792.
Boyles, Robert and Elizabeth Hammon, Jan. 9, 1801.
Brown, Wm. and Elizabeth Etherington, July 28, 1796.
Christfield, Gilbert and Mary Redgrave, Jan. 6, 1799.
Clayton, John and Isabella Simmonds, Jan. 26, 1790.
Colder [Colver?], Nathaniel and Sarah Spearman, Feb. 1, 1795.
Comegys, Abraham and Ann Smith, Dec. 10, 1793.
Conner, James and Elizabeth Campbell, Jan. 13, 1799.
Cooper, Ephraim and Mary Sartain, May 5, 1792.
Copper, Darius and Mary Watts, Nov. 24, 1799.
Crouch, Thomas and Mary Sewell, June 25, 1795.
Davidson, Wm. and Ann Jury, Oct. 22, 1795. "Returned."
Davis, John and Sarah Vansant, Feb. 23, 1797.
Davis, Wm. and Elizabeth Cherrington, Dec. 9, 1799.
Dawney, John and Marea Duyer, Jan. 5, 1804.
Dill, John and Hanny Dill, June 1, 1804.
Duffey, John and Martha Hance, Aug. 19, 1790.
Duyer, Wm. and Elizabeth Briscoe, May 11, 1797.
Eliason, Ebenezer and Rebecca Carnan, June 12, 1798.
Eliason, Elijah and Tobitha Bristow, Dec. 30, 1790.
Elliott, Benjamin and Margaret Crouch, Jan. 26, 1795.
Farmer, Thomas and Rachel Lasley, Sept. 9, 1795.
Fletcher, James and Comfort Messeck, Jan. 11, 1793.
Gears, John and Sarah Husler, Dec. 19, 1793.
Glenn, Peregrine and Mary Ann Briscoe, June 26, 1795.
Gonee, Rudolph and Elisabeth Heaver (Header), Oct. 27, 1796. "Returned."

* From original record in Burton Historical Collection, Burton Library, Detroit, Mich. and published through "its courtesy. Published also in Manuscripts From The Burton Historical Collection No. 2," pp. 52–57. (Probably Kent, Cecil, &c. marriages?)

Grace, William and Elizabeth Moore, July 9, 1789.
Grant, Jams and Catharine Reading, Jan. 31, 1802.
Hackett, Wm. and Cornelia Pennington, Oct. 12, 1793.
Haley, Jams and Mary Robinett, Oct. 12, 1789.
Harmon, John and Arimantha Eliason, Mch. 22, 1810.
Harper, Joseph and Martha Meeks, Aug. 30, 1804.
Hewett, Thomas and Mary Shawn, Mch. 28, 1790.
Hines, Edward and Elizabeth Copper, Dec. 30, 1802.
Hines, John and Susan Russel, Sept. 24, 1800.
Hinton, Jeremiah and Rebecca Melson, Dec. 29, 1799.
Horney, Wm. and Nelly McCarty, Sept. 22, 1798. "Returned this list."
Howard, Benjamin and Rachel Greenwood, Feb. 5, 1801.
Jackson, Tarbutt and Mary Rogers, Jan. 29, 1792.
Jarvis, Joseph and Elizabeth Barnaby, Dec. 10, 1796.
Jons, Simon Pryor and Sarah Galloway Thrift, Aug. 19, 1790.
Kendall, Wm. and Rebecca Johnson, May 27, 1800.
Kerbey, Caleb and Maria Sharpless, Aug. 31, 1800.
Kirk, John and Sarah Roberts, Dec. 27, 1789.
Logue, Wm. and Ann Smith, Jan. 1, 1795.
McDaniel, Wm. and Milicent Cornelius, Sept. 24, 1795.
McDowell, Wm. and Jean Dougherty, Aug. 24, 1790.
McFeely, John and Elizabeth Bateman, Dec. 28, 1800.
McNeal, Archabald and Frances Allen, Sept. 12, 1795.
Mahannah, John and Elizabeth Lasly, July 20, 1799.
Manliy, Nicholas George and Millicent Kinkiy, Dec. 23, 1789.
Manly, Jams and Lydia Liason, Mch. 13, 1790.
Manly, John and Susannah Cox, Apr. 15, 1790.
Meekes, Aquilla and Ann Cannell, Mch. 17, 1799.
Miers, Wm. and Jerusha Falconar, Aug. 18, 1791.
Mussey, Francis and Milcha Ussleton, May 11, 1801.
Oliver, Joseph and Rainey Gibbs, Feb. 4, 1792.
Ozier, Joseph and Elizabeth Stuart, May 1, 1798.
Pennington, Joseph and Ann Pennington, Mch. 2, 1797.
Pennington, Samuel and Sarah Etherington, Nov. 5, 1789.
Pope, Wm. and Elizabeth Hopkins, Nov. 9, 1801.
Read, Caleb and Polly Greenwood, Feb. 12, 1804.
Reed, John and Elizabeth Jeffers, Mch. 18, 1800.
Reed, Joseph and Elizabeth Hurtt, Aug. 30, 1797. "Returned this list."
Rochester, Richard and Rebecca Pratt, Jan. 1, 1795.
Roggester, John and Sarah George, Feb. 4, 1792.
Russel, Theophilus and Ann Tittle, Apr. 1, 1804.
Ruth, Christopher and Elizabeth Miers, Apr. 8, 1800.

Sappington, Lambert and Mary Wilson, Jan. 15, 1795.
Sappington, Nathaniel and Hannah Meeks, May 26, 1799.
Severson, Hance and Rebecca Price, Dec. 12, 1793.
Shahawn, Charles and Mary Vansant, Mch. 28, 1790.
Smith, Wm. and Ann Haward, Mch. 20, 1798.
Spencer, Labert W. and Ann Spencer, Sept. 13, 1804.
Stavely, John and Elizabeth Rayner, Jan. 26, 1802.
Taylor, John and Sarah Gay, Feb. 14, 1796.
Thompson, Wm. and Hosanna Pennington, Dec. 26, 1794.
Toenir, Moses and Elizabeth Cohee, Oct. 18, 1791.
Tompson, John and Catherin Homer, Oct. 18, 1791.
Vansant, Joshua and Ann Davis, May 10, 1798.
Walmsley, Thomas and Rebecca James, Apr. 22, 1790.
Watts, John and Elizabeth Ricketts, Nov. 30, 1800.
Way, George and Ann Tuttle, Mch. 19, 1801.
White, Wm. and Ann Redgrove, Jan. 8, 1797.
Young, Hugh and Elenor Durham, Dec. 23, 1790. (Harford Co.)
* Watson, William and Catharine Riley, 21 Oct., 1811.
William Watson died Oct. 28, 1815, aged 34.
Catharine Watson died Sept. 23, 1870.
Mary Jane Watson b. May 19, 1813.
William Geo. Watson b. Mch. 25, 1815.

List of Marriages by Publication in the Delaware State by Rev. George Moore

Fowler, Jesse and Lucretia McCrackin "was married Delaware State, Susex Co., Dec. the 20th, 1792."
Herrington, John and Hannah Marshel, Feb. 7, 1791. "York Co. State of Pa."
Ritch Peter and Rodey Hardinigth, May ye 3rd, 1789.

* In the same book, but not in the handwriting of Rev. Geo. Moore.

"List of Marriages by License in the State of Delaware in the Year 1788 by Me George Moore"

Appleton, Robart and Line Read, Sept. 16, 1790.
Bolton, Wm. and Mary Darling, Nov. 30, 1802.
Carnan, John and Rebecca Hynson, Dec. 13, 1798.
Clark, Wm. and Mary Mears, March 5, 1789.
Griffith, Benjamin and Mary Moore, Jan. 26, 1790.
Gutrey, Robard and Rachel Biddel, Feb. 22, 1790.
Haindsley, Ambroius and Ann Herrington, Nov. 2, 1788.
Kelley, Wm. and Jane Ray, Jan. 16, 1790.
Pollard, Wm. and Ann Egleson, June 18, 1790.
Robards, Benjamin and Nessa Rothwell, Oct. 8, 1789.
Wright, John and Maacha Low, Feb. 6, 1791. "York Co., State of Pa."

INDEX*

* Names of slaves are omitted. Figures in parentheses, "265 (2)," mean that the name occurs that number of times on the indicated page, but it is well to run through the entire page as this practice applies only to a part of the book.

The following imperfect records may assist some searchers:

D

H

I

J

K

L

M

O

P

Q

R

U

V

W

Y